# Lecture Notes in Artificial Intelligence 3336

Edited by J. G. Carbonell and J. Siekmann

Subseries of Lecture Notes in Computer Science

Dimitris Karagiannis   Ulrich Reimer (Eds.)

# Practical Aspects of Knowledge Management

5th International Conference, PAKM 2004
Vienna, Austria, December 2-3, 2004
Proceedings

 Springer

Series Editors

Jaime G. Carbonell, Carnegie Mellon University, Pittsburgh, PA, USA
Jörg Siekmann, University of Saarland, Saarbrücken, Germany

Volume Editors

Dimitris Karagiannis
University of Vienna
Faculty of Computer Science, Department of Knowledge Engineering
Brünner Strasse 72, 1210 Vienna, Austria
E-mail: dk@dke.univie.ac.at

Ulrich Reimer
Business Operation Systems
Esslenstr. 3, 8280 Kreuzlingen, Switzerland
E-mail: ulrich.reimer@bauer-partner.com

Library of Congress Control Number: 2004116218

CR Subject Classification (1998): I.2, H.2.8, H.3, H.4, H.5, K.4, J.1

ISSN 0302-9743
ISBN 3-540-24088-8 Springer Berlin Heidelberg New York

Springer is a part of Springer Science+Business Media

springeronline.com

© Springer-Verlag Berlin Heidelberg 2004
Printed in Germany

Typesetting: Camera-ready by author, data conversion by Olgun Computergrafik
Printed on acid-free paper     SPIN: 11362227     06/3142     5 4 3 2 1 0

# Preface

This book contains the papers presented at the 5th International Conference on Practical Aspects of Knowledge Management organized by the Department of Knowledge Management, Institute of Computer Science and Business Informatics, University of Vienna. The event took place on December 02–03, 2004 in Vienna.

The PAKM conference series offers a communication forum and meeting ground for practitioners and researchers engaged in developing and deploying advanced business solutions for the management of knowledge and intellectual capital. Contributions pursuing integrated approaches which consider organizational, technological and cultural issues of knowledge management have been elected for presentation. PAKM is a forum for people to share their views, to exchange ideas, to develop new insights, and to envision completely new kinds of solutions for knowledge management problems.

The accepted papers are of high quality and are not too specialized so that the main issues can be understood by someone outside the respective field. This is crucial for an interdisciplinary exchange of ideas. Like its predecessors, PAKM 2004 featured two invited talks.

It is a real joy seeing the visibility of the conference increase and noting that knowledge management researchers and practitioners from all over the world submitted papers. This year, 163 papers and case studies were submitted, from which 48 were accepted.

Many people were involved in setting up PAKM 2004. We would like to express our warm thanks to everybody who contributed to making it a success. First of all, this includes all the authors who submitted a paper to the review process, and the members of the program committee who made all the efforts to select the best papers and to ensure a high-quality program. Special thanks go to Prof. Dr. Hermann Krallmann and Prof. Dr. Dimitris Plexousakis for giving the keynote talks.

Most of the organizational work was done by Michaela Schein, reliable and industrious as always. She also managed the local organization. Our thanks also include the session chairs for their support in running a smooth conference, and all the participants who made the event possible in the first place.

Our wish is that all participants found it worthwhile to attend PAKM 2004 and returned home with many new ideas and valuable contacts.

Vienna, December 2, 2004
Dimitris Karagiannis
Ulrich Reimer

# Organization

**Co-chairs**

Dimitris Karagiannis, University of Vienna, Austria
Ulrich Reimer, Business Operation Systems, Switzerland


**Program Committee**

Xavier Boucher, École des Mines de St. Etienne, France
Kemal A. Delic, Hewlett-Packard, France
Juan Manuel Dodero, University Carlos III, Madrid, Spain
Joaquim Filipe, Escola Superior de Tecnologia Setubal, Portugal
Naoki Fukuta, Shizuoka University, Japan
Norbert Gronau, University of Oldenburg, Germany
Ulrich Geske, Fraunhofer Gesellschaft FIRST, Germany
Knut Hinkelmann, FH Solothurn Nordwestschweiz, Switzerland
Hans Hinterhuber, University of Innsbruck, Austria
Achim Hoffmann, University of New South Wales, Australia
Manfred Jeusfeld, University of Tilburg, Netherlands
Byeong Ho Kang, University of Tasmania, Tasmania
Niklaus Klaentschi, Swiss KM Forum, Switzerland
Edith Denman-Maier, Donau University, Krems, Austria
Vladimir Marik, Czech Technical University, Czech Republic
Frank Maurer, University of Calgary, Canada
Hermann Maurer, Technical University of Graz, Austria
Heinrich Mayr, University of Klagenfurt, Austria
Michele Missikoff, Italian National Research Council, Italy
Katharina Morik, University of Dortmund, Germany
Nikolaos A. Mylonopoulos, ALBA, Greece
Peter Reimann, University of Sydney, Australia
Debbie Richards, Macquarie University, Australia
Bodo Rieger, University of Osnabrueck, Germany
Isabel Seruca, Universidade Portucalense, Portugal
Marcin Sikorski, Gdansk University of Technology, Poland
Marcus Spies, Munich University, Germany
Steffen Staab, University of Karlsruhe, Germany
Rudi Studer, University of Karlsruhe, Germany
Ulrich Thiel, Fraunhofer Gesellschaft, Germany
A Min Tjoa, Technical University of Vienna, Austria
Klaus Tochtermann, I-Know Center, Graz, Austria
Robert Trappl, Medical University of Vienna, Austria
Erich Tsui, Computer Sciences Corporation, Australia
Roland Wagner, Johannes Kepler University, Linz, Austria
Fritjof Weber, University of Bremen, Germany
Rosina Weber, Drexel University, USA
Takahira Yamaguchi, Keio University, Japan

# Table of Contents

# The KMDL Knowledge Management Approach: Integrating Knowledge Conversions and Business Process Modeling

Norbert Gronau[1], Claudia Müller[1], and Mathias Uslar[2]

[1] University of Potsdam, Business Information Systems and Electronic Government,
14482 Potsdam, Germany
{NGronau,ClaMue}@rz.uni-potsdam.de
http://www.uni-potsdam.de/u/wvinf
[2] OFFIS e.V., Business Information and Knowledge Management, 26111 Oldenburg
Uslar@offis.de
http://www.offis.de/bi/

**Abstract.** This paper shows the KMDL Knowledge Management Approach which is based on the SECI and *ba* model by Nonaka and Takeuchi and the KMDL Knowledge modeling language. The approach illustrates the creation of knowledge with the focus on the knowledge conversions by Nonaka and Takeuchi. Furthermore, it emphasizes the quality of knowledge being embodied in persons and creates a personalization and socialization strategy which integrates business process modeling, skill management and the selection of knowledge management systems. The paper describes the theoretical foundations of the approach and practical effects which have been seen in the use of this approach.

## 1 Introduction

Knowledge management clearly has become more and more important since the beginning of the early nineties. Companies expect an improvement of the innovation capability and a significant increase in process efficiency. Globalization, increasing competition, more dynamic markets and shorter cycles in product development and innovation increase the need for a better adaptation to those environmental factors. These factors establish the need for a consequent adaptation of all business processes to existing and future market needs.

Knowledge processes are executed parallel but also linked to normal business processes in a ladder like structure. The knowledge processes are only slightly structured. Detecting, modeling, analyzing and finally optimizing those processes should be the long-term aim of a process-oriented knowledge management approach.

Knowledge and business processes are integrated and should be evaluated as a whole [1]. Business processes can be modeled and analyzed via the existing business process modeling methods. Furthermore, there are numerous approaches which take into consideration the knowledge within the company or the organization [21, 22]. Mapping static, explicit knowledge can only contribute little to a broad and integrated process-oriented knowledge management approach. Modeling the business processes and the processes of knowledge creation can ensure an effective and reasonable process-spanning knowledge flow.

The described problems and challenges have been the motivation to develop the knowledge modeling language KMDL (Knowledge Modeling Description Language)

D. Karagiannis and U. Reimer (Eds.): PAKM 2004, LNAI 3336, pp. 1–10, 2004.
© Springer-Verlag Berlin Heidelberg 2004

[2] in order to model knowledge-intensive business processes with the KMDL-based software tool K-Modeler. The tool implementing the language in an early version has been integrated into an approach which is based on the knowledge management philosophies of Nonaka, Takeuchi and Konno. The definition of the term knowledge is based on the very ideas of Nonaka and Takeuchi [18]. The knowledge is bound to a person, it is indeed personal knowledge. This so called tacit knowledge cannot be expressed by formal methods. It is based in the employee's occupation, the proficiencies of each employee and his ideals, values and experiences. It is possible to analyze and model this knowledge through KMDL even if it is not directly used in the operational business process.

## 2   Theoretical Foundation of the Approach

### 2.1   Definition of Knowledge, the SECI Model and *ba*

Nonaka and Takeuchi's thoughts and ideas are not only influenced by Japanese tradition but strongly by Michael Polanyi. Polanyi [20] defined the idea of a tacit knowledge embodied as personal knowledge. Therefore, Nonaka and Takeuchi distinguish between two types of knowledge: the tacit and the explicit knowledge. Tacit knowledge is personal knowledge which consists of mental models, beliefs and perspectives which cannot be easily articulated or shared. Explicit knowledge is formal, codified, systematic, articulated in writing/numbers, easy to communicate and shared; it is transmittable in a formal language and can be stored in databases or libraries [12].

The tacit knowledge is the more interesting knowledge when looking at knowledge-intensive business processes as we will see later. But yet, there are ways and possibilities to convert and combine tacit and explicit knowledge. Nonaka and Takeuchi mention four types of knowledge-conversions in the so called SECI model, the socialization, the externalization, the combination and the internalization.

The socialization is a conversion from tacit knowledge to tacit knowledge. Often it is done by sharing experience, just like apprentices of a craftsman learn their skills by watching a knowledge-worker can learn his needed abilities through on-the-job training. Even if possible, the socialization can be done without speaking or writing a single word.

The externalization is a conversion from tacit to explicit knowledge. By using metaphors, analogies or models one can express his tacit knowledge in a manner which can be understood by others. It is the essence of tacit knowledge which can then be handed over in a written form, yet it can be very difficult to externalize tacit knowledge, often it is simply impossible.

The combination is the conversion from explicit to explicit knowledge. Different kinds of explicit knowledge can be combined through media like telephone, mail, word processing by reconfiguring, categorizing and adding new information and context to the knowledge.

The internalization is the conversion from explicit to tacit knowledge. It is very close related to learning-by-doing. Experiences made through socialization, externalization or combination are internalized and put into one's own knowledge framework, they can become know-how or mental models and according to this, very important knowledge assets. It is very helpful it the explicit knowledge is in a written form like documents, handbooks or stories.

Those conversions are done regularly in everybody's daily life. Yet the idea is often neglected, because the conversions are bound to a place and depend on certain conditions and requirements. The idea has been adopted by Takeuchi and Konno [19]. The concept of *ba* creates the idea of this place. The *ba* is a shared location or place where relations can evolve. The place can be either physical (including bureau, shared workroom, mall) or virtual (email or teleconferences) or even mental (shared values, ideas, or ideals). The *ba* restrains itself from the ordinary human interaction by being a place of knowledge creation. Knowledge is bound to the *ba*, if it is dislodged from the *ba*, it simply becomes information. The *ba* is the framework where knowledge becomes the resource for creativity.

The model by Nonaka, Takeuchi and Konno establishes a logical framework which can be used to take a look at tacit and explicit knowledge, the conversions between those kinds of knowledge and therefore the creation of knowledge and the conditions and requirements for conversion to happen (the *ba*). It will serve as the basic framework for modeling a dynamic process of knowledge creation within the author's approach.

## 2.2  Definition of Knowledge-Intensive Business Processes

Several definitions of knowledge-intensive business processes have evolved. Remus first of all distinguishes four types of knowledge-oriented processes. A knowledge-intensive process is super-ordinate to the other processes in order to distinguish them from normal business processes [3]. The knowledge-intensive business process is a process which relies very much on knowledge like research and development processes. Remus defines two more processes which rely on knowledge [22]. The knowledge-process which is a process combining different knowledge activities like creating and distributing knowledge, for example the content management process and finally the knowledge-management process which tries to improve knowledge processes. The knowledge-intensive business process is subject to the definition of knowledge-intensive processes within this paper.

The literature defines several factors which are fundamental to knowledge-intensive business processes. In knowledge-intensive processes, knowledge contributes significantly to the values added within the process. The process has got many innovative and creative parts [5]. People within the process have a large scope of decision freedom, they can decide autonomous. The event flow of knowledge-intensive business processes is not clear form the very beginning, it can evolve during the process [3]. Many participants of the process have got different knowledge from different domains at different levels [11]. Like the flow, even the tasks within the process do not have to be clearly defined. A high level of communication between individuals is often part of the knowledge-intensive process. Knowledge which is part of the process has often a very short life-time [5], it is outdated very often, even though, it is more often very time-intensive to build up this knowledge [23]. Knowledge-intensive business processes often do not cover structured working rules and often lack metrics for evaluating the success of the process [4]. The IT-support for knowledge-intensive business processes is often not very sophisticated because it heavily relies on socialization and informal exchange [14]. A knowledge-intensive process should be a core process of the company and it should produce or add new knowledge to the organization's knowledge base [15]. A last criterion focuses on the very high costs which are often generated by knowledge-intensive processes.

Looking at these criteria, we can classify many processes, for example software development processes [17] or public administration processes as knowledge-intensive processes. The very vague and unstructured flows of knowledge cannot be modeled by conventional modeling tools. Important elements like the representation of tacit knowledge or the creation of knowledge through conversions cannot be modeled [7].

## 2.3 Knowledge Strategy

Hansen et al. have established the idea of the knowledge strategy [13]. They distinguish between two main strategies which are often combined but are in general two poles for knowledge management approaches. The *codification strategy* tries to track the knowledge of the employees or other stakeholders with interviews or analogue techniques and to save this knowledge by electronic means and measures within databases. By retrieving from those databases, knowledge can be used again and again within new processes and situations. According to the definition by Nonaka and Takeuchi, this so called "knowledge" is indeed just information. This approach is far more an information management approach than a real knowledge management approach. The focus is on documenting situational knowledge from projects in order to reuse this knowledge like lessons-learned or best-practice documents over and over again (the so called people-to-documents approach).

The are within the focus of this strategy. A successful strategy for knowledge management of knowledge-intensive processes should focus on a combined personalization and socialization strategy.

Looking at the previous paragraph, we can see that knowledge-intensive business processes deal very much with creating and using tacit knowledge from many participants. An integrated approach should focus first of all on the *ba*-concept of places or processes where knowledge is created, the difference between tacit and explicit knowledge and focus on the factors of knowledge-intensive processes which are very much driven and fulfilled by the SECI knowledge conversions. Furthermore, the general strategy should be a combination of personalization and socialization, we should be able to identify tacit knowledge bound to persons as well as identifying processes within the organization creating knowledge and supporting the creation by appropriate (knowledge management) solutions or practices. The three types of knowledge processes according to Remus should be supported, if it is possible to model and support knowledge-intensive processes, the subordinate processes can be modeled, too. Our approach to fulfill those requirements is the KMDL. second strategy is the *personalization strategy*, which focuses on tacit knowledge. This knowledge is bound to several experts within the process or company. The strategy tries to identify the experts and to connect or visualize them through methods like yellow pages or knowledge maps. The communication between experts should be improved. The codification strategy does not seem to be appropriate for knowledge-intensive processes; the personalization strategy can be suitable if it is expanded by some more elements which is sometimes called *socialization strategy* [6].

This strategy focuses on the exchange and creation of knowledge within groups. Knowledge is a social product made within an environment [24]. The settings of the environment and the organization.

# 3   The Knowledge Modeling Description Language

The elements and mechanisms have been discussed in several other publications and the literature [9, 10]; we will therefore only discuss the core elements which are basis to the mentioned practical benefits in the third section of this paper.

## 3.1   Objects

The actual implementation of the KMDL consists of six objects: information, task, role, role requirement, knowledge object and person. The relation of those objects can be seen in Figure 1.

The information object is used in a process like any other information or explicit knowledge. Information can be externalized easily. It can be saved to disk or written down in documents.

The task object is the core element of the process model. A task is defined in this context as an object within the business process having input and output and being a single step within the whole superior process. Knowledge-intensive processes often process a lot of information, the input and outputs of the task therefore are information objects.

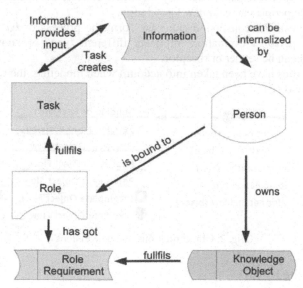

**Fig. 1.** Objects of KMDL

The role object is bound to tasks and roles execute the tasks. Roles can be taken and assigned to several persons. This provides the possibility to model the whole functional and personal company structure.

The role requirements are mainly used for skill management. Tasks require certain skills to be solved; those skills have to be provided by the persons taken the certain role. The complete role requirements define the tacit knowledge which is needed to fulfill the task assigned to the role. Every requirement is a tacit knowledge object. Though it is no physical object, we still define it as kind of internalized experience knowledge object.

Persons are bound and assigned to roles and are the owners of the knowledge objects. Knowledge objects are used to track the whole process-relevant (tacit) knowledge objects of a person. They are the foundation of everyone's knowledge base.

### 3.2 Knowledge Conversions and Relations

The four knowledge conversions according to the SECI model are represented within the notation as relations between the objects. It is possible to model several of the conversions properties, the most important we identified are frequency, completeness, number of participants, and conversions direction.

The frequency is an attribute how often people contact each other to share their knowledge. This can happen once, daily, twice a week or whatever. We can identify the necessity to support this process by looking at the frequency. We expect higher use when supporting frequent processes.

The completeness focuses on the level of socialized knowledge you can learn complementary knowledge from different persons to add to your knowledge base. Still, it is possible to externalize and socialize most of the knowledge.

The number of participants can vary within a conversion. When listening to a speech, multiple people can gain new knowledge.

The direction of the conversion can vary form the process or *ba*. A discussion, brainstorming, personal evaluation implicate different types of knowledge flows. Every recipient can be sender or receptor.

These properties have been taken into account when modeling; the relations can be seen in figure two.

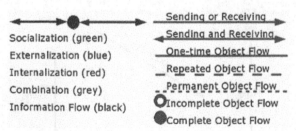

**Fig. 2.** Object relations and conversions

### 3.3 Views of the KMDL

Using those objects and relations, we can distinguish and model several views which show different aspects of business processes or the organization.

The task view shows an EPC-like view to the tasks which are involved in the whole process without any further information. We can use this view as an overview to identify all core tasks within the process.

The simple process view includes the tasks and the information coming in and out of the task. This is the level where it can be possible to import EPC models and include more information into the further views which better meets the requirements of modeling knowledge-intensive business processes.

The extended process view consists of the elements provided by the simple process view which have been enriched by the roles. It provides the advantage that we can view the roles associated with the tasks. Improper allocation and multi-allocations can be recognized.

The tacit process view shows the roles, the assigned persons and their knowledge objects which are subject to the role requirements. We therefore can get a view about alls requirements within the process or a view about all the knowledge objects provided by the matching employees.

The general view contains all the elements from the other views and integrates the whole views to a general view of the process which contains all the knowledge conversions and knowledge involved within the process.

# 4  Practical Aspects of the Approach

Normally, we must always consider the practical aspects of the approach. We have done several projects with the KMDL and developed several introduction models and features which provide the advantage for the whole approach. The following paragraph will summarize those benefits and provide an overview of non-striking benefits for the integrated approach for modeling knowledge-intensive business processes with the KMDL.

## 4.1  Procedural Model

We have already introduced several aspects which covered different domains of knowledge-intensive business processes like public administration, software development, IT-infrastructure, information systems in logistics business and corporate academies. The procedural model ensures the correct elicitation of all data needed and can be strongly adapted to the customers' processes and workers council requirements.

The model consists of several steps which can then again be subdivided. First of all, it is necessary to identify the knowledge-intensive processes. They can be defined by the customer but can also easily be identified using our criteria catalogue consisting of thirty factors. Having found the processes, we must do an analysis of the actual process executed. This is the most important point. We identify the tasks, assign the information objects to them, then identify the person and roles executing the task, specify their requirements and assign the person's knowledge objects to the role requirements. Afterwards, the process is modeled with our JAVA-based tool, the so called K-Modeler. The modeled processes are discussed afterwards with all partners, and then they are analyzed and hopefully optimized with the tool and the modelers' domain knowledge. Than the optimization can be directly executed within the company afterwards.

## 4.2  The K-Modeler Tool

The JAVA-based tool provides the possibility to model direct and via drag and drop on a canvas like design surface. The object can have attributes assigned to them which can be freely defined. A syntax check has been implemented to ensure that only formal correct models can be stored within the tools database. The processes tracked can be justified whether they include known anti-patterns which could be found in knowledge-intensive processes. We could identify knowledge monopolies, media breaches, not suitable knowledge objects which to not fit the role requirements, unsupported knowledge flow processes, unused knowledge, insufficiently used knowledge and so on.

## 4.3  Skill Management

The information about the person knowledge objects and the requirements of their roles can be used within skill management systems. It is possible to examine gaps between the requirements and the actual knowledge levels. This information can be used to start learning processes within the company to enhance the knowledge levels of the process-involved employees. The standard for the data used is HR-XML which provides a general format not only suitable for skill management systems but also for human resources information systems. The data tracked via the process modeling approach can support processes outside the knowledge-intensive domain. For example, an overview over the knowledge objects mostly used within the company can provide knowledge maps but also lead to finding core competences and processes with the corporation which can support a general business strategy [8].

## 4.4  Hyperlink Structure of Modeled Processes

It is possible to export all objects into a structured documentation in HTML or XML which provides an overview of all relevant data for a certain task. The task is shown with all information objects processed, all people linked with their role requirements in a hypertext-structure which can be browsed via normal internet browsers. It is a kind of process handbook which can easily be navigated. Linking resources like documents from DMS or CMS directly within these hypertext-documents ensures fast access to the relevant process information objects.

An export in XML format can be used to configure structures within those systems. Using this data in an electronic handbook furthermore ensures the topicality and validity of the data because it can easily be updated from the process tracked there is no need to reprint large documents over and over again.

## 4.5  Pre-configuration of Workflow or Document Management Systems

The process models can be exported to provide a pre-configuration of workflow management systems in order to reuse the modeled processes and to transmit the improved processes to the execution level. Document management systems can track the information documents created and used within the processes and link them via hypertext directly from the process model which can ensure a fast access to the relevant information for all employees or stakeholder within the business process.

## 4.6 Choosing Knowledge Management Systems

The knowledge conversions within the processes and the knowledge creation should be consequently supported by knowledge management systems. We have done a survey of knowledge management systems and tools [16] which ensures that we have a taxonomy which supports what type of knowledge creation and distribution is especially supported by which system.

## 4.7 Modeling Reference Processes Without Personal Data

Even when it is not possible to track all data due to workers council reasons and data protection, the approach still can contribute with modeled reference processes which show in an anonymous way how best practice processes can create knowledge and where conversions should appear. Furthermore, the skill catalogue for skill management systems can be created because all role requirements are needed skills which should be included in the catalogue.

# 5 Conclusion

The KMDL approach can be used as a very pragmatic and suitable platform for knowledge-intensive business processes. It covers various quick wins and factors which provide benefits for the business modeling approach and the companies analyzing their processes. It is possible to improve the processes and knowledge creation via various tools. The approach itself has been evaluated and improved in several projects and companies and should be established as one very suitable method to manage knowledge-intensive processes.

# References

1. Abecker, A., Hinkelmann, K., Maus, H., Müller H.-J.: Integrationspotenziale für Geschäfts-prozesse und Wissensmanagement. (in German) In: Abecker, A. (edt.): Geschäftsprozess-orientiertes Wissensmanagement. Springer-Verlag, Berlin Heidelberg New York (2002)
2. Arbeitsgemeinschaft Wissensmanagement: KMDL – Knowledge Modeler Description Language (in German), 2003. http://www.kmdl.de. Download 2004-07-20
3. Davenport, T.H., Jarvenpaa, S.L. and Beers, M. C.: Improving Knowledge Work Processes. Sloan Management Review, Summer (1996) 53–65
4. Davenport, T.H. and Prusak, L.: Working Knowledge. Harvard Business School Press (2000)
5. Eppler, M., Seifried P., Röpnack, A.: Improving knowledge intensive Processes through an Enterprise Knowledge Medium. In: PRASAD, J. (edt.): Proceedings of the 1999 Conference on Managing Organizational Knowledge for Strategic Advantage: The Key Role of Information Technology and Personnel. New Orleans (1999)
6. Fuchs-Kittowski, F., Reuter, P.: E-Collaboration für wissensintensive Dienstleistungen (in German). Information Management and Consulting (2002)
7. Gronau, N.: Modellierung von wissensintensiven Geschäftsprozessen (in German). In: Gronau, N. (edt.): Wissensmanagement: Potenziale - Werkzeuge - Konzepte. GITO-Verlag, Berlin (2003)

8. Gronau, N. and Uslar, M.: Creating Skill Catalogues for Competency Management Systems with KMDL. In: Khosrow-Pour, Mehdi (edt.): Innovations Through Information Technology. Idea Group Inc. (2004)
9. Gronau, N. and Weber, E.: Modeling of Knowledge Intensive Business Processes with the Declaration Language KMDL. In: Khosrow-Pour, Mehdi (edt.): Innovations Through Information Technology. Idea Group Inc. (2004)
10. Gronau, N. and Weber, E.: Management of Knowledge Intensive Business Processes. In: Desel, J., Pernici, B., Weske, M. (edt.): Business Process Management, Springer-Verlag, Heidelberg (2004)
11. Heisig, P.: GPO-WM - Methode und Werkzeuge zum geschäftsprozessorientierten Wissensmanagement (in German). In: Abecker, A. (edt.): Geschäftsprozessorientiertes Wissensmanagement. Springer-Verlag, Berlin Heidelberg New York (2002)
12. Hopfenbeck, W., Müller, M., Peisl, T.: Wissensbasiertes Management: Ansätze und Strategien zur Unternehmensführung in der Internet-Ökonomie (in German). Verlag Moderne Industrie (2001)
13. Hansen, M.T., Nohria, N., Tierney, T.: What's your strategy for managing knowledge? Harvard Business Review (1999) 106-116
14. Hoffmann, M.: Analyse und Unterstützung von Wissensprozessen als Voraussetzung für erfolgreiches Wissensmanagement (in German). In: Abecker, A. (edt.): Geschäftsprozessorientiertes Wissensmanagement. Springer-Verlag, Berlin Heidelberg New York (2002)
15. Hamel, G., Prahalad, C.K.: The core competence of the corporation. Harvard Business Review (1990)
16. Kalisch, A., Dilz S, Gronau N.: Anwendungen und Systeme für das Wissensmanagement: ein aktueller Überblick (in German), GITO Verlag, Berlin (2004)
17. Kidd, A.: The marks are on the knowledge worker. Human Factors in Computing Systems, Proceedings of the SIGCHI conference on Human factors in computing systems, (1994) 186–191
18. Nonaka, I., Takeuchi, H.: The Knowledge-Creating Company: How Japanese Companies Create the Dynamics of Innovation. Oxford University Press (1995)
19. Nonaka, I., Konno N.: The Concept of "ba": Building a foundation for knowledge creation. California Management Review (1998)
20. Polanyi, M.: Personal Knowledge: Towards a Post-Critical Philosophy. University of Chicago Press (1974)
21. Remus, U.: Integrierte Prozess- und Kommunikationsmodellierung zur Verbesserung von wissensintensiven Geschäftsprozessen (in German). In: Abecker, A. (edt.): Geschäftsprozessorientiertes Wissensmanagement. Springer-Verlag Berlin Heidelberg New York (2002)
22. Remus, U.: Prozessorientiertes Wissensmanagement. Konzepte und Modellierung (in German). Dissertation, Universität Regensburg (2002)
23. Schwarz, S., Abecker A., Maus H., Sintek M.: Anforderungen an die Workflow-Unterstützung für wissensintensive Geschäftsprozesse (in Germna). In: Müller, H.-J., Abecker A., Maus H., Hinkelmann K. (edt.): Proceedings des Workshops Geschäftsprozessorientiertes Wissensmanagement - Von der Strategie zum Content auf der WM 2001. Baden-Baden. (2001)
24. Shum, S. B.: Negotiating the construction of organizational memories. Journal of Universal Computer Science (1997) 899–928

# A JXTA-Based Framework for Mobile Cooperation in Distributed Knowledge Spaces

Bernd Eßmann, Thorsten Hampel, Joanna Slawik,
and Research Group "Spontaneous networking in virtual Knowledge Spaces"*

Heinz Nixdorf Institute, University of Paderborn
Fürstenallee 11, 33102 Paderborn, Germany
bernd.essmann@hni.uni-paderborn.de, hampel@uni-paderborn.de,
joanna.slawik@hni.uni-paderborn.de

**Abstract.** Computer supported cooperative knowledge management in mobile environments demands spontaneous interconnected applications supporting the users in their cooperation process. These applications often have to deal with heterogeneous network environments, the natural domain of peer-to-peer architectures. While several protocols and frameworks for peer-to-peer computing already exist (e.g. JXTA), opportunities for bringing cooperative objects and services together in shared knowledge spaces are not provided. This paper presents an architectural approach for an ad-hoc cooperation environment called *Swifff*. It provides distributed knowledge spaces based on the peer-to-peer framework JXTA. The paper points out basic needs for the desired cooperation system and presents related work in the field of CSCW. Additionally, it introduces our fundamental concepts and describes the architecture of our framework. This paper is concludes with a discussion of the solution we have achieved so far and gives a insight into our future research goals.

## 1 Introduction

Mobile cooperation needs to be independent from fixed places and existing network infrastructures. A possible solution for providing ubiquitous network environments with no need for centralized administration is to establish the so-called *ad-hoc networks* [1]. Ad-hoc networks seem to be the infrastructure of choice for supporting users in mobile environments, where no guaranteed connection exists. The major characteristics of this kind of networks include the ability of establishing network structures from scratch spontaneously and the connections are not reliable. Because of the dynamic nature of ad-hoc networks, hosts in these networks may come up or disappear without warning; even complete networks may be disconnected (*network partitioning*) [2].

Applications running on these networks need to be aware of the loss of connection to counterparts in the network. Strategies for network failures are especially

---

* Members: Böhle, Björn; Borowski, Marc; Flöthmann, Carsten; König, Andreas; Mischke, Stefan; Moritz, Stephan; Niehus, Dominik; Nörenberg, Franziska; Ortgiese, Simon; Pankratz, Stefan; Pawlak, Thorsten; Yan, Ling

D. Karagiannis and U. Reimer (Eds.): PAKM 2004, LNAI 3336, pp. 11–22, 2004.
© Springer-Verlag Berlin Heidelberg 2004

important for systems providing *computer supported cooperative work (CSCW) environments*. The embedded cooperation objects have to be stored and distributed over all involved hosts to reduce the risk of loosing access to all objects when one host goes down. In some cases this requires mechanisms to replicate and synchronize the knowledge space to be resistant to the partitioning of the network.

Our approach to the challenges of mobile CSCW environments is to provide a fundamental architecture supporting small highly portable devices in ad-hoc networks as well as powerful CSCW-servers in existing network infrastructures. The major services like network communication, distributed object repository, and user interfaces should be integrated in a flexible and modular way. This allows extending the basic architecture in future developments, an important feature since many of the mentioned problems are part of current research activities. This work focuses on the basic architecture, including a description of the essential modules for network communication, user interface communication, and persistence.

This paper is structured as follows: First, we will have a look at the fundamental problems of object management in mobile CSCW environments; then we will introduce systems, which deal with some aspects of the demands to mobile working environments; and in the subsequent two sections we will present our conceptual approach and give a brief description of the architecture of our system. We will end the paper with a short conclusion and future perspectives.

## 2   From Central Object Repositories to Peer-to-Peer Object Distribution

Client-server architectures are no longer useful in dynamic network infrastructures. The dedicated server is a single point of failure. When the server is disconnected from the network all clients are rendered useless. Fig. 1. shows objects stored on a central repository in the network as common in client-server architectures. Clients access original objects through proxy objects. These are just pointers to the original objects stored in the central server and its database. When disconnected from the server accessing the objects is no longer possible for clients.

The solution to avoid these shortcomings of ad-hoc networks is to use peer-to-peer architectures. Their goal is distribution of the working environment over all involved devices. This strategy avoids a complete breakdown of the working environment as a result of network disconnections and resources on all connected devices are still available.

In contrast to centralized stored objects in a server repository, distributed objects are spread all over the network. Fig. 2. illustrates a distributed repository where every device on the network can access objects on other connected remote devices. If one device is disconnected from the network the other devices may continue working with the remaining objects. This also works when loss of connections to parts of the network is experienced. This is the main advantage

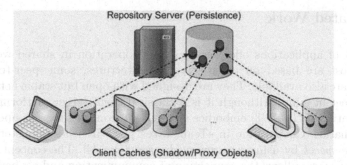

**Fig. 1.** Objects stored in a centralized object repository. Clients reference the original objects by proxy objects.

of peer-to-peer design with distributed resources in comparison to centralized client-server model in dynamic network environments.

Existing CSCW systems are dependent on dedicated servers and therefore, they are not useful in mobile environments. The major functionality of classical CSCW-systems depends on centralized services like user management, access control and persistent object repository. It is not easy to adapt these principles into the mobile domain. In mobile environments it is essential for each node to be able to take over the functionality of the dedicated server – permanent connections to all other nodes cannot be ensured. The major challenge of mobile collaborative working environments is to distribute needed data over the mobile devices. In case of a connection failure the access to objects in use has to be guaranteed.

In the following section we take a look at other projects related to peer-to-peer enabled collaborative working spaces. These include: complete existing peer-to-peer working space solutions; frameworks aimed at building mobile and/or peer-to-peer applications; and some interesting CSCW systems.

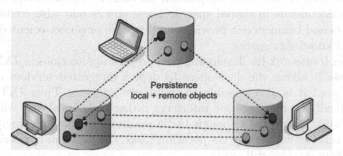

**Fig. 2.** A peer-to-peer based distributed object repository. Every peer may reference remote objects and provide objects to foreign peers.

## 3   Related Work

A variety of applications offer services for cooperation in shared workspaces. While most are based on client-server architectures, some peer-to-peer approaches are also available. They are designed with open but stable networks like the Internet in mind. Although it is a classical client-server platform the open source platform *sTeam* [3] embodies some useful concepts for our open cooperation scenarios. Cooperation in sTeam takes place in self-administered *virtual knowledge spaces* by using *primary media functions* [4]. The concept of virtual knowledge spaces allows the connection of communication and cooperative document management in a seamless way. On its architectural side sTeam uses a centralized server for persistent data storage and all management functions. Though the client-server architecture does not work well for dynamic network structures the core concepts are basis for our approach.

Peer-to-peer platforms are flexible according to the network infrastructure. Most peer-to-peer solutions are designed to distribute data, communication, or computing resources over the network. Nevertheless, even when called peer-to-peer, many of these platforms still use certain client-server structures for indexing the distributed data; connection management; and other functions. Due to the required Internet access most of these tools do not allow a data exchange in a dynamic ad-hoc network. [5] gives a survey over existing peer-to-peer systems.

A well-known peer-to-peer system designed for cooperative work is *Groove*[1]. Designed as a peer-to-peer CSCW platform it features a distributed persistence. This way the users are enabled to work together in a shared workspace. Looking at the architecture for synchronizing the distributed workspaces Groove still requires servers. According to its functionality Groove is extensible by plug-ins, which are not functionally interconnected.

For communication in heterogeneous network environments with several devices and applications the Park Labs developed *Speakeasy* [6]. They call their approach *recombinant computing*. This means providing fixed domain-independent interfaces and mobile code. Speakeasy is supposed to interconnect appliances in the environment like PDAs, multimedia devices, etc. in a peer-to-peer way. *Casca* is an application using the Speakeasy technology for cooperative work [7]. It allows discovering and selecting possible partners for collaborative work. Users may share documents in shared spaces. These spaces may also contain devices like printers and beamers but provides no semantic or object-oriented structure like virtual knowledge spaces.

Another framework for developing peer-to-peer applications is *JXTA* [8]. For this purpose it allows the developers to deploy integrated services and protocols. If desired it is also possible to build new services. Thus JXTA is open for many flexible communication interfaces rather than Speakeasy with its fixed communication interfaces. Although JXTA makes it possible implementing many separated services supporting cooperation tasks, the problem of missing linkage between these services still exists.

---

[1] http://www.groove.net

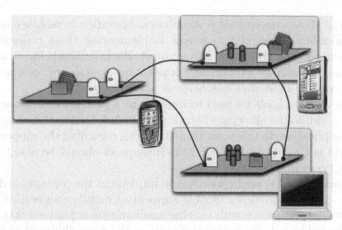

**Fig. 3.** Distributed knowledge space with interconnected areas, user objects and documents.

## 4   Distributed Knowledge Spaces for Mobile Cooperation

For seamless cooperation in mobile scenarios the cooperation environment has to be independent from existing infrastructures. This is true for the network environment and for the organizational structures. Important requirements for the cooperation environment are *self-administration* and *unrestricted structuring of knowledge*.

The concept of *virtual knowledge spaces* was already introduced in the section of related work when discussing the client-server CSCW platform sTeam. Virtual knowledge spaces allow cooperation partners the foundation of groups and associated areas for their cooperation. Gates may connect different cooperation areas, allowing the user, represented by a virtual avatar, to move from one area to another. Objects and groups in virtual knowledge spaces are persistent for use in later cooperation sessions. The main idea of the knowledge space metaphor is, that all different services, document and objects can refer to each other in an integrated way.

For transferring this concept to peer-to-peer environments where objects are distributed over the network the concept of virtual knowledge spaces has to be enhanced. We call the new idea of knowledge spaces scattered over the network *distributed knowledge spaces*. The area of cooperation is saved entirely on a device and may be replicated by collaborators. Gates are marked non-functional if the target area is not available. Fig. 3. shows a distributed knowledge space spread over several devices.

For short-term cooperation we presented the concept of *temporary groups and knowledge areas* [9]. They are especially useful in spontaneous face-to-face situations when a fast establishment of a cooperation setup is needed. After the cooperation session is closed the group and the area are deleted. Optionally, they may be included in persistent cooperation structures.

While the above concepts allow seamless cooperation in mobile environments without functional constraints, systems implementing these concepts have to take different network structures into account. Basic demands for an application implementing a mobility supporting cooperation system are *open architecture*, *automatic configuration*, and *spontaneous networking* [10].

To achieve these goals we need to implement a fundamental framework with a modular architecture allowing alteration of modules without having to change the whole application. In this context, restrictions regarding the supported object types should not exist. Additionally, the framework should be able to integrate new object types in the future.

As the main goal the application has to implement the concepts of distributed knowledge spaces to provide a flexible support of mobile cooperation scenarios. An appropriate persistence with caching mechanisms is fundamental to administer distributed knowledge spaces and ensures the accessibility of objects in the offline case.

On the network part a peer-to-peer approach is crucial for the spontaneous networking support. The peer-to-peer protocol requires service discovery for finding counterparts and configuring the communication mechanisms to remote instances.

The next phase will involve extending the persistence layer with replication and concurrency support. Development of interfaces to existing CSCW systems should be part of further work on the framework.

The first stage was the implementation of a fundamental framework with simple but powerful modules to support mobile cooperation. The next section describes this architecture.

## 5   Base Architecture for Peer-to-Peer Cooperation

The objective to create a mobility aware cooperation platform is therefore to implement the concept of distributed knowledge spaces. The technology basis is with a peer-to-peer architecture supporting multiple types of static and mobile devices. Thus the application has to be platform independent as well as using standardized interfaces and protocols. We chose JXTA for the peer-to-peer communication.

JXTA provides a framework for cross-platform peer-to-peer networking with minimal requirements to the device hardware. While one goal of JXTA is building up a peer-to-peer-based alternative to the Internet for us the JXTA network is only a means to an end for deriving a flexible peer-to-peer framework. Thus we use JXTA only as transport layer and for service discovery. The main feature for us is its network layer abstraction. Regardless of firewalls, routers or network address translators (NAT), the peers appear in a virtual network without any boundaries.

Another important design decision for our implementation is using XML as object description language. Like JXTA XML is software independent and furthermore JXTA uses XML for communication between the peers. XML is an industry standard and because it is extendable future expansions will be easy.

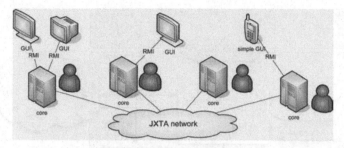

**Fig. 4.** Peer-to-peer connected Swifff cores each assigned to exactly one user. Optionally, the core can be used by one or more user interfaces.

The implementation of our architecture reflects the above advantages. To be as flexible as possible in providing different device specific user interfaces, our application is split into a core and a user interface part.

The communication interfaces are implemented as modules, which can be extended or exchanged. The graphical user interfaces visualize the objects in the knowledge spaces maintained by the core. It is possible to connect more than one user interface to the core while every core instance represents exactly one user of the cooperation environment. In fact it is possible to run a core instance without user interface. From the user interface point of view it may run on a mobile device without local core instance by using a remote one. Fig. 4. illustrates a possible scenario of users, where each is connected to exactly one core but using several or no connected user interfaces.

In the following section we want to discuss the core part and the communication modules of our peer-to-peer cooperation framework. The core is responsible for persistence and object management whereas the modules are mainly responsible for the network communication. For further information to the user interface concepts and implementation refer to [11].

Central component of the core concept is the *object management*. As a first requirement the structure of the objects should be independent of their content. Additionally the content of the objects should not be handled by the core itself but by additional code assigned to the object type. This code is loaded at runtime. This concept allows the extension of the system with new object types without touching the core's implementation.

The core is similar to microkernel architectures in order to substitute single parts if needed. Fig. 5. presents an architecture diagram with the vital *loader* and its persistence module *repository controller*. While the first one manages all object handled by the application, the last one manages the access to the local data repository. External communication is provided through the modules *GUI interface* and *JXTA interface*.

The GUI interface provides access for one or more user interfaces. It uses the *Java remote method invocation (RMI)* protocol, which provides a message scheme between the core and each GUI. The remote method calls are reduced to a necessary minimum. RMI is just responsible for transporting the communication

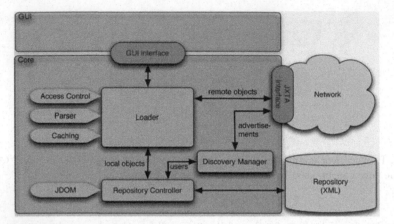

**Fig. 5.** The Swifff component architecture with external communication interfaces for the local GUI and the JXTA network.

data. So RMI may be replaced or supplemented by any other communication protocol if needed for special GUI implementations.

The *JXTA interface* is responsible for all network communication between the peers. It may be replaced or supplemented by a different communication layer in the future. We use the network layer abstraction of JXTA to get an adequate peer-to-peer communication. The *discovery manager* stands tight to the JXTA interface and handles the service discovery. If new potential cooperation partners arise, they are instantly made known in the knowledge space by creating a new user object. Each known user is monitored according to their online status.

The main object management module is the *loader*. All remaining modules are tied to the loader. The *loader* decides if objects are located local or remote. In the first case they are loaded through the *repository controller* from the local repository. In the latter case the *loader* tries to access them over the *JXTA interface* from the remote peer, which hosts the respective the object. This is transparent to the user interfaces. The user interface does not have to take into consideration where the objects are located.

The *caching module*, the *access control module*, and the *parser module* affect the *loader's* behaviour directly. The *caching module* provides performance optimizing for access to remote objects. Every time a remote object is requested for, it is looked up in the cache. The cached object is used if the remote object is the same or an older version. At this time the caching provides no concurrency control. Every time a more current object is detected on a remote peer it is immediately updated albeit the cached object was modified locally. In case of offline remote peers the cache provides their already received objects for further work. When reconnected the objects are synchronized again. Providing a more sophisticated caching module to the loader may change this behaviour.

The *access control module* checks the users permissions concerning a requested object. For this purpose objects provide an *access control list (ACL)*.

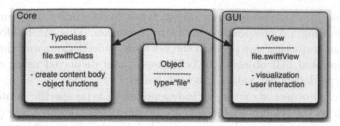

**Fig. 6.** Every object type may provide some views and code for manipulation.

The access rights are checked on every remote access to an object. Actually every access of a connected user interface is treated equally to a network access.

The core's internal object communication is based on XML. Thus the *parser module* provides XSLT as a query language to receive and filter objects. This feature is used for keeping the communication overhead as low as possible. The user interfaces only receive the object properties they really need to present to the user. Assuming reading data happens more often than writing this form of optimization is only done for read access.

The objects processed by the core may be stored in a local repository or on remote peers. The *repository controller module* handles all object operations to the local repository. It uses JDOM as XML document object model for managing the local objects. These objects are stored in the local object repository, which is for now a plain XML file. Dependent on the device's potentials the XML file may be replaced by a database management system (DBMS) or by a layer for distributed persistence. The distributed persistence layer can manage all objects in network by itself. In that case the framework would deal all objects to be stored locally.

Since the modular architecture makes our framework very flexible according its functionality, the design of the objects has to be flexible as well. Otherwise a change of functionality would fail because of static object structures. Thus we chose an open object structure, which allows new object types to plug-in.

Each object features a couple of fixed attributes and a list of associated objects. Because of these references to other objects a graph like structure evolves. Additionally each object type may feature optional attributes defined by the object type. While the default attributes can be found in any object and give an overview of the object properties, the type dependent attributes provide further information useful for each object type.

To display all object properties in the user interface each object type may provide an own visual plug-in we call *view*. The view is delivered to the graphical user interfaces in order to make the object's content visible. Further on the core requires also some extra piece of code for every object type to process the contained data. This code is loadable at runtime and provides functionality in order to manage the objects content. Fig. 6. shows an object type with its view. The management code is provided by the *typeclass*.

Our concept allows adding new object types to the cooperation environment just by providing a corresponding view and typeclass. This can be done at runtime without restarting any peers in the network. Indeed views and management code are optional. All objects can be browsed and displayed using default attributes; type dependent values can be ignored.

The overall object structure is independent to type-specific content and is derived just by the reference lists. The application does not check any constraints to the references because they are provided by the users notion. Again this approach is very flexible in terms of programming and expanding functionality in the future. Fig. 7. shows a representation of some objects in our system. The example consists of five objects. First there are two user objects representing the users Heidi and Peter. Peter's user object references a message received from Heidi and a file object pointing to a text document. The file itself references a note object, which actually is an annotation to the file. The example shows how strongly connected and atomic the objects are. An annotation for example is an attribute of an object represented by a separately saved object.

After introducing the framework architecture, the modules, and the object type concept, we will discuss the data flow of the core. There are three possible ways to route requested objects through the core. First the GUI interface may request for objects stored in the local object repository. Second the GUI interface can request for objects stored on a remote peer. Or third remote peers request for objects from your local repository through the JXTA interface.

When a user interface requests for an object it provides an XSLT query. The query is wrapped into a message and sent to the *GUI interface* via RMI. The *GUI interface* again unwraps it and passes it to the *loader*. Now the *loader* decides if the requested object is contained in the local object repository or on a remote peer.

For objects located in the local repository the query is passed to the *parser module*. The *parser module* requests for the objects from the *repository controller* and the *access control module* checks the result against the objects access control

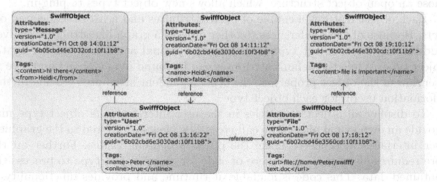

**Fig. 7.** The objects reference lists build up a strongly connected object structure in the knowledge space.

lists. Thereafter the *parser module* filters them according to the query. Finally a XML description of the filtered objects is passed back to the *loader*.

For the objects located on remote peers the query is passed to the *JXTA interface*. The query is wrapped in a JXTA message and sent to the apropiate peer. If a result returns the objects are send back to the *GUI interface*.

In the last case, if the *JXTA interface* receives queries from foreign peers it unwraps it from the message and passes it to the *loader*. From here the query is handled similar to the local user interface request and is routed through the modules mentioned above.

This data flow and the integration of a parser module together avoid an overhead of unnecessary object data passed to the user interface or the JXTA network. The sent object information satisfies the request precisely.

# 6   Conclusion

Because of the broad field of research questions affected by the development of a new mobility supporting collaboration framework, we decided as a first step to build a modular extendable architecture. This open architecture gives the opportunity to expand our system step by step with improved modules and additional functionality.

Another important aspect is the separation of user interface and system core in a network-transparent manner. Devices not able to compute the whole core's functionality can exploit other network-connected devices to provide the required core. So the system is able to scale from low-end devices like smart-phones to powerful devices like high-end laptops or even workstations and servers.

The flexible object design involves, but is not limited to, user interface design. Our concept allows developers to provide new object types with related views and functionality at runtime. A node, not knowing how to handle an object type, can load the views and functionality from other peers.

By using Java, XML, and JXTA we support a wide range of devices and operating systems. Additionally this ensures our solution to be based on open interfaces and standards. Of course later versions of our system may exchange or extend the communication protocols because of our open module architecture.

Since many research topics are affected by our system, not all functionality is fully implemented so far. There exist some fields of activities, which may solve typical problems of such dynamic environments. One field of activity deals with the term of saving data persistently even when the primarily providing device is leaving the network. There are attempts in *Swifff* to replicate every new object to several other peers. The intention behind this approach was to give a high grade of availability to the data stored in the *Swifff* community. Members of a team should be able to work on a shared object even when the object's owner has already left the network. From this demand a lot of known problems like concurrency control arise. Merging different versions of the same object from two peers is a known high-grade difficult matter.

Although some of this comprehensive functionality is missing, our approach provides a mobility-supporting cooperative environment based on open standards and open interfaces. Our *Swifff*-framework is therefore a first step to develop a peer-to-peer open architecture for distributed knowledge spaces. With its object distribution mechanisms and support for ad-hoc networks it allows us to research new forms of mobility in cooperative knowledge management.

## Acknowledgements

Joanna Slawik and Bernd Eßmann are members of the postgraduate program 776 "Automatic Configuration in Open Systems" funded by the German Research Foundation (DFG) and the Heinz Nixdorf Institute.

## References

1. Perkins, C.E.: Ad Hoc Networking, Addison Weseley (2001).
2. Feeney, L. M., Ahlgren, B., Westerlund, A.: Spontaneous Networking: An Application-oriented Approach to Ad Hoc Networking, in: IEEE Communications Magazin, Volume 39, (2001), 176-181.
3. Hampel, T., Keil-Slawik, R.: sTeam – Designing an integrative infrastructure for Web-based computer-supported cooperative learning, in: Proceedings of the tenth international conference on World Wide Web (2001), 76-85.
4. Hampel, T., Keil-Slawik, R.: sTeam: structuring information in team-distributed knowledge management in cooperative learning environments, in: Journal on Educational Resources in Computing (JERIC) Volume 1, Issue 2, (Summer 2001), Article No. 3 ACM Press.
5. Milojicic, D. S., Kalogeraki, V., Lukose, R., Nagaraja, K., Pruyne, J., Richard, B., Rollins, S., Xu, Z.: Peer-to-Peer Computing, Technical Report, http://www.hpl.hp.com/techreports/2002/HPL-2002-57R1.html, (2002).
6. Edwards, K. W., Newman, M. W., Sedivy, J. Z., Smith, T. F., Izadi, S.: Challenge: Recombinant Computing and the Speakeasy Approach, in: Proceedings of Mobicom '02. (September 2002), 279-286.
7. Edwards, K. W., Newman, M. W., Sedivy, J. Z., Smith, T. F., Balfanz, D., Smetters, D. K., Wong, H. C., Izadi, S.: Using Speakeasy for Ad Hoc Peer to Peer Collaboration, in Proceedings of CSCW '02, (November 2002), 256-265.
8. Gong, L. (2001): JXTA: A network programming environment, in: IEEE Internet Computing, Volume 5, (2001), 88-95.
9. Eßmann, B., Hampel, T.: Integrating Cooperative Knowledge spacess into Mobile Environments, in: Rossett, Allison: Proceedings of E-Learn, AACE Press, (2003), 2067-2074.
10. Eßmann, B., Hampel, T., Bopp, T.: A Network Component Architecture for Collaboration in Mobile Settings, in: Proceedings of the 6th International Conference on Enterprise Information Systems 2004 (ICEIS 2004), Porto, Portugal, Volume 4, (April 2004), 337-343.
11. Slawik, J., Eßmann, B., Hampel, T.: Shared Views on Mobile Knowledge – a Concept of a Graphical User Interface, to be published in: Lecture Notes in Computer Science, Springer Publishing House (2004).

# Towards an Evaluation Framework
# for Knowledge Management Systems

Folker Folkens and Myra Spiliopoulou

Institute of Technical and Business Information Systems
Otto-von-Guericke University Magdeburg

**Abstract.** Companies are not adequately able to assess the contribution of system infrastructure managing the admittedly most valuable asset, their knowledge. This paper presents a framework for ex-post evaluation of Knowledge Management Systems (KMS). The framework explained focuses on evaluation of knowledge management components and their functionality within an organization, so that appropriate integration techniques can be designed for each of those. For this purpose, the framework outlines dependencies and links between important corporate knowledge intensive entities for the purpose of evaluation. All phases of knowledge management in organizations are described and divided into functions of different corporation specific relevance, based on acknowledged categorization authored in literature. Improvement of inadequate knowledge methods, by evaluation and, as a possible result of assessment, integration/migration for more suitable methods of corporate knowledge management, defines the target of pigeonholing research to come.

**Keywords:** Knowledge Management Systems, Evaluation, Model, Framework, Information Systems Success

## 1 Introduction

Knowledge is the most important asset for companies today. It has become the most momentous resource and competitive advantage. As Drucker [8] stated, traditional factors of production (land, natural resources, labor, capital and so forth) have become secondary. The intellectual factor rose as the traditional ones shrunk and that process is continuing. Thus, knowledge is a key factor to focus on, to keep, to acquire, to create, to externalize, to share and to use. KMS are to support these tasks, though not necessarily all of them likewise, as will be discussed. When it comes to evaluation in knowledge management, there are two scopes, Intellectual Capital (IC) and systems managing knowledge. While IC evaluation assesses non-physical or intangible assets of a company [17], KMS evaluation stresses measurement of contribution of systems managing knowledge. We focus on the latter. While firms spend many resources and investing in infrastructure to support knowledge management, the effect of efforts made has neither been evaluated nor *proper* improvements fitting the company have been identified. Swaak and Lansink [25] argue that this is caused by insufficient instruments to measure and evaluate KMS. There are a lot of studies on metrics

D. Karagiannis and U. Reimer (Eds.): PAKM 2004, LNAI 3336, pp. 23–34, 2004.

in place, as will be discussed in the next section. Those studies use a number of metrics, each adapted to the given environment and needs. Unfortunately, it has not been possible to generalize metrics, so that each of the studies uses different ones, though subsets may be similar. Gable and Sedera [10] analyzed several Enterprize System Success studies, concluding, too, that varying results are a consequence of incomplete or inappropriate measures as well as lack of theoretical grounding, myopic on financial indicators or weakness in survey instruments employed. Metrics have been employed for assessment of system success, ex-ante and ex-post likewise. Since the system infrastructure to be evaluated is already in place for evaluation and later integration/migration in focus of this paper, ex-post evaluation is discussed here. Once lacks have been identified, those have to be corrected by new or improved methods. Other (probably non-technical) actions to take, i.e. organizational restructuring might be a choice but this is not of interest for now. The consequences of measurement results is another research issue to be discussed later.

Focusing KMS, the target for evaluation and measurement has been set: What is the contribution of the KMS in use and does it reach its potential? To answer these questions, metrics for measurement have to be formulated. Those metrics have to be knowledge management specific, since a knowledge management system has to be assessed. As stated before, a lot of studies on evaluation of systems using metrics had been done. Although, the metrics in each of the studies were formulated for the specific purpose. In this paper a framework for KMS evaluation is formulated, that approaches to provide a structure for metrics classification. Hereunto, knowledge management is firstly categorized into knowledge functions to associate metrics to those. Section 3.1 outlines which granularity is considered to be best and describes those knowledge functions. The model manifested in section 3 provides a framework specifically designed for evaluation of systems managing knowledge and thus, metrics for KMS evaluation have to be addressed. For that, firstly related work of areas is examined in the following section 2, followed by an explanation of knowledge management functions in section 3, that will picture cumulative knowledge management divided into functions. Thereafter, the framework of knowledge management system evaluation is described. Section 4 finally concludes this paper.

## 2    Related Work on System Evaluation

Many researchers evaluate KMS from an IS (Information Systems) point of view. DeLone and McLean created the most cited and accepted evaluation model [5, 6] in IS evaluation research so far. They analyzed relevant literature, which decades of research came up with regarding evaluation models and concluded those into a multidimensional model for IS evaluation. This model has been widely accepted, served as a basis for further evaluation research and has been used for empirical studies [3]. Nonetheless, the model was not designed to fit knowledge management purposes and it does therefore not consider knowledge management aspects. Maier and Hädrich [16] approached to suit the DeLone and McLean model to the demands of knowledge management for KMS evaluation. For this, they changed model components and assigned success factors to their two kinds of KMS: interactive systems and integrative systems. Interactive systems support humans communicating tacit knowledge, while integrative systems focus on aiding externalization and internalization using a central knowledge base (i.e. repository). There are other valuable approaches existent for KMS evaluation. Those are the deductive approaches Tobin's q [18] and Calculated Intangible Value [22] as well as the inductive analytical approaches Intellectual Capital Approach [22], Intangible Assets Monitor [24], Intellectual Capital Navigator [22], Balanced Scorecard [15] and Skandia Navigator [21], for which we agree with Maier and Hädrich to be insufficiently operationalized to accomplish KMS assessment. There, Kankanhalli and Tan [14] as well as Maier and Hädrich argue, that KMS success is evaluated at an abstract level that is influenced by an unmanageable and unstructured amount of factors. Furthermore Kankanhalli and Tan [14] provide a literature overview, where they analyzed measures and metrics for KMS evaluation. They found, that generalizable metrics are lacking, though they are desirable. Metrics are measures of key attributes that yield information about a phenomenon [23]. Metrics are well suited and even necessary to reveal coherences. In addition, several authors [2, 7, 13] argue that proper measurement requires adapted metrics.

Probst and Romhardt [20] divided knowledge management into several modules/functions. The widely acknowledged classification characterizes knowledge management in organizations by definition of functions/tasks[1] to accomplish. The classification model does not ground on a theoretical derivation. It was created in a practical environment, group discussions and interviews with practitioners. For this purpose, practice-orientation is intended to make KMS evaluation applicable. The Probst and Romhardt knowledge model has been widely accepted and will serve as a basis for the framework in discussion here. Furthermore, the classification encompasses a holistic concept of knowledge management and it serves as a basis for further research on systems for knowledge management. We take this categorization to build a frame for classification of factors for KMS evaluation. Thus, it will serve as a structure for existing metrics. The existing metrics are valuable, but extensive, not generalizable and not manageable because of the extent. This paper approaches to provide a structure for metrics towards KMS evaluation.

As opposed to other evaluation approaches, like the one of Maier and Hädrich [16], we seek to create an extendable framework for evaluation by integration of metrics. Furthermore, our frame bases on the Probst and Romhardt categorization of knowledge management functions [20]. We think that this classification represents corporate knowledge management best, as will be discussed in the next section. The framework is oriented on the corporate environment and targets, that will be reflected by the metrics used. Furthermore, Iversen and Kautz note that Implementation of metrics needs very clear goals as well as 'right'

---

[1] The terms "knowledge task" and "knowledge function" have been used in several articles likewise and mean the same. Here, we use the terminus "knowledge function".

metrics [13]. That is, metrics have to be adapted to the corporate goal and the evaluation purpose as will be taken into account and it is important in our point of view and further motivates the framework.

# 3 Evaluation of Knowledge Management Systems

The purpose of KMS is to support corporate knowledge management. Firstly, this section describes what knowledge management consists of and how to separate it into functions. Afterwards a framework is depicted, which bases on the functions given. This new approach assesses knowledge management functions and with this, the accomplishment of those by KMS.

## 3.1 Knowledge Management Functions

Focusing the different areas of knowledge management, some approaches to distinguish those will be encountered. These areas supported by knowledge management functions differ mostly in granularity. While Davenport and Prusak [4] identify three tasks of knowledge management, generation, codification/coordination and transfer, Probst [20] distinguishes eight tasks. Those tasks are functions of knowledge management to support the company. For the purpose of system evaluation, the knowledge management separation of Probst is the most appropriate one. The differentiating classification ensues a target oriented management. It structures the management process in logical tasks and provides clues for intervention. That can not be ensured using the grosser granularity of Davenport and Prusak for instance. Last but not least, the Probst separation is a proven mechanism to search for reasons for knowledge problems [20, 19, 12]. Therefore, this classification is appropriate to underlie the presented evaluation approach of this paper.

The importance of the functions given by Probst [20, 19, 12] differs significantly from one company to the next. Mertins and Heising [17] exposed significant differences regarding Knowledge Management Functions in organizations in their survey. Their findings[2] are embodied in Table 1. Through this, the distinction between the importance of knowledge management functions between diverse organizations is highlighted. Thus, organizations do have different demands on knowledge management functions, so that no generic evaluation method, that does not include those differences, is appropriate.

Recapitulating, knowledge management can be broken down into parts or functions to be supported [17, 12, 20, 19, 9]: knowledge identification, knowledge acquisition, knowledge creation, knowledge distribution, knowledge utilization

---

[2] Knowledge Management Functions have been adapted to a unique terminology regarding publications on that field/i.e. Mertins and Heising [17] refer to 'apply knowledge', while Probst and Romhardt [20] as well as Heinrich [12] call this 'knowledge distribution' and finally Alavi and Leidner [1] term it 'knowledge transfer'. The same slight difference appears with 'knowledge goals' and 'knowledge targets' or 'store knowledge' and 'knowledge preservation' etc.

**Table 1.** Importance of Knowledge Management Functions within various organizations. A 5-point Likert-scale has been used in the survey. The table aggregates the results of Mertins and Heising [17].

| Knowledge Management Functions | Important | Medium | Less Important |
|---|---|---|---|
| Definition of Knowledge Targets | 48% | 32% | 20% |
| Identification | 65% | 24% | 11% |
| Utilization | 96% | 3% | 1% |
| Creation | 84% | 8% | 8% |
| Distribution | 91% | 7% | 2% |
| Preservation | 78% | 16% | 6% |

and knowledge preservation. Knowledge evaluation and definition of knowledge targets are superordinate for evaluation of roles for knowledge functions in an organization. The definitions given below combine literature cited above. Although methods to support those functions have not yet been discussed in literature, we provide a first classification below. Additionally, a categorization is given, stating what the importance of each function usually depends on.

*Knowledge Identification* supports to make knowledge visible. The bigger the company the more difficult it is to identify existing knowledge. The lacking transparency causes inefficiencies, "uninformed" decisions/actions and redundancies. Effective knowledge management must accomplish transparency and support humans searching for knowledge. The importance of knowledge identification in a company depends on company objectives, infrastructure and company culture.

Ontologies, Knowledge Maps, Search Engines and information retrieval techniques in general are examples of appropriate methods to implement Identification.

*Knowledge Acquisition* supports to obtain knowledge. No company is able to produce all needed knowledge itself. Know-how, which a company can not develop itself, has to be acquired. That can be accomplished by acquiring innovative companies, recruiting experts, buying documents from outside sources, hire consultants, buy patents and so forth. Relationships with customers, suppliers, competitors and partners do also serve potential external sources for knowledge. KMS may point to external sources, if the desired knowledge is not available within the company. The importance of knowledge Acquisition depends on company culture and objectives.

Methods to implement Acquisition are i.e. data bases containing indices of external sources potentially valuable for the company.

*Knowledge Creation* supports to generate knowledge. Development of new knowledge in an organization focuses on creating new products, better ideas, more efficient processes or new skills. This cannot be bought on the market, it does not fit needs or is basically too expensive, so that development is desirable. Non-existent knowledge is usually generated in the research department. Nevertheless, creativity to develop new ideas or not yet present capabilities takes place throughout the company, so that knowledge creation is mostly not limited to just one (research) department. Furthermore, expert systems might help to develop, visualize or combine knowledge, so that new conclusions can be drawn and new knowledge can be created. It is essential that created knowledge will be preserved in any kind of "lessons learned" in a KMS, so that it will be available whenever needed. Importance of knowledge Creation depends on company culture, company objective and innovation/research efforts.

Methods to implement Creation are all kinds of data mining and learning tools [1].

*Knowledge Distribution* supports to share knowledge. Knowledge has to be made available throughout the company. Usage of knowledge requires availability. That is spreading and sharing know-how which is already present within the organization. This function goes hand-in-hand with knowledge identification, which supports spread of knowledge. The importance of knowledge distribution depends on the size of the company, infrastructure, company objective, culture and velocity of company regarding knowledge [4].

Suitable methods to implement Distribution are knowledge directories/maps, discussion forums and electronic bulletin boards as well as semantic annotation of documents and communication technology in general.

*Knowledge Utilization* supports to apply knowledge. Simple availability does not guarantee that present knowledge is indeed used. Knowledge Identification and Distribution is a precondition to successfully apply knowledge. This still does not ensure utilization, but the chance of usage of highly available and distributed knowledge does increase. Knowledge has to be trusted before routines or practices are changed due to better procedures for example. Ensuring the usage of KMS might positively influence applying new knowledge and prevent sticking to "unchangeable" old habits[3]. Furthermore, utilization means to assist knowledge workers to apply implemented knowledge. The importance of knowledge utilization depends on the complexity of problems, company culture, trust of knowledge sources and company infrastructure. Furthermore, the design of system interfaces may greatly influence Utilization [26].

Possible Implementation of Utilization is associated with expert systems, decision support systems and well designed user interfaces.

*Knowledge Preservation* supports to store knowledge. Companies often lose competencies due to reorganization processes or simply time. Knowledge preservation aims on retention of knowledge assets. Potentially valuable future knowledge has to be selected, structured, updated, made available and stored for time to come. This has to be accomplished by efficient storage media as well as KMS to access knowledge, to prevent valuable expertise to disappear. Selection of potentially valuable knowledge is of importance, since a huge amount of data, information/knowledge stored will eventually lack trust of people, if they do not

---

[3] This does not mean to *force* people to use a KMS, but to design the KMS in a way that it indeed serves the desired purpose and constitutes an advantage for people using it/applying the provided knowledge.

find *proper* knowledge in a huge database[4]. The importance of Preservation depends on the viscosity of knowledge to store [4], amount of knowledge accruing, company objective, infrastructure and culture.

Appropriate Methods to implement Preservation are efficient information retrieval techniques, organizational memory to manage experiences made in the past for future utilization as well as data bases and data warehouses.

*Definition of Knowledge Targets* defines knowledge importance roles. Concrete objectives deviate from roles, so that the definition of targets is superordinate. Those roles define the importance of any knowledge management function for the company. Thus, definition of targets goes hand in hand with evaluation. Skills and technology to be developed and integrated have to be identified beforehand through an appropriate evaluation. Although evaluation does include measurement of defined targets as well. Targets will be a result of the mutual evaluation procedure and company objectives.

*Knowledge Evaluation* assesses knowledge. Evaluation of roles and through this, the possible redefinition of importance roles may be a result, as stated above. Furthermore, the current concrete company objectives regarding knowledge management have to be evaluated as compared to technology supporting these objectives.

## 3.2 The Evaluation Framework

A significant part of this paper is dedicated to specification and exposure of the concept 'importance' and its linkage to knowledge functions. It has been made clear that such strategy is necessary for the evaluation of KMS.

The framework developed by the authors of this paper shows a holistic view of knowledge management system evaluation. It is a consolidation of the work of several cited authors as well as a concluding idea which bears on publications cited in section 2. The framework of knowledge management evaluation is based on the knowledge functions given in the previous section a holistic knowledge frame was created, which pictures knowledge management within a company. This will help to understand knowledge management within companies to develop methodologies for proper assessment of KMS in use. It applies to various fields like metrics definition or evaluation of corporate knowledge working efficiency. The semantics of the Unified Modeling Language (UML) is used to describe the model. UML, as the most widely accepted modeling semantic is well suited to clearly express dependencies and links between model components. Furthermore, the semantic is popularly understood, which makes it easier for the message to come across.

Let us begin with what the previous section came up with, knowledge functions. Companies do have different demands towards knowledge functions. A consultant company has another need for knowledge than a freight forwarder,

---

[4] This is often caused by bad precision and recall rates

for instance. The demanding for knowledge bases on the functions given before in this section. Concluding the findings of section 3.1, companies do have different demands, the "importance roles". An "importance role" expresses the specific demand for one of the knowledge functions of a company. For example, a company may have a higher demand for methods that implement the knowledge function "Identification". In table 1 of the previous section such differences of knowledge functions are outlined and that the demand for functions differs significantly. Knowledge Functions are implemented by knowledge methods as Figure 1 depicts. This means, knowledge methods are dedicated to functions and realize those. Some examples are given in section 3.1. All methods supporting one function summarized express the contribution to a function. A method can be dedicated to one or more functions and vice versa.

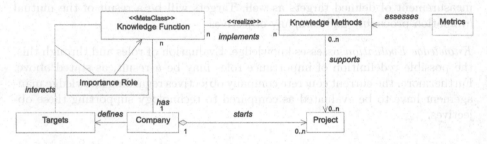

**Fig. 1.** Creating a context for Evaluation of KMS: Evaluation assesses Knowledge Functions and Importance Roles and knowledge methods to measure the real contribution of KMS.

Companies are different in their objectives, which is reflected in their targets. Targets have to be taken into account when selecting the importance of the knowledge functions. The result of this deliberation results into the importance role construct. To operationalize this, we take the target and map it to knowledge functions. Is of interest which knowledge function is important and which is less important to support accomplishment of the company target regarding knowledge management. Then chose appropriate methods that are dedicated to the functions, to support the needed functions. This procedure will be guided through by usage of metrics. Metrics are needed to assess knowledge methods which do implement functions including their importance represented by the importance roles. Functions and importance roles then reflect the targets of the company. There are two evaluation procedures implied. The importance role has to be set for each knowledge function by evaluation. Furthermore, assessment of knowledge methods represents the current contribution of the methods in use and with this, the KMS. Nonetheless, a concrete definition of metrics is not part of the framework so far. Further research will complete a more and more operational view for which we provide a first frame.

For the frame and the interaction itself, it is less important to qualify the metrics object in detail. Operationalizing the framework, it becomes much more

important. In the end, evaluation is all about metrics and measurement. At this
stage of abstraction, metrics do not have to be defined yet. Further work will have
to accomplish completing the puzzle. Nonetheless, the metrics context will be
defined here. There are three specializations that have to be taken into account,
Relevance, Quality and Availability that have to be measured for each knowledge
method. Relevance specifies the pertinence of the knowledge method, Quality
describes how good the method indeed fulfills the requirements and Availability
assesses if the method is on-hand for people who need it. Each of those specialized
metrics are dedicated to a set of metrics to assess methods. The selected metrics
take into account, that the relevance of the metrics is directly influenced by the
importance role of the dedicated knowledge function. That implicates a direct
relationship of targets and metrics used to express the corporate knowledge goal.
With this, the actual support of methods towards knowledge functions has to
be evaluated to discover the real contribution of methods in use.

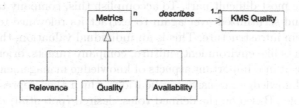

**Fig. 2.** Metrics for Evaluation of KMS.

Methods serve the purpose, in the end, to support knowledge intensive projects and thus, the company which performs the projects. The project construct
represents all kinds of knowledge tasks people or groups of people have to accomplish to succeed with their (knowledge intensive) assignment. That implicates
for metrics definition, that measurement has to assess the support and accomplishment of projects/support of humans regarding their assignment. Measures
regarding the KMS methods therefore include time savings, decision support or
goal achievement for instance.

Focusing the core message of the framework in figure 3, there are two kinds
of evaluation: The importance roles of knowledge functions, specific to the company, which have to be revalued and comparison of actual and desired contribution of methods. Knowledge importance roles of a company have to be discovered, so that appropriate methods can be applied to support functions properly.
Non-observance of knowledge roles may lead to overexpansion[5], wastefulness[6] or
squandering[7]. The framework therefore implicates, that each knowledge function
is implemented by methods. To assess these methods and its contribution to the
company, knowledge roles have to be revalued first. Determination of roles is

---

[5] Low efficiency and low effectivity [11].
[6] Low efficiency and high effectivity [11].
[7] High efficiency and low effectivity [11].

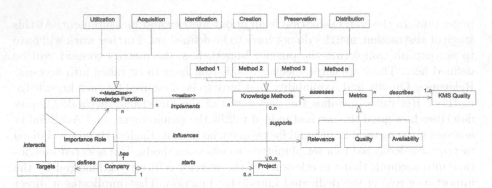

**Fig. 3.** The UML Evaluation Model for KMS describes links and dependencies of relevant components for system evaluation.

likely to be the most difficult part. To accomplish this, company targets have to be reviewed and scrutinized over again to extract its relevance towards knowledge and system infrastructure. This is an individual valuation, that reconsiders company aspects like environment, culture, company targets, orientation and so forth and turns it into important aspects of knowledge management. The conversion extracts knowledge intensive implications which then represent the entity 'importance role'. Based on the defined roles, desired (potential) contribution of functions has to be compared to the actual contribution. Measurement and thus comparison has to be accomplished by using metrics.

A set of metrics measures the efficiency and effectiveness of each function by assessing KMS methods implementing those. With this, the actual contribution of methods is assessed and compared to the desired/potential contribution: to meet requirements of importance roles of knowledge functions. These constructs are essential for evaluation of KMS.

The measurement of the constructs on which KMS quality depends, can be accomplished by using metrics. Currently, scholarship of metrics and generalizable measurement techniques in the field of KMS evaluation are lacking [17, 14, 16]. Therefore, more research on that field is needed and will follow, to apply the framework of KMS evaluation presented here.

## 4    Conclusion and Outlook

Systematic evaluation of benefits of KMS still falls behind. Users content themselves with success stories or surveys of satisfaction with KMS [16]. Despite multiple success stories it was not possible to sufficiently measure the success of KMS [25]. The framework presented in this paper outlines a first step towards holistic KMS evaluation. Therewith, this frame depicts a meta level, while metrics and measurement techniques have to be developed and applied with the framework. Furthermore, improvements of knowledge functions through methods enable maximum utilization, if evaluation concludes that there is an unused potential existent in the company, which would end up in a benefit. However, to avoid a competitive disadvantage, the required methods will have to be integrated. That can be accomplished through a possible migration of the KMS towards potential knowledge functions. Redevelopment or purchase of a suitable system might also be desirable. What to do best after a successful evaluation is dependent on the evaluation result, the constraints[8] as well as on the methods used. This paper draws a holistic picture of KMS evaluation and bespeaks links and dependencies in a frame. Although, further research is required to fill the frame. With this framework coming research pigeonholes to finally provide holistic methodology of KMS evaluation. Firstly, metrics will have to be specified to make the framework applicable. Secondly, an overview of knowledge methods available will help assigning methods to knowledge functions to be supported within the company. Thirdly, migration strategies will have to be discussed for integration of required knowledge methods. These issues characterize research requirements to come for holistic evaluation of KMS.

# References

1. M. Alavi and D.E. Leidner. Review: Knowledge Management and Knowledge Management Systems: Conceptual Foundations and Research Issues. *MIS Quarterly, Vol. 25, No. 1, 107-136.*, 2001.
2. J. Ballantine, M. Bonner, M. Levy, A. Martin, I. Munro, and P.L. Powell. Common Framework for the Evaluation Process of KBS and Conventional Software. *Knowledge-Based Systems Journal, Vol. 11, No. 2, 145-160.*, 1998.
3. J. Ballantine, M. Bonner, M. Levy, A. Martin, I. Munro, and P.L. Powell. The 3-D Model of Information Systems Success: the Search for the Dependent Variable Continues. *Information Resources Management Journal, Vol. 9, No. 4, 5-14.*, 2002.
4. T. H. Davenport and L. Prusak. *Working Knowledge - How Organisations manage what they know*. Havard Business School Press, 1998.
5. W.H. Delone and E.R. McLean. Information Systems Success: The Quest for the Dependent Variable. *Information Systems Research 3, 1 , 60-95.*, 1992.
6. W.H. Delone and E.R. McLean. Information Systems Success: Revisited. In *Proceedings of the 35th Annual Hawaii International Conference on System Sciences, Volume 8, 238*, 2002.
7. Chief Information Officer Department of the Navy. Metrics Guide for Knowledge Management Initiatives, 2001.
8. Peter Drucker. *Post-Capitalist Society*. Butterworth-Heinemann, Oxford United Kingdom, 1993.
9. R. Franken and R. Gadatsch. *Integriertes Knowledge Management. Konzepte, Methoden, Instrumente, Fallbeispiele*. Vieweg, Wiesbaden, 2002.
10. Guy G. Gable, Darshana Sedera, and Taizan Chan. Enterprise Systems Success: A Measurement Model. In *Proceedings of the International Conference on Information Systems 2003*, 2003.
11. L. J. Heinrich, I. Häntschel, and G. Pomberger. Diagnose der Informationsverarbeitung. *CONTROLLING, Vol. 3, 196-203.*, 1997.

---

[8] I.e. corporate environment, company culture, estimated return on investment and so forth.

12. Lutz J. Heinrich. *Informationsmanagement.* Oldenbourg Verlag München, 2002.
13. J. Iversen and K. Kautz. The Challenge of Metrics Implementation. In *Proceedings of the 23rd Information Systems Research Seminar in Scandinavia,* 2000.
14. A. Kankanhalli and B. C.Y. Tan. A Review of Metrics for Knowledge Management Systems and Knowledge Management Initiatives. In *Proceedings of the 37th Hawaii International Conference on System Sciences,* 2004.
15. Robert S. Kaplan and David P. Norton. *The Balanced Scorecard: Translating Strategy into Action.* Havard Business School Press, Boston, 1996.
16. R. Maier and T. Hädrich. Ein Modell für die Erfolgsmessung von Wissensmanagementsystemen. *WIRTSCHAFTSINFORMATIK, Vol. 43, No. 5, 497-508.,* 2001.
17. K. Mertins, P. Heisig, and J. Vorbeck. *Knowledge Management: Concepts and Best Practices.* Springer -Verlag, Berlin Heidelberg, 2003.
18. K. North, G. Probst, and K. Romhardt. Wissen messen - Ansätze, Erfahrungen und kritische Fragen. *zfo - Zeitschrift für Führung und Organization, Vol. 67, 158-166.,* 1998.
19. G. Probst, S. Raub, and K. Romhardt. *Managing Knowledge.* Springer -Verlag, Berlin Heidelberg, 1999.
20. G. Probst and K. Romhardt. Bausteine des Wissensmanagements - ein praxisorientierter Ansatz. *Handbuch Lernende Organisation, Gabler, Wiesbaden, 129-144.,* 1997.
21. D.J. Skyrme and D.M. Amidon. New Measures of Success. *Journal of Business Strategy, Vol. 40, 20-24.,* 1998.
22. Thomas Stewart. *Intellectual Capital: The New Wealth of Organizations.* New York, Currency/Doubleday, 1997.
23. D. W. Straub, D. L. Hoffman, B.W. Weber, and C. Steinfield. Measuring e-Commerce in Net-Enabled Organizations: An Introduction to the Special Issue. *Information Systems Research Vol 13, No. 2, 115-124.,* 2002.
24. Karl Erik Sveiby. *The New Organizational Wealth : Managing and Measuring Knowledge-Based Assets.* Berrett-Koehler, San Fransisco, 1997.
25. J. Swaak, A. Lansink, E. Heeren, B. Hendriks, P. Kalff, J.-W. den Oudsten, R. Böhmer, R. Bakker, and C. Verwijs. Measuring knowledge management investments and results; two business cases. In *Proceedings of the 59th AEPF Conference, Bremen,* 2000.
26. Ivo Wessel. *GUI Design.* Carl Hanser Verlag, München Wien, 2002.

# I-KNOW What You Will Know in Knowledge Management

## Current and Future Trends in Knowledge Management

Klaus Tochtermann[1,2], Gisela Dösinger[2], and Ines Puntschart[2]

[1] Graz University of Technology
[2] Know-Center Graz, Inffeldgasse 21a, 8010 Graz, Austria
{ktochter,gdoes,ipunt}@know-center.at

**Abstract.** The objective of this paper is to provide an indication about future trends in knowledge management. For this purpose a total of more than 380 papers submitted to the I-KNOW conference during the last three years were analyzed at different levels. This paper presents the methodology used which in addition to an intellectual analysis is also comprised of a computer-supported knowledge discovery analysis. The main insights gained by the analysis are that knowledge discovery, knowledge representation and knowledge distribution & sharing belong to the most intriguing topics of current and future research in knowledge management.

## 1 Introduction

As stated by the Center for Research on Information Technology and Organizations at the University of California (CRITO 2004) about two decades ago knowledge management evolved as a strategic task within companies as a response to downsizing and in parallel as a research topic dealt with by academics. Since then, industry and academia have put forth a great deal of technologies, solutions, models, methods, and lessons learned, all serving for an easier handling of knowledge. Diverse disciplines such as information sciences, organizational sciences, and even psychology and sociology - separately or in cooperation - have engaged in knowledge management. Today one can separate the research activities in this area along the following three lines: Technology-oriented knowledge management focuses on how to use information technologies as enabling technologies for knowledge management. Human-oriented knowledge management places the emphasis on human resource development and, finally, organizational knowledge management puts the organization itself and its culture in the centre of knowledge management.

The research community meets regularly at important, mostly international conferences to share experiences in these fields. Often special workshops/conferences exist for in-depth discussions in each of these areas (e.g., the International Semantic Web Conference 2004 for technology-oriented knowledge management ISCW 2004). Since the late nineties also conference series have established which are aiming at contributions which provide an integrated view on knowledge management. The most prominent of these conferences are the PAKM (Practical Aspects of Knowledge Management, www.dke.univie.ac.at/pakm2004/.), I-KNOW (International Conference on Knowledge Management, www.i-know.at), the European Conference on Knowledge Management (www.academic-conferences.org/eckm2004/eckm2004-home.htm) and the Professional Knowledge Management Conference (wm2005.iese.fraunhofer.de/).

D. Karagiannis and U. Reimer (Eds.): PAKM 2004, LNAI 3336, pp. 35–45, 2004.
© Springer-Verlag Berlin Heidelberg 2004

These conferences represent a huge treasure of information about current and future developments in knowledge management. Unfortunately, the research community gets only access to those contributions which are accepted by the international expert committees of these conferences. But the fact that a submission was rejected does not necessarily mean that the submission is of low quality – particularly if one takes into account that the acceptance rate of some of the conferences is below 40%. With this in background the analysis of future knowledge management trends on the basis of the conference proceedings can only provide a limited picture. Therefore, the objective of this paper is to present the analysis of all submissions we have received for the I-KNOW conference series in order to deduce what are "hot" current and future topics in knowledge management. The total of about 380 submissions for I-KNOW coming from more than 30 different nations during the last three years serves a sound statistical basis for our analysis.

The remainder of the paper is structured as follows: Section 2 briefly provides some background information about the I-KNOW conference. In Section 3 we describe the methodologies we used to analyse all submissions. Section 4 presents the main results of our analysis. Before Section 6 concludes the paper, Section 5 discusses related literature.

## 2  The I-KNOW Conference Series at a Glance

The I-KNOW is a conference series on knowledge management serving as an international platform on which attendees can present, discuss, and exchange their experiences in knowledge management. I-KNOW brings together practitioners and academics to learn from each other and to share experiences with one another. One aim of I-KNOW is to cover human-oriented, organizational as well as technology-oriented aspects of knowledge management acknowledging that all are integral parts of successful knowledge management tools, methods and strategies.

The I-KNOW conference series started in 2001 with about 150 attendees, grew to about 250 attendees in 2002, 300 attendees in 2003, and 340 attendees in 2004. After 2001 when only invited speakers gave presentations, a review process was established according to the common rules of international conferences (i.e. international expert committee, each paper is reviewed by at least three reviewers etc.). Since 2002 about 380 papers from more than 30 nations have been submitted to I-KNOW out of which on average 45% were accepted for publication in one of the conference proceedings.

## 3  Methodology

In order to systematically analyse more than 380 submissions, we had to decide on a sound methodology. This methodology consists of four steps:

*Step 1 – Selection of categorization schemes:* The purpose of this step is to bring all papers in some order which would facilitate the analysis.

*Step 2 – Categorization:* The purpose of this step is to categorize all papers into the categorisation schemes.

*Step3 – In-depth analysis:* The purpose of this step is to conduct an in-depth analysis of selected categories and to identify currently "hot" topics and future trends in knowledge management.

*Step 4 – Computer-supported verification of "hot" topics:* The purposes of this step are to apply computer tools for the analysis of "hot" topics and to verify the results of step 2 and partly of step 3.

## 3.1 Selection of Categorization Schemes

A systematic categorization of the 380 papers was considered to be a mandatory prerequisite for a sound analysis of the papers.

The first categorization scheme we used for ordering our papers was the distinction of whether a paper addresses human-oriented, organizational or technology-oriented aspects of knowledge management. With this classification we got a first rough idea about the main foci of our papers.

For the second categorization scheme we needed much finer categories as we wanted to categorize the thematic topics of the papers. Early candidates were the ACM Computing Classification System or an innovative knowledge and information management taxonomy as proposed by Giaglis (Giaglis 2002). These schemes, however, did not cover equally all aspects of knowledge management. For example, it is difficult to classify a human-oriented paper on knowledge management in the ACM scheme which was originally designed for computer science (ACM 1998). Such papers can only fall in the categories A0 (General Literature) or Am (miscellaneous). Of course these categories are too weak to really express what the paper is all about. Other categorization schemes are provided by various knowledge management portals (e.g. MetaKM 2004, KnowledgeBoard 2004). We saw again two main problems when applying them: firstly, the categorisation schemes are rather arbitrary and reflect the view of individual communities. Secondly, they do not sufficiently cover the broad range of topics our conference deals with. Since many of the contributions would have remained unclassified or improperly classified when using a classification scheme we decided for another approach: We classified the contributions according to different steps in knowledge processes and knowledge management concepts (e.g., Heisig 2001, Strohmaier 2003, and European Guide to Good Practice in Knowledge Management 2004). To achieve an appropriate scheme we went through different cycles during which we classified a sample of 45 contributions to continuously refined preliminary schemes. At the end of this process we came up with the following categories:

– Discovery, Search, Retrieval, Identification, Capturing, Analysis, Extraction
– Acquisition, Creation
– Storage
– Distribution, Sharing, Transfer, Exchange, Collaboration
– Utilisation
– Representation, Structuring, Synchronisation
– Presentation, Visualisation
– General.

For the sake of completeness we would like to mention that the few contributions (less than 2%) which address an overview on knowledge management could not be well categorized with this scheme. They fall into the category "general" and were not further considered. The following figure briefly shows an excerpt of our contribution-category-matrix:

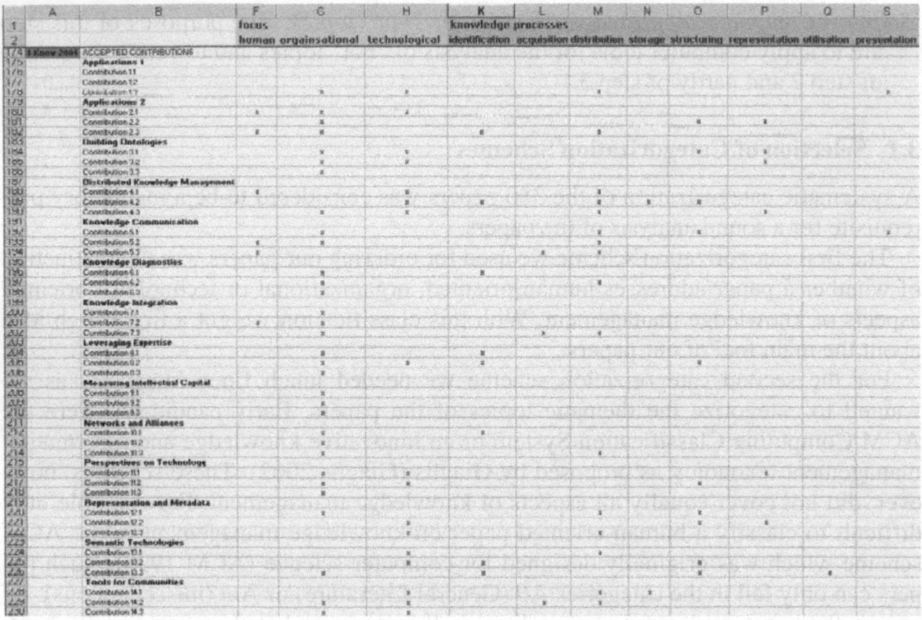

**Fig. 1.** Contribution-Category-Matrix (Note, that for ethical reasons the original titles of the papers on the left are made anonymous.)

## 3.2 Categorization

During a first step we classified the papers according to their title, abstract and keywords into one of the three categories human-oriented, organizational and technology-oriented aspects of knowledge management. A paper could fall into more than one category if it addressed more than one topic.

In a second step we analysed the content of each paper and categorized it into the above mentioned categories (i.e., discovery, acquisition, storage, distribution ...). Again, as a paper could address more than just one topic, it could fall into more than one category.

## 3.3 In-Depth Analysis

At the end of step 2 we had a contribution-category-matrix as shown in figure 1 plus the information of whether a contribution addressed human-oriented, organizational and/or technology-oriented aspects of knowledge management.

In a next step we conducted an in-depth analysis of the "most popular" categories to identify "hot" topics in knowledge management. In order to achieve this, we looked how many papers were categorized in each of the categories listed in section 3.1. For those categories with the most papers we checked again the content of the papers to identify which topics were the most intriguing ones in the category. The check of the main sections provided insights in topics which are currently of interest while the analysis of the sections on future work (if they existed) provides some indication of future topics.

### 3.4  Computer-Supported Verification of "Hot" Topics

In the area of knowledge discovery, tools exist to analyse huge document collections and to automatically cluster them according to obvious concentrations of documents and visualise them in two-dimensional satellite views. We have used one of our own tools, WebRat (Sabol et al. 2002) to check the results of step 3 against the computer-generated results.

## 4  Results

### 4.1  Results of the Categorization

Figure 2 shows how many contributions fall in which of the three categories human-oriented, organizational and technology-oriented knowledge management. In 2002 and 2003 most of the contributions addressed technology. Organizational issues were addressed by about half of the papers. Only a minority of the papers dealt with human-oriented aspects of knowledge management. The interesting trend is that in 2004 more papers addressed organizational than technology-oriented aspects. This is very much in line with the common trend that information technology should only be considered as enabling technology and that it supports rather than "is" knowledge management.

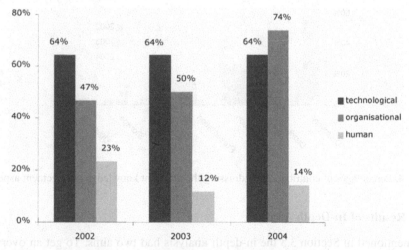

**Fig. 2.** Percentages of contributions addressing human-oriented, organizational and technology-oriented aspects of knowledge management (Note, one paper can fall into more than one category, this is why the numbers per year do not sum up to 100%.)

Figure 3 shows the distribution of the combination of technological-human and technological-organizational contributions. It is obvious that contributions covering technological-organizational aspects outreach by far technological-human aspects.

The next figure shows how the contributions were distributed among our categories defined in Section 3.1. In comparison to the others, three categories were strongly represented across all three years, namely knowledge discovery, knowledge distribution & sharing and knowledge representation. Knowledge discovery dominates the years 2002 and 2003 but was passed by knowledge distribution & sharing and knowledge representation in 2004. Over the years 68% (2002), 59% (2003), and 23% (2004) of the contributions were on knowledge discovery while for knowledge distribution & sharing the percentages were 32% (2002), 22% (2003), and 46% (2004), and for knowledge representation 23% (2002), 26% (2003), and 46% (2004). Knowledge presentation, acquisition, storage and utilization were hardly addressed over the years.

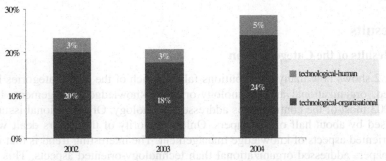

**Fig. 3.** Percentages of contributions dealing with combined aspects.

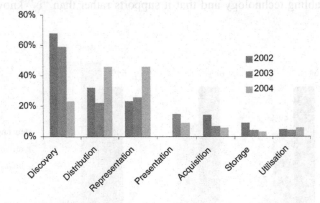

**Fig. 4.** Percentages of contributions addressing the different knowledge management aspects.

## 4.2  Results of In-Depth Analysis

As mentioned in Section 3.3 the in-depth analysis had two aims. To get an overview of 1) currently and 2) future "hot" topics in those areas which were addressed by most of the papers (namely knowledge discovery, knowledge distribution & sharing and knowledge representation).

The currently "hot" topics in *knowledge discovery* include

- Retrieval, with a focus on retrieval in heterogeneous and distributed knowledge spaces.
- Classification, that is the (semi-)automatic classification of knowledge objects (e.g., documents) in pre-defined classification schemes.
- Clustering, that is the clustering of search results according to similarity of the content and/or metadata of knowledge objects.

As future "hot" topics in this area we identified

- Structural Retrieval: The idea of structural retrieval is to enrich discovery algorithms with the information about the structure of a knowledge space (e.g. the location of a knowledge object in a hierarchy) in order to improve the result quality.
- Contextual Retrieval: The idea of contextual retrieval is to combine discovery technologies with information about the context (e.g., a user's expertise, role or task at hand) in which a user is seeking information.
- Cross-media Retrieval: Today's leading-edge techniques are focussing on isolated collections of multimedia data and are dealing only with single media types. Future research will address innovative cross-media exploration and retrieval techniques covering multiple media types and employing concepts at different semantic levels.

The currently "hot" topics in *knowledge distribution & sharing* include

- Collaboration, communication and networking; this covers technological (e.g., online community tools such as WIKI or weblogs) and non-technological tools (e.g., CoP) alike.

As future "hot" topics in this area we identified

- Peer-to-peer knowledge management: Today, research places the emphasis on centralized knowledge management approaches (e.g., designing, implementing and introducing a central knowledge management system in an organization). The open question for the future is how can knowledge management be decentralised and organized along communities without loosing the possibility to integrate the different community knowledge spaces (e.g., by ontology or taxonomy mapping).
- "Undiversified" knowledge management: Today the view on how knowledge management is interpreted in an organization, heavily depends on the unit (e.g. human resource development, IT, quality management) which is driving the knowledge management activities. The open question here is how can organizations generate a holistic view on knowledge management covering all diversified views which exist in the different units?

The currently "hot" topics in *knowledge representation* include

- Ontologies, metadata & taxonomies which are commonly seen as core enabler for sophisticated (technology-oriented) knowledge management, they all facilitate a greater machine interpretability of (web) content.
- Web services as de-facto standard for middleware to support machine-to-machine interaction over a network.
- Semantic web services to integrate web services with semantic web technologies.

As future "hot" topics in this area we identified

- Interoperable ontology infrastructures as a basis for semantic technologies. Today the use of ontologies is limited in that different ontologies may model the same concepts of a domain in different ways. Relating or even mapping ontologies of the same domain to one another is almost not possible. For the future interoperability between different ontologies of the same domain becomes increasingly important (e.g. concepts to relate different representations of the same "real world object" to one another and allowing their conversion to different ontologies).

- Semi-automatic ontology and taxonomy engineering: Today the engineering of ontologies and taxonomies is mainly carried out with little tool support and with centralized approaches (i.e. involve a small group of knowledge engineers and domain experts representing the user community). For the future methodologies and tools for distributed and collaborative ontology and taxonomy creation are considered to be of extreme importance.
- Interoperability of web services: Today web services have established as de-facto standard for middleware. For the future web services will become more composable, interoperable and should be able to negotiate with each other.

### 4.3 Results of Computer-Supported Verification of "Hot" Topics

To verify the results achieved in step 2 we have taken the contributions as input for our clustering and visualisation tool WebRat.

WebRat automatically analyses the content of the contributions (and not just titles, keyword and abstracts), extract most relevant terms by term frequency and displays the result on a two-dimensional similarity satellite map. Figure 5 displays the result of the computer supported verification. It clearly shows that WebRat identified almost the same important topics as were identified in step 2.

## 5  Related Work

Even though many studies aiming at future trends of knowledge management exist, we are not aware of a study which analysed a comparable number of scientific conference contributions. During our research we identified three different types of forecasts for knowledge management:

*Analyst studies:* Studies conducted by analysts such as Gartner, Forrester Research etc. are often based on polls in companies. For example, in a recent study Gartner states that "as enterprises better understand knowledge management (Gartner 2003), it will become a more practical and important part of doing business." This study predicts several ways in which knowledge management will become more concrete within the next 5 years: integration of knowledge management into key business processes and their applications, knowledge management as integral part of advanced information management, attention on collaboration, from transaction processing to extracting and exploiting knowledge, E-mail exploited for knowledge content, knowledge management as integral part of real-time management capabilities, and focus on internal innovation capability. These predictions imply – and point to the importance of – technological knowledge infrastructures.

*Consultation meetings:* A new concept of the EC is to adapt its work program of FP6 continuously according to the input provided by external experts. For knowledge management the consultation report 2004 for the strategic objective "semantic-based knowledge systems" is of great importance for the community (EC 2004). This report recommends focusing on semantic-based and context-aware systems integrating the functions of acquiring and modelling, navigating and retrieving, representing and visualising, interpreting and sharing knowledge. In accordance to our analysis knowledge identification, distribution and representation are mentioned.

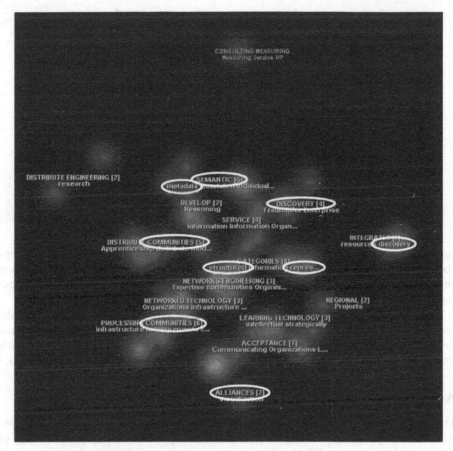

**Fig. 5.** Results of computer-supported verification; topics which were also identified in step 2 are highlighted by an ellipse.

*Project analysis:* Some researchers or group of researchers are trying to identify future trends by empirically analysing research projects in knowledge management. For example, (Giaglis 2002) belongs to this group. Figure 6 shows the certainly non exhaustive but indicative list of research themes identified by (Giaglis 2002). He also identified knowledge communication and knowledge identification (more precisely capturing) as being important for the future.

## 6   Conclusion

The objective of this paper was to identify current and future trends in knowledge management. In order to do so we analysed more than 380 papers submitted during 2002 and 2004 to the I-KNOW conference series. Our study reveals that - based on the material we analysed - knowledge discovery, knowledge representation, and knowledge distribution & sharing are among the most popular topics in knowledge management today and will probably stay important for the future. Since I-KNOW

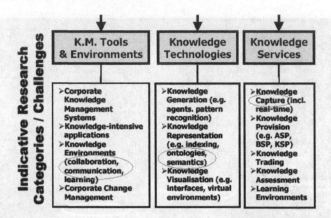

**Fig. 6.** Future research topics in knowledge management according to Giaglis.

can only cover parts of the entire knowledge management community, our findings should only be considered as indications. Still, as the section on related literature shows the findings of other types of similar studies underpin the importance of these topics.

We hope that this contribution will provide some orientation and guidance for the research community and particularly for young researches who are currently seeking future-oriented topics in knowledge management – be it for their master thesis, their PhD thesis or just because they like the fascinating topic of knowledge management.

## Acknowledgement

The Know-Center is a Competence Center funded within the Austrian K*plus* Competence Centers Program (www.kplus.at) under the auspices of the Austrian Ministry of Transport, Innovation and Technology.

## References

1. ACM (1998): ACM Computing Classification System, Version 1998: ttp://www.acm.org/class/1998/
2. CRITO (2004): http://www.crito.uci.edu/2/prlist2.asp?code=ITBkm
3. European Guide to Good Practice in Knowledge Management (2004): ftp://cenftp1.cenorm.be/PUBLIC/CWAs/e-Europe/KM/German-text-KM-CWAguide.pdf
4. EC (2004): Consultation Report for the Review and Update of the Strategic Objective 2.3.1.7 Semantic-based Knowledge Systems of the IST Work Program.
5. Gartner (2003): KM in 2004: Just Part of Doing business, Research Note.
6. Giaglis, G.M. (2002). Directions and trends in knowledge management research: results from an empirical analysis of European Projects. In Hlupic, V. (Ed.) *Knowledge and Business Process Management*, Idea Group Publishing. http://www.eltrun.gr/wrc/papers/Giaglis_KIM.pdf
7. Heisig, P. (2001). Business Process Oriented Knowledge Management - Methode zur Verknüpfung von Wissensmanagement und Geschäftsprozessgestaltung. *Proceedings of WM 2001*, 1. Konferenz Professionelles Wissensmanagement, Baden-Baden/Germany.
8. ISCW (2004): http://iswc2004.semanticweb.org/

9. KnowledgeBoard (2004): http://www.knowledgeboard.com/
10. MetaKM (2004): http://www.metakm.com/
11. Sabol V., Kienreich W., Granitzer M., Becker J., Tochtermann K., Andrews K. (2002): Applications of a Lightweight, Web-Based Retrieval, Clustering and Visualisation Framework; *Proceedings of the 4th International Conference on  Practical Aspects of Knowledge Management (PAKM)*, Wien/Austria.
12. Strohmaier M. (2003): A Business Process oriented Approach for the Identification and Support of organizational Knowledge Processes; *Proceedings der 4. Oldenburger Fachtagung Wissensmanagement*, Oldenburg/Germany.

# Decision Aid to Support the Building of Competencies Development Scenarios Within Networks of SMEs

Xavier Boucher and Emilie Lebureau

Ecole Nationale Supérieure des Mines de Saint-Etienne
158 cours Fauriel, F-42023 Saint-Etienne cedex
{boucher,lebureau}@emse.fr

**Abstract.** This paper aims at presenting the framework of a decision support system for the development of competencies in organizations through cooperation between Small and Medium Enterprises. Based on both qualitative and quantitative models linked to the concept of competence, this decision support system uses Analytic Hierarchical Process to arrange different collaborative action plans for the development of competencies. We propose to evaluate the development scenarios with five indicators based on a principle of equity applied to the competence increases of each partner within a network and to the costs and risks sharing. Finally, we apply this study to an industrial case.

**Keywords:** Competence, Networks of SME, Decision Support System, AHP.

## 1 General Introduction

After the research work of the late 1980's on organizational flexibility, and after the scientific contributions of the late 1990's on organizational reactivity, the management of firm's evolutions is clearly recognized as a major performance inducer. In this paper, our objective is to link together two important mechanisms for the evolution of a firm: the evolution of enterprise competencies and the evolution of the firm's borders. Indeed, we propose in that paper a regulation mechanism applied to management of opportunities of competencies exchanges and development, in the context of alliances.

Our work focuses on a specific type of inter-firm cooperation named in the literature «network of SMEs»: «defined as a specific form of network of two legally independent SMEs at least, which join together for a certain duration in order to carry out a common project, which requires to coordinate their behaviors» [6]. Thus, the relationships in this type of network are characterized by mutual investments and interdependencies, where equity and trust between the partners are essential. Moreover, these relationships are intended to be long lasting and they supply a very favorable context to competencies exchanges and developments.

Y. Doz and G. Hamel [3] point that «Companies often turn to alliances to win the learning race. These are often faster and more effective than alternative approaches to learning…Alliances are often the best way for companies to quickly acquire and deploy new skills». The approaches of «Resource-based view» initiated by B.Wernerfelt [13] and «Competence-based view» by R.Sanchez [8] are the more coherent for this exchange vision of inter-organizational exchanges and also for competencies development. The Winner /Winner relationship makes possible to increase individual per-

D. Karagiannis and U. Reimer (Eds.): PAKM 2004, LNAI 3336, pp. 46–58, 2004.

formances for each partner, induced by the collaborative growth. In that perspective, firms should consider cooperation as a central element of their competencies development processes.

However, in that inter-enterprises cooperation context, the management of competencies development processes becomes largely complex because of the multiple actors to consider with potentially divergent objectives. It becomes not only a question of increasing organizational learning for each firm but also a question of coherence in competencies management at the cooperation level. So, if there are potentially important productive gains, there is a need of accurate regulation mechanisms for the inter-organizational learning to ensure that the cooperation could be long lasting.

This paper focuses on that issue. We will develop a regulation mechanism for the competencies exchanges to search optimum gains on learning and costs for the partners and equity in the share of those gains within the network. Indeed, even if cooperation provides an interesting reduction of costs and risks linked to inter-organizational learning processes, we must not forget the necessity of balancing mechanisms in order to ensure equity between the partners on gains and losses. The notion of equity has been largely applied in the economic transactions, but we propose to formalize it for an application to the evaluation of inter-organizational learning processes.

This paper is structured in three parts. First, we begin by a brief statement on previous research work concerning the decision aid for the competencies development. In the second section, our conceptual contribution is developed in two parts: first, we structure the decision aid process studied, then we define the criteria helping the choice of collaborative action plans for the development of competencies in a network of SMEs. Finally, we will give a framework of Decision Support System applied to an industrial case of a network of SMEs in the Rhône-Alpes region in France.

## 2  Decision Support for Competency Development

Decision Support tools are essential components of enterprise modeling methodologies, helping to facilitate the management processes [12]. In our approach, the processes to be managed are the regulation and control processes of the competencies production system. M.Tokkeli & M.Tuominen [11] discuss the potential benefices of a group decision support system for promoting the technology selection processes taking part in the core competence management. But it is also necessary to take into account the immaterial resources in the competency development processes control. A.Drejer [2] presents a stairway pattern which integrates both technology, actors, and formal and informal management of a firm. Even if this pattern can be a basis for the competencies dynamic development, it is not implemented as a Decision Support System for the network of managers. The CRAI model and the systematical method of competencies identification initiated by M. Harzallah and F. Vernadat [5], are operational and exploitable for short-,medium- and long-term decision. However, the proposed IT-based competence model could be enriched in various ways to supply the users with decision support environment, in particular by "what-if" simulations. As for the competencies development processes control in inter-firm cooperation, O.Szegheo & S.A.Petersen [10] have developed a Model-based framework for extended enterprise engineering, where some criteria for partners selection are listed, and competencies are stocked in data bases. But this Model-based framework does not provides competencies development scenarios between partners of a network.

To complete these approaches, our objective is to develop a decision support that offers the managers thc possibility to have a comparative analysis of different collaborative action plans for the competencies development coordination within networks of partners:

- We propose competencies maps to the SMEs managers in order to help them for a comparative analysis in the development needs for each partner and in order to analyze the possibilities to fulfill their needs through inter-firm cooperation,
- We propose quantitative criteria which explicit objectives to be reached in the cooperation, especially the research of equity,
- Thus, our framework provides a real negotiation support, thanks to the information shared between the enterprises and to the clarification of the different points of view of the partners who have to build collective strategy of competencies development through cooperation.

## 3 Conceptual Contribution

We use the decomposition model of the decision making processes in three stages Intelligence – Design – Choice initiated by H.A.Simon. The added value of this model is to structure the decision making in the case of collective competencies development. Each stage can be rationalized and thus can supply added value for the managers. The intelligence stage provides an initial diagnostic: its objective is to evaluate each partner's competencies and their development needs that could be satisfied through cooperation. The design stage generates a set of actions which constitute collaborative action plans for the competencies development. Each possible collaborative action plan represents an alternative solution to satisfy the identified needs. Then, the result of the choice stage will be the selection of one collaborative actions plan for the competencies development thanks to a multi-criteria approach. Before detailing these three stages, we will introduce the competence model used as a basis for this work.

### 3.1 Preamble Concerning Competency Models

In this work, we will not only deal with actors' competencies but more generally with firms' competencies. We consider that every single competence emerges of course from an (several) actor(s) but also from a context, that is both a technological environment (i.e. material resources) and an organizational and socio-technical environment (that we describe as the concept of «professional situation»). In that perspective, we use in this paper, the s-a-r-C competency model explained by X. Boucher and P. Burlat [1]. This model formalizes that the competence emerges from the interaction between three components: "the professional situations, the actors, and the resources". These three components are also characterized by indicators (level of situation supervising, level of adequacy of actors, level of service of resources) so as to provide control parameters, later used for the competency development actions plan.

## 3.2 Intelligence Stage

The objective of this stage is to represent as well as possible the decision making environment. This environment is constituted by a set of competencies which characterizes each firm, their associated theoretical competence levels and the development needs expressed for each network of partner.

The two parts of this stage are based on audits[1] realizations which permit:

- **The formal competencies cartographies for each network of partners**

With the use of systems of reference or dictionaries of competencies[2], we can characterize each firm by sets of competencies. With the use of the s-a-r-C model, we can evaluate the level of competence called "theoretical competence level". This level is built on an aggregation[3] mechanism of three indicators. For each competence these indicators characterize actors (actor adequacy level), material resources (resource service level) and professional situation (situation mastery level).

- **The analysis of the competencies development needs**

Thanks to the quantifiable competence level approach, it is possible to analyze the gap between the actual competence level and the target competence level in the acquisition and control of a set of competencies that the managers wish to reach. This analysis helps in identifying the competencies development needs of each firm. Each need is characterized by the affected competence, the level gap to fill in, and the component(s) "situation, actor or resource" to be developed.

For the decision makers, this first stage contributes to the research of systematical approach applied with identical modalities for the different enterprises concerned. This rationalization holds added value because it permits a relative strategic positioning of firms, and because it offers the possibility of an exhaustive analysis of all the competence development needs regarding enterprises.

## 3.3 Design Stage

The objective of this stage is to answer to the needs identified during the intelligence stage by means of competencies development actions. This stage aims at gathering these actions into collaborative action plans for the competencies development, for various alternatives which are available. We will call these alternatives "competencies development scenarios". For one network of firms, these scenarios are generated in two steps: First, from a generic competencies development actions systems of reference, we deduce an exhaustive set of actions that are specific to the network; then constraints are applied to extract scenarios from actions combination.

- **Generic typology of competencies development actions**

The action types, written AT (Go, Cc, Ma), are defined by the three following attributes:

---

[1] All the cartography method is specified into the project GRECOPME II [4].

[2] For example we can refer to the French national dictionary of competencies proposed by the ROME (Répertoire Opérationnel des Métiers et de l'Emploi).

[3] For this aggregation we will use a fuzzy logical model initiated by X. Boucher & P. Burlat [1].

- Go, Goals: qualitative description of the application modality.
- Cc, Competency component: It is the component "actor, situation or resource" on which the action has an impact.
- Mdc, modes for the development of competences: In a cooperation context we consider two major modes for the development of competences:
  - The **cooperative mode** puts forth the opportunity for firms to take competence exchanges between one firm to the others. These exchanges have to be regulated by coordination mechanisms.
  - The **mutual mode** contents development actions supported collectively by the network, to satisfy all the partners' needs.

One of this approach interest is the comparative control of different modes for the development of competencies. A third mode is the autonomous mode (One partner autonomous Investment). We use this mode as a complement for the two others, when the cooperative mode and mutual mode have not been chosen during the decision making processes.

- **Sets of specific actions for each network**

Every action is notified $w_i$ (AT, $\{C_i\}$, $\{\lambda_j\}$, $\{\rho_i\}$, $f_i$)

- o  AT: type of this competencies development action.
- o  $C_i$: set of competencies impacted by the action. An action could impact one or more competencies.
- o  $\lambda_j$: set of costs induced by the action $w_i$ for the network.
- o  $\rho_i$: impacts of $w_i$ on evaluation level of the competence $C_i$ (impacts are distinct for each $C_i$ because they are on the component "actor, situation or resource" on which the competence is build) .
- o  fi: estimation of the action feasibility i.e. the risk evaluation of the action wi implementation[4], the risk to not really impact totally the component Cc of the Ci competence.

From the partner's needs (gaps between the target level of competence and the actual one) and the previous systems of reference for the development actions, we generate the set of competencies development actions notified $w_i$ for the $\{Ei\}$ enterprises of the network. This set, written $\Omega\{\{Ei\},\{wi\}\}$, is an exhaustive actions set potentiality implemented in order to satisfy the needs.

- **Scenarios generation**

However, actually, number of collaborative actions implementations are bound by budgetary and temporally network constraints, that hinder the realization of all the development actions included in $\Omega\{\{Ei\},\{wi\}\}$ in a single collaborative actions plan. Then decision makers should implement a sub-set of $\Omega$. Various possible sub-sets are generated by a combination between elements of $\Omega$. We call "scenarios" W(R) these possible sub-sets which constitute different alternatives of collaborative actions plans for the development of competencies in a SMEs network. The next stage will permit to choose one of the most pertinent collaborative action plans for the development of competencies.

---

[4] In the study case developed in section 3, costs and feasibilities are issued from basic refrence system usable for every firms.

**Table 1.** Generic Typology of competencies development actions AT

| Mdc / Cc | Cooperative mode | Mutual mode |
|---|---|---|
| **Actors** Ameliorate the actor adequacy level | • Inter-firm competence transfer for individual or collective actors (vocational sponsoring, common work, cognitive interactions…). <br> • Inter-firm share of employees. | • Mutual training of actors Know, Know-how, Know-be. <br> • Collective engaging at the network level. |
| **Resources** Ameliorate the resource service level | • Shared use of existing resources. <br> • Optimization of the technologies of a partner using the competences of another one. | • Investment on a resource in possession of the all network. <br> • Sub-contracting by the network of an optimization action on resources present by multiple partners. |
| **Situations** Ameliorate the situation mastery level | • Share of procedures or best practices on the rationalization processes. <br> • Share of procedures or best practices on the methods orientated on analysis, diagnosis and solving of problems. | • Audits realization for all the network of partners. <br> • Common Investment on methods. |

## 3.4 Choice Stage

This stage permits the selection of scenarios containing the most favorable actions to fulfill the competence development needs evaluated during the design stage. This scenario should satisfy the objectives of the network. In order to allow the choice, we propose quantifiable decisional criteria helping to make the comparative analysis of the scenarios. An important contribution of this work lies in the formalization of these decisional criteria permitting the treatment of the issue of equity which is so specific to networks of firms. Our approach makes possible to evaluate the potential «learning impact» of competencies development actions; consequently we are able to provide an indicator for the equity on inter-organizational learning processes. For the decisional analysis, we use a mathematic multi-criteria approach that better takes into account the preferences in term of competencies development of each partner.

### 3.4.1 Basis of the Choice Stage

This research work focuses on the construction of a decision support tool that help to manage the firms competencies development within collaborative network of firms. In our case we have to treat a P. $\gamma$ issue: we tend to obtain a classification of the scenarios thanks to decisional criteria and their weights.

The too previous stages provide basis data to this choice stage. For a network of firms, we already have sets of competences for the different firms, and the gaps between the evaluation of the level of competence[5] and the target level (objectives be to reached defining by each partner) that explicit the competence development needs.

Through actors or resources, an action $w_j$ can have a multiple-impact on several competencies, for instance when an actor or a resource is shared between various

---

[5] In reality there is too level of competence: the first evaluation is the "theoretical competence level" based on the aggregation of the s-a-r indicators that could be completed by a second evaluation «Measured competence level ». Only the first evaluation is viewed in this paper.

competencies. In that case, there is an interaction between the competencies, and the action $w_j$ has a higher global effect than when its impact touch only one competence.

**Table 2.** Main mathematical characteristics

| Data | Explanation |
|---|---|
| $\mu_{\tilde{Q}(E)}(C_i)$ | Resource service level in a competence $C_i$ for a firm E. |
| $\mu_{\tilde{A}(E)}(C_i)$ | Actor adequacy level in a competence $C_i$ by a firm E. |
| $\mu_{\tilde{S}(E)}(C_i)$ | Situation mastery level in a competence $C_i$ by a firm E. |
| $\mu_{\tilde{N}(E)}(C_i)$ | Theoretical competence level: $\mu_{\tilde{N}(E)}(C_i)=Min(\mu_{\tilde{S}(E)}(C_i),\mu_{\tilde{A}(E)}(C_i),\mu_{\tilde{Q}(E)}(C_i))$ |
| $\mu_{\tilde{O}(E)}(C_i)$ | Target on competence level in the acquisition and control of a competence $C_i$ by a firm E of the network. |
| $\rho_1$ | Performance indicator for a set of competences $\{C_i\}$ by a firm E<br><br>$\rho_1=1-\dfrac{1}{n}\sum_{i=1}^{n}\left\|\mu_{\tilde{N}(E)}(C_i)-\mu_{\tilde{O}(E)}(C_i)\right\|^{a}$ |
| $w_j$ | An action wj have an impact on the level $\mu_{\tilde{Q}(E)}(C_i)$ or $\mu_{\tilde{A}(E)}(C_i)$ or $\mu_{\tilde{S}(E)}(C_i)$. So the theoretical competence level pass from a $\mu_{\tilde{N}(E)}(C_i)$ a new value $\mu_{\tilde{N}'(E)}(C_i)$. The action of competence development create an increment $\Delta(E_i,w_j)$ of the theoretical competence level for a enterprise $E_i$ because $w_j$ is amelioration action ($\mu_{\tilde{N}'(E)}(C_i)\geq \mu_{\tilde{N}(E)}(C_i)$). |

[a] This performance indicator corresponds to the "pertinence" in [1], that concerns the appropriateness of the means implemented with respect to the targets.

### 3.4.2 Definition of the Decisional Criteria

Previously we have seen that even if the cooperation provides an interesting reduction of costs and risks linked to inter-organizational learning processes, we can not forget the necessity of equity between the partners to share the gains and losses. Thus the classification of the scenarios can be done in a systematical manner by the way of five objectives to be reached through the cooperation:

● **Optimization of the value created by the development actions: I1.** In a first time, we should know for each action the local impact on the amelioration of the competency components: In table 2, we show that the theoretical competence level is incremented from $\mu_{\tilde{N}(E)}(C_i)$ to the new value $\mu_{\tilde{N}'(E)}(C_i)$ after the action. Thus, for an actions set W(R) selected by the network of SMEs, we have a global increment of the theoretical competence level written:

$$\Delta(E,W(R)) = \sum_{i=1}^{n}\left(\mu_{\tilde{N}'(E)}(C_i)-\mu_{\tilde{N}(E)}(C_i)\right)$$

This increment allows to know the impact of competence amelioration due to the scenario W(R) for a partner E. Considering k enterprises, the indicator $I_1$ for the global competence gain induced by W(R) is given by:

$$I_1(W(R)) = \sum_{j=1}^{k}\Delta(E_j,W(R)) \tag{1}$$

- **Equity search in the competence gain: I2.** We deal here with the equity on the competence gains, which means an equity between the value transited by each partner to the network and the value he acquires with its own competence gains. In fact, we measure the homogeneity of the ratios between the transmitted value and the acquired value (one ratio for each partner). As an hypothesis, we consider that a "transfer of value" is an organizational learning action where a firm E induces a competence increase for its partners in the network, without any competence increase for E. We call "acquisition of value" the opposite mechanism.

We search to obtain that the global competence gain would be fairly shared between all the partners. For every action $w_j$ and for every enterprise $E_i$, we use the variable $v(E_i, w_j)$ to indicate if the action $w_j$ is a transfer of value (in that case $v(E_i, w_j)=1$) or an acquisition of value (in that case $v(E_i, w_j)=0$) for Ei. Considering m actions and k enterprises, the ratio R between the transmitted value and the acquired value for the firm $E_i$ is given by:

$$R(E_i) = \left( \sum_{j=1}^{m} (v(E_i, w_j) \times \Delta(E_i, w_j)) \right) / \left( \sum_{j=1}^{m} ((1 - v(E_i, w_j)) \times \Delta(E_i, w_j)) \right)$$

Within the network, the equity indicator $I_2$ gives an estimation of the dispersion on these ratios by a classical variance measure:

$$I_2(W(R)) = 1/(k-1) \sum_{i=1}^{k} (R(E_i) - M_R)^2 \text{ with } M_R \text{ the mean of the ratios.} \tag{2}$$

- **Costs reduction for the network: I3.** This function is the sum of the costs stemming from the implementation of the actions of competencies development, supported by the k enterprises of the network.

$$I_3 = \sum_{i=1}^{k} costs(E_i) \tag{3}$$

The different costs are determined thanks to a system of reference which specify the calculi parameters to provide for each action.

- **Equity search in the costs for the partners: I4.** We deal here with the equity on the costs stemming from the competence development actions. We use this indicator to not destroy links between partners inside the network because of overload costs. This equity is the image of the costs dispersion introduced for each firm in the cooperation actions. This indicator of equity I4 is calculated from the standard deviation of each partner $E_i$ costs to the average cost:

$$I_4 = 1/k \times \sqrt{\sum_{i=1}^{k} (cos\,ts\,(E_i) - Mc)^2} \text{ with } Mc = I_3/k \tag{4}$$

- **Optimization of the scenarios feasibility: I5.** This indicator represents the average feasibility for each action included in the development scenario.

$$I_s = \sum_{j=1}^{k} \frac{feasibility(wj)}{k} \tag{5}$$

The different feasibilities are determined thanks to a system of reference which specify the calculi parameters to provide for each action.

The notation in the choice stage is realized in a systematic manner thanks to the AHP (Analytic Hierarchical Process) developed by T.L Saaty [9]. The notation of the scenarios is effectuated by different weights for the five previous indicators attributed by the decision-makers. This method shows the advantages to modelize the articulation between the individual objectives of each partner and the collective ones of the network, to give a clear visualization in the decision-makers preferences, and to simulate different scenarios notations according to the weights affected to the five indicators. At the end of the notation, decision-makers obtain one development scenario permitting the amelioration of the competence level in their enterprise, according to both an individual strategy, by the definition of target levels, and a global one, by the cooperation criteria of the network.

# 4   Application

## 4.1   Computer Environment

To support the decision aid, the computer environment is structured in three elements: an enterprise modeling system, a data base, and a decision aid module.

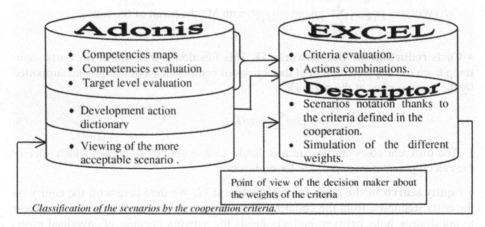

*Classification of the scenarios by the cooperation criteria.*

The enterprise modeling environment permits the creation and the generation of new models of enterprises where stays all the basis information for the decision aid. We have chosen the ADONIS software because it has a great flexibility and allows the development of specific libraries. ADONIS is interfaced with a data base, offering the openness of the software and its inter-connection with other modules. For the decision aid module, we use the DESCRIPTOR software to apply the method AHP.

## 4.2   Application to an Industrial Study Case

The case study presented here stems from a collaboration with a network of firms named ARTIC. ARTIC is a association that gathers about twenty firms from similar sectors. In order to manage the creation of tighter cooperation within the network,

ARTIC has initiated a cartography and an evaluation of its members' competencies. Its purpose is to set up collaborative processes of competencies increase. For reasons of confidentiality, the provided information is juggled.

We develop this study of cooperation over the case of 3 companies from the same sector (business computing). In order to compare the 3 companies each with another, a common system of competencies description in relation to their sector of activity has been settled. For each competence and each company, table 3 sets out:

- the target, $\tilde{O}_{(E)}$
- the theoretical competence level[6] $\tilde{N}_{(E)}$ constructed from the values obtained for situations, actors, and resources' indicators;
- the gap $e_1$ between the target and the theoretical competence level[7].

**Table 3.** Initial data of the study case ARTIC

| Compet-encies | Name:"To be able to... | Enterprise 1 | | | Enterprise 2 | | | Enterprise 3 | | |
|---|---|---|---|---|---|---|---|---|---|---|
| | | $\tilde{O}$ (E1) | $\tilde{N}$ (E1) | $e_1$ | $\tilde{O}$ (E2) | $\tilde{N}$ (E2) | e1 | $\tilde{O}$ (E3) | $\tilde{N}$ (E3) | $e_1$ |
| C1 | Conceive business software | 1 | 0,5 | 0,5 | 0,75 | 0 | 0,75 | 0,5 | 0,35 | 0,15 |
| C2 | Achieve programming | 0,5 | 0,5 | 0 | 0,5 | 0,5 | 0 | 1 | 0,72 | 0,28 |
| C3 | Master software adaptability and evolution | 1 | 0,63 | 0,37 | 0,5 | 0 | 0,5 | 0,75 | 0,4 | 0,35 |
| C4 | Control quality | 0,75 | 0,5 | 0,25 | 0,75 | 0 | 0,75 | 0,5 | 0,38 | 0,12 |
| C5 | Bring under control quality-costs-lead times | 1 | 0,5 | 0,5 | 0,75 | 0 | 0,75 | 0,5 | 0,5 | 0 |
| C6 | Keep in line with quality standards | 0,25 | 0 | 0,25 | 0,5 | 0 | 0,5 | 0,5 | 0 | 0,5 |
| C7 | Stage campaigns for quality continuous improvement | 0,5 | 0 | 0,5 | 0,5 | 0 | 0,5 | 0,5 | 0 | 0,5 |
| C8 | Achieve marketing | 1 | 0 | 1 | 0,25 | 0 | 0,25 | 0,5 | 0,5 | 0 |
| C9 | Manage customer relationship | 1 | 0 | 1 | 0,75 | 0,38 | 0,37 | 0,75 | 0 | 0,75 |
| C10 | Manage sales | 1 | 0,25 | 0,75 | 1 | 0,64 | 0,36 | 0,75 | 0 | 0,75 |

With a global analyze and a systematic manner, we can identify (1) the gap $e_1$ between the target and the actual level and (2) the situations, actors, and resources' indicators for each firm. Then (3) thanks to the generic typology of competency development actions shown in table 1, we can identify for the study case all the possible development actions in a mutualist mode or a cooperative one. Of course, for this identification, a number of logical or operational constraints are taken into account

---

[6] In this paper, only the theoretical competence level is provide.

[7] This gap is equal to the difference between the target and the theoretical competence level thus it is calculate by $e = (\tilde{O}_{(E)} - \tilde{N}_{(E)})$.

and can eliminate theoretically possible actions: for example, an enterprise with a gap $e_1$ at 0, doesn't apply an action in a mutualist mode ; but it can be at the origin of a «value-transfer» in a collaborative mode; an other example is when the differential on the indicators of each firm is high enough for the implementation of value-transfers to be possible; etc.

At an end we have got a dozen of possible actions[8] shown in the following table.

**Table 4.** Competencies development possible for ARTIC case

| Actions | Actions definition |
|---|---|
| $w_{1c}[A; C4; E_s 3; E_b1/ E_b2]$ | Inter-enterprise competencies transmission for individual actors |
| $w_{2c}[A; C8; E_s 3; E_b1/ E_b2]$ | Inter-enterprise competencies transmission for individual actors |
| $w_{3c}[S; C8; E_s 2; E_b1]$ | Best practices diffusion |
| $w_{4c}[A; C1; E_s1; E_b2/ E_b3]$ | Inter-enterprise competencies transmission for individual actors |
| $w_{5c}[A; C3; E_s3; E_b2]$ | Inter-enterprise competencies transmission for individual actors |
| $w_{6c}[S; C4; E_s1; E_b2/ E_b3]$ | Best practices diffusion |
| $w_{7c}[S; C9; E_s1; E_b2/ E_b3]$ | Best practices diffusion |
| $w_{8c}[A; C9/C10; E_s2; E_b1/ E_b3]$ | Inter-enterprise competencies transmission for individual actors |
| $w_{1m}[S; C1; E1UE2UE3]$ | Common Investment on methods |
| $w_{2m}[S; C4; E1UE2UE3]$ | Common Investment on methods |
| $w_{3m}[R; C4; E1UE2UE3]$ | Common Investment on one resource hold by the network |
| $w_{4m}[A; C9/C10; E1UE2UE3]$ | Mutual formation of the individual actors |

In this example, we consider that budget constraint restrict us to select 3 cooperative actions among 12 ones identified. The reader must remember that beyond selected cooperative actions, each company will supplement its action-plan with autonomous actions. Of course a change in this budget constraint would only modify the combinatory without modifying the proposed method. Thus in this case, there are 220 possible scenarios consisting of 3 actions ($C_3^{12}$) that we have to compare in order to establish the most relevant in the cooperation objectives.

For all the 220 scenarios, we calculate the five choice indicators thanks to the formula (1) to (5), and we apply the analytic hierarchical process. If the decision-makers give the same weight to each criterion i.e. they do not prefer one more than an other ; we obtain the following results on the software DESCRIPTOR:

| Evalués | Scores | SCENARIO GAIN_GLOBAL_I | SCENARIO EQUI_GAIN_I | SCENARIO COUT_GLOBAL_I | SCENARIO EQUI_COUT_I | SCENARIO FAISABILITE |
|---|---|---|---|---|---|---|
| ☐SCENARIO_59 | 75.79% | [1.5/2[ | [0.5/1[ | [15000/20000[ | [0.25/0.5[ | [0.08/0.12[ |
| ☐SCENARIO_116 | 74.74% | [1/1.5[ | [0.25/0.5[ | [15000/20000[ | [0/0.125[ | [0.08/0.12[ |
| ☐SCENARIO_90 | 74.74% | [2/2.5[ | [0.25/0.5[ | [20000/25000[ | [0.125/0.25[ | [0.04/0.08[ |
| ☐SCENARIO_175 | 72.63% | [1.5/2[ | [0/0.125[ | [20000/25000[ | [0/0.125[ | [0.04/0.08[ |
| ☐SCENARIO_58 | 72.63% | [1.5/2[ | [0/0.125[ | [20000/25000[ | [0.125/0.25[ | [0.04/0.08[ |
| ☐SCENARIO_190 | 72.63% | [1.5/2[ | [0.125/0.25[ | [20000/25000[ | [0/0.125[ | [0.04/0.08[ |

It is between these 6 scenarios that we find the better balance in the competence gains, costs, feasibilities and equity, since they obtain the three best notes. The final decision of the scenario to implement is to be taken by the network's managers. Their

---

[8]  w1c[A; C4; Es 3; Eb1/ Eb2] say that the action impact the actor for the competence C4, with the enterprises E1 et E2 as beneficiary-company and E3 as root-company.

decision could be oriented by a qualitative analyze of the better noted scenarios: the scenario_90 is better for the global competence gain, but it is the worth for the global costs, the scenario_59 et scenario_116 are comparable in term of global costs and feasibilities, and if we choose to favor equity on the competences gains and costs, we would prefer the scenario_175.

The analysis of scenarios also shows the influence of interactions between competencies. For instance the actions $w_{8c}$[A; C9/C10; $E_s2$; $E_b1$/ $E_b3$] and $w_{4m}$[A; C9/C10; E1UE2UE3] appear often in the best scenarios. It can be explained by the fact they impact two competences (this is the same actor that supports C9 and C10 competencies and has knowledge on these 2 competencies). The decision aid method presented here shows that interactions between competencies are a key element of our approach. Interactions between learning actions on actors, resources or situations within a same competence are taken into account in the calculation of the theoretical level of competence; and interactions between actions on distinct competencies (common actors or resources of distinct competencies) are taken into account in the calculation of actions impacts.

## 5 Perspectives

We have illustrate the formalizing of a decision aid on a tactical level, for the cooperative development of competencies. At the end of the decisional process, each enterprise of the network will benefit from the chosen collectives actions, that may be completed by autonomous actions to reach its proper targets. Some key points of the added value of that work can be highlighted: we situate this approach at a control level sufficiently high to look for a rationalization of the competencies development process ; we bring a contribution to the difficult question of the balance between local and global optimum within a network of firms; this approach provides the selective comparison between different modes for the development of competencies; different interactions between competencies can be taken into account.

It is clear that this research work lies on some restrictive hypothesis and keeps clear limitations at both a theoretical and operational level. Nevertheless, it opens the way to rich research on competence management focusing on the frontier between qualitative approaches (commonly used in that field) and quantitative models as proposed here.

## References

1. Boucher, X., Burlat, P.: Vers l'intégration des compétences dans le pilotage des performance de l'entreprise. Journal Européen des Systèmes Automatisés. Vol.37(3). (2003). 363-390.
2. Drejer, A.: How can we define and understand competencies and their development? Technovation, Vol.21. (2001), 135-146.
3. Doz, Y., Hamel, G.: Alliance advantage: the art of creating value trough partnering. (ed.) Harvard Business School Press, Boston (1998).
4. GRECOPME II: (GRoupement d'Entreprise Coopérantes: Potentialité, Moyens, Evolution). P.Burlat(coord.). Rapport final du projet de recherche GRECOPME II à la région Rhône-Alpes. Thématique prioritaire «Productique». Septembre 2003.

5. Harzallah, M., Vernadat, F.: IT-based competency modelling and management: from theory to practice in enterprise engineering and operations. Computer in Industry. Vol.48. (2002).157-179.
6. Peillon, S.: Le pilotage des coopération interentreprises: le cas des groupement de PME. Thèse de l'Ecole Nationale Supérieure des Mines de Saint Etienne. Octobre 2001.
7. Porter, M.: L'avantage concurrentiel des nations. InterEds. Paris (1993).
8. Sanchez, R., Heene, A., Thomas, H.: Dynamics of Competence-based Competition. Elsevier. (1996).
9. Saaty, T.L: The Analytic Hierarchy Process. New York. McGraw- Hill (1980).
10. Szegheo, O., Petersen, S.A.: Extended Enterprise Engineering – a model-based framework. Journal of concurrent engineering research and applications. Vol. 8. (2000). 32-39.
11. Tokkeli, M., Tuominen, M.: The contribution of technology selection to core competencies. International journal of production economics. Vol. 77. (2002). 271-284.
12. Vernadat, F.: EUML: towards a unified enterprise modelling language. 3rd francophone conference on Modelisation and SIMulation MOSIM'01. 25-27 April 2001. Troyes. France.
13. Wernerfelt, B.: A Resource-Based View of the Firm. Strategic Management Journal. Vol. 5. (1984). 171-180.

# MiNet: Building Ad-Hoc Peer-to-Peer Networks for Information Sharing Based on Mobile Agents

Takafumi Yamaya[1], Toramatsu Shintani[1], Tadachika Ozono[1], Yusuke Hiraoka[1],
Hiromitsu Hattori[1], Takayuki Ito[1], Naoki Fukuta[2], and Kyoji Umemura[3]

[1] Graduate School of Engineering, Nagoya Institute of Technology
Gokiso, Showa-ku, Nagoya 466-8555, Japan
{yamaya,hiraoka,hatto,itota,ozono,tora}@ics.nitech.ac.jp
[2] Department of Computer Science, Faculty of Information, Shizuoka University
836 Ohya, Shizuoka-shi, Shizuoka 422-8529, Japan
fukuta@cs.inf.shizuoka.ac.jp
[3] Department of Electronic and Information Engineering
Toyohashi University of Technology
1-1 Hibarigaoka, Tempaku-cho, Toyohashi, Aichi 441-8580, Japan
umemura@tutics.tut.ac.jp

**Abstract.** The Internet is a very popular for information sharing technology since users can share information in organizations and communities. In this paper, we present a flexible peer-to-peer networking technology for information sharing on the Internet called *MiNet*. In some certain communities, *MiNet* can construct an ad-hoc network for information sharing. *MiNet* enables users to share information based on mobile agents, which are implemented in a mobile agent framework *MiLog*. *MiNet* can construct ad-hoc peer-to-peer networks by encapsulating information and sending it as mobile agents that can migrate in *MiNet* beyond firewalls, proxies, and NATs in LANs. Therefore, *MiNet* can construct VPNs, which consist of several LANs covered by firewalls, etc. MiNet agents can automatically choose a destination platform according to its policies. We show the document sharing system MiDoc as an application based on *MiNet*. Since MiDoc is implemented using *MiNet*, MiDoc users can share any document among any LANs.

## 1 Introduction

The Internet is a very popular for information sharing technology since users can share information in organizations and communities. There are a lot of systems for information sharing in such organizations and communities, recently. Peer-to-peer architecture has received lots of attention. Today, such peer-to-peer systems as Napster [1], Gnutella [2], KaZaA [3], and FreeNet [4]) have many interesting technical aspects: decentralized control, self organization, adaptation, and scalability [8]. However, sometimes the information sharing system does not work well because of the firewalls, proxies, and Network Address Translation (NAT). In these cases, users can share information within firewalls, but they cannot share information beyond firewalls. For example, when a user goes on

D. Karagiannis and U. Reimer (Eds.): PAKM 2004, LNAI 3336, pp. 59–70, 2004.

a business trip, he/she cannot connect to an information sharing network that is operated within his/her company's LAN since that network in a common company is covered by firewalls. If the setting of the firewalls is changed to allow the connections from outside the company, users can connect to the network. However, they need authority to change the configuration, which they usually lack. Moreover, if the configuration is changed, the security of the company's network is threatened.

In this paper, we present a flexible peer-to-peer networking technology for information sharing on the Internet called *MiNet*. In some certain communities, *MiNet* can construct an ad-hoc network for information sharing. *MiNet* enables users to share information based on mobile agents, which are implemented in a mobile agent framework *MiLog* [5]. Each user has an MiNet platform and run it on his/her computer. a MiLog agent acts on the MiNet platform and manage its user's information. In *MiNet*, the function for sending/receiving the information is implemented as the agent's migration among platforms. The information is encapsulated as an mobile agent that can act autonomously as intelligent information. A MiLog agent can migrate via HTTP protocol, which is one of the most common protocols used on the Internet. Since an HTTP protocol is generally permitted to pass through firewalls because of their settings, the MiLog agent can pass the firewalls. An agent can migrate among different Local Area Networks (LANs) that are covered by firewalls, proxies, and NATs. *MiNet* can construct Virtual Private Networks (VPNs) that consists of several LANs based on mobile agent tunneling in which we use relay platforms established on the outside of each LAN. The relay platform is the *MiLog* platform, which behaves as a hub for LANs. The agents go back and forth between LANs via the relay platform. When an agent migrates to a platform in a different LAN, a destination platform doesn't need to be determined. An IP address of a destination platform is automatically detemined by negotiation among agent. A MiNet agent, which is implemented using *MiLog*, can select an appropriate destination platform by itself on a relay platform. Accordingly, a MiNet agent can behave like a Middle-Agent [6]. For example, when a *MiNet* agent must migrate to another platform for load balancing and the destination platform is not determined in advence, the agent checks the status of each LAN and automatically determines the destination platform. Therefore, *MiNet* can construct the VPNs without preparing IP addresses of other platforms in advance.

The rest of this paper is organized as follows. Section 2 presents an overview of *MiNet*, including a description of services and peer-to-peer network problems. A problem solving method is presented in Sections 3 and 4. Section 5 presents MiDoc, which is a document sharing system based on *MiNet*. Section 6 presents an evaluation of *MiNet*. Related work is discussed in Section 7, and Section 8 is the conclusion.

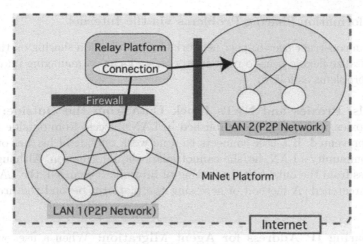

**Fig. 1.** An overview of *MiNet*.

## 2 Overview of MiNet

### 2.1 Features of MiNet

Figure 1 shows an overview of *MiNet*, which automatically constructs peer-to-peer networks among *MiNet* platforms. There are two types of peer-to-peer networks among *MiNet* platforms:

(i) a network among *MiNet* platforms within a LAN.
(ii) a VPN among *MiNet* platforms on different LANs.

Actually, type (ii) networks consist of some type (i) networks. A VPN is constructed as a hybrid peer-to-peer network. For example, in Figure 1, LAN 1 and LAN 2, which are covered by firewalls, could be used as one private network. A relay platform acts as a server for a hybrid peer-to-peer network. *MiNet* can construct ad-hoc networks for information sharing. *MiNet* can offer two main network services, which are described as follows:

*Automatic Network Construction.* *MiNet* platforms send their own information to other platforms and connect with others while *MiNet* platforms are online. A user can automatically join in a *MiNet* network without complex configurations. We use JmDNS [7] to send information to other platforms. JmDNS is a Java implementation of multicast DNS that can be used for service registration and discovery in LANs. Therefore, if a user connects his/her computer to LAN and run a MiNet platform, he/she can join in information sharing within a LAN.

*Naming Service for MiNet Platform.* *MiNet* can manage platforms by user of their name, which can be assigned to their platform. When a agent migrates, the platform's name is used. The *MiNet* naming service automatically adjusts name duplications. Since the platforms always use naming services in a *MiNet* network, *MiNet* can construct ad-hoc network without a physical IP address.

## 2.2 Information Sharing Problems via the Internet

*MiNet* can construct peer-to-peer networks for information sharing on the Internet. To realize flexble peer-to-peer networks, we focus on managing information sharing problems as follow:

**Firewalls, Proxies and NATs Block Data from the Outside:** If firewalls, proxies, and NATs are established in LANs, access from outside the network is prevented. If a user connects to a network outside of his/her organization's/community's LAN, he/she cannot share the information. Although users can access from the outside if the setting of firewalls is changed, the LAN security is threatened. A method of accessing the platform beyond the firewalls is required.

**A Preparing IP Address for Agent Migration:** When a user wants an agent to migrate to another platform, he/she must provide an IP address. However, users do not know the IP address of an appropriate platform for information sharing in advance. It is difficult for users to choose a destination platform explicitly. Agents should dynamically decide its destination platform.

# 3   The Migration Beyond Firewalls

## 3.1   The Migration Protocol of the MiNet Agent

In *MiNet*, communication among *MiNet* platforms is implemented as migration of mobile agents. MiNet agents are implemented using a mobile agent framework *MiLog* [5]. Since a mobile agent can migrate via HTTP protocols, MiNet agents can migrate among MiNet platforms without specific migration protocols, as shown in Figure 2. When a MiNet agent is sent to another platform, it is serialized into byte data, which can be sent to other platforms via HTTP. The byte data is deserialized into original MiNet agents at a destination platform, and then the agent can continuously act in other platforms. Since HTTP protocol is a very common Internet protocol, most firewalls accept HTTP data packets sent from the inside to the outside of a LAN. Therefore, MiNet agent can easily migrate to relay platforms that are outside of all LANs. If HTTPS are available in the network, MiNet agents can migrate on secure pathways.

## 3.2   A Migration Method Beyond Firewalls

Since firewall is security software, It can prevents unauthorized access from the outside of a LAN. HTTP protocol, a most important protocol, is usually authorized by firewall. So MiNet agents can pass through firewalls since it is sent to other platforms via HTTP. However, although a MiNet agent can go from the inside to the outside of a LAN, it cannot enter from the outside because of the settings of firewall. So *MiNet* uses a relay platform to indirectly connect to different LANs. MiNet agent reaches the relay platform, and wait for access

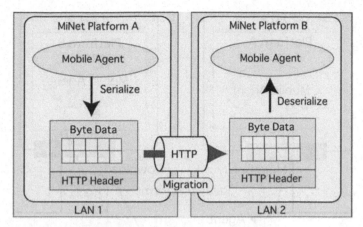

**Fig. 2.** A Migration of *MiNet* agent.

from a destination platform, which continuously monitors the relay platform. When a destination platform finds a MiNet agent that is trying to get there, it downloads the agent. Since most firewalls allow the downloading of data from outside of a LAN, MiNet agent can migrate among different LANs.

Figure 3 shows an example of the migration of a MiNet agent beyond firewalls. Here, an agent tries to migrate from platform A on LAN 1 to platform B on LAN 2. LANs 1 and 2 are covered by a firewall. An agent arrives at platform B via the relay platform. A detailed explanation follows:

**Step 1:** A agent migrates to the relay platform from platform A where the agent is serialized and sent via HTTP. Firewall allows the serialized agent to migrate to the relay platform.

**Step 2:** The serialized agent is deserialized on the relay platform, and the agent waits for access from other platform on the relay platforms.

**Step 3:** Platform B monitors the relay platform. Here, platform B sends a *scout agent* to the relay platform, continuously monitors whether an agent is trying to migrate to platform B.

**Step 4:** After finding the agent sent from platform A, scout agent of platform B signals platform B to download the agent. The agent is serialized again by the relay platforms and platform B downloads it. The relay platform cannot send the serialized agent to platform B since the firewall of LAN 2 prevents access from the outside. However, since the downloaded agent is requested by the platform in the inside of LAN 2, the serialized agent can pass through the firewall of LAN 2.

**Step 5:** Platform B deserializes the agent who finishes its migration process and can act continuously.

Note that in this section, we assume that the agent tries to pass thought firewalls. However, this migration method only applies to cases with proxies and NATs. All platforms must know the location of the relay platform on the Internet.

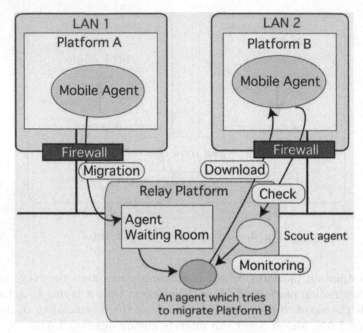

**Fig. 3.** An Migration of agents beyond the firewall.

## 4    Destination Determined by MiNet Agents

For a MiNet agent to migrate to another platform in a different LAN, a user must provide an IP address for the platform. However, it is difficult for common users to know IP addresses of platforms on the Internet in advance. It is sometimes difficult to know the IP address of a destination platform. For example, load balancing, it is impossible for users to know the platform of a high performance computer in advance. Even though users must dynamically select the destination platform based on the current status of other platforms, it is obviously a hard task for them.

MiNet agents automatically by solve this problem choosing a destination platform based on a brief negotiation among agents. They can dynamically select a destination platform and then construct appropriate VPNs without the IP addresses of other platforms. The relay platform actually behaves as a hub of all MiNet platforms. MiNet agents, which try to go through firewalls, must pass the relay platform. In *MiNet*, each platform sends a scout agent to the relay platform who has platform information and negotiates with agents sent from other platforms to the relay platform. Figure 4 shows on overview of migration based on such automatic platform selection. As shown in Figure 4, some scout agents are sent from the platforms on different LANs; the agent looking for an appropriate destination platform, called a *request agent*, negotiates with scout agents to determine his/her destination platform. During negotiations, each scout agent offers its platform's information to the request agent, who has the policy to de-

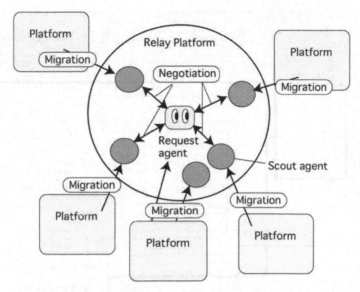

**Fig. 4.** An agent negotiation in the relay platform.

termine the destination. If a scout agent can offer appropriate information about the policy, the request agent selects the scout agent's platform as its destination. Then the selected scout agent sends a signal to its platform to download the request agent.

According to the method, MiNet agents can connect to platforms that are on different LANs without providing IP addresses of platforms by users. *MiNet* can automatically construct a scalable VPN on the Internet.

## 5   A Document Sharing System: MiDoc

### 5.1   Document Sharing System MiDoc

MiDoc is a document sharing system implemented by Java (J2SE)[16]. In MiDoc, users can collect and manage documents and associated metadata (e.g., title, authors' names, abstract, user's rating and user's review of the document). Furthermore, Users can register documents, and share documents and their metadata in a community (e.g., an university laboratory or a research group). In MiDoc, we implemented a Zero-Configuration network [13] by using *MiNet*. By employing MiNet, users do not need configuration to utilize the system. Fig. 5 shows a snapshot of MiDoc's interface. User's documents are listed on the right table, which users can open to see documents. Users can also access the documents of other users on the left table. By selecting user's name in the left table, selected user's documents are listed in the right table. Also, by double-clicking a one of other user's documents, a user can download the documents and add them the document to his/her list.

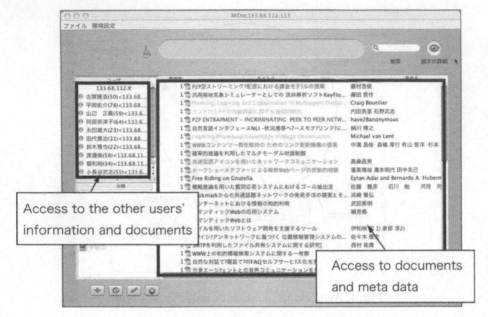

**Fig. 5.** The Snapshot of MiDoc.

In addition, MiDoc has the following features:

**Complementing Metadata of Documents**

When a user inputs a PDF file in MiDoc, MiDoc automatically extracts meta data from the PDF file as title and author's name.

**Portability**

The either MiDoc system and databases can be stored in a portable music player iPod [14][1] or in a USB flash memory. Thus, users can carry their MiDoc environment in an iPod or a USB flash memory. Users can launch their own MiDoc on any computer by connecting their iPod or USB flash memory to a computer. Also, users can read abstracts of documents anywhere by using an iPod. When a user discovers an interesting document, he/she marks it. Marked documents can be downloaded automatically the next time is launched.

**Searching Documents**

MiDoc finds the documents that contain the query words. In addition, MiDoc can search documents similar to the selected document. MiDoc measures similarity between two documents by using a co-occurrence-based thesaurus constructed from a document[15]. By using a co-occurrence-based thesaurus of a document, MiDoc can measure similarity in numerical terms. This function outputs a list of documents which similarity is over threshold.

---

[1] A portable music player. It can be used as a hard disk by connecting to a computer. By using an iPod, users can listen to music files and read text files.

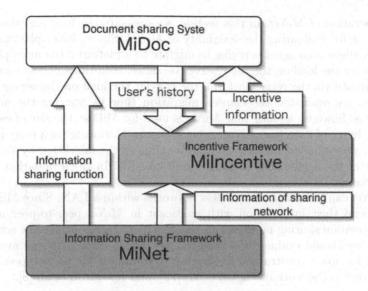

**Fig. 6.** The Architecture of MiDoc.

**Recommending Documents**

MiDoc can recommend documents that are interesting by the user. Users can input their feedback on each document by using a rating function called "my rate", which assesses on a scale of one to five, five being the best). MiDoc recommend a similar document with the document which my rate is high. We also employ using co-occurrence-based thesaurus constructed from a document[15] to measure similarity between two documents.

**Displaying Incentive**

MiDoc provides services, functions, rights to users as incentives to provide information. For example, the current MiDoc presents rankings and provides recommendation functions to users as an incentive. The current incentive function is managed by MiIncentive, whose

**MiDoc** has three layers of architecture. Fig. 6 shows the architecture of MiDoc. **MiNet** is the framework for an information sharing service. Document sharing on MiDoc is implemented by using MiNet's information sharing function. **MiIncentive** is the framework to manage incentive to users. MiIncentive users a user's history on MiDoc and information on a shared network such as other user's history. And, MiIncentive shows an incentive information. MiIncentive uses information on a shared network. **MiDoc** provides the interface for the document sharing system.

## 6   Evaluation

### 6.1   Experiment Setting

Since *MiNet* can construct VPNs using relay platforms, the performance of the server at the relay platform (relay server) is an important factor for comfortable operation of *MiNet*. In this section, we measure the load and the delay of the server for evaluating the scalability of *MiNet*. Since MiNet platforms check whether there is an agent is trying to migrate to a platform, the more platforms, the heavier the load on the relay server becomes. Additionally, the more agents that migrate via the relay platform, the heavier the load on the server.

First, we evaluated the elapsed migration time by varying the number of platforms. Since we assume that *MiNet* is used for MiDoc, the size of each agent is 100K bytes of data that migrates between two platforms via a relay platform. Second, we evaluated the elapsed migrate time of the migration by varying the number of the agents that migrate simultaneously. In this evaluation, we used 10 platforms.

*MiNet* can construct peer-to-peer networks within a LAN. Since MiNet platforms send their information with multicast in *MiNet* peer-to-peer networks, an information sharing network can be constructed without specific servers. Although we should evaluate the performance within each LAN, we avoid a discussion for space constraints. Evaluation of multicast for peer-to-peer overlays is included in the work of Miguel et al. [12]. and Rowstron et al. [8].

## 6.2  Experimental Results

Figure 7 shows the elapsed migration time by varying the number of platforms. The horizontal and vertical axes represent the number of platforms and elapsed time, respectively. The elapsed time increased as the number of platforms increased. That is to say, the load of the relay server increased. However, the elapsed time grew slowly. When there were 50 platforms, there was little influence on agent behavior. Therefore, there is no need to use so many relay platforms for smooth *MiNet* operation.

Figure 8 shows the elapsed migration time by varying the number of agents that migrate simultaneously. In this Figure, the horizontal and vertical axes represents the number of agents and the elapsed time, respectively. The elapsed

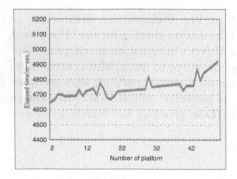
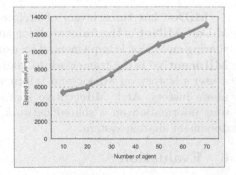

**Fig. 7.** The elapsed time of the migration where we varies the number of the platforms.

**Fig. 8.** The elapsed time of the migration where we varies the number of the agents.

time also increased as the number of agents increased. However, the elapsed time grew approximately linear to the number of agents. In other words, the time did not increase exponentially. When the number of agents is 70, the time is still about 14 sec. Therefore, the effect on the relay platforms is small even if many agents migrate simultaneously.

# 7   Related Work

There are many practical peer-to-peer systems that are used for file sharing: Gnutella [2], KaZaA [3], and Freenet [4]. However, there is no existing system that connects a system beyond firewalls. The Napster music service [1] provided much of the original motivation for the peer-to-peer system, but it is not a pure peer-to-peer system since its database is centralized. Although *MiNet* is not also a pure peer-to-peer system either, it is a pure peer-to-peer system within each LAN: *MiNet* is a hybrid peer-to-peer system that consists of pure peer-to-peer systems. There are other peer-to-peer systems: CAN [9], Tapestry [11], Chord [10], and Pastry [8]. The core of these systems is the same as *MiNet*.

# 8   Conclusion

In this paper, we presented *MiNet*, a peer-to-peer networking technology for effective information sharing based on mobile agents. *MiNet* can construct ad-hoc peer-to-peer networks by encapsulating information and sending it as mobile agents that can migrate in *MiNet* beyond firewalls, proxies, and NATs in LANs. *MiNet* can construct VPNs, which consist of several LANs covered by firewalls, etc. MiNet agents can automatically choose a destination platform according to its policies. *MiNet* could be used to construct a wide variety of peer-to-peer applications on the Internet (e.g., global file sharing systems). We showed MiDoc as an application based on *MiNet*. Since MiDoc is implemented using *MiNet*, MiDoc users can share any document among any LANs. Since *MiNet* can construct VPNs, uses can share the document among different LANs. We measured the load and the delay of the server for evaluating the scalability of *MiNet*. The result of the experiment was that there was no need to use so many relay platforms for smooth *MiNet* operation, and the effect on the relay platforms was small even if many agents migrate simultaneously.

A future direction of this study is to sophisticate the method of dynamic destination selection of MiNet agents.

# References

1. Napster. http://www.napster.com/.
2. Gnutella: http://www.gnutella.com/.
3. KaZaA: http://www.kazaa.com/.

4. I.Clarke, O.Sandberg, B.Wiley, and T.W.Hong. Freenet: A distributed anonymous information storage and retrieval system. In Workshop on Design Issues in Anonymity and Unobservability, pages 311-320, July 2000. ICSI, Berkeley, CA, USA.
5. N. Fukuta, T. Ito, and T. Shintani: "*MiLog*: A Mobile Agent Framework for Implementing Intelligent Information Agents with Logic Programming," In the Proceedings of the First Pacific Rim International Workshop on Intelligent Information Agents(PRIIA2000), pp.113-123, 2000.
6. K.Decker, K.Sycara, and M.Williamson: "Middle-Agents for the Internet," Proceedings of the 15th International Joint Conference on Artificial Intelligence, 1997.
7. JmDNS: http://jmdns.sourceforge.net/
8. A. Rowstron and P.Druschel, "Pastry: Scalable, distributed object location and routing for large-scale peer-to-peer systems." IFIP/ACM International Conference on Distributed Systems Platforms(Middleware), 2001.
9. S. Ratnasamy, P.Francis, M.Handley, R.Karp, and S.Shenker, "A scalable Content-Addressable Network." Proc. of the 2001 conference on applications, technologies, architectures, and protocols for computer communications, ACM Press,2001.
10. I.Stoica, R.Morris, D.Karger, F.Kaashoek, and H.Balakrishnan, "Chord:A scalable peer-to-peer lookup service for internet applications." in Proc of ACM SIGCOMM, San Diego, California, August, 2001.
11. B. Y. Zhao, L. Huang, J. Stribling, S. C. Rhea, A. D. Joseph, and J. Kubiatowicz, "Tapestry: A Resilient Global-scale Overlay for Service Deployment." IEEE Journal on Selected Areas in Communications, Vol. 22, No. 1, January, 2004.
12. M. Castro, M. B. Nones, A. Kermarrec, A. Rowstron, "An Evaluation of Scalable Application-level Multicast Built Using Peer-to-peer Overlays." The 22nd Annual Joint Conference of the IEEE Computer and Communications Societies, 2003.
13. Zero Configuration Networking (Zeroconf): http://www.zeroconf.org/
14. Apple-iPod: http://www.apple.co.jp/ipod/
15. S. Goto, T. Ozono, and T. Shintani, "A Method for Information Source Selection using Thesaurus for Distributed Information Retrieval.", In the Proceedings of the Pacific Asian Conference on Intelligent Systems 2001(PAIS2001),pp.272-277, Nov, 2001.
16. http://java.sun.com/j2se/

# Using Text Mining to Create Actionable Knowledge: Application to Network Failure Incident Reports

Joseph Williamson[1], Kevin Dooley[2], and Steven Corman[2]

[1] Electronic Data systems (EDS)
Herndon, Virginia, USA
joseph.williamson@eds.com
[2] Crawdad Technologies, LLC
Chandler, Arizona, USA
dooley@crawdadtech.com

**Abstract.** Leading in the innovation economy [1] requires an ability to create, comprehend, and utilize dynamic and distributed knowledge assets. This must be accomplished in a reliable, timely, and cost effective manner. Text mining technology has great potential to enhance knowledge management systems because it provides an objective analysis (reliable) of existing knowledge assets (cost effective) in a rapid manner (timely). We show, through a case study involving the analysis of computer network failure incident reports that deep analytics can be used to create actionable knowledge concerning the technical system, and entity extraction can be used to highlight the underlying social architecture of the system. Centering resonance analysis is employed to create a data model of each incident report, and hierarchical clustering, factor analysis, time series analysis, and social network analysis are used to generate insights into the management, execution, and control of the computer network system and its underlying social system.

## 1 Introduction

The potential benefits of knowledge management [2, 3] have led enterprises to strive to implement knowledge management initiatives for themselves in the hopes of achieving the idealized picture of an agile enterprise. Many of these initiatives have not achieved their desired results predominantly because of a management focus with the installation of an information technology solution with scant consideration for the social architecture of the enterprise and the ability to extract actionable knowledge from the information system.

In the agile enterprise, it is increasingly vital that we have the right knowledge we need anytime, anywhere, and in the form and context we desire in order to effectively do our job. Underlying this ability, we must be able to anticipate the need for a new capability and make it available to the rest of the enterprise so that it becomes an accepted offering without increasing the friction in delivery organizations. This artful weaving into the fabric of the enterprise of the right set of people focused at a task in hand, in the right work environment guided by the right kind of leadership and strategy. The only way this agility can emerge is through learning.

Agile enterprises rely on continuous improvement and innovation [4, 5]. Learning is emerging as a significant economic variable has been fuelled by factors such as the speed of technological change, trends towards globalization, and growing corporate

D. Karagiannis and U. Reimer (Eds.): PAKM 2004, LNAI 3336, pp. 71–81, 2004.

competitiveness [6]. Furthermore, organizational learning is seen as a critical complement to managerial theory, because it is through learning that complexity is managed [7]. These factors combine to propel learning to the forefront of corporate competitiveness [8, 9].

Despite our new Agora, boosting the ability for knowledge generation, codification, and transfer, knowledge generation and transfer within an enterprise remains a significant challenge. On the surface, certain factors contribute to this challenge such as economic constraints (the high cost of providing and maintaining tools and information sources on an enterprise-wide basis), lack of time, "infoglut" [10], heterogeneous information resources that are semi-structured and enormous, and misplaced or lost knowledge.

Knowledge is lost if it can not be found. As experienced people retire and today's workforce becomes even more mobile, the knowledge lost to an enterprise is not some half-remembered fact or blueprint. It is the absence of mythologies, the relationships of detail to purpose, and the patterns of rationale that make plain the choices and effects of a particular set of tradeoffs. When experienced individuals retire or relevant information cannot be located, assessing knowledge artifacts such as documents or the memory of a few individuals cannot restore the knowledge. It is their memory of the documents, even temporary working notes once used, which has the greatest payoff. The knowledge that was the rationale employed to formulate the decision (options and trade-off) is lost usually within the first two weeks.

The purpose of this paper is to show how one particular methodological approach – text mining – can be used to enhance the effectiveness of an organization's knowledge management system. Text mining technology is effective because it is an objective analysis (reliable) of existing knowledge assets (cost effective) in a rapid manner (timely). Current text mining systems are too focused however on the traditional "search and categorize" problems. In order for knowledge management systems to create value, they must point to actionable knowledge. In this paper we show how deep analytics can be used to generate actionable insight from text mining, and how entity extraction can be used to illuminate the organization's underlying social architecture.

## 2  Case Setting

The context of the text mining opportunity is an IT service management process managed by a global corporation; we will refer to the company as "Ajax". In managing global services operations, Ajax maintains a data base of incident reports that are written whenever a system outage or breakage occurs. Ajax has been in this business for a long time and considers this process critical to their organizational success, so the quality system surrounding these incident reports is "mature" [11] – reports are written up in a professional manner by IT domain experts. There is every attempt to provide information that can be later used for insight and knowledge generation. While not completely standardized, the reports generally describe the nature of the incident, a timeline of the failure and subsequent recovery actions, a diagnosis of what went wrong, and (often) specific actions plans to both correct the failure immediately, and to keep it from re-occurring. The maturity of the organization's quality system makes these reports an ideal candidate for further text mining.

There were 521 incident reports, each of length between 2-12 pages, with 6-8 pages being the norm. They represented failures in a distributed system – three different global locations, each under their own management structure. Note also that the incident reports themselves pertain to client IT systems, so while there may be, in some cases, multiple reports from the same site (and thus same IT system), the reports for the most part cover different IT systems, and thus the failures are indicative of systemic issues – common hardware and software, and common management, service, and maintenance processes.

## 3 Using Deep Analytics in Text Mining

Current text mining approaches rarely create insight or knowledge; rather, they are focused on facilitating the human use of information technology in order to create insight or knowledge. While increasing the productivity of information search is important to enterprise knowledge management, more significant opportunities exist. These shortcomings are especially acute when text is dynamic and represents the observable signature of a corresponding dynamic process.

A text is pre-processed and basic metrics (e.g. word frequency) are computed. These basic statistics are shallow analytics – representations that are useful as a starting point, but alone are far-less complex and information-rich than the phenomena that they are attempting to model. Shallow analytics can be further analyzed for patterns, leading to deep analytics. For example, the frequency of the word Microsoft in a text stream in a given time period is a shallow analytic; the alarm signal that is triggered when the occurrence of Microsoft in the text stream has significantly increased or decreased from previous levels is a deep analytic. Thus deep analytics are derived from shallow analytics – they involve a "second-order" induction. Finally, deep analytics are combined with domain knowledge to provide actionable insight.

Without deep analytics as a stepping stone, the link between shallow analytics and insight is absent. A human who is expert at modeling data can provide such a link, but the availability of such expertise is limited and not necessarily co-incident with domain expertise. As one executive shared with us recently, "I can't find qualified people to apply the type of analytics I need to in order to understand my content enterprise-wide". We believe the lack of deep analytics is a critical barrier that is standing in front of more widespread adoption of today's knowledge management and text mining systems – practitioners simply have limited time and ability to extract the "bullets of wisdom" themselves from shallow analytics.

In order to (eventually) automate the generation of deep analytics, it is necessary to design and validate an appropriate analytical methodology. The purpose of this case study is to demonstrate such a methodology, and validate its ability to generate useful knowledge.

### 3.1 CRA and Deep Analytics

We propose a four-step approach to employ deep analytics to the understanding of dynamic, textual content:

1. *Summarize content.* The first step is to understand the content of the textual data, both within each text and across a population of texts. We use a novel text model-

ing approach, Centering Resonance Analysis, or CRA [12] to determine the influence of words within a text.

2. *Correlate content*. After step one, each text's words have an associated metric (word influence). These metrics can be correlated with one another and with other variable or categorical data in order to detect patterns.

3. *Identify themes*. Themes are collections of words that have similar co-varying patterns of word influence. We use a data analysis protocol that ensures that themes represent temporally global rather than local phenomena. Themes help define the nature of the textual content beyond a collection of words.

4. *Examine patterns in themes: stability and correlation*. Because themes represent phenomena that cut across texts (and thus space and time), we can discover whether enterprise processes and systems are stable by examining thematic influence values over time using statistical process control charts, and possible causal connections between themes by using time series analysis.

The method we use for developing textual metrics is Centering Resonance Analysis, or CRA [12]. CRA models textual data and measures similarity between texts. CRA is being used for text mining for three reasons:

- CRA is more theoretically sound than traditional word frequency methods. CRA is grounded in a theory of human discourse, unlike frequency-based methods. Recent empirical work [13] has confirmed that CRA produces a metric that is much more statistically stable and well-behaved than any word-based metric, such as word frequency.
- CRA produces a more information-rich metric than traditional word frequency methods. Dooley et al. [13] report that CRA provided superior topic tracking performance compared to traditional word frequency methods such as TF-IDF.
- CRA is computationally feasible. Dooley et al. [13] report a CRA data architecture that is one-third the size of the raw compressed text. Additionally, benchmark tests indicated computational feasibility at a level of processing 36,000 pages per hour on a standard PC.

CRA represents a text as a network [14, 15]. In the resulting CRA Network, nodes represent words while edges indicate discursive connectivity between words. CRA draws on centering theory [16, 17] in assuming that competent authors/speakers generate utterances that are locally coherent by focusing their statements on conversational centers [18, 19]. A CRA Network is a data model that can be used to implement efficient and effective information retrieval and data mining systems. CRA creates a measure of a word's influence, which is a deep analytic in that it takes into account not just the occurrence of the word, but its location within the semantic network. Words that have high influence create coherence and meaning in the text [20, 21], connecting concepts that would otherwise not be connected. CRA uses resonance as a measure of discursive (structural) similarity between two CRA Networks. Resonance is a vector-correlation metric for applications depending on distance measures, such as searching, tracking, detection, and filtering.

CRA has been applied to a number of applications, including knowledge directories for strategic planning [22], customer service, group dynamics [23], media news tracking [24], organizational change [25], conversation [26], and academic discourse [27].

Two key issues demand an automated analysis of these reports. First, the number of reports and their length make it prohibitive that they could be analyzed using "traditional" qualitative data approaches. Humans can code qualitative data at a rate of 10-40 pages per hour. Thus, a single person would have taken one-quarter of a year to do such coding; and for such coding to be reliable, it would have to be done by multiple coders, making the cost prohibitive. Additionally, human coders are biased to see, and not see certain information. Second, such coding would still not uncover relationships across the reports. Statistical data would still need to be tallied in order to detect patterns, leading to insight and knowledge.

## 3.2 Results

1. *Summarize content.* As discussed, we applied CRA to the analysis of textual content. This produces a word-influence metric associated with each word in a text; words that do not occur in a given text are assigned a word-influence value of zero, in order to calculate corpus-level statistics. Average influence is the sum of a word's influence values across all texts, divided by the number of texts. Note that in order to maintain proprietary data in this case, specific names of vendors, products etc. have been made generic.

In order to facilitate the interpretation of the word influence values, an ontological dictionary was developed (using subject matter experts). The ontology specified specific words to be considered as indicative of the following categories: cause, product, application, and client. Not surprisingly, we find that both the distribution of word influence across the ontology, and within an ontological category is Pareto distributed. Figures 1 and 2 show that (a) the report content is mostly about causes – the ontological category of "cause", which contains words shown partially in Figure 2, has far greater representation than the other categories in terms of ranked influential words, and (b) within the category of causes, a few causes have high average influence, and many causes have much lower average influence. This data enabled Ajax to focus its IT investments and improvements on issues pertaining to applications, networks, and databases. It also found, for example concerning hardware causes, that "switch" had twice the average influence of "power", "router", and "firewall".

2. *Correlate content.* Word influence values, and average influence values, can be correlated with one another, and with other categorical or variables metrics of possible interest. Typically in text mining applications, the mode of statistical modeling is exploratory rather than confirmatory. Thus, one should (a) assume that some identified patterns will be false, and some true patterns will remain unfound, (b) use different methods to triangulate results, (c) use statistical methods that are robust to normality and independence assumptions, such as non-parametric methods, and (d) validate patterns based on domain-specific context and expertise.

Figure 3 shows the average word influence associated with the names of different vendors, stratified by location. The Figure shows that, for example, the name of Vendor-4 was more influential in reports from Site-3 than other sites, whereas the name of Vendor-5 was more influential in reports from Site-2 than Site-1 and Site-3.

3. *Identify themes.* Themes are collections of words that have similar patterns of influence across the reports. We employed principle components analysis with a varimax

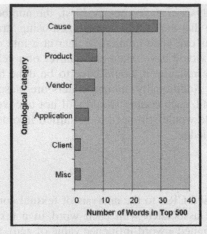

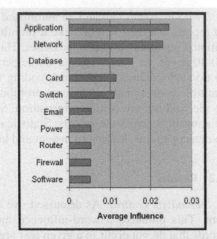

**Fig. 1.** What the reports are about         **Fig. 2.** Influence of words considered causal

rotation in order to identify themes. In order to ensure that themes represented temporally global rather than local phenomena, we only selected words that occurred in at
least ten percent of the reports. We also used extremely conservative limits for identifying factors; whereas normal practice identifies factors that have eigenvalues greater
than 1.0, we used 4.0 as a cut-off. Words with loadings of over 0.60 in absolute mag-
nitude were tagged for being a member of that factor. This yielded 14 factors, or
themes. Subject matter experts were then used to label the themes, based on the word
list comprising the theme. For example, the "Startup issue" theme was composed of
the words {location-A, slow, procedure-A, procedure-B}. This analysis helped Ajax
to see (literally) global problems that cut across different sites. Because these themes
were representative of different systems, sites, clients, and branch management, they
represented systemic causes that needed to be addressed accordingly.

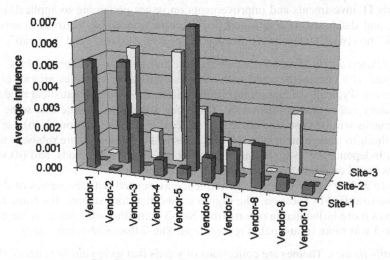

**Fig. 3.** Average influence of vendor by site

4. *Examine patterns in themes: stability and correlation.* While knowledge of the textual themes is useful, their knowledge utility increases when we examine patterns within and between themes. Several different statistical methods are useful here. The first step is to calculate a theme influence value for each text and theme, calculated as the average influence of the words within that theme, for that text. First, theme stability can be examined using statistical process control charts. The subgroup for the control chart was formed by aggregating theme influence values over a month's time (about three to ten reports). Second, themes influence values can be factor-analyzed themselves, to identify meta-themes. This was not done in this case, but could make sense if dozens of themes fall out from step #3. Third, time series analysis can be used to suggest possible causal patterns (Poole et al., 2000). Specifically, if influence of Theme (I) is significantly correlated with the influence of Theme (J) at a reasonable time lag (zero to three months), then we might presume that Theme (I) is a cause of, or leads to, Theme (J). Figure 4 shows a composite cause map, found by aggregating all of the pair-wise significant correlations. The arrow denotes direction of (possible) causality, and the number represents the time lag (in months). We can see that there are a number of causes (on top) that are "sources" of influence in the incident reports, and a number of causes that are downstream. Such an arrangement suggests a root causes-observable symptoms hierarchy. Such insight enabled Ajax to focus on systemic themes that were most likely to lead to the most overall improvement; the root causes are where the greatest leverage exists.

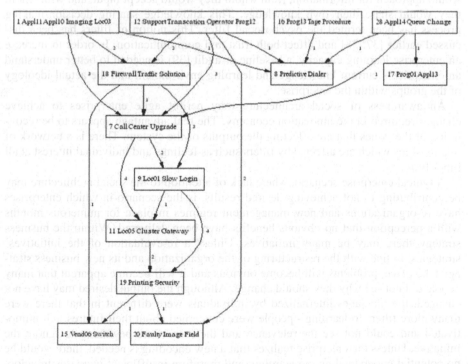

**Fig. 4.** Causal map of themes

## 4  Using Entity Extraction to Identify Social Architecture

Social Architecture was coined as a form of architecture being used when discussing the design and relationships within organizations e.g. General Electric [28] or when stressing the role of community in architecture [29]. It is seen to be very important when designing new organizational structures [30].

Social architecture is considered when discussing the requirements for effective self-managing teams [31], implying the relationships within the organizations will potentially support or destroy the teams. The term is employed when discussing the issues of connectivity within organizations and is identified as the social system as being one of the five key areas of connectivity, which can be managed in order to improve the information technology effectiveness within the organization [32].

In addition to the factors [33, 34] operating at the organizational level which appeared to provide the context for knowledge creation, the informal organization, the actual identity of the groups within the organization, always has psychological force and controls behavior. Identities are how we differentiate the world: Self and other, us and them, this and that etc., things with extension in space and/or time [35]. Identities are what we use to recognize and name the world [36]. The underlying process by which individuals share knowledge, which underpins organizational learning, knowledge creation and knowledge management, is intriguing and complex. As a general observation, knowledge is 'sticky', that is it does not easily flow from individual to individual. Instead, individuals seem to actively make decisions about who they would approach for information, from whom they would accept input, and with whom they would share their own knowledge. This knowledge sharing decision-making process has been termed the psychosocial filter. This notion of filters has been discussed earlier [37, 38] and affect both trust and communication. In order to increase an enterprise learning capacity, a baseline or audit [39] is needed to better understand an enterprise's current knowledge and learning environment and the actual ideology of the groups within the enterprise.

An awareness of social architecture may permit agile enterprises to achieve changes required in the innovation economy. The real advantage appears to be recognition of the issues that are affecting the outputs of the system. There is a network of relationships which are affected by filters such as feelings and individual interest at all times [40].

A typical enterprise scenario, where lack of attention to the social architecture may be contributing to not achieving desired results, is the scenario in which enterprises have re-organizations and new management regimes in place for numerous months with a perception that no obvious benefits have been delivered. Within the business strategy there may be many initiatives. Unless a re-evaluation of the initiatives' strategies, in line with the restructuring of the organization and its new business strategy take place, problems will become obvious and it will become apparent that many people did not see why they should change. Although the output desired may have not changed, the messages internalized by individuals were different in that there were many more filters to learning - people were concerned about their futures, felt unmotivated and could not see the relevance and therefore were beginning to ignore the initiative. Unless the enterprise realizes that a new encoding is needed, there would be no potential understanding, no learning, and therefore insufficient increases in velocity, visibility, or versatility...increases needed by an agile enterprise.

## 4.1 Identifying Social Architecture

We can extract the actual communication network embedded in the incident reports by applying entity extraction. Entity extraction involves scanning a text and identifying names and other proper nouns in either structured or unstructured formats. In this case study we formed a social network by first identifying all of the people mentioned in the reports (this can be difficult because of multiple ways in which the name of a single person can be represented), and then creating an edge (connection) between Person (I) and Person (J) if Person (I) and Person (J) are both mentioned in a particular report. The connections between people can be valued by the number of times the pair co-occur in an incident report. The subsequent social network can be visualized, and its overall structure and the role of particular individuals can be characterized.

Figure 5 shows the network extracted from the Ajax network incident reports. We see roughly three subgroups within the social network, representing the three branch offices; and there is varying connectivity between the subgroups. The subgroup to the right is rather isolated, and the subgroup in the middle is highly inter-connected (clique-ish). The individuals denoted by the blue dots have high "betweeness centrality", the same network-metric used to find word influence within a CRA Network. Individuals with high betweeness centrality connect subgroups that would otherwise be disconnected. In such a social architecture as this, these individuals are where global and systemic knowledge flows; they can act as effective liaisons and boundary spanners, or as ineffective gate-keepers. These insights enabled Ajax to (a) study the consequences of their existing social network and suggest changes, such as how to better connect subgroup three, (b) identify redundancies to manage information overload and divided responsibility, (c) identify important boundary spanners and retain and develop their skills.

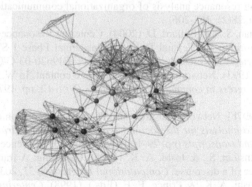

**Fig. 5.** Social network embedded in the incident reports

## 5 Conclusion

We have demonstrated that text mining, pushed to the level of deep analytics, is capable of producing significant insight into an organizational process and an informal organizational structure, and help the firm identify key issues, correlations, trends, and key people. Such deep analytics push text mining beyond search and categorize tasks, into the realm of business problem solving and thus value.

# References

1. Jeff Saperstein, Daniel, Dr. Rouach, Haney, Mary, Creating Regional Wealth in the Innovation Economy: Models, Perspectives, and Best Practices", Pearson Education, Inc., upper saddle River, New Jersey, 2002
2. M. Santosus & J. Surmacz, 'The ABC's of Knowledge Management', CIO Magazine, May 23, http:www.cio.com/forums/knowled-ge/edit/kmabcscontent.html# benefits, 2001
3. G. von Krogh, Ichijo, K. & Nonaka, I. *Enabling knowledge creation how to unlock the mystery of* tacit knowledge and release the power *of innovation,* Oxford, *Oxford university Press,* 2000.
4. W. H. Starbuck 'Learning by knowledge-intensive firms'. Journal of Management Studies, 29 (6), 713 – 740, 1992.
5. K.E. Sveiby  "The new organizational wealth: Managing and measuring knowledge-based assets". San Francisco: Berret Koehler Inc., 1997.
6. M. Easterby-Smith & Snell, R. & S. Gherardi, 'Organisational learning: Diverging communities of practice?'. Management Learning, 29 (3), 259 – 272, 1998.
7. C. Argyris, 'Prologue: Towards a comprehensive theory of management. In Moingeon, B., and Edmondson, A. (Editors) Organisational Learning and Competitive Advantage. London: Sage Publications, 1996.
8. A. P. De Gues, 'Planning as learning'. Harvard Business Review, March- April, 70 – 74, 1988.
9. C. K. Prahalad & G. Hamel, 'The core competence of the corporation'. Harvard Business Review, May - June, 79 – 91, 1990.
10. T. Berners-Lee, "Semantic Web," presentation at Extensible Markup Language 2000 Conf. (XML 2000), 6 Dec., 2000. http://www.w3.org/2000/Talks/1206-xml2k-tbl.
11. Dooley, K., Subra, A., and J. Anderson (2001), "Maturity and its impact on new product development project performance," Research in Engineering Design, 13: 23-29.
12. Corman, S., Kuhn, T., McPhee, R., and K. Dooley (2002), "Studying complex discursive systems: Centering resonance analysis of organizational communication," *Human Communication Research*, 28(2): 157-206.
13. Dooley, K., Corman, S., and Ballard, D. (2004), Centering Resonance Analysis: A Superior Data Mining Algorithm for Textual Data Streams, Final Phase I STTR Report, US Air Force Office of Scientific Research, Contract Number  F49620-03-C-0082.
14. Danowski, J. A. (1993). Network analysis of message content. In W. D. Richards & G. A. Barnett (Eds.), *Progress in communication sciences* (Vol. 12, pp. 197-221). Norwood, NJ: Ablex.
15. Carley, K. M. (1997b). Network text analysis: The network position of concepts. In C. W. Roberts (Ed.), *Text analysis for the social sciences: Methods for drawing statistical inferences from texts and transcripts* (pp. 79-100). Mahwah, NJ: Lawrence Erlbaum Associates.
16. Grosz, B. J., Weinstein, S., & Joshi, A. K. (1995). Centering: A framework for modeling the local coherence of a discourse. *Computational Linguistics, 21,* 203-225.
17. Walker, M. A., Joshi, A. K., & Prince, E. F. (Eds.). (1998). *Centering theory in discourse.* New York: Oxford.
18. G. McKoon and R. Ratcliff, "Memory based language processing: Psycho linguistic research in the 1990's," *Annual Review of Psychology*, vol. 49, pp. 25 -42, 1998.
19. Lecoeuche, R., Robertson, D., Barry, C., & Mellish, C. (2000). Evaluating focus theories for dialogue management. *International Journal of Human-Computer Studies, 52,* 23-76.
20. Kellerman, K., & Sleight, C. (1989). Coherence: A meaningful adhesive for discourse. In J. A. Anderson (Ed.), *Communication yearbook 12* (pp. 95-129). Newbury Park, CA: Sage.
21. Sperber, D., & Wilson, D. (1995). *Relevance: Communication and cognition.* Cambridge, MA: Blackwell.

22. Dooley, K., Corman, S., and R. McPhee (2002), "A knowledge directory for identifying experts and areas of expertise," *Human Systems Management*: 21(4): 217-228.
23. Choi, B-J., Raghu, T.S., Vinze, A., & Dooley, K. (2004), "Contrasting process models of the development of electronic business standards," under review at Management *Information Systems Quarterly*.
24. Dooley, K., and S. Corman (2002), "The dynamics of electronic media coverage," in B. Greenberg (ed.), *Communication and Terrorism: Public and Media Responses to 9-11*, Cresskill, NJ: Hamptom Press.
25. Lichtenstein, B., K. Dooley, and T. Lumpkin (2004), "Dynamics of organizational emergence: A longitudinal study of new venture creation," *to be published in Journal of Business Venturing*, 2004.
26. Dooley, K., Corman, S., McPhee, R., and T. Kuhn (2003), "Modeling high-resolution broadband discourse in complex adaptive systems," *Nonlinear Dynamics, Psychology, & Life Sciences*, 7(1): 61-86.
27. Dooley, K., and Corman, S. (2004), "Dynamic analysis of news streams: Institutional versus environmental effects," *Nonlinear Dynamics, Psychology, & Life Sciences*, 8(3): 403-428.
28. General Electric, 'Social Architecture', www.ge com/operatinq_system/architecture. Htm, 2001.
29. A.W. Batteau, 'The Social Architecture of Community Computing', www.benton.org/policy/Uniserv/Conference/bafteau.htmI, 1996.
30. R.M. Jacobs, 'Management and leadership as creative "social architecture, The Structure and Theory of Organization, www83.homepagevillanovaedu/richard.jacobs/MPA%208002/Powerpoint/f structural/ Index.htm, 2001.
31. W. Bennis, 'An interview with Warren Bennis'. Training, August, Vol 14, No. 8, pp. 33-37, 1997.
32. R.E. Kelley, 'Raising Corporate America's Connectivity Consciousness', PC Week, September 29, Vol 4, No. 39, C24, 1987.
33. W. H. Starbuck, 'Learning by knowledge-intensive firms'. Journal of Management Studies, 29 (6), 713 – 740, 1992.
34. I. Nonaka & H. Takeuchi, The Knowledge-Creating Company: How Japanese Companies Create the Dynamics of Innovation New York: Oxford Press, 1997
35. K. Lewin. Resolving Social Conflict and Field Theory in Social Science, American Psychology Association, 1997.
36. I. Wittgenstein, Philosophical Investigations, Routledge, 1991.
37. H. Saint-Onge, 'Tacit knowledge: The key to the strategic alignment of intellectual capital'. Strategy and Leadership, March/April, 10 – 14, 1996.
38. R.K. Wagner & R. J. Sternberg, 'Tacit knowledge in managerial success'. Journal of Business and Psychology, 1 (4), 301 – 312, 1987.
39. H.K. Rampersad, Total Performance Scorecard; een speurtocht naar zelfkennis en competentieontwikkeling van lerende organisaties, Scriptum Management, Schiedam, September, 2002.
40. C. Mabey, G. Salamann, & J. Storey, Strategic human resource management: a reader, London: Sage, 1990.

# Shared Views on Mobile Knowledge –
# A Concept of a Graphical User Interface

Joanna Slawik, Bernd Eßmann, Thorsten Hampel,
and Research Group "Ad-hoc networking in virtual Knowledge Spaces"*

Heinz Nixdorf Institute, University of Paderborn
Fürstenallee 11, 33102 Paderborn, Germany
{joanna.slawik,bernd.essmann}@hni.uni-paderborn.de,
hampel@uni-paderborn.de

**Abstract.** The term "distributed knowledge spaces" came more and
more into the focus of today's computer science as worldwide communication and cooperative work increase their influence. Our research group
has developed a framework called *Swifff*, which supports essential basics
for distributed working and knowledge management. This paper presents
the innovative concept of distributed shared views of the *Swifff*-GUI[1]-
framework. The framework is designed to combine different kinds of data
displayed in separate views within one interface. We will describe its open
architecture and its ability to add new views at any time. Therefore the
main goal of our approach is the extensibility of our interface concept.
We conclude with a short outlook on our future work.

## 1 Introduction

Being flexible and mobile has become increasingly important for many people in
today's modern information society. Fixed work stations lose more importance in
our community where global cooperation plays a fundamental role. Our personal
needs and behaviours adapt to this new possibilities of communication. Thus the
increasing complexity of features of mobile devices constantly inspires new user
desires.

Affordable mobile user-devices like cellphones, personal digital assistants
(PDAs) as well as laptops already have had a great impact on users for many
years and therefore form a substantial condition for the new independence in our
everyday life. These devices play the role of "personal digital assistants" in connection with the existing modern communication and information infrastructure.
With ad-hoc connected networks [11] even direct wireless cross-linking between
users is possible via their devices at any time and any location as this spon-
tanious peer-to-peer communication does not require any special infrastructure,
any action or effort by the user [5].

---

* Members: Böhle, Björn; Borowski, Marc; Flöthmann, Carsten; König, Andreas;
  Mischke, Stefan; Moritz, Stephan; Niehus, Dominik; Nörenberg, Franziska; Ortgiese,
  Simon; Pankratz, Stefan; Pawlak, Thorsten; Yan, Ling
[1] Graphical User Interface.

D. Karagiannis and U. Reimer (Eds.): PAKM 2004, LNAI 3336, pp. 82–93, 2004.
© Springer-Verlag Berlin Heidelberg 2004

**Fig. 1.** Knowledge space with devices, documents, persons and views.

A "distributed work space" arises from linking different devices, this means their owners, documents, tools and services stored on them. All these objects represent a virtual semantic *knowledge space* (Fig. 1) [9] where each participating user can manage his/her documents. At runtime these scattered virtual parts are joined together and embody data storage and knowledge management on equal peers with integrated synchronized ad-hoc peer-to-peer communication. The architecture below is based on strictly object oriented concepts.

For a better understanding we will sketch a future scenario for borderless distributed cooperative work within a peer-to-peer network. At university, data and information for a lecture are shared in a distributed work space that is accessible by different users. Technically seen, all connected users, for instance students and lecturers connect themselves ad-hoc to such a specific distributed working space representing several knowledge spaces. The lecturer there can publish tutorial materials and students can then access and download them from these knowledge spaces via their PDA, Tablet PC or laptop [4]. These connections are peer-to-peer.

Imagine, one student creates a document using a self-implemented tool but another student who needs the same document does not have the tool on their device. With traditional technologies the second student cannot read the document. Our system (*Swifff*: supporting cooperative work in distributed knowledge spaces) fetches the specific view (in this case the "doc-viewer") remotely from the author's device so that the receiver can work on the document through the view without having to install the application.

Later the author sends a to-do list together with its corresponding view, showing all the tasks the students have to accomplish. Every other student can also open and change this to-do list without having to install the list-view or save the document. During the lecture, students can exchange documents and if problems or questions occur they can be posted to a discussion or chat forum to all other users where the chat itself is distributed over all peers. In doing so, students can use different views according to their needs. For example, one student follows a forum and finds an interesting message. At the same time *Swifff* discovers that the message-author is online and enables the student to start a peer-to-peer-chat with the author by simply starting a chat-view within the forum.

This scenario shows that even when every student possesses their own resources (local files, own views and many more), they are empowered to work cooperatively by accessing all objects (i.e. documents, views, printers or similar), even if they are spread all over the knowledge spaces. This is done by exchanging and using different views even though they are not installed on their own devices.

Several requirements for working on these distributed knowledge spaces can be concluded from this scenario: In the first place, users of different kinds of systems and therefore graphical user interfaces (MS Windows, KDE, Gnome, PocketPC and many more) should be able to work together - thus *platform independence* resp. *portability* is necessary. Further, it would be helpful for users to be able to connect to the network on an ad-hoc basis so that factors like *mobility* and *flexibility* are ensured. Another important factor is *adaptability*. The GUI-layout has to be very flexible and customizable because of the users' various preferences and navigation habits. The user interface design requires reasonable structuring of data to avoid flooding the user with too much information. Further the presentation of these data should be adapted to the actual context. Finally, a distributed work space on such distributed knowledge spaces should allow the development of add-ons according to the user's needs and share them with other users. This makes *extensibility* and *modularity* important factors when designing such systems.

The goal of our research group at the University of Paderborn is to develop and design an application for cooperative work and knowledge management as outlined in the scenario. This paper is focused on the innovative framework for the *Swifff*-GUI within our architecture. Below is an analysis of related work, followed by a description of our concepts and ideas for views, and then a discussion of the GUI-framework.

## 2   Related Work

At the beginning of our work on the project *Swifff* we had a special look at various applications supporting CSCW (Computer Supported Cooperative Work). Especially their concepts of providing different views for the user interface are important for us as today's implementations of file browsers, document management systems or tools for CSCW usually provide only one view for navigation and presentation of its content. We would further like to emphasize that a view is not a dedicated read-only application like the MS PowerPoint-Viewer but a tool to provide a sight onto a subset of objects in knowledge spaces and even to work on these subsets and objects.

A classic CSCW System is *sTeam*[2] which is an open source project dealing with distributed cooperative working and communicating. It is based on a client-server architecture and therefore does not support peer-to-peer ad-hoc communication. It offers user administration and data storage. sTeam is platform-independent. There is a special client for almost every operating system included. The interface contains different views onto objects in knowledge spaces but they cannot be combined in one single work space, which would be suitable for our

---

[2] http://open-steam.org

scenario. Features like chat communication, mail and discussion forums provide a good fundament for cooperative work [8].

*Groove Workspace*[3] realizes cooperative work amongst users connected by a network on a peer-to-peer basis but still requires a connection to a dedicated server. Users are enabled to work cooperatively and if desired synchronously with programs, that are integrated into the system by plug-ins. The Groove user interface provides only one single view on the content. Furthermore Groove is not designed to be extended by user add-ons. For our scenario we want to structure information by different views which can also be implemented by users.

For communication in heterogeneous network environments with several devices and applications XEROX Park Labs developed *Speakeasy* resp. *Obje*. They call their approach *recombinant computing* [2] what means to provide fixed domain-independent interfaces, mobile code, and user-in-the-loop interaction. Speakeasy is supposed to interconnect appliances in the environment like PDAs, multimedia devices etc. in a peer-to-peer manner.

There is also an application available using the Speakeasy technology for cooperative work called *Casca* [3]. It allows discovering and selecting possible partners. The user may share documents with them in shared spaces in so called *conversespaces*. These spaces may also contain devices like printers and beamers but provide no semantic, object-oriented structure like virtual knowledge spaces. Casca again provides only one view onto a conversespace and does not allow to add newly created views. This is because Casca's main purpose is to provide far-ranging functionality, such as display sharing or remote control of peripheral devices, that the application was not explicitly written to support and not to provide different semantic sights onto its conversespaces.

Recapitulating our analysis we consider developing a whole new concept for a GUI-framework supporting spontaneous knowledge management in distributed ad-hoc networks.

## 3   Basic Concept of Views

A *knowledge space* is a virtual space with basic characteristics like: persistence of objects; facility for graphical representation; functionality for awareness; and cooperation of users and access control [9]. It contains all data and information that a user would like to share with others. Services like naming and messaging as well as device access to printers and scanners, for instance, can be parts or objects of knowledge spaces.

Therefore we consider knowledge spaces as (basic) sets of elements. These can be distributed on different devices (Fig.2). To individually or cooperatively manage shared knowledge, users have to be able to relate objects and services stored on different devices to each other. To visualize such related subsets of objects and services we need a special semantic view onto this subset which covers all scattered parts of that subset. Therefore different views onto these knowledge spaces are needed (Fig.3). One view per device or person is not sufficient as users can create numerous subsets of these knowledge spaces.

---

[3] http://www.groove.net

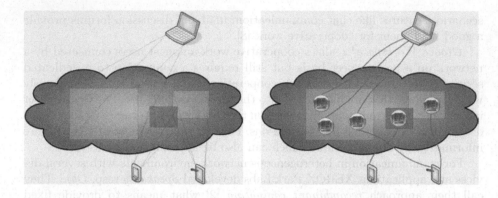

**Fig. 2.** Different views on knowledge spaces.

**Fig. 3.** Distributed views.

In addition to the content of the knowledge spaces we are dealing with information about semantic relationships between their objects. To each object we can assign static as well as dynamic attributes depending on current user properties or context (user device, network connection etc.). Static attributes are for instance, object's owner, file type resp. service while dynamic attributes consist of awareness information such as availability, capacity resp. bandwidth or device resources and the feasibility of presenting the content on the current platform. Using these attributes we are able to build subsets of objects with a specific relationship among them.

The *Swifff*-GUI is the layer for the graphical processing of subsets of objects in distributed knowledge spaces. So with the help of *Swifff*-GUI every user has an overview of existing objects even if they are stored on other users' devices, i.e. other knowledge spaces. Derived from our scenario, the requirements for our concept are *adaptability*, *portability* and *extensibility*. *Mobility* and *flexibility* are requirements resulting not only from the use of ad-hoc networking technology but also through platform independence and support of a variety of different user devices like PDAs and smartphones as well as laptops and desktop computers.

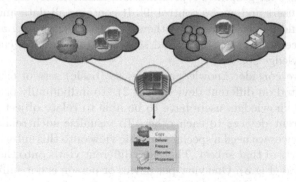

**Fig. 4.** View working on an object.

To realize these demands we have developed a concept that provides a framework for graphical user interfaces by using various views for different subsets of objects in knowledge spaces.

A *view* is therefore a graphical visualization of such a subset. This subset can contain objects from the entire space down to the content of a single object. This view provides user functions to show objects and their attributes; or to present, use and work on the object's content (Fig. 4).

The key concept of the *Swifff*-GUI is to provide the ability to display subsets of knowledge spaces through different views with regard to the object semantics as well as awareness information (Fig. 5). Different context-dependent views differ not only in the amount of objects they operate on but also on how information is structured and processed visually and the functions offered to the user. A view could e.g. be a chat console, an object browser or an agenda.

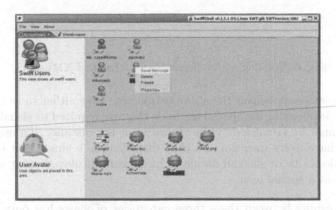

**Fig. 5.** Example screenshot of *Swifff*-GUI.

Therefore the user interface consists of a framework that controls a number of different views as shown in figure 6. Basically we distinguish three types of views:

- *Navigation views* offer methods to navigate through knowledge spaces that is to determine the current position regarding to a selected context and to select the subset of objects to operate on by a *spatial-* or *object view*. To enable this sorting and filtering methods are included. The contained history function is very useful to let the user fulfil his/her "path" up to the present state or to recall his/her previous "positions" by setting "landmarks" that also remains one of the context when set.
- *Spatial views* present a selected subset of objects. The information which is displayed together with each element as well as the arrangement of these objects itself is determined by the user and his/her context. Basically icons are used to represent different objects. General operations (as described below) apply to entire objects within this view.

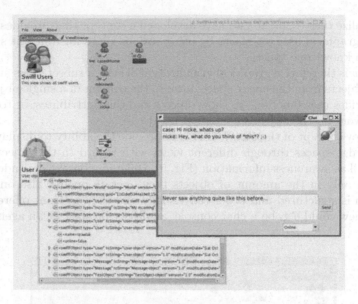

**Fig. 6.** Working with different views (chat and XML-tree).

- *Object views* supplement the above two views. They either show the content of a single object or use special methods that are required to visualize objects that cannot be visualized by the *spatial view*. For instance, if a user does not like to have every message of a chat displayed as a single text object – as *Swifff* does - he or she can decide to have them displayed using a chat view instead of a *spatial view*.

Distinguishing between these three categories of views has only subsidiary meaning. For intuitive interaction with the *Swifff*-GUI it is essential that the views are transparent to the user. The usage should be completely "view-type-independent".

To enable cooperative knowledge management on distributed knowledge spaces views support methods for *linking* and *annotating* objects within one view and even across views. By *linking* we do not mean creating a "pointer" as a reference to a remote object. Rather it means connecting two or more existing objects of different types, to establish a semantic relationship between them and to group objects within knowledge spaces beyond the limits of system-related attributes. *Annotating* helps users to deal with objects without having to open them or just to "publish" one's opinion without changing the object's content itself.

One central point of our approach is the ability of annotating objects and linking them together across views. Annotations made to an object in one view appear in any other view where this object occurs. Objects that are linked together open appropriate *object views* when referred to. For example, a user could mention another user's document during a chat, which a third user may drag & drop directly from the chat view to his/her agenda view to make it an entry of

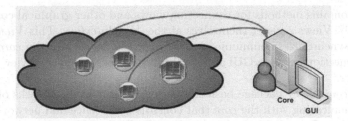

**Fig. 7.** Transporting views from knowledge spaces.

his/her agenda, without the need of opening a *spatial view* or explicitly resolving the link. Using attributed location awareness information, the *agenda view* as a default view for agenda entries, could automatically decide to either insert a reference to that document or to copy the entire document itself to the local persistence, a local part of the storage layer that is controlled by *Swifff*, e.g. hard drive or non volatile memory. Rules for this decision are taken from individual user preferences files. Even if one view is not available for a peer connected to *Swifff*, the system itself reloads this view from the respective remote peers and displays it.

Cooperative knowledge management between users is mainly supported by the *spatial view*. Thus it is a main advantage over conventional file browsers besides the consideration of awareness information and semantics. Additional to file sharing capability the *spatial view* supports direct user communication by written or spoken language through a chat or phone view and by a *synchronisation* and a *drawing* function (as used in sTeam's Shared Whiteboard [1]). The user is able to synchronize their current views especially the state of the *spatial view* or of the whole *Swifff*-GUI with that of other users. Using this mode one may use the *spatial view* as a whiteboard and operate on objects in front of the other user's eyes or just draw on it. This "global" function is useful mainly for demonstration purposes.

Consequently carrying out the object oriented approach of working within knowledge spaces we treat views as *Swifff* objects, too. This allows us to handle new types of objects requiring new views transparent for the use. If a view is not available at the user's device, *Swifff* will be able to search the knowledge spaces for this special "view object", fetch it across the network and launch it at runtime (Fig. 7). With this key feature we make *Swifff* itself part of the knowledge space.

## 4   The *Swifff*-Framework

In this section we will not describe *Swifff's* Java implementation and technical features of the ad-hoc communication in full detail since it concerns the work of a different division of our research group (the business logic called the *"core"*) [6]. Instead we want to focus on the architecture of the GUI-layout.

To realize the functionality mentioned earlier we use a fully modularized architecture. The front-end modules are gathered up in the *"visual"* package. This package contains methods for connecting views and other graphical components of the GUI. Views register themselves at the *ViewInterface*. This *ViewInterface* not only synchronizes communication between the views and the *core* modules (via a connection between GUI and *core*) but also presents special view functions to the user.

The *"controller"* package basically performs all non-visual tasks of the GUI like communicating with the *core* that controls persistence and network communication. Java Remote Method Invocation (RMI) is used as the communication layer. Since all *Swifff* objects are described by an XML document, the GUI requests objects using XSLT-queries that are sent to the *core*. An *XMLparser* is needed for DOM [7] conversion.

We decided to use SWT[4] as windowing toolkit because of its smart system integration and good performance relative to Java Swing or Java AWT. However, the consumption of system resources may become a problem on smaller devices.

The *SwifffShell* (Fig. 6) acts as a frame for active views (if they are not carried out in separate windows) and is therefore the central instance of user interaction. Graphically embedded in the *SwifffShell*, the *SwifffMenu* presents special view functions. Here the user will find general operations ("cut", "copy", "paste", "link", "annotate", "set properties" and "view selection"), basic navigation, window and network preference settings, as well as special functions added by different views. This *SwifffMenu* allows the user to find general operations in place independently from the selected view while at the same time having fast access to special functions.

As previously implied, selecting or launching views is also done within the *SwifffMenu*. In general, *object views* are opened automatically if needed as a "default". Besides that, the user is always able to open another *object view* by the *"ViewBrowser"* (Fig. 8), which is an *object view* we have included to "manage" views. The *SwifffMenu* also includes navigation elements that are added by the *navigation view*.

The *navigation view* represents the knowledge spaces as a tree structure with the current user focused at its root node and other connected users as child nodes (Fig. 8). We propose a hypergraph representation of the tree like in Hyperbolic trees [10] based on the Hypergraph Project[5] as it allows the user to flexible determine his/her region of interest without or before moving there (where "moving" means to explore a region by focusing it within a *spatial view*). Within this hypergraph the user is given an overview of all accessible objects of one or more contexts of his/her interest, such as belonging users, workgroups, services, file types etc. or semantic information of certain topics. Other objects can be displayed even though they may not be available to the user due to either nonexistent access rights or missing reachability in case of network connection. Nodes can be "land marked" for later reference.

A navigation history is given by marking edges according to the user's "path". We will add a simple gadget indicating the last four or five visited nodes in order to easily "jump" back to just visited contexts.

---

[4] Eclipse Standard Widget Toolkit.

[5] The HyperGraph Project http://hypergraph.sourceforge.net (July 2004).

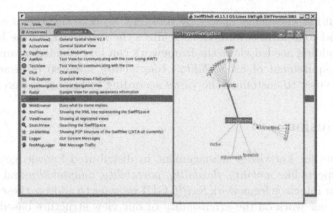

**Fig. 8.** ViewBrowser to manage registered views and HyperNavigationView.

**Fig. 9.** Passing views from one user to an other.

The *"ActiveView"* (working title for our implementation of a *spatial view*) typically occupies the largest area of the *SwifffShell*. Users may prefer to use it as background or a kind of "workbench" as they could do with every view. Objects within this view are visualized as icons. They are scalable and can be arranged freely or aligned depending on their attributes within the view. Standard operations as known from file browsers like sorting and filtering can be applied to all objects in the *spatial view*. This functionality is enhanced by the use of awareness and semantic information - if available and depending on the capabilities of the platforms that are involved - to group objects accordingly to their attributes in order to give an intuitive image of the focused region.

Activating an object (i.e. "double-clicking" in many platforms) invokes its default *object view* which in most cases will be an external application resp. a viewer application connected to that file type. In case of a native *Swifff* object an internal view opens locally if available. This is determined by the "default application" and the "object mime type" attributes. *Swifff* first tries to invoke the default application. If it fails, it tries to open the standard view connected to that object type. If this is not available at the user's device the GUI searches the XML tree that represents all knowledge spaces for a suitable "view object". If there is one available the GUI requests the *core* to fetch the view at runtime like any other object. The view is then passed to the GUI and opened (Fig. 9). If there is no view available, *Swifff* will ask for user assistance.

Representing knowledge spaces by different aspects and therefore splitting the displayed content to several views realizes the *modularity* of the framework. By simply adding needed views the framework can be extended at any time and fulfils the requirement of *extensibility*. *Adaptability* has also been achieved by allowing the user to customize the views according to his/her preferences.

## 5  Conclusion

The concepts for knowledge management in distributed knowledge spaces are based on aspects like *mobility, flexibility, portability, adaptability* and *extensibility*. With our interface framework *Swifff*-GUI we want to address these problems. We focused our work on the *extensibility* of our view structure based on a consequent object oriented approach. This enables us to add new views at runtime very easily without touching or changing the infrastructure itself. Currently a prototype for our framework has been implemented and successfully been tested in a laboratory setting.

Future work on our *Swifff*-framework can enfold into many different directions. The "dynamic" view concept of fetching views from remote and launching them at runtime could be extended to a complete new system feature our research group is currently working on. In the future the GUI and the *core* module can be launched from the web via webstart-technology. The only requirement is the local installation of a Java Runtime Environment. In such a scenario everything a user needs to spontaneously join knowledge spaces is his/her hardware with a standard web browser. The user connects to others who supply the software infrastructure needed to run *Swifff*. A user may transparently redirect one to other users with greater bandwidth if available. The usage acceptance of Java as a runtime environment for handheld devices (like the Java2MobileEdition[6]) helps to make this scenario possible.

Our work on this framework persuaded us of the great need of applications to support cooperative work for highly mobile users. With the support of the *Swifff* application and especially of the GUI-framework first steps have been taken to satisfy these essential needs for distributed knowledge management in ad-hoc peer-to-peer networks.

## Acknowledgements

Joanna Slawik and Bernd Eßmann are members of the postgraduate program 776 "Automatic Configuration in Open Systems" funded by the German Research Foundation (DFG) and the Heinz Nixdorf Institute.

Any icons shown within the presented figures are taken from the KDE Crystal Icon Set and are licensed under the GNU LGPL (http://artist.kde.org).

---

[6] http://java.sun.com/j2me/index.jsp

# References

1. Berteld, K.; Geissler, S.; Hampel, T.: Spatial Knowledge Organization in Cooperative Learning Environments - Combining Shared Whiteboard Technology with SVG, Proceedings of the E-Learn 2004, Washington DC, USA (2004).
2. Edwards, K. W., Newman, M. W., Sedivy, J. Z., Smith, T. F., Izadi, S.: Challenge: Recombinant Computing and the Speakeasy Approach, in: Proceedings of Mobicom '02. (September 2002), 279-286.
3. Edwards, K. W., Newman, M. W., Sedivy, J. Z., Smith, T. F., Balfanz, D., Smetters, D. K., Wong, H. C., Izadi, S.: Using Speakeasy for Ad Hoc Peer to Peer Collaboration, in Proceedings of CSCW '02, (November 2002).
4. Eßmann, B., Hampel, T.: Human Computer Interaction and Cooperative Learning, in Mobile Environments. Human Centred Computing - Cognitive, Social and Ergonomic Aspects. Proceedings of HCI International (2003) 694-698.
5. Eßmann, B., Hampel, T.: Integrating Cooperative Knowledge spaces into Mobile Environments, in: Rossett, Allison: Proceedings of E-Learn, AACE Press, (2003), 2067-2074.
6. Eßmann, B., Slawik, J., Hampel, T.: A JXTA-based Framework for Mobile Cooperation in Distributed Knowledge Spaces, to be published in: Lecture Notes in Computer Science, Springer Publishing House (2004).
7. Feeley, M. J., Levy, H. M.: Distributed shared memory with versioned objects, in: Proceedings of the Conference on Object-Oriented Programming Systems, Languages, and Applications, SIGPLAN Notices, Vol. 27, No. 10, ACM Press, (1992) 247-262.
8. Hampel, T., Keil-Slawik, R.: sTeam - Designing an integrative infrastructure for Web-based computer-supported cooperative learning, in: Proceedings of the tenth international conference on World Wide Web (2001), 76-85.
9. Hampel, T., Keil-Slawik, R.: sTeam: structuring information in team-distributed knowledge management in cooperative learning environments, in: Journal on Educational Resources in Computing (JERIC) Volume 1, Issue 2, Summer 2001, Article No. 3 ACM Press.
10. Lamping, J., Rao, R.: Laying Out and Visualising Large Trees Using a Hyperbolic Space, ACM, Proceedings UIST '94 (1994) 13-14.
11. Perkins, C.E.: Ad Hoc Networking, Addison Weseley (2001).

# Integrating Knowledge Management and Groupware in a Software Development Environment

Ricardo A. Falbo, Daniel O. Arantes, and Ana C.C. Natali

Computer Science Department, Federal University of Espírito Santo, Vitória – ES – Brazil
falbo@inf.ufes.br

**Abstract.** Knowledge is one of the organization's most valuable assets. In the context of software development, knowledge management can be used to capture knowledge and experience generated during the software process. In this process, collaboration technologies also play a central role. With groupware facilities, we have the basis for creating, increasing and capturing knowledge from group and organizational collaboration. First in this paper, we discuss the importance of knowledge management in software development, and how knowledge management and groupware facilities can be integrated into a software development environment (SDE). Then, we present an infrastructure to manage knowledge in ODE, an Ontology-based software Development Environment. This infrastructure deals with several knowledge items, including artifacts, lessons learned and packages of discussion, and considers knowledge capture, store, retrieval, dissemination, use and maintenance.

## 1 Introduction

Software development is a collective, complex, and creative effort. In order to produce quality software, software organizations are trying to better use one of its most important resource: the organizational software engineering knowledge.

Historically, this knowledge has been stored on paper or in people's mind. When a problem arises, we look for experts across our work, relying on people we know, or we look for documents. Unfortunately, paper has limited accessibility and it is difficult to update [1]. In the other hand, in a large organization, it can be difficult to localize who knows some matter, and knowledge in people's mind is lost when individuals leave the company. Important discussions are lost because they are not adequately recorded. Therefore, knowledge has to be systematically collected, stored in a corporate memory, and shared across the organization [2]. In other words, knowledge management is necessary.

Knowledge management (KM) can be viewed as the development and leveraging of organizational knowledge to increase an organization's value [3]. KM involves human resource, enterprise organization and culture, as well as the information technology, methods and tools that support and enable it [4]. A KM system facilitates creation, access and reuse of knowledge, and its main goals are to promote knowledge growth, communication, preservation and sharing.

In the context of software development, KM can be used to capture the knowledge and experience generated during the software process. Reusing knowledge can prevent the repetition of past failures and guide the solution of recurrent problems. Also, we cannot forget that collaboration is one of the most important knowledge sources

D. Karagiannis and U. Reimer (Eds.): PAKM 2004, LNAI 3336, pp. 94–105, 2004.

for software organizations. Then KM should be integrated with groupware applications. But, to be effective in the software development context, a KM system should be integrated to the software process. Since Software Development Environments (SDEs) can be viewed as software process automation, integrating collections of tools to support software engineering activities across the software lifecycle [5], it is natural to integrate groupware and KM facilities into a SDE.

This paper presents the KM infrastructure developed for ODE, an ontology-based SDE [6], and it is organized as follows: section 2 discusses the symbiosis between KM, groupware and SDEs; section 3 presents ODE's KM infrastructure; section 4 discusses related works, and, finally, in section 5, we report our conclusions.

## 2  KM, Groupware and Software Development Environments

Since nowadays knowledge is acknowledged as one of the most valuable organization's assets, it is important to manage organizational knowledge. KM combines tools and technologies to provide support to the capture, access, reuse and dissemination of knowledge, generating benefits for the organization and their members. In this context, collaboration technologies play a central role. KM applications form a continuum from low to high interaction complexity. Therefore, sharing knowledge requires using different interactive communication modes, according to the degree of shared contextual knowledge. In cases where knowledge can be explicitly encoded and recorded, or where the context is well-shared, collaboration technologies are useful in knowledge acquisition, combination, interpretation, and dissemination. Where knowledge is primarily tacit, these technologies can be used to support the personal interaction required for knowledge sharing, creation, and explication [3]. In fact, knowledge utilization and transfer cannot succeed without effectively supporting collaboration. On the other hand, collaborative problem solving, conversations, and teamwork generate a significant part of the knowledge assets that exist in an organization [7].

In the software development context, KM and groupware are quite essential. Using a KM approach, knowledge created during software processes can be captured, stored, disseminated, and reused. KM can be used to better support several activities, such as software process definition, human resource allocation, estimation, requirement analysis, quality planning, and so on.

Also, developing software is essentially a cooperative task. Developers act jointly to achieve the goal of producing a quality software product, and groupware applications, such as email, chat and forum, can be used to support interactions. The knowledge embedded in those interactions can also be captured, stored, disseminated, and reused. Thus, KM and groupware should be integrated. In fact, both KM and groupware should be integrated to the organizational process [8], which, in the case of software development, is the software process.

To deal with complex software processes, it becomes essential to provide computer-based tools to support software engineers to perform their tasks, and those tools must be integrated in a Software Development Environment (SDE). Consequently, SDEs, KM and groupware complement each other in supporting developers during the software process to produce better quality software.

In the next section, we discuss how KM and groupware facilities are integrated in ODE, an ontology-based software development environment.

## 3  Knowledge Management and Groupware in ODE

ODE (Ontology-based Development Environment) [6] is a process-centered SDE, that is developed grounded on ontologies. ODE's design premise is based on the following argument: if the tools in a SEE are built based on ontologies, tool integration can be improved. The same ontology can be used for building different tools supporting related software engineering activities. Moreover, if the ontologies are integrated, integration of tools built based on them can be highly facilitated [6].

ODE is developed based on some software engineering ontologies, such as an ontology of software process [9], an ontology of software metrics [10], and an ontology of software risks [11]. The most important of them is the software process ontology, since it describes the main concepts involved in software processes, such as process, project, activity, artifact, resource, procedure, and so on. The others ontologies are integrated to it, forming a net of concepts.

ODE is developed at the Software Engineering Laboratory of the Federal University of Espírito Santo, and it is implemented in Java. ODE has several tools developed based on its ontologies, such as tools supporting software process definition [6], estimation, resource allocation, risk analysis [11], quality control [6], documentation, and object modeling, among others. Figure 1 shows the software process definition tool. Looking to its interface, we can see that it is strongly based on the software process ontology, using its concepts, relations and constraints.

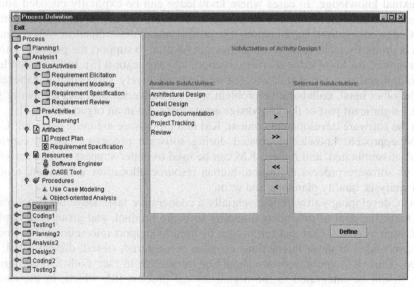

**Fig. 1.** ODE's Software Process Definition Tool

As pointed in section 2, KM can be used to better support several activities, and consequently several tools in a SDE can be improved by some KM facilities. To support developing such tool's KM facilities, a KM infrastructure was developed for ODE. This infrastructure is organized as shown in Figure 2. The *organizational memory* (OM) is at the core of the infrastructure, supporting knowledge sharing and reuse. Arranged around the OM, KM services are available, supporting activities of a general KM process, including creation, capture, retrieval, access, dissemination, use, and preservation of organizational knowledge.

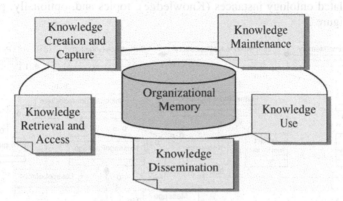

**Fig. 2.** ODE's KM Infrastructure

Ontologies are particularly important for KM. As pointed by Staab et al. [12], ontologies constitute the glue that binds KM activities together, allowing a content-oriented view of KM. Ontologies define the shared vocabulary used in the KM system, facilitating communication, integration, search, storage and representation of knowledge. In ODE's KM infrastructure, ontologies are used to structure the OM, as well as to support some knowledge services, such as search and dissemination. Following, the OM structure and the KM services of ODE's KM infrastructure are discussed in more details.

### 3.1 ODE's Organizational Memory

As pointed above, ODE's OM is structured based on ontologies. As shown in Figure 3, ODE's OM is composed of several knowledge repositories, which are grounded on at least one ontology. Knowledge repositories, in turn, store several types of knowledge items that are relevant to software development, including artifacts, lessons learned, and message packages. Also knowledge repositories contain ontology instances (treated as Knowledge), that are created by the knowledge manager. These are used to store general knowledge about the software engineering domain described through ODE's software engineering ontologies, and are used for indexing knowledge items. In fact, the ontology instances can be viewed as a type of knowledge item, since they are formally defined from ontologies, and they are used in several situations in ODE, such as for giving suggestions during process definition (figure 1). However, we decided not to threat them as knowledge items, because there are some KM services, such as knowledge use, that do not apply to them.

ODE's knowledge items are classified into formal and informal items. Formal items are artifacts created during the software process. Informal items include lessons learned and message packages. Lessons learned are reports describing successful solutions adopted to solve problems, or improvement opportunities. Message packages store important discussions made by developers during software projects developed using ODE. Lessons learned and message packages must be evaluated and, optionally adapted, before getting into ODE's OM. Also, those items are classified according to the indexing schema of ODE's informal knowledge items that includes defining related ontology instances (Knowledge), topics and, optionally, projects, as shown in Figure 3.

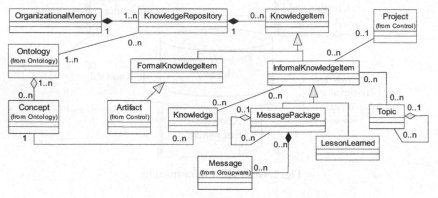

**Fig. 3.** ODE's Organizational Memory Structure (partial model)

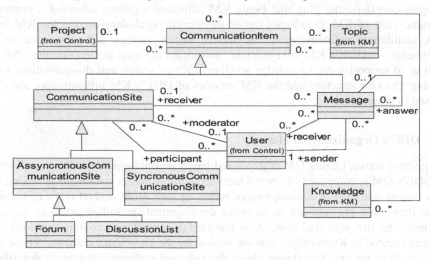

**Fig. 4.** ODE's Groupware Facilities

Message packages are obtained by evaluating and adapting the messages exchanged in ODE's groupware tools. Groupware in ODE includes an instant messaging tool, an email tool with discussion lists, and a forum tool. These communication sites store the exchanged messages, and are mapped in ODE's internal model to Synchronous Communication Site, Discussion List and Forum, respectively, as shown in Figure 4. Using these tools, developers must classify their messages, in order to allow them to be packaged later. Figure 5 shows an email being classified. According to the indexing schema of ODE's informal knowledge items, first the user should select which concepts of the ontology are involved in the message. Based on these concepts, ontology instances (objects from the Knowledge class) are presented. In figure 5, two concepts were selected (Activity and Artifact). Thus instances of these Knowledge classes can be used to classify this message. Also, as shown in figure 5, by default, Topics and Projects can be used to classify messages.

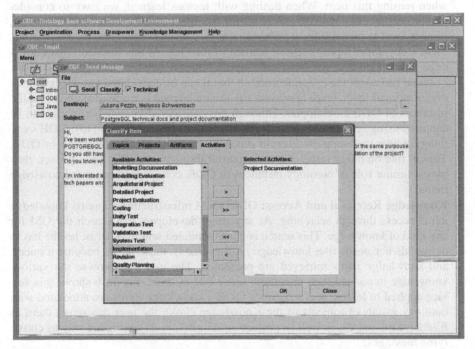

**Fig. 5.** Classifying messages in ODE's E-mail

Later, classified messages can be packed by the knowledge manager, deriving packaged discussions (*MessagePackage* in figure 3), that can be searched and reused by other developers. Integrating groupware and KM, the knowledge embedded in messages, that usually is dispersed in mailboxes of stand-alone email tools, or lost in instant messaging tools, can be captured, stored, disseminated, and reused.

### 3.2 ODE's KM Services

As shown in Figure 2, arranged around the OM, there are services supporting the following knowledge management activities:

- **Knowledge Creation and Capture:** As discussed previously, ODE's OM contains three types of knowledge items: artifacts, lessons learned, and discussion packages. Then, ODE offers facilities to capture each one of these knowledge types. Artifacts created during the software process are submitted to configuration management and become available in ODE's central repository. Discussion packages are created by packing messages exchanged in ODE's groupware applications. This is done using the indexing schema for informal knowledge items, discussed previously. Finally, ODE's KM infrastructure offers a service to register lessons learned. As an informal item, a lesson learned must be classified, indicating project in which it was created, ontology instances associated to the lesson, and topics. Moreover, the following information must be informed: *type* (good practice, improvement opportunity or informative lesson), *context* in which the lesson occurred, description of the *problem, solution* adopted and *expected results* when reusing this item. When dealing with lessons learned, we have to consider that project-level knowledge can be useful, but it is not always the case. Generally, project-level knowledge must be handled to become an organizational knowledge. First, a developer inputs a lesson learned in the OM. At this moment, this knowledge is not available for other developers. The knowledge manager must, first, evaluate and adapt the lesson learned so that it can be considered knowledge at the organizational level. Once approved, the lesson learned is made available. Finally, instances of ODE's ontologies, although not considered knowledge items, can be captured using applications for instantiating ontologies, or ODEd [13], ODE's ontology editor that supports domain ontology building and instantiation in ODE. Topics, like ontology instances, are captured through a specific tool. In fact, they play a similar role of ontology instances in ODE, concerning indexing knowledge items.

- **Knowledge Retrieval and Access:** ODE's KM infrastructure supports knowledge items access through searching. At any time, developers can search the OM for any kind of knowledge. This search is a user-initiated search. That is, he/she has to define his/her needs (the knowledge he/she wants), these needs become a query, and knowledge items retrieved are presented. The user can browse the various knowledge items and then select and reuse one of them. Figure 6 shows this service applied to lessons learned. Since ODE's knowledge items are annotated with ontology instances (objects of the Knowledge class), the user can select them as filters for the search, as well as projects and topics, in an analogous way as classifying messages.

- **Knowledge Dissemination:** Knowledge dissemination is particularly important when users are not motivated to look for information or when they are not aware of the need for information in the first place. While knowledge search is a user-initiated search, knowledge dissemination concerns system proactive aid. I.e. the system performs a search without requiring the user to explicitly formulate a query. In this case, software agents monitor the users' actions as they work and inform them about potential relevant knowledge items. As in knowledge retrieval, users can then browse the items, and select and reuse one of them.

- **Knowledge Use:** Once a search is completed and a knowledge item selected for use, the user must evaluate the item adequacy for helping knowledge maintenance. It includes some evaluation information, such as if the item was useful, problems that appeared when reusing it, and solutions applied.

- **Knowledge Maintenance:** For maintenance and evolution of the OM, it is necessary to take into account users' feedback. Based on the user feedback, the knowledge manager can decide which knowledge items are obsolete or which ones had never been used. To perform this task, the knowledge manager has an interface to search for knowledge items, and to exclude them. A software agent can be set to alert the knowledge manager to realize an OM's maintenance at defined time intervals, or when the OM has reached a defined size. The software agent can also suggest some knowledge items to be excluded based on some knowledge manager criteria.

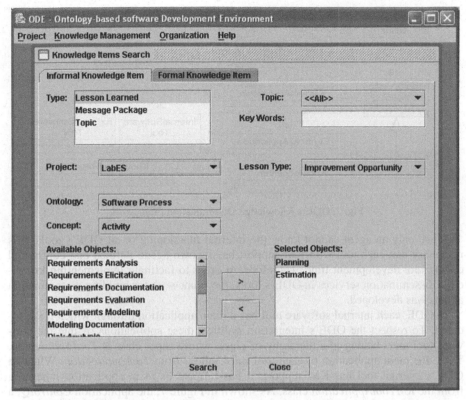

**Fig. 6.** ODE's Knowledge Retrieval Service applied for Lessons Learned

It is worthwhile to point out that ODE's KM services are classified in two types: general services and tool-specific services. General services include those related to knowledge capture, retrieval, use and maintenance. These services are called "general services", because they are provided by the environment, and they are available from the environment as much as from all its tools. Tool-specific services, in turn, concern knowledge dissemination. These services need to take into account features and working of a specific tool, because it is not possible to offer pro-active aid without knowing details about the task being supported by the tool. Thus, knowledge dissemination must be developed for each one of the ODE's tools.

Agents are used to implement the dissemination services. Each tool has an agent (or a community of agents) that monitors developers using it. When the agent perceives that there are knowledge items that can help the user, it acts, showing them. In order to support developing those agents, a framework for building agents was developed, as shown in Figure 7.

The dissemination service starts to be carried through the functioning of ODE's personal agent that monitories user action and verifies when a tool with KM support is initiated. From this moment, it is necessary that the tool specific agent follows user actions to know when to present knowledge and what is considered relevant knowledge for the task in hand.

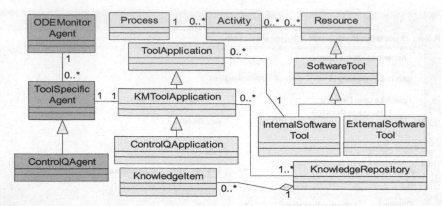

**Fig. 7.** ODE's Knowledge Dissemination Framework

Since only an agent cannot know the internal functioning of all ODE's tools, it is necessary that each tool with KM support has its own agent, defined and configured during tool development time. Therefore, in order to facilitate implementing knowledge dissemination services in ODE's tools, the framework for building dissemination agents was developed.

In ODE, each internal software tool has a main application through which it is executed. To respect the ODE's integration politics, these applications of internal software tool must belong to a hierarchy of class, whose super class is *ToolApplication*. Thus, the main application of each tool must inherit from *ToolApplication*. When an ODE's internal tool has KM support, it has to have its main application inheriting from the *KMToolApplication* class. As shown in Figure 7, the application *ControlQ*, a tool that supports software quality planning and control [6], inherits from this class. Both instances of the *KMToolApplication* class (that is, software tools main applications), and of the *ODEApplication* class (that is, the whole environment) have access to knowledge repositories.

Moreover, it is necessary to create a specialization of the *ToolSpecificAgent* class, associating it to the tool that it should support. In this specialization, it must be defined what to present (type of knowledge items) and when to present the knowledge, implementing the methods *searchKnowledge()* and *presentKnowledge()*, respectively. As shown in Figure 7, the *ControlQAgent* class implements the specific agent to support ControlQ tool. This specific agent is activated by the *ODEMonitorAgent* when ControlQ is initiated. Thus, the specific agent is able to act proactively, searching and disseminating knowledge.

## 4   Related Works

Several works have exploited the use of KM systems to support software engineering tasks, such as [2, 14]. Borges et al. [2] store and share the experience obtained in software process definition. To share this knowledge, an experience repository was built, containing the organizational standard process, as well as the artifacts and lessons learned obtained throughout the projects. In order to facilitate the storage and sharing of the experience, they built ProKnowHow, a tool that supports the standard software process tailoring procedure for each project, providing KM support.

In [14], a system for supporting experience management in Q-Labs, a multinational software improvement consultancy, is presented. The objective is to provide a "virtual office" for Q-Labs, and to allow Q-Labs consultant to benefit from the experience of every other Q-Labs consultants.

Looking to these works, we can find many common points. All of them, including ours, are based on the concept of Experience Factory [15], i.e. an organizational unit that supports reuse of experience and collective learning by developing, updating and providing, on request, past experiences to be used by project organizations. However, none of them is integrated to a Software Development Environment (SDE). Thus, it is worth to remember that this work was developed in the context of ODE, an ontology-based SDE. The remarkable feature of our work is proposing a KM approach actively integrated into the work process and collaboration practices of a SDE. A major goal is to capture information from the work process without extra effort for developers who can receive knowledge from an active organizational memory.

Observing structural aspects of a KM system, we also find many related works in the literature. Abecker et al. [16], for example, defined a KM approach with an organizational memory at the core of the KM system. Arranged around such an organizational memory, KM services provide actively knowledge to users. Our approach shares many of the definitions proposed by them. Thus, ODE's KM infrastructure has also the organizational memory acting as a central knowledge repository and around it, there are services for capturing, searching, disseminating, using and maintaining knowledge.

Ontologies have been pointed as crucial for KM systems. Benjamins et al. [17], for example, present a KM approach based on ontologies and use ontological engineering to organize and structure knowledge. Ontologies also play an important role in our approach, since they are used to structure ODE's organizational memory. But, in our approach, ontologies also give rise to knowledge items, since ontologies can be instantiated.

Several researches pointed out the benefits of software agents for several purposes in KM. Staab et al. [18], for example, present an approach for intelligent proactive knowledge dissemination. Agents work on knowledge created through the usual work tasks of the user and offer knowledge that may be relevant for his/her currently task. In our approach, agents also disseminate knowledge according to users' needs. But in contrast, we embed our agent support in specific steps of activities, based on its ontological distinctions, using semantic information to guide dissemination.

Finally, concerning groupware, there are several tools that have facilities to exchange, store, classify and index messages, but generally messages are not put in an organizational memory, but they are dispersed on users' mailboxes. On the other hand, in ODE, messages are packaged and stored as knowledge items that can be searched and disseminated like any other ODE's informal knowledge item.

## 5   Conclusions

Knowledge management systems facilitate access and reuse of knowledge typically by using several emerging technologies, such as ontologies and software agents. In this paper we presented an infrastructure for managing knowledge in a software development environment (SDE) called ODE.

In ODE's KM approach, knowledge workers constantly create new knowledge as they work. Some benefits of this approach can be pointed out: (i) With KM integrated to a SDE, it is easier for developers to create new knowledge. In this way, the organizational memory is not closed. It is always evolving. (ii) A major concern for KM in ODE is to capture knowledge during the software process without developers' extra effort. Thus, the KM system is actively integrated into the work process. An isolated KM system, on the other hand, can be a barrier to innovation, because it does not let workers share new ideas with their peers. Closed systems do not give organizations control over their own knowledge, since there is a gap between knowledge creation and integration. Innovations happen outside the KM system, and then it contains information that is chronically out of date and that reflects an outsider's view of work [8]. (iii) Developers (as knowledge workers) are no longer passive receivers of knowledge, but are active researchers, constructors, and communicators of knowledge. Knowledge can be constructed collaboratively in the context of the work. Attention to knowledge requires attention to people, including their tasks, motivation, and interests in collaboration. The heart of intelligent human performance is not the individual human mind, but groups of minds interacting with each other and with tools and artifacts [8]. (iv) A KM system must provide the information workers need, when they need it. ODE's KM based tools play an active role in knowledge dissemination. Software agents monitor the actions of users as they work, and inform them about potentially relevant knowledge for the task at hand.

In November 2004, ODE was implanted in a software house as a pilot project, and we expect that soon we can discuss actual results derived from its use, especially those concerning the practical usefulness of its KM approach.

## Acknowledgments

This work was accomplished with the support of CNPq and CAPES, entities of the Brazilian Government reverted to scientific and technological development.

## References

1. D.E. O'Leary, "Enterprise Knowledge Management", IEEE Computer Magazine, March, 1998.
2. L.M.S. Borges, R.A. Falbo, "Managing Software Process Knowledge", Proceedings of the International Conference on Computer Science, Software Engineering, Information Technology, e-Business, and Applications (CSITeA'2002), pp. 227 – 232, Foz do Iguazu, Brazil, June 2002.
3. M.H. Zack, M. Serino, "Knowledge Management and Collaboration Technologies", in Knowledge, Groupware and the Internet, Butterworth-Heinemann, 2000, pp. 303-315.
4. D.E. O'Leary, R. Studer, "Knowledge Management: An Interdisciplinary Approach", IEEE Intelligent Systems, January/February, vol. 16, No. 1, 2001.
5. W. Harrison, H. Ossher, P. Tarr, "Software Engineering Tools and Environments: A Roadmap", in Proc. of the Future of Software Engineering, ICSE'2000, Ireland, 2000.
6. R.A. Falbo, A.C.C. Natali, P.G. Mian, G. Bertollo, F.B. Ruy. "ODE: Ontology-based software Development Environment", Proceedings of the IX Argentine Congress on Computer Science (CACIC'2003), La Plata, Argentina, 2003, pp 1124-1135.
7. A. Tywana. Knowledge Management Toolkit: Orchestrating IT, Strategy, and Knowledge Platforms, 2nd edition, Prentice Hall PTR, 2002.

8. G. Fischer, J. Ostwald, "Knowledge Management: Problems, Promises, Realities and Challenges", IEEE Intelligent Systems, vol. 16, No. 1, January/February, 2001.
9. R.A. Falbo, C.S. Menezes, A.R.C. Rocha. "A Systematic Approach for Building Ontologies". Proceedings of the 6th Ibero-American Conference on Artificial Intelligence, Lisbon, Portugal, Lecture Notes in Computer Science, vol. 1484, 1998.
10. R.A. Falbo, G. Guizzardi, G., K.C. Duarte, "An Ontological Approach to Domain Engineering", in Proc. of the 14th Int. Conference on Software Engineering and Knowledge Engineering, SEKE'02, Ischia, Italy, 2002.
11. R.A. Falbo, F.B. Ruy, G. Bertollo, D.F. Togneri, "Learning How to Manage Risks Using Organizational Knowledge", Advances in Learning Software Organizations (Proceedings of the 6th International Workshop on Learning Software Organizations - LSO'2004), Melnik G. and Holz, H. (Eds.): LNCS 3096, pp. 7-18, Springer-Verlag Berlin Heidelberg, Banff, Canada, June 2004.
12. S. Staab, R. Studer, H.P. Schurr, Y. Sure, *Knowledge Processes and Ontologies*, IEEE Intelligent Systems, January/February, Vol. 16, No. 1, 2001.
13. P.G. Mian, R.A. Falbo. "Building Ontologies in a Domain Oriented Software Engineering Environment". Proceedings of the IX Argentine Congress on Computer Science, La Plata, Argentina, 2003, pp. 930 – 941.
14. M.G. Mendonça Neto, V. Basili, C.B. Seaman, and Y-M Kim, "A Prototype Experience Management System for a Software Consulting Organization", in Proc. of the 13th Int. Conference on Software Engineering and Knowledge Engineering, SEKE'01, Buenos Aires, Argentina, 2001.
15. V. Basili, G. Caldiera, H. Rombach. "The Experience Factory", Vol. 1 of Encyclopedia of Software Engineering, Chapter X, John Wiley & Sons. 1994.
16. A. Abecker, A. Bernardi, K. Hinkelman. "Toward a Technology for Organizational Memories", IEEE Intelligent Systems, Vol. 13., No. 3, pp. 40-48, 1998.
17. V.R. Benjamins, D. Fensel, A.G. Pérez, "Knowledge Management through Ontologies", Proc. of the 2nd International Conference on Practical Aspects of Knowledge Management (PAKM98), Switzerland, 1998.
18. S. Staab, H. P. Schurr. "Smart Task Support through Proactive Access to Organizational Memory". Knowledge-based Systems, 13(5): 251-260. Elsevier, 2000.

# Knowledge Management in Data and Knowledge Intensive Environments

Ashesh Mahidadia and Paul Compton

School of Computer Science and Engineering,
The University of New South Wales, Sydney, Australia
{ashesh,compton}@cse.unsw.edu.au

**Abstract.** In this digital age, it is now possible to electronically collect a large amount of data and business knowledge. However, the next crucial step is to make sense of these data and knowledge in order to improve business processes. Unfortunately, most of the tools available today are not capable of evaluating a large amount of available data against the current business knowledge, in order to automatically suggest improvements and help a decision maker in the process of revising current business processes. In this paper, we outline a new framework that assists a decision maker in the process of evaluating and then if required revising current business knowledge. The tool presented in this paper has been successfully applied to test and revise knowledge bases in the medical domain, using real world data and a domain expert.

## 1 Introduction

Recent advances in technology have resulted in massive amount of organizational and business related data being available to decision makers. At the same time, it is becoming increasingly essential to capture and effectively use available business knowledge to even survive, let alone improve business processes, in this ever-competitive global environment. Today decision makers need to deal with a large amount of data as well as available business knowledge, in order to understand and if possible improve business processes. Often, available data and business knowledge are interrelated and it is up to an expert to make sense of these relationships. Today, tools are available to allow decision makers to access a vast amount of relevant information more quickly and easily. However, such tools are generally **not** able to assist decision makers in the mammoth task of testing available business knowledge against a possibly vast amount of data, and importantly if required, such tools are not able to assist decision makers to revise the current business knowledge in order to explain all available data. Unfortunately, failure to do this may lead to a possible oversight of important business insights.

In this paper we describe a new framework and a tool, called **JustAid**, that allows decision makers to quickly and easily build the required knowledge bases, test these knowledge bases against available data, and importantly if required, revise knowledge bases in order to properly explain all available data. In other words, the system helps decision makers to interpret available data in terms of the current business knowledge. If the current business knowledge cannot explain all available data, the system will assist a decision maker in the process of revising the current business knowledge, in order to explain all available data. In the light of research work in situated cognition

D. Karagiannis and U. Reimer (Eds.): PAKM 2004, LNAI 3336, pp. 106–116, 2004.
© Springer-Verlag Berlin Heidelberg 2004

(Clancey 1997), we argue that a new generation of knowledge-based systems must support the incremental model building process, by allowing an expert to build, test and modify the current model on an on-going basis. JustAid achieves these goals by using an integrated framework that uses techniques from Machine Learning and Knowledge Acquisition, in a way that complements their strengths to overcome their weaknesses. JustAid provides an intuitive and easy to use graphical user interface that allows an expert to build and revise models using domain dependent constructs (causal relationships). This eliminates any need of a knowledge engineer and an expert is not required to know how models are internally stored and modified. We have used JustAid to build and revise causal qualitative models in the medical domain, using real world data and a domain expert. We argue that a similar approach can prove extremely useful in other domains where decision makers need to deal with a large amount of data and often incomplete and partial business knowledge (see Section 5).

## 2   The Nature of Human Knowledge

In this section we will discuss some of the important issues relating to the nature of human knowledge that are relevant to successfully realising knowledge management systems. We will restrict our discussion to building symbolic knowledge management systems. The early promise in 1980's of expert systems boom was not realised (Gaines 2000). This can be attributed to many reasons and they have been extensively discussed in Knowledge Acquisition (KA) literature over the last ten years. One of the main reasons we believe such early approaches did not succeed was their simplistic view regarding human knowledge (or expertise) and how easily it could be transferred. Some of these early approaches presumed that human knowledge is like a static "substance" that can be transferred from an expert to a machine, and the task of knowledge acquisition research is to devise tools that can help in this process.

(Clancey 1997; Menzies and Clancey 1998; Winograd and Flores 1987) have strongly argued against the above approach of building knowledge-based systems and suggested an alternative approach, now known as *situated cognition*. A situated cognition approach suggests that experts provide knowledge for a particular situation in hand (a context), and such knowledge may not be easily applicable in a different new situation (a new context). Clancey suggests that knowledge can be represented, but it cannot be exhaustively inventoried. Therefore, any model that represents what a person knows is just a partial model of their knowledge. Similarly, the context in which knowledge is applied can be represented, but importantly it cannot be objectively and exhaustively described.

Compton (Compton and Jansen 1989; Compton and Jansen 1990) has long argued for the similar case and suggested that experts normally provide *justifications* for their actions rather than explanations of how they reason. These *justifications* may vary depending on the context in which they are generated. For example, doctors' explanations to patients may be very different to their explanation to their colleagues.

Gaines (Gaines 2000) provides supporting arguments from philosophy, psychology, sociology, etc and argues that  "… human expertise arises in the context of human action as a pragmatic process of dealing with present contingencies knowing that there will be further opportunities to deal with consequences of our actions at a later stage.... . Human action takes place in a control loop with imperfect information at each decision point, and with the unfolding process continually changing the state of play." He further suggests that "In many situations, it is more important to act in a way that is not wildly wrong rather than to compute the optimum action, particularly when available information is inadequate, inaccurate, expensive to obtain, and so on. It is generally important to know who has the authority to act and who is accountable for monitoring the consequences, taking follow-up action, and so on."

The implications of the above and other similar arguments suggest that the nature of human behaviour and knowledge is not a *static entity* that can be bottled and reused easily. In fact these arguments indicate that the model representing an expert's knowledge will always be a partial model that may be able to explain the known situations (the contexts in which it was generated). However, we may need to revise this model to suit a new situation that was not considered before. That means, the task of knowledge management requires an on-going effort and we can never assume that the current knowledge base is complete. This highlights the following three crucial aspects that need to be addressed while building a knowledge management system (Menzies 1998; Menzies and Compton 1995):

- Ability to easily build a partial model for a given situation(s)
- Ability to easily test the current partial model
- Ability to easily modify the current partial model to suit a new situation

Thus, in the light of research work in situated cognition, we propose we should build tools that help an expert to cope with the situated nature of human knowledge. Experts are good at providing partial models for a given situation(s). However, it may not be easy for them to combine these partial models and generate consistent and coherent models that explain all the known situations. This task of integrating a new partial model with what is already known becomes harder with increase in the size of the current model. Therefore, we should develop tools that help an expert to quickly build partial models, test these partial models and integrate them with the current model. The aim should be to automate this incremental model building process as far as possible and allow an expert to focus on domain specific issues. Such tools can help in *amplifying* human expertise and over time may produce useful and relatively stable knowledge bases for a given problem.

For a long time, the nature of human knowledge and behaviour has been a major topic of research in the fields of philosophy, psychology, sociology, etc. The field of Artificial Intelligence is relatively new and therefore it might be understandable that researchers in this field have not yet properly addressed some of the issues regarding human knowledge and behaviour (Gaines 2000). We believe it is very important to draw relevant research works from different fields and consider them *seriously* while building intelligent systems. (Hoffmann 1998) argues that an expert's capabilities and limitations have to provide the guideline for the development of more suitable frameworks for AI and cognitive science. He draws relevant research work from different fields and outlines the possible reasons why some of the currently available techniques in AI are not proving useful in real world domains.

In the following sections, we will briefly highlight some of the issues involved in building intelligent systems that can automatically construct symbolic models from available data.

## 3  Automating Symbolic Knowledge Discovery

Machine Learning (ML) and Knowledge Acquisition (KA) are two key research areas in the field of Artificial Intelligence. They both aim to build intelligent systems by generating models of the system under study. In Knowledge Acquisition, these models are acquired from an expert(s) and in Machine Learning, they are automatically generated from data and in some cases partial model(s).

The majority of the learning algorithms in ML, so called data-intensive algorithms, use only data (and not partial models of the system) to automatically construct models of the system. The utility of such models is normally measured on unseen (new) data, and the primary aim here is to build models that perform well on unseen data. A user does not have any direct influence in the model construction process, and it is not possible to provide domain specific knowledge and ask a given learning algorithm to construct models using this knowledge. It is possible that the models constructed by such techniques might be significantly different to the way in which a human expert may perceive (understand) the problem. The field of Data Mining tries to discover useful patterns from large real world databases (Fayyad, Piatetsky-Shapiro et al. 1996), and is becoming increasingly popular in real world domains. Most of the learning techniques in Data Mining similarly use data-intensive algorithms (as described above) to automatically construct models of the system.

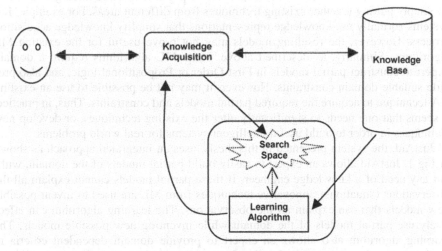

**Fig. 1.** The integrated framework used in JustAid

Few learning algorithms in ML, so called knowledge-intensive algorithms, can automatically construct models of the system using data and available partial model(s) of the system (De Raedt 1992; Kramer, Muggleton 1995; King, Muggleton et al. 1996; King and Srinivasan 1996). However, such systems normally require a user to construct partial models in the corresponding representation (typically in representations like First-Order logic, Propositional logic, etc). This means, a user (typically a domain expert) needs to have a sufficient knowledge about the required representation to construct partial models, which is normally not possible in many real world situations. Alternatively, a capable knowledge engineer is required for this task. However, the difficulties involved in communication between a knowledge engineer and a domain expert often complicates knowledge acquisition process, resulting in less than satisfactory outcomes (Musen, Fagan et al. 1999). Thus, the current knowledge-intensive algorithms are not easy to use and this is one of the reasons why one cannot find many real world applications of such algorithms. It seems that researchers in the ML field currently underestimate the difficulties involved in knowledge acquisition process to construct partial models (Mahidadia 2001). This knowledge acquisition process must be simplified to be able to use such systems for many real world problems.

## 4   Integrating Knowledge Acquisition and Machine Learning

Increasingly researchers from both the research areas, ML and KA, are realising that the task of building intelligent systems for real world problems may require techniques from both these research areas. The aim here should be to integrate them such that we can take advantages of their complementary strengths to overcome their weaknesses. Importantly, such integration should be at the heart of building any intelligent systems. This means, one needs to consider all the relevant issues from ML, KA and other disciplines from the very beginning of the development cycle of an intelligent system. In other words, it may not be possible to build intelligent systems by simply putting together existing techniques from different areas. For example, KA systems normally use knowledge representations that simplify knowledge acquisition process. However, the resulting models may not prove useful for the existing ML algorithms. Similarly, as described above, some ML algorithms require a domain expert to construct partial models in First-Order or Propositional logic, and also provide suitable domain constraints. However, it may not be possible to use an existing KA technique to acquire the required partial models and constraints. Thus, in practice, it seems that one needs to significantly alter the existing techniques, or develop new techniques in order to build useful intelligent systems for real world problems.

JustAid, the system presented in this thesis, uses an integrated approach as shown in Fig 1. JustAid allows an expert to easily build partial models of the domain, without any need of a knowledge engineer. If these partial models cannot explain all the observations (situations), innovative techniques from ML are used to invent possible new models that can explain all the observations. The learning algorithm can effectively use partial models of the domain while inventing new possible models. The learning algorithm also allows an expert to provide domain dependent criteria to guide the search process while looking for a new suitable model. Thus, JustAid uses domain knowledge in two different ways: initially to generate partial models and later to guide the search process while looking for a new suitable model. A simple user interface allows an expert to easily select any one of these possible new models and modify the current knowledge base. Importantly, an expert is not required to know how models are represented or modified.

## 5   Qualitative Models

The original goals of qualitative physics was to capture both the common-sense knowledge of a lay person and the tacit knowledge underlying the quantitative knowledge used by engineers and scientists (Forbus 1990). This requires reasoning with *incomplete knowledge* as well as *abstract knowledge* in a given domain.

In case of **incomplete knowledge**, we may not have detailed knowledge about a given domain. However we may still need to reason with whatever we know about the domain. This is particularly true for a lay person who wants to understand some new concept and has very little knowledge about it. It is also true in the early stages of model formation and revision in a new domain when a user may not have sufficient information about the system under study.

In case of **abstract knowledge**, we may have in-depth knowledge about the domain but may choose to reason with abstractions to avoid complexity and expensive computations. This is particularly true for engineering systems where we do know the exact relationships between different components of a given system, but may choose to reason at abstract level to avoid unnecessary complexity and computations.

Mainstream qualitative reasoning research focuses mainly on engineering problems (Bredeweg and Struss 2003). However, qualitative reasoning can also prove extremely useful for many other domains where decision makers do not have sufficient information available (incomplete knowledge) to solve a given problem. JustAid, the system presented here, uses causal qualitative reasoning to allow decision makers to reason with whatever little knowledge is available in a given domain. Note that, as discussed later, in JustAid the underlying models are represented in First-Order logic (Horn-clauses), and therefore if over time more precise information is available, it should not be difficult to incorporate additional causal relationships in to JustAid.. This will require one to write a "translator" that converts new domain relations to Horn-clause logic, and use it with the JustAid framework. See (Mahidadia 2001) for more in-depth discussion on this topic. In the following section we will briefly outline JustAid system. Space restrictions prevents us from discussing it in more detail here, please see (Mahidadia 2001) more in-depth discussion on JustAid.

## 6  JustAid

In JustAid, a user only deals with directed causal qualitative models throughout the process of model creation and modification. The graphical models are automatically converted into Horn-clause logic and a model-revision process is accomplished by a logic-based learner. As shwon in Fig. 2, the aim is to provide an intuitive and effective user interface that allows an expert to focus on the issues related to the domain and not worry about modeling constructs or underlying logical representation.

If a model cannot explain all the observations (data), model completion in JustAid is derived within a logical setting that forms the basis of Inductive Logic Programming (Mahidadia 2001). JustAid incorporates a new incremental learning technique that can learn definite clause logic programs from observations that are not in the form of definite clauses. Here we provide informal description of the learning technique used in JustAid.

If the current theory (model) cannot explain a given observation, we want to invent a new hypothesis such that the current theory along with this new hypothesis can explain an unexplained observation.

Abduction uses a general rule and the known conclusion to infer a specific fact that might be the cause of the known conclusion. That means, given a general rule (the

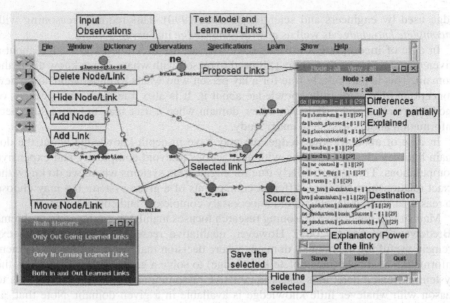

**Fig. 2.** Some of the features provided by the user-interface of JustAid

current theory), we can use abduction to infer a specific fact (an abducible) that might
be the cause of the known conclusion (unexplained effects). In other words, given a
general rule (the current theory), we can explain the known conclusion (effects) if we
can explain (derive) any one of the following:

- the known conclusion itself, or
- a possible abducible

Deduction can be used to infer possible facts given a general rule (the current theory) and a specific known fact (cause). All such inferred facts (call them deducibles)
are true and we can use them while constructing a new hypothesis.

The aim now is to use these deducibles and abducibles, and construct a new hypothesis that can explain the effects or an abducible. We also want to represent this
new hypothesis as a causal qualitative model and therefore we want to construct a
new hypothesis that can be represented as a directed causal link(s). Thus the overall
framework of the learning technique can be described as shown in Fig 3.

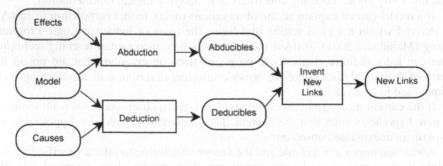

**Fig. 3.** Overall framework of the learning technique used in JustAid

## 6.1 Learning from Multiple Observations

The learning program should be able to find such common links that can explain more than one observation. JustAid uses the following two indicators to find common links that more than one observation (if possible). We say an **ExplanatoryPower**$_{effect}$ of a link represents the number of effects that can be explained by adding that link to the current model. We can use the above criterion and calculate ExplanatoryPower$_{effect}$ for every link we can induce for a given observation. Let's assume we have n unexplained observations.

Let us assume set S$_i$ contains all the new learned links for observation-i. Let us assume set S$_i$ also stores the maximum ExplanatoryPower$_{effect}$ for every link in set S$_i$. For example, let's assume there are two possible explanations for observation-i, and we need to induce the direct link from x to y for both these explanations for observation-i. Let us say, in the first explanation the ExplanatoryPower$_{effect}$ of the direct link from x to y is 1 (it can explain one effect) and in the second explanation it is 3 (it can explain 3 effects). The set S$_i$ needs to store 3 as the ExplanatoryPower$_{effect}$ for the direct link from x to y.

We can now merge all S$_i$'s and generate a set S$_{all}$ that contains all the learned links for all the observations. We can calculate ExplanatoryPower$_{effect}$ of a link in the set S$_{all}$ by adding values of ExplanatoryPower$_{effect}$ of that link in all S$_i$'s. Thus, the value of ExplanatoryPower$_{effect}$ in the set S$_{all}$ indicates the number of effects that can be explained by a given link in explaining all the observations.

Similarly, we can also introduce another indicator called ExplanatoryPower$_{observation}$. The aim here is to count number of observations that can be fully or partially explained by a given link. **ExplanatoryPower**$_{observation}$ of a link in the set S$_{all}$ is equal to the number of S$_i$'s that contains that link. We can now present the links in the set S$_{all}$ to an expert by ordering them in non-increasing (descending) order on the values of ExplanatoryPower$_{effect}$ or ExplanatoryPower$_{observation}$. If the links are ordered on ExplanatoryPower$_{observation}$, the output list will have all the common links (if any) at the top of the list. If the links are ordered on ExplanatoryPower$_{effect}$, the top of the output list will contain links that can explain many effects across all the observations. Depending on the domain knowledge, an expert can select a suitable link(s) from this ordered list and modify the current model. Thus, JustAid can use multiple observations along with the current theory and propose alterations that may require minimum changes (not necessarily optimal) to the current model.

## 6.2 Additional Biases in JustAid

JustAid allows an expert to specify explicit biases depending on the type of model being reasoned about and the particular experiment involved. The learning algorithm uses these explicit biases in reducing the search space while looking for a suitable hypothesis. After consultations with the domain expert in the area of neuroendocrinology, the following explicit biases are implemented in the JustAid learning system.

**Focus** – an expert can provide a sub-graph(s) in which they are interested. The source nodes and destination nodes of new learned links should be part of this sub-graph(s).

**Exclude Sub Models** – an expert can provide a sub-graph(s) that should not be changed. The source nodes and destination nodes of the new learned links should not be part of this sub-graph(s).

**Only Incoming/Outgoing Nodes** – an expert can specify node (nodes) for which the incoming or outgoing links are not possible.

**Impossible Links** – an expert can specify link (or links), which are not possible.

### 6.3 Experimental Results

To measure the effectiveness of JustAid to cope with increasingly incomplete models, we carried out the following experiments. Please note that, this is only one of many such experiments we carried out to evaluate JustAid's performance under a variety of circumstances. Again we refer reader to (Mahidadia 2001) for more in-depth discusses on this topic. Similar to the results outlined here, in all the cases JustAid performed well above the expectations.

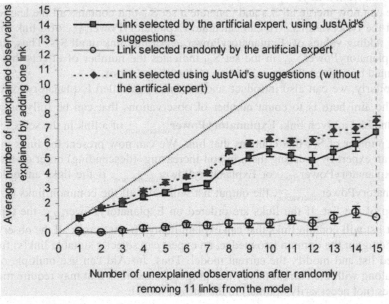

**Fig. 4.** Average number of unexplained observations explained by adding single learned link proposed by JustAid, for models of different sizes

First, we introduced artificial "model incompleteness" by random removal of links from a complete model. Such removals may result in a number of observations being unexplained. Note that, even after removing a link(s), we might be still able to explain a given observation provided we could find an alternative explanation path in the reduced model. That means, it does not follow that a large number of missing links would necessarily result in a large number of unexplained observations. This is particularly true if we have many redundant links in the model. Note that, a domain expert may want to keep these redundant links if such relationships do exist. This point notwithstanding, in this section we will discuss the model construction ability of JustAid for different number of unexplained observations.

For models where 11 links are removed (randomly) from the original model, Fig. 4 shows the average number of unexplained observations explained by adding one learned link selected by the *artificial* expert using JustAid's suggestions (ranking). It also shows the average number of unexplained observations explained by adding one link selected randomly from the suitable links (deleted links). The error bars in the figure represents the standard error of the mean (S.E.M)[1] for each number of unexplained observations. The figure also shows that JustAid is able to effectively find common links that can explain more than one observations.

# 7  Conclusion

We have described a new framework and a tool, called JustAid, that can assist decision makers in checking that their scientific models can explain available data and that can make useful suggestions to researchers about how to improve their models. Even with the very simple causal reasoning tools described here applied to real test cases, it has been possible to point out to a decision maker problems with their models and make useful suggestions as to how they can be improved. This has been possible because a decision maker is normally focused on a specific hypothesis, whereas a computer program will search through all the material available. The experience of interacting with such a system for the decision maker is not so much as interacting with a school master correcting mistakes, but interacting with a lateral thinker suggesting other things that need to be taken into account. The decision maker sees the program not as pointing out errors but in checking ramifications of the model that they would not normally consider. In our experiments, the decision maker found this interaction stimulating. If this sort of result can be found with the simple prototype we have described here, we anticipate that as these sort of tools become more developed they will have a central place in knowledge management systems.

# References

1. Bredeweg, B. and Struss P(2003). "Current Topics in Qualitative Reasoning", AI Magazine, Winter 2003, p 13-16.
2. Clancey W. J. (1997). *Situated Cognition: On Human Knowledge and Computer Representation*, Cambridge University Press, Cambridge, UK.
3. Compton P. J., and Jansen R. (1990). "A philosophical basis for knowledge acquisition." *Knowledge Acquisition*, 2, 241-257.
4. De Raedt L. (1992). *Interactive Theory Revision: an Inductive Logic Programing Approach*, Academic Press.
5. Fayyad U. M., Piatetsky-Shapiro G., Smyth P., and Uthurusamy R. (1996). *Advances in knowledge Discovery and Data Mining*, MIT Press, Cambridge, MA.
6. Forbus K. (1990). "Qualitative Physics: Past, Present, and Future." *Readings in Qualitative Reasoning about Physical Systems*, San Mateo, California, USA.
7. Forbus K. (1993). "Qualitative Process Theory: twelve years after." *Artificial Intelligence*, 59.

---

[1]  S.E.M = (standard deviation) / Sqrt(sample size)

8. Gaines B. R. (2000). "Knowledge Science and Technology: Operationalizing the Enlightment." *The Sixth Pacific Knowledge Acquisition Workshop*, Sydney, Australia.

9. Hoffmann A. (1998). *Paradigms of Artificial Intelligence: a Methodological & Computational Analysis*, Springer.

10. King R. D., Muggleton S. H., Srinivasan A., and Sternberg M. E. J. (1996). "Structure-activity relationships derived by machine learning: The use of atoms and their bond connectives to predict mutagenicity by inductive logic programming." *Proceedings of the National Academy of Sciences*, 93, 438-442.

11. King R. D., and Srinivasan A. (1996). "Prediction of rodent carcinogenicity bioassays from molecular structure using inductive logic programming." *Environmental Health Perspective*, 104((Suppl 5)), 1031-1040.

12. Mahidadia, A. (2001) "Helping Researchers to Construct Scientific Models", PhD Thesis, School of Computer Science and Engineering, University of New South Wales, Sydney, Australia

13. Menzies T. (1998). "Towards situated knowledge acquisition." *International Journal of Human-Computer Studies*, 49, 867-893.

14. Menzies T., and Clancey W. J. (1998). "Editorial: the challenge of situated cognition for symbolic knowledge-based systems." *International Journal of Human Computer Studies*, Vol. 49(No. 6), 767-769.

15. Menzies T. J., and Compton P. (1995). "The (Extensive) implications of evaluation on the development of knowledge-based systems." *Proceedings of the 9th Banff Knowledge Acquisition for Knowledge Based Systems Workshop*, Banff, Canada, 18.1-18.20.

16. Morik K., Wrobel S., Kietz J., and Emde W. (1994). *Knowledge Acquisition and Machine Learning*, Academic Press.

17. Muggleton S. (1992). "Inductive Logic Programming.", Academic Press, London.

# Knowledge Management in an Enterprise-Oriented Software Development Environment

Mariano Montoni, Gleison Santos, Karina Villela, Rodrigo Miranda,
Ana Regina Rocha, Guilherme H. Travassos, Sávio Figueiredo, and Sômulo Mafra

Federal University of Rio de Janeiro - COPPE Sistemas
Caixa Postal 68511 – CEP 21941-972– Rio de Janeiro, Brazil
Phone: +55-21-25628675 Fax: +55-21-25628676
{mmontoni,gleison,darocha,ght}@cos.ufrj.br

**Abstract.** Software Development Environments have evolved to support software developers activities, and to support organizations to achieve goals such
as productivity enhancement, quality improvement, cost reducing, and decrease
of time-to-market solutions. In this context, have appeared the Process-centered
Software Development Environments and, more recently, the Enterprise-
Oriented Software Development Environments. This paper presents the main
approaches adopted on the Taba Workstation, a software development meta-
environment, to support knowledge management in the context of Enterprise-
Oriented Software Development Environments: an ontology-based infrastructure, a knowledge acquisition tool, and a community of practice system.

## 1 Introduction

Software organizations have recently been re-engineering their business processes in
order to increase the maturity of their capability to develop software. The main goal
of most organizations is to increase the effectivity of software solutions developed to
support customer needs. In order to achieve this goal, organizations must be more
productive, increase the quality of software products, diminish project effort and
costs, and deal with the criticality of time-to-market for commercial products [1].

In this context, Software Development Environments (SDE) has been playing an
important role to support software engineers in the execution of software processes
through the application of specific procedures that combine integrated tools and techniques in accordance to particular software paradigms. Moreover, SDE are evolving
to integrate knowledge management activities within software processes aiming to
foster the institutionalization of a learning software organization [322].

The Taba Workstation was created from the perception that different domain applications have distinct characteristics that influence in the environment from which
software engineers develop software [2]. During the last years, the Taba Workstation
evolved to comply with the different levels of capability maturity models of software
organizations3. Therefore, the main objectives of Taba Workstation are: (i) to support the configuration of process-centered software development environments for
different organizations (Configured SDE); (ii) to support the automatic generation

D. Karagiannis and U. Reimer (Eds.): PAKM 2004, LNAI 3336, pp. 117–128, 2004.
© Springer-Verlag Berlin Heidelberg 2004

(i.e., instantiation) of software development environments for specific projects (Enterprise-Oriented SDE); and (iii) to support the management of organizational knowledge related to software processes.

The Taba Workstation is been largely used by software engineers of several Brazilian enterprises that constitute a community of practice for the software process domain. A Web-system named TabaCoP was developed and integrated into the Taba Workstation aiming to provide the basic infrastructure for the community to reach its full potential. The main objectives of the TabaCoP system are: (i) to facilitate the exchange of the community members' knowledge; and (ii) to enable the generation of a software process body of knowledge consistent across different organizations [3].

This paper will focus the main functionalities of the Taba Workstation and the TabaCoP systems. The next section presents some basic concepts related to SDE. The section 3 discusses knowledge management in the context of software organizations. The Taba Workstation infrastructure is presented in section 4. The section 5 discusses the use of the Taba Workstation in three groups of software organizations, and the role of the TabaCoP system in the Taba Workstation community. Finally, section 6 presents some conclusions and points out future work.

## 2 Software Development Environment

A Software Development Environment (SDE) is defined as a computational system that supports software development, maintenance and improvements. It is supposed to support individual and group activities, project management activities, enhancement of software products quality, and increase of the productivity, providing the means for the software engineers to control the project and measure the activities evolution based on information gathered across the development. SDE should also provide the infrastructure to the development and integration of tools to support the execution of software processes. Moreover, this infrastructure should maintain a repository containing software project information gathered across its life cycle.

Recent researches have demonstrated the necessity of standardization of software development methodologies in an organization aiming to increase the control and improve the results of the execution of software development processes [4, 51]. Therefore, SDE should not only support software engineers in the execution of software development processes activities, but also provide the means to execute these processes according to organizational software development standards.

The standardization of software processes can be achieved through the definition of a Standard Process, i.e., a basic process that guides the establishment of a common process across the organization [4]. This process is the base for the definition of software development processes specialized according to the software type (paradigm and technologies), and to the development characteristics (e.g., distributed or centralized development). These specialized processes can be used to define specific processes considering particularities of the software project, a.k.a., instantiated software processes1. Therefore, a SDE should be developed to guide software engineers in the execution of software processes instantiated to a specific software project.

Although it is recognized the importance of standardization of software processes, software organizations must cope with many difficulties that jeopardizes the institutionalization of standard processes, for instance, the dynamism of software processes, the necessity to apply new and evolving technologies, and the people turnover. Therefore, it is imperative for the organizations to manage their members' knowledge in an efficient way in order to guarantee the improvement of their processes execution and preservation of organizational knowledge [6, 7].

## 3   Knowledge Management in Software Organizations

The identification, maintenance and dissemination of different types of knowledge related to software processes (e.g., software process models, best practices and lessons learned) from one project to another are important to develop software with high quality and enhance software processes [8]. Software process models, for instance, explicitly represent knowledge about software development and describe not only the software development activities, but also the software products, necessary resources and tools, and best practices related to software processes execution [9]. Therefore, efficient management of such knowledge supports organizational learning and initiatives for software process measurement and improvement [10].

The fact that most software development organizations are process-centered provides many benefits (e.g., process-centered knowledge management systems can be designed to explicitly associate software process activities with knowledge necessary to execute it) [10]. Moreover, tacit and explicit members' knowledge related to software processes are valuable individual assets that must be captured and converted into the organizational level. The collected knowledge represents indicators of problems concerning the software process definition or the environment in which the software is being developed. This important knowledge can be used to learn about the software process and to provide the means for implementing organizational changes aimed to enhance business performance [11]. In order to acquire such knowledge efficiently, it is necessary to transform arbitrary experiences declarations in structured explicit representations through the execution of activities for knowledge acquisition, packaging, dissemination and utilization [12].

Lindvall et al. [13] present some benefits of a knowledge management program institutionalization: (i) efficient reuse of documented experiences; (ii) easiness to find solutions for problems within the organization; (iii) identification and storage of valuable experiences; and (iv) facility to propose measures to improve processes execution and increase software products quality. Basili et al. [14] and Ruhe [15] point out that by structuring and explicitly representing software process knowledge, it is possible to define efficient training programs that can increase employees' productivity and foster transference of innovative software engineering technology. Landes [16] also notes that knowledge management solutions efficiently support activities of organization members with poor experience in a specific area or domain.

Although most organizations recognize the importance of managing software process knowledge, the establishment of a knowledge management program is sometimes a laborious task. For instance, it is hard to convert tacit knowledge to explicit, and it is difficult to implement knowledge management solutions in a non-intrusive way. Weber et al. [17] point out problems with knowledge management systems, for instance, inadequacy of knowledge representation formats and lack of incorporation of knowledge management systems into the processes they are intended to support.

The next section details the Taba Workstation infrastructure designed to support the execution of software processes and the integration of knowledge management within these processes aiming to preserve organizational knowledge.

## 4   The Taba Workstation Ontology-Based Infrastructure

One of the greatest restrictions for knowledge sharing is the use of different concepts to describe a domain for different systems. The development of ontologies facilitates the sharing of a common terminology. The ontology is used to refer to a knowledge body, typically a common sense on one specific domain, using a vocabulary as representation [18]. In knowledge management systems, ontologies can be used to [19]:

- provide an appropriate precision level in search mechanisms, facilitating the identification of knowledge items in a knowledge base system;
- supply concepts that capture the nature of the desired knowledge, and;
- establish a common language and, thus, to prevent misconceptions in systems that provide means of contribution and use of knowledge withheld by experts.

The use of ontologies in the Taba Workstation infrastructure facilitates the communication between multiple users and the retrieval of knowledge stored in the environment. Considering communication, the defined ontologies reduces terminological and conceptual mismatch in a company. When retrieving knowledge items, the ontologies' supplies vocabularies whose terms are used as links among multiple knowledge/data bases contents. Moreover, when defining synonyms and acronyms for the concepts, ontologies provide linguistic equivalents, which may occur in text documents and can be used to classify and access non-formal knowledge.

The Software Engineering Ontology defines a common vocabulary to guide the registration/distribution of a company's knowledge map and software engineering knowledge in the Taba Workstation. A company's knowledge map defines for each employee its level of skills, knowledge and experiences. The Enterprise Ontology provides concepts and attributes related to the structure, behavior and knowledge owned by companies, defining a common vocabulary to guide the description of any company. This ontology is better explained in the following sub-section.

### 4.1   Enterprise Ontology

The enterprise ontology aims to supply a common vocabulary that can be used to represent useful knowledge for the software developers on the involved organizations in a software project. It supports the development of several case tools in the Taba Environment [22]. Among other factors, it can be useful for:

- supplying a structure that assists knowledge organization and guides knowledge acquisition on one or more organizations;
- easing the development of tools based on the ontology structure, reducing software development environments construction effort for different organizations;
- facilitating tools integration that manipulate ontology related knowledge , allowing the creation and sharing of databases generated based on the structure defined;

– allowing the reuse of organization's available knowledge;
– providing knowledge on the Organization that can assist the identification of the professionals with the abilities adjusted for composing a team in accordance with the project characteristics or to argue or guide the execution of a task.

The ontology explicit definition supported the identification of potentially useful terms and phrases, definition of ontology semantics and sub-ontologies (described in Figure 1) that describe concepts aiming to facilitate understanding, for example:
– how the organization is perceived in its environment;
– how the organization is structured, which are their objectives and how it behaves;
– how Organization's projects have been lead and how the desired and possessed abilities have been distributed into the organization;
– who are the available resources on the organization and how the distribution of authority and responsibility in the organization are accomplished.

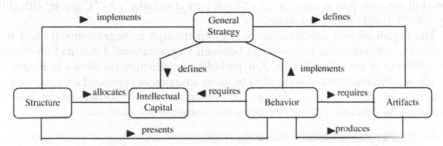

**Fig. 1.** Sub-ontologies of enterprise ontology.

## 4.2 Sapiens: A Corporate Yellow Page Tool to Support the Representation of Organizational Structure Knowledge

The analysis of corporative yellow pages has a great importance to human resources selection. Because usually most of the time the desired competence exists somewhere inside the Organization, being, however, necessary to expend much time to identify, find and have access to who possesses it [14]. The yellow pages support and optimize these tasks, stating a way not to only organize and keep control of the competences, but also to search for the human resources that possess them [20]. The corporative yellow pages are also important for stating a set of competences previously mapped, supplying a guide to the project manager, and sets the terms to be used [21].

Sapiens is a software tool for the representation of the organizational structure with the competences required along it [22]. Besides supporting staff allocation, including the competences of each professional, it also contains search and navigation mechanisms. This way, it is possible the creation of a culture of identification, acquisition and dissemination of the existing knowledge that can be used by the organization to know itself better and take off greater advantage of its potential. Sapiens intends to be generic, it means, independent of a specific organization or domain. It is based on the infrastructure defined for the Taba Workstation, making use of the enterprise ontology to describe the organizations that develop and maintain software for other companies or for its own use. Software developers can use it to find the most appropriate person to help in the solution of a problem inside the organization. The tool promotes the sharing of the organizational knowledge and the communication among the employees in a way to speed problems solution during the initial staff allocation phase of a software project. Moreover, it can be useful to support the activities of the Human Resources Department.

For each position in the organizational structure, it is possible to indicate which competences are necessary or relevant for its performance and to indicate which of these competences are obligatory or not. In a similar way, it is possible to indicate which competences a person owns. The association between people and competence, as well as between position and competence, is not always equal and must take in consideration a certain level of variation. This leveling of the competences allows the standardization of the different degrees of "expertise" existing for a specific ability. For each competence it is associated a specific scale of values. For example, a scale for a specific skill could be constituted of the following items: 1 - "Does not possess the skill nor took part at training"; 2 - "Took part at training"; 3 - "Capable with ability"; 4 - "Capable with great ability".

The organizational structure can be viewed through an organizational chart that shows the subordination relationships between Organizational Units and allows the visualization of each item details. A hyperbolic tree structure (as shown in Figure 2), which is indicated to the visualization of great amounts of organized data in a hierarchic form, is used to browse through the contents of the organizational database by exploring the relations between the items that compose this database.

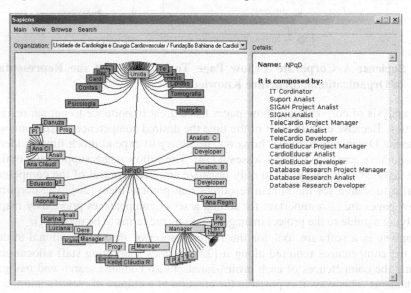

**Fig. 2.** Visualization of the organizational structure through the hyperbolic tree.

The initial root node is the Organization itself. From this point of view, the user can browse on its relations with the others items of the database. When the user clicks on some item its data are shown and the focused item and its relationships with the others items become more evident. For example, when the user clicks on an Organizational Unit, the existing positions inside of this unit appear in the center and, then, the user can see who are allocated to the positions and which competences are related to each one of the items. It is possible to make searches on the organization's database. There are some searches previously registered and the user can create a very new one if desired. Examples of available registered searches are: Who has a specific competence? Which are the competences for a person?

## 4.3 ACKNOWLEDGE: A Knowledge Acquisition Tool

In order to acquire, filter and package organization members' tacit and explicit knowledge related to software processes, an acquisition process was defined and a supporting tool named ACKNOWLEDGE was implemented and integrated into other tools in the Taba Workstation [3]. The main objective of this approach is to capture individual knowledge valuable for the organization, such as, domain knowledge (domain theory), business knowledge (best practices, knowledge about clients and new technologies), past experiences knowledge (lessons learned, common problems), and organization members' knowledge acquired during process execution.

The acquisition process was defined considering some important requirements collected from the literature: (i) allow acquisition of organization members' knowledge related to software processes, (ii) allow filtering of valuable knowledge before storing them in the organizational repository, (iii) guarantee that the representation format of the captured knowledge facilitates its reuse, (iv) guarantee that the captured knowledge content is easily understandable, and (v) guarantee that the new knowledge can be easily accessed and reused by organization members.

The ACKNOWLEDGE tool can be accessed from two icons located under the title bar of all tools from the software development environment. The integration of ACKNOWLEDGE to these tools avoids interruption of organization members normal routine during knowledge capture and reuse. Figure 3 presents the interface of a tool to support the risk management activity and the integration of ACKNOWLEDGE tool.

Organization members' knowledge can be acquired by clicking on the icon (🔆). A list of all knowledge types that can be acquired is presented to the user select which knowledge type is willing to register, for instance, ideas or lessons learned during the execution of the current activity. The acquired knowledge is stored in an intermediary base for further evaluation. The objective of this evaluation is to filter the intermediary base in order to identify the knowledge items relevant to the organization, i.e., the knowledge items, which reuse would improve members' activities execution, and, therefore, enhance organizational performance. By using the ACKNOWLEDGE tool, the evaluation committee coordinator selects members of the committee qualified for the filtering activity and notifies these members of the evaluation to be done. The ACKNOWLEDGE tool also supports the filtering activity by providing collaboration mechanisms for evaluation of the knowledge items over the Internet. Once the knowledge items have been evaluated, the knowledge manager can use the ACKNOWLEDGE tool to package and index the filtered knowledge into the organizational repository. Finally, all captured knowledge can be consulted by clicking on the icon (📀). Figure 4 presents the knowledge consulting interface.

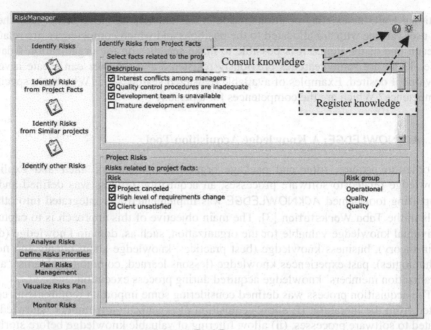

**Fig. 3.** Integration of **ACKNOWLEDGE** to a tool to support risk management.

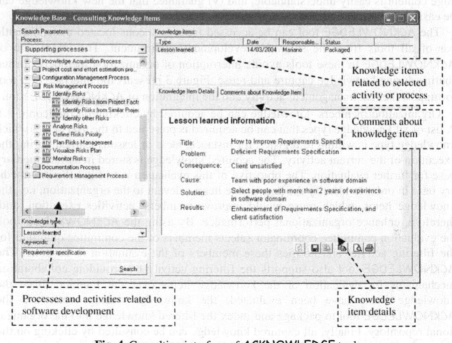

**Fig. 4.** Consulting interface of **ACKNOWLEDGE** tool.

In order to facilitate the search, some consulting parameters can be specified, such as, activity or process related to software development, knowledge type, and key words. The consulting interface also allows knowledge users to register comments about knowledge items. These comments are very useful during knowledge repository maintenance since they facilitate identification of knowledge items that have real value for the organization. Moreover, the comments add value to knowledge items turning them more reliable for knowledge users, and providing the means for establishment of a continuous learning cycle.

During the knowledge acquisition, the ontology concepts can be used to index the organizational knowledge memory. Later, during the knowledge search this same information can be used to assist the search for a specific knowledge.

# 5  The Taba Workstation Community of Practice

Since the end of 2003, the Taba Workstation and its tools have started to be used as support tools to the definition and introduction of software process based development approach in 28 small and medium-size Brazilian software companies organized in three different groups. For each group of companies, a standard software development process is defined based on their specific goals. These standard processes are, then, adapted to the culture and specific characteristics of each software company. Later an initial project is chosen to be developed using this process. The available tools in the Taba Workstation are used to support specific activities such as processes' definition, quality evaluation, process planning etc. After defining the software processes, organization employees are trained in software engineering and in the tools that will be used during the project. During this training people are motivated to adopt a knowledge based attitude, using the facilities provided by the tools and also to share their knowledge among them.

The members of the enterprises that are using the Taba Workstation constitute a community of practice for the software process domain. In order to provide the basic infrastructure for the community to reach its full potential, a Web-system named TabaCoP was developed and integrated into the Taba Workstation. The next section discusses the main functionalities of this system.

## 5.1  The TabaCoP System

The knowledge acquisition approach presented in section 4.2 evolved through the definition of a community of practice related to software process domain, and implementation of an infrastructure for the community to thrive. At the end of the execution of the knowledge acquisition process, all knowledge is stored in a community of practice repository accessible through the Web-based system TabaCoP [3]. This system was implemented to allow members of organizations using the Taba Workstation to access and use knowledge items stored in the community of practice repository. This approach provides the means for creating a continuously evolving body of knowledge consistent across different organizations.

The TabaCoP system supports the interaction of the community of practice members by providing functionalities such as discussion forums related to comprehensive topics, consulting of the knowledge repository, exchange of documents and files related to software process, synchronous and asynchronous discussions, knowledge items cross references so that knowledge located outside the repository can easily be located and accessed. Moreover, the system monitors the evolution, correction and usefulness of the knowledge repository over time.

The reuse of intellectual capital located in the community of practice repository facilitates the identification of valuable knowledge that could be used to support software process activities execution. Application of such intellectual capital from community of practice members, evaluation of the trustworthiness and reciprocity of the knowledge captured in the context of a specific organization, and reuse of this knowledge in different contexts allow the conversion of organizational knowledge into multi-organizational knowledge, and consequently foster the construction of a software process body of knowledge consistent across different organizations.

## 6  Conclusions

This paper presented the main approaches adopted on the Taba Workstation to support knowledge management activities: the use of an ontology-based infrastructure, a knowledge acquisition tool and a community of practice system. Several tools in the Taba Workstation are benefited from its ontology-based infraestructure. Among these tools, there are some for processes' definition, quality evaluation, process planning, requirements traceability, metrics collecting and planning, and so on. Most of the tools are process oriented and, thus, are benefited of ACKNOWLEDGE integration.

The Taba Workstation configured for specific enterprises are being used by more than 20 Brazilian companies supporting software development and software process improvements. The initial results regarding the use of these environments are promising. The environments are configured to support software process that adheres to CMMI Maturity Level 2. Ten enterprises using configured environments are expected to reach this maturity level by the beginning of 2005. The execution of an experimental study is been planned aiming to identify the return of investiment for the organizations using the Taba Workstation and to gather information useful to define strategies for evolving the environment.

Further information about Enterprise-Oriented Software Development Environment and its tools can be found at http://www.cos.ufrj.br/~taba.

## Acknowledgement

The authors wish to thank CNPq and CAPES for the financial support granted to the project Enterprise-Oriented Software Development Environments. We also wish to thank K. Oliveira, R. Falbo and M. Amaral for their contributions to this project.

## References

1. Pfleeger, S. L., 2001, Software Engineering: theory and practice, 2nd edition, Prentice-Hall, Inc., ISBN 0-13-029049-1.

2. Oliveira, K. M., Zlot, F., Rocha, A. R., Travassos, G. H., Gallota, C., Menezes, C., "Domain-oriented software development environment", Journal of Systems And Software, v.172, n.2, p.145 - 161, 2004.
3. Montoni, M., Miranda, R., Rocha, A. R., Travassos, G. H., 2004, "Knowledge Acquisition and Communities of Practice: an Approach to Convert Individual Knowledge into Multi-Organizational Knowledge", In: *Proc. of the 6th International Workshop on Learning Software Organizations (LSO'2004)*, pp. 110-121, Banff, Canada, June.
4. Eman, K. E., Drouin, J., Melo, W., 1998, "SPICE – The Theory and Practice of Software Process Improvement and Capability Determination", *IEEE Computer Society Press*.
5. ISO/IEC 12207:2000. Information technology – software process lyfe cycle.
6. Truex, D. P., Baskerville, R. And Klein, H., 1999, "Growing Systems in Emergent Organizations", *Communications of the ACM*, v. 42, n. 8 (Aug.), pp. 117-123.
7. Maidantchik, C., Santos, G., Montoni, M. A., 2004, "Organizational Knowledge: an XML-based Approach to Support Knowledge Management in Distributed and Heterogeneous Environments", In: *Proceedings of the 16th International Conference on Software Engineering and Knowledge Engineering SEKE'04*, pp. 427-430, Banff, Canada, June.
8. Houdek, F., Bunse, C.: Transferring Experience: A Practical Approach and its Application on Software Inspections, In: Proc. of SEKE Workshop on Learning Software Organizations, Kaiserslautern, Germany, Jun, (1999) 59-68
9. Holz H., Könnecker A., Maurer F.: Task-Specific Knowledge Management in a Process-Centered SEE, K.-D Althoff, R.L. Feldmann, and W. Müller (Eds): LSO, LNCS 2176, (2001) 163-177
10. Maurer, F., Holz, H.: Process-centered Knowledge Organization for Software Engineering, In: Papers of the AAAI-99 Workshop on Exploring Synergies of Knowledge Management and Case-Based Reasoning, Orlando, Florida, Jul: AAAI Press, (1999)
11. Decker, B., Althoff, K.-D, Nick, M., Tautz, C.: Integrating Business Process Descriptions and Lessons Learned with an Experience Factory , In: Professionelles Wissensmanagement - Erfahrungen und Visionen (Beiträge der 1. Konferenz für Professionelles Wissensmanagement), eds. Hans-Peter Schnurr, Steffen Staab, Rudi Studer, Gerd Stumme, York Sure. Baden-Baden, Germany. Shaker Verlag, Aachen, Mar (2001)
12. Birk, A., Tautz, C.: Knowledge Management of Software Engineering Lessons Learned, IESE-Report 002.98/E, Jan, (1998)
13. Lindvall, M., Frey, M., Costa, P., Tesoriero, R.: Lessons Learned about Structuring and Describing Experience for Three Experience Bases, K.-D Althoff, R.L. Feldmann, and W. Müller (Eds): LSO, LNCS 2176, (2001) 106-118
14. Basili, V., Lindvall, M., Costa, P.: Implementing the Experience Factory concepts as a set of Experiences Bases, In: Proceedings of the Int. Conf. on Software Engineering and Knowledge Engineering, Buenos Aires, Argentina, Jun, (2001) 102-109
15. Ruhe, G.: Experience Factory-based Professional Education and Training, In: Proc. of the 12th Conference on Software Engineering Education and Training, March, New Orleans, Louisiana, USA, (1999)
16. Landes, D., Schneider, K., Houdek, F.: Organizational Learning and Experience Documentation in Industrial Software Projects, Int. J. on Human-Computer Studies, Vol. 51, (1999) 646-661
17. Weber, R., Aha, D. W., Becerra-Fernandez, I.: Intelligent Lessons Learned Systems, International Journal of Expert Systems Research and Applications 20, No. 1 Jan (2001).
18. Chandrasekaran, B., Josephson, J. R., Benjamins, V. R., What Are Ontologies, and Why Do We Need Them?, IEEE Intelligent Systems & their applications, v. 14, n. 1 (Jan/Feb), pp. 20-26, 1999.
19. O'leary, D. E., Using AI in Knowledge Management: Knowledge Bases and Ontologies, IEEE Intelligent Systems, v. 13, n. 3 (May/Jun), pp. 34-39, 1998.

20. Alavi, M. and Leidner, D., Knowledge Management Systems: Emerging Views and Practices from the field, Proc. of 32nd Hawaii Int. Conf. on System Sciences, Hawaii, 1999.
21. Staab, S. Human Language Technologies for Knowledge Management. IEEE Intelligent Systems, vol. 16, n. 6 (November/December 2001), 84-88, 2001.
22. Santos, G., Villela, K. Schnaider, L. Rocha, A. R., Travassos, G. H., "Building ontology based tools for a software development environment", In: *Proc. of the 6th Int. Workshop on Learning Software Organizations (LSO'2004)*, pp. 19-30, Banff, Canada, June.

# Towards a Knowledge-Aware Office Environment

Leslie Carr, Timothy Miles-Board, Gary Wills,
Arouna Woukeu, and Wendy Hall

Intelligence, Agents, Multimedia Group
University of Southampton, Southampton, UK
{lac,tmb,gbw,aw1,wh}@ecs.soton.ac.uk

**Abstract.** The objective of the Semantic Web is to make the Web amenable to computer processing, and hence to improve the value that humans can obtain from it. One of the oft-touted user benefits is improved searching: better-described resources allow search engines to provide better-targeted search results. The aim of this paper is to investigate the way in which Semantic Web technologies can be applied to an office environment as the context in which people work and carry out day-to-day document tasks, focusing on the issues of creating and re-using knowledge-rich documents within that environment. To address these issues, we have analysed a business writing scenario and integrated an established commercial off-the-shelf office production environment with knowledge-aware services to assist the author in carrying out writing tasks within that scenario.

## 1 Introduction

Organisations have become increasingly concerned with knowledge management [1], amassing large intranets and multimedia information Web sites in order to capture their corporate knowledge [2] and use it to inform future discussions, decisions and activities. To put this into effect, organisations require a suitably sophisticated IT strategy and infrastructure, however without planning and support these knowledge-bases may be constructed and used in an unsystematic fashion which becomes impractical to manage as the intranet grows in size and complexity. Web and hypermedia design methods enable Web site designers to provide effective navigational access to information resources by cataloguing the kinds of available information; document management systems further help by managing metadata and providing classification and querying support to locate relevant information.

Beyond these dissemination facilities, the ways in which information is put to use varies with the role of each user within the organisation and also with the type and context of the information. To create new material, an author must be familiar with the context in which he or she is writing. Gaining this understanding from an intranet or Web site may come through browsing (navigation through link following) or searching (navigation through content matching). However, staff do not often have sufficient time for unbounded browsing and searching to evaluate the precise relevance of a large range of supplementary and supporting

D. Karagiannis and U. Reimer (Eds.): PAKM 2004, LNAI 3336, pp. 129–140, 2004.
© Springer-Verlag Berlin Heidelberg 2004

documentation. Take for example the situation where a manager is writing a policy statement; it is necessary to draw together information held in a number of business documents: corporate vision statements, corporate strategy documents, departmental policy documents, management summaries, financial reports and public relations statements *etc.*

While reading the content of those documents, the manager will also want to know their purpose (e.g. the intended audience) and authorship (e.g. the author's position of influence) in order to be confident about any judgements made about the documents. What they could reasonably ask of a semantically enriched support environment is to identify relevant material from appropriate documents, based on the context in which new material is being written. The new document should then be published in a form that facilitates reuse of the new knowledge embodied within it, and which provides explicit references to the sources of any reused knowledge, so that (for example) the connection between an institution's three critical success factors and the three section headings in the middle of its corporate strategy document can be identified.

The Semantic Web [3] provides the basis of just such an infrastructure by augmenting documents with explicit statements of semantics, allowing the Web (or an intranet) to be used for more than a human-browseable repository of information. The meaning of the published documents, knowledge about their authors and the reasons for their publication can all be made explicit (to one degree or another) and so be used to infer contextually appropriate knowledge. This paper reports the latest efforts of the Writing in the Context of Knowledge (WiCK) project[1] in investigating the use of Semantic Web technologies in a business-type environment, where authors create and re-use knowledge-rich documents. After considering related work that contributes to our understanding of how this union of technologies can be achieved (Sect. 2), we outline our approach to supporting the specific task of writing a funding proposal (Sect. 3), and finally introduce WiCKOffice, our knowledge-aware office environment which leverages knowledge-aware services to assist an author in such a scenario (Sects. 4 and 5).

## 2   Related Work

When writing new documents, trying to find and reuse the intrinsic knowledge held in other sources amongst an ever-rising mountain of material is at best impractical. Numerous efforts have contributed to our understanding of how this situation can be improved. ARIA [4], for example, supports email or web page authoring based on a semantically annotated photo database. By continuously monitoring the text typed by the author against a domain ontology, ARIA recommends photos from the database that seem appropriate to illustrate the various facets of the unfolding narrative. CREAM [5] helps the writer produce the text itself, by dragging and dropping knowledge fragments from an ontology browser into a text editor – for example a dropped slot inserts a text rendering of the slot value (with a link back to the source).

---

[1] http://wick.ecs.soton.ac.uk/

The potential research and commercial benefits of bringing these knowledge-aware processes into the office arena have not gone unnoticed. Microsoft Word, for example, is the most massively adopted product for authoring text documents [6]; authors can therefore adopt new knowledge-aware extensions without learning a new production environment and without sacrificing familiar features [7]. SemanticWord [6], a Microsoft Word-based environment, adds several toolbars to the standard interface which support the creation of semantic annotations in documents and templates according to selected ontologies (local or imported from the Semantic Web). Annotations are "carried over" in text cut/copy and paste operations, facilitating a level of knowledge reuse between documents. SemanticWord also offers a more proactive annotation feature which the author experiences through the Microsoft Smart Tags interface: as the author types the text content of the document, it is processed by an information extraction component which relates instances and values appearing in the text to ontology instances and types, visually highlighting the matched text in the document. Through the Smart Tags "action" menu, the author can examine the highlighted entities and convert them into semantic annotations.

Although provoking a range of reactions upon its release [8], Smart Tag technology has also been adopted by other office-based initiatives, including SemTalk [9] and OntoOffice [10]. As with SemanticWord, recognised concepts and instances are highlighted with Smart Tags. However, the kinds of action offered differs between systems: in SemTalk, for example, the author can access and edit the underlying ontological model; in OntoOffice, a search for context-relevant documents can be initiated.

Going beyond simply supporting writing in the context of an underlying ontology, the WiCK project has attempted to build on these initiatives by considering an office environment in which several knowledge-bases and knowledge-aware services exist and actively assist the author by providing targeted knowledge that would otherwise need to be searched for both manually and individually.

## 3   Scenario: Writing Funding Proposals

The task of writing a funding proposal is common in industrial and commercial environments; here, we consider a hypothetical funding proposal for a research project in an academic environment. The proposal is directed at the UK's Engineering and Physical Sciences Research Council (EPSRC), which has a well-defined procedure for submitting, reviewing, and selecting proposals for funding, and provides a standard form[2] (the Je-SRP1) and a comprehensive guidance document[3] on how to fill out the form, create the supplementary documentation, and submit it for consideration.

The Je-SRP1 form itself serves as an administrative summary of the research proposal, collecting together the relevant information about the hosting organisation, project investigators, project partners (for joint proposals), referees, staff

---

[2] http://www.epsrc.ac.uk/website/commonpages/downloads.aspx?CID=4482
[3] http://www.epsrc.ac.uk/website/commonpages/downloads.aspx?CID=8621

(including visiting researchers), and travel and equipment costs. The 'meat' of the proposal is contained in the supplementary document – the Case for Support – the composition of which is tightly defined in the guidance notes. The rules for the Case define the formatting (constraints on page length, font sizes *etc.*), the information content, and the structure of parts and sections where each of these pieces of information should be placed. The content of the Case includes previous research track records, proposed research programme and methodology, proposed dissemination routes, and justifications for each of the resources requested in the Je-SRP1 form.

## 4   Our Approach

In order to properly model the Je-SRP1 form and Case for Support document and the knowledge they contain, and hence be able to deploy it usefully in a computational environment more complex than a search engine, our scenario requires a number of ontologies. Firstly, we need to understand and model *what is being written about*. To meet the requirements for our scenario, we propose a *research ontology* to describe the stakeholders and activities who participate in research – the researchers, their publications, research interests, conferences and journals, and a *subject ontology* to describe the area in which we wish to conduct research, the problems that we wish to address and the methods, systems and approaches which have been described in the literature.

Having modelled the subject domain of the writing task, we next need to understand the 'design specification' for the writing task itself – *what needs to be written*. We therefore propose a *document ontology* to make explicit the semantic structure of the proposal documents – the pages, sections, paragraphs, forms, and fields. In order to explicitly model the *type* of information that the author must enter into each part of this structure, a *project ontology* capturing the activity of undertaking work – the ideas of work package, budget, personnel, milestones *etc.* – and a *proposal ontology* – describing the objectives, beneficiaries, funding call, and programme of activity for the project are proposed.

It follows that filling in the Je-SRP1 form is mainly a matter of choosing appropriate instances against the above ontologies from the knowledge-base. The initial fields on the form are for the host organisation's name and reference, and the name of the Principal Investigator. The explicit constraints on this information (according to the guidance notes) are that the host organisation must be of a specific type (e.g. UK Higher Education) and that the PI must be employed by the host organisation and must have a contract of the appropriate type (an academic, duration at least as long as the project lifetime). These simple constraints can easily be modelled as verification conditions on data entry, or as queries upon the knowledge-base to select an appropriate list of choices. Deconstructing the form in this way therefore provides an outline proposal ontology, with the guidance notes document supplying the constraints.

Creating the Case for Support document is more involved, as the author is required to construct a text, rather than enter data into clearly labelled spaces on a form. However the guidance notes indicate very clearly the kind of information that is expected in each part of the document. Examining the bullet points which give instructions for Part 1 of the Case for Support, we can see what basic information is required from the knowledge-base, in addition to the kind of processing and analysis which would need to be performed on it by computational services in order to provide valuable assistance to the author.

*Provide a summary of the results and conclusions of recent work in the technological/scientific area which is covered by the research proposal. Include reference to both EPSRC funded work and non-EPSRC funded work. Details of relevant past collaborative work with industry and/or with other beneficiaries should be given...* This specifies a literature review; the knowledge is described by the subject and research ontologies. A simple query of the knowledge-base would provide a list of potentially relevant papers, but a more advanced reasoning agent would be required in order to assist the author in evaluating the relative significance of the projects and papers.

Part 2 of the Case for Support requires a different kind of knowledge support, for instance within the *Program and Methodology* section: *Identify the overall aims of the project and the individual measurable objectives against which you would wish the outcome of the work to be assessed.* This information does not exist in the knowledge-base; it is invented as an integral part of the creation of a new research undertaking. However, authors may be assisted by seeing the aims and objectives of similar, recent or successful project proposals, especially if they do not have much experience of proposal writing to draw on. In other words a lack of personal experience could be supplemented by directed browsing of an institutional memory.

This brief examination of the EPSRC guidance notes shows how heavily the writing process (both apparently free-text content creation and information recall) is constrained and specified by the appropriate ontologies, opening the possibility of substantive help from a suitably equipped knowledge environment.

## 4.1  Proposed Architecture

Figure 1 illustrates our proposed knowledge-aware office environment, WiCKOffice, designed in response to the opportunities for functionality identified in the previous section. In this environment, knowledge is managed by two knowledge-bases, both based on the AKT 3Store platform [11]. The AKT knowledge-base models the UK Higher Education computer science community[4] (expressed using the AKT Reference Ontology[5]), and hence provides a suitable research ontology for our purposes. A WiCK knowledge-base hosts the additional ontologies. Instances for the proposal ontology are acquired from previous EPSRC project proposals; we envision Semantic Web agents trawling digital library archives and automatically constructing and populating the subject ontology. WiCK extensions to the Microsoft Office environment utilise key computational knowledge

---

[4] http://www.hyphen.info/
[5] http://www.aktors.org/publications/ontology/

134    Leslie Carr et al.

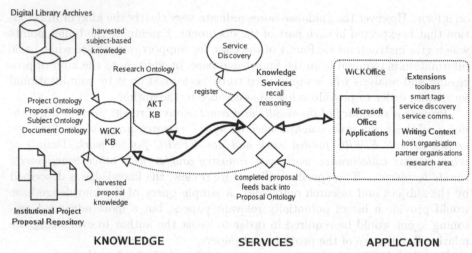

KNOWLEDGE                    SERVICES                    APPLICATION

**Fig. 1.** The proposed WiCKOffice knowledge writing environment.

services to assist the writing task, and to update the knowledge-bases when the writing task is completed (for example, new proposals becoming part of the "institutional memory").

## 5   WiCKOffice: A Knowledge Writing Environment

Based on the opportunities for functionality identified in the previous section, our modelling and development efforts to date have produced a coherent WiCKOffice environment in which several knowledge services are available to authors. A *knowledge fill-in* service and *knowledge recall* service are motivated by the need to provide timely and convenient access to knowledge, which would otherwise have to be manually 'looked up' on the institutional intranet. A third service, *in-line guidelines*, also assists recall by exposing guidelines and constraints captured from the design specification (the EPSRC guidance notes) that are relevant to the part of the proposal document currently being worked on, presenting them to the user via the Microsoft Office Assistant interface (Fig. 2).

### 5.1   Filling in Forms

The *knowledge fill-in* service assists the author in filling in the Je-SRP1 form. For example, the author can specify the (partial) name of the Principal Investigator and instruct the service to retrieve appropriate (in context) instances from the knowledge-base to automatically fill in the remainder of the required information.

The majority of the information required to provide an assisted knowledge fill-in service for the Je-SRP1 form is already provided by the AKT Reference Ontology (the *research* ontology in our scenario). However, leveraging this service is not as simple as filling each part of the form with an appropriate instance selected from the research ontology – different parts of the Je-SRP1 form "share"

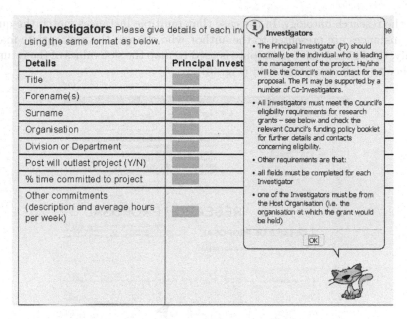

**B. Investigators** Please give details of each inv... using the same format as below.

**Investigators**

- The Principal Investigator (PI) should normally be the individual who is leading the management of the project. He/she will be the Council's main contact for the proposal. The PI may be supported by a number of Co-Investigators.
- All Investigators must meet the Council's eligibility requirements for research grants – see below and check the relevant Council's funding policy booklet for further details and contacts concerning eligibility.
- Other requirements are that:
- all fields must be completed for each Investigator
- one of the Investigators must be from the Host Organisation (i.e. the organisation at which the grant would be held)

[OK]

| Details | Principal Invest... |
| --- | --- |
| Title | |
| Forename(s) | |
| Surname | |
| Organisation | |
| Division or Department | |
| Post will outlast project (Y/N) | |
| % time committed to project | |
| Other commitments (description and average hours per week) | |

**Fig. 2.** In-line guidelines presented via the Microsoft Office assistant.

data about the same concept. For example, information relating to the Principal Investigator must entered in three different locations: section 1B (page 1) requires the PI's title, name, organisation, department, and commitments to other projects; section 2B (page 12) requires the PI's name (for the proposal declaration); and section 3B (page 13) requires the PI's contact telephone number, email address, fax number, *etc.*

We have therefore used Microsoft Office 2003's new "smart documents" feature to add *semantic structure* to the otherwise unstructured Je-SRP1 template in the form of an XML Schema derived from the document ontology. The XML Schema identifies each 'sub-form' of the Je-SRP1 and groups together related sub-forms (thus, for example, describing the fact that information about the PI is shared by sub-forms 1B, 2B, and 3B). Each individual form field is marked up with three attributes – the ID of the sub-form to which the field belongs, a boolean value indicating whether that field is a preferred search field (in the case of the Je-SRP1, the PI's first name and surname are good search terms for a person instance in the research ontology; knowing the PI's title may not so helpful), and finally a `filled-in-by` attribute which identifies the slot of the matching knowledge instance which should be used to actually provide a value for the field.

When the author partially fills in a sub-form (Fig. 3a) and presses the "Fill-In" button, the XML structure of the document is consulted to determine which fields are part of the current sub-form (and also which fields are part of other sub-forms that share data with the current sub-form). Fields in the current sub-form with an `is-search-field` attribute value of `true` are then used by the knowledge fill-in service to construct an RDQL query to extract matches from the research ontology. In the case that multiple instances match the query, these instances are presented to the author who chooses the appropriate match. Finally, the `filled-in-by` attribute is used to map the slot values of the returned instance to each associated field (Fig. 3b).

a. Author fills in partial details.

**B. Investigators** Please give details of each investigator below. Please provide the c using the same format as below.

| Details | Principal Investigator (PI) FILL IN |
|---|---|
| Title | Dr |
| Forename(s) | Les |
| Surname | Carr |
| Organisation | University of Southampton |
| Division or Department | Intelligence, Agents, Multimedia Group |

b. All sub-forms sharing data with current sub-form are populated from matching instance.

**Fig. 3.** Using the knowledge fill-in service to help complete the Je-SRP1 form.

Recently, the EPSRC rolled out its own assisted form filling system, the Je-S1 e-form[6], which provides some equivalent functionality to this service. Provided that each party has previously registered their details with the system, the author can select the host organisation, principal and co-investigators, referees and other staff from checklists and then download a partially completed JE-SRP1 form which contains all the required details of the selected parties, but still requires some unaided 'mandraulic' effort to complete in full. By contrast, we argue that the WiCKOffice approach of leveraging the functionality of multiple services operating over diverse *knowledge* sources (including, but not restricted to, employee data and information harvested from personal webpages and directories) not only allows authors to be aided in filling in *all* aspects of the Je-SRP1

---

[6] https://je-s.rcuk.ac.uk/

form but also potentially offers wider applicability (adding new types of form requires only that form's semantic structure be elicited according the document ontology) than a *data*-based application. By explicitly modelling the knowledge in proposal forms, we can also reasonably ask questions such as "which proposals has *Jane Doe* been involved in?" of an institution's document repository.

## 5.2   Knowledge in the Right Place at the Right Time

The *knowledge recall* service assists the author in quickly and conveniently recalling appropriate knowledge from the research environment. Example (contextual) queries include "what papers relevant to this proposal have been published recently?", or "what relevant projects has this person worked on?". In response to such queries, appropriate knowledge from the knowledge-bases is selected and inserted directly into the document in the form of 'potted' summaries.

As with the *knowledge fill-in* service, the AKT Reference Ontology provides the majority of knowledge utilised by this service. In the current implementation, given the name of a recognised person, project or place, the knowledge recall service assists the writer in recalling facts about it. We have seen that recent incarnations of Microsoft Office already provide a mechanism for recognising terms and presenting available "actions" associated with that term to the user in the form of Smart Tags. However, in the case of the Case for Support document, the author's information requirements depend on the section or part of the document currently being worked on. For example, the author might expect that typing "Les Carr" in the *Previous Research* section would make available options to "auto-summarise" or browse those facets of Les Carr's previous research history most relevant to the current proposal, whereas typing "Les Carr" in the *References* section would make available options to insert Les Carr's most recent and relevant publications, and typing "Les Carr" in the *Researcher Curriculum Vitae* section would make available options to insert a "mini CV" with information appropriate to the proposal (with links to knowledge sources in each case). However, prior to the release of Microsoft Office 2003, the actions made available through Smart Tags have been static; Office 2003 allows the set of available actions to be determined dynamically when the author activates (clicks on) a Smart Tag [13].

An XML Schema derived from the document ontology is again used to make explicit the structural semantics of the Case for Support document. When the author activates a WiCK Smart Tag by clicking on a highlighted term in the text, the XML structure of the document is consulted to work out which part of the document the text appears in (e.g. Background, References) and the actions offered by available services which are appropriate to the type of knowledge required in that section are presented (Fig. 4). We therefore describe this service as providing knowledge in the right *place* (i.e. appropriate to the author's current location in the document) at the right *time* (when a name of a recognised person, place or project is typed by the author).

The principal investigator for this
proposal, Wendy Hall, has been
involved in a number of projects
in this area, including ...

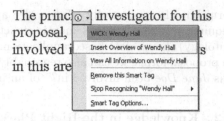

a. Name recognised as author types.

b. Available actions in Previous
Research section.

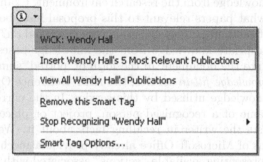

c. Available actions for recognised text "Wendy Hall" in References section.

**Fig. 4.** Using the knowledge recall service, via the WiCKOffice Smart Tag.

## 5.3 Planned Future Services

Two further knowledge-based services are currently under development within
the project proposal writing scenario. Using an appropriate proposal ontology,
an *augmented experience* service provides the author with access to the "institutional memory" of previous research proposals, thereby augmenting the author's
own experience of proposal writing ("what works? what doesn't work?"). For
example, the author is assisted in evaluating the most important beneficiaries
of the proposed research by being shown the beneficiaries put forward by other
proposals (with an indication as to whether those proposals were subsequently
approved or otherwise).

An *assisted writing* service attempts to assist the author in making higher-
level decisions about relevant content to include in the proposal by suggesting
appropriate instances from the subject ontology (for example, relevant projects,
papers, resources) based on both the writing context and the text that the author has already written. For example, this service uses an internal bibliometric
reasoning engine to detect that although the author has referred to a number of
*knowledge acquisition*-related projects in the *Background* section[7] of the Case
for Support, one statistically significant project has not yet been mentioned, and
so offers to create a summary of the project from the relevant instances in the

---

[7] Guidance notes: "Demonstrate a knowledge and understanding of past and current
work in the subject area both in the UK and abroad."

knowledge-base (gathering details of key personnel and publications) and inserts the information into the appropriate sections of the Case document.

# 6 Conclusions and Future Work

Semantic Web technologies are beginning to build large, flexible knowledge stores which can be leveraged for diverse purposes within an organisation. This paper has reported the latest efforts of a project to assist authors in creating and re-using knowledge-rich documents within such an environment. This paper has three contributions. First we have analysed the knowledge flow in an business writing task, specifically the creation of a project proposal aimed at a funding body, in this case a research council. Secondly we have identified that this task can be constrained and specified by five ontologies: a *research ontology* (stake-holders and activities participating in research) and *subject ontology* (the area in which we wish to conduct research) capture *what we are writing about*; a *document ontology* (proposal structure), *project ontology* (the activity of undertaking work) and *proposal ontology* (objectives, beneficiaries, funding call *etc.*) model *what needs to be written*. Finally, we have used the above to integrate an office environment with knowledge-aware services to demonstrate that with a suitable set of ontologies and a supportive knowledge-aware environment, an author can be assisted in producing knowledge-rich documents.

Our future work plans, aside from continued implementation of our integrated office environment, include a more detailed focus on the processes and mechanisms by which the knowledge provided by the AKT and WiCK knowledge-bases can be updated and maintained as more and more research proposals are produced. We also plan to carry out a systematic user evaluation – academics who write research proposals as part of their day-to-day work are a readily exploitable human resource in our department. Lastly, we are also working on a writing methodology for creating more complex, knowledge-rich documents such as multi-faceted Web sites and hypertexts.

# Acknowledgements

This work has been funded in part by the EPSRC Knowledge Writing in Context (KWiC) project (GR/R91021/01) – now known as *Writing in the Context of Knowledge (WiCK)* – and the EPSRC Advanced Knowledge Technologies IRC (GR/N15764/01) in the UK.

# References

1. Shadbolt, N.R., Milton, N.: From Knowledge Engineering to Knowledge Management. British Journal of Management **10** (1999) 309–322
2. Heath, I., Wills, G., Crowder, R., Hall, W., Ballantyne, J.: A New Authoring Methodology for Large-Scale Hypermedia Applications. Multimedia Tools and Applications **12** (2000) 129–144

3. Berners-Lee, T., Hendler, J., Lassila, O.: The Semantic Web. Scientific American (2001)
4. Lieberman, H., Liu, H.: Adaptive Linking between Text and Photos Using Common Sense Reasoning. In: Proceedings of the Conference on Adaptive Hypermedia and Adaptive Web Systems, Malaga, Spain. (2002) 2–11
5. Handschuh, S., Staab, S.: Authoring and Annotation of Web Pages in CREAM. In: Proceedings of the Eleventh International World Wide Web Conference, Honolulu, Hawaii, USA. (2002)
6. Tallis, M.: Semantic Word Processing for Content Authors. In: Proceedings of the Knowledge Markup & Semantic Annotation Workshop, Florida, USA. (2003) Part of the Second International Conference on Knowledge Capture, K-CAP 2003.
7. Tallis, M., Goldman, N.M., Balzer, R.M.: The Briefing Associate: Easing Authors into the Semantic Web. IEEE Intelligent Systems **17** (2002)
8. Hughes, G., Carr, L.: Microsoft Smart Tags: Support, ignore or condemn them? In: Proceedings of the ACM Hypertext 2002 Conference, Maryland, USA. (2002) 80–81
9. Fillies, C., Wood-Albrecht, G., Weichardt, F.: A Pragmatic Application of the Semantic Web using SemTalk. In: Proceedings of the Eleventh International World Wide Web Conference, Honolulu, Hawaii, USA. (2002) 686–692
10. ontoprise GmbH: OntoOffice Tutorial. http://www.ontoprise.de/documents/tutorial_ontooffice.pdf (2003)
11. Harris, S., Gibbins, N.: 3store: Efficient Bulk RDF Storage. In: Proceedings of the 1st International Workshop on Practical and Scalable Semantic Systems (PSSS'03), Sanibel Island, Florida. (2003) 1–15
12. Fillies, C.: On Visualizing the Semantic Web in MS Office. In: Proceedings of the 6th International Conference on Information Visualisation (IV'02), London, England. (2002) 441–446
13. Kunicki, C.: What's New with Smart Tags in Office 2003. MSDN OfficeTalk (2003) Available from http://msdn.microsoft.com/library/en-us/dnofftalk/html/office01022003.asp.

# Evaluation of an Approach to Expertise Finding

Yee-Wai Sim and Richard Crowder

Intelligence Agents Multimedia Group
School of Electronics and Computer Science
University of Southampton, Southampton SO17 1BJ, UK
rmc@ecs.soton.ac.uk

**Abstract.** This paper presents an approach to locating an expert through the use of existing organizational information. This approach was realised through an Expert Finder framework developed by the authors. The framework enables the relationships of heterogeneous information sources to experts to be factored in to the modelling of an individuals' expertise. The framework also provides an architecture that can be easily adapted to different organizations. The framework has been applied to a real world application and been evaluated using the notions of precision and recall.

## 1 Introduction

Many organisations require systems that gather corporate information and make it available to employees in order to resolve specific problems or queries. This allows organizations to capitalise on their best knowledge, leading to higher levels of productivity and competency, [1]. When employees collaborate, they initially rely on their own experiences, but as knowledge transfer occurs during task activities, a dynamic knowledge creation process takes place. With the correct tools organisations can acquire and analyse knowledge from individuals, in order to learn from their successes and failures. As businesses and companies become larger and more geographically dispersed, this collaboration space has now becoming more virtual then physical; hence it is becoming increasingly difficult for organisations to know where their best knowledge is and even more difficult for them to *know who knows what*. A survey of a number of different approaches to People–Finding is to be found in the paper by Beccerra–Fernandez, [2].

The recognition for the need to augment the expertise finding behaviour has resulted in the development of a number of Expert Finders. An Expert Finder is considered to be repositories that attempt to manage knowledge by, holding pointers to experts, who possess specific knowledge. As discussed latter in this paper there are problems of maintaining and retrieving expertise in these systems, relating to the exploration of heterogeneous information sources, the methodology used to analyse expertise, and system interoperability.

In many organisations there is a need to develop a framework for providing up-to-date information for expertise modelling. This is because people in organisations accumulate knowledge through task achievements [1] and this output

D. Karagiannis and U. Reimer (Eds.): PAKM 2004, LNAI 3336, pp. 141–152, 2004.
© Springer-Verlag Berlin Heidelberg 2004

is a valuable source for capturing knowledge that relates to an individual's expertise. In practice this output is the documentation (reports, memorandums, e-mails, etc.) generated during a project or similar activity. Exploiting meta data information from these documents can draw inferences to derive or update the knowledge about expertise associated of an individual.

## 2     Approaches to Expert Finding

Any Expert Finder requires a rang of information relating to an individual, for example;

- Level of knowledge or experience possessed.
- Performance of an individual compared to others in a related field.
- Current availability of an individual.
- Contact information of individuals who posses the required knowledge.

To manage an Expert Finder, their is a need for tools that gathers and consolidates this information in a form that is accessible by the Expert Finder. The availability of large electronic repositories in organisations, have led to the development of a autonomous approach to collect and analyse information when locating experts. The literature details are number of systems that undertake a fully automatic approach to expert finding, including, *Who Knows* [3], *Agent Amplified Communication* [4], *ContactFinder* [5], *Yenta* [6], *MEMOIR* [7], *Expertise Recommender* [8], *Expert Finder* [9], *SAGE* [2] and the *KCSR Expert Finder* [10]. In a review of these systems, problems related to heterogeneous information sources, expertise analysis support, and interoperability were identified.

**Heterogeneous Information Sources.** Experts can be used as effective and reliable information filters to locate useful information. This implies a role for Expert Finders in providing the expert-oriented access to an organisation's information system, thus mining an organisation's information system is a suitable path for an implicit source for expertise evidence.

In order to effectively explore the organisational information space for expertise evidence, Expert Finders need the ability to handle the heterogeneity of the widely distributed information sources. This is reflected by the wide variety of expertise evidence used, including, emails [4,11], bulletin boards [5], program codes [8,9], Web pages [4,6,7,12], and technical reports [3,10,13]. Hence, a framework that is flexible enough to address this problem is required.

The systems proposed by Crowder [10] and Mattrox [13], used a raw document indexing technique to capture a documents' concepts. These systems ignored the documents' structural elements (e.g. title, abstract, etc.) and treated all the text as a *bag of words*. Since this technique only captures the concept-to-document relationships, a different approach is needed to capture concepts related to expertise, as in an Expert Finder, the analysis of the documents should focus more on how they relate to experts rather than how they relate to the concepts they contain.

The authors propose that the heterogeneity of information sources should be used as an indicator to reflecting experts' competencies. How well these expertise indicators (e.g. indexed terms) reflect expertise is mainly a factor of how the source in which these indicators occur relates to the expert. This idea is based on the assumption that terms found in different types of documents indicate expertise differently, irrespective of their statistical traits. For example, the occurrence of a term in the title of the document shows a different distance to a persons actual expertise, compared to its occurrence anywhere in the body of the document. Therefore, the relationship of expert-to-document needs to be determined before extracting indexed terms from the document.

**Expertise Analysis Support.** The system developed by McDonald [8] incorporates a user-customisable expertise filtering process. Such a process takes a set of unfiltered names recommended by the system, and then reorders and removes items to generate a refined recommendation. Support for this filtering process can be provided by accessing the database that maintains personal and organisational relevant data, e.g. departmental affiliation.

A user seeking individuals as sources of information and/or as individuals who can perform given organisational functions, imposes their own requirements on the Expert Finder's functionality. Hence it is the users who should select the appropriate filters depending on their needs, and the system should only support the expert finding process by providing analysis functionality. This means that including the ability to rank experts using different user-customisable criteria (rather than the mere provision of a linear listing based on pre-determined criteria) can considerably enhance the expert finding applications. For example, a filter which represents the working relationships among experts can be used for catalysing collaboration in co-authoring documents or launching projects. In cases where users require knowledge that can only be shared through the human dimension, a filter based on the physical distance between departments can be employed.

Another approach that can support users in expertise analysis is to increase the system's transparency. This can be achieved by providing interfaces to access the expertise evidence, together with the expertise recognition logic. For example, the system can supply the scores for ranking the experts along with the associated expertise evidence. It allows users to evaluate the validity of the system's recognition logic. This in turn permits the incorporation of functionality, which can assist the users in evaluating and exploring the expertise evidence, i.e. spotting anomalies in the expert finding process, giving users greater trust in the system.

**Interoperability.** The majority of the Expert Finders surveyed focus on solving a particular problem, resulting in a closed standalone solution. However, Expert Finders can and should be integrated into other organisational systems and should be readily transferable from application to application and be interoperable with other systems, [14].

## 3   A Framework for an Expert Finder

In order to address the problems discussed above, the authors propose the frame-work, shown in Figure 1, for an Expert Finder. The framework consists of a collection of components for expertise evidences extraction, expertise modelling, querying, expertise matching and user interface. These components are flexible enough to address different organisational environments. The functionality of the proposed frame work is as follows:

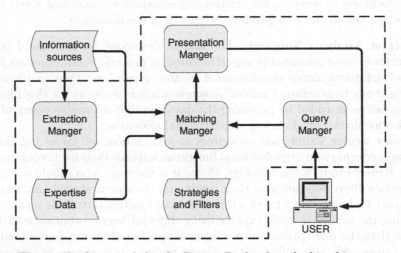

**Fig. 1.** The framework for the Expert Finder described in this paper.

*Expertise Extraction.* The extraction manager is responsible for identifying po-tential information sources containing expertise evidence. This will typically include shared or personal workspaces, document storage systems, or e-mail archives. It is recognised that each repository attached to the Expert Finder will require a customised API. However this is less complex that a custom system for each organisation or part of an organisation.

*Expertise Modelling.* Regardless of the origin of the information sources, i.e. shared or personal, the extracted evidence will be need to be stored on a server for use by the Expert Finder. However, in order to address the heterogeneous information sources problem presented above, the process of building the exper-tise model needs to detail the relationship of a given source to an expert. For instance, the occurrence of a term in the title of a document should be given a higher weighting, compared to its occurrence in the body of a document, this approach is discussed in Section 4.1.

*Expertise Matching.* The matching manager is initiated by a user request. Through the query manager, the user can select the strategies and/or filters required in selecting expertise for their needs. In order to achieve the goal of selection, the matching manager provides access to the information space that maintains personal and other data, (i.e. departmental affiliation) which can be used as criteria. Based on these criteria, the set of candidate experts are re-ordered to a specified rank and/or deleted from the set to produce a refined list of experts. As an example, users may wish to remove individuals who left the organisation. This can be achieved by using the human resource database to identify dates of employment.

*User Interface.* At the conclusion of the process a ranked list of experts coupled with evidence (e.g. documents) retrieved for expertise modelling is submitted to the user. As described earlier, increasing the system's transparency can provide by providing the expertise recognition logic and expertise evidence to the users, this in turn increaser the users' trust in the system.

## 4   A Prototype Expert Finder

The prototype Expert Finder was developed as part of an ongoing project at Southampton whose objective was to develop tools to support the activities of the design engineering, particularly in areas of knowledge capture, sharing and reuse. The *Relational Expert Finder System* based on the framework discussed earlier has been implemented in Java, the key features are summarised below.

### 4.1   Expertise Extraction

To implement the prototype system, we used data supplied by a major UK man-ufacturer, in the form of their internal publication database. This corresponds to a total of over 170,000 entries, covering a time period of fifty years. All the records in the database were entered manually, and ranged from technical re-ports to departmental memoranda. In practice neither the data source could be guaranteed to be correctly maintained nor can the entries in any fields be guaranteed to be valid and/or consistent. The supplied data was placed into a database management system with Structured Query Language (SQL) support. Careful design was required due to the database size, otherwise, accessing the resource could be very time consuming and the responses resulting from queries could easily overwhelm the system. A considerable amount of effort was taken to remove inconsistent or duplicated entries from the database, to improve the performance of the expertise modelling.

**Expertise Modelling.** Expertise models were created using text modelling algorithms based on the vector space model. The vector space model has advan-tages over other text modelling methods in overcoming overfitting, and dimen-sionality large problems, [15]. This means the model can easily adapt to dynamic environments where additions to the database are frequent. TFIDF is a popular function employed by most vector space modelling applications, [16].

However, the TFIDF function ignores the document's structural elements, i.e. title or body, and treats all the text contained in that document as a bag of words, e.g. unstructured text. In view of this, the authors modified the TFIDF function to account for the structural elements,

$$w'(t_k, d_j) = w(t_k, d_j) + s_j$$

where $w'(t_k, d_j)$ denotes the weight of the term $t_k$ in a document $d_j$, $w(t_k, d_j)$ denotes the weight of $t_k$ in $d_j$ calculated by the TFIDF function, and $s_j$ denotes the weight of the structural element in which $t_k$ occurs at least once. The value of $s_j$ was determined heuristically as part of the development process. As part of the process the raw documents were process by a number of tools to extract the text under the various headings, i.e. project name, authors, report abstract, etc., [17]. The equation above reflects the fact that the more often a term occurs in a document's major structural elements, such as title,abstract, etc. the more it is representative of its contents, and the more documents in which the term occurs, the less discriminating it is. The $w'(t_k, d_j)$ term is normalised for the purpose of comparison during the expertise matching process. It should be noted that, in this application, stemming is not performed on the text in the data source, since it produces ambiguous results, particularly when dealing with technical terms. The finalised expertise models will contain indexes resulting from the calculation of term space coverage and application of dimension reduction mechanisms, and are stored prior to expertise matching.

**Expertise Matching.** The querying process as currently implemented uses the AND Boolean operator. Using the query terms together with the AND operator, expertise models containing the query terms are identified, and then combined by taking the intersection of the sets of expertise models retrieved earlier. In order to simplify the query input interface, a query is made without any formal syntax, hence if *crack propagation* is entered it was interpreted as being a request that matches *crack* AND *propagation*.

In using the Expert Finder the users should select the appropriate expert finding strategies according to their needs, and the Expert Finder should only provide analysis functionality. This can be achieved by providing an interface to access the expertise recognition logic, i.e. how expertise is identified using various strategies. The system implementation includes two expert finding strategies. The first strategy is based on the concept of organisational awareness [18], in which the system only considers an individual as an expert if they are linked to a large number of relevant documents. However such an approach tends to reflect the interests of experts instead of their competency levels, and is only appropriate for users who seek individuals as sources of information.

The second strategy identifies experts by the importance of terms (supplied by the user) in documents. The importance of such terms is calculated using a vector space algorithm, as defined by the equation above. This algorithm not only reflects the importance of terms in relation to their occurrences in a set of documents, it also indicates the terms' importance in relation to the document structures Therefore, the computed terms' importance can then be used as indicators for experts' competency. This strategy, coupled with or without the first strategy, can be used to find individuals who can perform given organisational functions, such as collaboration in co-authoring documents or launching projects.

Two filters were implemented to refine the list generated from the above strategies. If the number of experts returned by the system overwhelms the user, then a filter is used to display only the top twenty experts in the recommendation list. Since the database covers over fifty years of work, the information will be out-dated for certain queries or requirements. In view of this, users are also given the option to filter the list of experts by document publication dates.

**User Interface.** After the expertise matching process has been completed, the ranked experts' names with their associated scores are displayed. The scores for ranking the experts are supplied to assist the users in analysing the recommendation. An interface is also provided to access the list of documents selected for expertise recognition, and the documents are grouped by authors for browsing purposes. This approach not only satisfies users' requirements in locating experts as information sources, it also allows users to evaluate the expertise recognition logic for themselves, hence, giving them greater trust as regards the recommendation.

## 4.2  Evaluation

Expertise retrieval effectiveness can be measured in terms of the information retrieval notions of *precision* and *recall*. In this paper, *precision* is defined as the probability that a random expert suggested in response to a query is correct; analogously, *recall* is defined as the probability that, if a random expert is recommended in response to a query, this decision is accepted. Neither precision nor recall make any sense in isolation, as it is widely recognised that higher levels of precision may be obtained at the price of a low recall. Hence, the evaluation requires a combined effectiveness measure, determined by precision and recall. The question then arises as to how the combined measures can be used to determine whether *system A* is better than *system B*. Generally, *system A* is assumed to be better than *system B* if, at every recall point, *system A*'s precision value is higher than *system B*'s, [16]. If this does not hold, then the precision values for selected recall values are averaged and compared.

Effectiveness is computed as an *11-point interpolated average precision* [19], this measure is widely adopted in the case of document-pivoted categorisation. For obtaining estimates of precision and recall relative to multiple decisions when two or more queries are submitted, microaveraging was adopted as a global evaluation method, [20].

The evaluation allowed us to compare the effectiveness of the proposed system against the system previously reported by Crowder and Hughes, [10]. However, this system approach the modelling of expertise differently as the *KCSR Expert Finder* ignores such structural information by representing its expertise models using full-text indexes. In order for the experimental results on the two Expert Finders to be directly comparable, the experiments were performed using identical source databases and queries.

**Test Data.** The effectiveness of an Expert Finder can be evaluated by users relative to specific contexts. The most likely context is their experience accumulated from the workplace. In order to measure the effectiveness of the *KCSR Expert Finder* and the *Relational Expert Finder System* in retrieving experts,

**Table 1.** Exemplar questions obtained from the user community. For each question the users also provided a number of recommendation of whom they considered to be experts across the company.

| Number | Sample Question |
| --- | --- |
| 1 | What are the operational issues of a specific systems? |
| 2 | What is the condition of specific parts at overhaul? |
| 3 | How does oil behave in hydraulic seals? |
| 4 | What are the positive characteristics to be noted when checking a simulation? |
| 5 | The procedure for modelling a turbine component for analysis. |
| 6 | Defining a turbine component ratio. |
| 7 | Requirements for an impact containment casing. |
| 8 | What are the properties of this material. |
| 9 | What are the resistant loads in designing a specific component? |

a set of questions that can provide contextualised problem statements was obtained. A total of nine possible users, drawn from the upper half of the company's engineering career structure, were interviewed to obtain sample questions and names of the individuals who they believed to have the expertise in answering these questions. The sample queries, Table 1, were chosen, as they gave a good spread of topics, ranging from the general to the highly specific.

**Results.** The experts recommended by the *KCSR Expert Finder* and *Relational Expert Finder System* were compared with those identified by the user community. It was noted that:

- In the initial evaluation queries based on questions 1, 2 and 6 failed to return any matches with both systems.
- Queries based on questions 3,4,5 and 8 failed to return any matches with the *KCSR Expert Finder*.
- Matches were obtained between both Expert Finders and the user community for Questions 7 and 9. Figure 2, show how the expertise retrieval precision varies with recall thresholds.

In order to compare the systems' effectiveness in finding the overall values for each of the precision-recall curves were calculated, Table 2. Additionally, the global effectiveness values using the microaveraging method, values of **0.12** for the *KCSR Expert Finder* and **0.28** for the *Relational Expert Finder System* were obtained. These values were used to determine whether the result of the comparison between the two Expert Finders were significant.

In the precision-recall curves shown in Figure 2, the *Relational Expert Finder System's* precision values are higher than the *KCSR Expert Finder's* at every recall threshold. In question 9, the difference in the precision values between the two Expert Finders is most evident. As seen in Table 2, the *Relational Expert Finder System* has a higher success rate in retrieving experts who were recognised by the users community. Using the *KCSR Expert Finder's* microaveraged effectiveness value as the reference in identifying experts who have the relevant

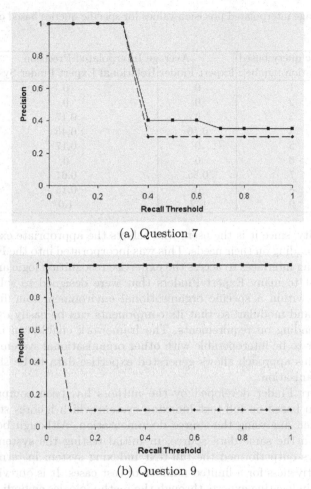

(a) Question 7

(b) Question 9

**Fig. 2.** Precision-recall curves showing comparative results between the *KCSR Expert Finder* – dotted line – and the *Relational Expert Finder System* – solid line, for two specific searches.

expertise for a specific interpretation of the sample questions, the improvement is 16%, which is statistically significant.

## 5   Concluding Comments

We have presented an approach to using capturing organisational knowledge for expert finding. A framework for Expert Finders is proposed by the authors that extends the relationships between information sources and expertise models. We have noted two significant activities for why experts need to be located, either users seek experts as sources of information or as collaborators in specific activities. Hence, we suggested that the Expert Finder should provide analy-

**Table 2.** Average interpolated precision values for specific queries based on the sample questions.

| Specific query based on question number: | Average Interpolated Precision | |
|---|---|---|
| | Expert Finder | Relational Expert Finder System |
| 1 | 0 | 0 |
| 2 | 0 | 0 |
| 3 | 0 | 0.17 |
| 4 | 0.16 | 0.45 |
| 5 | 0 | 0.17 |
| 6 | 0 | 0 |
| 7 | 0.55 | 0.61 |
| 8 | 0 | 0.15 |
| 9 | 0.2 | 1.0 |

sis functionality, since it is the users who selects the appropriate expert finding strategies depending on their needs. This was incorporated into the Expert Finders by providing interfaces to access the expertise recognition logic and evidence.

In contrast to many Expert Finders that were designed to solve a particular problem within a specific organisational environment, our framework is both flexible and modular; so that its components can be easily extended and replaced depending on requirements. The framework enables an implemented Expert Finder to be interoperable with other organisational systems via appropriate API. This approach allows generated expertise data to be shared across across an organisation.

The Expert Finder developed by the authors has been compared with a similar system based on full-text indexing system which ignores structural information when analysing the source documentation. Although both of these systems shared the same data source, in initial testing the system developed by the authors outperformed the full-text indexing system in terms of expert retrieval effectiveness for a limited number of test cases. It is our view that the improvement in locating experts through the methodologies embodies in the *Relational Expert Finder System* will translate to a reduction in costs within an organisation as the correct expert is located more rapidly.

Although the approach demonstrates that the mechanism for extracting expertise data can be automated, it however trades the problems of increased workload and subjective self-assessments with the problem associated with 'dirty' data. The authors invested a considerable amount of time and effort to formulate techniques for validating data and folding it to a format that can be processed by the systems. As such, the validity and consistency of the data plays an important role in determining the performance of expertise retrieval, and should be considered when deploying an Expert Finder.

## Acknowledgement

The authors acknowledge the studentship for Yee–Wai Sim from the Faculty of Engineering, Science and Mathematics, University of Southampton.

# References

1. Shadbolt, N.R., O'Hara, K.: Aktuality: An overview of the aims, ambitious and assumptions of the advanced knowledge technologies interdisciplinary research collaboration. In Shadbolt, N.R., ed.: Advanced Knowledge Technologies: Selected Papers 2003. AKT (2003) 1–11

2. Becerra-Fernandez, I.: The role of artifical intelligence technologies in the implementation of People–Finder knowledge mangement tools. Knowledge Based Systems **13** (2000) 315–320

3. Streeter, L.A., Lochbaum, K.E.: An expert/expert locating system based on automatic representation of semantic structure. In: Proceedings of the Fourth IEEE Conference on Artificial Intelligence Applications, Computer Society of the IEEE, San Diego, CA (1988) 345–349

4. Kautz, H.A., Selman, B., Shah, M.: Referral Web: Combining socail networks and collaborative filtering. Communications of ACM **40** (1997) 63–65

5. Krulwich, B., Burkey, C.: The ContactFinder agent: Answering bulletin board questions with referrals. In: Proceedings of the Thirteenth National Conference on Artificial Intelligence and Eighth Innovative Applications of Artificial Intelligence Conference. Volume 1., Portland, OR (1996) 10–15

6. Foner, I.N.: Yenta: A multi-agent referral-based matchmaking system. In: Proceedings of the First International Conference on Autonomous Agents, Marina del Rey, CA (1997) 301–307

7. Pikrakis, A., Bitsikas, T., Sfakianakis, S., Hatzopoulos, M., DeRoure, D., Hall, W., Reich, S., Hill, G., Stairmand, M.: MEMOIR - software agents for finding similar users by trails. In: Proceedings of the Third International Conference and Exhibition on the Practical Application of Intelligent Agents and Multi-agents, London, UK (1998) 453–466

8. McDonald, D.W., Ackerman, M.S.: Expertise recommender: a flexible recommendation system and architecture. In: ACM 2000 Conference on Computer Supported Cooperative Work. ACM, New York (2000) 231–40

9. Vivacqua, A.S.: Agents for expertise location. In: Proceedings of the AAAI Spring Symposium on Intelligent Agents is Cyberspace, Standford, CA (1999) 9–13

10. Crowder, R., Hughes, G., Hall, W.: An agent based approach to finding expertise. In Karagiannis, D., Reimer, U., eds.: Proceedings Fourth International Conference on Practical Aspects of Knowledge Management. Volume LNAI 2569. Springer-Verlang, Berlin Heidelberg (2002) 179–88

11. Kanfer, A., Sweet, J., Schlosser, A.: Humanizing the net: Social navigation with a 'know-who' e-mail agent. In: Proceedings of the Third Conference on Human Factors and the Web, Denver, Co (1997) Available at http://archive.ncsa.uiuc.edu/edu/trg/human/.

12. Cohen, D., Prusak, L.: Networks and communities. In Cohen, D., Prusak, L., eds.: Good Company: How Social Capital Makes Organizational Work. Harvard Business School Press (2001)

13. Mattox, D., Maybury, M., Morey, D.: Enterprise expert and knowledge discovery. In: Proceedings of the 8th International Conference on Human-Computer Interaction (HCI International'99), Munich, Germany (1999) 303–7

14. Crowder, R., Bracewell, R., Hughes, G., Kerr, M., Knott, D., Moss, M., Clegg, C., Hall, W., Wallace, K., Waterson, P.: A future vision for the engineering design environment. A future sociotechnical scenario. In: International Conference on Engineering Design, ICED2003, Stockholm (2003)

15. Joachims, T.: Estimating the generalization performance of a SVM efficiency. In: Proceedings of the Seventeenth International Conference on Machine Learning, Stanford, CA (2000) 431–438
16. Sebastiani, F.: Machine learning in automated text categorization. ACM Computing Surveys **34** (2002) 1–47
17. Sim, Y.W.: Capturing Organisational Knowledge from Documentation for Expert Finding. PhD thesis, School of Electronics and Computer Science, University of Southampton (2004)
18. Maybury, M., Amore, D., House, R.: Awareness of organizational expertise. Technical papers, MITRE (2000)
19. Salton, G.: Advanced information-retrieval models. In Salton, G., ed.: Automatic Text Processing. Addison-Wesley Publishing Company (1989)
20. Lewis, D.D.: Evaluating text categorization. In: Proceedings of Speech and Natural Language Workshop. (1991) 312–318

# Collaborative Knowledge Transfer
# by Annotating Documents

Ruth Cobos[1] and Johann Schlichter[2]

[1] Escuela Politénica Superior, Universida d Autóoma de Madrid, 28049, Madrid, Spain
ruth.cobos@uam.es
[2] Institute for Informatics, Technische Universität München, 80290 Munich, Germany
schlichter@in.tum.de

**Abstract.** This paper deals with how document annotations contribute in knowledge transfer processes. An approach to support the collaborative process of transferring knowledge among several user communities by annotating documents is presented.

## 1 Introduction

There are several open issues in the Knowledge Management area. A very interesting research issue in this area is the Knowledge Transfer. Knowledge transfer is an important component of knowledge management [5]. Ladd et.al. refer to this issue in [9] as follows: "knowledge transfer is nominally concerned with the process of moving useful information from one individual to another person".

In relation to this matter, Hermann Maurer states in [12] that the knowledge resides in the heads of people, but this can be mapped into "shadow" knowledge residing in computer. In other words, the knowledge that people have in mind may be transferred to others using computing resources.

It is generally known that documents are the common method of collaborating and communicating. There is some evidence that documents are used for transferring information, concepts and ideas from one individual to another, or within a group [15]. Thus, the document creation and improvement process can be used for sharing and exchanging knowledge, i.e., for knowledge transfer.

However, it is important to take into account that the authoring of a proper document is a complex and time-consuming task, for single authors as well as joint authors [13]. Several studies have confirmed that the use of collaborative annotations to documents is very useful in the task of improving documents [4]

Several approaches demonstrate the necessity of having annotation management functionality in document management systems [2]. Moreover, we have more and more evidences of the usefulness of annotations in document based collaboration for transferring knowledge and for providing a way of interaction among users [1].

One of the main aims of this research consists in studying and analysing the usefulness of annotating documents, and how this functionality may contribute to the knowledge transfer among several virtual communities of users [16]. With user communities we refer here to communities of practice [17]. Lueg [10] also calls them "knowledge communities".

D. Karagiannis and U. Reimer (Eds.): PAKM 2004, LNAI 3336, pp. 153–158, 2004.

This paper is structured as follows: In section 2 we introduce the relation between document annotation and knowledge transfer. Then, in section 3 we explain our proposed approach. The remaining sections give a brief summary and references.

## 2   The Usefulness of Document Annotations in Knowledge Transfer

There is an agreement on the potential value of annotations in document based collaboration [2]. In fact, there are more and more systems that support annotations. We can find several approaches that deal with annotations and that show us its different applications. In this paper, we want to show that document annotations contribute in knowledge transfer processes.

An annotation, or note for short, reflects the knowledge of the note author about the information represented in the annotated document. In some sense a note has as a purpose to convert implicit (tacit) knowledge, that someone has in mind, into explicit knowledge. The knowledge associated with the note could be useful in several ways, for example, helping to understand the content of the document and making it more useful for future tasks [14].

On one hand, there are some notes that are useful for doing summarisation, while others highlight important parts of a document. In fact, this type of notes is the result of *notetaking* processes, that is a common behaviour while reading. These notes are often helpful for other readers [18].

On the other hand, the knowledge of the note could be very useful for the document author in the task of improving the original document by creating another, improved version. Taking into account the two perspectives, we see that notes are the "bridge between reading and writing" [11], in other words, they are useful for knowledge transfer among users.

A note may be seen as an interaction between his/her author with the author of the annotated document. From this point of view, we can say that notes are useful for providing interaction among users. The interaction among people helps in the knowledge transfer [1]. Then, in some sense the interaction – which is represented by a note – supports the knowledge flow from the note author to the document author. If notes are public, the knowledge flow may extend to other people who may read these notes.

To sum up, there is a knowledge flow between the note author and the single/joint document authors, as well as a knowledge flow between the note author and the readers of the document and the note. Moreover, the document author is not just a passive recipient of the knowledge flow, he/she even actively applies the conveyed knowledge to improve the document;thus, he/she interprets and internalises the knowledge.

## 3  Design and Implementation of a Distributed Document Annotation Management Platform

Communities have a shared community space, which is used for information exchange and collaboration. These communities can work together helping each other in a common task. Taking into account these community characteristics, our approach supports community members to share documents within a community space as well as across community spaces. They collaborate using the knowledge attached to these documents in form of annotations, comments, suggestions, opinions, valuations, etc.

As we said in the previous section, the additional knowledge of these contributions may be useful for potential document readers of the community as well as for the document author in the task of improving the document. Thus, there are different types of knowledge flows: between document authors, between document author and readers, between note author and document authors and between note author and note readers in the context of the document.

We propose a platform to support the collaborative process of transferring knowledge between members of one or several communities by the use of annotations in the document improvement task. We list the most important design and implementation issues of this platform in subsections 3.2 and 3.3. In subsection 3.1 we discuss the knowledge elements that are relevant for the document improvement task.

### 3.1 Knowledge Elements That Take Part in the Document Improvement Task

The document evolves through a sequence of document versions, which are checked and evaluated by the members of the communities having the required access permissions. A document version which may be the basis for a further improvement process is shared by all selected community spaces. The document is composed of "document parts". Notes and ratings may be attached to the whole document or to the document parts.

A note expresses an idea. It is very important that each note expresses only one idea, in order to facilitate the classification i.e. its purpose. A rating expresses the degree of agreement one of one user with the annotated knowledge element (the whole document or a document part). A rating may have an "agree" or "disagree" value.

The document author may derive a new document version of the previous one at any time. Thus, it is possible to have several document versions available. Between a document version and the following one there is a new knowledge element: the "dialogue". This dialogue is a sequence of notes (dialogue notes) between the document author and other users.

"Notes" and "dialogue notes" are different knowledge elements. Notes are related to the document content. If the document author takes them into account it may be assumed that the new document version will be an improvement compared to the previous one [4]. Dialogue Notes are related to the similarities and differences between two document versions. These notes reflect the different opinions of several users about the document evolution process. They can be very useful in order to understand the process.

Every knowledge element that we can find in the community space may be public or private. A public knowledge element is visible in all relevant community spaces. A private knowledge element is visible only in the community space of its author. Each knowledge element is physically present only in one community space. If a knowledge element is public, then there are references to it in other community spaces.

## 3.2  Design Requirements and Considerations

We have used scenario-based design [3] for this approach. Our proposed approach has to support the following design requirements and considerations:

- Providing a community space to each community, where its members may share their collective knowledge, interacting, communicating and matchmaking between them. Moreover, in each community space all shared documents and their associated knowledge element are easily accessible.
- Informing all users about what is happening in his/her community space.
- Dealing with cross references between knowledge elements that are distributed between several community spaces.
- Providing information propagation. In the case of public knowledge elements, it is very important that when a public knowledge element is updated in one community space then this change needs to be properly propagated to other community spaces using the reference links.
- Managing relations of knowledge elements to users. There is the trivial relation "document – user (author of document)", but we can find other interesting relations such as "document – user (user is citing a document through a note)", because users can annotate, use, cite, etc. documents. This may be an interesting source for some social network analysis.
- Providing access to any document of the sequence of document versions, that is, accessing a relevant version depending on the desired moment of the document evolution process.
- Managing the transfer of notes and ratings between document versions. When a new document version is created, what about the notes and ratings that were related to the previous document version? Some notes or ratings may be relevant for the new document version, so the approach has to deal with this matter.
- Providing the necessary operations to all users for participating in the document improvement process, such as the functionalities of sharing a document, of annotating a whole document or a document part, etc.

## 3.3  Distributed Document Annotation Management (DiDoAM) Platform

The goal of the Distributed Document Annotation Management (DiDoAM) Platform is to support the collaborative process of improving documents between several communities. It is being developed based on the Cobricks-2 Platform Toolkit (*http://www.cobricks.de/*) [8].Cobricks-2 (Bricks for Supporting Collaboration in Teams and Communities) is a java-based community support system, which has been developed at Technische Universität in München. It supports building and operating interoperable Cobricks-based community platforms.

Cobricks-2 provides architectural landscapes for collaboration support, interfaces and standards for data structures (ontologies). Cobricks-2 elements are categorized according to ontologies. The knowledge elements of subsection 3.1 are mapped to Cobricks-2 elements through the extension of these ontologies. The use of ontologies facilitates the assignment of meta data to knowledge elements. In fact, more and more web systems and knowledge management systems use ontologies to describe system knowledge and to make explicit the document semantics [6][7].

All knowledge elements of all community spaces from DiDoAM Platform are in the same knowledge repository due to the Cobricks-2 implementation. This functionality facilitates the management of cross references between knowledge elements of different community spaces. For the same reason, it is possible and easy to provide the information propagation on the Platform.

Cobricks-2 stores knowledge in a way that provides enough information for extracting relations of knowledge elements to users. This is an interesting functionality that our proposed approach offers to users. Another interesting functionality is to provide a document view at any moment of its evolution process. To achieve this, DiDoAM Platform provides a "reconstruct" of the context of a document at any time, that is, what its content and related knowledge elements are.

We use the term "reconstruct" because in addition to the changes that the document experiences during its evolution, associated knowledge elements may be propagated between document versions. Thus, knowledge elements might lose the original context.

Concerning this last issue, when there are notes or ratings of a document part and this document part is not updated in the new document version, they will be transmitted to the document part of the new document version. The remaining ratings will not be transmitted. However, whether the remaining notes are transmitted or not, it depends on the decisions of all communities, which are made through ratings.

## 4  Summary

In this paper, we have discussed the usefulness of document annotation, and how it may contribute to the knowledge transfer among several virtual user communities.

We have presented a Distributed Document Annotation Management (DiDoAM) Platform. It supports the collaborative process of transferring knowledge among several communities by the use of annotations. DiDoAM manages two kinds of notes: notes to documents and dialogue notes. The first ones are useful for motivating the document author in the document improvement task by creating a new document version. The document evolves through a sequence of document versions. Dialogue notes are useful for comparing two document versions. These comparisons may be useful for extracting information about how the document evolution process is going.

## Acknowledgements

We are very grateful to the researchers of the Computer Science Group Informatik K̦ Applied Informatics / Cooperative Systems,  of the Institut für Informatik (TUM).

## References

1. Al-Hawamdeh, S.: Knowledge management: re-thinking information management and facing the challenge of managing tacit knowledge. Information Research, 8(1), paper no. 143, October 2002.

2. Cadiz, J.J., Gupta, A., Grudin, J.: Using Web Annotations for Asynchronous Collaboration Around Documents. Proc. of the Conference on Computer-Supported Cooperative Work (CSCW 2000), Philadelphia, PA USA. (2000) 309–318

3. Carroll, J.M.: Scenario-based Design. John Wiley &Sons, Inc. New York., 1995

4. Cobos, R., Pifarré M., Alamá, X Aprendizaje    entre iguales en la red: Anßsis de la asistencia del sistema KnowCat en el trabajo en grupo. Proc. of the V Congreso Internacional de Interacció Persona-O rdenador. Lleida, Spain (2004) 341–350

5. Davenport, T.H., Prusak, L.: Working knowledge: How organizations manage what they know. Boston: Harvard Business School Press (2000)

6. Fensel, D., Angele, L., Decker, s., Erdmann, M., Schnurr, H., Staab, S., Studer, R., Witt, A.: On2broker: Semantic-based access to information sources at the WWW. Proc. of the Intelligent Information Integration Workshop (III 99) during IJCAI 99. Stockholm, Schweden (1999)

7. Haustein, S., Morik, K., Pleumann, J.: The Infolayer – A Simple Knowledge Management System Put to Use in Academia. Proc. of the 3$^{rd}$ International Conference on Knowledge Management (I-Know-03), Graz, Austria, Springer (2003)

8. Koch, M.: Community-Unterstützungssysteme – Architektur und Interoperabilität. Professorial dissertation, Institut für Informatik, TUM, December 2003

9. Ladd, D.A., Ward, M.A.: An Investigation Of Environmental Factors Influencing Knowledge Transfer. Journal of Knowledge Management Practice, Vol. 3, August (2002) 8–17

10. Lueg, C.: Where is the Action in Virtual Communities of Practice? Proc. of the (German Computer-Supported Cooperative Work Conference D-CSCW 2000), Munich, Germany (2000)

11. Marshall, C.C.: Toward an ecology of hypertext annotation. Proc. of the ACM Hypertext 98, Pittsburgh, PA USA (1998) 40–49

12. Maurer, H. The Heart of the Problem: Knowledge Management and Knowledge Transfer. Proc. of the ENABLE'99, Espoo, Finland (1999) 8–17

13. Neuwirth, C.M., Kaufer, D.S., Chandhok, R., Morris, J.H.: Computer Support for Distributed Collaborative Writing: A Coordination Science Perspective. Proc. of the Conference on Computer-Supported Cooperative Work (CSCW 94), Chapel Hill, NC, USA (1994) 145–152

14. O'Hara, K., Sellen, A.: A comparison of Reading Paper and On-Line Documents. Proc. of CHI 97, Los Angeles, USA (1997) 335–342

15. Rodriguez, H.: Designing, evaluating and exploring Web-based tools for collaborative annotation of documents. Ph. D. thesis, TRITA-NA-0312, Royal Institute of Technology, June 2003

16. Schlichter, J., Koch, M., Chengmao, X: Awareness The Common Link Between Groupware and Communityware. Community Computing and Support Systems, Ishida, T. (ed), Springer Verlag (1998) 77–93

17. Wenger, E.: Communities of Practice: Learning, Meaning and Identity. Cambridge, UK: Cambridge University Press. First Paperbak Edition 1999

18. Wolfe, J.: Effects of Annotations on Student Readers and Writers. Proc. of the Fifth ACM conference on Digital Libraries, San Antonio, Texas, USA. (2000) 19–26

# Representing Knowledge Gaps Effectively

Alan Belasco, Jon Curtis, Robert C. Kahlert,
Charles Klein, Corinne Mayans, and Pace Reagan

Cycorp Inc, 3721 Executive Center Drive S#00, Austin TX 8731
{belasco,jonc,rck,klein,cmayans,pace}@cyc.com

**Abstract.** In knowledge acquisition, one typically encounters two difficult situations: First, there are times when the system requests information that, due to a lack of information, the user is not in a position to provide at the level of precision requested. Second, there are situations where the system cannot capture information at the level of precision the user wishes to provide. We describe the techniques that have been developed for CYC to address these two cases during the extension of a variety of domains.

## Introduction

In this paper we describe a Subject Matter Expert (SME) usable knowledge acquisition system that is used to extend the breadth of CYC's common sense knowledge verticals, some of them by half a million facts over the last two years. Increasing knowledge base verticals requires tools that allow for very high knowledge entry rates. Previous research suggests that entry rates drop when either the users or the system hit upon a knowledge gap. We therefore developed and deployed strategies to mitigate either contingency. We achieved average entry rates of 96 facts per hour, for entry sessions four hours long on average.

## Knowledge Acquisition System Description[1]

For the purposes of extending CYC's knowledge verticals, a client-server knowledge acquisition system was developed. As the backend server, we used Cycorp's CYC knowledge base, inference engine and natural-language subsystem; as the front-end client, we developed a template-based knowledge acquisition tool known as the "Factivore." In the following, we will describe both components briefly.

### Cyc 10

CYC Version 10 is a knowledge base system designed for efficiently manipulating and reasoning with a large ontology (over 2.4 million assertions, 200000 terms and 9000 relationships). Its symbolic representation language, CycL, is based on first order predicate calculus with higher-order and modal extensions.

---

[1] The key elements of the components described were developed by David Baxter, Tony Brusseau, Chris Deaton, Keith Goolsbey, Kevin Knight, Doug Lenat, Pierluigi Miraglia, Stephen Reed, Dave Schneider, Anuroopa Shenoy, Michael Witbrock, Ming X and the authors.

D. Karagiannis and U. Reimer (Eds.): PAKM 2004, LNAI 3336, pp. 159–164, 2004.

CycL contains both atomic and functionally-defined terms. As part of its higher-order extensions, CycL allows assertions in the Cyc knowledge base to occur as terms (arguments) for meta-assertions. CycL assertions are grouped into reasoning contexts called *micro-theories*, which in turn form hierarchies of assumption inheritance[2].

## The "Factivore" Knowledge Acquisition Tool

The "Factivore" knowledge acquisition interface (see Figure 1) is the main tool employed for extending knowledge verticals. It presents a tabular user interface that is driven by fact-entry templates described in CYC's knowledge base.

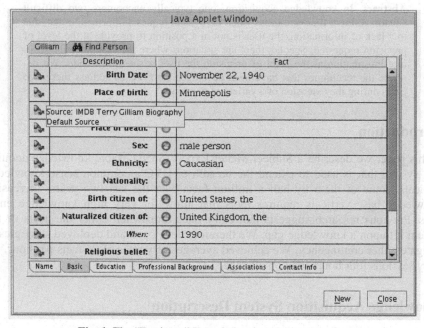

**Fig. 1.** The "Factivore" Knowledge Acquisition Interface

One or more of the rows in the presented form correspond to argument positions in the underlying fact templates;the current topic of discussion, the so-called *focal term*, is implied by the title bar. Users either select possible values from drop-down lists or enter them, in which case CYC's natural language parsing mechanisms attempt to map the string entered via CYC's English lexicon to the appropriate CycL term. [2][3]

As previously indicated, all properties of the individual fact templates are described in the knowledge base itself, including the organization of the tabbed panels, the presentation order of the templates, the types of entities that are permissible, whether new entities can be introduced or only existing ones selected, and how often a fact can be stated. In the future, CYC will adjust the interface as it understands more about the focal term, pre-filling input fields or adding additional questions.

---

2   A substantial, taxonomic portion of Cyc's knowledge has been exported into OWL;a smaller version of the knowledge base, OpenCyc, is already freely available and freely usable (at http://www.cyc.com/2004/06/04/cyc).

Because knowledge verticals typically combine information from a variety of document sources, each individual fact can be associated with a source. These sources are also described via appropriate "Factivore" templates and represented in the knowledge base. Inside CYC, each source is associated with it a micro-theory that represents the semantic content of the document; source assignments determine into which micro-theory the facts are placed (see tool-tip in Figure 1).

## Representing What Users Do Not Know

When entering information from individual sources, Subject Matter Experts (SMEs) attempt to capture their meanings as accurately and with minimal information loss. Consider the following example from a fictitious source, selected for expository purposes: "Brandishing AK-47s, the kidnappers pulled the diplomat from his car."

While this sentence names the type of weapon employed, it provides no information about the exact number of weapons that the kidnappers employed. However, the underlying fact template, as represented in CYC, expects not only the weapon type but also a non-negative integer.

```
(relationInstanceExistsCount Kidnapping4 weaponsUsed
AK47Gun number)[3]
```

At this point, SMEs have three choices: They can skip the question; they can enter a number by making an educated guess; or, they can enter "unknown." Skipping the question altogether violates the stated goal of capturing the meaning. One would want this kidnapping to be in the result set if CYC was queried for criminal activities involving AK-47s. Making an educated guess is a more helpful but equally inaccurate description of the source, since it omits the fact that there was a lack of information in the source. The remaining choice is then to allow the SME to enter "unknown" and to make this information productive[4].

The knowledge base description of a fact template includes information describing what should be done when a SME's input is malformed in specific ways. These repair strategies are called *reformulation rules* and are semantically guided descriptions for how to perform syntactic transformations on the input. These rules target a CYC component appropriately called the *Reformulator*, a generic CycL to CycL transformer that uses semantic indicators to select applicable and valid transformations from a set of rules encoded in the knowledge base.

In the current situation, the Reformulator would produce the strictly weaker but inferentially productive fact:

```
(relationInstanceExists Kidnapping4 weaponsUsed AK-47)
```

Adding this fact ensures that this crime will be in the result set when querying for kidnapping events involving AK-47s, yet it is syntactically different – and thereby appropriately semantically distinct – from the case where exactly one AK-47 was employed:

---

[3] Meaning that, in the event Kidnapping4, the count of AK47s playing the role of the weapons used was *number*.

[4] The user interface of the "Factivore" provides a way for inserting a sentinel "unknown" value, which is mapped to a value appropriate for the specific template to forestall ambiguity.

```
(relationInstanceExistsCount Kidnapping4 weaponsUsed
AK47Gun 1)
```

In addition, the "Factivore" makes a meta-assertion about the added fact, linking it to the original SME-authored formula and to the reformulation rule used to affect the syntactic transformation. Using this two-step method of transforming the user's input and recording the transformation itself allows the "Factivore" to successfully add knowledge contained in the source – that AK47s were used in the kidnapping – yet retain what amounts to the SME's identification of a knowledge gap. In effect, the meta-assertion and its subject retain the knowledge that the source did not provide all of the information the system desired[5].

## Representing What CYC Does Not Know

### Acquiring "Need to Know" Information
In a situation of knowledge acquisition, the system will very often not know what the SME has to teach. Typical entities for which the system is unlikely to have complete coverage are persons, companies, cities and villages. Therefore, it is of particular importance to deal gracefully with missing knowledge, especially when high rates of knowledge acquisition are desired.

In some situations it is appropriate for the system to assist the SME in drilling more deeply into a subject immediately, such as when describing the board members of a commercial organization; here the "Factivore" can simply create the missing officers and launch additional knowledge acquisition windows for describing them. In practice, one wants to restrict this approach to the important cases, because feedback indicates that topic-shifts disrupt the SMEs' focus and reduce the overall entry rate.

Conversely, there are situations where unrecognized entities indicate an entry error, such as misspellings. Whether the CYC system enforces that its input be valid and recognized, or not is again dependent on the template definition in the knowledge base, which in turn is driven by whether CYC knows that it can make the assumption that it knows all of the instances of a type[6].

Again, it may not be worth the time of a subject matter expert to flesh out minor details. For these cases it is sufficient to allow the SME to create a stub-term that denotes the appropriate information and has the appropriate type to make the resulting fact semantically well-formed (see row three in Figure 1):

```
(placeOfBirth JosephStalin
    (InstanceNamedFn "Gori, Georgia"
        GeographicalRegion))
```

A stub-term consists of a type-specifying "function" and its arguments: a natural language string used to introduce the entity, and a collection that "types" the resulting term – in this case a geographical region named "Gori, Georgia." The word "func-

---

[5] Should the SME find the number later, then CYC's Truth Maintenance System will automatically remove the dependent meta-assertion when the old assertion is replaced during the edit operation.

[6] For example, if the SME attempted to supply the month in which a meeting took place, a misspelling of "December" would not trick the CYC system into thinking that a new month has been introduced, since it knows – and knows that it knows – all of the Julian months.

tion" is employed loosely here;there is no guarantee that the string designation of the entity is in fact unique (and therefore invertible), as a true function would require: the string "Gori" may denote any of a number of cities.

The representation makes use of CYC's ability to reason about the result types of functional terms; we simply state that the type of entity denoted by the functional term is the type of the $2^{nd}$ argument. This is, however, insufficiently descriptive in the cases where the SMEs want to introduce a new subtype, such as a new type of weapon. Here we employ a different, type-denoting function:

```
(relationInstanceExists Kidnapping4 weaponsUsed
(SubCollectionNamedFn "Stazer" Weapon))
```

Stub-terms were originally developed for semantically integrating external knowledge sources such as SQL databases [1] for use during inference. In databases, string denotations are the predominant type of information, and many terms have to be classified while processing an SQL result set without access to SMEs to answer questions.

**Resolving the "Need to Know" Information**
At this level of representation, it is no longer possible to distinguish misspellings from new entities; therefore, all stub terms are reviewed and triaged by the ontological engineers at Cycorp overseeing the construction of the knowledge verticals. The stub-terms therefore function as markers in the workflow between the SMEs and the ontological engineers. The proper typing and the descriptive natural language of the functional term, plus its example usage make it straightforward for the ontological engineer to properly place the missing term in CYC's ontology.

Reviewing these terms provides critical feedback on what the SMEs are trying to represent and helps to identify limitations in the usability of the Factivore forms.

A particularly noteworthy class of stub terms are neither ontology gaps nor input errors but cases of SMEs pushing the envelope of the template infrastructure. Consider the following example:

```
(objectFoundInLocation MackTheKnife (InstanceNamedFn
"some bar in London or Paris" GeographicalRegion))
```

An appropriate CycL representation of the SME's intended statement would be:

```
(thereExists ?BAR
(isa ?BAR Bar)
(or (geographicalSubRegions ?BAR CityOfLondonEngland)
(geographicalSubRegions ?BAR CityOfParisFrance))
(objectFoundInLocation MackTheKnife ?BAR))
```

A solution to this class of problem is not within the scope of our current research, but some preliminary approaches suggest themselves. In order to be able to transform the first representation into the second representation, it seems important to recognize that the SME is completing a natural language sentence that the presentation of the template in the "Factivore" is suggesting to them, for example "Mack the Knife is hiding in _____.", a very focused parsing problem.

If the representation of the natural language syntax tree for the suggested sentence were a property of the template, then the natural language processing system could attempt to parse the SME's completion of the sentence in the syntactic context of the overall sentence:

```
(TheDisjunctiveCoordinationSet
  (NLQuantFn-3 Some-NLAttr
    (NLNumberFn Singular
      (SubcollectionOfWithRelationToFn Bar
        in-UnderspecifiedContainer CityOfLondonEngland))
  1) CityOfParisFrance)⁷
```

This reduces the problem to adding to the Reformulator's rule set so that an appropriate representation can be computed from these parts, a relatively straightforward task. Again, meta-assertions would track the dependency between what the SME entered and how the statement was interpreted and made inferentially productive by CYC.

## Conclusions and Outlook

Even when a knowledge acquisition system and its users cannot completely understand each other, there is valuable information to be gained from what *can* be understood. We argue that the explicit representation of the exchange between SMEs and system can result in natural system interactions and high rates of knowledge acquisition, as well as the production of inferentially productive knowledge up to a maximum set by the incompleteness of information.

This approach to representing knowledge gaps in the information contained in a source or the result of system misunderstanding, also serves to treat gaps as markers in the knowledge acquisition workflow;they  represent to-do items for either the SME to investigate or the system to learn about.

More generally, such knowledge-gap markers can function as workflow markers for CYC itself, enabling CYC to focus its efforts in its general striving to extend what it knows. Each stub-term indicates an ontology gap that CYC can actively seek to fill. Each missing information piece is an indication that the wrong source or SME was consulted, allowing CYC to remain on the lookout for more details about the entity described. Such learning could happen through interaction with more appropriate users or even through CYC performing research on its own. Preliminary work at Cycorp is currently experimenting with ways in which CYC can try to harvest knowledge about novel terms for itself from the World Wide Web and other text sources. After all, the first step to achieving wisdom lies in knowing what one does not know.

## References

1. Chip Masters, Zal Güngüdü, "Structured    Knowledge Source Integration: A Progress Report". *Proceedings of the Internationa Conference on Integration of Knowledge Intensive Multi-Agent Systems (KIMAS 03)*. Piscataway, N.J.: IEEE Press. (562-566), 2003.
2. Michael Witbrock, David Baxter, Jon Curtis, et al, 'An Interactive Dialogue System for Knowledge Acquisition in Cyc"in *Proceedings of the IJCAI-2003 Workshop on Mixed-Initiative Intelligent Systems*, Acapulco, Aug 9, 2003.
3. Burns, K., and Davis, A. 1999. "Building and Maintaining a Semantically Adequate Lexicon Using Cyc", in E. Viegas, *Breadth and Depth of Semantic Lexicons*, Kluwer.

---

⁷ Notice that the interpretation as shown here treats the phrase as if it had been "some bar in London or in Paris", i.e. it gets confused about the attachment.

# Security Design, Organization Dynamics and Performance: More than Meets the Eye

James A. Sena[1] and Abraham B. (Rami) Shani[2]

[1] Professor of Management Information Systems, Industrial Technology Chair
California Polytechnic State University, San Luis Obispo
+1 805 756 2680
jsena@calpoly.edu

[2] Professor of Management, Management Area Chair
California Polytechnic State University, San Luis Obispo and
The Fenix Program, Stockholm School of Economics, S-113 83 Stockholm, Sweden
+1 805 7561756, +46 70 3900391
ashani@calpoly.edu

**Abstract.** This manuscript explores the gap between organizational processes and security design. We begin with a presentation stressing the need for improved security in the corporation. Organizational processes, such as work design, creativity and innovation, culture, learning and change are considered in organizational design. The way the organization is designed and coordinated determines its ability to achieve its goals. Many factors influence the behavior and performance of the organization including the context, purpose, people, and structure as they interface with the core transformation and management support processes to set up the organization's performance level. All factors are affected by security.

## 1 Introduction

Most everything of tangible value in today's society (and many intangibles as well) is stored in digital form somewhere. Without the knowledge to defend our digital assets, we are lost, and our potential loss grows larger everyday as we pour the contents of our lives into databases, PDAs, personal computers, and Web servers, through routers, hubs, switches, cell phones, gateways, copper, coax, the air itself. The need for security has existed since introducing the first computer. The paradigm has shifted in recent years, though, from terminal server mainframe systems, to client/server systems, to the widely distributed Internet [1].

Although security is important, it has not always been critical to a company's success. With a mainframe system, you were protecting your systems from resource abuse – either authorized users hogging resources or unauthorized users gaining access and using spare resources. Such abuse was damaging because system resources were costly in the early days of mainframes. As technology developed and the cost of system resources decreased, this issue became less important. Remote access to systems outside a company's network was almost nonexistent. Moreover, only the underground community had the knowledge and tools needed to compromise a mainframe system.

Client/server technology developments led to a myriad of new security problems. Processor utilization was not a priority, but access to networks, systems, and files

D. Karagiannis and U. Reimer (Eds.): PAKM 2004, LNAI 3336, pp. 165–174, 2004.

grew in importance. Access control became a priority as sensitive information, such as human resources and payroll, was being stored on public file servers. Companies did not want such data to be public knowledge, even to their employees, so new technologies such as granular access control, single sign-on, and data encryption were developed. As always, methods of circumventing and exploiting these new applications and security products quickly arose. During the client/server era, access into the corporate network was usually had only a few dial-up accounts. This did open some security holes, but the risk to these accounts could be easily mitigated with procedures such as dial-back and access lists. Branch offices communicated with one another over dedicated leased lines.

Then came the Internet – the open access worldwide network – and everything changed. The growth of e-mail and the World Wide Web soon led companies to provide Internet access to their employees. Developing an e-business initiative for your company became critical to stay competitive in the changing marketplace. With the increased use of the Internet, information, including security information, became accessible to the general public. Because the Internet is a public network, anyone on the Net can "see" other system on it. As use of the Internet grew, companies began to allow increased access to information and networks over the Internet. This approach, although beneficial for business, was inviting to attackers.

Recent events have led information security to become a significant focus in the way an organization conducts its business. The majority of businesses today have at least a rudimentary security program in place, and many programs are evolving and growing in maturity. As these programs have grown, so has the need to move beyond the view that security is just a technical issue. Security today should be integrated with the fabric of a business. In doing so, information security programs need to move from tactical implementations of technology to strategic partners in business. [1] Although companies were committed to develop a complete information security program they may not have integrated them into the framework of their businesses.

## 1.1 The Case for Information Security Scrutiny

Some companies have taken an enlightened view of security. They believe that to be successful, they must show their customers that security and protecting information assets are core business function. Security by design means that it is not an afterthought in the design process; instead, it is one of the requirements that designers use when starting a project. Secure in deployment means that products will be shipped and ready to use in a way that will not compromise the security of the customer or other products.

In the broadest definition, an information security program is a plan to mitigate risks associated with the processing of information. The security profession [1] has defined the basics of security as three elements:

1. *Confidentiality:* Preventing unauthorized use or disclosure of information. Privacy is a closely related topic that has lately been getting greater visibility.
2. *Integrity:* Ensuring that information is accurate, complete, and has not been modified by unauthorized users or processes.
3. *Availability:* Ensuring that users have timely and reliable access to their information assets.

These three elements are the basics around which all security programs are developed. The three concepts are linked together in information protection. The idea that information is an asset that requires protection, just like other asset of the business, is basic to understanding these concepts.

In an annual study [2] conducted by the Computer Security Institute: ninety percent of respondents (mainly large corporations and government agencies) detected computer security breaches during that year; seventy percent reported a variety of serious computer security breaches except the most common ones of computer viruses, laptop theft, or employee "Net abuse"; eighty percent acknowledged financial losses caused by computer breaches;  forty-four percent were willing and able to quantify their financial losses. The losses from these 223 respondents totaled $455,848,000; the most serious financial losses occurred through theft of proprietary information (26 respondents reported $170,827,000) and financial fraud (25 respondents reported $115,753,000). For the fifth year in a row, more respondents (74 percent) cited their Internet connection as a frequent point of attack than those who cited their internal systems as a frequent point of attack (33 percent).

## 2   Organization Processes and Security Considerations

Understanding and managing organizational processes, such as work design and redesign, creativity and innovation, culture, learning and change seems to absorb a significant time and energy in today's business environment. Some managers argue that in reality their job virtually consist entirely in managing change [3]. Change comes about in many ways. We have described in some detail the changing face of information commerce among organizations based on introducing information communication technologies. These technologies have changed the way we work; they have altered the cultures within our firms.

The way the organization is designed and coordinated has major effect on the organization's ability to achieve its goals. Many factors influence the behavior and performance of the organization. These elements, as Shown in Figure 1, can be grouped into six categories. The context, purpose, people, and structure interface with the core transformation processes and management support processes to set up the organization's performance level. All factors are affected by security. It is these factors, given their security is properly addressed, that determine the ongoing success of the organization.

### 2.1   Context

Context refers to the entire organization including size, technology, and environment. Contextual dimensions affect the other categories, such as structure and work processes, and later organization performance. The environment has a two tier perspective: the task environment and the global environment. The task environment consists of the firm's immediate relevant environment such as all customers, suppliers (of labor, knowledge, information, money, materials, and so on), markets, competitors, regulators, ands associations that are relevant to the business' current services and products. The global environment includes all the other possible environmental factors in which the organization functions, such as political, educational, economy, demographic characteristics, societal structure, laws, and the many global impacts of doing business today.

We have already introduced the internet. Its opportunities are virtually unlimited and challenging from a company perspective. Most of the primary tasks of doing business across the network have been addressed. But commerce and communication through the internet continues to be a major security threat. Viruses and other external threats have and continue to shut down entire systems of electronic communication in and among organizations; records in databases are compromised; private and delicate communications become not so private. The global environment and the choice of technology are intertwined.

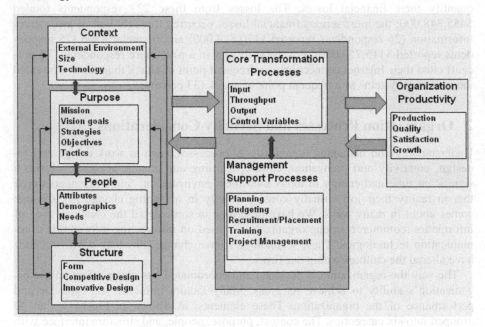

**Fig. 1.** Organizational Performance Factors

## 2.2 Purpose

In defining the purpose category, we consider how the organization interprets the environment to develop statements of mission, vision, goals, strategies, objectives, and tactics. Although the firm's mission may change slowly, important signals to employees are gained from formal communications from management about goals and priorities. Most business organizations have strategic plans that incorporate information technology. Frequeintly the information technology part does not include a security plan. Instead security is assumed to be inherent in the information technology infrastructure.

Strategically executive management needs to be certain that all threats, external and internal, have been addressed through an information security plan and policy. The portal to the outside world is a series of defenses such as an outer firewall, an intermediate area in between to filter internet traffic, and another firewall to control the liaisons between the company and the outside world. The next step is to verify that the operations in the organization have security measures in place. Decisions for grouping users and providing access rights and the ability to modify critical data are frequently delegated to a security specialist. Such a specialist likely does not view the workings of the organization in a macro sense and is not vested with the authority or knowledge to align the corporate structure with the security structure.

## 2.3 People

Organizations have members with diverse attributes, demographic characteristics, and needs. Attributes include knowledge, skills, and abilities and learning styles and problem-solving styles. In many organizations, the collective knowledge sharing and learning becomes an organizational capability that is difficult for other companies to duplicate. Demographic characteristics are also important in building capabilities and improving organizational performance. If organizations are to thrive, they must address employee needs, so employee satisfaction is potentially as important as the satisfaction of other stakeholders.

As companies are confronted with global competition, e-commerce, industry consolidation, new partnerships and alliances, and the like, there is an increased need for internal and external coordination and collaboration. In this context, decisions are made on a decentralized basis, by teams that can use the best information at hand. One answer is a shift toward viewing the organization as "teams of teams," or the team-based organization [4].

Employees are the most difficult part of security management to address and control. Security policies do not always follow the chain of command or the formal/informal systems of communication. In many cases there is a lack of support or conflict over the enforcement and enactment of security policies. Sometimes the security manager will attempt to enforce policies for all without an attempt to temper enforcement with judgment. Enforcement to the security manager includes penalizing the people who break the rules. Other managers look at security policies the same way they look at all policies and weigh the punishment with the crime. Access control violations are compared to violations of accounting policy and the myriad of other rules that exist in the workplace today. Executive management has to weigh all types of policies with the other goals and objectives of the business. This is not too different from the security manager's decisions e about access controls and authorization. The security manager has to weigh the "need to know" against the "want to know," where the line always requires greater access to information than the former. The convergence of the executive manager and the security manager decisions is in the balancing of their goals and objectives. One way to improve communication between the executive team and the security area is security area is to link decisions to find common goals and objectives and then work on disagreements.

Organizations [5] invest heavily in the latest firewalls, intrusion detection systems, and other advanced security technologies; yet losses from security incidents continue to grow each_year. The problem is not so much with security technology as it is with the lack of security awareness among users. Information security professionals have to deal with breaches caused by users opening an e-mail attachment_with a virus that reproduces itself across the enterprise, forgetting to backup critical files, using weak passwords, losing laptops with confidential data, or being tricked into giving up their passwords through social engineering techniques. Security experts acknowledge that an organization's first line of defense is the front-line employees who interact with customers, process their information, and pass it along to others in the delivery chain. Many discussions of security and privacy compliance mention that successful initiatives require sweeping cultural changes, including changes in operational processes and behaviors.

## 2.4  Structure

The term structure has many meanings. Research studies on organizations have identified structural variables such as levels in the hierarchy, formalization (the written documentation, as in policies and procedures manuals, job descriptions, and the like), standardization (the extent to which activities must be performed in a uniform manner), and centralization (at what decision levels). Form of structure refers to the method of grouping employees together into work units, departments, and the organization.

As the organization grows, differentiation of specialty units occurs, with managers appointed for each unit. Functional organizations tend to be efficient and work well when the business situation and outside environment are stable. Employees then take on increasingly complicated tasks and grow through special assignments and applications of their skills. On the negative side, people in functional organizations may develop parochial viewpoints, and interdepartmental cooperation can be poor. Department goals differ, and decisions are pushed up the hierarchy, slowing deliberations and blocking needed changes. As the company's products and customers expand, other forms of structure may appear attractive to top management.

With increasing company size, product divisions or other self-contained units are created to replace the functional organization. With greater diversification of products and greater diversification in customers and markets served, a company may choose to reorganize according to its major products. When this occurs, each product group gains discretion to design, produce, and distribute its products in ways that are consistent with the competitive environment. If the new product groups are organized in the same basic way (R&D, manufacturing, accounting, marketing), it can be argued that nothing new has occurred. The product groups still appear functional, and people may behave in the same ways. If the structure and support processes change to stress multispecialty teams or other forms of teamwork, a truly new form might exist.

## 2.5  Core Transformation Process

The core transformation process is the conversion process turning inputs into output. Looking at it from a strictly technical systems view input combined with technology produces "throughput" or product-in-becoming" [6]. Throughput is the state of the product at an earlier stage of development. Management and employees must apply technology and control variances so that the core transformation process is sound. Security is endemic in the core transformation process. At every stage measures must be in place to insure that the customer orders are received, the billing information is secured, communications with vendors for purchases, processing of the orders, and the distribution and collection are assured. The means to secure (authenticated) transaction has been addressed in many systems and is provided by software vendors and the communication industry. It is the responsibility of each company to insure that they have incorporated these features into their internal systems.

## 2.6 Management Support Processes

Before, companies chose to centralize management support groups at the corporate level. Staff members were then deployed to provide support or needed corporate controls. The reaction from lower management was negative, as staff personnel demanded time and resources in carrying out their roles in divisions and departments of the company. The staff members carried the corporate perspective of control, relative to true service and support to managers and employees in the field. Today, the situation is much improved in most corporations, because of two developments in organization design. First, corporations have experienced waves of downsizing as a strategic move and to cut costs. Frequently, there are fewer and smaller corporate staff work units, and service groups. A second development in organization design is physical location of staff groups. When service groups are located with operations groups, there is a greater sense of cooperation, teamwork, and identity with operations managers and work teams. Under the *distributed organization* divisions and departments are encouraged to develop support groups that are close to the real operations action. For example, rather than locate a corporate-wide Information Technology group at headquarters, in a multi-division firm, one division might have such a group to serve its own needs and to serve all other company divisions. When this idea is extended to other staff support groups, a situation emerges where divisions help each other and bring in new ideas, methods, and technologies to improve operations throughout the company.

Management may view their information systems infrastructure as an inevitable evil rather than as a critical business process [7]. Many times this is attributable to a lack of understanding and communication. For a company, information systems are expensive assets. Management must clearly understand their information systems environment to manage this asset as they would other business asset. The planning process will significantly improve the communication between management and information systems. Management hopes to gain a better understanding of their current systems, and identify potential risks and opportunities. Information Systems will better understand the business direction and the role of technology.

The information systems direction must be aligned with business drivers and must also conform to boundary conditions imposed by the business environment. Boundary conditions may limit what can be done. Information is a valuable resource, and it is important to increase its value for the corporation. Planning and managing the information flow throughout the organization can reduce labor, data redundancy, and inconsistency, besides increasing the quality and accuracy of the information.

Developing systems that provide the business with a competitive advantage must be the focus rather than simply satisfying the wheel that squeaks the loudest. Some information systems managers are efficient in developing a strategic plan by taking their top computer technicians and outlining the technical architecture of the future. When these technicians complete their planning, they may have an ideal technical plan, but one which management may not totally understands, let alone approve. These plans tend to accumulate dust on someone's bookshelf and never affect the direction of information systems or the business. The plan must show management ideas, styles, and objectives. To be successful, the entire organization must support the information systems objectives.

# 3  Observations

## 3.1  Security as a Competitive Edge

A properly implemented security infrastructure [8] can become a competitive advantage, providing protection to corporate assets. If a company's main competitor is looking to launch e-business initiatives, the company with the stronger security infrastructure will be more successful. Why? First, the company with the weaker security infrastructure might be reluctant to launch e-business projects because it is concerned with security and does not know how to adequately protect itself. Second, and more commonly, the weaker company will ignore the security aspect of online business and then wonder why it suffered a successful, damaging attack against its systems. This inattention can lead to the compromise of critical sensitive data – such as, customer credit cards or business bank account numbers – and the subsequent loss of customers. The company with the superior security environment can safely launch an online business initiative, knowing that its corporate security infrastructure is strong enough to protect it. If its systems do happen to be compromised, the business response plan in place should reduce the damage.

## 3.2  Management Buy-In

Security programs should involve all aspects of the organization. Management support and organization buy-in are key to the success of a security infrastructure. A program works best when it is built around a framework of established policies, standards, and procedures. If implemented properly, a security infrastructure will help curtail practices that seem to have become the norm in most organizations, such as employees writing down passwords on notepaper and storing the notes under their keyboards or mouse pads. It can also stop social engineering and physical attacks, such as the fake help desk call asking to reset a password or dumpster diving. A comprehensive security program also must address business partners who create potential security breaches by improperly securing their own networks and systems, leaving them as backdoors into your network.

## 3.3  Recognition that Security is Key to the Business

The inexorable drive of companies to reduce costs and enhance productivity has entailed increased reliance on the Internet. Information security is a pervasive concern for all companies, not simply those that rely to a varying extent on the Internet to conduct business. An accurate gauge [9] of losses resulting from IT security incidents needs to be established. Given the tight corporate budgets, IT managers, risk managers, and finance policy makers require reliable quantitative estimates on enterprise IT security.

Studies [10] have shown that IT can be a major source of productivity gains. The results are likely to be variable, depending on the specific IT investment at the firm level. Productivity improvements may arise from competitive pressures, which can lead to process innovations, which involve deployment of information technology. If IT investment is not for a business process innovation, chances are that little gain in productivity can be anticipated or will occur.

# 4 Directions for Future Research

## 4.1 Organization Design, the Design for Security and Planned Change

As the field of security design matures, the need to develop security design theory [SDT], security design principles [SDP] and a comprehensive planned change process would be the next stage in the field's development. Security design theory is a developing body of academic literature that requires further development and articulation. Its main stream activity is dedicated to advanced research in the field. The security design principles are the pragmatic and applied cousin of security design theory. Specific sets of design principles [11] have been advanced over the last five years that guide the actual design or redesign of an existing organization or the design of a new organization – the actual architecture of the firm's security. The relationship between security design theory and security design principles is both implicit and explicit. Though it is not SDP, SDT does inform SDP. ON occasion, SDP and SDT are tightly coupled. At other times the relationship is tenuous.

The third subfield is security design planned change process [SDPCP]. This emerging subfield is devoted to the change and development process of creating or transforming an organization. Specific sets of phases and steps are being advanced to guide the redesign process for existing organizations or the design for new organizations. SDPCP provides a comprehensive planned change process with analytical tools and methods that have been developed to facilitate the transformation of an organization to a security-designed-based entity. The design process, methods and tools need to be further developed and elaborated.

The relationship among SDPCP, SDT and SDP is important. Our knowledge and understanding of the complexity of the interface requires systematic research to insure that the field advances to the next level of development and practice.

## 4.2 Security Design and Continuous Improvement

In our model we indicated that organizational productivity depends on the alignment and dynamics among context, people, structure, core transformation processes and management support processes. The complexity of these relationships requires continuous improvement efforts. Firms around the globe are increasing their engagements in a variety of continuous improvement programs and system-wide change efforts. At a basic level continuous improvement is a purposeful and explicit set of principles, and activities within an organization designed to achieve positive and continuous change in deliverables, operating procedures, and systems by the people that actually perform these procedures and systems. A careful review of the reported continuous improvement and system-wide change efforts centering about security reveals the need to develop a unified set of SDT, SDP and SDPC. This development signifies that security design would be moving through the stages of introduction, experimentation and evaluation towards the general acceptance and implementation stage.

### 4.3 Security Design and Collaborative Research

Collaborative research is defined as *an emergent and systematic inquiry* process embedded in a true *partnership* between researchers and members of a living system in which behavior, social, organizational and management scientific knowledge is *integrated* with existing organizational knowledge for the purpose of generating actionable knowledge [12]. At a basic level, collaborative research brings about the challenge to balance the interdependence among actors, academic research and actual application, knowledge creation and problems solving, and inside and outside inquiries, It is a partnership among a variety of individuals forming a "community of inquiry" and is viewed as an emergent inquiry process that differs from the notion of scientific research as being a closed, linear and planned activity.

The ultimate success of knowledge creation and security design and organization design depends on how different actor groups and micro-communities relate through the knowledge creation process. Collaborative research is viewed as an enabler for the understanding of security design since it provides methods, mechanisms and processes for the interactions between the micro communities of knowledge and other relevant individuals inside and outside the organization for the purpose of creating new actionable knowledge.

## References

1. Wylder, John, Strategic Information Security, Auerbach Publ (2004)
2. Ernst & Young, LLP, Global Information Security Survey (2002) cited in www.vnunet.com (9/20/2002). (2002)
3. Shani, A. B. (Rami) and James Lau, Behavior in Organizations, McGraw-Hill Irwin, New York (2005)
4. Mohrman, S. A,. Cohen, S. G. and Mohrman, Jr., A. M., Designing Team-Based Organizations: New Forms for Knowledge Work, San Francisco: Jossey-Bass (1995).
5. Guenther, Melissa, Security/Privacy Compliance: Culture Change, EDPACS, June (2004)
6. Taylor, J.C. and Felten, D.P., Performance By Design: Sociotechnical Systems in North America, Englewood Cliffs, N.J: Prentice Hall (1993).
7. Cassidy, Anita, A Practical Guide to Information Systems Planning, (Chapter 1), CRC Press (1998 )
8. Andress, Amanda, "How to Integrate People, Process, and Technology "in Surviving Security, Second Edition, CRC Press Company ( 2004)
9. Raval, Vasant, Window on the World / Security, Society, and Skepticism, Information Strategy: The Executive's Journal 45 l46 Winter (2003)
10. Raval, Vasant, Executive Insights / Productivity and Information Technology Information Strategy: The Executive's Journal 38 Fall (2003)
11. Daft, Richard L. Organization Theory and Design, Thompson Learning  (2004) "The Impact of Information Security Incidents on Share Holder Value: Event Study Evidence, ," Ernst & Young, LLP. September (2002)
12. Adler, Nicholas, Shani, A.B. (Rami), and Styhme, Alexander, Collaborative Research in Organizations, Sage, 2004

# Knowledge Exploitation from the Web

David Riaño[1], Antonio Moreno[1], David Isern[1],
Jaime Bocio[1], David Sánchez[1], and Laureano Jiménez[2]

[1] Departament d'Enginyeria Informàtica i Matemàtiques
Universitat Rovira i Virgili
43007 Tarragona, Catalonia, Spain
{drianyo,amoreno,disern,jbocio,dsanchez}@etse.urv.es
[2] Department of Chemical Engineering and Metallurgy
University of Barcelona
08028 Barcelona, Catalonia, Spain
laure.jimenez@ub.edu

**Abstract.** In the framework of Knowledge Management, the Internet can be a valuable source of information to produce new Knowledge. Here, an ontology-based web search system to ease the enterprise managers in the process of discovering new knowledge from the documents in the Internet is introduced. By means of a graphical user interface, the user of the system supplies an ontology in RDF to describe the domain of interest, and sets up some predefined parameters in order to constrain the search corpus. A distributed intelligent process works to achieve the levels of quality and quantity about the results that the user established. Several ideas about how to use this system and its application to seven real domains are also supplied.

## 1 Introduction

Knowledge Management (KM) can be defined to encompass the strategy, the processes, and the technology employed to enable an enterprise to acquire, create, organise, share, and make actionable knowledge needed to achieve the vision of the enterprise. These complex tasks have been traditionally tackled with the use of *first generation knowledge management* (FGKM) tools that are oriented to the administration of information structures in order to deal with the knowledge that benefits the enterprise. These tools are mainly based on information technology and strategic management. Nowadays, the approach to KM is by means of *second generation knowledge management* (SGKM) tools which are oriented to the development of knowledge structures that are captured from the enterprise experiences. Contrarily to FGKM, SGKM systems do not consider valuable knowledge as something that already exists, but something that emerges from the enterprise activities and that must be managed along a *knowledge life cycle* process that is divided into three sequential steps[1] [8]: knowledge production, knowledge validation, and knowledge integration.

*Knowledge production* involves the creation of new knowledge, such as new ideas, insights and innovation spawned by interaction between people or groups and the acquisition of knowledge from outside sources. *Knowledge validation* is the next step, during which potential new knowledge is subjected to expert review and proc-

---

[1] Other authors define different knowledge life cycles; e.g. Davenport and Prusak [10] consider the steps of knowledge generation, codification and transfer.

D. Karagiannis and U. Reimer (Eds.): PAKM 2004, LNAI 3336, pp. 175–185, 2004.
© Springer-Verlag Berlin Heidelberg 2004

esses that test its reliability and value in practice. Knowledge that passes these tests is then integrated, or implemented, within the organisation in the *knowledge integration* step.

One of the main problems in knowledge production is that knowledge is not always easily expressed by means of a formal representation language. This fact makes a distinction between what is called *explicit knowledge* (it can be expressed in words and numbers and shared in the form of data, scientific expressions, specifications, manuals, etc.) and *tacit knowledge* (it is far to be reduced to explicit expressions and cannot be articulated, but it can be learned, acquired or managed).

## 1.1 Using Ontologies for Knowledge Management

Knowledge engineering in KM is closely related to the concept of ontology. In this framework, an *ontology* is a conceptualisation of a knowledge domain in a model that defines a structure of concepts and concept relationships which are relevant to the domain. Ontologies are explicit knowledge structures that can be shared [1].

These structures can be used to represent declarative or procedural knowledge about the domain of interest of an enterprise. *Declarative knowledge* (or know-what) consists of the factual assessments an organisation makes about itself and its capabilities in the context of its marketplace and operating environment. *Procedural knowledge* (or know-how) takes the form of business processes that the organisation executes in the areas of marketing, manufacturing, personnel, R&D, etc.

## 1.2 An Ontology-Based Internet Search Tool

KM is not only related with the internal knowledge of a enterprise, but also with its context in the local, the national, and the world wide market. Declarative and procedural knowledge about competitors, their products, their policies, their success, etc. can be very valuable for the manager of a company. Political changes, the publications of new laws, norms, or standards, the appearance of new materials or the development of new production technologies describe also a sort of knowledge that has to be managed for the benefit of the own company. Nowadays, the Internet is the best window to show and find public information all around the world. Unfortunately, although computer browsers that access this information are efficient in the tasks of web page search and retrieval, they are not so good in the tasks of processing such information (e.g. page selection, knowledge production, validation and integration). This is so because these search tools use to work with a limited keyword-based description of the domain of interest of the user, and not with a semantic representation of the relationships between these keywords (i.e. concepts) or a description of the concepts in terms of their properties and synonyms.

Here, an ontology-based search system is introduced that explores the Internet to find relevant pages related to the different concepts in an ontology. The retrieved pages are textual instances of the concepts, but conditioned to the meaning of the concept in the whole ontology. The content of the pages related to a particular concept are analysed in order to rank them according to a relevance function which takes into account the properties describing the user desired profile of such concept.

This system is introduced as a decision support tool that can ease and fasten the process of knowledge production and validation by means of a friendly user interface.

The system was tested with seven public ontologies: *employment, petrol oil, biotechnology, sustainability, axens processes, wastewater,* and *technology.* For each one, the system was used for knowledge mining from the web. Particularly, it was used to acquire new explicit knowledge, to validate this knowledge on the basis of the relevance of the pages producing it, and to discover tacit knowledge and make it explicit.

Section 2 describes the ontology model that the search system is able to work with. Then, the system is introduced in section 3 where some ideas about how to exploit the system for knowledge production are highlighted. Section 4 describes the use of the system to produce knowledge in seven alternative application domains. The paper finishes with a section containing some conclusions.

## 2 Domain Representation as an Ontology

Knowledge production is the process by which new knowledge is created from a variety of sources: people and groups, reports, intranet and Internet documents, information systems, etc. When the source of information used in knowledge production is textual or oral, natural language processing scientists call it a *corpus.* Knowledge production can be guided by a description of the area of interest defined by the enterprise manager that shows what the manager is willing to search about in the selected corpus. An *ontology* is an explicit formal specification of how to represent objects, concepts and other entities that exist in such area of interest, and the relationships that hold among them. These use to be *class-subclass* relationships. For example, the *petrol oil* ontology in figure 1 describes an area of interest with concepts as *fuel, oil, diesel (fuel),* or *unleaded (fuel)* that are related in a taxonomy of petrol products. This could be used by the manager of a petrol company to define the area of interest that filters the knowledge that he wants to obtain from the web pages of a rival company.

Each concept included in the ontology can be refined with the use of *properties.* The properties of a concept describe the sort of features that the manager is looking for. So, for example, *price* is a property of the concept *fuel,* meaning that the manager is interested in the production of knowledge about the cost of fuel. If this ontology was used in a corpus of *stock exchange markets,* the knowledge would be about petrol company stocks, but if the corpus was in *production processes,* the knowledge would be about fuel refinement costs. Concepts and properties can have *synonyms* related.

There are many formal languages for representing ontologies [3]: XOL [7], SHOE [5], RDF [4], OIL [2], OWL [4], and others. Here, the RDF notation has been selected because it is simple and flexible, and it allows property inheritance. Some other languages as OIL or OWL sacrifice the RDF simplicity by adding some particularities to deal with more general ontology models. In RDF, concepts are represented as classes, concept properties as attributes, and concept relationships as *subclassof* attributes.

## 3 An Ontology-Based Search System

Ontologies and corpuses are the main inputs of the web search system. Ontologies represent an area of interest that has been defined by a company manager or selected

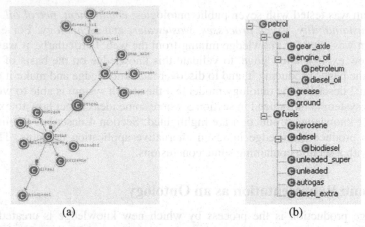

(a)                                      (b)

**Fig. 1.** *Petrol Oil* ontology: (*a*) graphical representation and (*b*) taxonomic representation

from an ontology repository (e.g. www.daml.org, protege.stanford.edu, and prise-serv.cpe.surrey.ac.uk). The corpuses are the web search space from which the manager wants to produce knowledge about the domain described by the selected ontology. Once an ontology and a corpus are decided, the search system looks in the corpus for web pages related to the ontology, retrieves them, evaluates their contents, ranks them according to the relevance to the manager interest, and displays them in a graphical interface that helps the user to produce new knowledge.

The system has several control parameters to restrict some aspects of the search as the system response time and response extension, the minimum relevance of the results, etc. All these aspects are described in more detail in the next subsections.

### 3.1  The Search Parameters

Before the system starts working, a set of parameters must be supplied. These parameters are divided into two groups: *control parameters* and *corpus parameters*. There are five control parameters (*deadline, search engine, number of links, search agents,* and *threshold*) that can be used to restrict some properties of the search as the expected response time, the search engine used, the response extension, the degree of parallelism of the search process, and the expected quality of the results.

There are also three corpus parameters (*web site, language,* and *country*) to define the search space by means of reducing it to all the pages in a particular web site or domain (e.g. *.org, .edu, .com,* etc.), or restricted to a particular language (e.g. *English, Spanish, French,* etc.), country or region (e.g. *European Union, USA, Japan,* etc.).

All the parameters have a default value as table 1 shows. In the corpus parameters, the default value indicates that the search is on all the web without any restriction.

### 3.2  The Search Engine

The search system uses the APIs of Google and Altavista as search engines wrapped by an intelligent system that cuts the domain ontology into pieces (sub-ontologies)

**Table 1.** User parameters to customise the web search process

| Parameter name | Description | Default |
|---|---|---|
| *Deadline* | Time allowed to retrieve, rank and sort web pages | 20 sec. |
| *Search Engine* | Google or Altavista | Google |
| *Number of links* | Links to be retrieved for each ontology concept | 20 |
| *Search Agents* | Number of IAs to be used in the search process | 1 |
| *Threshold* | Minimum rate to be attained by a page to be shown in results | 50% |
| *Web Site* | The search is restricted to the given web site | - |
| *Language* | Language in which retrieved web pages must be written | - |
| *Country* | Country of origin of retrieved web pages | - |

according to the degree of concurrency indicated by the *search agents* parameter, and scatters these pieces between the available search processes running in the computers involved in the process. Then, each search process works to obtain as many relevant pages as the parameters *number of links* and *threshold* respectively indicate. The search engine API used is the one indicated by the *search engine* parameter.

There is a component of the system that predicts whether the number of pages for a particular sub-ontology is adequate. This component works in parallel to the rest of the system in order to modify sub-ontologies with an inadequate number of pages. The process generalizes these sub-ontologies in such a way that the number of pages retrieved can be complemented with some other new relevant ones.

The contents of the pages retrieved are analysed and the relevance of the page is calculated in terms of the sub-ontology concepts and properties appearing in the documents. The relevance is used to rank the pages and to discard those pages with an unacceptable quality. Any text file format is analysed (html, doc, pdf, ps, txt, etc.).

The overall process is restricted by the *deadline* parameter and it stops when this time is reached. This means that the most restrictive the time is, the higher probability there is to have less pages than required.

### 3.3 The Relevance of the Results

A concept in an ontology is defined by a description and a context. The description of a concept is represented by the concept *name* (and synonyms, if there are) and the concept *properties* (and synonyms). The context of a concept is represented by the *names of the ancestors* of the concept (and synonyms) and the *inherited properties* (and synonyms) of the ancestors. For example, the description of the concept *kerosene* is {kerosene, kerosine} for name and synonyms, and {flash point, duration} for properties, and the context is {*fuels, oil, petrol*} for the ancestor names and synonyms and {octane index} for the inherited properties.

Whereas the web pages retrieved by the search engine for a concept only depend on the names of the concept and the ancestors, the quality of these pages is computed with all the properties, inherited or not, of the concept.

Equation 1 shows the quality function that measures the relevance of a page, where $p$ stands for the evaluated page, and $A_c$ for the set of properties of the concept $c$.

$$R(p, A_c) = \frac{number\ of\ properties\ in(p, A_c)}{total\ number\ of\ properties(A_c)} \times 100 \tag{1}$$

This evaluation takes into account only the presence or the absence of each property, but it does not count the number of times that the property appears.

When we tested the system we noticed that during the analysis of concepts with a certain depth in the ontology (4-5-6 levels) it was quite difficult to find web pages containing a high percentage of the properties. For this reason, the above function is normalised with respect to the greatest quality obtained for a concept of the ontology, as equation 2 indicates.

$$\bar{R}(p, A_c) = \frac{R(p, A_c)}{\max_c R(p, A_c)} \tag{2}$$

### 3.4 The Uses of the Search System

Although the search system as it is now is not able to produce new knowledge, it can be used to ease the process of knowledge mining that a company manager may require, and therefore it belongs to what is called *business intelligence*. The system has two potential approaches to knowledge production: one which is based on the analysis of the quantity of links retrieved for each concept and their relevance, and another one which is about the interpretation of the contents of the retrieved pages. As the second approach is still not completely solved in our system, only the possible practical uses of the first approach will be reported here. Two alternative points of view are presented in the next paragraphs. On the one hand, the possible uses of the system when the input (i.e. ontology and parameters) and the output (retrieved pages) of the system change. On the other hand, the possible uses of the system from the perspective of the company department using it.

*Ontology:* according to the sort of concepts in an ontology, the system is able to help the user in the production of declarative knowledge, procedural knowledge, or both. If the concepts in the ontology represent static concepts as company products the system will help the user to produce declarative knowledge, but if the concepts in the ontology represent dynamic concepts as company processes, then the knowledge produced will be procedural.

*Parameters:* the wise use of the corpus parameters will permit the user to focus the production of knowledge in the desired context: personal, departmental, in a company, local, regional, national, or international. For example, the system can be used to compare the laws that concern the domain of interest of a company for different countries, and help a manager to decide where to open a new factory.

*Retrieved pages:* the number of pages retrieved for each concept and their normalised relevance can supply much information about the domain of interest. For example, if no pages about one concept are retrieved from the web pages of a company or the pages retrieved are irrelevant, this reinforces the tacit fact that this company does not produce, sell or offer the product, service or technology that the concept represents. On the contrary, if there are many web pages about one concept of the ontology, the product, service or technology that the concept represents is an important explicit element of the analysed company. When this simple idea is extended to a whole ontology, the implications are very interesting. So, for instance, if a company is in the process of merging another one and the manager has an ontology representing the domain of what the merger is expected to be, then if both companies offer the same products, services or technologies this means that the union of both companies will become a stronger competitor in the same marketplace. On the contrary, if the pages retrieved for each one of the two companies are related to different concepts in the ontology, then the companies complement one another, and the unification will produce the growing of the marketplace. This functionality can be extended to help enterprise managers to find and decide about the company that better fits their needs, according to the interests of the manager represented by an ontology.

*Company department:* the system can be applied differently according to the interest of the departments of a company. So, in the department of Human Resources it is possible to generate knowledge about where the best professionals to cover the company vacancies can be found (country, university, etc.), or what are the alternative hiring procedures or models. In the Marketing department the manager can produce knowledge about market maps related to the ontology of the company products or services. The study can start with all the internet were the most relevant geographic zones or countries can be detected. Focused on these zones or countries, the most relevant companies, organisations, universities, etc. can be detected, and from them the departments involved in such products or services and even the persons related to them. Finally, for the Production and R&D departments it is also possible to use the system to detect new products or technologies. For example, if we have an ontology with a parent concept representing a sort of product or technology and the sons representing particular products or technologies, we can use the system to search every month about this ontology in the web. If we detect that the number of pages retrieved for the parent concept has increased significantly, and the sum of the retrieved pages for the son concepts remains the same or is reduced, then a feasible explanation that has to be studied in detail is that some new product or technology has appeared replacing the previous ones.

These uses of the search system are a sample of possible applications to help managers to produce knowledge in their domains of interest. In the next section, some experiences about the use of the search system to produce new knowledge in concrete domains are described.

## 4  Applications

The search system has been tested for producing new knowledge in seven domains of interest: *employment* in chemical engineering, *petrol oil, biosensors, technologies* in chemical engineering, *processes, wastewater,* and *sustainability*. These ontologies have been obtained from public repositories in the internet as the DAML repository at www.daml.org, the Prótegé repository at protege.stanford.edu, and the hTechSight repository at prise-serv.cpe.surrey.ac.uk [6], and some of them have been modified to permit a proper check of the system.

*Employment* is a model of the concepts involved in the description of educational and professional sectors where jobs are offered in the area of chemical engineering. *Petrol oil* shows a classification of the sort of fuels and oils derived from the petroleum. *Biosensors* is designed to describe the concepts related to companies and products that work on biosensor technology. *Technologies* is concerned about several areas in the chemical engineering technology as process design or thermodynamics. *Processes* contains concepts about the treatment of petroleum residues. *Wastewater* describes concepts about the available legislations in the EU and in the USA about water cleaning, and also about methods to manage water pollutants. Finally, *sustainability* is about technologies that may be applied in any industry to accomplish better ecological measures, and also about tools and methods to be applied in those technologies.

**Table 2.** Domain ontology features

| Ontology name | No. classes | Avg. depth | Max. depth | Attributes? | Synonyms? | D/P |
|---|---|---|---|---|---|---|
| *Employment* | 23 | 5.0869 | 7 | No | Yes | D |
| *Petrol Oil* | 17 | 3.7647 | 5 | Yes | Yes | D |
| *Biosensors* | 19 | 4.3636 | 6 | Yes | Yes | D |
| *Technologies* | 24 | 4.6666 | 6 | Yes | No | P |
| *Processes* | 15 | 3.7333 | 5 | No | No | P |
| *Waste water* | 49 | 4.8867 | 6 | Yes | No | D/P |
| *Sustainability* | 46 | 4.6739 | 6 | No | No | D/P |

For each ontology, table 2 supplies extra information as the number of classes of the RDFS document (i.e. *concepts*), the average and maximum depth of the ontology concepts, whether the ontology has attributes or synonyms, and the kind of knowledge this ontology contains: *D* for declarative and *P* for procedural.

In the rest of this section we describe, using several case studies, how the search system can be used to extract different kinds of knowledge and perform diverse types of analysis of documents related to the concepts of a certain domain ontology.

## 4.1   Case Study 1: Biosensor Companies and Application Areas in Europe

Biosensors are analytical tools consisting of biologically active material used in close conjunction with a device that will convert a biochemical signal into a quantifiable electrical signal. They have many advantages with respect to other traditional sensors (simplicity, low-cost, fast response time, etc) and many potential applications (agriculture, horticulture, veterinary, pollution, water contamination, clinical diagnosis, biomedicine, etc.). The area of biosensors evolves very rapidly and the management of the new emerging knowledge is something relevant to satisfy the market requirements for small and medium enterprises. Here, the system introduced in section 3 is used to generate knowledge about the more important biosensor companies and areas of application of biosensors in European countries with a high impact of this technology.

For this case study we concentrate on the concepts of the *Biosensors* ontology defined in the IST project *hTechSight* (prise-serv.cpe.surrey.ac.uk/techsight/). First, we use the system to study the number of results provided on the concept *biosensor company* (which obtains more than 22,500 references in Google) restricted to some country domains in Europe (.uk 763, .de 627, .it 145, .es 82, .fr 52, .fi 58, .pt 10, .lv 1). From the analysis of these results we can notice that "*the United Kingdom seems to be the country with more presence of biosensor companies in Europe*". The system also supplies the names of some of "*the most relevant biosensor companies in the UK: Cybersense Biosystems Ltd, BIVDA, The Generics Group, and MCA Services*".

In a further step, we can search pages related to the whole *Biosensor* ontology on each one of the above companies (i.e. www.cysense.com, www.bivda.co.uk, www.generics.co.uk, and www.mcaservices.co.uk). The ontology contains classes about possible areas of application of biosensors: *health-care, industry, environment* and *veterinary*. By comparing the pages obtained from each company in each of these classes, we may produce different kinds of knowledge: the areas of application of each company can be made explicit from their web pages (e.g. *"The Generics Group is a technology consulting development and investment organisation focused in health-care biosensors and not in other sort of biosensors"*), the areas in which there is a shortage of manufacturing companies is obtained from tacit facts as the absence of relevant pages in certain ontology classes (e.g. *"there are not relevant companies in the UK related to the application of biosensors to veterinary"*), areas in which different companies are competing (e.g. *"the Generics Group and Pinebridge are two companies competing on health-care biosensors"*) or areas in which companies are complementary. In these two latter cases, knowledge is implicit in the distribution of web pages among different classes in the ontology.

## 4.2 Case Study 2: Petrol Companies, Research Groups and Institutions

Petrol is used to produce some of the materials that have a higher impact on the world wide national and international policies and economies. The companies of the sector have to be aware of the global evolution and also about the strategies of their partners and competitors. Here, we use the search system to find knowledge about state-of-the-art the current most relevant companies, research groups and other related institutions in the areas of petroleum and derivatives.

In this case study, the ontology in figure 1 is used to analyse the world wide companies, research groups and other related institutions, restricted to the domains .com, .edu and .org. With the first analysis we detect several *"well known petrol companies as Texaco, Esso, BP, Shell or Total, and"* also some others *"less known companies as Bharat Petroleum"* (www.bharatpetroleum.com) that cover important topics in the ontology as petrol, fuels, kerosene, unleaded, diesel, grease, engine_oil or petroleum. With the second analysis, knowledge about research groups in the petroleum area is produced. For instance, we found references to the web site of The College of Earth and Mineral Science (www.ems.psu.edu) at Penn State University, the Biology department (www.bio.unc.edu) at North Carolina University, and the Department of Earth and Atmospheric Sciences (www.geo.cornell.edu/eas) at Cornell University. Finally, closed related organisations like *Planet Ark* (www.planetark.org), an ecologist organisation covering several topics about fuels, and *Clean Air* (www. cleanairnet.org) an Asian organisation that promotes technologies for the improvement of the air quality around the world were found under some fuel nodes as petrol, unleaded, autogas, diesel, biodiesel and grease. From these results, we can infer knowledge about *"the organisations working on the effects of fuel and derivatives in the environment"* and *"the sort of concern of such organisations with respect to the concepts in the ontology"*. For example, this case study can conclude that the *"ecological organisations are more concerned about the petrol derived fuels than about the petrol derived oils"*.

### 4.3   Case Study 3: Sustainability in Environmental-Aware Companies

Sustainability is defined as a process or state that can be maintained indefinitely, and which integrates an appropriate balance between a viable economy, protection of the environment and social well-being.

Here, the *sustainability* ontology contains technologies, tools and methods to improve the level of sustainability of a company. These are summarised in environmental risk assessment, analysis of the life cycle of a product or process, ecodesign, and process simulation. The search system in section 3 has been used to find the most frequent web domains. Among those which have been found (.com, .edu, .gov, and some others which are proper to countries), the first two ones are the most frequent.

The *wastewater* ontology includes concepts about legislation on water quality and pollutants. The ontology distinguishes between EU and US legislations. In the EU, four countries have been studied: France, Germany, Ireland, and Spain. In the ontology four concepts about wastewater legislation have been analysed in detail: energy, paper, plastic, textile and sodium. The study shows that "*for all the EU countries, the relative importance order of all the concepts about wastewater legislation is always the same: energy, paper, plastic, textile and sodium, being energy the most important*". Moreover, "*the relative order of importance of the EU countries for all the concepts are always the same: Germany, France, Spain, and Ireland*".

## 5   Conclusions

In the last years the Internet has become the most important source of information. Companies use it for advertising their products and services, universities and research institutions for showing new emerging technologies and knowledge, and governments for forecasting information about legislation. All this kind of information can be relevant to enterprise managers. In this paper, an ontology-based search system to assist them in the process of knowledge production from Internet has been introduced.

In the context of the concept of organisational learning [9] defined as the ability to learn faster than your competitors, some abilities of the search system are: discovery of new marketplaces, market needs, technologies and products; analysis of the competitors and allies; promotion of investments that yield higher rates of innovation or added value; detect the situation of the own company in the world, etc.

The search system has been tested using seven domain ontologies that defined the area of interest of the knowledge to be produced. Among all the results obtained, only those which are interesting to show the capabilities of the system have been introduced and commented as case studies. In these cases the knowledge produced as a results of the use of the system has been made explicit as sentences in italic.

Another purpose of the paper has been to show the flexibility of the system in the way it can be adapted to the requirements of the enterprise manager: enterprise alliances, market analysis, national and international legislation, etc.

As a result of the tests made, the most important lessons learned have been:

- It is very important to have a detailed characterisation of the area of interest in the domain ontology. Thus, a set of domain experts should have agreed on the structure of the domain and the terminology used.

- It is also necessary to think about the different ways in which a class or an attribute may be named, and use synonyms to describe them.
- The presence of relevant attributes in each class is crucial, since they allow the system to distinguish among good and bad pages.
- Final users of the system have to be experts in the domain, and in the different types of knowledge that can be acquired from the system response.
- The system is most useful when used in an iterative fashion (e.g. first making a general search on the concepts of the ontology, and then possibly refining the search on a particular concept on the web pages of a specific company).
- The system provides interesting results, but in most cases it is the final user who has to analyse them, extract some kind of knowledge and proceed with a more specific search.

The work presented is part of a work in progress and the results preliminary. In the future, the system will be extended with some functionalities for knowledge extraction and integration. Knowledge extraction will be used to automatically analyse the contents of the retrieved documents in order to generate new knowledge that will be optionally added to the domain ontology during the knowledge integration process.

## Acknowledgements

This work has been partially funded by the EU Project *hTechSight* (IST-2001-33174, [6]). D. Sánchez would like to acknowledge the support of the *Departament d'Universitats, Recerca i Societat de la Informació* of Catalonia.

## References

1. M. S. Abdullah, I. Benest, A. Evans, C. Kimble, Knowledge modelling techniques for developing KM systems, 3rd European Conf. on KM, Dublin, Ireland, 2002: 15-25.
2. D. Fensel, I. Horrocks, F. Van Harmelen, S. Decker, M Erdmann and M. Kein. OIL in a nutshell. Lecture Notes in Artificial Intelligence, Vol. 1937, Springer-Verlag, (2000).
3. A. Gómez-Pérez, O. Corcho. Ontology languages for the semantic web, IEEE Intelligent Systems, 54-56, 2002.
4. A. Gómez-Pérez, M. Fernández-López, O. Corcho. Ontological Engineering: with examples from the areas of KM, e-commerce and the semantic web, Springer Verlag, UK, 2003.
5. J. Heflin and J. Hendler. Searching the Web with SHOE. In AAAI-2000 Workshop on AI for Web Search. (2000).
6. h-Techsight Consortium. Deliverable D4.Sample Ontologies for representative trial domains. http://prise-serv.cpe.surrey.ac.uk/techsight/deliverables.asp, 2002.
7. P. D. Karp, V. K. Chaudhri, and J. Thomere: XOL: An XML-Based Ontology Exchange Language, v0.3, (1999). ftp://smi.stanford.edu/pub/bio-ontology/OntologyExchange.doc.
8. M. W. McElroy, The new knowledge management: complexity, learning and sustainable innovation, Elsevier, 2003.
9. P. M. Senge, The fifth discipline: the art & practice of the learning organization, Currency and Doubleday, 1990.
10. T. Davenport, L. Prusak, Working Knowledge: How Organizations Manage What They Know, Harvard Business School Press, 1998.

# Developing an Integrated Retrieval System for Web Databases

Jeong-Oog Lee, Heung Seok Jeon, Hyun-Kyu Kang, and Jinsoo Kim

Dept. of Computer Science, Konkuk University,
322 Danwol-dong, Chungju-si, Chungcheongbuk-do, 380-701, Korea
{ljo,hsjeon,hkkang,jinsoo}@kku.ac.kr

**Abstract.** The majority of the information on the Web is dynamic content provided through linkups with databases. Therefore, we need an integrated information retrieval system that can effectively combine and access a vast resource of dynamic web contents linked with databases. The integrated Web information system proposed in this paper is based on the concept-based semantic network. Also, the concept-based semantic network allows a user to easily obtain the desired information from several autonomous databases without prior knowledge of the schema by providing only a semantic query language. One of the major characteristics of the integrated database system based on the semantic network and semantic query language is that a single ontology can be used for various information sources.

## 1 Introduction

As the amount of digitized information has rapidly increased along with developments in Web-based technology, interest in efficient information retrieval has also grown, fuelled in no small part by the popularity of such search engines as Yahoo and AltaVista.

However, while most of these search engines have good recall rates, their often-low precision rate is becoming a problem. The recall rate refers to the amount of information the search engine turns out after a user enters a query. The precision rate, on the other hand, refers to the number of relevant information (information that really answers the user's query) among the recalled information. In the past, when information was not easily available, the recall rate was more important than the precision rate. These days, however, with so much information flooding the Internet and the World Wide Web, the precision rate has become more important. The majority of the information on the Web is dynamic content provided through linkups with databases. Although retrieval methods using a query language based on natural human language are being tested, there are still many technological issues to resolve. The retrieval method using keyword matching, utilized by current search engines, is often insufficiently precise, usually turning out irrelevant search results. Accordingly, the creation of an integrated Web information system, through which a user may have an effective access to the integrated information by structural query language like

D. Karagiannis and U. Reimer (Eds.): PAKM 2004, LNAI 3336, pp. 186–197, 2004.
© Springer-Verlag Berlin Heidelberg 2004

SQL via integration of the dynamic Web contents linked up with databases, is now an urgent concern.

The integrated Web information system proposed in this paper is based on the concept-based semantic network. The concept-based semantic network is the semantic network that expresses the relationship between the concept and the schema of information in order to explore and resolve semantic heterogeneity among component databases. Also, the concept-based semantic network allows a user to easily obtain the desired information from several autonomous databases without prior knowledge of the schema by providing only a semantic query language, SemQL [1]. The SemQL processor allows a user to gain access to the desired information independent of the query language and the location of the component database. The SemQL processor decides the information source most suitable to the user's query, how to obtain the desired information, and the methods to efficiently retrieve such information from the Web databases. One of the major characteristics of the integrated database system based on the semantic network and semantic query language is that a single ontology can be used for various information sources.

The ontology is based on the WordNet and provides multiple domains instead of a single domain. This approach is more efficient in terms of extendability and flexibility than existing multiple database systems.

The rest of this paper is organized as follows. Section 2 explains how we can build semantic networks. The role of WordNet and the global semantic network in resolving semantic heterogeneity are introduced in section 3. And then, section 4 shows the procedure of semantic query processing. In section 5 and 6, some experimental results and comparisons with previous works are introduced, respectively. Finally, in section 7, we offer our conclusions.

## 2  Semantic Networks

### 2.1  Classification of Semantic Heterogeneity

Semantic heterogeneity is the differences in the way the real world is modeled in the databases, particularly in database schemas [2]. Fig. 1 illustrates semantic heterogeneity. Since a database is defined by its schema and data, semantic heterogeneity can be classified into schema heterogeneity and data heterogeneity [3]. Schema heterogeneity mainly results from the use of different structures for the same information and the use of different names for the same structures. For example, in fig. 1, component database $CDB_2$ uses one table, Student, for information about students, while the same information is represented by two tables, Undergraduate and Graduate, in $CDB_1$. Data heterogeneity is due to inconsistent data in the absence of schema heterogeneity.

As our focus is only on the schema conflicts, we assume that data conflicts such as different representations for the same data are already conformed. We have defined the types of conflicts considered in this paper as *Entity versus entity structure conflicts (EESC)*, *Entity versus attribute structure conflicts (EASC)*,

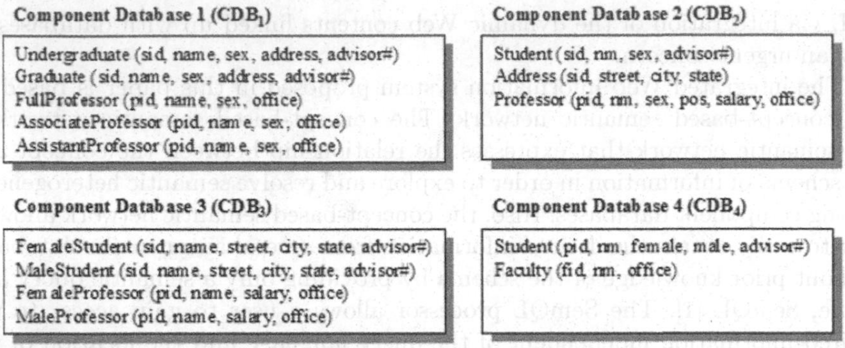

**Component Database 1 (CDB₁)**

Undergraduate (sid, name, sex, address, advisor#)
Graduate (sid, name, sex, address, advisor#)
FullProfessor (pid, name, sex, office)
AssociateProfessor (pid, name, sex, office)
AssistantProfessor (pid, name, sex, office)

**Component Database 2 (CDB₂)**

Student (sid, nm, sex, advisor#)
Address (sid, street, city, state)
Professor (pid, nm, sex, pos, salary, office)

**Component Database 3 (CDB₃)**

FemaleStudent (sid, name, street, city, state, advisor#)
MaleStudent (sid, name, street, city, state, advisor#)
FemaleProfessor (pid, name, salary, office)
MaleProfessor (pid, name, salary, office)

**Component Database 4 (CDB₄)**

Student (pid, nm, female, male, advisor#)
Faculty (fid, nm, office)

**Fig. 1.** Example of database schemas.

*Entity versus value structure conflicts (EVSC), Attribute versus attribute structure conflicts (AASC), Attribute versus value structure conflicts (AVSC), Entity versus entity name conflicts (EENC)* and *Attribute versus attribute name conflicts (AANC)* [1].

## 2.2 Approach to Information Sharing

In this paper, we used WordNet as linguistic knowledge to represent and interpret the meaning of the information, to integrate information, and to give users an efficient access mechanism to the integrated system. The basic idea is to make a semantic network for each component database and to use WordNet to provide mappings between the semantic networks.

In WordNet, the semantic relations are expressed with a semantic pointer between synonyms, which also create a strongly linked vocabulary network. Fig. 2 shows part of the vocabulary network in diagrams. Each vocabulary maintains the vocabulary concept arrayed in a relative position compared with other vocabularies.

Using WordNet and the descriptions of the database objects, a concept-based semantic network for each component database can be created. A semantic network provides mappings between concepts in WordNet and information in the database schema [4]. Fig. 3 depicts a partial semantic network for $CDB_2$. In WordNet, each synset is granted a unique concept number. In the *Concept* field in Fig. 3, the entity concept and the attribute concept are combined and expressed in *Entity Concept.Attribute Concept*. In the *WNConcept* field, the concept numbers are combined into *Entity Concept Number.Attribute Concept Number*. The *Entity* field expresses the database object corresponding to the entity concept, while the *Attribute* filed expresses the database object corresponding to the attribute concept. After constructing semantic networks for component databases, a global semantic network can be created with the semantic relations in WordNet and the semantic networks. A global semantic network provides semantic knowledge about a distributed environment.

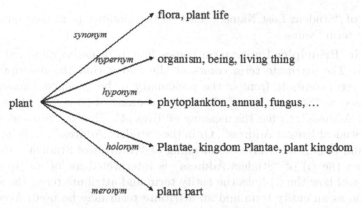

**Fig. 2.** Example of vocabulary network expressing the semantic relations for 'plant'.

| Concept | WNConcept | Entity | Attribute |
|---|---|---|---|
| student.name | 07617015.04778525 | Student | nm |
| studnet.gender | 07617015.03910916 | Student | gender |
| professor.salary | 07504465.09556237 | Professor | salary |
| professor.office | 07504465.03052755 | Professor | office |
| ⋮ | ⋮ | ⋮ | ⋮ |

**Fig. 3.** A partial semantic network for $CDB_2$.

## 2.3    Description of Schema Information

To incorporate information from various component databases, the multidatabase system needs to understand the meaning of the information in each component database, and each component database should express information in a unified manner. To do so, the component database administrator prepares the description of the database schema. A semantic network of component database is created according to the semantic relations between the prepared description and WordNet. The semantic network provides ideas among entities, attributes, value domains, and WordNet. The whole semantic networks are integrated into the global semantic network for the multidatabase system. The description is prepared using the rules on syntactic and semantic principles. The semantic rule, which is an agreement regarding the vocabulary content contained in the description, enables semantic delivery. The syntactic principle, on the other hand, specifies the array among words within the description.

**Semantic Rule:** Meaning is concerned with components (vocabulary) included in the description. The component units are entity term, attribute term, and qualifier term. For example, in a description of "Student Last Name," the component, 'Student' is an entity term. The attribute term is the component indicating the attribute of the entity. The qualifier term is the component added to the entity term and attribute term in order to identify the description. In the case of "Student Last Name," 'Last' is the qualifier term that qualifies the attribute term 'Name'.

**Syntactic Principle:** Entity term comes first in a description and followed by a dot. The attribute term comes at the end within the description. The qualifier term comes in front of the vocabulary to be qualified. Student Name is expressed as "Student.Name". Here, the meaning of (.) is 'of'. Meanwhile, in "Student.Address", (.) has the meaning of 'lives at'. That is, "Student.Address" means "Student lives at Address". Or in the "Student.Address", (.) is interpreted as 'of', and thus it may have the meaning of "Address of Student". Regardless of whether the (.) of "Student.Address" is interpreted as 'of' or 'lives at', or regardless of how the (.) links the entity term and attribute term, the same dot expression as an entity term and an attribute term may be used. Accordingly, the following can be defined:

"In $E_1.A_1$ and $E_2.A_2$, if $E_1 = E_2$ and $A_1 = A_2$, then $E_1.A_1 = E_2.A_2$ can be asserted."

Here, '=' indicates similar relations, and $E_1$ and $E_2$ indicate entity terms, while $A_1$ and $A_2$ show attribute terms.

## 3 Detection of Semantic Heterogeneity

### 3.1 The Role of WordNet in Detecting Semantic Heterogeneity

The approach in this paper uses semantic relations in WordNet for detecting semantic heterogeneity. It links the schema information in each database to the lexical concepts in WordNet, and identifies the semantic relations related to the lexical concepts. By understanding the relationships between schema information using the identified semantic relations, one can detect semantic heterogeneity.

Fig. 4 shows how the hyponymy semantic relation in WordNet can be used in detecting *entity versus entity structure conflicts (EESC)*. According to the hyponymy semantic relation in WordNet, one can find that 'professor' is a hypernym of 'full professor', 'associate professor', and 'assistant professor'. Therefore,

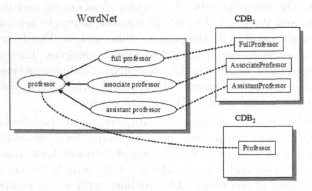

**Fig. 4.** Detection of EESC using hyponymy semantic relation.

the entity *Professor* in $CDB_2$ is semantically equivalent to the set of entities, {FullProfessor, AssociateProfessor, AssistantProfessor}, in $CDB_1$. The other semantic conflicts can be resolved in the same way.

## 3.2   The Role of the Global Semantic Network

We have developed a global semantic network, which specifies the semantic relations among entities, attributes, and value domains in all the component databases. Once a global semantic network is constructed, the system can resolve semantic heterogeneity based on it [4].

The global semantic network is constructed by merging semantic networks, one for each component database. Fig. 5 shows a partial state of merging two component databases, $CDB_1$ and $CDB_2$.

| Concept | WNConcept | Entity | Attribute | DB |
|---|---|---|---|---|
| undergraduate.identification number | 07655357.04841846 | Undergraduate | sid | $CDB_1$ |
| undergraduate.name | 07655357.04778525 | Undergraduate | name | $CDB_1$ |
| undergraduate.sex | 07655357.03910916 | Undergraduate | sex | $CDB_1$ |
| : | : | : | : | |
| student.identification number | 07617015.04841846 | Student | sid | $CDB_2$ |
| student.name | 07617015.04778525 | Student | nm | $CDB_2$ |
| studnet.gender | 07617015.03910916 | Student | gender | $CDB_2$ |
| : | : | : | : | |

**Fig. 5.** A partial state of merging two component databases, $CDB_1$ and $CDB_2$.

Given a query, the concepts contained in the query are extracted first. Then, one can identify component databases that possess all the extracted concepts using the global semantic network (providing access knowledge), and the original query is reformulated into sub-queries according to the schema information of identified component databases (providing semantic knowledge).

This paper's approach is well adapted in open and dynamic environments. As the process of each component database being integrated into the multidatabase system is done without intervention of other component databases, it is very easy for component databases to change their schema information and for new information sources to participate in the system.

## 4   Semantic Query Processing

Fig. 6 shows an integrated retrieval system for Web databases using ontology technology and multiagents [5, 6, 7]. The *User Interface Agent* parses the user's query, extracts concepts in the query using ontological concepts and relations, requests for query processing, and displays the processed results to the user. The

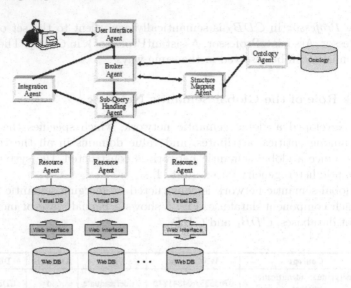

**Fig. 6.** An integrated retrieval system for Web databases.

*Ontology Agent* manages the ontology and cooperates with the *Broker Agent* and *Structure Mapping Agent*. The *Broker Agent* identifies the relevant Web databases using information received from the *User Interface Agent* and the *Ontology Agent*. The *Structure Mapping Agent* generates the mappings between concepts in the original query and information of the identified Web databases. The *Sub-Query Handling Agent* reformulates the original query into multiple sub-queries for each Web database according to the mappings generated by the *Structure Mapping Agent*. The *Resource Agent* resides in each Web database and executes the sub-query received from the *Sub-Query Handling Agent* according to the schema information of the Web database in which it resides, and then sends the results to the *Integration Agent*. The *Integration Agent*, in turn, manages the intermediate results from various Web databases and presents the integrated results to the users.

In this section, we introduce an example query scenario to demonstrate the procedure of our proposed semantic query process. The example query is to find information on female students living in 'New York'. We assume that the user who issues the query only knows the concepts about what he or she wants, but does not know the detailed schema structure for each component database.

QUERY: Find those female students who live in 'New York'
The query can be posed as follows:
    SELECT student.name
    WHERE student.gender = 'female' AND student.city = 'New York'

The *User Interface Agent* parses the query and extracts concepts from the query {student, name, gender, female, city}. The *Broker Agent* then identifies the relevant component databases, $CDB_1$, $CDB_2$ and $CDB_3$, which posses all the concepts. The mappings in-between concepts in the original query and represen-

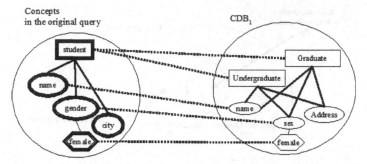

**Fig. 7.** Part of the mappings in-between concepts in the original query and representations in the relevant component databases.

tations in the relevant component databases are generated. Fig. 7 shows part of the mappings.

Now, the *Sub-Query Handling Agent* reformulates the original query into three sub-queries for $CDB_1$, $CDB_2$ and $CDB_3$ according to the mappings. Thus, the sub-query for $CDB_1$ might be:

SELECT name
FROM Undergraduate
WHERE sex = 'female' AND address LIKE '%New York%'
UNION
SELECT name
FROM Graduate
WHERE sex = 'female' AND address LIKE '%New York%'

After the *Sub-Query Handling Agent* reformulates the original query into sub-queries, and sends them to $CDB_1$, $CDB_2$, and $CDB_3$, respectively. The *Resource Agent* returns the results to the *Sub-Query Handling Agent*. Finally, the *Integration Agent* merges the results from the three component databases and presents the integrated results to the users.

## 5   Experiments and Evaluation

To evaluate the proposed approach for information sharing in multidatabase systems, we have conducted some experiments on several Web databases. Applying the method of the retrieval performance evaluation for Web documents [8], the experiments have been conducted in the aspect of retrieval performance, which measures how effectively the user's semantic queries are processed through the proposed methods.

For experiments, we have chosen four Web databases related to plant information. Using the constructed system, a global semantic network merging four component databases was created and all the possible queries were prepared for experiments based upon all the concepts in the component database schemas. Afterwards, each query was processed by the SemQL processor, the results were analyzed, and the retrieval performance was evaluated.

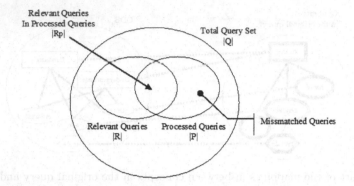

**Fig. 8.** The relations among relevant queries (R), processed queries (P), and relevant queries in processed queries (Rp).

$R_{CDB_i}$ is extracted from the set of total queries, Q, which must be processed by $CDB_i$. $P_{CDB_i}$ is a set of queries processed by $CDB_i$, after each query in Q is processed through the SemQL processor. $Rp_{CDB_i}$ is a set of queries that are included in the intersection set of $R_{CDB_i}$ and $P_{CDB_i}$. The relations among these sets are shown in Fig. 8.

$Recall_{CDB_i}$ ($=|Rp_{CDB_i}|/|R_{CDB_i}|$) is the ratio of the actually processed queries among the set of relevant queries to $CDB_i$. $Precision_{CDB_i}$ ($=|Rp_{CDB_i}|/|P_{CDB_i}|$) is the ratio of relevant queries to $CDB_i$ to the set of queries which are actually processed by $CDB_i$.

Fig. 9 shows recall and precision rates for each component database in graphical form. The recall rate for $CDB_1$ is 96.43% and very excellent, while the recall rate for $CDB_2$ is 49.09% and is not good compared to that of $CDB_1$. This is because almost all the input fields of the Web interface for $CDB_1$ are structured to enable users to select one of the values for each input field (see Fig. 10(a)), while all the input fields of the Web interface for $CDB_2$ require users to insert values in the fields (see Fig. 10(b)). That is, $CDB_1$ provides more schema infor-

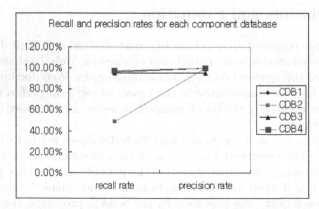

**Fig. 9.** Recall and precision rates for each component database.

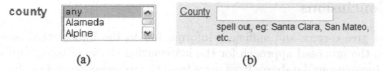

**Fig. 10.** Part of web interfaces for (a) $CDB_1$ and (b) $CDB_2$.

mation than $CDB_2$. In the case of precision rates, the experiments show very excellent precision rates in all the component databases. This means that the SemQL processor exactly reformulates the original query into sub-queries that are for component databases identified during the procedure of query processing.

As the experiments have been conducted in the laboratory level with four Web databases in the real world, if the proposed approach is applied to an unspecified number of the general databases, both the recall rate and precision rate are more or less expected to decrease. However, if sufficient schema information of each Web database is provided, the proposed approach for information sharing among heterogeneous databases can potentially become one of the most effective methods for information integration.

## 6   Comparisons with Previous Works

As the proposed approach in this paper does not require the construction of a global view, it is easy to construct an information integration system. Also, the proposed approach provides a semantic query language, SemQL, which enables the user to issue queries to a number of component databases with the user's own concepts. With this kind of approach, users can make queries on their terms even if they do not know all the database schemas [1].

In several research works such as SIMS [9], HERMES [10], InfoSleuth [11], etc., new approaches have been developed for integrating information using new technological developments such as agent technology [12], domain ontologies [13], intelligent mediator [14], and high-level query languages [15], in dynamic and open environments. These approaches were designed to support flexibility and openness. However, a common assumption on these dynamic approaches is that the users have preexisting knowledge for integrating information, which might be a burden to the users.

The proposed approach provides common domain knowledge using WordNet as knowledge base, so that each information source can be merged into the system without specific domain knowledge of other sources. That is, each information source can describe its domain knowledge and construct its own semantic network independent of other information sources, which enables each information source to be easily merged into the system. This kind of approach guarantees the autonomy of each information source and gives users needing to integrate information an easy and efficient method for information integration. Also, it enables a number of information sources to be merged into the information integration system, so that it gives the system good extensibility.

# 7  Conclusions

If users give correct and sufficient information to the information integration system, the proposed approach for the information sharing among autonomous and heterogeneous databases frees users from the tremendous tasks of finding the relevant information sources and interacting with each information source using a particular interface. Furthermore, the proposed approach has the advantage of source independence by describing the meaning of the information in terms of general linguistic knowledge, which means that the multidatabase system can efficiently update the global semantic network when the component databases are changed, added, or deleted. Moreover, the integrated retrieval system based on the semantic network enables multilingual information retrieval. The reason is because an original query in the final processing stage is indicated in a concept number, which is equivalent to the word concept, not in a word form, whatever language query the user enters. For an instance, fig. 11 shows the queries on the information of plants growing in wetland. Although the query on the left side is in Korean and the query on the right is in English, they are processed in the same concept number as shown in the center. For this reason, the two queries made in two different languages generate the same result.

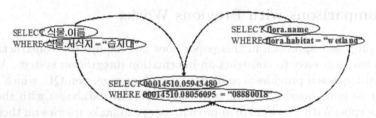

**Fig. 11.** An example of possibility of cross-language information retrieval in the proposed system.

# References

1. J. O. Lee, D. K. Baik, "SemQL: A Semantic Query Language for Multidatabase Systems", Proc. 8th International Conf. on Information and Knowledge Management (CIKM-99), 1999.
2. M. Garcia-Solaco, F. Saltor, and M. Castellanos, "Semantic Heterogeneity in Multidatabase Systems", in Object-Oriented Multidatabase Systems: A Solution for Advanced Applications, ed. O. A. Bukhres, A. K. Elmagarmid, pp. 129-202, Prentice Hall Inc., 1996.
3. W. Kim, J. Seo, "Classifying Schematic and Data Heterogeneity in Multidatabase Systems", IEEE Computer, vol.24, no.12, pp. 12-18, 1992.
4. J. O. Lee, D. K. Baik, "SemNet: A Semantic Network for Integration of Databases", Lecture Notes in Computer Science, LNCS 1749, Springer-Verlag, 1999.
5. Marian Nodine, Jerry Fowler, Brad Perry, "An Overview of Active Information Gathering in InfoSleuth", InfoSlueth Group, 1998.
6. Maurizio Panti, Luca Spalazzi, Alberto Giretti, "A Case-Based Approach to Information Integration" , Proceedings of the 26th VLDB conference, 2000.

7. J. Hammer, H. H. Garcia-Molina, K. Ireland, Y. Papakonstantinou, J. Ullman, J. Widom, "Information translation, mediation, and mosaic-based browsing in the tsimmis system", In Proceedings of the ACM SIGMOD International Conference on Management of Data, 1995.
8. R. Baeza-Yates, B. Ribeiro-Neto, Modern Information Retrieval, Addison-Wesley, 1999.
9. C. A. Knoblock, Y. Arens, and C. N. Hsu, "Cooperating Agents for Information Retrieval", Proc. the second International Conf. on Cooperative Information Systems, 1994.
10. S. Adali, K. S. Candan, Y. Papakonstantinou, and V. S. Subrahmanian, "Query caching and optimization in distributed mediator systems", Proc. ACM SIGMOD International Conf. on Management of Data, 1996.
11. R. Bayardo, W. Bohrer, et al, "InfoSleuth; agent-based semantic integration of information in open and dynamic environments", ACM SIGMOD Record, vol.26, no.2, 1997.
12. M. Genesereth and S. Ketchpel, "Software Agents", Communications of ACM, 37(7), 1994.
13. T. Gruber, "The role of a common ontology in achieving sharable, reusable knowledgebases", Proc. 2nd International Conf. on Principles of Knowledge Representation and Reasoning, 1991.
14. G. Wiederhold, "Mediators in the Architecture of Future Information Systems", Computer, 25(3), Mar., 1992.
15. T. Finin, R. Fritzson, D. McKay, R. McEntire, "KQML as an Agent Communication Language", Proc. 3rd International Conf. on Information and Knowledge Management, 1994.

# Incremental Knowledge Management
# of Web Community Groups on Web Portals

Yang Sok Kim, Sung Sik Park, Byeong Ho Kang, and Young Ju Choi

School of Computing, University of Tasmania
Hobart, Tasmania, 7001, Australia
{yangsokk,sspark,bhkang,Y.J.Choi}@utas.edu.au

**Abstract.** The concept of the web portal was introduced in around 1998 when the web became a standard medium for accessing information. While HTML-based static web pages were also popular, people used the search engine websites, or specific web pages, such as the personal web page or the web browser company default page, as their web portals. Since their inception, providing information for users has been the most important function of web portals, and many of them try to provide adapted information to different users. Offering this level of service is difficult because of the quantity of information and the various types of information classification for different user groups involved. In most web portals, the collection and classification of the information is still carried out manually. Automation of this task requires domain-specific classification knowledge, which is not easy to acquire. Automated web information management and publication system has been developed using the Multiple Classification Ripple Down Rules (MCRDR) knowledge acquisition engine. Various prototype web portals are being developed and the evaluation study proves the potential of the out-of-box style web portal generation tool for the adapted service.

## 1 Introduction

Web portals provide a single, integrated point of access to web-based information and are intended to be used as access points, rather than as an information provider in themselves. Web technology is moving from the static information-based, using HTML, to the dynamic, using the server-side technology. Web portal sites service the user directly and have recently incorporated adapted information and community services for the common interest groups. Web portals also make an important contribution to the facilitation of organisational knowledge management [1].

A major challenge of web portal technology is to provide the right information as soon as it is published on the web [2]. This is not easy because information providers usually allow access to web information in a passive way. As such, users cannot know what the new information is until they visit the websites. To support right time information provision, web portals require appropriate content aggregation and distribution functions. The right information provision means that the content that the web portals provide should be customized to the users' information needs. Web portals originally focused on individual customisation, but nowadays interest group level customisation has become more important. This has occurred because web portal communities have grown more popular, and the information needs for specific communities have increased accordingly.

D. Karagiannis and U. Reimer (Eds.): PAKM 2004, LNAI 3336, pp. 198–207, 2004.

In this research, we propose a new web portal management method. We use an integrated web information management tool, called the Personal Web Information Management System (PWIMS) [3]. PWIMS supports content aggregation through web page monitoring, so that new information is collected from the target website without prior protocol agreement. Contents are also distributed through content posting such as web page posting and email posting. Individual and group personalization is performed by rule-based document classification.

The body of this paper is organised as follows: In section 2, we will examine requirements for Web information portals. We will explain the MCRDR based knowledge management system and method in section 3. In section 4, we will explain PWIMS. Web portal implementation experience will be discussed in section 5. Finally, section 6 concludes the paper and discusses remaining issues and possible future work.

## 2   Web Information Portal and Its Required Services

There are many types of web portals, including public portals, enterprise portals, market place portals, and portals that are specialised according to the user they serve and the service they offer. Wege [1] specifies a common set of web portal services: customisation; content aggregation; content syndication; multi-device support; single sign on service; portal administration; and user management. From the knowledge management point of view, customisation and content aggregation services are more important than any other services. Furthermore, although Wege does not include content distribution service in his common set, content distribution is critical when users want to share information with other users [4].

The first of the common set of web portal services, customisation, is usually performed by generating adaptive WebPages or personalized WebPages. There are many portals that support the construction of personalized web pages in the portals, for example 'My' pages. The main drawback of current portal services is their lack of generality and adaptability [5-7]. Another customisation method involves adaptive web systems, which adapt content in accordance with user models. Researchers in adaptive web systems have explored many user modeling and adaptation methods [8]. Although adaptive web and personalised web contribute to enhance customisation, they do not sufficiently support knowledge-based customisation. This means that content can only be presented on the basis of user's domain knowledge. Rule-based document classification provides a solution to the problems associated with explicit knowledge-based customisation because it directly encodes human experts' knowledge into the system. On the other hand, rule-based systems have a knowledge acquisition bottleneck problem, which makes it difficult to implement rule-based systems[9]. The Multiple Classification Ripple-Down Rules (MCRDR) overcomes the bottleneck situation with its incremental knowledge acquisition method and local validation and verification with cases technique [10, 11]. Kim et. al [12] proposed a document classifier, which is implemented with the MCRDR method and supports personalised knowledge base construction. A detailed explanation of this will be given in section 3.

Content aggregation may be performed by humans but it is very difficult, time-consuming, and expensive. Content syndication can be used for content aggregation but it needs prior protocol agreement between sender and receiver. Protocol includes rich site summary (RSS), news industry text format (NITF), and NewsML, an XML-based standard used to represent and manage news through its life cycle [1]. Web monitoring systems can be used without any protocol agreement. The monitoring systems collect newly uploaded information from websites that have been specified by users [13-17].

Content posting can be used to distribute Web portal contents in various ways, including through content pushing[18], Web page posting, e-mail posting and contents syndicating [3]. Among these methods, Web page posting has become the dominant method because of the prevalence of Portal communities and their desire to present specialized information in their community WebPages.

## 3   MCRDR Document Classifier

Fig. 2 represents a knowledge base structure (KBS) and storage folder structure (SFS). KBS has n-ary tree structure and each node represents three different types of rules; the groundbreaking, refining and stopping rules. A groundbreaking rule is created under the root node to make a new branch under root node (e.g., rule 1 ~ 4 in Fig. 1). A refining rule is created under the groundbreaking rules or other refining rules to make an exception to the current rule (e.g., rule 5 ~ 8, 10 in Fig. 1). A stopping rule is created under the ground breaking rule, refining rule, or stopping rule. If the stopping is fired by a case (document), the case is not classified into the folder that its parent rule indicates (e.g., rule 9 in Fig. 1).

The choice of representation can have an enormous impact on human problem-solving performance [19, 20]. The mediating knowledge representation should be optimised for human understanding rather than for machine efficiency. To improve the KA process, it is suggested that appropriate representational devices should be available to the expert and knowledge engineer [21]. This would provide an appropriate medium for experts to model their valuable knowledge in terms of an explicit external form. We use common folder structures as a mediating representation because users can easily build a conceptual classification model by using folder manipulation. The MCRDR approach differs from the traditional knowledge engineering approach because it assumes there is no mediate person (knowledge engineer). Rather, the domain experts or users directly accumulate their knowledge by using KA tools.

A classification recommendation (conclusion) is provided by the last rule satisfied in a pathway. All children of satisfied parent rule are evaluated, allowing for multiple conclusions. The conclusion of the parent rule is only given if none of the children are satisfied. For example, the current document has a set of keywords with {a, b, c, d, e, f, g, i}. The system evaluates all the rules in the first level of the tree for the given document features (rules 1, 2, 3, 4 and 11 in Fig. 1.). It then evaluates the rules at the next level, which are refinements of the rule satisfied at the top level, and so on. The process stops when there are no more children to evaluate, or when none of these rules can be satisfied by the document features at hand. In this instance, there are 4 rule paths and 3 classifications (classes 5, 6 and 8). Rule 9 represents a stopping rule. If it did not exist, rule 4 would be fired. The system classifies nodes (F_5, F_6 and F_8) into the storage folder structures (SFS) in accordance with the inference results.

KA and inference are inextricably linked in the MCRDR method, so some KA steps depend on the inference and vice versa [11, 22, 23]. The KA process consists of the following sub-tasks: 1) initiating the KA process, 2) choosing the KA method, and 3) validating new rules. The KA process is initialised by users when they dissatisfy the system's inference result. The users' decision for initialising new KA processes depends on the range of convenience [21]. There are two different forms of KA initialisation. In the first, the KA is initiated when the system recommends incorrect class or no class 17] and users initiate a new KA process (human initiated KA). In the other form, the KA is initiated when users conduct an operation in the SFS, for example move or copy some pre-classified documents to another folder (system initiated KA). KA methods depend on the rule types that will be created: refinement KA, stopping KA, and groundbreaking KA.

Cornerstone cases are the documents that are used for the rule creation. When domain experts initiate the KA process, the MCRDR classifier generates a keyword set. Once the domain experts have selected a folder, the classifier retrieves all cornerstone cases. The difference list consists of keywords from new documents that do not exist in the selected cornerstone cases. Difference lists will be recreated if domain experts select further cornerstone cases that cannot be classified as belonging to this folder. If domain experts select a keyword or keywords from the difference list, the classifier generates duplicated case lists from storage. The duplicated case lists will then be used to classify new folders. Domain experts add keywords until the only cases remaining in the duplicated list are those that would be reclassified by a new rule. Cornerstone cases and difference lists help domain experts when they validate new rules and verify reclassification of cases. This has been shown to guarantee low cost knowledge maintenance [11, 22]

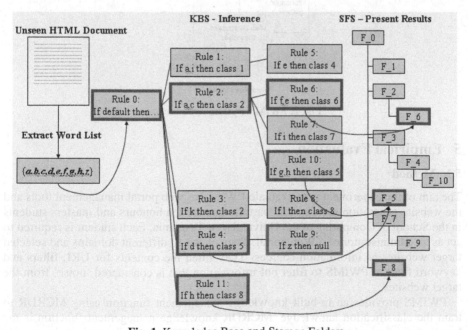

**Fig. 1.** Knowledge Base and Storage Folders

## 4  PWIMS

PWIMS is a stand-alone personalized Web information management system. The system consists of three main components as follows (shown in Fig.2):

- Web Information monitoring system: gathers information from target Web pages
- Web document classification system: knowledge management component that enables users to organise the monitored information. It is implemented with MCRDR knowledge acquisition methods.
- Web information distribution system: disseminates the obtained information by using personalized content posting, including e-mail notification and Web page posting.

PWIMS support dynamic and personal web portals easily. It collects information that is needed from the user-specified websites by using the web monitoring function. Users classify the collected documents with the MCRDR document classifier. This classified information is automatically synchronized with the web portal contents using the content posting function.

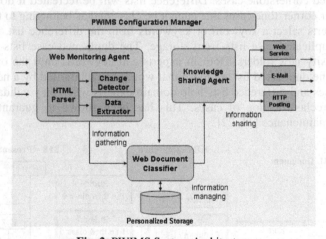

**Fig. 2.** PWIMS System Architecture

## 5  Empirical Evaluation

### 5.1  Method

The aim of the experiment is to evaluate PWIMS as web portal management tools and the website generation system. The participants are ten honours and masters students in the School of Computing at the University of Tasmania. Each student is required to act as an administrator of a Web portal. They chose 10 different domains and selected target websites as information sources. They filled the contents for URL filters and keyword filter in PWIMS to filter out information that is considered 'noise' from the target websites.

PWIMS provides an in-built knowledge management function using MCRDR to train the classification knowledge. MCRDR knowledge management function is the key to providing adapted information for the various groups of users in the sample portal websites. A website generation system, using PHP and MySQL database is also given to students to generate the dynamic Web portal sites. When the new pages (information) appear on the Web, the PWIMS collects and classify these.

In PWIMS, there is a Web posting module with auto form filling functions. This function simplifies the transference of information and it is compatible with many different platforms. Thus the PWIMS fills the form from the website generation system with the classified information when the information is classified in PWIMS. The duration of the experiment is one month (May, 2004). Table 1 summarizes the target domain and monitoring Web pages. The total number of target website is 95 and the total number of monitoring pages is 122. The average number of target websites is 14 and the average number of monitoring pages is 17. There are 1.21 monitoring pages per website on average.

**Table 1.** Web monitoring configuration

| Domain | Number of Site | Number of Monitoring Page | Site Name |
|---|---|---|---|
| Networking & Telecommunication | 14 | 14 | Australian IT, Zdnet, Wireless week, News.com, Cisco, Newsfactor, Amazon, 3Gportal, Computer world, Wireless, IT world, CNN, Searchnetworking, BBC |
| World News | 5 | 5 | CNN, BBC, News.com.au, VOA, Reuters |
| Business | 9 | 10 | CNN, Finance news, Trade international centre, Yahoo (America, UK, Australia), Forex Market News, Insurance news net, Insurance journal.com |
| English Football | 6 | 14 | SkySports, BBC, Football365, Premier League,Team talk, The World Game |
| Travel | 10 | 15 | Lonelyplanet, CNN, Airliners.net, Asiatraveltips.com, Nwitimes.com, Travel deals, Air Newzealand, All Frequent Flier Deals, Star-alliance,exoticvacationinfo.com |
| Computer Security | 12 | 20 | BBC, CCR, CNET, CNN, ComputerWorld, eWeek, F-Secure, InternetWeek, Networking Pipe Line, Network World Fusion, News Factor, Secutriteam |
| Cricket | 10 | 10 | ABC, BBC, Channel 4 Cricket, CricInfo, Cricket 365, Cricket Online Org, CricketNet, India Times, Slam Sports, Yahoo UK |
| Racing | 11 | 11 | SKYSports, Motor Sports, Daily F1, Renaut F1 Team, ITV News, Racing, United State F1, BBC, CNN, Mercury, Formula 1 |
| Security | 14 | 14 | TrendMicro, Microsoft, Security Focus, The Register, Symatec, Securina, Sophos, NetworkAssociates, LinuxSecurity, Australian, Secure Mac, Debian, VirusList,OSVDB |
| Computer Games | 4 | 9 | GameSpot *Discontinued*, GamesRadar, PlanetGamecube, GameSpy GBA, IGN |
| Total | 95 | 122 | |
| Average | 14 | 17 | |

## 5.2  Results

### 5.2.1  Content Aggregation and Content Usage

Table 2 shows content aggregation results of PWIMS Web monitoring system. On average, 1,950 articles are collected and 621 articles are classified by participants (31.9%). The number of monitored articles in each domain varies greatly and is dependent on the domain characteristics and target websites. For example, Cricket (376) and Racing (469) has fewer monitored articles than Business (4959). However, the World News has a smaller number of monitored articles (434) than Business, even though their target websites are similar. This is because the PWIMS in World News has superior filtering contents. The result shows that pre-filtering information can reduce the information to be classified. The article usage rate (number of classified articles / number of monitored articles) of each domain varies greatly; the minimum rate is 8.0% and maximum rate is 100%. A lower rate is obtained because lots of irrelevant information is filtered out before classification. Conversely, an higher rate means collected information is regarded as very relevant information. This happens because some users specify their information needs very narrowly whereas other users specify the needs broadly. It does not mean, however, that narrow information specification is better than broad specification. Rather, users' information gathering behaviors are simply very different and the system should these activities.

**Table 2.** Content Aggregation and Content Usage

| Domain | Number of Monitoring Page | Monitored Articles | Average articles per page | Classified Articles | Article Usage Rate |
|---|---|---|---|---|---|
| Networking & Tele-communication | 14 | 4,225 | 301.8 | 336 | 8.0% |
| World News | 5 | 434 | 86.8 | 391 | 90.1% |
| Business | 10 | 4,959 | 495.9 | 1,297 | 26.2% |
| English Football | 14 | 499 | 35.6 | 301 | 60.3% |
| Travel | 15 | 4,576 | 305.1 | 1,585 | 34.6% |
| Computer Security | 20 | 2,321 | 116.1 | 215 | 9.3% |
| Cricket | 10 | 376 | 37.6 | 213 | 56.6% |
| Racing | 11 | 469 | 42.6 | 469 | 100.0% |
| Security | 14 | 1,187 | 84.8 | 948 | 79.9% |
| Computer Games | 9 | 458 | 50.9 | 458 | 100.0% |
| Total | 122 | 19,504 | 159.9 | 6,213 | 31.9% |
| Average | 12.2 | 1950 | 159.9 | 621.3 | 31.9% |

### 5.2.2  Knowledge Acquisition

In totally 1,263 rules are created by users and the average number of rules of each domain is 126. To add one rule only takes a few minutes, so 180 rules (the average number of rules) can be built within 5-7 hours, after the three to four weeks spent collecting articles to train the system. Some of the domains work reasonably well with a small number of rules; 16 in "Computer Security", and 23 in "Travel". The number of rules needed often depends on the characteristics of domain and the style of classifications. If the number of classification is small, or the terms in the domain are well standardized, only a small number of rules will be required for classification. For example, in travel domain the user classifies documents based on the geographical names such as Australia, New Zealand, and China. In this case very small number of rule suffices for classification.

Another decision factor that affects knowledge acquisition activity is the classification preference. Some users want to classify document more general classification criteria, while others classify documents using specific criteria. This is not also neither a good nor bad sign; it only reflects different knowledge management behavior. The knowledge management system should therefore support these requirements.

**Table 3.** Knowledge Acquisition Results

| Domain | Classified Articles | Number of Rules | Articles per Rule | Precision Rate |
|---|---|---|---|---|
| Networking & Telecommunication | 336 | 168 | 2.0 | 78.77% |
| World News | 391 | 155 | 2.5 | 83.92% |
| Business | 1,297 | 160 | 8.1 | 80.70% |
| English Football | 301 | 122 | 2.5 | 81.00% |
| Travel | 1,585 | 23 | 68.9 | 85.00% |
| Computer Security | 215 | 16 | 13.4 | 87.70% |
| Cricket | 213 | 270 | 0.8 | 98.00% |
| Racing | 469 | 168 | 2.8 | 91.00% |
| Security | 948 | 46 | 20.6 | 95.10% |
| Computer Games | 458 | 135 | 3.4 | 90.71% |
| Total | 6,213 | 1,263 | 4.9 | |
| Average | 621 | 126 | 4.9 | 87.19% |

### 5.2.3 Classification Performance

In this research, we use precision rates to estimate the performance of classification. Overall classification accuracy is 87%, which is quite high considering the limited time, and the range of these rates is 78.77% ~ 98.00%. We usually assume that if we acquire more knowledge of specific domain the precision rate will improve. But there is no consistent relationship between the number of rule and the precision rate according to experiments results. Rather, the knowledge management activity and the knowledge base are domain specific and there is no consistent relationship between knowledge base size and the performance of classifier. For example, whereas the "Networking and Communication" and "Racing" domain have same number of rule and very similar number of articles per rule, the precision rate very different: the former is 78.77% and the latter is 91.00%.

## 6 Conclusion

We have suggested a new Web portal management tool, which is based on the MCRDR knowledge acquisition method. This study shows that the web information management system PWIMS, using MCRDR knowledge acquisition method, can be used to provide adapted contents for various Web portals. Furthermore, the dynamic web page generation system with the support of knowledge management system can be an effective way of maintaining dynamic web portals for various groups of users.

This study also confirms the findings of previous studies that MCRDR allows the domain knowledge to be maintained by the domain expert without the help of computer engineers or knowledge engineers. MCRDR is an incremental KA method and is used to overcome the traditional KA problem. Our classifier uses common folder structures as a mediating knowledge representation to facilitate KA. Users can construct their conceptual document classification structures using folder manipulation. In our system, the KA and inference process is inextricably linked, so some KA steps depend on the inference and vice versa. The KA process begins when the classifier suggest 'no folder' or 'incorrect folders' or users activate some function in folders such as copying or moving cases. Experiment results show that users can create their document classifier very easily with a small number of cases and our system successfully supports incremental and robust document classification. Incremental KA based classification works well in domains where the information increases continu-ally, as is the case with Web information.

It is difficult to apply the machine learning studies in the real world application because it is hard to collect a well trained data set [12, 24]. This does not mean, however, that we are dismissing machine learning and its usefulness in web information management. To the contrary, we view our approach as complementary to the machine learning technique. We will undergo further work to research how the incremental KA approach may be combined with machine learning techniques most effectively [25, 26]. We believe our approach can help construct a cost-efficient fine training data set in the initial stage.

# References

1. Wege, C., Portal Server Technology. IEEE Internet Computing, 2002. 6(3): p. 73-77.
2. Priebe, T. and G. Pernul. Towards integrative enterprise knowledge portals. in Twelfth International Conference on Information and Knowledge Management. 2003. New Orleans, LA, USA: Publisher ACM Press  New York, NY, USA.
3. Park, S.S., S.K. Kim, and B.H. Kang. Web Information Management System: Personalization and Generalization. in the IADIS International Confernece WWW/Internet 2003. 2003.
4. Alavi, M. and D.E. Leidner, Knowledge management systems: issues, challenges, and benefits. Communications of the AIS, 1999. 1(2).
5. Manber, U., A. Patel, and J. Robison, Experience with personalization on Yahoo! Communications of the ACM, 2000. vol.43, no.8: p. 35-39.
6. Bellas, F., D. Fernandez, and A. Muino. A flexible framework for engineering "my" portals. in 13th conference on World Wide Web. 2004. New York, NY, USA: ACM Press New York, NY, USA.
7. Rossi, G., D. Schwabe, and R. Guimaraes. Designing personalized web applications. in tenth international conference on World Wide Web. 2001. Hong Kong, Hong Kong: ACM Press  New York, NY, USA.
8. Brusilovsky, P. and M.T. Maybury, From adaptive hypermedia to the adaptive web. Communications of the ACM, 2002. 45(5): p. 30 - 33.
9. Feigenbaum, E.A., Knowledge engineering: The applied side of artificial intelligence. Annals of the New York Academy Sciences, 1984. 246: p. 91-107.
10. Kang, B., P. Compton, and P. Preston. Multiple Classification Ripple Down Rules : Evaluation and Possibilities. in 9th AAAI-Sponsored Banff Knowledge Acquisition for Knowledge-Based Systems Workshop. 1995., Banff, Canada, University of Calgary.

11. Kang, B.H., W. Gambetta, and P. Compton, Verification and validation with ripple-down rules. International Journal of Human-Computer Studies, 1996. vol.44, no.2: p. 257-269.
12. Kim, Y.S., et al. Adaptive Web Document Classification with MCRDR. in International Conference on Information Technology: Coding and Computing ITCC 2004. 2004. Orleans, Las Vegas, Nevada, USA.
13. Lu, B., S.C. Hui, and Y. Zhang. Personalized Information Monitoring Over the Web. in FIRST INTERNATIONAL CONFERENCE ON INFORMATION TECHNOLOGY & APPLICATIONS (ICITA 2002). 2002. BATHURST, AUSTRALIA.
14. Liu, L., C. Pu, and W. Tang. WebCQ: Detecting and Delivering Information Changes on the Web. in International Conference on Information and Knowledge Management (CIKM). 2000. Washington D.C.: ACM Press.
15. Pandey, S., K. Ramamritham, and S. Chakrabarti. Monitoring the dynamic web to respond to continuous queries. in International World Wide Web Conference. 2003. Budapest, Hungary.
16. Tang, W., L. Liu, and C. Pu. WebCQ Detecting and Delivering Information Changes on the Web. in Proc. Int. Conf. on Information and Knowledge Management (CIKM). 2000.
17. Tan, B., S. Foo, and S.C. Hui, Web Information Monitoring: an Analysis of Web Page Updates. Online Information Review, 2001. 25(1): p. 6-18.
18. Brandt, S. and A. Kristensen. Web push as an internet notification service. 1997.
19. Hahn, J. and J. Kim. Why are some representations (sometimes) more effective? in 20th International Conference on Information Systems. 1999. Charlotte, North Carolina, United States: Association for Information Systems Atlanta, GA, USA.
20. Larkin, J. and H. Simon, Why a diagram is (sometimes) worth ten thousand words. Cognitive Science, 1987. 11: p. 65-99.
21. Ford, K.M., et al., Knowledge acquisition as a constructive modeling activity. International Journal of Intelligent Systems, 1993. vol.8, no.1: p. 9-32.
22. Kang, B.H., P. Compton, and P. Preston, Validating incremental knowledge acquisition for multiple classifications. Critical Technology: Proceedings of the Third World Congress on Expert Systems, 1996: p. 856-868.
23. Compton, P. and D. Richards, Generalising ripple-down rules. Knowledge Engineering and Knowledge Management Methods, Models, and Tools. 12th International Conference, EKAW 2000. Proceedings (Lecture Notes in Artificial Intelligence Vol.1937), 2000: p. 380-386.
24. Mladenic, D., Text-learning and Related Intelligent Agents. Applications of Intelligent Information Retrieval, 1999.
25. Wada, T., et al. Integrating Inductive learning and Knowledge Acquisition in the Ripple Down Rules Method. in 6th Pacific Knowledge Acquisition Workshop. 2000. Sydney, Australia.
26. Suryanto, H. and P. Compton. Intermediate Concept Discovery in Ripple Down Rule Knowledge Bases. in 2002 Pacific Rim Knowledge Acquisition Workshop. 2002. Tokyo, Japan.

# Automatic Generation of Taxonomies from the WWW

David Sánchez and Antonio Moreno

Department of Computer Science and Mathematics
Universitat Rovira i Virgili (URV)
Avda. Països Catalans, 26. 43007 Tarragona, Spain
{dsanchez,amoreno}@etse.urv.es

**Abstract.** In this paper we present a methodology to extract information from the Web to build a taxonomy of terms and Web resources for a given domain. This taxonomy represents a hierarchy of classes and gives to the user a general view of the kind of concepts and the most significant sites that he can find on the Web for the specified domain. The system uses intensively a publicly available search engine, extracts concepts (based on its relation to the initial one and statistical data about appearance), selects and categorizes the most representative Web resources of each one and represents the result in a standard way.

## 1 Introduction

In the last years, the growth of the Information Society has been very significant, providing a way for fast data access and information exchange all around the world through the Word Wide Web. However, human readable data resources (like electronic books or web sites) are by definition unstructured: there is not a standard way of representing information in order to ease access to it.

Although several search tools have been developed (e.g. search engines like Google), when the searched topic is very general or we don't have an exhaustive knowledge of the domain (in order to set the most appropriate and restrictive search query), the evaluation of the huge amount of potential resources obtained is quite slow and tedious. In this sense, a way for representing and accessing in a structured way the available resources depending on the selected domain would be very useful. It is also important that this kind of representations can be obtained *automatically* due to the dynamic and changing nature of the Web (hand made Directory Services like Yahoo are always incomplete and obsolete and require the work of human experts).

In this paper we present a *methodology to extract information from the Web to build automatically a taxonomy of terms and Web resources for a given domain.* During the building process, the most representative web sites for each selected concept are retrieved and categorized. Finally, a polysemic detection algorithm is performed in order to discover different senses of the same word and group the most related concepts. The result is a hierarchical and categorized organization of the available resources for the given domain. This hierarchy is obtained automatically and autonomously from the whole Web without any previous domain knowledge, and it represents the available resources at the moment. These aspects distinguish this method from other similar ones [18] that are applied on a representative selected

D. Karagiannis and U. Reimer (Eds.): PAKM 2004, LNAI 3336, pp. 208–219, 2004.

corpus of documents [17], use external sources of semantic information [16] (like WordNet [1] or predefined ontologies), or require the supervision of a human expert. A prototype has been implemented to test the proposed method.

The idea that represents the base for our proposal is the *redundancy of information* that characterizes the Web, allowing us to detect important concepts for a domain through a statistical analysis of their appearances.

In addition to the advantage that a hierarchical representation of web resources provides in terms of searching for information, the obtained taxonomy is also a valuable element for building machine processable information representations like *ontologies* [6]. In fact, many ontology creation methodologies like METHONTOLOGY [20] consider a taxonomy of terms for the domain as the point of departure for the ontology creation. However, the manual creation of these hierarchies of terms is a difficult task that requires an extended knowledge of the domain obtaining, in most situations, incomplete, inaccurate or obsolete results; in our case, the taxonomy is created automatically and represents the state of the art for a domain (assuming that the Web contains the latest information for a certain topic).

The rest of the paper is organised as follows: section 2 describes the methodology developed to build the taxonomy and classify web sites. Section 3 talks about the way of representing the results and discusses on the main issues related to their evaluation. The final section contains some conclusions and proposes some lines of future work.

## 2  Taxonomy Building Methodology

In this section, the methodology used to discover, select and organise representative concepts and websites for a given domain is described.

The algorithm is based on analysing a large number of web sites in order to find important concepts for a domain by studying the *neighbourhood* of an initial *keyword* (we assume that words that are near to the specified keyword are closely related). Concretely, the immediate anterior word for a keyword is frequently *categorizing* it, whereas the immediate posterior one represents the *domain* where it is applied [19]. These concepts are processed in order to select the most adequate ones by performing a statistical analysis. The selected ones for the *anterior* words are finally incorporated to the taxonomy. For each one, the websites from where it was extracted are stored and categorized (using the *posterior* words), and the process is repeated recursively to find new terms and build a hierarchy.

Finally, in order to detect different meanings or domains to which the obtained classes belong, an algorithm for word sense discovering is performed. This process is especially interesting when working with polysemous keywords (to avoid merging results from different domains). The algorithm creates clusters of classes depending on the websites' domains from where they where selected.

The resulting taxonomy of terms eases the access to the available web resources and can be used to guide a search for information or a classification process from a document corpus [3, 4, 12, 13], or it can be the base for finding more complex relations between concepts and creating ontologies [8].

This last point is especially important due to the necessity of ontologies for achieving interoperability and easing the access and interpretation of knowledge resources (e.g. Semantic Web [21], more information in [10]).

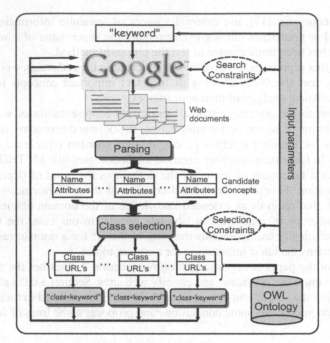

**Fig. 1.** Taxonomy building methodology

## 2.1 Term Discovery, Taxonomy Building and Web Categorization Algorithm

In more detail, the algorithm's sequence for discovering representative terms and building a taxonomy of web resources (shown on Fig. 1) has the following phases (see Table 1 and Fig. 2 and 3 in order to follow the explanation example):

- It starts with a *keyword* that has to be representative enough for a specific domain (e.g. *sensor*) and a set of parameters that constrain the search and the concept selection (described below).
- Then, it uses a publicly available search engine (Google) in order to obtain the most representative web sites that contain that keyword. The search constraints specified are the following:
  - *Maximum number of pages returned by the search engine*: this parameter constrains the size of the search. The bigger is the amount of documents evaluated, the better are the results obtained, because we base the quality of the results in the redundancy of information (e.g. 1000 pages for *sensor* example).
  - *Filter of similar sites*: for a general keyword (e.g. *sensor*), the enabling of this filter hides the web sites that belong to the same web domain, obtaining a set of results that represent a wider spectrum. For a concrete word (e.g. *neural network based sensor*) with a smaller amount of results, the disabling of this filter will return the whole set of pages (even sub pages of a web domain).
- For each web site returned, an exhaustive analysis is performed in order to obtain useful information from each one. Concretely:

- Different types of non-HTML document formats are processed (pdf, ps, doc, ppt, etc.) by obtaining the HTML version from Google's cache.
- For each "*Not found*" or "*Unable to show*" page, the parser tries to obtain the web site's data from Google's cache.
- *Redirections* are followed until finding the final site.
- *Frame-based* sites are also considered, obtaining the complete set of texts by analysing each web subframe.

- The parser returns the useful text from each site (rejecting tags and visual information), and tries to find the initial keyword (e.g. *sensor*). For each matching, it analyses the immediate anterior word (e.g. *temperature sensor*). If it fulfills a set of prerequisites, they are selected as *candidate concept*. The posterior words (e.g. *sensor network*) are also considered. Concretely, the parser verifies the following:
  - Words must have a minimum size (e.g. 3 characters) and must be represented with a standard ASCII character set (not Japanese, for example).
  - They must be "relevant words". Prepositions, determinants, and very common words ("stop words") are rejected.
  - Each word is analysed from its morphological root (e.g. *optical* and *optic* are considered as the same word and their attribute values - described below - are merged: for example, the number of appearances of both words is added). A stemming algorithm for the English language is used for this purpose.

- For each candidate concept selected (some examples are contained in Table 1), a statistical analysis is performed in order to select the most representative ones. Apart from to the text frequency analysis, the information obtained from the search engine (which is based in the analysis of the whole web) is also considered. Concretely, we consider the following attributes:
  - *Total number of appearances* (e.g. minimum of 5 for the first iteration of the *sensor* example): this represents a measure of the concept's relevance for the domain and allows eliminating very specific or unrelated ones (e.g. *original*).
  - *Number of different web sites that contain the concept at least one time* (e.g. minimum of 3 for the first iteration of *sensor*): this gives a measure of the word's generality for a domain (e.g. *wireless* is quite common, but *Bosch* isn't).
  - *Estimated number of results returned by the search engine with the selected concept alone* (e.g. maximum of 10.000.000 for *sensor*): this indicates the word's global generality and allows avoiding widely-used ones (e.g. *level*).
  - *Estimated number of results returned by the search engine joining the selected concept with the initial keyword* (e.g. a minimum of 50 for the *sensor* example): this represents a measure of association between those two terms (e.g. "*oxygen sensor*" gives many results but "*optimized sensor*" doesn't).
  - *Ratio between the two last measures* (e.g. minimum of 0.0001 for *sensor*): This is a very important measure because it indicates the relation intensity between the concept and the keyword and allows detecting relevant words (e.g. "*temperature sensor*" is much more relevant than "*optimized sensor*").

- Only concepts (a little percentage of the candidate list) whose attributes fit with a set of specified constraints (a range of values for each parameter) are selected (marked in **bold** in Table 1). Moreover, a relevance measure (1) of this selection is computed based on the amount of times the concept attribute values excede the selection constraints. This measure could be useful if an expert evaluates the taxonomy or if the hierarchy is bigger than expected (perhaps constraints where too loose), and a trim of the less relevant concepts is performed.

$$relevance = \frac{2*\dfrac{\# Appearances}{Min\_Appear} + 3*\dfrac{\# Dif\_Webs}{Min\_Dif\_Web} + \dfrac{Google\_Ratio}{Min\_Ratio}}{6} \tag{1}$$

- For each concept extracted from a word previous to the initial one, a new keyword is constructed joining the new concept with the initial one (e.g. "*position sensor*"), and the algorithm is executed again from the beginning. This process is repeated recursively until a selected depth level is achieved (e.g. 4 levels for the *sensor* example) or no more results are found (e.g. *solid-state pressure sensor* has not got any subclass). Each new execution has its own search and selection parameter values because the searched keyword is more restrictive (constraints have to be relaxed in order to obtain a significant number of final results).
- The obtained result is a hierarchy that is stored as an ontology with is-a relations. If a word has different derivative forms, all of them are evaluated independently (e.g. *optic*, *optical*) but identified with an *equivalence* relation (see some examples in Fig. 2). Moreover, each class stores the concept's attributes described previously and the set of URLs from where it was selected during the analysis of the immediate superclass (e.g. the set of URLs returned by Google when setting the keyword *sensor* that contains the candidate term *optical sensor*).
- In the same way that the "previous word analysis" returns candidate concepts that could become classes, the posterior word for the initial keyword is also considered. In this case, the selected terms will be used to describe and classify the set of URLs associated to each class. For example, if we find that for an specified URL associated to the class *humidity sensor*, this keyword set is followed by the word *company* (and this term has been selected as a candidate concept during the statistical analysis), the URL will be categorized with this word (that represents a *domain of application*). This information could be useful when the user browsers the set of URLs of a class because it can give him an idea about the context where the class is applied (see some examples in Fig. 2: *humidity sensor company, magnetic sensor prototype, temperature sensor applications…*).
- Finally, a refinement process is performed in order to obtain a more compact taxonomy and avoid redundancy. In this process, classes and subclasses that have the same set of associated URLs arc merged because we consider that they are closely related: in the search process, the two concepts have always appeared together. For example, the hierarchy *"wireless -> scale -> large"* will result in *"wireless -> large_scale"* (discovering automatically a *multiword* term, [16]), because the last 2 subclasses have the same web sets. Moreover, the list of web sites for each class is processed in order to avoid redundancies: if an URL is stored in one of its subclasses, it will be deleted from the superclass set.

An example of the resulting taxonomy of terms obtained by this method with the set of parameters described during the algorithm description and for the *sensor* domain is shown in Fig. 2. Several examples of candidate concepts for the first level of search and their attribute values are shown on Table 1. Moreover, for the most significant classes discovered, examples of the Web resources obtained and categorized are shown in Fig. 3 (note that several types of non-HTML file types are retrieved).

**Table 1.** *Candidate concepts* for the *sensor* ontology. Words in **bold** represent all the selected classes (merged ones -with the same root- in *italic*). The other ones are a reduced list of some of the rejected concepts (attributes that don't fulfil the selection constraints are represented in *italic*). The 10 most relevant classes are also represented in **bold** in the last column

| Concept | #Appear. | #Differ. pages | #Search Results | #Joined Results | Result Ratio | Relev. |
|---|---|---|---|---|---|---|
| **airborne** | 5 | 3 | 751000 | 2190 | 0.0029 | 5.66 |
| **autonomous** | 6 | 4 | 938000 | 960 | 0.001 | 2.73 |
| **based** | 7 | 4 | 8520000 | 7220 | 8.47E-4 | 2.54 |
| **chemical** | 15 | 9 | 4260000 | 5410 | 0.0012 | 4.5 |
| **digital** | 20 | 16 | 6610000 | 1270 | 1.92E-4 | 4.32 |
| **distributed** | 11 | 8 | 5440000 | 4600 | 8.45E-4 | 3.47 |
| **field** | 9 | 6 | 7120000 | 5120 | 7.19E-4 | 2.79 |
| **humidity** | 6 | 5 | 1500000 | 14900 | 0.0099 | **17.73** |
| **intelligent** | 16 | 6 | 3230000 | 3220 | 9.96E-4 | 3.72 |
| **light** | 14 | 7 | 7040000 | 26400 | 0.00375 | **8.35** |
| *magnetic* | *123* | *96* | *2960000* | *2130* | *7.19E-4* | *25.39* |
| *magnetics* | *5* | *4* | *2970000* | *6650* | *0.00223* | *4.71* |
| **motion** | 14 | 11 | 6350000 | 36300 | 0.0057 | **12.26** |
| **oxygen** | 25 | 14 | 2330000 | 93600 | 0.040 | **70.66** |
| **position** | 7 | 5 | 7360000 | 27700 | 0.0037 | **7.46** |
| **pressure** | 8 | 8 | 6420000 | 53000 | 0.0082 | **15.53** |
| **smart** | 11 | 8 | 6890000 | 7310 | 0.0010 | 3.73 |
| **special** | 7 | 3 | 8340000 | 6100 | 7.31E-4 | 2.18 |
| **tactile** | 5 | 3 | 146000 | 1730 | 0.0118 | **20.50** |
| **temperature** | 24 | 17 | 5980000 | 113000 | 0.0188 | **35.76** |
| **wireless** | 71 | 47 | 5420000 | 23700 | 0.0043 | **19.73** |
| optimized | 8 | 5 | 1190000 | *11* | 9.24E-6 | 0.0 |
| bosch | 7 | *1* | 1870000 | 6570 | 0.00351 | 0.0 |
| original | 2 | *1* | 7350000 | 979 | 1.33E-4 | 0.0 |
| involving | 6 | 3 | 3810000 | 222 | *5.82E-5* | 0.0 |
| level | 2 | 2 | *18420000* | 18000 | 9.77E-4 | 0.0 |
| common | *3* | 3 | 6900000 | 1750 | 2.53E-4 | 0.0 |

## 2.2  Polysemy Detection and Semantic Clustering

One of the main problems when analyzing natural language resources is polysemous words. In our case, for example, if the primary keyword has more than one sense (e.g. *virus* can be applied over "malicious computer programs" or "infectious biological agents"), the resulting taxonomy could contain concepts from different domains (one for each meaning) completely merged (e.g. *"computer virus"* and *"immunodeficiency virus"*). Although these concepts have been selected correctly, it could be interesting that the branches of the resulting taxonomic tree were grouped it they pertain to the same domain corresponding to a concrete sense of the immediate "father" concept. With this representation, the user could be able to consult the hierarchy of terms that belongs to the desired sense for the initial keyword.

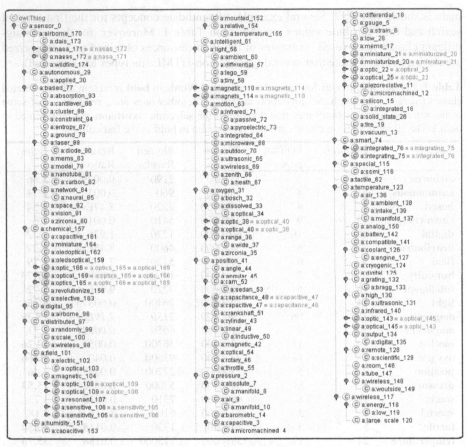

**Fig. 2.** *Sensor* taxonomy visualized on Protégé 2.1: numbers are class identifiers

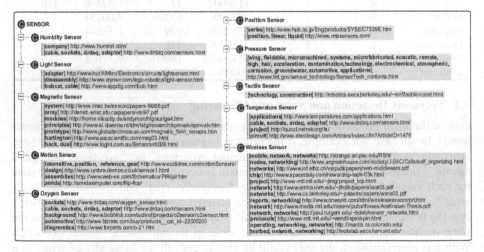

**Fig. 3.** Examples of categorized URLs for the 10 most relevant subclasses of *sensor*

Performing this classification without any previous knowledge (for example, the list of meanings, synonyms for each sense or a thesaurus like WordNet [1]), is not a trivial process [16, 17]. However, we can take profit from the context where each concept has been extracted, concretely, the documents (URL) that contain it. We can assume that each website that talks about a given keyword is using it in a concrete sense, so all candidate concepts that are selected from the analysis of a single document pertain to the domain associated to a concrete keyword's meaning. Applying this idea over a large amount of documents we can find, as shown in Fig. 4 for the *virus* example, quite consistent semantic relations between the candidate concepts.

So, if a word has N meanings (or it is used on N different domains with different senses), the resulting taxonomy of terms of this concept will be grouped in a similar number of sets, each one containing the elements that belong to a particular domain. The classification process is performed without any previous semantic knowledge.

In more detail, the algorithm performs the following actions:

- It starts from the taxonomy obtained from the described methodology. Concretely, all concepts are organised in an is-a ontology and each term stores the set of webs from which it has been obtained and the whole list of URLs returned by Google.
- For a given term of the taxonomy (for example the initial keyword: *virus*) and a concrete level of depth (for example the first one), a classification process is performed by joining the terms which belong to each keyword sense. This process is performed by a SAHN (*Sequential Agglomerative Hierarchical Non-Overlapping*) *clustering algorithm* that joins the more similar terms using as a similitude measure the number of coincidences between their URLs sets:
  - For each term of the same depth level (e.g. *anti, latest, simplex, linux, computer, influenza, online, immunodeficiency, leukaemia, nile, email*) that depends directly on the selected word (*virus*), a set of URLs is constructed by joining the stored websites associated to the class and all the sets of their descendent classes (without repetitions).
  - Each term is compared to each other and a similitude measure is obtained by comparing their URLs sets (2). Concretely, the measure represents the maximum amount of coincidences between each set (normalised as a percentage of the total set). So, the higher it is, the more similar the terms are (because they are frequently used together in the same context).

$$dist(A, B) = Max\left(\frac{\#Coin(URL(A), URL(B))}{\#URL(A)}, \frac{\#Coin(URL(B), URL(A))}{\#URL(B)}\right) \quad (2)$$

  - With these measures, a similitude matrix between all terms is constructed. The more similar terms (in the example, *anti* and *computer*) are selected and joined (they belong to the same keyword's sense).
  - The joining process is performed by creating a new class with those terms and removing them individually from the initial taxonomy. Their URL's sets are joined but not merged (each term keeps its URL set independently).
  - For this new class, the similitude measure to the remaining terms is computed. In this case, the measure of coincidence will be the minimum number of coincidences between the URL set of the individual term and the URL set of each

term of the group that forms the new class (3). With this method we are able to detect the most subtle senses of the initial keyword (or at least different domains where it is used). Other measures like taking into consideration the maximum number of coincidences or the mean have been tested obtaining worse results (they tend to join all the classes, making difficult the differentiation of senses).

$$\# Coin(Class(A,B),C) = Min(\# Coin(A,C), \# Coin(B,C)) \qquad (3)$$

- The similitude matrix is updated with these values and the new most similar terms/classes are joined (building a dendogram like the one shown in Fig. 4). The process is repeated until no more elements remain unjoined or the similitude between each one is 0 (there are no coincidences between the URL sets).
• The result is a set (with 2 elements for the *virus* example) of classes (their number has been automatically discovered) that groups the terms that belong to a specific meaning. The dendogram with the joined classes and similitude values can also be consulted by the user of the system.

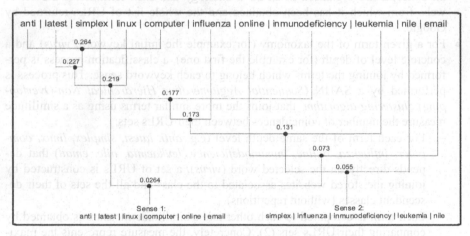

**Fig. 4.** Dendogram representing semantic associations between the classes found for the keyword "*virus*". Two final clusters are obtained: Sense1 groups the classes associated to the "*computer program*" meaning and Sense 2 for the "*biological agent*" meaning

## 3   Ontology Representation and Evaluation

The final hierarchy of terms is stored in a standard representation language: OWL [14]. The *Web Ontology Language* is a semantic markup language for publishing and sharing ontologies on the World Wide Web. It is designed for use by applications that need to process the content of information and facilitates greater machine interpretability by providing additional vocabulary along with a formal semantics [21]. OWL is supported by many ontology visualizers and editors, like Protégé 2.1 [15], allowing the user to explore, understand, analyse or even modify the ontology easily.

In order to evaluate the correctness of the results, a set of formal tests have been performed. Concretely, Protégé provides a set of ontological tests for detecting inconsistencies between classes, subclasses and properties of an OWL ontology from a logical point of view. However, the amount of different documents evaluated for obtaining the result and, in general, the variety and quantity of resources available in the web difficults extremely any kind of automated evaluation. So, the test of correctness from a semantic point of view can only be made by comparing the results with other existing semantic studies (for example, using other well known methodologies) or through an analysis performed by an expert of the domain.

Anyway, several points could be improved in the current method (from the example of Fig. 2) like the detection of the presence of common meaningless words (like *based*), the detection of *multiword* terms (*low->energy*) or equivalences between classes (possible acronyms, relations at different levels for the same class: e.g. *airborne sensor* and *airborne digital sensor* or very common sub hierarchies like *optic*).

## 4  Conclusion and Future Work

Some researchers have been working on knowledge mining and ontology learning from different kinds of structured information sources (like data bases, knowledge bases or dictionaries [7]). However, taking into consideration the amount of resources available easily on the Internet, we believe that knowledge extraction from unstructured documents like webs is an important line of research. In this sense, many authors [2, 5, 8, 10, 11] are putting their effort on processing natural language texts for creating or extending structured representations like ontologies. In this field, term taxonomies are the point of departure for many ontology creation methodologies [20].

The discovery of these hierarchies of concepts based on word association has a very important precedent in [19], which proposes a way to interpret the relation between consecutive words (*multiword* terms). Several authors [11, 16, 17] have applied a similar idea for extracting hierarchies of terms from a document corpus to create or extend ontologies. However, the classical approach for these methods is the analysis of a relevant corpus of documents for a domain. In some cases, a semantic repository (WordNet [1]) from which one can extract word's meanings and perform linguistic analysis or an existing representative ontology are used.

On the contrary, our methodology does not start from any kind of predefined knowledge of the domain, and it only uses publicly available web search engines for building relevant taxonomies from scratch. Moreover, the fact of searching in the whole web adds some very important problems in relation to the relevant corpus analysis. On the one hand, the heterogeneity of the information resources difficults the extraction of important data; in this case, we base our methodology on the high amount of information redundancy and a statistical analysis of the relevance of candidate terms for the domain. Note also that most of these statistical measures are obtained directly from the web search engine, fact that speeds up greatly the analysis and gives more representative results (they are based in the whole web statistics, not in the analysed subset) than a classical statistical approach based only in the texts. On the other hand, polisemy becomes a serious problem when the retrieved resources obtained from the search engine are only based on the keyword's presence (even some authors [16, 17] have detected this problem in the corpus analysis); in this case, we propose an automatic approach for polisemic disambiguation based on the clusterization of the selected classes according to the similarities between their information sources (web pages and web domains), without any kind of semantic knowledge.

The final taxonomy obtained with our method really represents the state of the art on the WWW for a given concept and the hierarchical structured and domain-categorized list of the most representative web sites for each class is a great help for finding and accessing the desired web resources.

As future lines of research some topics can be proposed:

- To ease the definition of the search and selection parameters, an automatic pre-analysis can be performed from the initial keyword to estimate the most adequate values. For example, the number of results for a concept can tell us a measure of its generality, which indicates the need of more restrictive or relaxed constraints.
- Several executions from the same initial keyword in different times can give us different taxonomies. A study about the changes can tell us how a domain evolves (e.g. a new kind of *sensor* appears).
- For each class, an extended analysis of the relevant web sites could be performed to find possible attributes and values that describe important characteristics (e.g. the *price* of a *sensor*), or closely related words (like a *topic signature* [9]).
- The same methodology applied to discover subtypes of the initial keyword can be useful for finding concrete instances of classes (e.g. *manufacturer names* of a specific *sensor type*), using some simple rules like the presence of capital letters [19].
- The described methodology is useful when working in easily categorised domains (where concatenated adjectives can be found). However, in other cases, a more exhaustive analysis has to be performed (like finding out the verb of a sentence or detecting the predicate or the subject). Following this way, more complex semantic relations could be found, and ontological structures could be constructed.

## Acknowledgements

We would like to thank David Isern and Jaime Bocio, members of the *hTechSight* project [4], for their help. This work has been supported by the "*Departament d'Universitats, Recerca i Societat de la Informació*" of Catalonia.

## References

1. WordNet: a lexical database for English Language. http://www.cogsci.princeton.edu/wn.
2. Ansa O., Hovy E., Aguirre E., Martínez D.: Enriching very large ontologies using the WWW. In: proceedings of the Workshop on Ontology Construction of the European Conference of AI (ECAI-00), 2000.
3. Alani H., Kim S., Millard D., Eal M., Hall W., Lewis H., and Shadbolt N.: Automatic Ontology-Based Knowledge Extraction from Web Documents. IEEE Intelligent Systems, IEEE Computer Society, 14-21, 2003.
4. Aldea A., Bañares-Alcántara R., Bocio J., Gramajo J., Isern D., Jiménez J., Kokossis A., Moreno A., and Riaño D.: An ontology-based knowledge management platform. In: Workshop on Information Integration on the Web (IIWEB'03) at IJCAI'03, 177-182, 2003.
5. Alfonseca E. and Manandhar S.: An unsupervised method for general named entity recognition and automated concept discovery. In: Proceedings of the 1st International Conference on General WordNet, 2002.
6. Fensel D.: Ontologies: A Silver Bullet for Knowledge Management and Electronic Commerce. Volume 2, Springer Verlag, 2001.

7. Manzano-Macho D., Gómez-Pérez A.: A survey of ontology learning methods and techniques. OntoWeb: Ontology-based Information Exchange Management, 2000.
8. Maedche A., Volz R., Kietz J.U.: A Method for Semi-Automatic Ontology Acquisition from a Corporate Intranet. EKAW'00 Workshop on Ontologies and Texts, 2000.
9. Lin C.Y., and Hovy E.H.: The Automated Acquisition of Topic Signatures for Text Summarization. In: Proceedings of the COLING Conference, 2000.
10. Maedche A.: Ontology Learning for the Semantic web. Volume 665, Kluwer Academic Publishers, 2001.
11. Velardi P., Navigli R.: Ontology Learning and Its Application to Automated Terminology Translation. IEEE Intelligent Systems, 22-31, 2003.
12. Sheth A.: Ontology-driven information search, integration and analysis. Net Object Days and MATES, 2003.
13. Magnin L., Snoussi H., Nie J.: Toward an Ontology–based Web Extraction. The Fifteenth Canadian Conference on Artificial Intelligence, 2002.
14. OWL. Web Ontology Language. W3C. Web: http://www.w3c.org/TR/owl-features/.
15. Protégé 2.1. Web site: http://protege.stanford.edu/
16. Voosen P.: Extending, trimming and fusing WorNet for technical documents. In: Proceedings of the NAACL Workshop on WordNet and Other Lexical Resources, Pittsburgh, 2001.
17. Sanderson M., Croft B.: Deriving concept hierarchies from text. In: Proceedings of the 22nd Annual International ACM SIGIR Conference on Research and Development and Information Retrieval. 1999, Berkeley, USA.
18. Hwang C.H.: Incompletely and Imprecisely Speaking: Using Dynamic Ontologies for Representing and Retrieving Information. In: Proceedings of the 6th International Workshop on Knowledge Representation meets Databases. 1999, Sweden.
19. Grefenstette G.: SQLET: Short Query Linguistic Expansion Techniques: Palliating One-Word Queries by Providing Intermediate Structure to Text. In: Information Extraction: A Multidiciplinary Approach to an Emerging Information Technology, volume 1299 of LNAI, chapter 6, 97-114. Springer. International Summer School, SCIE-97. 1997, Italy.
20. Fernández-López M., Gómez-Pérez A., Juristo N.: METHONTOLOGY: From Ontological Art Towards Ontological Engineering. Spring Symposium on Ontological Engineering of AAAI. Standford University, 1997, USA.
21. Semantic Web. W3C: http://www.w3.org/2001/sw/.

# Corporate Innovation Engines: Tools and Processes

Kemal A. Delic and Mark T. Fulgham

Hewlett-Packard Comp.
{kemal.delic,mark.fulgham}@hp.com

**Abstract.** Inventiveness is one of the most important human traits present in the history of human race. Companies and their respective legal entities have created the context in which several individual acts of invention should be streamlined into common purpose, individual, group, and company benefit. Therefore, in modern terms, we talk about innovation as a process which follows an IP lifecycle. Corporations rely upon IP artifacts (patents, copyrights, trade & service marks, trade secrets) to protect and restrict competition relative to their investments in products, services, processes, and facilities. In this paper we introduce: 1. the subject of corporate innovation and describe the organization 2. processes behind corporate innovation activities and 3. the conceptual architecture of the corporate innovation management system. Then, we will briefly describe the practical aspects of IP exploitation and discuss overall benefits in section four and close with our outlook and future challenges for IP management.

## 1 Brief History of Patents and Intellectual Property

The long history of patents goes back to the 15th century when the famous builder of Florence's Santa Maria del Fiore cathedral, Philippo Brunelleschi asked the Florentine Republic to give him an exclusive but limited monopoly for two years to exploit his invention about transporting merchandise upstream of river the Arno (see Fig. 1: Patent application from year 1421). Later on, in Venezia in 1474, some merchants obtained commercial monopolies, called also patents. The statute of monopolies issued in England in 1647 has probably defined patents as a much more sophisticated legal artifact. In modern terms, patents are also a sort of monopoly giving a holder commercial rights to exploit the patent for 20 years after it being granted. With advances of different technologies we have seen different types of intellectual property being articulated, developed and legally protected as patents, copyrights, trade and service marks and trade secrets [1].

The folklore image of the lone, brilliant, money-disinterested inventor (not far from the mad scientist caricature) has prevailed in public opinion. Thomas Alva Edison changed this opinion when he established the first innovation lab systematically focusing on practical inventions that changed the prevailing public image. Edison also became history's most prolific inventor, with more than a thousand patents.

Corporate R&D labs, generally speaking, adhere to the theme established by Edison's lab. These days we are seeing profound transformations within corporate R&D labs. They are transforming into leaner structures with innovative cross-company collaboration. We believe the large corporations and incubation start-ups budget and sponsor research and development that supports their brand and capital valuation.

D. Karagiannis and U. Reimer (Eds.): PAKM 2004, LNAI 3336, pp. 220–226, 2004.

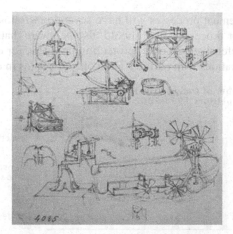

**Fig. 1.** First known patent write-up by Philippo Brunelleschi (1421)

Similar to the Medici family's sponsored activities in medieval Tuscany creating personal wealth and public benefit. International treaties and bodies are defining, overseeing, and regulating the IP market(s). The estimated value of the IP market today is around 100 billion dollars. IBM corporation has been the leading IP company for the last 10 years making an average of ~ 1.5 B$ in revenues from IP. In this paper we introduce:

1. the subject of corporate innovation and describe the organization
2. processes behind corporate innovation activities and
3. the conceptual architecture of the corporate innovation management system.

Then, we will briefly describe the practical aspects of IP exploitation and discuss overall benefits in section four and close with our outlook and future challenges for IP management.

## 2  Corporate Innovation: Organization and Processes

Inventiveness is one of the most important human traits present in the history of human race. Companies and their respective legal entities have created the context in which several individual acts of invention should be streamlined into common purpose, individual, group, and company benefit. Therefore, in modern terms, we talk about innovation as a process which follows an IP lifecycle. Corporations rely upon IP artifacts (patents, copyrights, trade & service marks, trade secrets) to protect and restrict competition relative to their investments in products, services, processes, and facilities. We can benchmark the stage of maturity of the business by its ability to gather, transform, and exploit distinctive ideas into intellectual capital that is transformed into property and business practice. New product creation with distinctive features being protected with patent(s) is the most classical illustration of the patent benefit. It is an idea which has certain, distinctive features of being non-obvious, useful and innovative which is embodied as patent, being made publicly available while giving the owner exploitation rights. These rights might be sold, exchanged or imposed thanks to the well-established rules. A single patent may create a revenue stream (crown-jewel patent) or be bundled into patent portfolios.

Mature IP management processes will have several portfolios of patents relating to products, services, or processes. One should also be aware that patent portfolios can be used either for defensive purposes (protecting products, for example) or offensive purposes as in negotiations with partners and competitors (as in cross licensing deals).

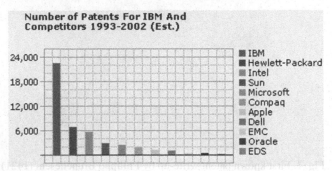

**Fig. 2.** Patents spread within IT industry

The Information Technology industry is marked by high inventiveness and special skills in exploiting inventions in hardware, software and business processes. This can be illustrated by the number of patents granted to the major IT players during the last 10 years (see Fig. 2). They all own strong patent portfolios that are exploited in a variety of ways and exhibit specific cultural attitudes regarding IP. Depending upon the industry segment, one can claim that it's more about the culture of inventiveness then about the mechanics of protection and monetization of IP artifacts.

If we summarize the principal concerns for corporate inventiveness we observe the identification of prolific inventors and their engagement on the most fruitful topic(s) as key success factors. This is based on empirical evidence revealing that the majority of patent filings are made by a tiny population of inventors. It is not easy to identify them, even with detailed patent analytical tools, or engage them on predefined topics without invention workshops sponsored within and among companies.

Invention workshops create the environment for vaguely defined concepts to transform into ideas that go through an internal review to classify them as internal inventions or IP filings worthy of on-going investment. Note that patent filings and IP portfolio management are not inconsequential expenses. This is a delicate process which is often regarded as an art rather than a science requiring joint involvement of skilled technologists, law, and financial experts. The final decision is usually reached as the negotiated consensus.

Corporate innovation, generally speaking, align to three distinct waves.(see Fig. 3).

The first wave (stable businesses/products) aims at making revenue and managing predictable growth. The second wave (expanding markets) aims at growth within an emerging market with revenues oriented at new name accounts. The third wave (innovation) has no revenue or growth objectives. The third wave focuses on establishing beachhead(s) in future markets enabling corporate evolution and long-term survival. It is intuitively clear that different mind-sets are necessary for the executives, managers and employees in these respective three waves. This is not to say that inventiveness should not be spread across the entire company, more to the point it should be focused. Creation of the IP around existing products and services will be

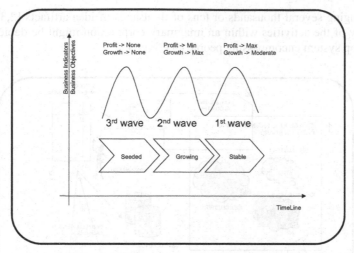

**Fig. 3.** Three waves of the corporate innovation

characteristic for the first two waves which we call "incremental inventiveness" while "disruptive inventiveness" is the characteristics of the third wave (or layer).

Another way to look into this domain is to see it as technology development landscapes. Closely related with technology evolution, we have seen an always-increasing interest to create an endless stream of inventions which will protect future company rights.

The technology development processes closely follow three waves of ascending order maturity:

*Invention* – ideas and innovations formulized, documented, and where desired, submitted for patent application.

*Process* – formalizing the method and repeatable activities that yield differing details but similar objectives (i.e. business process re-engineering lifecycle and or methodology).

*Experience* – human factors, aesthetics, and image recognition associated with the Invention and or Process (i.e. packaging, presentation, and overall appearance).

Having said this, we assert that corporate processes perform investment hedging as evidenced by converging thousands of ideas into a small manageable set of programs, most of which will fail, and very few of which may exhibit the possibility to recover all costs incurred. Therefore, beside well-organized and profoundly-thought programs, we need a special system for supporting IP activities. The architecture of such a system is sketched in the following section.

## 3  Technical Support for Innovation: An Architecture

Supporting large-scale innovation efforts requires the deployment of adequate technical means capable of effectively and efficiently managing corporate-wide activities. Assuming the involvement of several hundreds or thousands of individuals means also managing several thousands or tens of thousands of idea artifacts [2,3]. The generic flow of the activities within an imaginary corporation might be depicted as the closed loop system encompassing people (see Fig. 4).

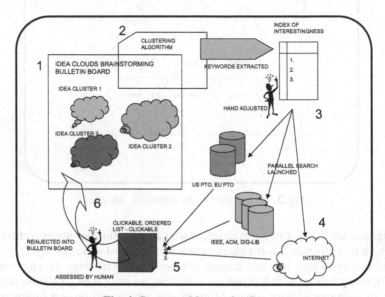

**Fig. 4.** Conceptual Innovation Process

We assume the existence of brainstorming bulletin-boards which seed initial ideas which can then be discussed in depth within a "community-of-interest" (1). Once we have enough harvested ideas, we may deploy clustering algorithm(s) (2) which will arrange ideas into natural groupings and assess interestingness into an ordered list (3). After being inspected and manually adjusted and abstracted, ideas will be confronted with prior-art artifacts in patent repositories, academic libraries and open Internet (4). Parallel search results will be collated and arranged into appropriate ordered lists and re-injected into the bulletin-board, making visible to original author of the idea what is known in the outside world (5). This may re-trigger yet another cycle (6) of discussions articulating better initial ideas or starting something entirely new. As ideas are being sharpened, we may decide to either: trigger periodic review of the ideas looking for the patentable ones or encourage idea authors to do some additional work and to file an invention disclosure for review committee.

Typically, corporations will have IT systems for such purposes and will carefully maintain repositories of ideas and invention disclosures. Still, additional legal work is necessary, in which in-house lawyers will work with external attorneys on patent filings and maintenance. It is a lengthy and expensive process intermixing legal, financial, and technological aspects. Yet another team will typically take care of the company patent portfolio's exploration and maintenance. Pipeline-wise thinking will hint at the corporate organization here: one part will take responsibility for seeding, spearheading and harvesting ideas, while another part will concentrate on valorization and monetizing of the patent portfolios.

## 4 Exploring IP Markets and Exploiting Patent Portfolios

Understanding of the market value of the corporate patent portfolios is a critical and intricate business endeavor [4]. It requires special skills, business knowledge and extraordinary intuition. Highly abstracted, this activity will imply bundling of the patents into portfolios and finding appropriate way of monetizing them: either through licensing or sales. But before doing this, one should explore the situation in the IP markets. This could be done through the deployment of some useful (slicing and dicing) tools and services within the IP landscaping (see Fig. 5).

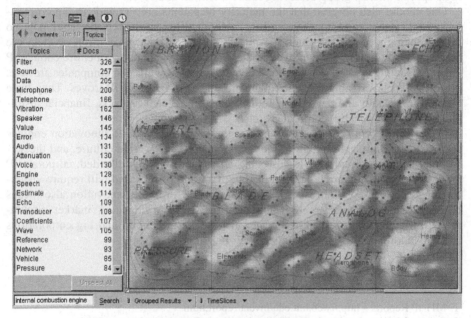

**Fig. 5.** IP Landscape Explorer

After creation and abstraction of the company portfolios, one may compare and position appropriately its offering. It will also imply that the value depends on how heavily populated the target domain already is. The street value of a granted patent is in the order of hundreds of thousands of dollars, while patent portfolios will have a multimillion street price tag. Crown jewel patents are typically carefully guarded and eventual infringements watched. Having seen a heavy involvement of lawyers and typical amounts involved in patent disputes, one can only guess what is really at stake here.

As we have mentioned, it is the UN-sponsored World IP Organization (http://www.wipo.int/) which is taking care of regulations and rules governing IP activities and markets. More than 180 countries are signatories to international IP treaties and acts. They cover around 90% of the world's countries and regulate the work of a large groups of lawyers, legal counsels, patent engineers etc. It may look as if there is a well-established order, but we still see some future great challenges lying ahead of WIPO.

## 5  Future Outlook and Key Challenges

US and EU patent offices are filing, examining and granting the majority of the world's patents. The US office alone grants nearly 200.000 patents per year. The processes are different in US and Europe as well as the cost and processing speed. The methods of examination are different and patenting subject matter is treated differently. So, for example, business processes could be patented in US and not in Europe. There is yet another big unresolved question/dispute in Europe about software patents. On the top all this, the open-source, world-wide movement is representing a special interest group deserving future attention and care.

One should also observe that the majority of patents are granted to big corporations while one should not disregard the individual inventors as well. They hope to protect their inventions as patents, while in reality, a huge proportion of them are never monetized, used nor deployed in the real business context. An entire cottage IP industry is being created on these lone-inventors hopes, while big companies are sole, powerful IP players able to create, maintain and valorize their IP troves. They have the power, breadth and persistence to deal with IP as legal artifacts, financial instruments and (high-density) corporate assets.

We conclude with the observation that the modern corporate innovation engines are fed by the intricate mixture of the the company's innovation culture, and the serendipity of some gifted individuals being embedded within well-oiled, corporate IP process. This should surely be combined with a grain of luck and will require visionary talent of well-positioned corporate executives. Corporate innovation also means business-longevity and possibly survival in constantly changing market circumstances, by guaranteeing company renewal [5]. The race is on and big corporations are daily adding tens of new patents to their patent portfolios.

## References

1. MIT IP Reports – http://web.mit.edu/invent/report.html
2. Stewart McKie – Let Innovation Thrive, Intelligent Enterprise, January 2004
3. Stewart McKie – Practical Tools for New Ideas, Intelligent Enterprise, February 2004
4. Kevin Rivette & David Kline – Rembrandts in The Attic, HBS Press, 2000
5. Geoffrey A. Moore – Darwin and the Demon, HBR, July/August 2004

# Integration of Business Process Support with Knowledge Management – A Practical Perspective

Birger Andersson[1], Ilia Bider[2], and Erik Perjons[1]

[1] Royal Institute of Technology, Department of Computer and Systems Sciences,
Forum 100, SE-164 40 Kista, Sweden
{ba,perjons}@dsv.su.se
[2] IbisSoft AB, Box 19567, SE-104 32 Stockholm, Sweden
ilia@ibissoft.se

**Abstract.** For knowledge management to be of use in an organization, it should be seamlessly incorporated in everyday business activities. Large parts of an organization's activities, especially on the operational level, are structured around business processes. Therefore, knowledge management needs to be integrated with these processes, which means that a computerized system that supports business processes should also support knowledge management. This paper reports on the experiences of implementing an integrated business process support system and knowledge management system into an organization. The implementation is the subject of a research project. The project's objective is to work out techniques for developing integrated process and knowledge management systems, and investigate effects of introducing such a system in operational practice, e.g., effects on productivity, internal cooperation, and democracy in organizational life.

## 1 Introduction

The paper discusses achievements and setbacks of an ongoing research project that concerns computerized Knowledge Management Systems (KMS) aimed at managing operational knowledge [15]. As operational we consider the knowledge required for handling daily operations, e.g., knowledge on operational goals, polices and procedures, current state of affairs, and past experience. The project has two main objectives:

- Investigate approaches to building such KMS, and introducing them into operational practice
- Evaluate results of introduction of such systems in operational practice

The project uses the methodology of action research [4], i.e., it employs a combination of theoretical studies with an experimental work where the experimental part plays a decisive role; all theoretical findings are to be tested in practice. The test is being done in a real operational environment with all its complexity. Our main assumptions for the project are as follows:

1. For the knowledge management to be of use in an organization, it should be seamlessly incorporated in everyday business activities. Thus we need an integrated system that supports both daily operations and knowledge management.

D. Karagiannis and U. Reimer (Eds.): PAKM 2004, LNAI 3336, pp. 227–238, 2004.

2. Operational knowledge is structured around business processes, such as processing an order, insurance claim, or bug in a software system. Therefore, for a business support system to be able to automatically gather and distribute knowledge, both the business and support system should be process-oriented. Practical introduction of KMS is difficult without process-orientation of the organization.
3. An important prerequisite for a KMS will function in practice is that a majority of the organization staff actually use the system in a major part of their daily work.

According to the action research theory and the above assumptions, the following main steps are needed for achieving the project's objectives:

1. Choosing or developing an approach for modeling business processes suited for the task.
2. Developing a computerized business process support (BPS) system that includes some elements of knowledge management and has a potential to be gradually developed to a full-featured knowledge management system.
3. Introducing the system in the operational practice, and at the same time making basic steps towards process-orientation of the pilot organization.
4. Choosing or developing an approach to introduction a more advance knowledge management features into the system, and testing it in the practice.
5. Choosing an approach for measurement of results of introduction of the system in practice. This includes choosing metrics and developing objective (through the system log) and subjective (through interviews and surveys) means of measurement.

Up to now, steps 1 and 2 are fully completed, step 3 is on-going, and steps 4 and 5 are in the stage of research in progress. The goal of the paper is to discuss the results of the completed steps and review directions of the research in progress.

This paper is structured in the following way. In section 2, we shortly describe the organization where we do our field investigations. Section 3 discusses selection of an approach to business process modeling. Section 4 describes the general architecture of our integrated BPSS/KMS. Section 5 discusses some problems of introducing the system into operational practice. Section 6 describes our research in progress, and finally, Section 7 presents some concluding remarks.

## 2  Pilot Organization

As a pilot organization the project has "Association of Tenants, Region West Sweden" (in Swedish: Hyresgästföreningen, Region Västra Sverige), abbreviated to HGF. HGF is a non-profit interest organization that unites more than 60 000 tenants and has as its primary goal guarding the interests of its members. The regional office, which is used as the main pilot site, has about 50 employers whose task is to provide service to the members and to the "field-level" organizations. The service is provided in a number of areas, such as:

• Giving legal and practical advice to the HGF's members.
• Conducting rent negotiation with the property owners on behalf of the members.
• Lobbying, i.e., influencing decisions made by authorities.

Most of business processes in the pilot organization are of administrative nature, such as negotiation, conflict management, lobbying, etc. We call such processes loosely structured to stress that for these processes, it is difficult to pre-determine the order of activities. This term has connotation with the concept of ill-defined problems in AI, see, for example, [16], and with such terms as ad-hoc, emergent and dynamic workflows, see for example [9]. The nature of the processes in the pilot organization was one of the main factors when choosing an approach to business process modeling to be used when developing a support system.

## 3   Selecting an Approach to Business Processes Modeling

According to a general definition of a business process, see, for example [7], a business process is a partially ordered set of activities performed to reach a well-defined goal. A process engages a number of participants, which can be divided into two categories: "passive" and "active" participants. Passive participants are consumed, produced or changed through the execution of activities, for example, a document being written, an organization being reorganized, or a patient treated in the hospital. Active participants, or agents, are those participants that perform activities aimed at the passive participants. Human beings, as well as artifacts can fill both the roles of "passive" and "active" participants.

There are many different methods of modeling business processes that could be used in the project. Below, the most common ones are grouped in four categories based on the way they reflect the business process dynamics (for details see [6]):

1. *Input/output flows*. The focus is on passive participants that are being consumed, produced, or changed by the activities. A typical notation here is IDEF0 [8].
2. *Workflows*. The focus is on time ordering of activities performed by active participants. Examples of notation here are Petri nets [1] and IDEF3 workflow diagrams [11].
3. *Agent-related workflows*. The focus is on agent cooperation, i.e., order in which active participants get and perform their part of work. An agent-related workflow adds a new, agent dimension to the time dimension of an ordinary workflow. A typical notation here is Role-Activity Diagrams [12].
4. *State-flows*. The focus is on changes produced by activities executed in the frame of a given process instance. Some changes may concern the state of passive participants, e.g., their form, shape, or physical location. Other changes may concern the state of active participants, e.g., a state of the mind of a human agent trying to find a solution for a complex problem. A typical example of the state-flow notation is IDEF3 state-transition diagrams [11]. However, the state-transition diagrams exploit the state-flow view only partially. For a more extensive exploitation of the state flow view, the state-flow modeling method from [3, 10] can be used.

Administrative processes that exist at the pilot site do not have predefined passive participants, except documents of general nature, nor do they have a very well defined distribution of responsibilities between the members of staff, i.e., task assignment can be done "on the fly". In addition, they belong to loosely structured processes, i.e., it is difficult to establish the exact order of their activities. Based on the specific nature of the business processes in question, we found the state-flow as most appropriate view for building a business process support for the pilot organization. More details on how to choose an appropriate approach for the business task at hand see in [6].

In addition, the first three views are in essence type-oriented. They are intended for describing normative behavior of business process, and they pay less attention to the development of particular business process instances in time. The fourth view is in-stance-oriented and requires tracing the changes in the part of reality that concerns a particular process instance (see below). The latter is of great importance for knowl-edge management as it facilitates both easy distribution of knowledge on the current state of affairs and automatic gathering of past experiences.

Based on the above deliberations, the state flow view has been chosen as a basis for building a support system suitable for the project. More specifically, the flavor of the state-flow technique described in [3, 10] was adapted. As this favor is not wide spread in the theory and practice of Business Process Management, below we present basic notions on which it is built.

The main concept of the state-flow modeling method is a process's *state*. A proc-ess's state is aimed to show how much has been done to achieve the operational goal of the process and how much is still to be done. A state of the process is represented by a complex structure that includes attributes, and references to various active and passive participants of the process, such as process's owner, documents, etc. A state of the process does not show what activities have been completed to reach it;it only shows the results achieved so far.

The process is driven forward through a set of stipulated states until its goal has been reached, e.g., a delivery has been paid for. The operational goal can be defined as a set of conditions that have to be fulfilled before a process can be considered as finished. A state that satisfies these conditions is called a *final state* of the process.

The process is driven forward through *activities* executed either automatically or with a human assistance. Activities can be planned first and executed later. A *planned activity* records such information as type of action (goods shipment, compiling a pro-gram, sending a letter), planned date and time, deadline, name of a person responsible for an action, etc.

The process's state is used as a primary tool in deciding on what should be done to reach the process's goal from the current state. All activities planned and executed in the frame of the process should be aimed to minimize the difference between the current state and the projected final one. However, in some cases, a *history* of the process's evolution in time is important when deciding on actions. The history is defined as a time-ordered sequence of all previous states.

Let's include in the process's state all activities currently planned for this process. As a result, the process's *generalized state* beside its *passive part* (attributes and ref-erences mentioned above) will get an *active part*. The active part, i.e., the process's plan, will be responsible for moving the process forward. Making the plan an integral part of the generalized state allows us to define the notion of valid state that can be applied not only to the final states of the process, but also to any intermediate state. For example, a process that is not in the final state, but has no activities planned for moving it to the next stipulated state can, for many types of processes, be considered to be in an invalid state. Formal rules, so called *rules of planning*, can be defined to specify what planned activities could/should be added to an invalid state to make it valid. The use of these rules can be combined with manual planning.

When an activity is executed, a process changes its state. Changes concern both the passive and active parts of the state. The active part, i.e., the plan, changes due to the disappearance of the executed activity from the process plan and some new activities can be planned instead of it. Changes in the state constitute an internal time axis of the process. To link this axis to real time, an event is registered each time an activity is executed. A *registered event* is a record that links the change in the state to the reality outside the process. For example, it can record the time when the event happened (and/or was registered), the "id" of responsible for the event, his/her comments, etc.

## 4   Architecture of a Support System

The heart of the integrated KMS/BPS we built based on the state-oriented view on business processes consists of:

- Historical database that automatically stores information on all events and all past states of all processes, documents, and other business objects.
- Principle of dynamic and distributed planning. Dynamic means planning when needed, distributed means planning to each other. Planning for each other constitute a communication channel between process participants along business process instances. Planning can be partly manual, partly automatic.
- Navigational system that allows the end user to freely navigate through the space of interconnected processes in the present and past.

  The system, among other things, provides:

- A virtual calendar that allows the users to plan tasks to each other, and gives immediate access to all information required for completing individual tasks. The latter includes information on the currents situation and all relevant events and documents in the past and future.
- Automatic support of history recording that allows not only to see what happened (i.e., events) in the past, but also how things looked like at that time (i.e., state of the processes, documents and other business objects).
- Document management that facilitates getting access to any internal or external document without knowing its name or storage placement. The documents are found through association to their usage (e.g., purpose of creation) in some process. In addition, via support of history, all internal documents are automatically versioned.

Current version of the system called *ProBis* the system is built as a client/server solution, where clients run under Microsoft Windows, and a server runs an SQL DBMS, Oracle, or MS SQL Server. The historical database is implemented as a set of stored procedures and triggers. User interface is built with the help of Prolifics application development tool from Prolifics, Inc. More details on the architecture and implementation of the system could be found in [5].

Besides supporting business processes, *ProBis* provides two basic elements of KMS:

1. When assistance is required from a member of the staff, it is requested through planning an activity for him/her in the frame of this process instance. This is done in the same manner independently whether he/she was engaged in the process before or not. This activity automatically appears in his/her virtual calendar. When executing this activity, he/she automatically gets all the knowledge on the current

state of the process, its history and the future (other activities planned for the process). No extended communication with the colleagues previously engaged in the process is required for this end.

2. The full history of previously completed processes is easily available through a number of associations, like time-frame, documents used, received or produced, or people engaged in the process (own staff as well as external contacts). This historical database can be effectively used for finding past experience that can help in finding solution for current problems.

## 5   Introduction of Support System in the Operational Practice

### 5.1   Background

Prior to building *ProBis* for our pilot site, an extensive job of business process analysis was undertaken in order to discover and describe business processes existing at HGF. Each process has been analyzed by an specially composed project group that consisted of a number of domain experts from HGF, and two business analysts from our own staff. The role of the experts in the domain was to provide information, and verify the suggested business model. The role of the business analysts was to initiate discussions, ask questions and provide the drafts of the model for review. The analysis was conducted according to a methodology described in [3].

In parallel with the analysis projects, a simplified version of the *ProBis* system has been built and introduced in one particular department of the pilot organization. The system, called *ReKo*, supported recruiting of new members to the interest organization (more details on the recruiting process see in [3]). The system had reduced functionality because most of the participants of the process were working outside their office. For example, the planning capability has not been built in the system.

It took about half a year to build the system. It took one year before the organization started to use it in their operational practice and fully substituted the previously used technique based on Microsoft Excel sheets. The main reason for a one-year delay was (natural) resistance to organizational changes. To overcome the resistance, a competition was used at one point to show the advantages of the new system to the administrative personal. The goal of the competition was to test who can complete certain tasks quicker: an experience office worker with the old technique or non-experienced person (our own member of staff) with the new technique. Winning the competition was one of the many steps to overcome the natural resistance.

After one more year, the recruiting staff became fully acquainted with the system and understood advantages of working in a more structured way. By the end of the second year, the statistics showed growing numbers of new members, which was attributed to better order in recruiting activity imposed by the system.

### 5.2   Problems Encountered

The full-featured *ProBis* system was delivered during 2003 in the module-by-module fashion. Modularization was envisaged to make the introduction easier. All modules were built on the same principles and they shared common user-interface. The rationale behind this was that by the time the next module was introduced, the workers would already know how to deal with the system by learning the previous module. Due to organizational difficulties, the implementation plan failed, and the operational test of the system started only after practically all modules had been delivered and installed.

Based on previous experience of introducing a support system into this organization, some delays were expected in the introduction process. However, the difficulties of introducing a system aimed at functioning through the whole organization showed to be much greater than in case of introduction of a system in a single department. It was expected that it would be easy to introduce a system built on the results of the detailed analysis project. This expectation never materialized.

Some of the introduction problems were purely organizational; they were not unique to introduction of *ProBis*, and they are often encountered during introduction of new information systems. To this class of problems, for example, belong:

- Bad planning of the introduction, e.g. absence of a formal responsible for introduction of each module.
- Unwillingness on the part of the management to press their staff to use the system
- Assigning people that were not part of the analysis project to test the system
- Insufficient quality of training programs.

Another not-unique problem was users' expectations. Part of the personnel had very little experience of using computers in general, and business systems in particular. This situation, in itself, was predictable. What was not predictable was lack of willingness to learn. Current users expect a system to be so intuitively clear that even an inexperienced user can "mouse click" him/herself to understanding the system. Our user-interface did not meet this expectation.

In addition, a number of conceptual problems that are specific to BPSS/KMS in general, and *ProBis* in particular, have been discovered. Understanding of business process orientation in theory does not automatically imply understanding of how it will look like in practice. The following problems are examples in this category:

- Use of planning in general. People are usually not accustomed to plan their operative work in details, unless absolutely necessary, such as in cases where other people are involved.
- Use of planning as a way of communication. People are not accustomed to plan tasks for their colleagues or managers.
- Level of details on the computer screens. Though the level of details was agreed on the analysis stage, the members of the analysis team did not fully understand that this would be the level of details to work when using the system. The screens have to many details for the initial phase.

## 5.3  Solutions

After analysis of the encountered problems, a number of measures were undertaken to speed up the introduction of *ProBis* in HGF's operational practice. These measures concern both adjusting the system, e.g., changing the user-interface, and improving the organizational structure of the introduction project at the customer site.

Up to now the following measures has already been completed:

- The complexity of the screens that represent the states of various business processes has been significantly reduced. This was done by temporarily hiding part of the information fields. These fields will be opened later when the end-users are more ready for extended complexity.
- Planning and registering requirements have been eased so that the system does not force the end-users to introduce new activities in the project plan, or add comments to the history records. These requirements can be introduced on the latter stage.
- User-interface has been completely redone to making it more in line with the other systems used in the office.

When redesigning user-interface, a particular care has been taken to make the basic concepts of the process-orientation more explicit for the end-users. For example, one of the main ideas on which *ProBis* is built is execution of a planned activity in the frame of a process instance. This includes three steps:

1. introducing changes in the process state
2. planning new activities instead of the executed one
3. registering an event of current execution

We found that the end-users had difficulties to understand what actually happens with the planned activity under execution. To show it explicitly, a following visualization has been used, see Figure 1. Both activities planned for a process instance and the events already registered in the frame of this process are represented as two list boxes adjacent to each other. The left box represents planned activities, and the right box represents completed events. To start the execution of a planned activity, the end user presses the "⅗ button placed between th e boxes, alternatively drags this activity from the right box to the left one. The planned activity disappears from the "plan" box and appears in the event box with a specially designated icon (lightening). After all changes in the process state are completed, the user presses the "save" button ("Spara"). At that moment the "lightening" icon is substituted by a "green tick" icon for events/completed activities. This visualization gives the end-user clear understanding as to what happens with the planned activity.

# 6   Research in Progress

## 6.1   Activating Knowledge

One of the main goals of the project is to make the operational knowledge active [2], i.e., make the system to suggest solutions rather than force the user to search the knowledge base for a suitable solution. Our way of activating knowledge is based on the idea of *rules of planning* suggested in the state-flow model of business processes, see Section 3, and [5, 10]. The rules specify what activities could/should be added to an invalid generalized state to make it valid. Using these rules, the process is driven forward in the following manner. First, an activity from the process plan is executed and the state of the process is changed. Then, the plan is corrected to make the generalized state valid. Rules of planning can be roughly divided into three categories:

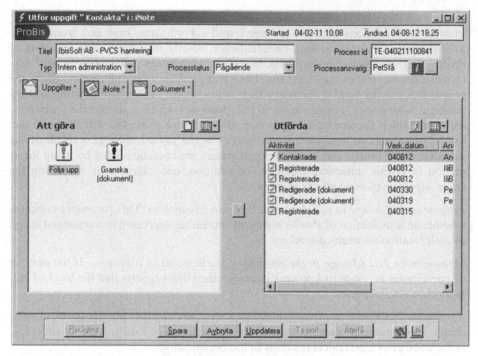

**Fig. 1.** Screen dump from *ProBis*

- *Obligations*. Given current state and, possibly history, and other planned activities, certain activities should be present in the plan.
- *Prohibitions*. Given current state and, possibly history, and other planned activities, certain activities should not be present in the plan.
- *Recommendations*. Given current state and, possibly history, and other planned activities, certain activities are normally planned for the process instances of the type in question.

While obligation and prohibitions can be enforced automatically by adding/deleting activities, recommendations give to the human participants a choice to follow or not to follow them based on their understanding of the situation. Besides what should be planned, rules of planning should also help to determine when things should be done and by whom, i.e., help in assignment of human resources.

The current version of *ProBis* does not provide the means for automated planning; this part is under development. The earlier versions of the system (see [5]) had some automated planning capability, but it was hard coded in the system. Current research is devoted to creating a formal language for expressing rules of planning. Having such a language, hard coding can be substituted by an interpreter.

## 6.2  Devising Metrics and Means for Measurement of Results

One of the goals of the project is to investigate how an integrated BPSS/KMS affects the efficiency of a workplace and the impact it has on the relations between colleagues on the workplace, i.e., what are consequences on productivity, efficiency, transparency, relations between managers and subordinates, man and woman, etc. This investigation is based both on qualitative, mainly interviews with the users of ProBis, and quantitative information, based on information gathered in ProBis' historical database. For example, ProBis' historical database store information about the people that use the system, including their roles, gender, and which department they belong to; which users communicate in the processes; which activities the users perform; and which documents they produce. Below, three examples will illustrate the use of parameters to measure *social changes in the organization* as a result of the introduction of ProBis and how these parameters are operationalized by using information in ProBis' historical database. In addition, one example of measuring the *knowledge management effects* is given.

*Parameter 1: Change in collaboration between co-workers.* This parameter concerns whether an introduction of *ProBis* results in increased, decreased or unchanged levels of collaboration between co-workers.

*Measurement 1.1: Change in the number of participants in a process.* If the number of participants in a standard process increases then this suggests that the level of collaboration also increases.

*Parameter 2: Change in the organizational structure (mainly the hierarchical relations).* This parameter concerns whether the introduction of *ProBis* leads to a decrease in the number of hierarchical relations in the organization.

*Measurement 2.1: Change in the number of superiors engaged in processes.* If co-workers can manage processes without engaging their superiors then this will result in a flatter organization.

*Measurement 2.2: Change in the number of activities planned by sub-ordinates to their superiors.* If the number of sub-ordinates that plan activities for their superiors increase, then this will result in a flatter organization.

*Parameter 3: Change in co-workers level of involvement.* This parameter concerns whether the introduction of *ProBis* leads to an increase in the co-workers level of involvement or commitment.

*Measurement 3.1: Change of who initiates processes.* If the number of processes is initiated by a larger number of co-workers, then the level of involvement in the organization is increasing. Considerations about the types of processes initiated must be taken here.

*Parameter 4: Change of frequency of use of past experiences.* This parameter concerns whether the introduction of *ProBis* leads to an increase of use of past experiences.

*Measure 4.1: The number of times a completed process has been viewed by the workers.* Increased viewing suggests that workers are more willing to find and learn from past experiences.

# 7  Conclusion

In the introduction, we stated that successful introduction of computerized operational knowledge management requires:

1. Seamless integration of business process support with knowledge management
2. Process-orientation
3. Extensive use of the system

None of the above ideas are exceptionally new; actually they currently constitute the major topics of international workshops and conferences devoted to KMS. Integration of KMS with BPS is discussed in e.g., [2, 13, 14, 17]. The main observation is that business processes are context-giving, structuring elements prevalent in most organizations making the integration of KMS, or Organizational Memory Information System (OMIS), with business process support systems natural.

We do not have any detailed knowledge on research projects that are building a practical case in order to test them according to the action research theory. Our project is aimed to fill this gap. From the theoretical/conceptual point of view our approach to integrating knowledge management with business process support differs from those of others, at least, in one of the following two aspects:

- Our starting-point is not that a computerized KMS can help in driving business processes more efficiently, but rather that process-orientation of an organization is an important prerequisite for introduction of a computerized KMS.
- We use the state-flow view on business processes, which we believe has certain advantages when developing integrated KMS/BPS, at least, for loosely structured business processes.

So far, the project has encountered some difficulties, which was to be expected. However, none of these difficulties have been unsolvable, and we do not expect any really critical problems to arise in the nearest future. We do hope that the experiences we have gathered so far is of interest for both practitioners and the scientific knowledge management community, considering that reports on real introduction of integrated BPSS/KMS into operational practice of organizations are scarce.

## Acknowledgements

The project described in this paper is currently supported by the Swedish Agency for Innovation Systems (Vinnova). The authors would like to thank all people who participated in the project, our colleagues, as well as the experts in the field, especially, Tomas Andersson, Alex Durnovo, and Rogier Svensson.

## References

1. Aalst W. v. d., and Hee K.v.: *Workflow Management – Models, Methods, and Systems*, MIT Press, 2002.
2. Abecker A., Bernardi A., and Sintek, M.: Enterprise information infrastructures for active, context-sensitive knowledge delivery. In: *ECIS'99 Procs. of the 7th European Conf. on Information Systems*, 1999.

3. Andersson, T, Andersson-Ceder, A, and Bider, I: State Flow as a Way of Analyzing Business Processes - Case Studies, *Logistics Information Management*, MSB University Press. Volume 15, No 1, pp. 34-45, 2002. http://www.ibissoft.se/English/Cases.pdf.
4. Baskerville R., and Myers, M.D.: Why Action Research and Information Systems?, *MIS Quarterly*, Volume 28, No 3, September, 2004.
5. Bider I.: *State-Oriented Business Process Modelling: Principles, Theory and Practice*, PhD Thesis, DSV, Stockholm University/Royal Institute of Technology, 2002.
6. Bider I., *Choosing Approach to Business Process Modeling – Practical Perspective*, Research Report, IbisSoft AB, 2002, Revision 2003. http://www.ibissoft.se/English/Howto.pdf.
7. Hammer, M., and Champy, J.: *Reengineering the Corporation - A Manifesto for Business Revolution*, Nicholas Brealey Publishing, London, 1994.
8. IDEF0: *Integration Definition for Function Modelling (IDEF0)*, Draft Federal Information Processing Standards, 1993. http://www.idef.com/Downloads/pdf/idef0.pdf
9. Jøgensen H.D., and Carlsen S.: Emergent  Workflow, Integrated Planning and Performance of Process Instances, In: *Workflow Management '99*, Münster, Germany, 1999.
10. Khomyakov, M., Bider, I. Achieving Workflow Flexibility through Taming the Chaos. In: *OOIS 2000 - 6th international conference on object oriented information systems*, pp. 85-92, Springer, 2000. http://www.inconcept.com/JCM/August2001/bider.html
11. Mayer R. J., Menzel C.P., Painter M.K., deWitte P.S., Blinn T., Perakath B.: *IDEF3 Process Description*, Capture Method Report, Information Integration for Concurrent Engineering (IICE), Interim technical report, 1995.
12. Ould, M.A.: *Business Processes- Modelling and Analysis for Reengineering and Improvement*, Wiley, 1995.
13. Pavassiliou, G., Ntioudis S., Abecker A., Mentzas, G. A.: Supporting Knowledge-Intensive Work in Public Administration Processes, *Knowledge and Process Management*, Vol. 10, No 3, pp. 164-174, 2003.
14. Reimer U., Margelisch A., Staudt, M.: EULE: A Knowledge-Based System to Support Business Processes. *Knowledge-Based Systems*, Vol.13, No.5, pp. 261-269, 2000.
15. Rigallo, A., Valente, G.: Operational Knowledge Mangement: A Way To Manage Competence, *exp*, Vol 2, No 2, December, 2002. http://exp.telecomitalialab.com
16. Simon, H. A.: "The structure of ill-structured problems", *Artificial Intelligence*, No 4, pp. 181-201, 1973.
17. Wargitsch, C., Wewers, T., and Theisinger F: Organizational-Memory-Based Approach for an Evolutionary Workflow Management System - Concepts and Implementation. In: J.R. Nunamaker, editor, *Procs. of the 31st Hawaii Int. Conf. on System Sciences*, Volume 1, pp. 174-183, 1998.

# Towards a Systematic Approach
# for Capturing Knowledge-Intensive Business Processes

Matthias Trier[1] and Claudia Müller[2]

[1] TU Berlin, Franklinstrasse 28/29,
10587 Berlin, Germany
Trier@sysedv.cs.tu-berlin.de
[2] Universität Potsdam, August-Bebel-Strasse 89,
14482 Potsdam, Germany
Clamue@rz.uni-potsdam.de

**Abstract.** Business process oriented Knowledge Management (KM) has two objectives: the design of KM Processes and the support of knowledge-intensive Business Processes. Existing approaches focus integrated Knowledge- and Process Management Systems, the support of processes with KM Systems, or the analysis of knowledge-intensive activities. All these applications require a systematic approach for the documentation of existing processes. Available procedural models propose steps for process oriented KM projects, but they rarely describe their implementation in concrete practical applications. That is why this contribution introduces a new process-oriented KM (POKM) project approach developed in corporate projects. A special focus is put on a detailed method for capturing knowledge intense processes which extends the existing broad perspective on KM projects. It allows for insights into questions like how to comprehensively capture expert processes, how to store the collected information in a structured way, and how to design supporting instruments and materials in order to generate a high quality data set, which subsequently is utilized to derive Knowledge Management measures.

## 1 Introduction

Starting in 2001, the disciplines of Knowledge Management and Business Process Management merge towards an integrated process oriented Knowledge Management approach. Next to two other application scenarios, Abecker identifies a field of research, which utilizes the modelling of business processes to enable the derivation of Knowledge Management measures [1]. These three application scenarios require some or all of the following project stages: Systems Design (consisting of Systems Planning, Analysis, and Implementation), Systems Usage, and Systems Evolution. This contribution focuses on the first stage of Systems Design. To exactly classify different research approaches, it can be further segregated into three different layers. On the top layer, strategic business process oriented Knowledge Management is a top-down perspective, which derives knowledge objectives from the long-term business objectives. The bottom layer deals with KM design based on communication analysis and diagnosis. It primarily deals with communication aspects of knowledge work and develops appropriate methods or tools. It is thus very hard to be separated from the middle layer, where Abecker allocates approaches of business process oriented design, where methods and tools for business process analysis are extended to meet the new requirements of Knowledge Management. This middle layer is dealing

D. Karagiannis and U. Reimer (Eds.): PAKM 2004, LNAI 3336, pp. 239–250, 2004.
© Springer-Verlag Berlin Heidelberg 2004

with modelling methods derived from business process management and the modelling of existing processes to find potential for improvement. The existing approaches which belong to this category are introduced now. After identifying a lack of specification in current models, a related procedure is introduced. It has been developed in two corporate projects and focuses a special method for capturing knowledge-intensive business processes, which will be the main contribution of this paper.

## 2    Generic Approaches to Process Oriented KM

To create a systematic method for capturing knowledge-intensive business processes, the existing related KM approaches have been analysed and the following three are now introduced: BPO-KM, PROMOTE, and CommonKADS.

The first selected approach is BPO-KM (in German: GPO-WM®). It proposes a method for a process-oriented analysis and design of Knowledge Management solutions [2]. Within this procedure of eight steps, the KM Audit analyses the fundamental conditions including the evaluation of existing IT systems, the analysis of the information- and knowledge culture, and the determination of the demand for information and knowledge. The main focus of this step is the identification of potential for improvement of the existing utilisation of knowledge in the business context. The subsequent step analyses knowledge-intensive processes to identify strengths and weaknesses or possible improvements. Further, the process- and task-related demand for knowledge is identified. Unfortunately, the procedural model does not propose any methods which explain how to capture and model processes on a detailed level and hence, this approach results in a rather strategic analysis of business processes and concentrates on the identification of strengths and potentials for the utilization of knowledge.

Another approach is the PROMOTE method, which integrates strategic planning with the evaluation of Knowledge Management and Business Process Management [3]. The intended scope of the approach covers the analysis, the modelling, and the execution of knowledge-intensive processes. It extends the more general method of Business Process Management Systems (BPMS) including strategic decision, reengineering and resource allocation, and workflow and performance evaluation [3]. The additional KM related steps are creating awareness for enterprise knowledge, discover knowledge processes, create operational knowledge processes and organisational memory, and evaluate enterprise knowledge. The second element, discovering knowledge processes, deals with capturing knowledge-intensive business processes. In the underlying reengineering stage of the BPMS method, process knowledge is getting documented. It consists of the sequence of activities and its related employees, organizational units, necessary data, application systems, and resources. The PROMOTE method now extends this process knowledge to additionally capture functional knowledge, consisting of the identification of knowledge-intensive activities, the description of relevant knowledge flows and the identification of knowledge flows between persons and processes. Although this approach introduces a systematic orientation for the necessary elements to be captured in knowledge-intensive business processes, a detailed description of how to elicit these additional items in a KM project and a discussion of the actual pitfalls in the practical implementation would be beneficial.

Next to the process oriented KM models introduced, the established Knowledge Engineering approach CommonKADS could influence a method for the capturing of knowledge-intensive business processes. Although its objective of constructing a program that can perform a difficult task adequately is completely different [4], its process of Knowledge Acquisition can be regarded as similar, because Knowledge Acquisition includes the elicitation, collection, analysis, modelling, and validation of knowledge for Knowledge Engineering and Knowledge Management projects [5]. The according Knowledge Acquisition (KA) techniques have been developed to help with the elicitation of knowledge from an expert. Obviously, they focus the same problem of examining and analysing knowledge-intensive business processes. However, the special methods for documenting the expertise of a knowledge worker are not completely applicable in business process oriented KM. This is supported by Abecker, who comments, that the method contains only a few KM-specific concepts and focuses technical infrastructures [1]. Another example for the divergence can be derived using the interview structure for domain-knowledge elicitation provided by CommonKADS [4,6]. It consists of the steps identifying a particular sub-task, ask the expert to identify "rules" used in this task, take each rule, and ask when it is useful and when not. Thus, it gives no special procedure to ask for the topics of expertise and their relation to the process.

These procedural models are just some examples of the multitude of available approaches. They all provide a comprehensive theoretical model which can help to plan and execute a process oriented KM project. However, their practical execution in corporate settings necessitates detailed procedural specifications of how to actually execute the proposed steps. Further methodical discussions and foundations are required for issues like how to comprehensively capture expert processes, how to store the collected information in a structured way, and how to design supporting instruments and materials in order to ensure a high quality data set, which subsequently is utilized in every type of KM project to derive management measures.

After briefly introducing a procedure for process oriented Knowledge Management developed in two corporate projects, this contribution focuses on a method for capturing the expert knowledge in knowledge-intensive business processes. Further, it discusses the practical insights and challenges involved in eliciting the environment of a knowledge worker and documenting the data sets necessary for process oriented Knowledge Management.

# 3  Practical Challenges – Experiences from Corporate Projects

Every capturing method is dependent on the actual project objective as it determines the actual data to be elicited. To define such objectives for the capturing method described in the next section, the applied procedural model for KM projects is now being introduced. It has been developed in 2001 to guide the process oriented KM (POKM) projects conducted [7] and meanwhile has been confirmed by the approaches introduced in the literature (see section above).

## 3.1  The POKM Model

The general approach for process oriented Knowledge Management (POKM) assumes that KM has to be demand driven. This implies that the location of the knowl-

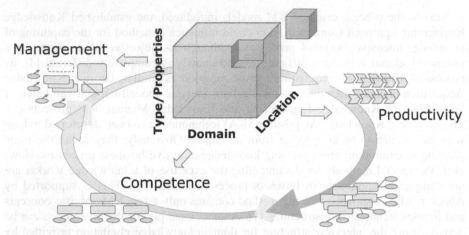

**Fig. 1.** The overall process oriented KM project procedure

edge has to be identified first (see Fig. 1). It is usually the business process, where the experts apply their knowledge to generate productivity for the company. Hence, the analysis of the actual business processes leads to the identification of domains of expertise or competence. In detail, this is done by identifying the topics connected to the knowledge-intensive business process. The properties of the actual topics identified help to classify knowledge types. Examples are tacit or explicit knowledge, or knowledge of facts versus knowledge about methods or references. Finally, these documented properties of the identified topics define the KM-related management interventions. They help to transform the existing scenario towards the new concept. Obviously, defining and documenting the appropriate properties increases the quality of the suggested organisational changes. The measures derived could include improved documentation and according means to access the documents, competence management with targeted qualification programs, appropriate management of the corporate expertise portfolio, the introduction of electronic means for the identification of knowledge carriers (i.e. yellow pages), or the improvement of connectivity between the workforce. Next to identifying such opportunities, the acceptance of the proposed changes has to be estimated. This is strongly related to the employee's evaluation of the current situation and the informal culture of the department under consideration (as a company can have multiple cultures).

The topic property analysis should be augmented by a situational analysis of the overall processes which investigates, if the knowledge is available in time (delays, limited time periods), at the right location, and in the right form (understandable). Further it can be analyzed, if the knowledge is dependent on agents and exposed to instability (frequent updates needed), if it is reused in the processes, and if the agents have appropriate expertise [4,6].

Summarizing, this practical KM procedure consists of the four stages identifying processes, capturing processes and topics together with the topic's properties and structure, conduct an analysis of topic properties and of the overall processes to finally derive management interventions. Within this framework, the instruments for capturing the actual topics specify stage two. To further determine the requirements for the data structure to be documented in this stage, the following generic KM entity model has been adopted. It further serves as an easy model to structure and improve the communication with the company and the creation of the target concept.

## 3.2  The KM Entity Model

To ensure a complete documentation of the existing processes and a structured discussion of the KM measures derived, a generic KM Entity Model has been developed for the practical project work [8]. It assembles all relevant objects together with their interrelationships on the most aggregated level and hence defines an abstract meta-structure for the data collected in knowledge-intensive business processes.

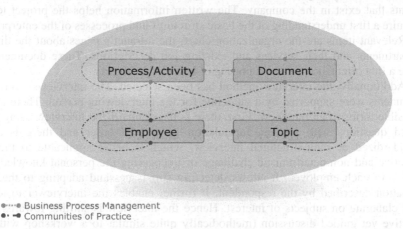

**Fig. 2.** The KM Entity Model

The respective entities are Process/Activity, Document, Employee, and Topic (see Fig. 2). Connecting these four main entities automatically helps to focus the relevant relationships between them. This helps to derive necessary insights like which author is connected with other authors, who is responsible for a process, or what documents about which topics are needed to carry out an activity. The model can now help to create a shared understanding of the participants and to communicate the main task of the POKM project: the creation of transparency about the KM entities and their connections by capturing the structure of topics, documents and employees.

Looking at the entities another insight can be derived. The importance of the approach of business process modeling for Knowledge Management can be identified, because it models the process (as a sequence of activities), the attached responsible person and the documents necessary for the transactions. In the recent modeling approaches for knowledge-intensive business processes, this conventional approach has been extended. The main innovation has been the introduction of topic elements into process models [9].

Having defined the generic entities and relations to be modeled and the overall KM project procedure, the actual process of capturing the expertise of the knowledge worker in the knowledge-intensive business process can now be systematically supported as described in the next section.

### 3.3  A Method for Capturing Knowledge-Intensive Business Processes

Theory separates between two possible methods, the access to existing secondary data and the generation (or capturing) of novel data using primary data collection methods. The latter can include workshops as a special form of group interview, questionnaires or observations [10]. These approaches are also discussed in the related literature on Knowledge Acquisition, which differentiates between protocol-analysis-techniques and protocol-generation techniques [5]. Both strands have been combined in the data collection strategy applied in the POKM projects. First, a secondary data collection using the inventory method is conducted before semi-structured interviews are employed.

The inventory method is based on the collection and analysis of all relevant documents that exist in the company. The written information helps the project team to acquire a first understanding of the basic structures and processes of the enterprise.

Relevant items are the organization chart, the intranet's pages about the different departments and their services and existing job descriptions. These documents can give a first orientation for the capturing of knowledge objects.

Additionally, the interview method has been selected. The interviews with the respondents were supported by a guideline for the interviewing person. There are two possible forms of an interview. First, there is the standardized interview using predefined questions with a given formulation in a fixed order and there is a non-standardized or semi-structured interview, which is better applicable to the more iterative and non-deterministic challenge of uncovering the personal knowledge domains of each employee. It allows detecting soft issues and adapting to the actual situation described by the respondent. It further enables the interviewer to identify and elaborate on subjects of interest. Hence the interview is shifting towards a productive yet guided discussion (methodically quite similar to a workshop with a restricted number of respondents) [10]. The necessary duration for capturing the knowledge domains and knowledge objects in the interviews has been limited to about 60 to 90 minutes. The preferred location has been the actual workplace in order to create a better impression of the expert's environment.

To guide the interviewers and to assure the completeness and comparability of each protocol (as they have to be integrated into a consistent model), an interview guide should be created, released and consistently be used by the team. The following interview guide introduces a procedure which has been applied and tested in practice (see Fig. 3). It includes five sections which specify the procedure for capturing knowledge-intensive business processes within the POKM project.

The first and introductory section of the interview introduces the project and its objectives as well as the benefits for the employee. Here informal questions help to establish a pleasant and trustful atmosphere ('breaking the ice'). It has been useful to communicate several advantages of participating in the project. This includes the public recognition of the respondent's fields of expertise, new knowledge about how problems can be solved, or opportunities to collaborate and exchange knowledge with people having a similar background.

The second section constitutes the main part and is broken down into eight subsections. Their main objective is to find out business tasks and relate topics to it. Next to the topics, the properties of the domains of expertise have to be documented in order to prepare for the derivation of management instruments in the last stage of the pro-

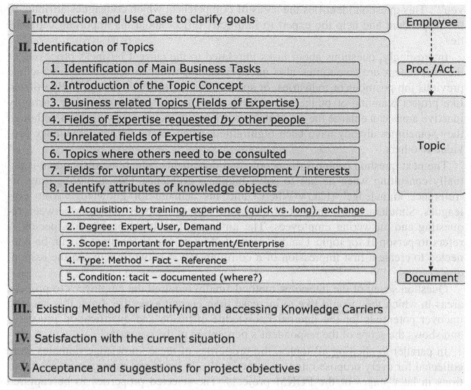

**Fig. 3.** Procedural Guide for capturing Knowledge intense Business Processes and its relation to the KM Entity Model

ject. The three elements process activities, related topics, and topic attributes should be captured in parallel in order to track the complete information about relations between the items.

Although it is quite easy to find out a limited set of three to five main business tasks of the respondent in subsection one, the subsequent steps of eliciting topics are difficult. In order to help the employee to understand the term topic, it was useful to give some first examples. Here, the interviewer team communicated, that it is interested in 'knowledge about something', e.g. knowledge about intranet maintenance, knowledge about the initiation of internal projects, knowledge about facility costs, knowledge about the buying behaviour of a certain customer, etc.

After explaining the element of interest for the project in question two, several areas where explored to identify a list of topics. As often, the required topics can not simply be asked and collected directly, a set of questions has been developed to help the interviewer in his discovery and elicitation process. Question three therefore is: 'Which of the topics you deal with in this process activity do you regard as interesting for other people?'. Strongly related and very helpful to view this area from the opposite perspective was question four: 'For which of your business topics people are getting in contact with you personally, by mail or by phone – What do they ask you?'. This question identifies the areas of competence, which colleagues attribute to the respondent and help the expert to indirectly reflect about his important capabilities.

Interestingly, questions about tasks unrelated to the current business processes of the respondent are sometimes also uncovering important topics. Examples include previous job positions or industries, or special abstract methods not currently utilized like project planning or budgeting methods. Examining such unrelated or currently inactive areas can enlarge the set of items achieved in the previous question, although they sometimes already have been highlighted, when asking for the knowledge provided to others.

The next question captures the people and documents, which the respondent is actually consulting when he has to solve business problems. This is highlighting his 'reference knowledge' (Know-Where) and his demand for knowledge from colleagues. Simultaneously, this set of questions help to uncover networks between requesting and answering employees. The answers of multiple people (i.e. person A refers to person B for topic 1 and is contacted by person B for topic 2) can be connected to create a first impression of a communication network between the respondents.

Question seven of the interview method finally required the employees to propose areas in which they would like to increase their current expertise. Later this helps to uncover potentials for the internal knowledge diffusion and qualification processes and shows the scope of the respondent's perception of the company.

In parallel to eliciting all topics, the properties of these knowledge domains were collected for every proposed item to improve the derivation of management interventions in later stages of the POKM projects. The selected properties to be captured included five elements: the way of acquisition, the degree of expertise, the scope of relevance, the type of knowledge, and the condition of the topic.

The first set of properties is related to the way by which the respondent acquired his expertise in the topic under consideration. This could be either done by training, by practical experience over time, or by exchanging with other colleagues. A further investigation can be done to document the effort needed to acquire the sufficient knowledge about the topic in order to find topics of importance which are hard to develop.

The next set of properties turned out to be very complex and included the evaluation of the degree of the respondent's expertise in every topic. This can be used as a proxy for the importance of the expert-topic-tupel and later helps to determine a limited number of important experts. The objective is to estimate the relevance of the topics proposed. Here the following interesting practical insights have been achieved.

The first approach of sorting the tasks and knowledge objects into issues of high or low level of expertise failed. The respective scaling approach reached from 1 for a domain which has been theoretically learned and practically applied often to 5 when the expert has only basic knowledge about that topic. Although this allows a detailed capturing of the levels of expertise, it was criticised and finally neglected by the workforce. They attributed an evaluation of their performance to this method and found it detrimental to their open and friendly corporate culture. They did not want to be assessed in such a numerical and quantitative way as it allowed to statistically compare the employees instead of respecting their overall contributions.

A second approach requested to sort the topics of expertise into a model of concentric circles in order to visually enable the employees to highlight the topics of biggest expertise and importance and hence put core competencies into the centre. However, this approach did also not succeed, which shows the difficulties of separating common routine tasks from expert tasks. The problem was to compare important expertise, which is used only rarely, with less exclusive topics which are used frequently.

Thus, it was finally decided to just work with two options: common topics versus topics of expertise. In addition to question four, two further questions were developed to help allocating topics into this dichotomy. The respondents were asked whether they do really 'feel home' in that topic and help others or whether it is just another topic related to their work, but where they not yet feel completely confident about. This question relates to the issue whether the knowledge of the employee in this topic is sufficient to consult others on that topic.

To define the scope of each topic, i.e. whether it is relevant for the enterprise, it can be identified, if the people who request topics from the respondents are coming from other departments. Further, the supervisor of the respective respondent can be consulted to rank the scope and the importance of the topics. From his broader perspective it can better be decided, in which fields the expert is most valuable to his or other departments. The supervisor usually already has some insights into the topics, because he discusses important fields for qualification in the semi-annual or annual employee development meeting together with the experts.

On an abstract level, a topic can be demanded and could hence be regarded as having a negative degree of expertise. For example, questions six and seven of the interview guide usually uncover topics, where there is such a demand for more knowledge: The respondent asks colleagues or wants to develop own skills. The employee can further be asked whether such topics are vital or nice to have. Later this demand can be matched with the expertise 'supply' of others.

The fourth important attribute of each topic is its type of knowledge. This could either be methodical knowledge (know how to do something), fact knowledge (know what) or reference knowledge (know where). This helps in the fourth step of the overall POKM project to identify the appropriate ways of managing the knowledge domains. For example, the employee knows where documents or people about certain engineering standards can be consulted. If this access should be important, it can be analysed how to reduce the effort and time to access this information. Similarly, the condition of the knowledge domain refers to the question, if the knowledge about the topic is tacit. A practical problem is that tacit knowledge objects could not easily be identified as they are often were not consciously perceived by the respondents. Here, the interviewer utilized the learning curve as a proxy for identifying tacit expertise: How long took the activity when conducted for the first time as opposed to now? How can this increase be explained (i.e. by which knowledge could it be achieved)?

If tacit elements are found, it could be analysed, if the tacit knowledge might be explicable and thus could be documented. If it is already explicated in a document, the subsequent question has to find out the location and the name of the document and has to explore if the respondent has been the author. This can later establish the relationship between the KM entities topic, document, and employee.

After the main part of identifying the relevant topics, in the third section of the interview guide the respondent was asked about the existing methods for identifying and accessing important knowledge carriers. This helps to understand the employment of different communication channels in the company ("By which media do you connect to the expert or the document?"). Further it allows a first insight about probable media which can be used for the resulting KM services, for example how promising would be an extension of the intranet functionality.

At the end of the interview the employees should express their expectations for the project. The project can use such answers to identify new aspects, derive priorities, and receive feedback to ideas proposed by the interviewer in the introductory sections. In the final section, the respondents evaluated the existing information structures and infrastructures. This is a very project specific question which requires preparatory supply of necessary documents from the preceding inventory method.

Next to this procedural guide for the interview, a tabular instrument was developed to aid the documentation of the topics' attributes (see Fig. 4). This allows to completely cover the generic KM entities [8] and their relations because every attribute can be associated to every topic to every business process and finally to every employee.

| our interview-partner: | | | |
|---|---|---|---|
| | Name | Tel | Date |
| | First name | e-mail | Duration |
| | Div. | Location | Interviewer |
| | List main Business tasks | | |

| Process Activities | Topic / Topic Map | Acquisition | | | Degree | | | Scope | Type | | | Condition |
|---|---|---|---|---|---|---|---|---|---|---|---|---|
| | | Basic Foundations | | | Consulting-level | Demanded | | relevant for Department or Enterprise | Method | Facts | Reference/ Name | explicit doc., implicit, explicable |
| | | via Training | Experience | Empl-exchange | | MUST | Helpful | | | | | |
| Projekt-planning | Project Activity Duration Estimation | | X | | X | | | D | X | | | expl.Doc. |
| | | | | | | | | | | | | |
| | | | | | | | | | | | | |
| | | | | | | | | | | | | |
| | | | | | | | | | | | | |
| | | | | | | | | | | | | |
| | | | | | | | | | | | | |
| | | | | | | | | | | | | |
| | | | | | | | | | | | | |

**Fig. 4.** Tabular tool for capturing properties of topics and their connection to processes

To improve the identification of priority topics among the hundreds of topics identified, three coloured diamond symbols were introduced to emphasize certain types of knowledge domains. A green diamond indicates topics with very limited distribution. Sometimes, only one respondent knew about a topic, which is very dangerous for the company. Red diamonds marked rare topics which were classified as important for external departments. Finally, a blue diamond represents topics which are not properly documented (i.e. explicated), but are relevant for the company. Using such symbols not only defines a limited set of very essential topics but also helps to identify key experts. However, it should be recognized that not every culture lends itself to an open publication of these priorities. It could cause a detrimental competition for special status and hence should only be visible to the personnel department.

## 4 Conclusion

This contribution first introduced a classification for approaches related to process oriented Knowledge Management. Within this field the BPO-KM, the PROMOTE, and the CommonKADS approach have been briefly reviewed. It could be concluded, that although the available procedural models discuss, what steps are important for KM projects, they hardly document how to actually execute the steps proposed in such practical applications. That is why this contribution introduced a practical method for process oriented KM (POKM) projects developed in two corporate cases. Together with a generic model of the relevant KM entities to be elicited and their relationships, this project procedure can set the framework for the specification of a detailed method for capturing knowledge intense processes. It extends the existing broad perspective on KM projects and approaches issues, like how to comprehensively capture expert processes, how to store the collected information in a structured way and how to design supporting instruments and materials in order to generate a high quality data set, which subsequently is utilized to derive Knowledge Management measures. It does not want to propose the only solution to the issue of how to capture knowledge-intensive business processes, but emphasizes the need for a discussion of a more detailed description within current KM project approaches. In the end, the capturing process determines the quality of the elicited dataset and is hence of major relevance for the success of the overall process oriented KM project.

## References

1. Abecker, A., Hinkelmann, K., Maus, H., Müller, H.J.: Integrationspotenziale für Geschäftsprozesse und Wissensmanagement (in German). In: Abecker, A., Hinkelmann, K., Maus, H., Müller, H.J. (eds.): Geschäftsprozessorientiertes Wissensmanagement: Effektive Wissensnutzung bei der Planung und Umsetzung von Geschäftsprozessen (in German). Springer-Verlag, Berlin Heidelberg New York Tokio (2002) 1-22
2. Heisig, P.: Wissensmanagement in industriellen Geschäftsprozessen (in German). Industrie Management 3, Gito-Verlag, Berlin (2003) 22-25
3. Hinkelmann, K., Karagiannis, D., Telesko, R.: PROMOTE – Methodologie und Werkzeuge für geschäftsprozessorientierten Wissensmanagement (in German). In: Abecker, A., Hinkelmann, K., Maus, H., Müller, H.J. (eds.): Geschäftsprozessorientiertes Wissensmanagement: Effektive Wissensnutzung bei der Planung und Umsetzung von Geschäftsprozessen (in German). Springer-Verlag, Berlin Heidelberg New York Tokio (2002) 65-90
4. Schreiber, G.: Online Presentation on CommonKADS.
   http://www.commonkads.uva.nl/frameset-commonkads.html (1997) Download 2004-07-01
5. Milton, N.: Information on Knowledge Acquisition.
   http://www.epistemics.co.uk/ Notes/37-0-0.htm (2003) Download 2004-07-01
6. Schreiber, G., Akkermans, H., Anjewierden, A., de Hoog, R. Shadbold, N., van der Velde, W., Wielinda, B.: Knowledge Engineering and Management, The CommonKADS Methodology. The MIT Press, Cambrigde (2000)
7. Trier, M.: Wissensmanagement und Geschäftsprozesse - Potentiale, Methoden und Anwendungsbeispiele (in German). Keynote Presentation for Berlin Meeting of GfO, Berlin (2002)

8. Trier, M.: IT-gestütztes Management virtueller Communities of Practice (in German). Extended Abstract of DoIT-Kongress Karlsruhe 2003.
http://www.integrata-stiftung.de/ files/p14_trier.pdf (2003) Download 2003-12-12

9. Gronau, N., Palmer, U., Schulte, K., Winkler, T.: Modellierung von wissensintensiven Geschäftsprozessen mit der Beschreibungssprache K-Modeler (in German) In: Reimer, U. Abecker A., Staab S., Stumme G., (eds.): Professionelles Wissensmanagement – Erfahrungen und Visionen (in German). Proceedings GI 2003  (2003) 315-322

10. Krallmann, H., Frank, H., Gronau, N.: Systemanalyse im Unternehmen: Vorgehensmodelle, Modellierungsverfahren und Gestaltungsoptionen (in German). 4th edn. Oldenbourg Verlag, Munich Wien (2002)

# The Concept of Elimination of Barriers to the Implementation of Integrated Systems with the Use of I-CASE Tools

Witold Chmielarz

The University of Warsaw, Faculty of Management
vitec@post.pl

**Abstract.** The main objective of this paper is the analysis of the possibilities of overcoming barriers to the implementation of integrated systems with the use of specialised software supporting the implementation process (modelers and constructors) and the use of reference models in integrated systems. Firstly, the basic implementation problems are identified. Subsequently, we shall move on to discuss the possible steps to overcoming these barriers with the use of I-CASE tools and knowledge contained in reference models, and the concept of a knowledge management system supporting this process.

## 1 Introduction

Empirical research shows that there is a simple relationship between the complexity and innovativeness of a project and the feasibility of its implementation. The more innovative and complex a project is, the more likely it is that its implementation will be delayed or even discontinued. In the case of integrated systems, this rule applies now to as many as 70% - 80% of the projects. Obviously, the implementation firms use their best efforts to prevent it, but most of their actions are focused on two main directions:

improvement of tools supporting the process of automatic analysis, design and implementation of systems, mainly with the aim to use knowledge management tools in the process,
improvement of interpersonal relations management as part of project management.

This paper is focused on the former group of issues and methods of preventing most frequent implementation problems.

The following diagram illustrates the relationship between the complexity of a project and the feasibility of its implementation.

The following procedure can be followed in order to overcome barriers and threats to the implementation of an integrated system [1]:

Undoubtedly, the first step to overcome implementation barriers is to identify the areas where such barriers appear, and the reasons why they appear.
The second step is to define the methods of removing these barriers.
The third step is to identify the barriers which can be eliminated or at least significantly reduced using the methods of knowledge management contained in the intelligent tools supporting the process of designing and changing the systems.

D. Karagiannis and U. Reimer (Eds.): PAKM 2004, LNAI 3336, pp. 251–258, 2004.
© Springer-Verlag Berlin Heidelberg 2004

The next step is to identify the tools and methods used to assist the designer and implementator in this respect.

The last step is to create a concept of automation of the process of preventing barriers to integrated systems implementation.

The successive stages of this procedure are presented in the next sections of this paper.

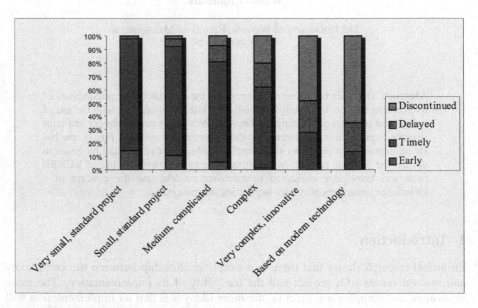

**Fig. 1.** Relationship between project complexity and success of its implementation

## 2   Identification of the Areas Where Implementation Barriers Appear

The following table summarises the most frequent implementation barriers, the reasons why they occur and the methods of their prevention [3].

**Table 1.** Problems and reasons why implementation barriers occur

| Types of problems | Reasons |
|---|---|
| **Organisational problems** | |
| 1. *Problems with the correct assessment of a company's condition*<br>• A lack of organisational documentation<br>• A lack of technical documentation<br>• Inadequate assessment of the resources | • Insufficient information at the client<br>• Documentation not updated properly, a lack of a management system, people, wrong solutions<br>• A lack of HR policy |

| Types of problems | Reasons |
|---|---|
| **2. Problems with the correct analysis of the needs**<br>• A lack of a company development vision at the client<br>• A lack of precise goals<br>• A lack of operating procedures | • A lack of awareness of the company's needs |
| **3. Problems with preparation of a reliable implementation schedule (plan)**<br>• Correct assessment of the amount of time necessary for the implementation | • Incorrect analyses<br>• Excessive rush<br>• Desire to win tender procedures |
| **4. Problems with defining the necessary conditions of efficient implementation**<br>• Undefined or unfeasible requirements<br>• A lack of methodology or procedures | • Incorrect analyses<br>• Undefined requirements<br>(including the working hours of end-users) |
| **5. Problems with application of implementation methodology** | • Unfamiliarity with the methodology<br>• Deviations from the methodology |
| **6. Problems with correct preparation of documentationk** | • Poorly qualified staff<br>• Problems with timcly preparation of documentation<br>• Frequent changes of the concept |
| **7. Problems with users and their selection** | • A lack of substitute staff<br>• Allocation of inadequate end-users<br>• Late identification of a problem<br>• Psychological barrier – a need to change the method of work |
| **8. Problems with consultants and their selection** | • Shortage of consultants on the market<br>• Inadequate company policy (no training)<br>• Outflow abroad |
| **9. Problems with training** | • A lack of ready-made training courses<br>• A lack of training programmes<br>• Inadequate training plans<br>• Poor training efficiency – no discipline<br>• Savings on the project |
| **10. Problems with project execution** | • Frequent changes of execution plan, scope etc.<br>• Imprecise contract<br>• Changes among project staff |
| **Psychological problems** | |
| **11. Problems with reaching understanding between the consultants and end-users** | • Cultural differences<br>• Wrong composition of the implementation team<br>• Clash of personalities<br>• Conflicts within the client's team<br>• A lack of division of responsibilities within the implementation team |

| Types of problems | Reasons |
|---|---|
| 12. *A lack of understanding of the implementation needs* | • No information about the implementation objectives <br> • No global vision – excessive focus on details |
| 13. *Hostile attitude of employees* | • Fear of losing jobs <br> • A lack of motivation <br> • A lack of faith in the success of the project <br> • Fear of the need to improve qualifications |
| **Financial problems** | |
| 14. *A lack of means* | • Insufficient IT budget <br> • Temporary problems on the market |
| 15. *Pseudo-savings* <br> • Purchase of a limited version of the system <br> • Purchase of an older version <br> • Giving up training | • Misunderstanding of the needs <br> • A lack of reserves |
| **Technological problems** | |
| 16. *Excessive customisation – tailoring of the system to the client's needs* | • Misunderstanding of the system's logic <br> • Wrong definition of the needs |
| 17. *A lack of security* | • Disregard for safety |

## 3   The Role of I-CASE Tools in Solving Implementation Problems

CASE tools are useful in solving many of the problems presented above. Below we discuss the application of such tools in solving the aforementioned problems [2,3].

- Re: problem 1. Preliminary training of end-users in CASE methodology helps them understand the consultants' expectations as to the scope and quality of the required data.
- Re: 2. In-depth training of end-users in CASE methodology is recommended. Subsequently, the main procedures describing the elementary business processes at the client's company should be prepared by the client in cooperation with the consultants. Ideally, the client should develop such procedures using its own resources (as much as possible) with as little assistance from the consultants as possible. In this way, end-users are forced to get to know the tool well and, first and foremost, study the existing and planned procedures in depth. This approach has the following advantages: involvement of the client in the implementation from the very beginning, understanding of the main ideas and assumptions of the implementation – a common platform of understanding, making the client partly responsible for the implementation and reduction of involvement of the consultants.
- Re: 3. CASE is used indirectly – the use of this tool for problems 1 and 2 has resulted in obtaining good quality „as is" and „to be" analyses and ensured compliance with the methodology.

- Re: 6. Problems with preparation of documentation – the application of CASE has measurable advantages – the whole processes are automatically documented as they are developed. All changes to the processes introduced during the implementation are also documented. Moreover, the tools of certain vendors allow automatic configuration of the system for end-users. As a result, a considerable part of the documentation is automated.
- Re: 8. The use of CASE allows significant reduction of the time needed for implementation and the time of work of the consultants. As a result, the existing resources (the consultants) are utilised better.
- Re: 9. Problems with training. In this case, the use of CASE tools may be the best solution. On the basis of the previously developed business processes (item 2), the training needs of the client are defined, and the end-user training is focused on the aforementioned processes only. In this case, it is sufficient to study the implementation plan and determine when end-users should be trained in the particular processes. Training is based on previously prepared (item 2) models of business processes. This approach allows elimination of unnecessary elements from training, thus increasing the absorption of the remaining material. As a result, training becomes more effective and can be shorter.
- Re: 11. Problems with understanding – end-users and other employees of the client involved in the implementation, including the management (items 1 and 2), obtain knowledge about the CASE tool used. Subsequently, a ready-made (predefined) solution is presented and discussed. In this way, the existing and modified business models containing all basic processes functioning at a given company become a platform of understanding.
- Re: 12. Presentation of processes subject to changes with the use of CASE helps the employees understand the objectives and needs of the implementation.
- Re: 13. If the implementation process becomes faster and more efficient, the results are achieved earlier, which has an encouraging effect and increases faith in success.
- Re: 16. Excessive customisation – presentation of the existing and planned business processes allows end-users to understand their nature and find the optimum solution, which increases the chances for avoiding unnecessary and costly customisations.

The analysis presented above shows that there are several important factors which allow elimination of problems occurring during system implementation. The main one is the use of CASE tools, which is useful in 10 out of 17 cases. The second important element is the application of the remaining part of implementation methodology (which is often integrated with a CASE tool). The third factor concerns the HR issues to be considered during the implementation. The fourth one is finance.

## 4  Decision-Making Support Model for Implementation Processes

Further research should focus on development of a model which would allow automatic reduction of the effect of barriers on the implementation process.

Collection of data for the management of such a process has been presented earlier in this paper. Identification of barriers on the one hand, and identification of the methods of eliminating them on the other suggest that plans of transformation of barriers into solutions for the individual, predefined cases should be developed in the next step. However, this process is extremely difficult for the following reasons:

- The amount of data in the implementations of integrated systems is now growing exponentially. A lot of such data must be stored for a long time, while masses of new data are added continuously (parameterisation of applications – the system cannot start until thousands of parameters are entered),
- Only a small portion of this data is subsequently used for making decisions,
- A growing amount of external information, which nowadays changes rapidly, has a significant impact on internal decisions,
- Data necessary for decision-making can be accumulated in different computer subsystems, databases, formats and languages (both programming and human),
- There are great many tools supporting data selection for management purposes,
- Security, quality and integrity of data in a system constitute a critical success factor for systems implementation in the economic reality.

One could expect that the application of knowledge management solutions would solve such problems related to automation of the solutions of identified problems with integrated system implementation. Transformation of data into knowledge, which is necessary to make decisions, can take very different forms. The following diagram shows a generalised method of transformation. Data is initially accumulated in a database. Subsequently, following preliminary processing, it is stored in data warehouses. In order to make the knowledge contained in such data available for management purposes, the data undergoes transformation to prepare it for a detailed analysis. This analysis is performed with the use of automatic search tools. The final transformation stage involves a comparison of data found with models (of behaviour, reactions) stored in intelligent systems, which allow interpretation of the obtained comparisons. The ultimate outcome of such comparisons is an assessment of usefulness of generalised information for management purposes and accumulation of such information, along with data, in the knowledge base.

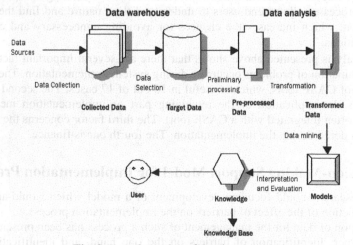

**Fig. 2.** Transformation of data into knowledge

The process of bringing out useful knowledge from mass data is called knowledge management. Knowledge management is the effective use of information-handling techniques by the user to improve the efficiency of organisation management processes.

The process of behavioural models development seems the most difficult step towards transformation of information into knowledge. In this case, it involves allocation of alternative solutions for every implementation barrier: on the one hand, solutions aimed at preventing barriers with the use of I-CASE tools, and on the other – social methods (management of the Company's human potential). Adding the interpretation of these solutions (putting them in a specified business context), and an assessment of their feasibility (or probability of success) in every analysed case leads directly towards automation of decisions made in the process, and indirectly – towards construction of a tool supporting this process. In a deterministic case (full identification) it can be based on creating cause-and-effect relations between the blackboards of barriers and methods of their prevention (or at least reduction of their effects); in a non-deterministic case – blackboard architecture based on diluted models [4]. The following diagram illustrates the former case.

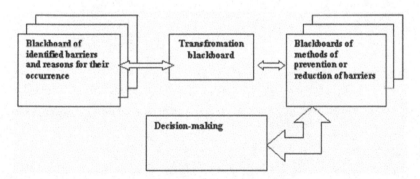

**Fig. 3.** The concept of a model of transformation of models into a knowledge base

Development of this concept will lead to construction of a tool supporting the decision-making process for the end-user and allowing automatic selection of a method minimising the limitations of the integrated systems implementation process.

# References

1. Chmielarz W., P. Krajewski: Mechanizmy dostosowań w implementacji systemów wspomagających zarządzanie na przykładzie BaaN Orgware; in the materials for the conference: "Interakcja Człowiek-Komputer'99"; Gdańsk, 1999, pp. 225-236,
2. Chmielarz W.: Model procesu zarządzania potencjałem społecznym w etapie planowania projektu informatycznego, in the materials for the conference: "Human-Computer Interaction 2001 (Interakcja Człowiek-Komputer'2001) w reorganizacji procesów gospodarczych i tworzeniu zintegrowanych systemów informacyjnych" edited by B. Kubiak, A. Korowicki,; Gdańsk, 2001, pp. 343-358,

3. Krajewski P.: Modelowanie z wykorzystaniem narzędzi CASE na potrzeby wdrożenia ZSWZ klasy ERP, in the materials for the conference: "Human-Computer Interaction 2001 (Interakcja Człowiek-Komputer'2001) w reorganizacji procesów gospodarczych i tworzeniu zintegrowanych systemów informacyjnych" edited by B. Kubiak, A. Korowicki,; Gdańsk, 2001, pp. 541-550.
4. Orłowski C.; E. Szczerbicki „Application of Blackboard Architecture in Concurrent Environment for IT project Management", in: "Komputerowo Zintegrowane Zarządzanie", edited by R. Knosala, WNT, Warszawa, 2004, vol.II, pp. 249-254.

# XAROP: A Midterm Report in Introducing a Decentralized Semantics-Based Knowledge Sharing Application

Christoph Tempich[1], Marc Ehrig[1], Christiaan Fluit[2], Peter Haase[1],
Esteve Lladó Martí[4], Michal Plechawski[3], and Steffen Staab[1]

[1] Institute AIFB, University of Karlsruhe, 76128 Karlsruhe, Germany
{ehrig,haase,staab,tempich}@aifb.uni-karlsruhe.de
[2] Aduna, Amersfoort, The Netherlands
Christiaan.Fluit@aduna.biz
[3] Empolis, Warsaw, Poland
Michal.Plechawski@empolis.pl
[4] Fundación IBIT
esteve@ibit.org
http://swap.semanticweb.org

**Abstract.** Knowledge management solutions relying on central repositories sometimes have not met expectations, since users often create knowledge ad-hoc using their individual vocabulary and using their own individual IT infrastructure (e.g., their laptop). To improve knowledge management for such decentralized and individualized knowledge work, it is necessary to, first, provide a corresponding decentralized IT infrastructure and to, second, deal with specific problems such as security and semantic heterogeneity. In this paper, we describe the technical peer-to-peer platform that we have built and summarize some of our experiences applying the platform in case study for coopetitioning organizations in the tourism sector.

## 1 Introduction

Knowledge management solutions relying on central repositories sometimes have not met expectations, since users often create knowledge ad-hoc using their individual vocabulary and using their own individual IT infrastructure (e.g., their laptop). [1] provide an explanation for the failed cases. They argue that traditional knowledge management systems take on a traditional managerial control paradigm, while subjectivity and sociality are essential features of knowledge creation and sharing. From that point they overhaul the traditional architecture of knowledge management systems towards a more decentralized architecture.

This general observation is supported by our own case study, which we pursued in the course of the SWAP project[1]. The case study is in the tourism domain of the Balearic Islands. The needs of the tourism industry there are best described by the term 'coopetition'. On the one hand the different organizations *compete* for customers against each

---

[1] http://swap.semanticweb.org/

D. Karagiannis and U. Reimer (Eds.): PAKM 2004, LNAI 3336, pp. 259–270, 2004.

other. On the other hand, they must *cooperate* in order to provide high quality for regional touristic issues like infrastructure, facilities, clean environment, or safety – that are critical for them to be able to compete against other tourism destinations. Working based on traditional, centralized knowledge management systems is infeasible, since no single organization can control all processes.

Although the need for decentralized knowledge management solutions is obvious, the field of solutions is still very limited. Two technologies are currently emerging as candidate solutions. On the communication level peer-to-peer (P2P) networks provide the means to connect the different participants (*cf.* [2]) while ontologies can provide the necessary expressivity on the representation level [3].

As for peer-to-peer networks one can distinguish three separate levels: *viz.* infrastructure, application and community level(*cf.* [4]). The P2P infrastructure provides basic mechanisms to communicate, security mechanisms, resource identification and peer identification. The P2P application provides services to the users supporting their process needs. P2P communities comprise the social activities which are enabled by the P2P paradigm.

Our use of ontology-based knowledge representation lies orthogonal to the three levels of the P2P network. The use of semantic descriptions of data sources stored by peers and indeed of semantic descriptions of peers themselves alleviates current problems on all three levels as we will show in the remainder.

In this paper we describe our experiences in introducing a peer-to-peer based knowledge management application. The application is built around and takes advantage of ontologies at the three different levels mentioned before. Before we start to explain this interaction, we briefly introduce the organizational setting of our case study (Section 2). From the case study we have derived several technical requirements (Section 3) for our application. The requirements led us first to an architecture for a semantically enriched peer-to-peer application (Section 4), and second to a number of new methods (Section 5). We finalize the paper with a summary of the case study (Section 6) and lessons learned (Section 6), a reference to the related work (Section 7) and the conclusion (Section 8).

## 2   Organizational Context

The case study we consider here is based in the tourism sector of the Balearic Islands. A number of organizations participating in the case study want to collaborate on some regional issues. Therefore they now collect and share information about *indicators* reflecting the impact of growing population and tourist fluxes in the islands, their environment and their infrastructures. Moreover, these indicators can be used to make predictions and help planning. For instance, organizations that require *Quality & Hospitality management* use the information to better plan, for example, their marketing campaigns. As another example, a governmental agency, a Balearic Government's coordination center of telematics, provides the local industry with information about *new technologies* that can help the tourism industry to better perform their tasks.

Due to the different working areas and objectives of the collaborating organizations, it proved impossible to set up a centralized knowledge management system or even a completly centralized ontology. The case study partners asked explicitly for a system without a central server, where knowledge sharing is integrated into the normal work, but where very different kinds of information could be easily shared with others.

## 3   Requirements

From a technical point of view, the different organizations can be seen as one or many independently operating nodes within a "knowledge" network. Nodes can join or disconnect from the network at any moment and can live or act independently of the behavior of other nodes in the system. A node may perform several tasks. The most important one is that it acts as a peer in the network, so it can communicate with other nodes to achieve its goals. But apart from that it may act as an interface to interact with the human user of the network, or it may access knowledge sources to accomplish its tasks. One node may have one or more knowledge sources associated with it. These sources contain the information that a peer can make available to other peers. Examples are a user's filesystem and mail folders or a locally installed database.

A node must be designed to meet the following requirements that arise from the task of sharing information from the external sources with other peers: *Integration:* Each piece of knowledge requires metadata about its origin. To retrieve external information, the metadata needs to capture information about where the piece of information was obtained from. This information will allow to identify a peer and locate resources in its repositories.

*Information Heterogeneity:* As each peer may use its own local ontology, the distributed information is inherently heterogeneous. Mappings may be required, e.g. to overcome the heterogenous labelling of the same objects. However, in most cases some of the defined structures are very similar to each other. A general process is needed to identify commonalities and make them explicit.

*Security:* Some information may be of private nature and should not be visible to other peers. Other information may be restricted to a specific set of peers.

*Presentation:* In a peer-to-peer network queries are forwarded to different peers. Due to different network latencies and resources on the answering machines, answers can come at any time. Hence, the interface must help the user to distinguish between recent and old results, must update itself from time to time and should visualize where results come from.

*Network Efficiency:* In peer-to-peer systems a general problem is, to distribute the queries in the network. Since, the number of messages increases exponentially with the number of hops a query is allowed to travel, intelligent query routing algorithms are required when the size of the network grows.

## 4   The SWAP Platform

In the SWAP project, we have build the generic platform SWAPSTER to account for the general need of sharing semantic-based information in P2P fashion[2]. Based on SWAP-

---

[2] Bibster [5] is another solution for a different case.

STER we have developed a semantic and P2P based knowledge management solution appropriate for the case study sketched above. The latter is called XAROP i.e. Catalan for syrup.

XAROP nodes wrap knowledge from their local sources (files, e-mails, etc.). Nodes ask for and retrieve knowledge from their peers. For communicating knowledge, XAROP transmits RDF structures [6], which are used to convey conceptual structures (e.g., the definition of what an indicator for airtravel is) as well as corresponding data (e.g., data about the number of arrivals by plane). For structured queries as well as for keyword queries, XAROP uses SeRQL, an SQL-like query language that allows for queries combining the conceptual and the data level and for returning newly constructed RDF-structures.

In the following we describe only the XAROP components that we refer to later in this document.

*Knowledge Sources:* Peers may have local sources of information such as the local file system, e-mail directories, local databases or bookmark lists. These local information sources represent the peer's body of knowledge as well as its basic vocabulary. These sources of information are the place where a peer can physically store information (documents, web pages) to be shared on the network.

*Knowledge Source Integrator:* The Knowledge Source Integrator is responsible for the extraction and integration of internal and external knowledge sources into the Local Node Repository. This task comprises (1) means to access local knowledge sources and extract an RDF(S) representation of the stored knowledge, (2) the selection of the RDF statements to be integrated into the Local Node Repository and (3) the annotation of the statements with metadata.

*Local Node Repository:* The local node repository stores all information and its meta information a peer wants to share with remote peers. It allows for query processing and view building. The repository is implemented on top of Sesame [7].

*User Interface:* The User Interface of the peer provides individual views on the information available in local sources as well as on information on the network. The views can be implemented using different visualization techniques (topic hierarchies, thematic maps, etc). One part of the user interface is the *Edit* component. The *Edit* component allows the user to supervise the mapping process and enables light weight ontology engineering.

*Communication Adapter:* This component is responsible for the network communication between peers. Our current implementation of the Communication Adapter is build on the JXTA framework [8].

*Information and Meta-information.* Information is represented as RDF(S) statements in the repository. The SWAP meta model[3] (*cf.* [9]) provides meta-information about the statements in the local node repository in order to memorize where the statements came from and other meta-information.

Besides the SWAP meta data model the SWAP environment builds on the SWAP common ontology[4]. The SWAP common model defines concepts for *e.g.* File and

---

[3] http://swap.semanticweb.org/2003/01/swap-peer#
[4] http://swap.semanticweb.org/2003/01/swap-common#

Folder. Purpose of these classes is to provide a common model for information usually found on a peer participating in a knowledge management network.

*Querying for Data.* SeRQL [10] is an SQL like RDF query language. The main feature of SeRQL is the ability to define structured output in terms of an RDF graph that does not necessarily coincide with the model that has been queried. This feature is essential for defining personalized views in the repository of a XAROP peer.

# 5   Method Description on the Three P2P Levels

In this section we explain some of the methods that are most crucial to the XAROP knowledge management solution at the infrastructure, application or community level. Because of space restriction we skip over parts that are only of longer term interest, such as scalability towards a larger P2P network, which we have explore in another case study in somewhat more depth [5].

## 5.1   Infrastructure Level: A Distributed Security Framework

Security considerations are of particular concern within a peer-to-peer framework. Users of a P2P system want to be sure that they give access to local resources only to trusted persons. Furthermore, they want to define different access control levels to their local knowledge, since they might trust different participants to various extent. While these consideration in themselves are difficult to handle, the security mechanism in a P2P system must be straightforward to define.

For authentication we use a public-key infrastructure (PKI) infrastructure with certificate authorities established within XAROP. A certain XAROP node acts as a root certificate authority for the XAROP system, all other peers will configure this node as trusted root certificate authority. In small networks, this certificate authority will issue certificates directly for users, whereas in large networks, it is possible to build a hierarchy of certificate authorities. The certificate creation will be done offline, on the configuration level. Certificates themselves will not be transmitted within the standard SWAP user interface.

The access control model has to be based on rules, since we cannot demand from users that they will enumerate privileged users for each local resource. The rules have to base on strict facts with proven origin (i.e. signed by the peer that generates a fact). A simple rule gives access for a single document (*e.g.* SWAP.doc) to a single, fixed person (*e.g.* Esteve). More complex rules are based on knowledge about both people and resources (All people involved in SWAP project can download all documents from my SWAP folder). All access control rights have to be explicit. Otherwise we assume that access is not allowed.

Further, the right to decide about the access properties of peers can be delegated to other peers. A person that we delegate the right to can be fixed or described by a similar pattern, forming a chain of trust (*e.g.* All people, about which Esteve said that they are involved in SWAP, and Mariusz said that they work for empolis, can download all my documents about SWAP). The access properties have to be digitally signed by the peer who assigned them.

*Example for IBIT.* IBIT needs access control based on organization boundaries. On the other hand, it is not acceptable for an average user to be forced to create and maintain organizational information by herself. Using the described security model for the IBIT case an average user has to define (1) their administrator and (2) access control rules for his local resources. Administrators, define and maintain information about (1) organizational structures and (2) user membership to organizations.

## 5.2  Application Level: Dealing with Semantic Heterogeneity and Visualization

**Heterogenity.** Semantic mapping between ontologies is a necessary precondition to establish interoperation, i.e. overcoming the heterogeneity between peers using different ontologies. When we tried to apply existing tools [11, 12] to our scenario, we found that existing mapping methods were not suitable for the ontology integration task at hand. They have laid focus exclusively on improving the effectiveness and neglected efficiency, which becomes an issue already with the ontologies required in the context of Xarop. It is not sufficient to provide its user with the best possible mapping, it is also necessary to answer his queries within a few seconds – even if the two peers use two different ontologies and have never encountered each other before.

We briefly introduce the process that our approach follows [13]. It is started with two ontologies, which are going to be mapped onto one another, as its input. Mapping one ontology onto another means that for each entity (concept, relation, or instance) in ontology, we try to find a corresponding entity, which has the same intended meaning, in ontology. *Feature engineering* transforms the initial representation of ontologies into a format digestible for the similarity calculations such as RDFS. In a naive approach all entities of the first ontology are compared with all entities of the second ontology (*search steps*). However, in our approach we use heuristics to lower the number of candidate mappings. In specific, this means to compare pairs with similar labels or pairs for which neighboring entities have been assigned a mapping. The *similarity computation* measures are needed to compare the features of ontological entities. The features need to be extracted from extensional and intensional ontology definitions such as URIs, RDF/S primitives such as *subclass*, or domain specific features. Extremely costly features, in terms of runtime complexity, are replaced by less costly features. Then "String Similarity" measures the similarity of two strings on a scale from 0 to 1 based on Levenshtein's edit distance [14]; "SimSet" is used to compare sets of entities based on measures used for multidimensional scaling [15]. In general, there are several similarity values for a candidate pair of entities. These must be aggregated into a single aggregated similarity value. This is achieved through a summarization and normalization of adjusted similarity values. A similarity value above a certain threshold finally implies a mapping (*interpretation*). Several *iterations* of similarity calculations are needed to receive meaningful results. The returned output is a mapping table.

In first evaluation runs we have shown that our approach for identifying mappings between two ontologies is on a par with other good state-of-the-art algorithms concerning the quality of proposed mappings, while outperforming them with respect to efficiency. Using an approach combining many features to determine mappings clearly leads to significantly higher quality mappings. The here used approach is faster than standard prominent approaches by a factor of 10 to 100. This makes the presented method a valid approach for the Xarop scenario.

**Visualization.** We have developed the Cluster Map [16], for visualizing populated, light-weight ontologies as used for XAROP. It visualizes the instances of a number of selected classes from a hierarchy, organized by their classifications. Figure 1 shows an example Cluster Map, visualizing documents, classified according to topics discussed in those documents. The dark gray spheres represent ontology classes (the topics), with an attached label stating their name and cardinality. When a subclass relation holds between two classes, they are connected by a directed edge. The light yellow spheres represent instances. Balloon-shaped edges connect instances to the class(es) they belong to. Instances with the same class membership are grouped in clusters. Our example contains two clusters, one of them showing overlap between the two classes. Cluster Maps contain a lot of information about the instantiation of the classes, specifically exploiting the overlaps between them. For example, figure 1 shows that the "original lucerne" folder class has a significant overlap with the "swap idea". Such observations can trigger hypotheses about the available information and the domain in general. The graph layout algorithm used by the Cluster Map is a variant of the well-known family of spring embedder algorithms. Its outcome results in the geometric closeness of objects indicating their semantic closeness: classes that share instances are located near each other, and so are instances with the same or similar class memberships.

The Cluster Map is embedded in a highly interactive GUI, which is designed for browsing-oriented exploration of the populated ontology. Users can subsequently create visualizations of a number of classes by marking the check boxes in the class tree on the left pane. The software can animate the transition from one visualization to the next, showing how the instances are regrouped in clusters. Through interaction a user can also retrieve information about the specific documents that are contained in a class or cluster.

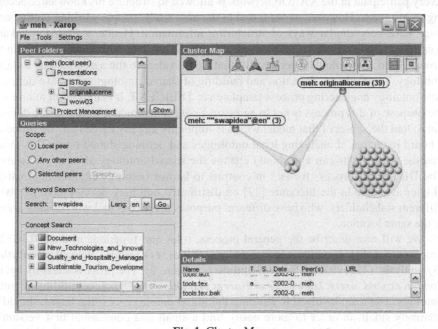

**Fig. 1.** Cluster Map.

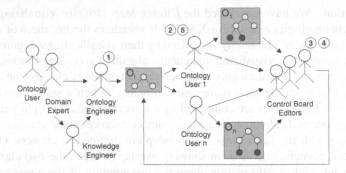

**Fig. 2.** Roles and functions in distributed ontology engineering.

Further the visualization can be fine-tuned in several ways, in order to support certain tasks, or improve scalability. In the context of XAROP it was important to account for the particularities of P2P systems. Hence, the results are marked with the peer name they are coming from. Results are added to the Cluster Map incrementally, since not all peers answer at the same time. New results are highlighted. The search can be stopped when the user is satisfied. Thus it provides the usability requirements needed for the XAROP system.

### 5.3 Community Level: The Distributed Ontology Engineering Process

Every participant in the XAROP network is allowed to structure his knowledge according to his needs. However, as we found in the case study, people working on the same issue have very similar ways of structuring information. Hence, a first step towards community building is to raise awareness about the existing commonalities within the group. From an ontological perspective that is equivalent to the agreement on a shared ontology. To enable the detection and building of shared ontologies we have defined a new ontology engineering process template *viz.* DILIGENT. It is important to note that the purpose of this process is not to agree on a conceptual model for the entire domain, but to find the subset of that model which is implicitly already agreed on. We introduce a board in charge of analyzing local ontologies and defining shared ones. This means that the participants can and should change the shared ontology after its publication. The DILIGENT process focuses in contrast to known ontology engineering methodologies available in the literature [17] on distributed ontology development involving different stakeholders, who have different purposes and needs and who usually are not at the same location.

We will now describe the general process, roles and functions in the DILIGENT process (cf. [18]). It comprises five main activities: (1) **build**, (2) **local adaptation**, (3) **analysis**, (4) **revision**, (5) **local update** (*cf.* figure 2). The process starts by having *domain experts, users, knowledge engineers* and *ontology engineers* **build**ing an initial ontology. The team involved in building the initial ontology, *viz.* the board, should be relatively small, in order to more easily find a small and consensual first version of the shared ontology. Moreover, we do not require completeness of the initial shared ontology with respect to the domain. On the first sight it seems contradictory that the case study partners do not want to share a common infrastructure but a shared ontology. However, the existence of a shared domain, overlapping or related competencies within organizations and the need for carrying out certain functions in cooperation suggests that it is possible to develop ontologies shared by the different sub-communities.

Once the product is made available, users can start using it and **locally adapting** it for their own purposes. Typically, due to new business requirements, or user and organization changes, their local ontologies evolve in a similar way as folder hierarchies in a file system. In their local environment they are free to change the reused shared ontology. However, they are not allowed to directly change the ontology shared by all users. Furthermore, the control board collects change requests to the shared ontology.

The board **analyzes** the local ontologies and the requests and tries to identify similarities in the users' ontologies. Since not all of the changes introduced or requested by the users will be introduced[5], a crucial activity of the board is deciding which changes are going to be introduced in the next version of the shared ontology. The input from users provides the necessary arguments to underline change requests. A balanced decision that takes into account the different needs of the users and meets user's evolving requirements[6] has to be found. The board should regularly **revise** the shared ontology, so that local ontologies do not diverge too far from the shared ontology. Therefore, the board should have a well-balanced and representative participation of the different kinds of participants involved in the process.

Once a new version of the shared ontology is released, users can **update** their own **local** ontologies to better use the knowledge represented in the new version. Even if the differences are small, users may rather reuse e.g. the new concepts instead of using their previously locally defined concepts that correspond to the new concepts represented in the new version.

# 6   The Case Study

More concretely four organizations including 21 peers took part in the case study and it is expected that the total number of organizations will grow by 7 to a total of 28 peers until September 2004.

*Early Experiences.*   In a collaboration effort the KEEx [2] system was distributed among the participants in an early stage of the project. In the distributed version of KEEx users could share file, email and bookmark folders and the corresponding documents with the participants. Additionally to a keyword based query mechanism they could look at the contents of other participants folders. Furthermore they were able to provide manual mappings between their own folders and remote folders. This made it possible to query for remote documents by means of the local folder structure. From this early experiment we could draw two main conclusions which led us to our current solution. Our first conclusion was, that keyword based querying is not sufficient in the

---

[5] The idea in this kind of development is not to merge all user ontologies.

[6] This is actually one of the trends in modern software engineering methodologies (see Rational Unified Process).

context of the case study, since three different languages were in use and the search suffered from low precision. The performance of the search was improved by the use of a folder based approach. Our second conclusion was, that some users are willing to provided mappings between their structures and remote structures, but the additional effort to keep them updated is prohibitive.

*Current Status.* With XAROP users can share different kinds of folders and the corresponding documents. In the setup phase of the application users must define which information they want to share with whom. Additionally to the security infrastructure we introduced a small but shared ontology, to reduce the cost of mapping provision. Local documents can be associated automatically and manually with the concepts of the shared ontology. Participants can thus query for the content of others also with the concepts of the ontology. The shared ontology can be extended by the participants individually. The manual association task between documents and concepts was eased in two ways. Firstly, users could associate entire folder sub trees with certain concepts. Secondly, users could import their local folder structures and use the mapping tool to search automatically for correspondences between their local structures and the shared ontology. The mapping tool can also be used to search for correspondences between local and remote structures. When all participants had worked with the system for several days the board – comprising two domain experts and two ontology engineers – came together to analyze the changes made to the common ontology. The board could identify several concepts which are shared implicitly by all users. After some discussion the board decided to slightly change the shared ontology and redistribute a new version.

*Lessons Learned.* The case study helped us to better comprehend the use of ontologies in a peer-to-peer environment in general. The first lesson we learn is that security is the single most important issue in inter-organizational knowledge exchange. Without appropriate security mechanism users are not willing to share any information. Additionally to the implemented security mechanisms the participants would also like to know, who downloads which information. The possibility to grant access to certain documents on a 'per-query' base, was also requested. They could thus decide on query time which documents to share with whom.

On the application level we made the observation that the combination of keyword based and concept based search helps users to refine their query according to their information needs. At this point the ease of use of our user interface is very important. However, we must still work on the system and make it more light weight since not all participants work with the latest available computer equipment. Our mapping algorithm provides first suggestions for possible mappings very early, although these might be revised when the algorithm proceeds. This behavior was appreciated by most users.

Regarding the community level, the shared ontology was quickly accepted. Even so our users did understand the ontology mainly as a classification hierarchy for their documents and did not create instances of the defined concepts. Our expectation that the collaborative ontology engineering effort raised community awareness was met. Some of the participants changed their own folder structures in order to adhere to the commonly defined shared ontology. Other participants extended and changed it a bit. Later on this was the input for a refinement of the original ontology.

In spite of the technical challenges, user feedback was very positive since (i) the tool was integrated into their daily work environment and could be easily used and (ii) the tool provided very beneficial support to perform their tasks.

# 7 Related Work

Knowledge management in Peer-to-Peer systems is the topic of various active research projects. Edutella [19] provides an RDF-based infrastructure for exchanging metadata in P2P applications. The Edutella Query Service is intended to be a standardized query exchange mechanism for RDF metadata stored in distributed RDF repositories. The Edutella project focuses on the education community. The Edamok project [2] also deals with distributed knowledge management in Peer-to-Peer systems and provides advanced facilities for mapping knowledge structures. However, neither of the systems is accompanied with an overall process for decentralized knowledge management on the community level. [20] presents a commercial P2P solution. They emphasize the organizational difficulties and the security concerns of the participants when introducing their P2P application. The system does not provide semantics-based representation of knowledge, and thus allows only for keyword-based queries.

# 8 Conclusion

In this paper we have described a solution for the recently recognized problem of decentralized knowledge management. We have developed a semantics based P2P knowledge sharing platform. In this platform, we introduced an appropriate security mechanism on infrastructure level. On the application level we introduced new mapping and visualization techniques. To foster community building we have defined a distributed ontology engineering process. We have described how the different methods have been applied in a concrete case study in the tourism domain. The results of our early experiments in introducing the application in the case study show the promises of our work. We could derive several lessons learned which will drive the future development of XAROP.

While we have addressed a broad range of problems in decentralized knowledge management, there are some issues to be addressed as part of future work. For example, query routing is currently not an issue within the XAROP system since the number of users is still small and simple query routing mechanism work effectively. However, in bigger networks, as they are found in the Bibster case study (the second system build on Swapster) efficient query routing is crucial. The interested reader may find some ideas of how to deal with such scalability issues in the description of the Bibster system [5].

# Acknowledgements

Research reported in this paper has been partially financed by EU in the IST project SWAP (IST-2001-34103) and the IST project SEKT (IST-2003-506826). In particular we want to thank the other people in the SWAP team for their collaboration towards SWAPSTER.

# References

1. Bonifacio, M., Bouquet, P., Traverso, P.: Enabling distributed knowledge management: Managerial and technological implications. Novatica and Informatik/Informatique **III** (2002)
2. Bonifacio, M., Bouquet, P., Danieli, A., Donà, A., Mameli, G., Nori, M.: Keex: A peer-to-peer solution for distributed knowledge management. In Tochtermann, K., Maurer, H., eds.: Proceedings of the 4th International Conference on Knowledge Management (I-KNOW'04), Graz, Austria, Journal of Universal Computer Science (J.UCS) (2004) 43–52
3. D. O'Leary: Using AI in knowledge management: Knowledge bases and ontologies. IEEE Intelligent Systems **13** (1998) 34–39
4. Schoder, D., Fischbach, K.: Peer-to-Peet Netzwerke für das Ressourcenmanagment. Wirtschaftsinformatik **45** (2003) 313–323
5. Haase, P., Broekstra, J., Ehrig, M., Menken, M., Mika, P., Plechawski, M., Pyszlak, P., Schnizler, B., Siebes, R., Staab, S., Tempich, C.: Bibster – a semantics-based bibliographic peer-to-peer system. In: Proc. of the 3rd Int. Semantic Web Conf. (ISWC 2004). (2004)
6. Klyne, G., Carroll, J.J.: Resource Description Framework (RDF): Concepts and abstract syntax. http://www.w3.org/TR/rdf-concepts/ (2003)
7. Broekstra, J., Kampman, A., van Harmelen, F.: Sesame: A generic architecture for storing and querying RDF and RDFSchema. In Horrocks, I., Hendler, J., eds.: Proc. of the 1st Int. Semantic Web Conf. (ISWC 2002), Springer (2002)
8. Gong, L.: Project jxta: A technology overview. Technical report, Sun Microsystems Inc. (2001)
9. Ehrig, M., Haase, P., van Harmelen, F., Siebes, R., Staab, S., Stuckenschmidt, H., Studer, R., Tempich, C.: The SWAP data and metadata model for semantics-based peer-to-peer systems. In: Proceedings of MATES-2003. First German Conference on Multiagent Technologies. LNAI, Erfurt, Germany, Springer (2003)
10. Broekstra, J.: SeRQL: Sesame RDF query language. In Ehrig, M., et al., eds.: SWAP Deliverable 3.2 Method Design. (2003) 55–68 http://swap.semanticweb.org/public/Publications/swap-d3.2.pdf.
11. Noy, N.F., Musen, M.A.: The PROMPT suite: interactive tools for ontology merging and mapping. International Journal of Human-Computer Studies **59** (2003) 983–1024
12. Doan, A., Domingos, P., Halevy, A.: Learning to match the schemas of data sources: A multistrategy approach. VLDB Journal **50** (2003) 279–301
13. Ehrig, M., Staab, S.: Qom – quick ontology mapping. In: Proceedings of the ISWC 2004, Hiroshima, Japan (2004)
14. Levenshtein, I.V.: Binary codes capable of correcting deletions, insertions, and reversals. Cybernetics and Control Theory (1966)
15. Cox, T., Cox, M.: Multidimensional Scaling. Chapman and Hall (1994)
16. Fluit, C., Sabou, M., van Harmelen, F.: Supporting user tasks through visualisation of lightweight ontologies. In Staab, S., Studer, R., eds.: Handbook on Ontologies in Information Systems, Springer-Verlag (2003)
17. Gómez-Pérez, A., Fernández-López, M., Corcho, O.: Ontological Engineering. Advanced Information and Knowlege Processing. Springer (2003)
18. Pinto, S., Staab, S., Sure, Y., Tempich, C.: OntoEdit empowering SWAP: a case study in supporting DIstributed, Loosely-controlled and evolvInG Engineering of oNTologies (DILIGENT). In Bussler, C., et al., eds.: 1st Euro. Semantic Web Symposium, ESWS 2004. (2004)
19. Nejdl, W., Wolf, B., Qu, C., Decker, S., Sintek, M., Naeve, A., Nilsson, M., Palmér, M., Risch, T.: EDUTELLA: A P2P networking infrastructure based on RDF. In: Proc. of the 2002 WWW Conference, Hawaii, USA (2002) 604–615
20. J. Schmücker and Wolfgang Müller: Praxiserfahrungen bei der Einführung dezentraler Wissensmanagement Lösungen. Wirtschaftsinformatik **45** (2003) 307–311

# Managing Knowledge Assets for NPD Performance Improvement: Results of an Action Research Project

Daniela Carlucci[1] and Giovanni Schiuma[1,2]

[1] Lieg, Dapit, University of Basilicata, Via dell'Ateneo Lucano,
85100 Potenza, Italy
{carlucci,schiuma}@unibas.it
http://www.unibas.it/lieg/index.html
[2] Centre for Business Performance, Cranfield School of Management,
Cranfield Bedfordshire MK 43 0AL, UK
giovanni.schiuma@cranfield.ac.uk

**Abstract.** This paper explores the fundamental issue of how Knowledge Management (KM) initiatives impact on business performance. Reflecting on the management literature enabled the definition of a conceptual background which has been tested and developed by an action research project. Drawing on the results of this project the paper proposes a framework to support managers in defining, planning, implementing and evaluating KM initiatives for performance improvement.

## 1 Introduction

In the present competitive context knowledge has been recognised as the main distinguishing factor of business success [7]. Today many organizations accredit their core competencies and capability differential [10], [25] essentially to their cognitive resources and consider knowledge as the differentiating competitive lever in knowledge economy [19]. In such an environment, over the past decade, starting from the beginning of '90, a new managerial paradigm, named Knowledge Management (KM), is emerged, resulting in many related contributions both theoretical and practical. The development of this research stream has lead to different results. At the beginning the attention has been mainly paid on the relevance of knowledge as the foundation of competitive advantage. In particular, focusing on the importance of knowledge as a strategic resource for company competitiveness, a number of contributions have analysed the differences between information and knowledge as well as the forms and nature that knowledge resources can take within an organisation. Dicotomic classifications have been proposed and the distinction between tacit and codified knowledge is emerged as key one [20]. Afterwards, as the research in the knowledge paradigm has grown, the focus has moved on an understanding of the approaches and tools for KM. This is resulted in a number of contributions analysing both the meaning and the approaches of KM as well as the tools and the organisational characteristics to plan and implement KM projects [6]. In the last years the interest of both academics and practitioners is focusing on the understanding of the benefits provided by KM initiatives, both in the short-term and long-term, which can justify KM investments. In fact, even if organizations recognize the value of knowledge and the importance of its management, they appear unable to evaluate the return on investment in knowledge [5] and, more generally, to estimate the value generated by KM initiatives in terms of

D. Karagiannis and U. Reimer (Eds.): PAKM 2004, LNAI 3336, pp. 271–281, 2004.

impact on business performance. Therefore organisations often embark on KM initiatives without a clear idea of what business benefit they could expect. More generally organizations need not only to measure KM impacts on performance but to improve its ability to exploit and create knowledge in order to increase the value for its stakeholders. For this reason a better understanding about the link between KM and business performance is very important. Understanding the link support the validation of KM investment and can contribute to explain what knowledge should be managed and developed within an organisation to achieve performance improvement.

In order to provide an understanding of how KM initiatives contribute to company performance improvement and value creation mechanisms different researches have been performed. These seem to be classifiable in three main categories: mapping, impact evaluating and value chain descriptive research studies. The mapping research studies [1] appear mainly focused on an analysis of the nature, forms and evolution stages of the KM initiatives within companies. The impact evaluating studies can be further sub-divided in two categories, those which investigate on the base of surveys the impact of KM initiatives on organisational performances [12], [15], and those which are focused on the definitions of approaches and tools to measure the business impact of KM initiatives [8], [21], [23]. Finally, the value chain descriptive studies, adopting a cause-effect relationship approach, aim to interpret how KM initiatives can support companies in improving process and/or business performance [4], [17]. Despite, the above studies provide interpretative frameworks to understand how KM initiatives can impact on companies performance, there is still a lack of understanding of how managers can develop KM initiatives which in turn generate corporate value and business performance improvement. The aim of this paper is to define a normative model, which drives managers towards the definition, planning, implementation and evaluation of KM initiatives which allow company business performance improvement. For this reason the "Knowledge Asset Value Spiral" (KAVS) is proposed. It is the result of an Action Research (AR) project developed within a world leader company in sofa production located in South Italy. In the first section of this paper, the conceptual foundations of the "KAVS" are introduced. An interpretation of KM and a descriptive framework – the Knowledge Value Chain – which provides an interpretative theoretical picture to understand and analyze the implementation of KM initiatives aimed to improve performance and deliver value, are presented. In the second section the AR project is outlined and finally, the managerial framework derived from the AR project is presented.

## 2   Knowledge Management
## and Business Performance Improvement

Over the past decade the acknowledgment of knowledge as a strategic resource at the basis of company competitive success has led to the development of a wide literature on KM. From the analysis of this literature two main characteristics of KM arise. The first characteristic is related to the process nature of KM. All definitions of KM, although in different forms, highlight how KM involves processes. These can take different forms according to the needs and characteristics of the organization system in which they are implemented. The second characteristic of KM is related to its aim. KM, independently from the process nature, is aimed to create value for the organization. Therefore the process nature and the value-creation aim are the two characteristic facets of the KM. Moreover, the analysis of the literature suggests three interpretative dimensions of KM: strategic, managerial and operational. Those correspond to the organizational levels of KM implementation. The *strategic dimension* considers the set of approaches that highlight the strategic importance of knowledge and its management in a company's strategy [11], [27]. The strategic perspective highlights that the definition of any KM strategy, in order to be successful, has to be aligned with the company's strategy. This has great relevance in the definition and implementation of KM initiatives, since stresses the importance to define KM projects in accordance with the company's strategic objectives. The *managerial dimension* comprises approaches and methodologies of organizational knowledge assessment and management. This interpretative dimension has involved the development of models which allow managers to drive the implementation of KM processes within the organization. The analysis of literature reveals two streams of study: knowledge creation and knowledge assessment. The first one, knowledge creation, begins with the seminal work of Nonaka [20] who introduces the concept of the 'Knowledge creating company' and defines KM approaches and models both of descriptive and prescriptive nature. The 'Knowledge Process Wheel' [16] proposes a taxonomy of KM processes[1]. Knowledge assessment is aimed to provide methodological approaches and tools to identify and value the intellectual capital of a company. The literature about the assessment of intellectual capital counts a number of contributions [2], [3], [24], [26]. The *operational dimension* of KM includes the set of organizational and managerial activities and projects such as teamwork, meetings, benchmarking of best practices, community of practice, and so on. This dimension also includes projects to implement ICT tools designed for development and use of knowledge.

On the base of the above insights derived from the literature review, we propose the following KM working definition: 'The KM is a managerial paradigm which considers knowledge as a resource at the basis of a company's competitiveness, it identifies the capabilities to generate value for a company's stakeholders with the explicit and systematic implementation of approaches, techniques and tools for the assessment and management of knowledge assets'. This definition is helpful to understand both the contents and the aims of KM as well as for addressing the development and implementation of KM initiatives within companies. It highlights that KM is at the basis of the company's ability to generate value and therefore represents one of the pillars of competitiveness. In order to better understand the link between the KM and business performance, we have reviewed the performance management literature focusing on how performance management models address the role of KM. The analysis of the most important performance measurement and management models, such as the Balanced Scorecard [13], [14], the Business Excellence Model and the Performance Prism [18], although differently, shows how KM sustains the dynamics of organizational learning, innovations and continuous improvement of performances in organizational processes and then how the development and management of knowledge assets is at the basis of company business performance. The

---

[1] This model identifies seven main processes of knowledge management: knowledge generation, knowledge codification, knowledge application, knowledge storing, knowledge mapping, knowledge sharing and knowledge transfer.

analysis of the performance measurement and management models allows us to draw the following conclusions. Improvement in business performance equals an increase in value generated for the key stakeholders of an organization. The generated value is the result of an organization's ability to manage its business processes. The effectiveness and efficiency of performing organizational processes are based on organizational competencies. KM enables an organization to grow and develop organizational competencies. Therefore, the cognitive nature of organizational competencies allows us to state that their improvement takes place through KM and that KM is at the heart of business performance improvement and value creation. All these formulated assumptions derived from theory represent the foundation of the Knowledge Value Chain [4], that provides an interpretative framework of the links between KM and value creation.

The above insights stress the role of KM as a paradigm to drive managers towards an improvement of the organization value creation mechanisms which in turn allow a continuous company performance improvement. In such regard, O'Dell and Grayson [21] maintain that in order to generate value by KM, companies need to "focus", on the basis of a set of opportunities or challenges that drive their particular business, the knowledge area in which KM initiatives can be implemented in order to improve business performance. For this reason organisations need a managerial framework which drives the definition and implementation of KM initiatives. In order to define such a framework, we have carried out an AR project. In particular on the base of the literature review, we have applied, tested and further developed the insights gathered and summarised in the above three KM perspectives and in Knowledge Value Chain.

## 3 An Action Research Project: Improving NPD Performance by KM Initiatives

The Action Research (AR) is a methodological approach which allows both to provide a solution to a specific practical problematic situation within an organisational context and contribute to develop a research theory. An AR project starts from the definition of a general idea both at theoretical and practical level. It is based on a spiral cycle of four main phases: diagnosing, planning, acting, evaluating[2]. Different types of AR can be adopted. Grundy's [9] provides a useful taxonomy of AR projects. According to this taxonomy we have decided to develop a technical as well as practical AR project. Our AR project can be considered technical since we started the research with a theoretical background that we were interested to test and develop. In particular, we were focused on an understanding of how the KM initiatives should be defined and planned in accordance with the company's strategy; how to identify and map the organisation knowledge areas to be developed; how to choose and design the

---

[2] Initially, in the diagnosis phase, the problem to be investigated is defined and diagnosing data are collected. Afterwards, on the base of an analysis of the possible solutions to the problem, an action plan is defined (planning) and subsequently it is implemented (acting). Finally the results of the project implementation are collected and analyzed in order to perform an evaluation and to define the new diagnosis stage. The spiral cycle is ended when the investigated problem is solved.

KM processes and projects to be implemented in order to maintain and develop the organisation knowledge domain at the basis of company competitiveness; and finally how to evaluate the value provided by the implementation of the KM initiatives against the company strategic objectives. We decided to develop an AR project for the following reasons: i) the management literature stresses that KM is strongly affected by the context in which is implemented, thus any research investigating the KM has to take into account the organisational context. This is a fundamental characteristic of the AR which uses the company as a physical laboratory for developing and testing the research hypothesis; ii) adopting the AR we had the opportunity to verify within an organisation the insights provided by the KM literature and to develop new hypothesis as well as to test them on field by a learning by doing and experimenting process; iii) through the AR project we have improved our knowledge on KM and we extracted from practice, in accordance with an inductive approach, insights to be combined with those based on a theoretical deductive approach; iv) the AR has been seen as a useful approach to overcome the reluctances, prejudices and resistances that the implementation of KM initiatives often involves. In fact, the participative approach characterizing AR allowed to create a consensus on the development and implementation of KM initiatives.

Once the theoretical background to be investigated has been defined, we looked for a company interested in testing and developing a model to support the definition and implementation of KM initiatives. For this reason we have involved a leader company in sofa production located within an industrial district in South Italy. This choice has been supported by the relevance that KM initiatives cover within this company. In fact, even if the sofa production is a traditional manufacturing process in a mature industry, it can be considered as a knowledge intensive process. The sofa is a product with highly stylistic contents and a limited life cycle. Moreover its production is based on worker's craftsmanlike skills. The companies operating in sofa industry, in order to gain or sustain competitive advantage, are pushed to continuous innovate their products and manage the know-how of some key individuals, such as designers, prototypists and assemblers (i.e. those workers who, on the base of their tacit know-how, assemble the different parts of a sofa providing to the product stylistic and functional characteristics). We have proposed the research project to the large company and after an analysis of the role of knowledge in the different company's departments, we agreed with the top management to carry out the AR project within the R&D department, focusing on the New Product Development (NPD). From this perspective the AR project can be considered a practical project in addition to a technical one. The literature defines as practical AR projects those where the researchers and the managers mutually identify and analyse a specific operative problem to be solved by the research. In fact, once we agreed to launch the AR project, first the organisational department where to perform the project was chosen and afterwards some operative problems to be solved were identified. However, since the AR project's aims were to define the managerial stages to go through in order to develop effective and efficient KM initiatives for company performance improvement, the operative problems were defined in general terms. In particular, we fixed as project target the improvement of NPD performance. Over nearly two years of research, which is still on going, we have implemented two AR spiral cycles. In the following the main insights of each AR cycle are presented.

Diagnosing phase. In this phase researchers and organisation managers identified some relevant problems affecting the NPD performances. At this stage, first, some focus groups were managed involving the top management of the organisation. The aim was to understand from strategic point of view what were the most important NPD performance areas to be improved. In this phase of the research we were looking for an analysis of the links between company's strategy, business performance improvements and the KM strategy to be implemented. Interviewing managers we discovered that in the past, some KM projects failed because of a lack of alignment between company's strategy and KM initiatives and/or a poor commitment of top management. Once the NPD performance areas to focus on were defined, we managed others focus groups with the managers of the R&D department in order to define some specific NPD operative problems to be investigated. At this level we stressed that two main performance dimensions affecting the efficiency of NPD process were the reduction of product design activities as well as prototyping time, and the improvement of the conformity of the prototype to the standards of the designed product. Consistently with the prescriptions of the AR we performed a diagnosis, i.e. an analysis, of the causes affecting the identified performance dimensions. For this reason, in order to collect data and information, structured and unstructured interviews, focus groups, direct observations and document analysis were used. Both managers and employees working in the NPD process were involved. This analysis has revealed that the implementation of a KM initiative has to be integrated with the implementation of auditing approaches and tools. This is of fundamental importance in order to define the informative base for the decision-making process about the KM initiatives to be implemented. In our research, we have identified some problems affecting the NPD process performance. In the following they are outlined: i) poor knowledge sharing between prototypists and designers and lack of an effective knowledge interface between the design area and the prototype area; ii) low level of designers' know-how about the technical and structural features of a sofa; iii) lack of codified rules and procedures to drive both designers and prototypists in their activities; iv) lack of ICT tools to support information/knowledge storage, processing and managing.

Planning phase. In this phase we defined the KM initiatives to be implemented. Adopting the classifications available in the management literature, we analysed the forms and the nature of the knowledge at the basis of NPD process. Moreover the possible KM approaches to be implemented for improving NPD performance were investigated. For this reason we adopted the knowledge processes taxonomies as well as the insights gathered from the analysis of both the case studies and the research results reported in the literature. However we discovered that in order to implement effective and efficient KM initiatives some approaches and tools to link the performance improvement targets and the KM initiatives were necessary. In particular, we found that was necessary first to identify the knowledge assets to be managed as well as their links with the performance improvement targets, and afterwards to define the KM projects to be implemented for the knowledge assets development. Moreover, in order to evaluate the relevance of KM initiatives and to account their value within the organisation was important to define measures and indicators for monitoring the improvement of process performance. In our research, we adopted two main performance indicators to assess the NPD performance improvements: (1) design/prototype time for a new sofa model; (2) level of conformity, measured on the base of an appropriate list of features, of the prototype with the drawing of the designed product. In order to identify the knowledge resources at the basis of NPD performance improvements, the Knowledge Asset Map[3] [16] has been adopted and further extended by the definition of a "matrix of direct dependences"[4]. These tools allow the identification and selection of the knowledge assets at the basis of process performance improvement. For the improvement of NPD performance, we have identified the following relevant knowledge assets: i) technical expertise of designers; ii) problem solving capability of designers as well as of prototypists; iii) ICT infrastructure and particularly design software; iv) teamworking culture; v) codified procedures. The AR project has highlighted that when managers are looking for knowledge resources to lever on, they need to identify the key value knowledge assets value driver, i.e. those organisational knowledge resources which are key value drivers for performance improvement and which require to be managed with priority. For this reason, we have developed the Knowledge Asset Value Creation Map[5] (KAVCM). It has been defined on the base of managers' need to have a tool to assess the importance of a knowledge asset against a specific performance objective. It provides a visual representation of the links between knowledge assets and performance improvement targets. For the improvement of NPD performances we have selected, adopting the "KAVCM", the following key knowledge assets: the teamworking culture, codified knowledge on prototyping procedures and knowledge physical infrastructure. The identification of the key knowledge assets has to be followed by the definition of the KM initiatives to be implemented. The AR project has shown that in order to drive managers towards the definition of a KM project, they need to understand what are the most suitable KM processes for developing the identified knowledge assets. For this reason the Knowledge Process Wheel [16] can be adopted. Implementing this framework two main KM processes were identified as relevant for the development of the key knowledge assets: the knowledge sharing and knowledge codification process. The definition of KM processes have proved to be particularly useful to define the KM initiatives. For improving NPD performance we planned to implement two main KM projects aimed to define a knowledge interface infrastructure to support the develop-

---

[3] The Knowledge Asset Map is an Intellectual Capital assessment model based on the concept of "knowledge asset" which is a company's asset which incorporates knowledge to acquire or to produce economic benefits for the organizational system. The model proposes a classification of organizational knowledge assets on the distinction between Stakeholders Resources e Structural Resources.

[4] In the matrix, the knowledge assets, classified in accordance with the Knowledge Asset Map are listed in rows, while along the columns are listed the defined performance objectives. Using the matrix, managers judge, adopting a binomial approach (i.e. filling the cell of the matrix with Yes or Not), if a knowledge asset is important or not for the achievement of each objective.

[5] The "KAVCM" shares the visual representation of the Strategy Map based on the Balanced Scorecard. The "KAVCM" shows and assesses how knowledge assets are linked to performance objectives and how different knowledge assets are linked each other in order to create value. Knowledge assets and performance objectives are depicted on nodes linked each other by arrows. In the tool the assessment of the strength of the links between knowledge assets and organizational performance is based on the application of AHP method.

ment of a teamworking approach between designers and prototypists, and a knowledge repositories where to collect and manage codified rules and procedures of the NPD process.

Acting phase. In this phase the KM projects have been implemented. In order to implement successful KM initiatives we noticed that has great relevance to identify a champion of the KM project. Someone who supports the project and stimulates the involvement. This role should be covered by a top manager who has the leadership to promote commitment around the KM initiatives. For the improvement of NPD process we performed two main KM projects. The first has involved the definition of new design standards based on the introduction of a sofa designed drawings in a 1:1 scale. Today, once the designers have completed their process they draw a detailed picture of the external stylistic characteristics of a sofa and afterwards the drawing is analysed by a team of designers and prototypists. This allows a prompt feedback about problems of the designed sofa as well as support a knowledge sharing process, by socialisation mechanisms based on face-to-face interactions, between designers and prototypists. The second project has been aimed to define a design sofa manual based on knowledge ICT infrastructure. Today, it collects and makes easily available codified rules and procedures on the design and prototype activities. It is continuously update and developed by the implementation of a knowledge codification process. This is performed by an externalisation process which involves designers and prototypists. It is important to stress that once the methodology to carry out the externalisation process was set up, in order to start the project the top management had to stimulate the creation of a knowledge sharing oriented culture. The implementation of the KM projects have proved that it is of fundamental importance to support any KM initiative by creating a strong KM-oriented culture within the organisation.

Evaluating phase. This is the last phase of the AR spiral cycle and it is aimed to assess the results of the research. In our research the evaluation of the KM initiatives has been performed on the base of a continuous monitoring of NPD performances. This has been carried out both by adopting a performance measurement system of the sofa NPD performances and by gathering information from managers, designers and prototypists through structured and unstructured interviews. Some of the main performance improvements involved by the implementation of KM projects can be summarised as follow: the reduction of the time to develop a new model of sofa, particularly the time for performing the NPD process of a sofa has been today reduced of 30%; an improvement of the stylistic/functional conformity of the prototype to the product design; the reduction of 20% of the time to carry out the sofa prototype wooden structure. The research has stressed the importance of adopting performance measurement system to assess the value generated by KM initiatives. Accounting the benefits of the implementation of KM projects creates consensus, attention and involvement around KM, but also it can help managers to design future KM projects or improve the current KM initiatives.

## 4   The Knowledge Asset Value Spiral

The results of the AR project can be summarized into a framework, the Knowledge Asset Value Spiral (KAVS). It provides managers with a structured framework to define, plan, implement and evaluate KM initiatives aimed to improve company busi-

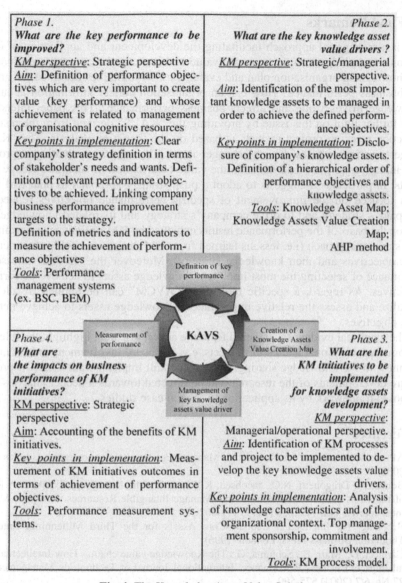

| Phase 1. | Phase 2. |
|---|---|
| **What are the key performance to be improved?** | **What are the key knowledge asset value drivers ?** |
| *KM perspective*: Strategic perspective | *KM perspective*: Strategic/managerial perspective. |
| *Aim*: Definition of performance objectives which are very important to create value (key performance) and whose achievement is related to management of organisational cognitive resources | *Aim*: Identification of the most important knowledge assets to be managed in order to achieve the defined performance objectives. |
| *Key points in implementation*: Clear company's strategy definition in terms of stakeholder's needs and wants. Definition of relevant performance objectives to be achieved. Linking company business performance improvement targets to the strategy. Definition of metrics and indicators to measure the achievement of performance objectives | *Key points in implementation*: Disclosure of company's knowledge assets. Definition of a hierarchical order of performance objectives and knowledge assets. |
| *Tools*: Performance management systems (ex. BSC, BEM) | *Tools*: Knowledge Asset Map; Knowledge Assets Value Creation Map; AHP method |
| Phase 4. | Phase 3. |
| **What are the impacts on business performance of KM initiatives?** | **What are the KM initiatives to be implemented for knowledge assets development?** |
| *KM perspective*: Strategic perspective | *KM perspective*: Managerial/operational perspective. |
| *Aim*: Accounting of the benefits of KM initiatives. | *Aim*: Identification of KM processes and project to be implemented to develop the key knowledge assets value drivers. |
| *Key points in implementation*: Measurement of KM initiatives outcomes in terms of achievement of performance objectives. | *Key points in implementation*: Analysis of knowledge characteristics and of the organizational context. Top management sponsorship, commitment and involvement. |
| *Tools*: Performance measurement systems. | *Tools*: KM process model. |

**Fig. 1.** The Knowledge Asset Value Spiral

business performance. It is based on the fundamental assumption that a KM strategy has to be aligned with the company's strategy and any KM initiative has to be derived from the definition of strategic business performance objectives. The "KAVS" allows the identification of the knowledge value drivers at the basis of company business performance improvement, the visualization of how they contribute to organizational performance and the definition of the KM projects to be implemented in order to develop the key knowledge assets value drivers. The "KAVS" is briefly presented below.

## 5  Final Remarks

KM is a managerial approach facilitating the development and application of organisational knowledge in order to create value and increase the competitive advantage. But how can an organisation plan and evaluate a KM initiatives designed for improving business performance? How can an organisation collect information about how knowledge drives value and affects business performance? This paper intended to shed further light on this issue by providing the "KAVS" derived from the results of an action research project as well as based on the literature analysis. The "KAVS" suggests various phases driving manager in identifying and evaluating appropriate KM initiatives to grow and maintain the value contribution of such knowledge based assets. In particular it suggests to adopt a push strategy approach to plan KM initiatives focused on the improvement of specific performance objectives related to a company's strategy and to drive company's strategy and its related knowledge strategy on the basis of the performance results achieved by KM initiatives, according to a pull strategy approach (i.e. lessons learned from KM initiatives could orient performance objectives and then knowledge strategy). Moreover the "KAVS" stresses the importance of selecting the most important knowledge assets to achieve performance objectives. As regard, a specific tool, the "KAVCM" can be applied. It allows to visualize and assess the relative importance of knowledge assets to achieve performance objectives.

The empirical evidences, gathered from the action research, highlight the relevance of some organisational and cultural facets, e.g. the board involvement and the cultural openness to the knowledge sharing, for a successful implementation of KM projects. Future developments of the research will be directed towards a deeper analysis of the proposed framework by its application to several case studies.

## References

1. APQC: Measurement for Knowledge Management http://old.apqc.org/free/articles (2001; 2002)
2. Bontis, N., Dragonetti, N.C., Jacobsen, K. Roos, G.: The Knowledge Toolbox: A Review of the Tools Available to Measure and Manage Intangible Resources. European Management Journal Vol. 17 No. 4 (1999) 391-402
3. Brooking, A.: Intellectual Capital: Core Assets for the Third Millennium Enterprise. Thompson Business Press, London (1996)
4. Carlucci, D., Marr, B., Schiuma, G.: The Knowledge value chain – How Intellectual Capital Impacts Business Performance. International Journal of Technology Management Vol. 27 No. 6/7 (2004) 575-590
5. Chong, C. W., Holden, T., Wilhelmij, P., Schimdt, R.A.: Where does knowledge management add value?. Journal of Intellectual Capital Vol.1 No.4 (2000) 366-380
6. Davenport, T. H., Prusak, L.: Working knowledge: How organizations manage what they know. Harvard Business School Press, Boston (1998)
7. Drucker, P.F.: Post - Capitalist Society. Butterworth Heinemann, Oxford (1993)
8. Firestone, J. M.: Estimating Benefits of Knowledge Management Initiatives: Concepts, Methodology and Tools. Journal of the KMCI Vol. 1 No. 3 (2001) 110-129
9. Grundy, S.: Three modes of action research. Curriculum Perspectives Vol. 2 No. 3 (1982) 23-24

10. Hall, R.: A framework linking intangibles resources and capabilities to sustainable competitive advantage. Strategic Management Journal Vol. 14 (1993) 607-618
11. Hansen, M. T., Nohtria, N., Tierney, T.: What's Your Strategy for Managing Knowledge?. Harvard Business Review March-April (1999) 106-116
12. Heisig, P., Mertins, K., Vorbeck, J.: Knowledge Management. Concepts and Best practices in Europe. Springer-Verlag, New York (2001)
13. Kaplan, R.S., Norton, D.P.: The Balanced Scorecard - Measures That Drive Performance. Harvard Business Review Vol. 70 No. 1 (1992) 71-79
14. Kaplan, R.S., Norton, D.P.: The Balanced Scorecard - Translating Strategy into Action. Harvard Business School Press Boston, MA (1996)
15. KPMG: Etude Européenne KPMG sur la Gestion des Connaissances, Enquête 2002/2003 sur la Gestion des Connaissances. KPMG Knowledge Advisory Services Amstelveen, Pays Bas (2003)
16. Marr, B., Schiuma, G.: Measuring and Managing Intellectual Capital and Knowledge Assets in New Economy Organisations. In: Bourne, M. (ed.), Handbook of Performance Measurement, Gee, London (2001)
17. McElroy, M. W.: The New Knowledge Management: complexity, learning and sustainable innovation. Butterworth-Heinemann, Burlington (2002)
18. Neely, A., Adams, C., Kennerley, M.: The Performance Prism: The Scorecard for Measuring and Managing Business Success. Financial Times Prentice Hall, London (2002)
19. Nonaka, I., Takeuchi, H.: The Knowledge-creating Company: How Japanese Companies Create the Dynamics of Innovation. Oxford University Press, New York (1995)
20. Nonaka, I.: The Knowledge Creating Company. Harvard Business Review November- December (1991)
21. O'Dell, C., Grayson, J.: If only we new what we knew: the transfer of internal knowledge and best practice. The Free Press, New York (1998)
22. Ortiz, A.: KM on steady state?, KM needs Action Research. Proceedings of 3° European KM summer school 7-12 September San Sebastian Spain (2003)
23. Robinson, H.S., Anumba, C.J., Ahmed, M.A.G., Carrillo, P.C.: IMPaKT: A Framework for Linking Knowledge Management to Business Performance. Electronic Journal of Knowledge Management Vol. 1 No. 1 (2003) 1-12
24. Roos, J., Roos, G., Dragonetti, N.C., Edvinsson, L.: Intellectual Capital: Navigating the New Business Landscape. Macmillan, London (1997)
25. Stalk, G., Evans, P., Shulman, L. E.: Competing on capabilities: the new rule of corporate strategy. Harvard Business Review march – april (1992)
26. Sveiby, K.E.: The New Organizational Wealth: Managing and Measuring Knowledge-based Assets. Barrett-Kohler Publishers, San Francisco (1997)
27. Zack, M.: Developing a Knowledge Strategy. California Management Review Vol. 41 No. 3 (1999) 125-145

# Knowledge Management in the Semiconductor Industry: Dispatches from the Front Line

Brian Donnellan

Brian Donnellan, Centre for Innovation and Structural Change,
National University of Ireland, Galway
brian.donnellan@nuigalway.ie

**Abstract.** The semiconductor industry is characterized by products with a high level of intellectual property content, long product development cycles, designed by very scarce engineering talent. Because of the knowledge-intensive nature of the development process barriers to market entry are extremely strong. The foundation of many semiconductor company's successes has been the research and development of new products, with a range of products being sold to thousands of customers in many different horizontal and vertical markets. There are a number of knowledge management challenges facing corporations in the semiconductor industry: how to improve the sharing of knowledge and best practices across the organization, how to quickly develop solutions to technical problems and hence reduce time-to-market, and how to accelerate innovation rates by bringing diverse views and experience to bear. This paper will describe some of these challenges. The research is based on a case study of a leading semiconductor company with worldwide operations.

**Keywords:** Knowledge Management, Knowledge Management Systems, New Product Development, Innovation.

## 1 Introduction

Leading proponents of Knowledge Management (KM) in the semiconductor industry include Hewlett Packard (HP) and Texas Instruments (TI). Thomas Davenport describes how Hewlett Packard have adopted a strategic approach to KM [1]. He describes KM initiatives in using Lotus Notes. HP established three different 'knowledge bases' for educators in the company. Three projects involving HP's Product Processes Organisation were described. One involved competitor information for HP's Components group. The goal of the second project was to create a web-based interface to primary and secondary research information. The third system managed international marketing information.

Carla ODell describes how Texas Instruments (TI) attempted to identify and transfer internal best practices [2]. In 1993 TI's former CEO, president and chairman of the board, the late Jerry Jenkins initiated a project to create a common methodology and common language which would be used to provide best practices across the company. One of the earliest and simplest facilitators of knowledge sharing was the standardisation of the company on Microsoft applications in the early 1990's, which enabled individuals to share documents through attachments and file transfer. In 1995, 200 Texas Instruments employees worldwide were set up to use a 'Best Prac-

D. Karagiannis and U. Reimer (Eds.): PAKM 2004, LNAI 3336, pp. 282–291, 2004.
© Springer-Verlag Berlin Heidelberg 2004

tice Knowledge Base' in Lotus Notes. A practice is documented in the system with a title, a short narrative and contact information. Each practice is categorised for retrieval by: (i) quality criteria (ii) process and (iii) keywords.

This paper will examine current KM issues in the semiconductor industry. The analysis will be grounded in the experiences of a leading company in the industry. The organizational context for this study is a semiconductor new product development group comprised of 430 staff members. The group is based in Ireland and is part of a larger multi-national corporation. The corporation is a world leader in the design, manufacture, and marketing of high-performance analog, mixed-signal and digital signal processing integrated circuits (ICs) used in signal processing applications. Founded in 1965, it employs approximately 8,800 people worldwide.

**Table 1.** Structure of this Paper

| Section | Topic |
|---|---|
| 1 | **Introduction:** This section will give some background and motivation for this research. |
| 2 | **The Semiconductor Industry:** This section will give an overview of the semiconductor industry and indicate some of the KM challenges faced by firms in that industry. |
| 3 | **KM Challenges faced by firms in the Semiconductor Industry:** There are some KMS challenges faced in the semiconductor industry. They will be described in this section. |
| 4 | **Examples of KMS in the Semiconductor Industry:** Companies have responded to the KMS challenges associated with NPD by developing portfolios of KMS applications. Some examples will be given. |
| 5 | **Summary, Conclusions** |

## 2 The Semiconductor Industry

The semiconductor industry has grown considerably over the last 30 years to the point where it is now constitutes over \$100B in worldwide sales. This growth has been achieved in a very dynamic, turbulent, operating environment. Specifically, the following dynamics are currently impacting semiconductor firms:

- A difficult and uncertain economic environment, where many customers continue to experience flat or declining growth
- Increased outsourcing of manufacturing by semiconductor manufacturers and their customers
- Increased complexity, fragmentation and globalization of markets
- Ever compressing product lifecycles in many product segments
- Continued rapid technology evolution and the ability of manufacturers to respond to and invest in these changes

Consequently, semiconductor firms are faced with many business challenges:

- The selling process for component suppliers is becoming increasingly complex in this multi-tier, multi-party and global ecosystem.
- Manufacturers are under pressure to win more designs than ever.

- Lack of visibility into the demand chain makes opportunity management, account management and forecasting inherently difficult.
- Managing the complex interactions with their distribution partners, including managing sales reporting, inventory, and liabilities.
- Pressure to decrease costs without sacrificing customer or partner loyalty

To address these challenges, semiconductor companies need new strategies to assure their success or even survival during these times of increased competition and economic uncertainty.

## 3   KM Challenges Faced by Firms in the Semiconductor Industry

The "resource-based" view of the firm emphasizes the importance of a firm's resources, including intellectual capital, as its source of sustainable competitive advantage. Grant states "what distinguishes the Knowledge Economy from previous economies is the sheer accumulation of knowledge by society, the rapid pace of innovation and, most important, the advent of digital technologies that have had far-reaching implications for the sources of value in the modern economy" [4]. He identifies four aspects of management practice in NPD organizations that are being impacted by the emergence of the Knowledge Economy:

**a) Property rights in knowledge**
Recognition of the value of proprietary knowledge has increased the amount of intellectual property legislation by legislatures and judicial systems over the past two decades. The enforcement of intellectual property in the form of patents, copyrights, and trademarks has become a central asset-management activity [5].

**b) Accelerating knowledge creation and application**
Companies engaged in NPD have struggled to shorten their NPD cycles. For example, the fundamental force behind Intel's sustained success is its "time pacing" - the time pacing of NPD though continual minor innovation with periodic "mid-life kickers", together with a nine-month fabrication cycle [6].

**c) Converting tacit into explicit knowledge**
Kogut and Zander coined the term "paradox of replication" to describe where the codification of knowledge required for internal replication may also facilitate replication of that knowledge by other firms [7]. The challenge facing KM practitioners appears to be how to build barriers to external replication through linking internal systems to knowledge that cannot be replicated by outsiders [8].

**d) Competing for standards**
Over the last two decades, there has been a change in attitude towards the role of industry standards. Firms are now more willing to sacrifice short-term financial gains for long-term benefits derived from standardization processes. These strategies can imply that firms have to form collaborative projects with customers, competitors and government agencies to achieve a standardization goal. These types of projects, by their nature, place a lot of emphasis on KM capabilities.

Ramesh and Tiwana analysed the NPD process for a Personal Digital Assistant operating system, and went on to develop a prototype system to support collaborative

NPD [9]. Court, Culley et al. investigated the use of information in NPD teams and reported on the use of information technology to support the NPD process [10]. They analyzed the methods by which the NPD team members retrieve, apply and subsequently transfer their information. A significant finding was that even though team members have access to IS tools and services, they still preferred to use manual and verbal methods of communication and information retrieval. These preferred formats may suggest that computer information accessing and storage is still at the infancy stage and therefore used with some reluctance by design teams. A key challenge appeared to the researchers to be the extensive use of personal information stores and the absence of easy-to-use indexing systems.

Anderson et al. looked at the design activity in Rank Xerox and illustrated how collaborative, inter-actional, and organizational ordering are not addressed by the information technology infrastructure in the Design Dept. at Rank Xerox [11]. Adler et al. argued for a process-oriented approach to NPD and used a case study of a fictitious company, which represented a composite of a number of companies studied by Adler [12]. He claimed that the process oriented approach, which had cross-functional teams as a central element, led to the creation of best practice templates which in turn led to greater efficiencies in NPD. Van de Ven and Polley empirically demonstrate how the early stages of NPD projects can be accounted for by using principles drawn from chaos theory – providing potential future insight into the front end of NPD efforts that traditionally have proven elusive [13]. Scott proposed a framework that decomposed the NPD process into three phases and then classified the types of knowledge and IS appropriate for each phase [14].

## 3.1 Demands for Increased Productivity in New Product Development

NPD processes may have short product and process life cycles. These cycles are getting shorter and they are compressing the available time window for recouping the expenses associated with NPD. This places a premium on the ability to effectively capture knowledge created during the process so that it can be re-used in the next generation of products to reduce development time. This capture-reuse cycle is a key enabler for productivity improvements in the design phase of NPD. Underlying the growth has been a fundamental driver of market growth called Moore's Law. Moore's Law is an historical observation by Intel executive, Gordon Moore, that the market demand (and semiconductor industry response) for functionality per chip (bits, transistors) doubles every 1.5 to 2 years. He also observed that MPU performance (clock frequency (MHz) × instructions per clock = millions of instructions per second (MIPS)) also doubles every 1.5 to 2 years. Moore's Law has been a consistent macro trend and key indicator of successful leading-edge semiconductor products and companies for the past 30 years.

However it has been estimated that productivity (where productivity = dollar value-add per unit of engineering effort in the U.S. Semiconductor Industry 1986 – 1995, source: U.S. census and bureau of labour and statistics) among electronic design engineers doubles every 36 months [15]. The competitive pressure to improve productivity and thereby reduce the NPD cycle time is huge. Since the challenges associated with capturing and reusing knowledge are, by their nature, knowledge management challenges – this is one of the key KM challenges being posed by NPD.

KMS responses to this challenge range from the application of knowledge "codification" systems to knowledge "personalization" systems [16].

## 3.2   Internal Knowledge Transfer

Today's NPD organizations need to facilitate knowledge transfer across internal organizational boundaries. The drive to enable this knowledge transfer may stem from any one of a number of factors: the existence of "virtual teams" that are geographically dispersed, the re-organization of NPD activities from a linear to a concurrent model or the need for stronger communication flow between organizational units that had been disconnected heretofore e.g. sales and manufacturing.

### 3.2.1   Virtual NPD Teams

NPD organizations can be distributed across geographical boundaries. The NPD activity that spans these centers requires the teams to share their knowledge across team boundaries. It also creates a need for KMS infrastructure to support and promote knowledge sharing. The challenges posed by distributed teams may arise from cultural differences. The appreciation of cultural differences across geographically dispersed teams may be a key factor in the success of those teams. There are at least four ways in which culture influences the behaviours central to knowledge sharing in NPD teams:

  a) Culture shapes assumptions about what knowledge is and which knowledge is worth managing. Sackman empirically demonstrated four different kinds of cultural knowledge: "dictionary" knowledge, "directory" knowledge, "recipe" knowledge and "axiomatic" knowledge [17]. Hedlund and Nonaka contrasts U.S. and Japanese practices of managing knowledge [18]. The basis for the contrast is the cultural difference between U.S. and Japanese firms.
  b) Culture defines the relationships between individual and organizational knowledge, determining who is expected to control specific knowledge, as well as who must share it and who can hoard it. This relationship is influenced by what some researchers refer to as the presence of an atmosphere of "care" in a company. "Care" can be characterized by an active empathy, access to help and lenience in judgement. Von Krogh and Roos stress that knowledge nurturing and creating organizations should be caring organizations [19]. Culture can also promote unique attitudes toward communication and information, which in extreme cases can restrict knowledge transfer to the point of organizational demise as demonstrated by Brown and Starkey [20].
  c) Culture creates the context for social interaction that determines how knowledge will be shared in particular situations. Reducing harsh bureaucratic structures and increasing informal communication may empower creativity and innovation by promoting spontaneity, experimentation and freedom of expression [21]. This culture entails an almost total removal of many of the values that underpinned the re-engineering and "right sizing" management culture of the early 1990's. For example, knowledge cultures value a "fat" middle management layer for professional support and a tolerance for the functional inefficiency that a messy, chaotic creative process implies [22].

d) Culture shapes the processes by which the new knowledge with its accompanying uncertainties is created, legitimated, and distributed in organizations. In this context Hayduk developed a framework of organizational practices to foster knowledge sharing that is based on sensitivities to the national culture in which a firm finds itself located [23].

### 3.2.2 Cross-Functional Collaboration

Many NPD projects require cross-functional collaboration. The nature and importance of this collaboration is described by Wheelwright and Clark as follows:

"Outstanding product development requires effective action from all of the major functions in the business. From engineering one needs good designs, well-executed tests, and high quality-proto-types; from marketing, thoughtful product positioning, solid customer analysis, and well-thought-out product plans; from manufacturing, capable processes, precise cost estimates and skilful pilot production and ramp-up. *Great products and processes are achieved when all of these activities fit well together. The firm must develop the capability to achieve integration across the functions in a timely and effective way.*" p.165 [24]

The patterns of communication are described in Table 2. The ends of the spectra represent opposites in integration. On the left is a communication pattern that is sparse, infrequent, one-way, and late. One the right, the communication is rich, frequent, reciprocal, and early. This is the preferred mode of communication for NPD organizations because collaborating engineers meet face to face with their colleagues early in the design process and share preliminary ideas with sketches, models, and notes.

**Table 2.** Communication between Functional Groups in NPD [24]

| Communication Dimension | Range of Choice | |
| --- | --- | --- |
| Richness of Media | Sparse: documents, computer networks | Rich: face-to-face, models |
| Frequency | Low: One-shot, batch | High: piece-by-piece, on-line, intensive |
| Directions | One-way: monologue | Two-way: dialogue |
| Timing | Late: completed work, ends the process | Early: preliminary, begins the process |

### 3.3 Cross-Institutional Collaboration

Cross-institutional collaboration is also becoming quite common in NPD processes. The need for this type of collaboration arises when organizations seek to collaborate with sources of knowledge, which are external to it. For instance a firm may want to work with an internationally recognized centre-of-excellence in an academic institution with which it has no formal relationship. Cases where NPD teams want to work closely with external standards organizations are also becoming more prevalent. In such cases knowledge has to be combined from participants across multiple collaborating organizations.

### 3.4  Transient Team Membership

NPD teams are staffed with people who may possess much sought-after skills and expertise. Consequently there can be high turnover rates in NPD organizations, as firms compete for staff with highly rated R&D experience. The resulting transient existence of teams results in a reduction in organizational knowledge unless there is a repository for knowledge rather than a dependence on knowledge that is solely situated in the minds of individuals.

There is also a requirement that some staff turnover should exist for NPD teams to be effective. The rate of movement of staff members across organizational boundaries has been shown to have an effect on NPD team output. Katz explored the relationship between the mean tenure of NPD teams, the degree of external communication, and performance [25]. In his study of 50 NPD teams in a large American corporation, he found that initially group performance increased with increasing mean tenure of the group, but this relationship reversed and performance dropped off after five years. The decline in performance was significantly correlated with a decline in external communication and a growth in so-called Not-Invented-Here (NIH) behavior [26].

## 4  Examples of KM Initiatives in the Semiconductor Industry

Semiconductor firms have responded to the KMS challenges associated with NPD by adopting a dual approach. On one hand, a portfolio of KMS applications are being developed. On the other hand, peer reviews that are an integral part of the stage-gate process are being leveraged as knowledge-sharing opportunities.

### 4.1  NPD Meta-knowledge

"Conventional explanations view learning as a process by which a learner internalizes the knowledge, whether "discovered," "transmitted" from others, or "experienced in interaction" with others." (p.47) [27]. However, before one can initiate such a process, whether through discovery or interaction, there must be a mechanism by which people can easily find out what knowledge is being created in the organization and by whom. The knowledge being sought is, in fact, knowledge about knowledge or "meta-knowledge" [28], [29].

Meta-knowledge attempts to provide answers to questions such as "Where can I get information about a particular technical topic? How can I find out more about this topic? Is there work in progress in this organization on this topic?" KMS applications address these challenges by making it easy for members of the technical staff to publish and locate technical reviews, notes, articles etc. - items which previously may have required several emails and phone calls to track down.

### 4.2  Catalogs

A "Catalog", in this context, is an application that generates a list of previously designed products in the product development community. The catalog would enable product development staff to quickly find out if products were previously designed that were similar to those currently under development. The entries are created and owned by the product development staff. Each entry in the catalog represents is a potentially reusable circuit design. Catalog entries, depending on their utility, are potential candidates for inclusion in a repository. The problems that were identified in the NPD process that were to be addressed by catalogs are:

(a) a lack of awareness of what previously designed circuit blocks had been created and might be available for reuse in future projects
(b) a mechanism by which product development staff could easily make their products more easily "discovered" by members of the product development organization outside of their own organization unit

## 4.3  NPD Design Repositories

A "Repository", in this context, provides a store of previously design products that could be reused throughout the corporation. Each of the repository's elements has an extensive support kit associated with it i.e. thorough documentation, contextual information about previous usage, data formats compatible with existing NPD systems, validation data, interface information, etc. The goal of the repository is to provide a library of robust and supported reusable circuit designs available for download, obtained from both internal and external sources. The repository contains previously designed products packaged in a format suitable to delivery as intellectual property to either internal groups or external groups (or both). The repository is a structured repository for formal knowledge containing previously used circuits that were internally developed and externally procured circuits that may also be re-used in future products. Its purpose corresponds, generally, to what Hansen termed a "codification" strategy where the value of the repository lies in "connecting people with reusable codified knowledge" [16] or to what Swan termed a "cognitive" strategy where the primary function of the repository is to codify and capture knowledge so that the knowledge can be recycled (Swan, Newell et al. 1999).

## 4.4  Implications for Practitioners

The underlying philosophical approach to the firm's knowledge management initiative was that knowledge management should be integrated into the daily work of people in the organization. A number of steps were taken in the development and implementation of the knowledge management process that were designed to promote the integration of the process into the daily working of the organization:

- **Focus:** progress in the initiative was systematically monitored in a balanced scorecard that captured different facets of organizational performance
- **Alignment:** the placing of the knowledge management process in a framework with other key business processes promoted alignment with those processes. Decisions were made on all the business processes in a collective manner with some mutual adjustment where necessary to achieve an overall consistency in strategic direction.
- **Instruments:** There were specific KM services and enabling technologies provided to promote and facilitate knowledge management. These included the types of KMS applications described elsewhere in this paper.
- **Communities:** Communities-Of-Practice were set up which proved to be powerful mechanisms for disseminating knowledge across organizational boundaries.

## 5  Summary and Conclusions

This paper has provided an overview of the knowledge management challenges faced by firms in the semiconductor industry. The industry was characterized by products with a high level of intellectual property content, long product development cycles, designed by very scarce engineering talent. Examples were provided of knowledge management applications designed to overcome some of these challenges. The research was based on a case study of a leading semiconductor company with worldwide operations.

## References

1. Davenport, T.H., *Ten Principles of Knowlede Management and Four Case Studies*. Knowledge and Process Management, 1997. **4**(3): p. 187-208.
2. O'Dell, C. and G. Jackson, *If Only We Knew What We Know: Identification and Transfer of Internal Best Practices*. California Management Review, 1998. **40**(3): p. 154-174.
3. Moore, G. *Keynote Address*. in *International Solid State Circuits Conference*. 2003. San Francisco.
4. Grant, R., *Shifts in the World Economy: The Drivers of Knowledge Management*, in *Knowledge Horizons: The Present and the Promise of Knowledge Management*, C. Despres and D. Chauvel, Editors. 2000, Butterworth-Heinemann: Boston. p. 27-55.
5. Grindley, P. and D. Teece, *Managing intellectual capital: licensing and cross-licensing in semiconductors and electronics"*. California Management Review, 1997. **39 (Winter)**: p. 8-41.
6. Brown, S.L. and K.M. Eisenhardt, *Competing on the Edge: Strategy as Structured Chaos*. 1998, Boston: Harvard Business Press.
7. Kogut, B. and U. Zander, *Knowledge of the Firm, Combinative Capabilities, and the Replication of Technology*. Organisation Science, 1992. **3**(3): p. 383-397.
8. Schultze, U. *Investigating The Contradictions In Knowledge Management*. in *IFIP*. 1998.
9. Ramesh, B. and A. Tiwana, *Supporting Collaborative Process Knowledge Management in New Product Development Teams*. Decision Support Systems, 1999. **27**(1-2): p. 213-235.
10. Court, A.W., S.J. Culley, and C.A. McMahon, *The Influence of Information Technology in New Product Development: Observations of an Empirical Study of the Access of Engineering Design Information*. International Journal of Information Management, 1997. **17**(5): p. 359-375.
11. Anderson, B., G. Button, and W. Sharrock. *Supporting The Design Process Within An Organisational Context*. in *ECSCW'93*. 1993. Milan.
12. Adler, P.S., et al., *Getting the Most Out of Your Product Development Process*, in *Harvard Business Review*. 1996. p. 134-152.
13. van de Ven, A.H. and D. Polley, *Learning While Innovating*. Organisation Science, 1992. **3**(1): p. 92-116.
14. Scott, J.E. *The Role of Information Technology in Organizational Knowledge Creation for New Product Development*. in *Second Americas Conference on Information Systems*. 1996.
15. Collett, R., *A Strategic Analysis of the Emerging Market for IP and The Role Of Design Re-Use 1998-2002*, in *Presentation to VSIA Membership*. 1998.
16. Hansen, M., N. Nohria, and T. Tieney, *What's your strategy for managing knowledge?* Harvard Business Review, 1999. **March-April**(1999): p. 106-116.
17. Sackmann, S.A., *Cultures and Subcultures: An Analysis of Organisational Knowledge*. Administrative Science Quarterly, 1992. **37**(1): p. 140-161.

18. Hedlund, G. and I. Nonaka, *Models of Knowledge Management in the West and Japan*, in *Implementing Strategic Process: Change, Learning and Cooperation*, P.L.e. al., Editor. 1993, Basil Blackwell: Oxford. p. 117-144.
19. von Krogh, G. and J. Roos, eds. *Managing Knowledge : Perspectives on Cooperation and Competition*. 1996, Sage: London.
20. Brown, A.D. and K. Starkey, *The Effect of Organisational Culture on Communication and Information*. Journal of Management Studies, 1994. **31**(6): p. 808-828.
21. Graham, A.B. and V.G. Pizzo, *A question of balance: case studies in strategic knowledge management.* European Management Journal, 1996. **14**(4): p. 338-346.
22. Baskerville, R. and J. Pries-Heje. *Managing knowledge capability and maturity.* in *IFIP 8.2 and 8.6 Joint Working Conference on Information Systems*. 1998. Helsinki.
23. Hayduk, H. *Organizational Culture Barriers to Knowledge Management.* in *Association for Information Systems - Americas Conference*. 1998.
24. Wheelwright, S. and K. Clark, *Revolutionizing Product Development*. 1992, New York: Simon and Schuster Inc.
25. Katz, R., *The effects of group longevity on project communication and performance*. Administrative Science Quarterly, 1982. **27**: p. 81-104.
26. Brown, S.L. and K.M. Eisenhardt, *Product Development: Past Research, Present Findings, and Future Directions*. Academy of Management Review, 1995. **20**(2): p. 343-378.
27. Lave, J. and E. Wenger, *Situated learning: Legitimate peripheral participation*. 1991, Cambridge: Cambridge University Press.
28. Swanstrom, E., *MetaKnowledge and MetaKnowledgebases*, in *The Knowledge Management Handbook*, J. Liebowitz, Editor. 1999, CRC Press: London.
29. Kehal, M., *Searching For An Effective Knowledge Management Framework*. Journal Of Knowledge Management Practice, 2002(February, 2000).

# Incremental Knowledge Acquisition for Building Sophisticated Information Extraction Systems with KAFTIE

Son Bao Pham and Achim Hoffmann

School of Computer Science and Engineering
University of New South Wales, Australia
{sonp,achim}@cse.unsw.edu.au

**Abstract.** The aim of our work is to develop a flexible and powerful Knowledge Acquisition framework that allows users to rapidly develop Natural Language Processing systems, including information extraction systems. In this paper we present our knowledge acquisition framework, KAFTIE, which strongly supports the rapid development of complex knowledge bases for information extraction. We specifically target scientific papers which involve rather complex sentence structures from which different types of information are automatically extracted. Tasks on which we experimented with our framework are to identify concepts/terms of which positive or negative aspects are mentioned in scientific papers. These tasks are challenging as they require the analysis of the relationship between the concept/term and its sentiment expression. Furthermore, the context of the expression needs to be inspected. The results so far are very promising as we managed to build systems with relative ease that achieve F-measures of around 84% on a corpus of scientific papers in the area of artificial intelligence.

**Keywords:** Incremental Knowledge Acquisition, Knowledge-based systems, Natural language processing.

## 1   Introduction

The development of sophisticated Natural Language Understanding systems, including information extraction, is usually a rather time-consuming and expensive process. For a new application, usually large parts of the system have to be redesigned in order to take relevant domain-dependent wordings into account. The particular task to be accomplished, e.g. the particular information to be extracted will also require an often substantial tailoring of the system.

In this paper, we present KAFTIE (Knowledge Acquisition Framework for Text classification and Information Extraction), an incremental knowledge acquisition framework that strongly supports the rapid prototyping of new NLP systems, that require classification of text segments and/or information extraction tasks. Our framework is inspired by the idea behind Ripple Down Rules [2] and allows for the incremental construction of large knowledge bases by providing one rule at a time. An expert just needs to monitor the system's performance on text and intervenes whenever the system does not perform as desired. The intervention will be based on a concrete text segment which

D. Karagiannis and U. Reimer (Eds.): PAKM 2004, LNAI 3336, pp. 292–306, 2004.

the expert uses to specify rule conditions which are met by that text segment in order to formulate an exception rule to the rule that produced the undesirable system performances. Alternatively, the experts could modify an existing rule to cover the new case at hand provided the KB is still consistent.

Another strength of KAFTIE which makes it powerful and easy to use on NLP domain is its flexible annotation-based rule language and a customizable Shallow Parser.

We apply KAFTIE to the two tasks of extracting advantages and disadvantages of concepts or actions in technical papers. An advantage/disadvantage is detected when a positive/negative sentiment is expressed towards the concept or action. For example, given the following sentences:

*There is some evidence that Bagging performs worse in low noise settings.*
*It is more efficient to use Knowledge Acquisition to solve the task.*

The tasks are to detect that the algorithm *Bagging* and the action *to use Knowledge Acquisition to solve the task* have been mentioned with negative and positive sentiments respectively. These tasks are challenging and will be described in more details in the experiments section.

In this paper, we will first describe the underlying methodology of our framework and how to realize it on natural language domains. We will then illustrate the process by giving examples on how the knowledge base evolves. We will present experimental results and conclude with future works.

## 2 Methodology

In this section we present the basic idea of Ripple-Down Rules which inspired our approach.

**Knowledge Acquisition with Ripple Down Rules:** Ripple Down Rules (RDR) is an unorthodox approach to knowledge acquisition. RDR does not follow the traditional approach to knowledge based systems (KBS) where a knowledge engineer together with a domain expert perform a thorough domain analysis in order to come up with a knowledge base. Instead a KBS is built with RDR incrementally, while the system is already in use. No knowledge engineer is required as it is the domain expert who repairs the KBS as soon as an unsatisfactory system response is encountered. The expert is merely required to provide an explanation for why in the given case, the classification should be different from the system's classification.

Say, the system's classification was produced by some rule $R_A$. The explanation would refer to attributes of the case, such as patient data in the medical domain or a linguistic pattern matching the case in the natural language domain. The new rule $R_B$ will only be applied to cases for which the provided conditions in $R_B$ are true and for which rule $R_A$ would produce the classification, if rule $R_B$ had not been entered. I.e. in order for $R_B$ to be applied to a case as an exception rule to $R_A$, rule $R_A$ has to be satisfied as well. A sequence of nested exception rules of any depth may occur. Whenever a new exception rule is added, a difference to the previous rule has to be identified by the expert. This is a natural activity for the expert when justifying his/her decision to colleagues or apprentices. A number of RDR-based systems store the case which triggered the addition of an exception rule along with the new rule. This case, being called the *cornerstone case* of the new rule $R$, is retrieved when an exception to $R$ needs to be entered. The cornerstone case is intended to assist the expert in coming up with a justification, since a valid justification must point at differences between the cornerstone case and the case at hand for which $R$ does not perform satisfactorily.

This approach resulted in the expert system PEIRS used for interpreting chemical pathology results [6]. PEIRS appears to have been the most comprehensive medical expert system yet in routine use, but all the rules were added by a pathology expert without programming or knowledge engineering support or skill whilst the system was in routine use. Ripple-Down Rules and some further developments are now successfully exploited commercially by a number of companies.

**Single Classification Ripple Down Rules:** A single classification ripple down rule (SCRDR) tree is a finite binary tree with two distinct types of edges. These edges are typically called *except* and *if not* edges. See Figure 1. Associated with each node in a tree is a *rule*. A rule has the form: *if* $\alpha$ *then* $\beta$ where $\alpha$ is called the *condition* and $\beta$ the *conclusion*.

Cases in SCRDR are evaluated by passing a case to the root of the tree. At any node in the tree, if the condition of a node $N$'s rule is satisfied by the case, the case is passed on to the exception child of $N$. Otherwise, the case is passed on the $N$'s if-not child. The conclusion given by this process is the conclusion from the last node in the RDR tree which fired. To ensure that a conclusion is always given, the root node typically contains a trivial condition which is always satisfied. This node is called the *default* node.

A new node is added to an SCRDR tree when the evaluation process returns the wrong conclusion. The new node is attached to the last node evaluated in the tree provided it is consistent with the existing rules. If the node has no exception link, the new node is attached using an exception link, otherwise an *if not* link is used. To determine the rule for the new node, the expert formulates a rule which is satisfied by the case at hand.

# 3   Our Approach

While the process of incrementally developing knowledge bases will eventually lead to a reasonably accurate knowledge base, provided the domain does not drift and the experts are making the correct judgments, the time it takes to develop a good knowledge base depends heavily on the appropriateness of the used language in which conditions can be expressed by the expert.

Some levels of abstraction in the rule's condition is desirable to make the rule expressive enough in generalizing to unseen cases. To realize this, we use the idea of annotation where phrases that have similar roles are deemed to belong to the same annotation type.

## 3.1   Rule Description

A rule is composed of a condition part and a conclusion part. A condition has an annotation pattern and an annotation qualifier. An annotation is an abstraction over string

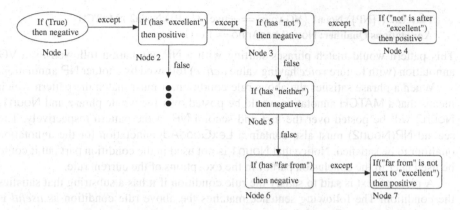

**Fig. 1.** An example SCRDR tree with simple rule language to classify a text into positive or negative class. Node 1 is the default node. A text that contains *excellent* is classified as *positive* by Node 2 as long as none of its exception rules fires, i.e., the text does not contain *not, neither* nor *far from* so Node 3,5,6 would not fire. A text that has *not excellent* is classified as *negative* by Node 3 while it is classified as *positive* by Node 4, if it contains *excellent but not*. If it contains *far from excellent* then it is classified as *negative* by Node 6.

tokens. Conceptually, string tokens covered by annotations of the same type are considered to represent the same concept. Annotations contain the character locations of the beginning and ending position of the annotated text in the document along with the type of annotations and a list of feature value pairs.

The pattern is a regular expression over annotations. It can also post new annotations over matched phrases of the pattern's sub-components . The following is an example of a pattern which posts an annotation over the matched phrase:

({Noun} {VG} {Noun}):MATCH

This pattern would match phrases starting with a Noun annotation followed by a VG followed by another Noun annotation. When applying this pattern on a piece of text, MATCH annotations would be posted over phrases that match this pattern.

An annotation qualifier is a conjunction of constraints over annotations, including newly posted ones. An annotation constraint may require that a feature of that annotation must have a particular value:

VG.voice == active
Token.string == increase

A constraint can also require that the text covered by an annotation must contain ( or not contain) another annotation or a string of text:

NP.hasAnno == LexGoodAdj
VG.has == outperform
VG.hasnot == not

A rule condition is satisfied by a phrase if the phrase matches the pattern and also the annotations qualifier is satisfied. For example we have the following rule condition:

**Pattern:** (({NP}):Noun1 {VG.voice == active} ({NP}):Noun2 ):MATCH
**Annotations Qualifier:** Noun2.hasAnno == LexGoodAdj

This pattern would match phrases starting with a NP annotation followed by a VG annotation (with feature *voice* having value *active*) followed by another NP annotation.

When a phrase satisfies the above rule condition, it must match the pattern which means that a MATCH annotation would be posted over the whole phrase and Noun1, Noun2 will be posted over the first and second NP in the pattern respectively. The second NP(Noun2) must also contain a LexGoodAdj annotation for the annotation qualifier to be satisfied. Notice that Noun1 is not used in the condition part but it could be used later in the conclusion part or in the exceptions of the current rule.

A piece of text is said to satisfy the rule condition if it has a substring that satisfies the condition. The following sentence matches the above rule condition as *useful* is annotated by the LexGoodAdj annotation:

[NP Parallelism NP][VG is VG][NP a useful way NP] to speed up computation.

with following new annotations posted:

[MATCH Parallelism is a useful way MATCH]
[Noun1 Parallelism Noun1]
[Noun2 a useful way Noun2]

but the following do not match:

(1) [NP Parallelism NP] [VG is VG] [NP a method NP] used in our approach.
(2) [NP Parallelism NP] [VG has been shown VG] [VG to be VG ] very useful.

Sentence (1) matches the pattern, but it does not satisfy the annotation constraints. Sentence (2) does not match the pattern.

The rule's conclusion contains the classification of the input text. In the task of extracting positive attributions, it is *true* if the text mentions an advantage or a positive aspect of a concept/term and *false* otherwise.

Besides classification, our framework also offers an easy way to do information extraction. Since a rule's pattern can post annotations over components of the matched phrase, extracting those components is just a matter of selecting appropriate annotations. For example, we can extract the concept/terms of interest whenever the case is classified as containing a positive aspect by specifying the target annotation. A conclusion of the rule with the condition shown above could be:

**Conclusion:** true
**Concept Annotation:** Noun1

The rule's conclusion contains a classification and an annotation to be extracted. It is deemed to be incorrect if either part of the conclusion is incorrect.

## 3.2   Annotations and Features

**Built-in annotations:** As our rules use patterns over annotations, the decision on what annotations and their corresponding features should be are important for the expressiveness of rules. We experimentally tested the expressiveness of rules on technical papers and found that the following annotations and features make patterns expressive enough to capture all rules we want to specify for various tasks.

We have Token annotations that cover every token with *string* feature holding the actual string, *category* feature holding the POS and *lemma* feature holding the token's lemma form.

As a result of the Shallow Parser module, which will be described in the next section, we have several forms of noun phrase annotations ranging from simple to complex noun phrases, e.g., NP(simple noun phrase), NPList ( list of NPs) etc. All forms of noun phrase annotations are covered by a general Noun annotation.

There is also a VG (verb groups) annotation with *type, voice* features, several annotations for clauses e.g. PP (prepositional phrase), SUB (subject), OBJ(object).

An important annotation that makes rules more general is Pair which annotates phrases that are bounded by commas or brackets. With this annotation, the following sentences:

> *The EM algorithm (Dempster , Laird , & Rubin , 1977 ) is effective.....*
> *...the algorithm, in noisy domains, outperformed.....*

could be covered by the following patterns respectively:

> {Noun}({Pair})?{Token.lemma == be}{LexGoodAdj}
> {Noun}({Pair})?{Token.lemma == outperform}

Every rule that has a non-empty pattern would post at least one annotation covering the entire matched phrase. Because rules in our knowledge base are stored in an exception structure, we want to be able to identify which annotations are posted by which rule. To facilitate that, we number every rule and enforce that all annotations posted by rule number $x$ have the prefix RDRx_. Therefore, if a rule is an exception of rule number $x$, it could use all annotations with the prefix RDRx_ in its condition pattern or annotations qualifier.

**Custom annotations:** Users could form new named lexicons during the knowledge acquisition process. The system would then post a corresponding annotation over every word in those lexicons. Doing this makes the effort of generalizing the rule quite easy and keeps the knowledge base compact.


## 3.3   KAFTIE

Our Knowledge Acquisition Framework for Text classification and Information Extraction allows users to easily and quickly develop knowledge bases to classify a text segment into a number of categories as well as extracting relevant information for those categories. For each category $C$, a SCRDR tree will be acquired which determines whether a text segment is classified as class $C$ and which phrases in the text segment are extracted for the class $C$. Each SCRDR tree is composed of a number of nodes each containing a rule as described in section 3.1.

As our approach has the objective of ensuring the incremental improvement of a system's capabilities, all text segments which KAFTIE had already given conclusions (i.e. classification and information extracted) to the satisfaction of the user need to be treated in the same way after any modification to KAFTIE's knowledge base. To ensure this, KAFTIE checks automatically for any potential inconsistencies with previous conclusions of text segments for each modification that a user makes.

## 4   Implementation

We built our framework KAFTIE using GATE [4]. A set of reusable modules known as ANNIE is provided with GATE. These are able to perform basic language processing tasks such as POS tagging and semantic tagging. We use *Tokenizer, Sentence Splitter, Part-of-Speech Tagger and Semantic Tagger* processing resources from ANNIE. *Semantic Tagger* is a JAPE finite state transducer that annotate text based on JAPE grammars. Our rule's annotation pattern is implemented as a JAPE grammar. We also developed additional processing resources for our tasks:

**Lemmatizer:** a processing resource that puts a *lemma* feature into every Token annotation containing the lemma form of the token's string. Lemmatizer uses information from WordNet [7] and the result from the POS Tagger module.

**Shallow Parser:** a processing resource using JAPE finite state transducer. The shallow parser module consists of cascaded JAPE grammars recognizing noun groups, verb groups, propositional phrases, different types of clauses, subjects and objects. These constituents are displayed hierarchically in a tree structure to help experts formulate patterns, see e.g. Figure 2. The Shallow Parser module could be refined as needed by modifying its grammars.

All these processing resources are run on the input text in a pipeline fashion. This is a pre-processing step which produces all necessary annotations before the knowledge base is applied on the text.

## 5   Examples of How to Build a Knowledge Base

The following examples are taken from the actual KB as discussed in section 6. Suppose we start with an empty knowledge base (KB) for recognizing advantages. I.e. the KB

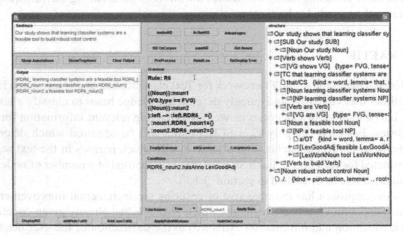

**Fig. 2.** The interface to enter a new rule where the rule is automatically checked for consistency with the existing KB before it gets committed. Annotations including those created by the shallow parser module are shown in the tree in the *structure* box.

would only contain a default rule which always produces a *'false'* conclusion. When the following sentence is encountered:

*Our study shows that learning classifier systems are a feasible tool to build robust robot control.*

Our empty KB would initially use the default rule to suggest it does not belong to the *Advantages* class. This can be corrected by adding the following rule to the KB:

**Rule:R6**
(({Noun}):RDR6_noun1 {VG.type==FVG}
({Noun.hasAnno == LexGoodAdj}):RDR6_noun2):RDR6_
**Conclusion:** true
**Target Concept:** RDR6_noun1

This rule would match phrases starting with a Noun annotation, followed by a VG annotation (with feature *type* equal to *FVG*) followed by a Noun annotation. Furthermore, the second Noun annotation must contain a LexGoodAdj annotation covering its substring. As there is a LexGoodAdj annotation covering the token *feasible*, the phrase *learning classifier systems are a feasible tool* is matched by **Rule6** and *learning classifier systems* is extracted as the concept of interest. When we encounter this sentence:

*Given a data set, it is often not clear beforehand which **algorithm will yield the best performance**.*

Rule **R6** suggests that the sentence mentions *algorithm* with a positive sentiment (the matched phrase is highlighted in boldface) which is not correct. The following exception rule is added to fix that:

**Rule:R32**    ({Token.lemma==which}{RDR6_} ):RDR32_
**Conclusion:** false

This rule says that if the phrase matched by **Rule6** follows a *which* token, then the sentence containing it does not belong to *Advantages* class. However, when we encounter the following sentence

*The latter approach searches for the subset of attributes over **which naive Bayes has the best performance**.*

Rule **R6** suggests that *naive Bayes* has been mentioned with a positive sentiment but its exception rule, **R32**, overrules the decision because the phrase that matches **R6** (annotated by RDR6_) follows a token *which*. Obviously, *naive Bayes* should be the correct answer since the token *which* is used differently here than in the context in which **R32** was created. We can add an exception to **R32** catering for this case:

**Rule:R56**  ( {Token.string==over} {RDR32_} ):RDR56_
**Conclusion:** true
**Target Concept:** RDR6_noun2

# 6   Experimental Results

We have applied our framework KAFTIE to tackle two different tasks of recognizing sentences that contain positive and negative attributions of a concept/term as well as extracting the concept/term[1]. These tasks are challenging as the analysis of positive and negative sentiments towards a concept requires deep understanding of the textual context, drawing on common sense, domain knowledge and linguistic knowledge. A concept could be mentioned with a positive or negative sentiment in a local context but not in a wider context. For example,

*We do not think that X is very efficient.*

If we just look at the phrase *X is very efficient*, we could say that *X* is of positive sentiment, but considering a wider context it is not.

The task of extracting negative attributions may appear similar to the task of extracting positive attributions, but it is more difficult in this domain. One reason is because when authors mention a disadvantage of a concept, they sometimes talk about its positive aspects first. For example:

**These innovations** *proved very useful in increasing the CS efficiency , but* **inadequate for our needs**

The negative sentiment towards *These innovations* is not next to the term it attributes to. Therefore, recognizing and extracting *These innovations* with its negative sentiment is more difficult compared to its positive sentiment.

A corpus was collected consisting of 140 machine learning papers and journals downloaded from citeseer, and converted from PDF into text. Even though these papers are from the same domain, we have to stress that the topics they cover are rather diverse and include most areas within machine learning. We randomly selected 16 documents of different authors and grouped them into 2 corpora. The first corpus has 3672 sentences from 9 documents and the second corpus contains 4713 sentences from 7 documents.

For each task, a knowledge base(KB) is built using the first corpus. The two KBs are built independently, at different times. Quality of the built KBs will be evaluated against the second corpus.

## 6.1 Experience with the Knowledge Acquisition Process

Building KBs using our framework is easy and quick. Most of the time spent is on going through the corpus, sentence by sentence, to determine if a sentence belongs to the class of interest but is not picked up by the KB. After the expert identifies the sentence of interest and the phrase to be extracted, it takes about 2 minutes to come up with a new rule or change an existing rule. This process involves first creating a pattern and then modifying it, if needed, until the pattern covers the sentence at hand.

While the particular choice of generality or specificity of a rule's pattern affects to some degree the convergence speed of the knowledge base towards complete accuracy, it is not that crucial in our approach. This is because suboptimal early choices are naturally patched up by further rules as the knowledge acquisition process progresses. Where a too general rule was entered a subsequent exception rule will be created, while a subsequent if-not rule patches a too specific rule. However, to help speed up the convergence of the KB, we do allow experts to change rules (usually to make it more general) while automatically ensuring the KB is consistent.

---

[1] The phrase *positive/negative sentiment or attribution* and *advantage/disadvantage* of a term are used interchangeably.

In fact, for the two tasks follow, we tried to formulate more general rules for the first task (Advantages) and more specific rules for the second task (Disadvantages). The performance of the two KBs on an unseen test corpus reveals a similar F-measure of above 80%. Looking at it more closely, we achieved a lower precision and a higher recall for the first task but a higher precision and a lower recall for the second task on the same corpus. This is quite intuitive as if we make rules very specific to the case, we would have a good precision but unlikely to cover other cases, hence a low recall.

## 6.2   Performance of Knowledge Bases

For each of the two tasks of recognizing positive and negative attributions of concepts/terms, we built a KB based on the first corpus and will test it on the second corpus. A sentence is deemed correctly suggested by the KB if the KB classifies the sentence to the right class and the concept/term of interest is also at least partly extracted. We do not require the full phrase containing the concept/term to be extracted to accommodate for the imperfection of our shallow parser as well as other pre-processing modules. For example:

*Randomized C 4.5 performed badly in this setting.*

Our KB correctly classifies this sentence into the *Disadvantage* class and extracts phrase **5** as the term of interest rather than **Randomized C 4.5**. We still consider this correct. Ultimately, users would inspect extracted phrases and can easily pick up the full phrase if it is not fully extracted.

**Recognizing Positive Attributions:** For this task, we build a knowledge base to determine if a sentence belongs to the *Advantages* class and also to extract the concept/term of interest. Given a sentence, the fired rule from the KB would give a *true* conclusion if the sentence is considered to be of *Advantages* class and *false* otherwise.

Using the first corpus we have built a KB consisting of 61 rules. Applying the knowledge base to the second corpus (4713 sentences), it classifies 178 sentences as belonging to the *Advantages* class. Checking the accuracy, 132 cases are correct. That gives a 74% (132/178) precision. It misses 18 cases giving a recall of 88% and an F-measure of 80.4%. Examples of sentences returned by the KB with the extracted concepts in bold face are:

*Again,* **EM** *improves accuracy significantly.*
*In this low dimensional problem it was more computationally efficient* **to consider a random candidate** *set.*

**Recognizing Negative Attributions:**   This task is similar to the task of *recognizing positive attributions* except we would like to extract phrases that have been mentioned with a disadvantage or a negative sentiment.

Using the first corpus, we build a KB of 65 rules for this task. When applying to the second corpus (4713 sentences), it classifies 132 sentences as belonging to the *Disadvantages* class. Out of them 114 sentences are correctly classified resulting in a precision of 86.4%. In the corpus, there are 25 cases that should be classified into the *Disadvantages* class but are missed by the KB. That gives a 82% recall and an F-measure of 84.1%.

Some examples of sentences in the *Disadvantages* class returned by the KB with extracted terms in bold face are:

**The mechanism in ICET for handling conditional test costs** *has some limitations.*

*The development of Foil was motivated by a failure we observed when* **applying existing ILP methods to a particular problem** *, that of learning the past tense of English verbs.*

Notice that the second example above is quite tricky to extract.

**Query-directed Advantages and Disadvantages Extraction:** To verify the quality of our approach, we look at an application scenario of finding advantages and disadvantages for a particular concept/term e.g. *decision tree*. The literal string *decision tree* appears at least 720 times in the corpus of 140 journals and papers. We only consider sentences that are classified into *Advantages* or *Disadvantages* class by the KBs and have the string *decision tree* in the extracted *target annotation*. Clearly, this simple analysis would miss cases where the actual string is not in the sentence but is mentioned via an anaphora instead. Future work will address this point.

The two KBs described above suggested 22 sentences for the *Advantages* class and 9 sentences for the *Disadvantages* class that have *decision tree* in the target annotation. These sentences were from 7 documents of 5 different authors. Some examples are:

**Advantages:**
*Results clearly indicate that* **decision trees** *can be used to improve the performance of CBL systems and do so without reliance on potentially expensive expert knowledge*
**Disadvantages:**
*Rule sets are relatively easy for people to understand, and rule learning systems outperform* **decision tree learners on many problems** *.*

Among the suggested sentences, 12 (out of 22) sentences of the *Advantages* class are correct and 7 (out of 9) sentences of the *Disadvantages* class are correct. That gives 55% and 78% accuracy for the *Advantages* and *Disadvantages* classes respectively. We will analyze why the accuracy is not very good for the *Advantages* class in the next section.

## 6.3   Analysis of KB Errors

Inspecting misclassified sentences of the above experiment for the *Advantages* class reveals that 6 of them are from the same document (accounting for 60% of the error) and are of the same type:

*...what is the probability that [RDR1_ [RDR1_noun2 the smaller decision tree RDR1_noun2] is more accurate RDR1_ ].*

which does not say that the decision tree is more accurate if we consider the sentential context. This misclassification is due to the fact that we have not seen this type of pattern during training which could easily be overcome by adding a single exception rule.

A number of misclassifications is due to errors in modules we used, such as the POS tagger or the Shallow Parser, that generate annotations and features used in the rule's condition. For example, in

*Comparing classificational accuracy alone , assistant performed better than cn 2 in these particular domains.*

*performed* is tagged as VBN(past participle), rather than VBD(past tense), causing our Shallow Parser not to recognize *performed* as a proper VG. Consequently, our rule base did not classify this case correctly. We also noticed that several errors came from noise in the text we get from the pdf2text program.

Overall, errors appear to come from the inaccuracy of pre-processing modules or the fact that rules' patterns are either overly general or too specific. This is not crucial in our approach and in fact highlights a strength of KAFTIE - it allows experts to enter exception rules for the refinement of existing rules.

## 6.4 Exception Rules Structure

Apart from the default rule, every rule is an exception rule which is created to correct an error of another rule. An SCRDR KB could be viewed as consisting of layers of exception rules where every rule in layer $n$ is an exception of a rule in layer $n - 1$ [2]. The default rule is the only rule in layer 0. A conventional method that stores rules in a flat list is equivalent to layer 1 in our SCRDR KB. The KB for the *Disadvantages* class has 32, 33 and 1 rules in layers 1, 2 and 3 respectively. The KB for the *Advantages* class has 25, 31 and 4 rules in layers 1, 2 and 3 respectively. Having more than one level of exceptions indicates the necessity of the exception structure in storing rules. An example of 3 levels of exception rules has been shown in section 5.

# 7 Related Work

## 7.1 Ripple Down Rules (RDR)

Unlike domains where traditional RDR has been applied, the number of attributes is arbitrary large in natural language domains. It is therefore impossible to just compare the cornerstone case against the current misclassified case for a list of attributes that are different for the creation of new exception rules. In our framework, KAFTIE, the rule that misclassified the case, in addition to its cornerstone case, is presented to the experts to form a new exception rule. Furthermore, in order to reduce the number of duplicated or *similar* rules and to speed up the KB's convergence, existing rules could be modified as long as the KB remains consistent.

Ripple Down Rules have also been applied to sentence and relation classification tasks [14, 8]. There are several shortcomings with these approaches. Firstly, patterns used in these works are simple utilizing only words, word groups and POS. Moreover, a pattern in an exception rule cannot refer to the exact matched phrases of the parent rule. That limits the capability of expressing exception rules. In this work we addressed these shortcomings by defining patterns over annotations. Annotations subsume all features used in previous work, as well as enable the reference to the matched phrase of the parent rules.

---

[2] Rules in Figure 1 are presented in layers structure

## 7.2   Knowledge Acquisition Versus Machine Learning

Our approach takes a knowledge acquisition approach where experts create rules manually. This differs from machine learning approaches that automatically learn rule patterns [16, 9, 1], or learn implicit rules (not expressed as patterns) to classify sentiment expressions [13, 17] or for the task of information extraction [16]. We strongly believe that our approach is superior to automatic approaches since an expert needs to spend their time to classify the sentences even where machine learning approaches are taken. This is also corroborated by some very recent studies comparing Machine Learning with Knowledge Acquisition using the same corpus of text and showing vast differences in accuracy in the range around 40% for Machine Learning depending on the used method and 80%+ for Knowledge Acquisition [15].

If the expert has to classify the sentences anyway, it does not take much more time to also provide some explanations on some of the sentences for why they should be classified differently to how the current knowledge base classified the sentence. I.e. the knowledge acquisition process comes almost for free compared to the effort of manual sentence classification required for both, our knowledge acquisition as well as for machine learning approaches.

For the two tasks presented in section 6, it took one expert about 10 hours to build one KB based on a corpus of 3672 sentences. However, most of the time was spent in looking at sentences to determine if they belong to the class of interest and which phrase in the sentence needs to be extracted. This amount of time is also needed for the tagging of training data for other techniques that attempt to learn rules automatically from examples. The actual time required to build a knowledge base consisting of 65 rules by one expert is only about 2 hours in total.

We believe that our approach leads to a significantly higher accuracy based on a given set of sentences than could be achieved by machine learning which would only exploit a boolean class label as expert information for each sentence [15]. As a consequence, the total number of sentences an expert needs to read and classify in order to achieve a certain classification accuracy can be expected to be much less with our approach than a machine learning approach. Similar findings for medical knowledge bases have been obtained in systematic studies for Ripple Down Rules [3]. Many other researchers [12, 10] share the same view by manually creating patterns and lexicons in their approaches. We take one step further by helping experts to incrementally acquire rules and lexicons as well as control their interactions in a systematic manner.

## 7.3   Information Extraction

Allowing a pattern to be a regular expression over annotations, the expressiveness of our rule language is at least as good as existing IE systems (e.g. [9, 16], see [11] for a survey). Our framework combines the following valuable features of those IE systems: it allows syntactic and semantic constraints on all components of the patterns including the fields to be extracted. Further, it can accommodate both single-slot and multi-slot rules. Finally, it can be applied to a wide variety of documents ranging from rigidly formatted text to free text.

## 7.4 Sentiment Analysis

Most of the related work on sentiment analysis has focused on news and review genres [12, 17, 10, 13]. We demonstrated KAFTIE's effectiveness on a corpus of technical papers as it appears more challenging but the framework is domain independent. A majority of existing approaches only analyze co-occurrences of simple phrases (unigrams or bigrams) within a short distance [10, 13] or indicative adjectives and adverbs [17]. In contrast to that, we look at more complex patterns in relation to the subject matter to determine its polarity. One reason for this difference might be that those applications tend to classify the polarity of the whole article assuming that all sentiment expressions in the article contribute towards the article's subject classification. In this work, we identify sentiment expressions to extract the subject of the expression as well as its sentiment classification. [12] has a similar goal as ours but they do not consider the surrounding context of the sentiment expression which could affect the subject's polarity.

## 8 Conclusion and Future Work

In this paper, we presented KAFTIE, an incremental knowledge acquisition framework that allows users to rapidly develop new text classification and information extraction systems. We demonstrated the effectiveness of KAFTIE using two sample tasks of extracting information from scientific papers regarding advantages of concepts/terms as well as disadvantages.

Our experiments so far were very encouraging and showed that KAFTIE can be a very valuable support tool for the rapid development of advanced information extraction systems operating on complex texts as present in scientific papers.

The performance of the resulting information extraction system, after 10 hours of knowledge acquisition (expert time), have shown that the knowledge bases built using the framework achieved precisions of at least 74% and recalls up to 88% on an unseen corpus. It should be noted that all documents in the corpus are from different authors covering different topics. This suggests that it would be feasible to quickly build new knowledge bases for different tasks in new domains. Although it appears easy for experts to create rules, it would be desirable if the experts are presented with possible candidate rules to choose from. Even when the suggested rules are not correct to be used as-is, using them as a starting point to create the final rules should be helpful. Future work will address the problem of using machine learning techniques to automatically propose candidate rules to be used in a *mixed initiative* style [5]. Furthermore, we plan to investigate a method to suggest to the experts existing rules in the KB that *nearly* match the case at hand for possible modification of those rules.

## References

1. F. Ciravegna. Adaptive information extraction from text by rule induction and generalization. In *17th International Joint Conference on Artificial Intelligence*, Seattle, 2001.
2. P. Compton and R. Jansen. A philosophical basis for knowledge acquisition. *Knowledge Acquisition*, 2:241–257, 1990.

3. P. Compton, P. Preston, and B. Kang. The use of simulated experts in evaluating knowledge acquisition. In *Proceedings of the Banff KA workshop on Knowledge Acquisition for Knowledge-Based Systems*. 1995.

4. H. Cunningham, D. Maynard, K. Bontcheva, and V. Tablan. Gate: An architecture for development of robust hlt applications. In *Proceedings of the 40th Annual Meeting of the Association for Computational Linguistics(ACL)*, Philadelphia, PA, 2002.

5. D. Day, J. Aberdeen, L. Hirschman, R. Kozierok, P. Robinson, and M. Vilain. Mixed-initiative development of language processing systems. In *Fifth ACL Conference on Applied Natural Language Processing*, Washington, DC, 1997.

6. G. Edwards, P. Compton, R. Malor, A. Srinivasan, and L. Lazarus. PEIRS: a pathologist maintained expert system for the interpretation of chemical pathology reports. *Pathology*, 25:27–34, 1993.

7. C. Fellbaum, editor. *WordNet - An electronic lexical database*. MIT PRESS, Cambridge, MA, 1998.

8. A. Hoffmann and S. B. Pham. Towards topic-based summarization for interactive document viewing. In *Proceedings of the 2nd International Conference on Knowledge Capture(K-Cap)*, Florida, 2003.

9. J. Kim and D. Moldovan. Acquisition of linguistic patterns for knowledge-based information extraction. *IEEE Transactions on Knowledge and Data Engineering*, 7(5):713–724, 1995.

10. S. Morinaga, K. Yamanishi, K. Tateishi, and T. Fukushima. Mining product reputations on the web. In *Proceedings of the Eighth ACM International Conference on Knowledge Discovery and Data Mining(KDD)*, pages 341–349, 2002.

11. I. Muslea. Extraction patterns for information extraction tasks: A survey. In *The AAAI Workshop on Machine Learning for Information Extraction*, 1999.

12. T. Nasukawa and J. Yi. Sentiment analysis: Capturing favorability using natural language processing. In *Proceedings of the 2nd International Conference on Knowledge Capture(K-Cap)*, Florida, 2003.

13. B. Pang and L. Lee. Thumbs up? sentiment classification using machine learning techniques. In *Proceedings of the Conference on Empirical Methods in Natural Language Processing(EMNLP)*, pages 79–86, 2002.

14. S. B. Pham and A. Hoffmann. A new approach for scientific citation classification using cue phrases. In *Proceedings of Australian Joint Conference in Artificial Intelligence*, Perth, Australia, 2003.

15. S. B. Pham and A. Hoffmann. Extracting positive attributions from scientific papers. In *7th International Conference on Discovery Science*, Italy, 2004.

16. S. Soderland. Learning information extraction rules for semi-structured and free text. *Machine Learning*, 34(1-3):233–272, 1999.

17. P. Turney. Thumbs up or thumbs down? semantic orientation applied to unsupervised classification of reviews. In *Proceedings of the 40th Annual Meeting of the Association for Computational Linguistics(ACL)*, pages 417–424, 2002.

# Ontologies Help Finding Inspiration:
# A Practical Approach
# in Multimedia Information Management

Silvia Calegari and Marco Loregian

Dipartimento di Informatica, Sistemistica e Comunicazione,
Università degli Studi di Milano Bicocca,
via Bicocca degli Arcimboldi 8,
20126 Milano, Italy
{calegari,loregian}@disco.unimib.it

**Abstract.** Students working in inspirational learning environments need some help with finding new ideas. An ontology-driven selection facility was developed in the ATELIER project for automatically extract appropriate material from a large knowledge base. This paper introduces the ATELIER project and describes the algorithm we studied for presenting inspirational material to students while using the system. A scenario and literature contextualization are also given.

## Introduction

Students in inspirational learning environments, like the ones we studied in the ATELIER[1] project, have at their disposal thousands of documents and they risk getting lost in such a wide information base. Multimedia file description through metadata and the use of such metadata for information retrieval and resource sharing are well-established practices. Problems arising from these approaches are related to finding appropriate content description and the time-consuming task of properly querying a database in order to find what is needed. To support students in creative practices we developed an ontology-driven selection facility for moving from a document to another in a creative path without involving users in typing and explicit query writing. The aim is to awake creativity and inspiration into learners setting the focus on creative tasks instead of computer use. The paper is structured as follows: background for our research is initially discussed introducing the model of learning we claim to be suitable for the environment ATELIER project has been developed in, then the project structure itself is shortly described and some of the digital devices available to system users are presented. A scenario introduces our approach and then the discussion turns to the details of the algorithm we studied and implemented. Evaluation of the approach is given referring to two quantitative experiments we lead after our

---

[1] Architecture and Technology for Inspirational Learning Environments, IST-2001-33064, http://atelier.k3.mah.se

D. Karagiannis and U. Reimer (Eds.): PAKM 2004, LNAI 3336, pp. 307–318, 2004.
© Springer-Verlag Berlin Heidelberg 2004

students work. Computational cost and performance are presented. Some other relevant works we found in literature are presented for introducing our scope. Finally some conclusions are drawn.

# 1 Background

The background for our research is the ATELIER project. The aim of the ATE-LIER project is to build a digitally enhanced environment supporting creative learning. Learning contexts analyzed are those of architecture and interaction design students[2]. A common software infrastructure integrates many kinds of device (e.g. large displays, RFID technology, barcodes... ). Moreover knowledge management facilities supporting the whole infrastructure itself are available. These management functionalities act as glue for the system, keeping information collected within the environment coherent both from logic and pragmatic point of view. There are basically two kinds of application: the first one is for indexing items in a shared database according to a dynamically generated and evolving ontology [1] and the second is for helping users in finding inspiration through material previously inserted by themselves or someone else. The first part of this process (i.e. building and maintaining an ontology inside a learning environment) will not be treated in this paper. Interested reader may refer to [1] fore more details. Next a brief introduction to what we call "inspirational learning" is provided.

## 1.1  Learning Model

According to Kolb's model [2, 3] of experiential and inspirational learning, meaning is generated by the combination of two cyclic phases. The concrete world of experience and the personal sphere of insights operate in turn and interleave in order to refine learner's knowledge and understanding. The process of learning starts with the immersion of the person in a concrete experience from which as many observations as possible are gathered and perceptions are stored. Architecture students usually take trips for visiting sites and collect multimedia data that is later taken into the digital environment. During this phase they already face problems they are dealing with and implicitly choose some particular view for the solution, eventually finding some more ideas on the site. Experiential learning can thus be envisioned as a recurrent process of adaptation to change, based on a rigorous process of transformation. Inspirational learning is, on the other hand, an inner process that takes place in the student. New ideas are elaborated while awareness grows and focus is gained on most relevant topics and knowledge fragments. This phase is neither constrained to experience-making nor any other particular activity and can be stimulated in many different ways. Meaning usually emerges from the "systemic interaction" [2] of insights gained through inspirational learning with concepts learned through experiential learning. Both these phases are supported by the ATELIER project at various degrees.

---

[2] We made experiments with architecture students at the Academy of Fine Arts in Vienna (Austria)

**Fig. 1.** *(left)* The Jacket, a visit map and some pictures. *(right)* The Texture Painter.

## 2   The ATELIER Project

The ATELIER software infrastructure was thought for supporting a hetero-geneous environment, rich of different devices manipulating both tangible and digital information and material. Physical artifacts of course populate every room that is not purely virtual, so they have to be seriously taken into account. Physical items are addressed in the ATELIER workspace in two different ways: with barcodes and Radio Frequency Identification (RFID) tags. Both solutions are also used for associating commands to tangible objects. Digital artifacts are stored, whenever they enter the workspace, in a hyper-media database [4] that allows a hierarchical organization of information in a non-linear structure. Some more details of these mechanisms for collecting and storing information are now given. As briefly stated while dealing with experience in learning, architecture students usually start their projects with visits to sites of interest outside their workplace.

The *Jacket* is a wearable device which assemblies the functionalities of digital camera, sound recorder and path recorder (by the use of GPS signals). Data is temporarily kept on a PDA until the students get back to the academy. Once at home files are uploaded to a server and organized according to temporal and spatial logics: all data collected during the visit to a particular site is grouped and displayed in a three dimensional path. This is possible by the GPS informa-tion. Moreover, document description can further be enriched by freely chosen metadata. Besides of time, place and author information, what will be more useful for next discussions is an ontology-based description in the form of some appropriate keywords. The author, or the person who is uploading documents, can choose keywords from the ontology. The ontology is dynamically enriched, meaning that new keywords can be used for describing a document and tools are also available for re-organizing concept hierarchy. What follows is the descrip-tion of another system component that is not used for recording or managing information but for the purpose of making it available to end users.

The *Texture Painter* consists of a projector, a camera and a wooden brush. Some software tracks brush movements in front of the camera and this infor-mation is used to virtually paint, with some digital texture projected by the beamer, a physical model that is placed in front of the camera. While painting a texture palette, with ten different textures, is displayed and users choose one of them by placing the brush upon the selected slot in the palette. Functionalities for altering textures (rotating, scaling...) are also available to extend graphical possibilities. The Texture Painter may also be connected to RFID tag readers, so to be controlled using physical objects (e.g. textures can be switched or even printed using a card with that particular meaning). Using the Texture Painter mixed objects [5, 6] are created, properties of physical models are deeply investigated and students, architecture students in particular, are moreover allowed to experiment and to test different possibilities before realizing final (colored, textured) models of objects they are working on. The following scenario presents the typical situation for which our algorithm was tailored.

## 3   Scenario: Exploring Multimedia Information

*Fabio is painting a model with the Texture Painter but he is not totally satisfied of the texture combination. He asks the system for a new texture placing the Random Pick card on the tag reader and then a picture is randomly fetched from the hypermedia database for substituting the currently selected texture on the model. The new picture is still not fitting Fabio's artistic will so he requests another one.*

The problem arising from random picking images from the hypermedia database is that it is not proved to be an inspirational process. A database typically contains thousands of pictures dealing with so many topics that the user could get annoyed by meaningless pictures being presented before finding something that fits a bit to his intentions. No convergence is ever granted for this unpredictable process. Two other ways for relating pictures are currently available in the system. The first is to search for color matching pictures. Picking pictures with the same color configuration is a well-known strategy and often implemented search facility [7], it is anyway not so much inspirational as the color layout has to be made explicit. It is much more to try to navigate a conceptual map. Pictures or digital elements in general can be conceptually linked using the ontology and the association database (the combination of these two components generates a consistent knowledge base for the ATELIER environment).

*Fabio painted the central part of his model using a texture with a rose but that flower is not the one he had in mind or the result is not what it was meant to be. He puts the Ontology Pick card on the tag reader and then the ontology engine analyzes the current picture. That picture depicts a rose, that is a flower, and no other metadata is provided. The ontology then extracts from the database all the pictures that deal with flowers and picks one among them. The new picture depicts a flower on the branch of a cherry tree. Still it is not the most suitable one, because of the color layout, so another one is searched. The set of pictures dealing with flowers, cherries and branches is extracted from the database and one with a maple leaf is chosen. Again the search is repeated and different pictures follow on the texture palette: a Canadian flag, an Italian flag, Italian food, red tomatoes...*

The surprising effect is granted by the degree of randomness that is used together with the relevance weighting mechanism used to make ontology engine extract useful items from the hypermedia database. Other surprising factors have not been mentioned in the scenario yet, as they are much more hidden inside the mechanism. They will be shown in next section.

# 4   The Algorithm

We started our problem analysis by considering which properties of each document could have been considered of interest for bringing inspiration to a user and why. First it has to be said that ATELIER room and information system are shared across a small number of members of the same workgroup, working on the same project and sharing a common goal: the making up of a complex project and its final presentation. For this reason it can be stated that all material available in the database can freely[3] be distributed to other members, without any privacy constraint. For this reason *authorship* has to be considered as a relevant factor when displaying material to any user. Most of the times it can be assumed that if something that does not belong to the user who is querying the system is displayed it would probably appear as something rather new to the student. Another relevant property for a document is its *age*. Even if projects usually last for short periods, a semester at most, it can happen that documents generated at the beginning of the work, and then rich of ideas that have probably been left apart during later stages, would carry much more new, or forgotten, stimulus to the user. On the other hand, old documents might be obsolete and annoying: this factor has to be taken into consideration too. Recently created information will probably be still fresh in user's memory and will probably carry not much inspiration to him. The right balance between old and new information has to be found.

The algorithm we adopted will now be discussed presenting execution steps and formulas we used. The core concept of the algorithm is the distance function. Distance is evaluated between documents and an enriched keyword set. Distance is weighted according to other factors (such as age and authorship): documents are ranked according to this relevance measure. Another item used during the algorithm is a *log-file* (i.e. search history) that is used for storing the last the selection queries sent to the database service, in order to track implicit correlation among keywords: if two or more words are very often used together than they will probably be related to the same set of concepts.

A start document is given as an input: keywords are extracted from it and used to start the algorithm. Identification (the name) of the person who is using the service is needed, since results will be tailored for him. A first search is executed on the database to retrieve all documents matching with at least one of the keywords that describe the input document. Meanwhile the history file

---

[3] This feature can easily be handled by group management facilities, which are already available in our system, but algorithm discussion would uselessly result in a more complicated description

is analyzed to compute correlation among keywords, counting how many times keywords were used together to query the database. Original keyword set is then enriched with keywords from these other sources:

- Keywords other than the original ones that were used for describing documents retrieved from the database.
- Keywords recursively extracted from query history file. If a keyword is in the set then all words that were used together with it at least once will be added too, and so for the new added ones until no more correlations may be found.

All these new terms are provided with a recursion level that will be used later to evaluate their distance from the original query. Original keyword level is one, while keywords coming only from database documents (and not present in history correlation matrix) have recursion level set to *null*: reason for this choice will be clear later. This enriched keyword set is then pruned by the use of the ontology. Rules for keeping a candidate keyword in the query set are:

- The keyword must be present in the ontology: this condition should be satisfied for each keyword since document metadata is checked at insertion time and unknown keywords are automatically added to the ontology.
- There must be a direct path of accepted keywords connecting each candidate keyword to one of the original ones. Only keywords having a child or father already accepted can be accepted.

The refined query is then used to search database again: a document vector ($w$) is created. $w$ is a bi-dimensional vector containing the weight of each document with respect to the keyword set, creation date and author's name. Weight is computed as follows:

- $a_j$ is defined as the number of documents created by the author of the search divided by the number created by other people (both number plus one, in order to avoid null values and division by zero)

$$a_j = \frac{1 + \left|\{d \mid author(d) \wedge d \in Docs_j\}\right|}{1 + \left|\{d \mid \neg author(d) \wedge d \in Docs_j\}\right|}$$

- $m$ is the position of the document having the creation date closest to the average between the oldest and the newest document. Value $m$ splits the document set in two sub-sets that may be different in size.
- The value for the median document at position $m$ is $w_{m,j} = 1/a_j$ and for all others the value of $w_{i,j}$ is given by

$$w_{i,j} = \frac{Dist(m,i)}{1 + \left|\{x \mid (date(x) > M \wedge date(i) < M) \vee (date(x) < M \wedge date(i) > M)\}\right|} \cdot \frac{1}{a_j}$$

where the denominator is one plus the cardinality (meaning the number of documents) of the subset not containing the document $i : date(i)$ stands for the date of the document at position $i$ while $M = date(m)$.

A keyword vector $k$ is also created: each keyword of the enriched query is weighted according to some factors:

$$k_i = \frac{\sum_{j=1,\, j \neq i}^{n} h_{i,j}}{l_i^2}$$

- Correlation between it and other keywords (based on query history, numerator): $h$ is the matrix describing correlation of keywords in the history of the system. $h_{i,j}$ thus says how many times keywords $i$ and $j$ were used together.
- Keyword originality or recursive insertion level[4]: $l_i$ is the recursive level of keyword $i$. Keywords having $l = null$, meaning they were not present in the history file or not used with other ones, will have this weight set to the average weight of other words.

Lower bound for $k_i$ is zero when a keyword without correlation with other words is in the query: it might happen, for example, if the word came from document, was accepted by ontology and was present in history file but never used with other query keywords.

Distance $d(x, k)$ between documents and the keyword vector is computed using cosine distance:

$$d(x, k) = \frac{\sum_{i=1}^{n} (w_{x,i} \cdot k_i)}{\sqrt{\sum_{i=1}^{n} w_{x,i}^2 \cdot \sum_{i=1}^{n} k_i^2}}$$

Relevance calculation comes last for sorting documents and distance, computed at the previous step, is multiplied by the percentage of the keyword set that the single document is able to cover.

$$R(x) = d(x, k) \cdot m(x, k)$$

Relevance is used to sort documents in decreasing order. At the end of this process one document is randomly picked among the top ten. This random selection is necessary to avoid entering in loops and eventually bouncing between the "best" documents.

## 5   Evalutation

It is hard to quantify inspiration. We received a positive feedback every time our software service was used but this is not enough to measure its performances in term of surprise factors. In order to quantify this evaluation we ran two experiments, using two different multimedia data sets and two different ontologies, tracked iterated executions of the algorithm and analyzed interesting behaviors.

---

[4] It is a penalty factor and thus set in the denominator. The higher the level the greater can be considered the semantic distance between the keyword and the original query.

**First experiment.** The first experiment was conducted on a restricted set of images but using a large ontology. The hypermedia database was filled with just 215 items that were described using an ontology with 1006 different terms. The history file was 100 lines long, meaning that exactly one hundred queries were made to ontology database before-hand. All pictures were collected on the same day but by five different authors: it was the documentation of a one day trip of a small workgroup. A document was randomly selected to be the seed for the simulations. Ten simulations were started, each consisting of 100 ontology-picks in sequence. We estimated surprise capability by counting how many times it happened that all keywords from a document were dropped after one single pick and how many times it happened after two picks. Results are presented in Table 1 below. It can be seen that it was quite infrequent that all keywords were lost from a document to the following one, meaning that some kind of coherence was always kept all along the sequence but also, on the other hand, that it has been quite frequent that all keywords were lost after two steps: this shows that the crossing of the data base was rather quick.

**Table 1.** First experiment.

|            | 1  | 2  | 3 | 4 | 5  | 6 | 7 | 8  | 9 | 10 | avg  |
|------------|----|----|---|---|----|---|---|----|---|----|------|
| $1^{st}$ step | 0  | 4  | 1 | 1 | 5  | 0 | 0 | 2  | 1 | 0  | 1,4  |
| $2^{nd}$ step | 12 | 13 | 6 | 3 | 31 | 2 | 9 | 10 | 7 | 14 | 10,4 |

**Second experiment.** The methodology of this experiment was the same of the previous, but with some differences in the data set. This time the picture set was composed of 20882 items, many times more than in the first experiment, while the ontology was composed of only 122 terms. Items were collected in a six months long period by seven different people: this was the work of two small workgroups along a student-project time. Results are presented in Table 2 below. It can be seen that this time, with one hundred executions of the algorithm in a row and repeating it again for ten times, it never happened that all keywords got lost from an item to the following one. It also came much more seldom that all keywords were lost at a two distance, though it still happened 3,4% of the times. We explain this loss in variability by observing that in this experiment there was a huge amount of items that were indexed using a very small set of keywords and so it got much more hard for the algorithm to discover new paths to be followed because of the higher similarity among large set of documents. Nevertheless, also looking at execution logs, we saw that the evolution in the

**Table 2.** Second experiment.

|            | 1 | 2 | 3 | 4 | 5 | 6 | 7 | 8 | 9 | 10 | avg |
|------------|---|---|---|---|---|---|---|---|---|----|-----|
| $1^{st}$ step | 0 | 0 | 0 | 0 | 0 | 0 | 0 | 0 | 0 | 0  | 0   |
| $2^{nd}$ step | 3 | 4 | 3 | 3 | 1 | 4 | 5 | 4 | 3 | 4  | 3,4 |

inspirational process was still present, even if slower and more gradual than in the previous experiment, where new elements could abruptly come into scene with great surprise of the user.

We can also observe that such a behavior is also functional to the learning process we envision. At a first stage, the one presented with the first experiment, students are looking for inspiration in the little material they have at their disposal and they might be looking for new connections among documents. After six months they will be focusing on their final presentations and need to get proper support, and feedback, from the system. The system should then present them various material in the first stage while it should restrict its scope in the later one, not bothering users with documents that might be irrelevant at this stage.

## 5.1   Performance Evaluation and Complexity Analysis

Some considerations can be made, apart from inspirational measures, also regarding algorithm complexity and execution speed. Our implementation proved to be quite performing, behaving almost in real time within the ATELIER system. Slowness was only carried by loading time when dealing with huge pictures (one Megabyte or more in size) that had to be transferred along a LAN and displayed using Java$^{TM}$ image processing.

The algorithm complexity can be evaluated by memory occupation and computational cost. We will focus, as it is much more critical from our point of view, on the latter one considering the response time from both the database and ontology access as an unitary operation. We define:

- $dSize$ as the size of the documents final list;
- $kSize$ as the size of the final keywords;
- $historyVectorSize$ as the size of the keyword vector into history file without duplicate values.

The computational cost of $w$ (bi-dimensional vector) is $O(dSize \cdot kSize)$, corresponding to the cost of the $a_j$ function. In fact, the median value calculation requires $O(log(dSize))$ and both $Dist(m, i)$ and the subset cardinality calculation costs are $O(dSize - 1)$. The keyword vector $k$ requires $O(kSize \cdot historyVectorSize)$, while the cost of cosine distance calculation is $O(dSize \cdot 3kSize2)$. In detail we have that the access cost to document bi-dimensional vector is $O(dSize \cdot kSize)$, for each document the numerator calculation cost is $O(kSize)$, while the denominator calculation cost is $O(kSize \cdot kSize)$. The computational cost for the relevance value is $O(dSize \cdot kSize)$. Therefore the dominant computational cost is $O(dSize \cdot 3kSize2)$.

Let us note that in case of low $kSize$ cardinality (e.g. the first experiment), or when $\frac{kSize}{dSize} \ll 1$ (e.g. second experiment) the algorithm shows a quasi-linear time behaviour.

# 6   Related Works

Large hypermedia bases require content description facilities to help users not get lost or stuck inside their own information. Content analysis, be done by humans or by machines, is a complex task involving the analysis of meaning [8]. What our approach aims to do is not document classification but just a selection according to given meta-information. The more complex problem of dividing documents into classes according to their content is a widely treated subject in artificial intelligence and machine learning. Techniques such as neural networks, decision trees [9], support vector machines [10] and nearest neighbor [11] are well known and widely in use. Much more similar problems are treated in object-based navigation [12], conceptual linking [13] and conceptual navigation [14]. Object-based navigation [12] is based upon object characteristics: contents of the objects and relationships among them. In such an approach users specify a set of objects and their relationships. The system dynamically creates queries processing user's input and determines links based on matching between these queries and some indices. Conceptual linking [13] is on the other hand a technique that refers directly to the World Wide Web: it tries to overcome limitations given to automatic link discovery by a purely lexical string matching. Conceptual linking, as treated in [13], relies on ontology management facilities the same way we did in our project. Conceptual navigation [14] goes a step further: not only links among documents are discovered but user profile is taken into account to build a path that users can follow to browse available documents. Different strategies for such a mechanism are available and ontology is still the key to make them work. What we did in our work is even beyond conceptual navigation as we consider not only user's profile and behavior but also system configuration and history to help students in finding suitable contents for their research.

Our model has been applied to multimedia files domain but it is not the only possible choice. It is possible to enable search engines to provide query results: document concepts are so far expressed mostly by keywords and thus it is easy to group documents into clusters of documents sharing the same keyword description. It has been shown [15] that different documents need to be linked in many dimensions (according their content, format, location and so on) to achieve the necessary scope wideness required by non-trivial Web applications. In the Conceptual Hypermedia System (CHS) [16] a conceptual schema for hypertext structure and behavior has been defined. In that model documents sharing the same metadata are considered similar and links among them become the reference concepts. Most of web-based systems for document retrieval (e.g. search engines) use ontologies to provide domain-restricted description of documents [17]. Problems arising are that several non-relevant results could be prompted and that document retrieval is not possible when documents do not contain the user-specified keywords. The approach we are proposing gives a solution for those problems: the ontology can be used to automatically redefine a query with an expansion mechanism. The original query to the database, that is implicitly given by an active document description, is extended in order to broaden the search scope and then results are refined and ranked relying on service knowledge both of system's and user's context. A similar approach is used in ONTOLOGER [18], a system for usage-driven management of information in ontology-based web portals. ONTOLOGER considers, in its inner evaluations, user activities to understand what she should mostly be interested in. It is done by profiling each user as it is a single-user system, on the other hand, as we have been developing a cooperative system we had to consider the whole student project community and to take so into account the whole system behavior and user knowledge at the same time.

## 7    Conclusion

In this paper we propose a novel approach for the retrieval of multimedia information within inspirational learning environments. This model has been developed in the ATELIER project. The aim is to support architecture and interaction design students work, find new ideas and inspiration. We thus developed an ontology-driven selection facility for opportunely navigating the knowledge-base. In our work we not only consider user profile and behavior but also system configuration and history to help students in finding suitable contents for their research. The algorithm has been implemented using the Java$^{TM}$ language and has been embedded in the ATELIER architecture as an independent external service, so to be available to every component in the environment. The Ontology Pick service itself has been tested under particularly intense situation and with large amounts of data stored in the whole system. In our intentions it had to fulfill some minimum requirements in terms of usefulness, not to be just a random presentation or screensaver-like software tool to be added into the environment. As we showed with experiments, we tried to quantify and evaluate inspiration we are able to convey. Apart from the positive subjective comments we received and personal opinions, we think we succeeded or goals. Nevertheless some improvements can still be made. For example we would like to be able to deal with document contents rather than just with their descriptions and be able to somehow deal with user feedback (e.g. through some kind of result rating mechanism).

## Acknowledgements

This paper was written within the ATELIER project (IST-2001-33064) and we want to thank in particular all the people who allowed us to go deep into the behaviors of architecture students at the Academy of Fine Arts of Vienna.

## References

1. Loregian, M., Telaro, M.: Dynamic ontologies and cooperative learning. In: Supplements to Proceedings of COOP 2004, Hyères Les Palmiers, France, May 11-14, 2004. (http://klee.cootech.disco.unimib.it/Atelier/loregian-telaro.pdf). (2004)

2. Bawden, R.: The community challenge: The learning response. In: Invited Plenary Paper, 29th Annual International Meeting of the Community Development Society 27-30th July, Athens, Georgia. (1997)
3. Kolb, D.A.: Experiential learning experience as the source of learning and development. Prentice Hall (1984)
4. Pehkonen, P.: Hypermedia Infrastructure for location-based multimedia. PhD thesis, Oulu University (2002)
5. De Michelis, G.: Mixed objects. In: Appliance Design Journal. to appear (2004)
6. De Michelis, G.: The design of interactive applications: A different way. In: Proc. International Workshop on Ambient Intelligence Computing, CTI press (2003)
7. Matkovic, K., Neumann, L., Siglaer, J., Kompast, M., Purgathofer, W.: Visual image query. In: Proc. Smart Graphics 2002. (2002) 116–123
8. Borko, H., Bernick, M.: Automatic document classification. J. ACM **10** (1963) 151–162
9. Lewis, D.D., Ringuette, M.: A comparison of two learning algorithms for text categorization. In: Proceedings of SDAIR-94, 3rd Annual Symposium on Document Analysis and Information Retrieval, Las Vegas, US (1994) 81–93
10. Joachims, T.: Text categorization with suport vector machines: Learning with many relevant features. In: Proceedings of the 10th European Conference on Machine Learning, Springer-Verlag (1998) 137–142
11. Yang, Y., Liu, X.: A re-examination of text categorization methods. In Hearst, M.A., Gey, F., Tong, R., eds.: Proceedings of SIGIR-99, 22nd ACM International Conference on Research and Development in Information Retrieval, Berkeley, US, ACM Press, New York, US (1999) 42–49
12. Hirata, K., Mukherjea, S., Okamura, Y., Li, W.S., Hara, Y.: Object-based navigation: An intuitive navigation style for content-oriented integration environment. In: UK Conference on Hypertext. (1997) 75–86
13. Carr, L., Hall, W., Bechhofer, S., Goble, C.A.: Conceptual linking: ontology-based open hypermedia. In: World Wide Web. (2001) 334–342
14. Crampes, M., Ranwez, S.: Ontology-supported and ontology-driven conceptual navigation on the world wide web. In: Proceedings of the eleventh ACM on Hypertext and hypermedia, ACM Press (2000) 191–199
15. Ellis, D., Furner, J., Willett, P.: On the creation of hypertext links in full-text documents: measurement of retrieval effectiveness. J. Am. Soc. Inf. Sci. **47** (1996) 287–300
16. Carr, L., Hall, W., Bechhofer, S., Goble, C.A.: Conceptual linking: ontology-based open hypermedia. In: World Wide Web. (2001) 334–342
17. Choi, O., Yoon, S., Oh, M., et al.: Semantic web search model for information retrieval of the semantic data. In: Web Communication Technologies and Internet-Related Social Issues - HSI 2003, Lecture Notes in Computer Science, Vol. 2713 (2003) 588–593
18. Stojanovic, N., Gonzalez, J., Stojanovic, L.: ONTOLOGER: a system for usage-driven management of ontology-based information portals. In: Proceedings of the international conference on Knowledge capture, ACM Press (2003) 172–179

# Enhancing Knowledge Management
# Through the Use of GIS and Multimedia

Petros Belsis[1], Stefanos Gritzalis[1], Apostolos Malatras[2],
Christos Skourlas[3], Ioannis Chalaris[3]

[1] Department of Information and Communication Systems Engineering
University of the Aegean, Karlovasi, Samos, Greece
{pbelsis,sgritz}@aegean.gr

[2] Department of Electronic Engineering, Centre for Communications Systems Research
University of Surrey, UK
a.malatras@surrey.ac.uk

[3] Department of Informatics, Technological Education Institute, Athens, Greece
{cskourlas,ixalaris}@teiath.gr

**Abstract.** Knowledge is probably the most important capital for an organization, constituting thus its management an issue of high significance. The majority of existing solutions utilize static sources for knowledge (document repositories), allowing for minimum support for tacit knowledge that is an outcome of an on demand cooperation with an appropriate expert. In this paper we describe a system that introduces the concurrent integration of Multimedia and Geographical Information Systems (GIS) functions in Knowledge Management (KM) applications. In most Knowledge Management systems one of the real challenges is expert's knowledge utilization. Towards this direction, we exploit possible technological prospects and we present the architecture of a prototype developed to implement selected innovative KM components by embedding state-of-the-art multimedia Java-based applications integrated in parallel with GIS functionality.

## 1 Introduction

The learning process and potential ways to establish a supporting framework have been for long of primary interest to both the academic and entrepreneurial world. Knowledge has become a key resource [1], [6] for both organizations and individuals. Faced with global competition and increasingly dynamic environments, organizations are being advised to assemble people of diverse talents and deploy their expertise to gain access to new areas of knowledge and new technologies. Innovative techniques and advanced technology features are emerging on a daily basis, on every area of expertise making the effective handling of knowledge a difficult task. Therefore, there is an obvious necessity for exploiting this knowledge with the assistance of technological means and supporting it with learning techniques to allow its dissemination in order to enhance individual and organizational performance.

GIS technology integrates common database operations such as query and statistical analysis with the unique visualization and geographic analysis benefits offered by maps [10], [18]. Among other things, a GIS facilitates the modeling of spatial networks and provides a number of tools for the analysis of spatial networks [7]. The incorporated capability of GIS to perform spatial analysis can be considered as similar

D. Karagiannis and U. Reimer (Eds.): PAKM 2004, LNAI 3336, pp. 319–329, 2004.

to the decision capabilities of decision support systems (DSS)[16], enhancing therefore their distinguished significance to support basic organizational tasks. Furthermore, the integration of state of the art multimedia technologies such as Voice over IP (VoIP) through Java-based applications provides a framework for expert's knowledge utilization [2], [3].

In this paper we attempt to enhance KM functions with GIS and multimedia functions. The rest of the paper is organized as follows. In section 2 we present the main technological challenges in KM implementations and we present how new technologies can be helpful, describing our contribution in relation to contemporary KM approaches, while in parallel we introduce the benefits of introducing GIS into KM techniques. In Section 3 related systems to the one proposed by us are studied and in section 4 we present the architecture of our prototype and a concise description of it. Section 5 concludes the paper, evaluating the benefits of our prototype and providing directions for further work.

## 2  Benefits of KM

Philosopher Polanyi [26] distinguishes knowledge in two types: tacit, which is embedded in the human brain and cannot be expressed easily, and explicit knowledge, which can be easily codified [6]. Codified knowledge can be managed through several types of applications like document management applications, intranets, repositories and databases provided with proper querying mechanisms.

Bhatt [4] argues about the distinction between individual knowledge and organizational knowledge, which yet are interdependent. In complex situations, where organizational tasks are highly interdependent and individuals do not possess necessary levels of expertise to solve interdisciplinary problems, people are required to cooperate with others to share their knowledge and expertise. Knowledge management is an emerging discipline that promises to capitalize on organizations' intellectual capital [21]. As a concept, KM appeared in the beginning of the previous decade. Among the potential benefits from establishing specific techniques to manage knowledge, according to a major study that took place over several worldwide-distributed organizations [5], we can distinguish:

❑ Improved decision making
❑ Improved efficiency of people and operations
❑ Improvement of innovation
❑ Improved products/services

Among KM benefits we could also distinguish enhanced collaboration and communication, new knowledge creation, knowledge retention and increased knowledge availability and access [21].

Knowledge management technology is not a single technology, but rather a broad collection of techniques that need to be adopted and integrated [6]. Some of these technologies, e.g. those derived from "artificial intelligence" tools, are not new. Some are useful not only for managing knowledge, but also managing data and information – as is true for intranets and the Web. Relatively to technology, broad repertoires of techniques have been developed [17], namely:

❑ Personalization: it is the activity of knowledge sharing through person-to-person contacts. This can be facilitated by investment in current IT systems.

❑ Codification is the activity of capturing existing knowledge and placing this in repositories in a structured manner.
❑ Discovery is the activity of searching and retrieving knowledge from repositories and databases, such as using the Internet and intranet systems.
❑ Creation / innovation is the activity of generating new knowledge, vital if an organization is to remain competitive. The role of the human factor is essential and there are almost no indications that it can be substituted by technology, at least in the near future.
❑ Capturing /monitoring is the activity of capturing knowledge as people carry on their normal tasks such as interacting with other people.

Implementation of IT-related KM can be built on the following cornerstones: Corporate environment, knowledge retrieval and knowledge transfer. Corporate environment refers to utilizing to the maximum extent the intellectual assets of an organization. Knowledge retrieval is mainly enhanced by database and information retrieval technologies, while as far as knowledge transfer is concerned we can identify more than a few degrees of freedom and innovation concerning the potential techniques and technologies that can be applied.

Our approach tries and succeeds in supporting the aforementioned cornerstones by capturing tacit knowledge and supporting the creation of new knowledge through the provision of means that support interaction between human networks of experts [15]. Towards this direction we attempt to exploit GIS and multimedia capabilities, for which we provide support through Java-based applications.

## 3 Knowledge Processing Systems and GIS

The proliferation of GIS technologies has lead to their exploitation in a diverse set of research fields including KM. Most recent work has concentrated on the development and application of methods and tools for the combination of knowledge processing and environmental informatics through the use of GIS techniques [23]. Moreover, in the area of Knowledge Management, a number of challenges concerning the development of efficient systems, focus on supporting the capture of knowledge through the socialization process [14]. The socialization process can be supported through the capabilities that multimedia applications can offer. It is for that reason that we believe that the parallel use of multimedia operations integrated in GIS applications can enhance the socialization process. This is especially the case in geographically dispersed organizations, where the consequences of distribution of human assets can be minimized through the use of GIS with multimedia-integrated capabilities. This can be achieved by combining the geographically related information (locating the expert) with the capability of establishing contact with her through the integration of multimedia functionality in our prototype.

Worth mentioning examples of systems in the area of environmental informatics with knowledge management oriented capabilities are: the DIWA system [11] aims in maintaining and using a web-archive for environmental documents. Its current version though does not support the use of archived knowledge but only components using explicit knowledge [23]. HIRN (Hypertext Information Retrieval Network) is an internet-based environmental information system for environmental regulations and laws [20]. The basic characteristic of this system is that it demands from the user to codify manually tacit knowledge so that it can be transferred to other users. These systems as somebody could easily distinguish, implement partially selected explicit knowledge management related activities, lacking the concurrent integration of both explicit and tacit knowledge management activities.

The idea of intelligent maps for knowledge retrieval is described in [23]. With the assistance of intelligent maps, conceptual navigation can be applied [24]. This means that users select geo-objects on the map to define the geographical relationship; the system then returns all knowledge resources, which match this relationship. In a second step, users define textually other relationships to filter the resources of interest. The drawback of this approach is that the query interface would be a mixture of an interactive, graphical interface and a textual interface. The subject tree contains all thematic relationships of knowledge resources, which are indexed with the respective geo-reference. Users select one or more entries in the subject tree to define the the-matic relationship for their query.

Multimedia cartography and GIS applicability for knowledge management are described also in [8]. 2-D or 3-D maps are used in a way similar to the use of conventional maps. The aim is to provide a sense of an environment able to provide information retrieval through sophisticated indexing and classification methods.

In our approach the geo-objects are being viewed as a reference to available experts, which upon selection via the map interface, provide through a user interface the ability to acquire further information about the expert's specialization area and specific skills, and upon selection to access the multimedia communication application, acquiring on-line information about specific topics of interest.

## 4 System Description and Architecture

One of the primary functions of a system that manages knowledge is documented knowledge handling. In order to achieve this, a repository has been created which aims to store codified knowledge. Access to the multiple documents related to the same subject can be facilitated through a search engine, implemented for this specific reason, which has the ability to bring documents related to the keywords provided by the user. Nevertheless, the real challenge is tacit knowledge utilization. Creation of knowledge [17] is one of the vital areas for the organization to remain competitive and the role of the human factor is essential. Our application focuses on providing the means to experts and users to cooperate with each other, either with an asynchronous communication module that enables the communication by users being able to send messages to groups of experts or synchronously by using multimedia components. An additional important factor of the proposed architecture is the multilingual document retrieval aspect that enables the users to search within knowledge repositories and perform specific queries upon them without having to worry about the language considerations (Figure 1). Tacit knowledge is not only exploited at runtime when a user communicates with an expert through the multimedia or the messaging application. We provide support for the recording of this knowledge in order for it to be exploit-able in future cases. When such a communication occurs the expert upon completion registers the details of this interaction into a properly defined document (XML is used for this process) and stores it to the Data Store used by the Document Retrieval module. The user has subsequently access to explicitly encoded tacit knowledge.

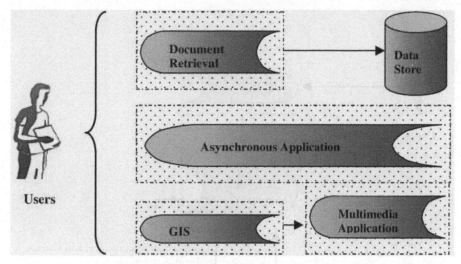

**Fig. 1.** General description of the KM system

The various knowledge sources that constitute the foundations of the system can be located in the same path or can be distributed throughout a network. The distribution of knowledge sources applies not only to the multimedia, but also to the document retrieval aspect, since documents need not be co-located. To support this feature we have used a simple directory server, where all knowledge sources such as a document database or a knowledge expert's multimedia module register. This architectural notion is borrowed from directory services like Jini [25]. Thus the user actually interacts with the directory server to gain access to a remote knowledge source, though she can view information for a knowledge source before the communication by querying the directory server. Knowledge retrieval and the distributed framework are presented in Figure 2.

The goal of the system is to enable users and knowledge experts to communicate with each other using audio and video techniques in a real-time environment, enhanced by the parallel presence of a GIS component. The user pursues in this way to gain knowledge regarding a domain that she is not aware of. The users are given the capability to select the most appropriate expert to collaborate with through a number of experts being presented in a GIS working space. Thus the user can base her selection in criteria like expert's background and expert availability since this information is made available to the user through the graphical interface that the GIS application environment supplies. In what follows we will present the functionality of the system by means of an example scenario, where a user contacts a knowledge expert and uses real-time, two-way video and audio communication to solve a problem.

Describing the functionality of the GIS environment implemented is considered to be outside the scope of this paper, yet an inexperienced user can consider it to be a type of interactive map. Figure 3 depicts the view of the system, where three different experts are presented on the GIS interface so that the user can select one to communicate with.

If the user clicks on an available knowledge expert's location a popup menu appears that allows the user to either view information regarding that particular expert,

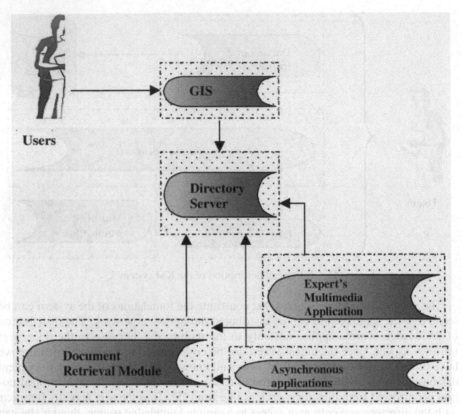

**Fig. 2.** Distribution Of Knowledge Sources And Knowledge Retrieval Mechanism

or to commence a Live Video conference with the expert. In the case of the latter the system in the background translates the expert's geographic location into an IP location using a custom directory service and then informs the expert that a user is attempting to communicate with her. The next step is for both parties of the upcoming communication to configure the sound and video devices that they will be using.

After having configured the device-related options, the user and the knowledge expert are given the option to set their preferences regarding the video and audio streaming, namely the quality of the received and transmitted streams, the size of the video frames and the volume of the audio input. The communication is now ready to commence. By using the associated controls, the user and the expert can start, pause and stop their live video chat.

To prove our point of view that the convergence of GIS and multimedia technologies with KM techniques can lead in the design of more effective KM applications and tools, we have implemented a prototype system that incorporates the set of the aforementioned technologies. The system is implemented entirely by using Java [13] and can thus be considered as highly interoperable with many diverse platforms, provided that the Java Runtime Environment is installed. The system architecture can be conceptually divided in 4 major components.

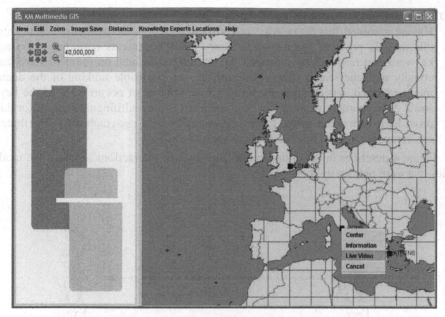

**Fig. 3.** User interface of the system – GIS Aspect

❑ KM module

The KM module is responsible for handling all the knowledge information from various sources, mostly experts around a particular domain. The grouping of the various knowledge fields and the unified presentation of them to the users of the system is a feature that this module is designed to support. Also the KM module provides a means to locate knowledge sources and identifying them, enabling the communication capability with them on behalf of the user.

❑ GIS module

The GIS module is responsible for providing the functionality of a standard GIS to the system. The users are capable, through this module, to access multi-layered maps where in conjunction with the KM module, knowledge information is presented as well. The basis for this module is the layered architecture it adopts directly from the GIS background. We have extended the notion of this architecture to encompass layers that are not directly map-related to support knowledge sources representation on the interactive maps. We can identify two sub-modules to this module: the GIS interface and the service module that handles all network connection and discovery issues required for the communication between the knowledge expert and the user.

❑ Multimedia module

The multimedia module is responsible for enabling the direct and in real-time communication between the user and a knowledge expert that she has selected through the GIS interface. The communication can be either by Voice over IP or in a more elaborate way it can be a live video chat with the knowledge expert as long as both parties are online. The RTP (Real Time Protocol) protocol is extensively used to enable the best communication possible [22].

❑ Multilingual Document Retrieval module
Having assumed that knowledge is codified in semi-structured text documents, this module provides the means to query these documents regarding a certain keyword and responds by returning the documents located on the data store that comply with the search string. A simplistic yet extensible ranking of the documents returned is performed according to the number of occurrences of the keyword. An important parameter to be considered is the multilingual support for this procedure, which can prove to be very significant in geographically distributed environments like the one we chose to view.

Figure 4 describes in detail the architecture and the interactions amongst the modules that were previously mentioned.

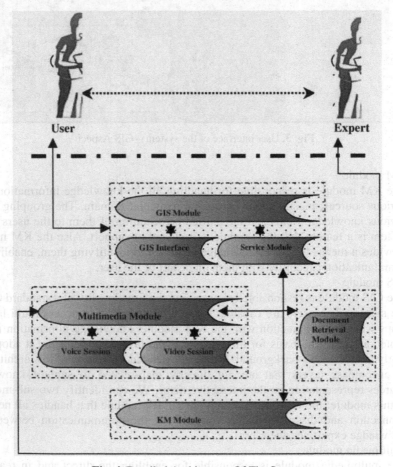

**Fig. 4.** Detailed Architecture Of The System

The JDK version used for the implementation of this system was 1.3 but tests proved that there is no version incompatibility with more recent JDK releases. The system has been tested on both Unix-like and Windows operating systems. The graphical user interfaces of the entire system, ranging from the user to the expert and administrator views were implemented using Java Swing. To enable the GIS capabilities of the system an open source Java library from BBN Technologies was used, titled OpenMap [19]. OpenMap is actually a JavaBean Component that was used to enable GIS features in the application. The version of OpenMap used was 4.5 and for the purposes of this specific applications some alterations were made in the original source code in order to accommodate the need to load data on the GIS interactive map through relational databases and XML [9] files. The video and voice communication modules were implemented using the Java Media Framework API [12] and by grasping the benefits of the RTP protocol over the UDP transport, while the KM module is a set of Java classes with no dependency on external libraries.

## 5  Conclusions – Further Work

The research domain of knowledge management can grasp a plethora of benefits through the use of multimedia GIS. Knowledge management systems enhanced with geographic capabilities presented in a user-friendly manner with the deployment of multimedia techniques can aid users of such systems in extracting and handling knowledge in a more effective way. Two aspects of multimedia GIS systems are fundamental for the amelioration of current knowledge management systems:

❑ Visual aids
❑ More practical data presentation

The exploitation of multimedia GIS in knowledge management systems implies the delivery of the data in the knowledge management system that have a geographic perspective (i.e. addresses) in a more concise and helpful way, by presenting them on maps. In this way the user can be assisted in extracting knowledge through the use of the map, by selecting for example to deal only with the information located in her vicinity. The primary concept behind GIS is their layered architecture, where multiple layers are combined and a unique view is delivered to the user. This notion can be easily adapted to the knowledge management realm by providing users of such systems one single view of the whole of the data, rather than projecting a series of varying views usually in a spreadsheet manner like existing knowledge management systems perform. Considering the Human-Computer Interaction factor, this visual representation of data is more effective for users and will subsequently result in higher performance metrics.

In our current system prototype we have used GIS to present the locations of nearby certain knowledge domain experts, with whom the users of the systems can interact using the video / chat system module. Expanding this research to support better and more multimedia options does not lie within our research agenda. We consider this as a mere implementation issue, which can be developed by a group of software engineers. Our prototype serves as a proof of concept and a roadmap to future systems that integrate multimedia GIS capabilities into knowledge management systems.

Our prototype, innovates on combining both GIS characteristics and the possibility of making experts from remote locations available to all organization members. Through the current implementation and the graphical interface, the geo-referenced objects of the GIS refer to expert location and through the distributed multimedia components experts make their experience available the moment it is needed, in contrast with existing related systems that focus mainly on explicit knowledge reuse.

In our future work we are looking of ways of integrating the notion behind GIS into the knowledge management domain. That is how to combine knowledge into group of layers and visually presenting them to the users, without the necessity of knowledge having a geographic reference. Another index apart from the combination of longitude/latitude can be used to bind knowledge layers and the exploitation of this index can lead to more successful knowledge systems and more efficient knowledge systems users.

## Acknowledgments

This work was co-funded by 75% from E.E. and 25% from the Greek Government under the framework of the Education and Initial Vocational Training Program – Archimedes.

## References

1. Bell D. (1976). "The Coming of Post-Industrial Society", Basic Books, New York, NY, 1976.
2. Belsis P., Chalaris A., Malatras A., Drakopoulos I. (2004a). "Supporting the learning process through knowledge based systems". Proceedings of Workshops on Computer Science Education, Jan. 2004, pp. 43-49, Nis, Serbia.
3. Belsis P., Gritzalis S., Skourlas C., Drakopoulos I. (2004b). "Implementing Knowledge Management techniques for security purposes", Proceedings of the ICEIS 2004 conference, vol.2, pp. 535-540, April 2004, Portugal.
4. Bhatt G., (2002). "Management Strategies fro individual and organizational knowledge", Journal of Knowledge Management, vol. 6, number 1, 2002, pp. 31-39.
5. Chase R. L. (1997). "The knowledge-based Organization: An International Survey", The Journal of Knowledge Management, vol. 1, No 1, 1997.
6. Davenport T., S. Volpel (2001). "The rise of knowledge towards attention management", Journal of knowledge management, vol. 5, No 3, 2001, pp 212-221.
7. Derekenaris, G., Garofalakis, J., Makris, C., Prentzas, J., Sioutas, S., Tsakalidis, A. (2001). Integrating GIS, GPS and GSM technologies for the effective management of ambulances. Computers, Environment and Urban Systems, vol. 25 (2001), pp. 267-278
8. Dodge, M. (2000), An Atlas of Cyberspaces
   http://www.cybergeography.org/atlas/atlas.html
9. Extensible Markup Language Specification (XML),
   http://www.w3.org/XML/, accessed March 2004
10. Franklin, C. (1992). An introduction to geographic information systems: linking maps to databases. Database, 15(2), pp.12-21.
11. Henning, I., Ebel, R., Tauber, M., Tochtermann, K., Pursche, K., Kussmaul, A., Schultze, A. (1999). Internetbasiertes Dokumentenmanagement heterogener Umweltdokumentbestände, in [Rautenstrauch/Schenk, 1999], pp. 376-388.
12. Java Media Framework (JMF),
    http://java.sun.com/products/java-media/jmf/index.jsp, accessed March 2004.
13. Java Technology, http://java.sun.com, accessed March 2004
14. Kida, K., Shimazu, H., (2002), "Ubiquitous Knowledge Management – Enabling an office work scheduling tool to corporate knowledge sharing", Proceedings of the IEEE Workshop on Knowledge Media Engineering, Japan.

15. King W., Marks P., McCoy S., (2002). "The most important issues in Knowledge Management", Communications of the ACM, Sept. 2002, vol.45, No. 9
16. Mennecke, B., Crossland, M., (1996), "Geographic Information Systems: Applications and Research Opportunities for Information systems Researchers", Proceedings of the 29th International Conference on System Sciences, Hawaii.
17. Milton N., Shadbolt N., Cottam H., Hammersley M, (1999). "Towards a knowledge Technology for Knowledge Management", Int. J. of Human-Computer Studies, (1999) 51, pp. 615-641.
18. Muller, J. C. (1993). Latest developments in GIS/LIS. International Journal of Geographic Information Systems, 7(4), 293-303.
19. Open Systems Mapping Technology, OpenMap TM, http://openmap.bbn.com, accessed March 2004
20. Riekert, W.-F., Kadric, L. (1997). A Hypertext-based Information Retrieval Network for Environmental Protection Regulations. Proceedings of the 11th Symposium on Environmental Informatics, Straßburg, Metropolis Pub. Marburg, pp. 475-482.
21. Rus I., Lindvall M., (2002). "Knowledge Management in Software Engineering, IEEE Software, vol. 3, pp.26-38, 2002.
22. Schulzrinne, H., Casner, D., Frederick, R. & Jacobson, V., (2003). RTP: A Transport Protocol for Real-Time Applications, IETF RFC 3550, July 2003
23. Tochtermann T., Maurer H. (2000). "Knowledge Management and environmental informatics", Journal of Universal Computer Science, vol. 6, no. 5 (2000), pp. 517-536
24. Veltman, K. H. (1997). Frontiers in Conceptual Navigation, International Journal on Knowledge Organization ISSN 0943-7444, 24 (4), pp. 225-245.
25. Waldo, J. (2000) & The Jini Technology Team, "The Jini Specifications", Addison-Wesley Pub Co., 2000.
26. Polanyi M. (1966). "The Tacit Dimension", Routledge & Kegan Paul, London, 1966.

# Mediating Ontologies for Communities of Practice

Marc Spaniol and Ralf Klamma

RWTH Aachen, Informatik V, Ahornstr. 55, D-52056 Aachen, Germany
{mspaniol,klamma}@cs.rwth-aachen.de
http://www-i5.informatik.rwth-aachen.de/lehrstuhl/i5/index.html

**Abstract.** Knowledge management technologies are widely used in organizational information systems. However, the knowledge representations in these systems reflect the formal organization more than informal structures like communities of practice. To overcome the gap between the informal and formal knowledge structures within an organization, we can apply ontology mediation techniques which can detect similarities and dissimilarities between two or more different ontologies which reflect the current practice of terminology use in a community of practice. In this paper, we compare such ontology mediation techniques and introduce a semi-automatic ontology mediation system for communities of practice called *COSMO*. This system can be used to facilitate informal organizational structures within formal organizational information systems like workflow management systems.

## 1  Communities of Practice and Knowledge Management

Knowledge management for communities of practice is discussed widely in the area of information systems [6, 45, 17, 44]. It is often argued that knowledge management tools for communities of practice should support the tacit side of knowledge whereas formal information systems handle its explicit side. While the distinction between tacit and explicit knowledge itself is subject of discussion [30, 20, 18] we do not see any reasons to exclude communities of practice from the use of formal information systems. But, we claim that formal information systems should be more sensible for the needs of communities of practice.

Knowledge emerges in communities of practice by discursive assignment of sense. Communities of Practice (CoP) [46] are characterized by common conventions, language, tool usage, values, and standards. But this is an ongoing and never ending process. The development of a common practice which defines the community integrates the negotiation of meaning among the participating members as well as the mutual engagement in joint enterprises and a shared repertoire of activities, symbols, and artefacts. Some of these artefacts are possibly stored in formal information systems and shared among the members of one CoP or with members of other CoPs by means of formal descriptions like workflow or learning objects. Sharing formal descriptions in a CoP or between CoPs might raise several issues: First, members of a CoP might have different educational of professional backgrounds leading to a different interpretation of

D. Karagiannis and U. Reimer (Eds.): PAKM 2004, LNAI 3336, pp. 330–342, 2004.

artefact descriptions. Second, artefacts familiar to one member or CoP might be confusing, marginal, misleading etc. for other members of a CoP. Third, local contextualisation of artefacts by members or in CoPs within classification hierarchies, work lists, etc. might be useless or confusing for other members or in other CoPs.

KM applications in workflow management systems, e-learning applications, or help desk tools incorporate the risk that naming, description, and classification of newly created content is not necessarily unambiguous for all members of a CoP or other CoPs. These conceptual differences lead to non addressable and therefore, non shareable content in KM applications. From a KM application point of view a major requirement is that applications should be robust against unwished misinterpretation of content. Unfortunately, this wanted robustness leads in many cases to a fixed interpretation schema of content in KM applications called ontology [13]. All content is shareable only by means of the fixed ontology often developed by a person called ontology engineer [40]. While in many cases this level of support in sharing knowledge may be sufficient we think that CoP need a more dynamic, localized and reflective support in knowledge sharing with formal information systems. From a CoP point of view ontologies should be local to CoP or even to every member of a CoP and if sharing is wanted this has to be negotiated between the members of a CoP or between CoPs. Consequently, the formal descriptions have to be compared and similarity measures have to be applied as a basis of these negotiations. In the light of this new requirement, ontology mediation techniques are possibly of interest. Tools for a detection of conflicting concepts and a semi automatic mediation of ontologies can be a first step towards dynamic knowledge sharing. Moreover, the disclosure of conflicts, redundancies, and misaddressing can help foster the ongoing discursive assignment of sense in CoPs via networked KM systems. However, this is still a preliminary solution since the ontology itself might be confusing to the members of a community. Therefore, effective and efficient methods are needed that allow individuals to work with domain depending ontologies and mediate them when collaborating.

In this paper we discuss techniques for community based ontology mediation for communities of practice. The rest of the paper is organized as follows: In the next section we introduce and compare techniques used for ontology mediation. After that, we give an overview on related research. Then we present our system for a Community Oriented Semiautomatic Matching of Ontologies (*COSMO*) and afterwards compare its results with similar approaches. The paper closes with conclusions and gives an outlook on further research and opportunities to integrate *COSMO* in KM applications.

## 2   Ontology Mediation Techniques

Basically there are three approaches to ontology mediation. Ontologies might be manually, semi-automatically, or automatically mediated. Any of these strategies comprises more or less the risk of being too complex (e.g. time consuming, man power) on the one hand and of being inexact (e.g. superficial domain knowledge, inappropriate terminology) on the other hand. In addition, this often leads to a terminology covering the lowest common denominator of a community vocabulary, still comprising terms that are misleading to members of a community. Hence, we analyze techniques for a self-regulating ontology in inter- and intra-community practice. Therefore, we will now survey these techniques of ontology mediation regarding the following aspects:

- *Understandability.* By means of understandability we check in how far concepts can be mediated between ontologies without being mistakable.
- *Mediation complexity.* This criteria compares the cost for mediating between different ontologies.
- *Conceptual comprehensiveness.* The last criterion deals with the comprehensiveness of concepts that are covered by the mediation process.

The **manual ontology mediation** process is performed by a "so called" ontology engineer. An ontology engineer is needed in many cases because the mediation needs an expert in the field of computer science. The reason is that ontology design and maintenance require in depth knowledge on ontology languages and formalization aspects, usually overstraining users of KM application not working in a computer science domain. Therefore, the ontology engineer analyzes the environment of a community and gets (if possible) in contact with its users. In addition, the ontology engineer is usually assisted by a domain expert to understand the semantic interpretation of concepts in a particular community. Finally, the ontology engineer tries to mediate between all important aspects of a community, like in so-called top ontologies [28]. Due to previous complexity, the manual mediation can be applied in cases of specific application areas only. Experiments have shown that large ontologies can't even be created efficiently without the assistance of design tools [12]. However, in general, manual mediation is the only choice to obtain full conceptual comprehensiveness. Consequently, a manual process is very expensive and time consuming.

Approaching **ontology mediation semi-automatically** means to extract basic concepts of an ontology by automated tools that allow a following adaptation by the user(s). In this case, the work done by an ontology engineer is replaced by a computation based on previously described rules about the formal descriptions captured within the ontology. This process can be compared with semi-automatic ontology creation as found in [41] as it concludes with a final manual adaptation step. Usually, the most common terms of a community ontology are derived from domain specific documents. This results in a better understanding of the ontology basis covering the automatically detected most significant concepts of a community and their interrelationship. By comparing the conceptualizations of similar documents in various ontologies, the differences of conceptualizations can be computed and a mediation is being proposed. Depending on the area of application the tool support differs in comprehensiveness, but in general the approach is applicable to ontologies of any size. Finally, this technique ends up with an individual validation step afterwards.

The **automatic ontology mediation** method is based on tools that are similar to those applied in semi-automatic ontology mediation and creation [10]. This technique is fully automated and doesn't require any manipulation of a potentially unskilled user with respect to computer science means. In particular, this method is used in cases that cover application domains with many concepts and covering various application areas, which can't be distinguished by a particular domain language. It is also applied in domains where it seems to be unlikely that a common terminology can be agreed on a-priori. The advantages of an automatic ontology mediation are its flexibility with respect to underlying documents and its scalability. However, the main drawback is that a completely automatic resolving of conflicts deriving from different individual conceptualizations is often faulty since their interpretation heavily depends on the individual semantic. To cope with this problem, the mediation usually covers a few "uncritical" core concepts only.

Comparing the previously discussed strategies we can summarize that manual and semi-automatic techniques are most suitable to obtain understandable ontologies. The reason therefore is that a purely automated mediation can't detect high level semantics. This shortcoming requires (up to now) manual manipulation (options). With respect to mediation complexity the situation is quite different. Here, automated techniques have a clear advantage, since a completely manual mediation is too complex and time consuming. Regarding conceptual comprehensiveness, none of the techniques is perfect. Anyhow, manual and semi-automatic strategies are better than automatic. The reason is that a manual adaptation makes it possible to mediate between concepts having a not so close correlation, which might not be detected automatically. However, this implies a risk that the correlation of concepts might be misinterpreted. Recapitulating, a semi-automatic ontology mediation best meets the requirements in an intra-respectively inter-community setting. Its main advantages compared with the other strategies are the comparatively minor complexity of mediation and the options of manual adaptations that allow best as possible conceptual comprehensiveness and understandability.

## 3   Related Work

We'll now give a brief overview on related work in the field of ontology mediation. In this aspect we'd like to stress on the differences between content transformation and mediation [34, 26]. Content transformation is an adaptation of content covering a wide spectrum of users, e.g. by adapting link structures of web sites due to usage statistics. Contrary, content mediation is an individual modification and adaptation of ontological conceptualizations with respect to the user's explicit (e.g. stored in a profile) or implicit (e.g. individual activity traces) preferences including information about the terminology used. Related research can be found in the following projects. An integration of heterogeneous information sources on the basis of a top level ontology can be found in DOME [9]. In Donden [42] collaborative ontology creation is being supported. 1:1Pro is an approach for the extraction of dynamic user profiles for an integration in push/pull services [2]. Another approach for the dynamic extraction of user profiles is OBI-WAN [35]. In IndexFinder [33] dynamic user profiles are applied for an adaptive linking structure of web sites. Addressing of movies on the basis of a domain specific terminology is supported by MovieTool [24]. In addition, the MultiMedia Message Box $M^3$ [21] supports the presentation of versatile multimedia content based on metadata descriptions in MPEG-7 [3]. Hunter's MetaNet system is an attempt for an automated interoperability among metadata languages [15]. Artequakt [1] aims at the automated creation of multimedia presentations, like Cuypers [25]. InfoSleuth serves as a unified query system for heterogeneous data sources [4]. SMOOTH [5] serves as a multimedia presentation system based on application dependent taxonomy. Saccol's approach aims at the integration of heterogeneous XML documents based on a manually created ontology [7]. A related attempt is the work of Omelayenko [31] with an additional naive Bayes analysis. Techniques for ontology management are used in OntoLearn, ConSys, and SymOntoX, which are used for a collaborative ontology creation and data integration [28]. A project for the integration of heterogeneous ontologies can be found at [37]. PromptDiff is a system for change detection in different versions of an ontology [29]. CodeBroker is a tool for a context aware support of programmers on behalf of interest profiles and user models [47]. The aim of GLUE is the detection of rules for an automated matching between ontologies [11].

## 4   COSMO

In the following, we'll describe the algorithms used in *COSMO* for the mediation of ontologies in communities of practice. As figured out before, the main problem is that a mediation technique has to "decide" whether two concepts are similar to each other or not [43, 48, 36]. Since a completely manual ontology mediation can be applied efficiently only in very small ontologies, we will now present an alternative to solve this shortcoming by combining human interpretation with a computer assisted mediation. To overcome the gap between conceptualizations having the same semantic and being expressed unequal, *COSMO* makes use of mediator ontologies. The idea behind mediator ontologies is twofold by considering the individual terminology inherent in an ontology as well as an upcoming integration step by mediating concepts. To assure quality, *COSMO* detects concepts matching fully or partially. The computed value indicates the matching probability of concepts with a final manual editing option for the user. Emerging difficulties in communications are eased by the usage of implicit and explicit ontologies. The implicit ontologies are computed during runtime from the previously described user descriptions. They represent the ontology inherent in a particular description and contain the terminology used in a community. Contrary, the explicit ontology is given by WordNet, which represents a domain independent thesaurus. Both types of ontologies are managed within *COSMO* by the use of graph structures that are used for the upcoming computation of the semantic similarity. Figure 1 gives an overview on the *COSMO* architecture and

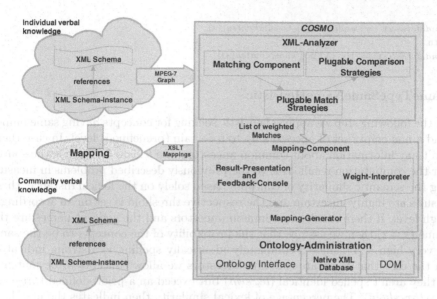

**Fig. 1.** Computational results of *COSMO* in comparison to human anticipation

the components mentioned above applied for computing the semantic similarity of concepts in ontology mediation. The semantic similarity expresses the closeness/distance between concepts in an ontology or between ontologies. It depends heavily on the context and is perceived asynchronously. That means, depending on the overall context, terms might be semantically closer than in another setting. For instance, the concept "nail" is more closely related to "hammer" in a tool kit setting than to "hand" in a manicure context.

*COSMO* uses fix point methods that make use of four heuristics being applied step by step to find the set of potential candidates being similar in source and target ontology represented by a mediator ontology. The computation result (only if there are any matching candidates) is a set of potential matching candidates denominated with a matching probability. Per iteration, for each concept of the source ontology the algorithm seeks the set of potential matching candidates originated in the target ontology. Those concepts that have a lower probability in being a matching candidate than an a-priori defined threshold value requires are pruned directly. We will now explain in detail the heuristics applied in *COSMO* that involve natural language aspects like polysems, holonyms, and hypernyms as well as lexical, structural, and thesaurus dependencies.

## RetrieveKnownMatchesHeuristic

This is the most simple heuristic of *COSMO*. The candidate set of concepts $t$ in the target ontology $T$ to be matched with a concept $s$ of the source ontology $S$ is denoted by $candidates(s)$. In the first computational step all matches are extracted, which have been learned from previous matchings ($knownmatch(s)$).

$candidates(s) := candidates(s) \cup candidates_1(s)$
with
$candidates_1(s) := \{(x, y) \mid x \in knownmatch(s)\}$

## SameTypeSameNameHeuristic

In the following step we apply a heuristic seeking for concepts having same names and a non empty set of ancestors up to a certain (predefined) level. In case there isn't any information about common ancestors, the lexical distance is the source for the computation result. Due to the previously described problems in measuring the semantic similarity of concepts based solely on the lexical distance, these results are highly uncertain and the respective threshold is set on an accordingly high level. If there aren't any common ancestors and the concept names are the same ($s = t$) then we assume that the probability of the concepts to be the same is very high ($t, 1$), since a completely identically spelling is a strong indicator. In the case that there are common ancestors we allow concepts to be matched if they aren't spelled identical ($lexsim$) but exceed an a-priori defined threshold ($lexthreshold$). The percentage of lexical similarity then indicates the matching probability. In many other cases the set of candidates isn't augmented. The usage of the applied heuristic appears to be useful since communities of practice communicating with each other need a small but certain conceptual intersection to facilitate any conversation.

$candidates(s) := candidates(s) \cup candidates_2(s)$
with

$$candidates_2(s) := \begin{cases} (t, 1) & \text{if} \quad s = t \\ & \wedge\, ancestor(s) \cap ancestor(t) \neq \emptyset \\ (t, lexsim(s, t)) & \text{if} \quad ancestor(s) = ancestor(t) \\ & \wedge\, lexsim(s, t) \geq lexthreshold \\ \emptyset & \text{else} \end{cases}$$

having
$s \in ontology(S); \; t \in ontology(T)$
and
$0 \leq lexthreshold \leq 1; \; lexsim \in [0; 1]$

## StructuralComparisonHeuristic

The structural comparison heuristic in *COSMO* is the most sophisticated operation. It gathers recursively semantic information about a particular concept based on the thesaurus applied. These information consist of synonym, hypernym, and hyponym relationships up to a certain but adjustable threshold. In addition, for all hypernyms applied all their synonyms are considered as potential matching candidates, too. After the first internal computation step in gathering all semantic information about a concept from our source ontology, denoted by $seminfo(s)$, the concept itself and any of its semantic related concepts are tested for their appearance in the target ontology. Thereby, only those concepts are considered ($name(candidates(s))$) which aren't yet candidates. In the case that there are any possible candidates in the target ontology which are similar to one of the original concepts' semantic similar expression, these concepts with their respective probability are considered to be a matching candidate. Here, as before it might be considered useful to apply a threshold to remove those concepts falling below a required similarity value.

$candidates(s) := candidates(s) \cup candidates_3(s)$
with
$candidates_3(s) := \{(t, lexsim(t, s)) \mid t \notin name(candidates(s)) \wedge t \in seminfo(s)\}$
having
$s \in ontology(S); \ t \in ontology(T)$
with
$seminfo(s) = synonyms_{dist}(s) \cup hypernyms_{dist}(s) \cup hyponyms_{dist}(s)$
$name(candidates(s)) = x; \ x \in ontology(T)$
and
$dist = $ maximum distance of synonym, hypernym, and hyponym relations

Obviously, this computation tends to be very time consuming if the degree of synonym, hypernym, or hyponym relationships to be analyzed is set to a high value. When doing so, the number of concepts to be compared increases exponentially with the maximum distance to be searched and may lead to an intolerable computation time, especially in real time applications. Even more, this heuristic should be applied on somehow similar or compliant structures only, since results might be misleading.

## SingleUnmatchedSibling

The idea behind this heuristic is quite intuitive. In the last step we now seek for concepts that have been matched in one of our previous computations and have a single holonym left. Then we consider both holonyms to be similar, assigned with the same similarity value as the initial concept.

$candidates(s) := candidates(s) \cup candidates_4(s)$
with
$candidates_4(s) := \{(c, lexsim(c, s)) \mid t \in name(candidates(h)) \wedge$
$\qquad\qquad c \in holonyms(t) \wedge s \in holonyms(h) \wedge$
$\qquad\qquad |holonyms(t)| = |holonyms(h)| = 1 \wedge$
$\qquad\qquad c \notin name(candidates(s))\}$
having
$h, s \in ontology(S); \ c, t \in ontology(T)$
and
$name(candidates(s)) = x; \ x \in ontology(T)$

COSMO has been evaluated with synthetic as well as real documents. To compare the results of COSMO with those of related publications we now stick to synthetic data that has been produced by a human integrator in the context of WordNet. Figure 2 shows the results of 28 word pairs that are frequently compared in tests on semantic similarity [14]. For a better readability the results of figure 2 are ordered with descending consensus in human anticipation. The results of COSMO are very satisfying with respect to the fact that they are computed during runtime. That means, in a non real time scenario the results of COSMO can be even more precise by increasing the pruning level of our heuristics. This allows *COSMO* to detect even not so closely related concepts but leads to a longer computation time in return. Compared with two other strategies (path resp. information distance) used for computing the semantic similarity of concepts, the results of *COSMO* are very promising. It is closer to human intuition than path distance is. In comparison to applying a purely information based approach, *COSMO* requires less effort because there is no need to do an extensive analysis of domain specific documents.

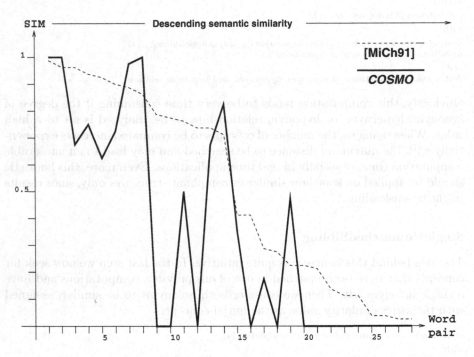

**Fig. 2.** Computational results of *COSMO* compared with human anticipation in [27]

## 5    Conclusions and Outlook

In this paper we presented and discussed an approach for KM applications to mediate ontologies for communities of practice. Our results obtained from tests of word pairs used in *COSMO* for a mediation and comparison of "synthetic" ontologies show that it leads to very good results. We have conducted two case studies with the *COSMO* system. First, we applied the mediation system in the ATLASFlow help desk environment managed by electronic circulation folders [22, 38, 19]. Second, we extended and used *COSMO* in a community aware adaptive environment for mobile tourist information [32].

In ATLASFlow multimedia content describing failures in using information technology could be uploaded via a web browser and annotated with metadata. For each user an individual editor was described by analyzing the metadata and their preferred ontologies. Some users e.g. preferred to describe failures by means of the CIM schema DMTF (http://www.dmtf.org). All these metadata were stored, transformed and re-used with MPEG-7 which served as a framework for unifying other metadata standards [16, 23]. *COSMO* served as a mediator between different work places translating terms in the different metadata standards according to simple rules learned in a few runs. Surprisingly, the multimedia content of the help desk has been used for lectures for the use of information technology inside the organization by explaining the misuse of the system.

In the tourist information scenario, ontology information from the communities was used to build stereotypes of users for adapting content to their needs. Additionally, technical content adaptation information was used to describe the capabilities of the mobile devices. Both was described by MPEG-21 [8] resp. MPEG-7 [23]. When content from a server should be delivered to a mobile device upon request or upon automatic location of the system using GPS, a pre-clustered static profile computed by the extended version of *COSMO* was applied to adapt the content to the specific needs of the user and the device. By giving feedback in forms of ratings the order of adapted content delivered to the device is influenced. These are very basic examples how ontology mediation techniques can be used to deliver more specific content to users. Particularly the second case study has demonstrated how costly the computation of such mediation can be. Thus, we decided to use static ontologies on the server side.

In future, we seek for possibilities to speed up the computation time, especially on handheld devices such as PDAs or cellular phones with load balancing techniques including parallelization of server side computations and the development of agent-based brokerage based on content transformation with parameterized XSLT scripts [38]. Further research in *COSMO* aims at an additional consideration of the structural dependencies of concepts. Right now, the mediation of ontologies is based on the semantic similarity of concepts. In some cases this is not sufficient, since the usage of concepts and their semantics might also depend on their interrelationship with neighboring concepts. For instance, the use of the concept "nail" related with the concept "hammer" might indicate a tool kit setting instead of a manicure context. Therefore, we are currently trying to embed strategies to measure the structural similarity such as tree comparison algorithms [39] in *COSMO*, too. By doing so, we are hoping to improve mediation even between those concepts that are not so closely related to each other.

## Acknowledgements

This work was supported by the German National Science Foundation (DFG) within the collaborative research centers SFB/FK 427 "Media and Cultural Communication", SFB 476 "IMPROVE", and by the 6th Framework IST programme of the EC through the Network of Excellence in Professional Learning (PROLEARN) IST-2003-507310. We'd like to thank our colleagues for the inspiring discussions.

# References

1. Alani, H., Dasmahapatra, S., O'Hara, K., Shadbolt, N.: Identifying Communities of Practice through Ontology Network Analysis. *IEEE Intelligent Systems March/April* (2003), pp 18-25.
2. Adomavicius, G., Tuzhilin, A.: Using Data Mining Methods to Build Customer Profiles. *IEEE Computer Februar* (2001), pp 74-82.
3. Avaro, O., Salembier, P.: MPEG-7 Systems: overview. *IEEE Transactions on Circuits and Systems for Video Technology 11, 6* (2001), pp 760-764.
4. Bayardo, R. J., Bohrer, W., Brice, R., Cichocki, A. et al.: InfoSleuth: Agent-based Semantic Integration of Information in Open and Dynamic Environments. *Proc. of the ACM-SIGMOD Intl. Conf. on Management of Data* (1997), pp 195-206.
5. Böszörményi, L., Hellwagner, H., Kosch, H.: Multimedia Technologies for E-Business Systems and Processes. *Proceedings of E-Business Processes* (2001).
6. Bressler, S. E., Grantham Sr., C. E.: Communities of Commerce: Building Internet Business Communities to Accelerate Growth, Minimize Risk, and Increase Customer Loyalty. *McGraw-Hill Professional Publishing* (2000).
7. de Brum Saccol, D., Heuser, C.: Integration of XML Data. *Bressan, S. et al. (eds.): VLDB 2002 Workshop EEXTT and CAiSE 2002 Workshop DIWeb - Revised Papers, Springer-Verlag Berlin Heidelberg* (2003), pp 68-80.
8. Burnett, I., Van de Walle, R., Hill, K., Bormans, J., Pereira, F.: MPEG-21: Goals and Achievements. *IEEE Multimedia, 10, 4* (2003), pp 60-70.
9. Cui, Z., Jones, D., O'Brien, P.: Issues in Ontology-based Information Integration. *Gomez-Perez, A. et al. (eds.): Proceedings of the IJCAI-01 Workshop on Ontologies and Information Sharing* (2001).
10. Cristani, M., Cuel, R.: A Comprehensive Guideline for Building a Domain Ontology from Scratch. *Proceedings of I-KNOW'04, Journal of Universal Computer Science J.UCS* (2004), pp 205-212.
11. Doan, A., Madhavan, J., Dhamankar, R., Domingos, P., Halevy, A. Y.: Learning to match ontologies on the Semantic Web. *VLDB Journal, 12, 4* (2003), pp 303-319.
12. Doerr, M., Hunter, J., Lagoze, C.: Towards a Core Ontology for Information Integration. *Journal of Digital Information 1, no. 8* (2003).
13. Gruber, T.: What is an Ontology? *Knowledge Acquisition* (1995).
14. Mc Hale, M. L.: A Comparison of WordNet and Roget's Taxonomy for Measuring Semantic Similarity. *Computation and Language, Sept.* (1998), pp 115-120.
15. Hunter, J.: MetaNet - A Metadata Term Thesaurus to Enable Semantic Interoperability Between Metadata Domains. *Journal of Digital Information 1, no. 8* (2001).
16. Hunter, J.: An Overview of the MPEG-7 Description Definition Language (DDL). *IEEE Transactions on Circuits and Systems for Video Technology, 11, 6* (2001), pp 756-772.
17. Huysman, M., Wenger, E., Wulf, V.: Communities and Technologies: Proceedings of the First International Conference on Communities and Technologies; C&T 2003. *Kluwer Academic Publishers, Dordrecht* (2003).
18. Jimes, C., Lucardie, L.: Reconsidering the tacit-explicit distinction - A move toward functional (tacit) knowledge management. *Electronic Journal of Knowledge Management, 1, 1* (2003), pp 23-32.
19. Klamma, R.: Multimediatechnologien für das Verbesserungsmanagement. *atp - Automatisierungstechnische Praxis, 5* (2004), pp 52-60.

20. Klamma, R., Schlaphof, S.: Rapid Knowledge Deployment in an Organizational-Memory-Based Workflow Environment. *Hansen, H. R. et al.: Proceedings of the 8ᵗʰ European Conference on Information Systems (ECIS 2000), Vienna, Austria* (2000), pp 364-371.
21. Kosch, H., Döller, M.: Content-based Indexing and Retrieval supported by Mobile Agent Technology. *Tucci, M. (eds.): Multimedia Databases and Image Communication, Second International Workshop MDIC 2001, LNCS 2184* (2001), pp 152-165.
22. Klamma, R., Peters, P., Jarke, M.: Workflow Support for Failure Management in Federated Organizations. *Blanning, R. W., King, D. R.: Proceedings of the 31ˢᵗ Hawai'i Conference on System Sciences, IEEE Computer Society Press* (1998), pp 302-311.
23. Klamma, R., Spaniol, M., Jarke, M.: Digital media knowledge management with MPEG-7. *The Twelfth International World Wide Web Conference, (WWW 2003), Poster Session, 20-24 May 2003, Budapest, Hungary* (2003).
24. Kunieda, T., Wakita, Y.: XML-schema Dynamic Mapped Multimedia Content Description Tool. *Kunii, H. S. et al. (eds.): Conceptual Modeling - ER 2001, 20th International Conference on Conceptual Modeling* (2001).
25. Little, S., Geurts, J., Hunter, J.: The Dynamic Generation of Intelligent Multimedia Presentations through Semantic Interferencing. *The Sixth European Conference on Research and Advanced Technology for Digital Libraries, ECDL 2002, Rome, September* (2002).
26. Liu, J., Wong, C. K., Hui, K. K : An Adaptive User Interface Based on Personalized Learning. *IEEE Intelligent Systems, March/April* (2003), pp 52-57.
27. Miller, G. A., Charles, W.G.: Contextual Correlates of Semantic Similarity. *Languages and Cognitive Processes 6, no. 1* (1991), pp 1-28.
28. Missikoff, M., Navigli, R., Velardi, P.: The Usable Ontology: An Environment for Building and Assessing a Domain Ontology. *Horroks, I. et. al. (eds.): ISWC 2002. Springer-Verlag, LNCS 2342* (2002), pp 39-53.
29. Noy, N. F., Musen, M. A.: PROMPTDIFF: A Fixed-Point Algorithm for Comparing Ontology Versions. *Proceedings of the National Conference on Artficial Intelligence* (2002).
30. Nonaka, I., Takeuchi, H.: The Knowledge-creating Company. *Oxford University Press, Oxford* (1995).
31. Omelayenko, B. : Integrating Vocabularies: Discovering and Representing Vocabulary Maps. *Horroks, I., Hendler, J. (eds.): The Semantic Web - ISWC 2002, Springer-Verlag, LNCS 2342* (2002).
32. Özmen, O.: Behavior Patterns for a Community Aware Content Adaption for Mobile End Devices. *Master thesis, RWTH Aachen* (2004).
33. Perkowitz, M., Etzioni, O.: Adaptive Web Sites: Concept and Case Study. *Artificial Intelligence, no. 118* (2000), pp 1-2.
34. Perkowitz, M., Etzioni, O.: Adaptive Web Sites: an AI Challenge. *IJCAI (1)* (1997), pp 16-23.
35. Pretschner, A., Gauch, S.: Ontology Based Personalized Search. *Proceedings of the 11ᵗʰ IEEE Conf. on Tools with Artificial Intelligence* (1999), pp 291-298.
36. Resnik, P.: Semantic Similarity in a Taxonomy: An Information-Based Measure and its Application to Problems of Ambiguity in Natural Language. *Journal of Artificial Intelligence Research* (1999).
37. Rodriguez, A., Egenhofer, M. J.: Determining Semantic Similarity among Entity Classes from Different Ontologies. *IEEE Transactions on Knowledge and Data Engineering, no. 15* (2003), pp 442-456.

38. Schmitz, D.: Adressierung digitaler Medien mittels Community-basierter Agenten-technik. *Proceedings of: Informatiktage, Bad Schussenried, Germany, November 8-9* (2003) (in German).
39. Selkow, S. M.: The Tree-to-Tree editing Problem. *Information Processing Letters, 6(6)* (December 1977), pp 184-186.
40. Staab, S., Mädche, A.: Axioms are Objects, too - Ontology Engineering beyond the Modeling of Concepts and Relations. *Proceedings of the ECAI 2000 Workshop on Ontologies and Problem-Solving Methods, Berlin, August 21-22* (2000).
41. Tempich, C., Pinto, S., Staab, S., Sure, Y.: A case study in supporting DIstributed, Loosely-controlled and evolvInG Engineering of oNTologies (DILIGENT). *Proc. of I-KNOW'04, Journal of Universal Computer Science J.UCS* (2004), pp 225-240.
42. Takaai, M., Takeda, H., Nishida, T.: Distributed Ontology Development Environment for Multi-agent Systems. *AAAI-97 Spring Symposium Series on Ontological Engineering* (1997), pp 149-153.
43. Tversky, A.: Features of Similarity. *Psychological Review, 84* (1977), pp 327-352.
44. Wang, J.-C., Chen, C.-L.: An Automated Tool for Managing Interactions in Virtual Communities - Using Social Network Analysis Approach. *Journal of Organizational Computing and Electronic Commerce, 14, 1* (2004) pp 1-26.
45. Werry, C., Mowbray, M.: Online Communities - Commerce, Community Action, and the Virtual University. *Hewlett-Packard Professional Books, Prentice-Hall* (2001).
46. Wenger, E.: Communities of Practice - Learning, Meaning, and Identity. *Cambridge University Press, Cambridge, UK* (1998).
47. Ye, Y.: Programming with an Intelligent Agent. *IEEE Intelligent Systems, May/June* (2003), pp 43-47.
48. Zhang, K., Wand, J., Shasha, D.: On the Editing Distance between Undirected Acyclic Graphs and Related Problems. *International Journal of Foundations of Computer Science 7, no. 1* (1996), pp 43-58.

# Cross Media Retrieval in Knowledge Discovery

Mathias Lux, Michael Granitzer, Wolfgang Kienreich,
Vedran Sabol, Werner Klieber, and Walter Sarka

Know-Center Graz, Inffeldgasse 21a,
8010 Graz, Austria
{mlux,mgrani,wkien,vsabol,wklieber,wsarka}@know-center.at
http://www.know-center.at

**Abstract.** Recent trends show that more and more digital cameras, video cameras and DVD recorders are sold and the number of emails and other messages sent increases each year. For example it is estimated that there will be nearly 300 million digital image capture devices in use worldwide through 2004, capturing about 29 billion digital pictures [12]. Users not only produce huge amounts of content, but this content is also spread over many different media types and document formats. Storing all contents implicates a great extent of documents in large, heterogeneous data repositories. Performing effective retrieval in heterogeneous repositories requires new approaches: documents in different formats containing different media types have to be transformed to a common denominator, and relations between contents of different media types must be established. This allows direct comparison of contents of different media types. In this paper we present a prototype called *Magick* that implements such an approach to cross-media retrieval.

## Introduction

Taking a look at the term *cross media* reveals its heritage from the publishing community. It defines that content, the actual essence to publish, is delivered using different media. Taking for example a daily newspaper, cross media publishing can mean that all content is provided as hypermedia documents on the internet or using emails with digital document attachments.

In information retrieval and knowledge discovery the term cross media means an equal treatment of the essence, the actual meaning of the content, independent from the media used for deliverance. In many cases information retrieval methods are used on data repositories containing emails, editable and non editable textual documents and hypermedia documents. In case of multimedia retrieval the actual retrieval is done on multimedia data like images, audio or video. Cross media retrieval combines all kind of data for collective retrieval, not taking care of the format or media used for the actual retrieval but using information and multimedia retrieval methods on the data itself.

The use case in which needs for cross media retrieval can be identified is not unimaginable. Taking for example a multimedia database like a digital museum or the personal files of a user, also referred to as personal digital library, we can identify huge data bases containing digital images, documents, audio and video files and of course semantic interconnections between these documents of different media.

D. Karagiannis and U. Reimer (Eds.): PAKM 2004, LNAI 3336, pp. 343–352, 2004.
© Springer-Verlag Berlin Heidelberg 2004

# Related Work

Most of the research work done on information and multimedia retrieval does not combine documents of different media types treating them as equal. Clustering and multidimensional scaling were already applied on Hypermedia documents and Internet content using common search engines for information retrieval in the kartOO visual search [2] and the Vivisimo clustering engine [3]. A combination of clustering and MDS was for example presented in the WebRat project [8] which is a visual meta search engine: Clusters of search results were identified, similarity placement for the visualization of the clusters and documents was performed and the labels of clusters were extracted and displayed. All these meta search engines can only handle textual documents.

Other projects like Musescape [1] handle one specific media format, in case of Musescape the retrieval is limited to audio files and even more specific music files. Other examples for multimedia but single media retrieval are the SMOOTH video database [11] which allows annotation and retrieval of video data, based on the multimedia description standard MPEG-7 and supported by automatic video segmentation and the image retrieval prototype, described and evaluated by Rodden et. al., that organizes images by their similarity using content based image retrieval features and self organizing maps [6].

Jones and Lam-Adesina investigated cross media retrieval (or mixed-media retrieval in their terminology) in a very specific context by combining text, spoken text and scanned image documents search in [5]. Their approach was not as general as the one described in this paper because all three mentioned media types which were integrated in the mixed media retrieval can be converted to a text document either by speech recognition or OCR methods. A method for integrating images and audio files in general like music files or digital photos was not discussed.

# Knowledge Discovery

Knowledge Discovery (KD) refers to the overall process of finding and identifying data of interest, extracting and generating knowledge from the raw data, and presenting the results in an adequate and convenient way to the user. More precisely this process can be subdivided in following steps:

- Data acquisition: finding, selecting and retrieving data of interest.
- Preprocessing (data transformation): cleaning, formatting and preparing the data for further processing.
- Analysis (mining): extraction of explicit and detection of implicit knowledge from the raw data.
- Storing (optional step): storing of all or only a part of the gathered data and generated knowledge for later reuse.
- Presentation: Presenting and/or visualizing results for exploration, interpretation and evaluation by the user.
- Gathering feedback (optional step): KD may also be an iterative process where user's feedback is utilized to improve the process.

Magick, the prototype discussed in this paper, uses the *KnowMiner* framework to perform for performing the knowledge discovery tasks let alone the presentation of results. The KnowMiner framework is an extendable, configurable, general-purpose knowledge discovery software package. It was implemented in Java for portability, offers standardized, XML-based input/output capabilities and was primarily designed for handling human-readable cross-media information. KnowMiner acts as a bridge between data repositories and the front-end Magick: finding relevant information available in different formats stored in heterogeneous repositories, as well as providing powerful means of analysis, orientation and navigation in large cross-media data repositories are typical areas of application. The framework's functionality includes advanced methods and techniques from domains of information retrieval, data mining and information visualization. Due to plug-and-play architecture of its modules implementation of high-quality, high-performance knowledge discovery solutions, and/or integration of KnowMiner functionality into existing systems takes place in an efficient, straightforward manner.

Figure 1 shows an example of how a knowledge discovery solution can be implemented employing the KnowMiner framework. In this example three different data sources are accessed. A connector is assigned to each source to retrieve data and transform different document formats and data types into a unified GML-format. An application based on the KnowMiner framework analyses, processes and transforms this data and makes the results of this process accessible to a front-end through a standardized (SOAP-based) interface. The framework does not offer any visualization or presentation tools itself. However, its functionality, configurability and standardized interfaces ensure that a presentation layer can be implemented atop the framework with a minimum effort. Although still in development KnowMiner was already employed for implementing real-world knowledge discovery solutions.

Particular emphasis was given to cross-media capabilities of the framework, which were of central interest to Magick, the prototype described in this paper. Two operations are particularly prominent in this context: format normalization and content normalization. Format normalization transforms different document formats (such as Word, PDF, HTML) to a unified format and transforms different data formats describing the same data type (for example JPEG, PNG, GIF or bitmap for pictures) to a single format for that data type. This operation transforms all data into a KnowMiner-specific, XML-based GML-format representing a common denominator for all supported document formats and media types.

Content normalization transforms data entities in GML format into data structures similar to well-known feature vectors so they can be compared. As relations between contents of different media types belonging to the same data entity are tracked, and through definition of combined comparison metrics for data entities KnowMiner is able, in certain cases, to establish relations between data entities even if they contain completely different media (data) types. For example: a picture of a dog can be evaluated to be similar to a text about dogs if there is another data entity containing a dog picture accompanied by additional text describing the picture. It is obvious that using annotations and enriching documents with metadata can play a crucial role here. One of the intentions behind developing Magick was to investigate how to effectively employ annotations and metadata to improve cross-media knowledge discovery.

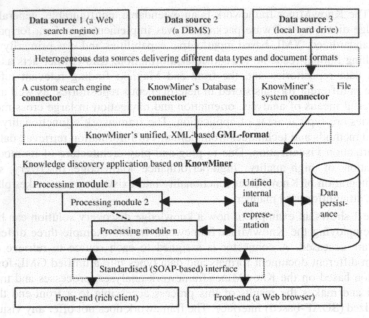

**Fig. 1.** Example: architecture of a knowledge discovery solution based upon KnowMiner

## Magick

Using the KnowMiner Framework for a specific use case we created Magick, an application for cross media clustering and visualization. Assuming that a common web page contains text and images, we applied clustering and multidimensional scaling to a set of data containing textual and image documents of various formats whereas the textual content is outnumbered by the images and documents of different media are semantically related. For example a web page about a specific topic like "medieval castles" contains some describing text, some photos and outlines of prominent castles, which allows splitting up the web page in one text document and a number of images with relations between images and text documents. Taking some web pages like above examples we can quickly build up a cross-media data repository. As annotation is already a common practice along the creation process of media, e.g. the enrichment of web pages with keywords or adding short descriptive words and texts to images, we also take for granted that all documents are at least in some way annotated with metadata like a creation date, an author and a subject or some keywords.

The use case can be described through the following user requirements: A user wants to browse a set of documents, e.g. a list of search results from a web search. The user wants to identify focal points of the set and the interconnection between these focal points like categorizing similar documents and combining them to subsets. As a tool for browsing the user needs an interface which visualizes those subsets and documents and the interconnections between the subsets and their members. An example can be given as follows: A user searches for the term "enterprise" on the Internet. The query returns numerous cross media which are taken from different contexts as the term is used in the Star Trek science fiction stories as name of a starship, in the name of Sun's Java 2 Enterprise Edition (short J2EE) or as common name for business ventures. These contexts can be seen as focal points that should be detected automatically by the application.


## Architecture

Using the features and tools of the KnowMiner Framework the main work consisted of interconnecting and configuring existing modules and creating a visualization of the results. The main components and their dependencies can be shown in a simplified manner in following flow diagram.

In the import module the media type and format of each data item is identified and appropriate import plug-ins are instantiated. This allows a pluggable import support and easy integration of additional media types and formats. After the loading process data and metadata are *normalized* as part of the import process, which means that all relevant data and metadata is converted to a unified internal format. This ensures that each data processing module like the clustering and multidimensional scaling modules can handle the data independent from its original format and media type. After the data processing the results are visualized, a controller component configures and controls the processes and the data flow. A Java Swing interface allows user interaction like result browsing and setting of parameters.

For implementation of the data processing modules we used a complete-link hierarchical clustering and a force directed placement algorithm for multidimensional scaling as described and evaluated in previous projects (see [7] and [8]). The similarity measurement between single documents is based on the document metadata. For each media type the available metadata elements were mapped to Dublin Core metadata elements, e.g. EXIF creation date or file creation date for digital photos was mapped to the date element in Dublin Core or the author element in Adobe's XMP standard for PDF files or the file owner was mapped to the Dublin Core element author. So for all documents, regardless of their media type, a Dublin Core based metadata was available. In this project following terminology was used: All documents have a representation in the Dublin Core *feature space*, where they can be compared to each other and similarity and distance values could be computed. In addition to the Dublin Core feature space media specific feature spaces were implemented and used for similarity and distance calculations between documents of the same media type: The EXIF feature space for digital photos, the IPTC feature space for annotated images and two additional content based image retrieval feature space based on the MPEG-7 descriptors ScalableColor and ColorLayout (see also [4]). All the similarities calculated in different feature spaces are combined and weighted to create a parameterized overall similarity upon all feature spaces For example the content based image retrieval and the EXIF feature space are used although text documents in the processed data repository do not have content based image retrieval features or EXIF annotations. In case of similarity measurement between two text documents or a text document and an image only those features spaces, in which both objects have representations, are considered for computations.

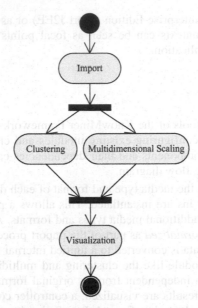

**Fig. 2.** Main components of Magick identified by their processing task in an activity diagram

## Interface

Conclusions from previous projects like WebRat and Infosky (see [7] and [8]) have shown us the importance of an intuitive and easy-to-handle interface. The visualization has to show the user the results of the clustering and the multidimensional scaling and the interconnections between the results of both processing modules. We used two well-known and well evaluated visualization approaches which are described in detail in [9]. The clustering results are displayed as tree, the results of the multidimensional scaling process are visualized using the landscape metaphor. The combination of both visualization techniques happens through highlighting in the landscape visualization on selection in the tree using concentric circles to give the impression of a group island or a mountain ridge. A similar combination of the tree and the landscape visualization was used in the Infosky project [8] were the tree hierarchy had up to 14 levels. Recent browsing and searching usability tests have shown that the tree visualization without the landscape is the fastest way for browsing, the slowest is the landscape visualization alone, while the combination tends to be much faster than a landscape-only visualization but still being slower than the tree alone. The main benefit of the combination of both is that, as shown by Infosky usability tests, there were 2.5 times less  search time outs, meaning the requested item could not be found by the user, than in the stand alone tree visualization, which implicates that more problems can be solved with a combined visualization, see also [10].

Due to simplification and rapid development in the Magick prototype only a one level hierarchy was used for clustering results although the used HAC algorithm could produce an arbitrary number of levels (described in [13]).

On the above picture the resulting visualization of the processing of 171 digital photos and 29 HTML documents is shown. The images are displayed as thumbnails.

The HTML documents are visualized as icon images of text scrolls. To navigate through the landscape visualization zoom and panning controlled by mouse were implemented, the size of the icons can be changed continuously.

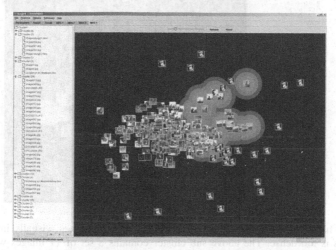

**Fig. 3.** Screenshot of the Magick visualization: Using Java Swing on the left hand side the tree visualization was implemented. On the right hand side the landscape is shown

## Conclusions

Evaluating the above setting the first conclusion is that clustering alone on the meta-data all objects have in common, which is in this case a subset of the well known Dublin Core elements, results in much too dense clusters. This is due to a small number of comparable elements and the disadvantageous distribution of similarities. The distribution can be visually arranged by using content based image feature spaces with a small weight. This allows correcting the similarities between images by pulling together visually similar images and pushing away images from text documents. However, if the weight for the content based image feature space is set too high, objects of different media types are pushed away too much, like text documents are moved to the edges of the landscape and images get positioned in the center. The usage of content based image feature spaces also makes the landscape visually more attractive because clusters with obvious intuitive color and color distribution similarity are displayed next to each other, e.g. pictures with different semantic content but blue background become neighbors.

The landscape and the tree visualization allow the user to identify focal points of the data set by visually comparing the density and size of the clusters. The interface and visualization technique have been tested, as already mentioned above, in the Infosky project, although the usage with cross media data sets has not yet been evaluated. The integration of additional media types and feature spaces is supported through a modular architecture of the KnowMiner framework. Based on the Dublin Core and the ID3 feature space MP3 audio files can already be integrated.

While evaluating the overall performance and correctness of the methods we also discovered some special tasks the prototype can be used for. Objects with missing or

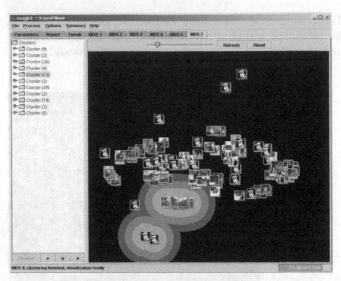

**Fig. 4.** The highlighted cluster in the visualization, which combines, visually interpreted, two sub clusters is too dense. The above sub cluster contains a set of 11 images which can't be investigated by the user because the overlap each other too much

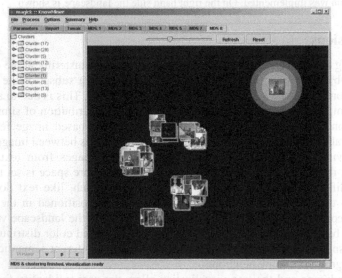

**Fig. 5.** In the upper right corner of the landscape visualization a single outlier marks an object that does not have any EXIF metadata

extraordinary different metadata descriptions can be easily found using the landscape visualization - they will be represented as outliers. Using the prototype on image only data sets the feature spaces allow clustering and multidimensional scaling based on color similarity or special metadata elements. In case of digital photos the data objects can be processed upon their flash settings, their date or the digital camera preferences which allows a separation between indoor and outdoor photos or photos shot with flash, at daylight or artificial light without extra annotation of the images.

The runtime performance of the clustering is cubic although the algorithm can be accelerated to a quadratic runtime. The multidimensional scaling, performed with a sampling-accelerated force directed placement algorithm has quadratic runtime. Additionally a constant number of iterations with a traditional, cubic runtime algorithm is performed to refine the results. The runtime for the creation of the similarity matrix is also quadratic. All other modules like import and visualization have linear runtime. The overall memory usage is quadratic because of the similarity matrix.

For usage in a non prototype environment the whole application has to be optimized for runtime, especially the import and the calculation of the similarities can be speed up by employment of faster clustering algorithms and caching of normalized documents, which could be done easily because an XML Format and a XML-Java binding for the normalized documents has been defined and could be cached after the import process.

## Future Work

Besides the integration of additional media formats like audio and video documents hierarchical data repositories should be considered as starting point for Clustering and multidimensional scaling. Many existing data repositories are already organized in a hierarchical way, which could be of great benefit for further improvement of processing complexity. In addition to this a way for summarizing and labeling the clusters has to be found regardless of the media types of their members through representative images and keywords.

Providing all available parameters confuses the user too much. Already supported profile generation and loading should be used by an expert to create user specific profiles or cut down the number of parameters to one or two sliders which are semantically described for the users like e.g. a slider to specify the level at which the visual similarity interferes the actual process without setting each single parameter.

Evaluating the distribution of object similarities in different feature spaces the parameters can be corrected automatically in specific cases. A lot of research can be done in evaluating the possibilities of these techniques in cross media retrieval.

The whole prototype can also be implemented as client-server application for outsourcing the computation modules to a powerful server and displaying the results on a thin client. And last but not least the application could be used for the World Wide Web by spidering homepages and generating a sitemap or an overview about a subset of a homepage.

## References

1. Tzanetakis, G.: Musescape: A Tool for Changing Music Collections into Libraries, 7th European Conference, ECDL 2003 Trondheim, Norway, August 17-22, 2003 Proceedings, Lecture Notes in Computer Science, Volume 2769/2004, Springer Verlag Heidelberg, pp. 412 - 421

2. KartOO Technologies: KartOO Visual Meta Search Engine, 2004,
   uri: http://www.kartoo.com, last visited: 15<sup>th</sup> April 2004
3. Vivisimo Inc.: Vivisimo Clustering Engine, 2004,
   uri: http://www.vivisimo.com, last visited: 15<sup>th</sup> April 2004
4. Lux, M., Becker, J., Krottmaier, H.: Semantic Annotation and Retrieval of Digital Photos,
   in Proceedings Short Papers, Hg., CAiSE '03 Forum, University of Maribor Press: Klagenfurt,2003, 85-88.
5. Jones, G.J.F., Lam-Adesina, A.M.: Musescape: A Tool for Changing Music Collections
   into Libraries, 6th European Conference, ECDL 2002, Rome, Italy, September 16-18,
   2002. Proceedings, Lecture Notes in Computer Science, Volume 2769/2004, Springer
   Verlag Heidelberg, pp. 412 - 421
6. Rodden, K., Wojciech, B., Sinclair, D., Wood, K.: Does organisation by similarity assist
   image browsing? Proceedings of the SIGCHI conference on Human factors in computing
   systems, Seattle, Washington, United States, p. 190 - 197, 2001
7. Andrews, K., Kienreich, W., Sabol, V., Becker, J., Droschl, G., Kappe, F., Granitzer, M.,
   Tochtermann, K., Auer, P.: The InfoSky Visual Explorer: Exploiting Hierarchical Structure
   and Document Similarities, Palgrave Macmillan, 2002, 166-181
8. Granitzer, M., Kienreich, W., Sabol, V., Dösinger, G.: WebRat: Supporting Agile Knowledge Retrieval through Dynamic, Incremental Clustering and Automatic Labelling of Web
   Search Result Sets, Linz, Austria: 1st Workshop Knowledge Management for Distributed
   Agile Processes (IEEE Workshop Enabling Technologies), 2003.
9. Andrews, Keith, "Visualising Information Structures: Aspects of Information Visualisation", Professorial Thesis, Graz, Austria: IICM, Graz University of Technology, 2002. uri:
   ftp://ftp.iicm.edu/pub/keith/habil/visinfo.pdf
10. Andrews, K., Kienreich, W., Sabol, V., Granitzer, M.: Interactive Poster: Visualising Large
    Hierarchically Structured Document Repositories with InfoSky, submitted to InfoVis 2003.
11. Bachlechner, A., Böszörményi, L., Hanin, C., Hofbauer, C.,Kosch, H., Lang, M., Riedler,
    C., Tusch, R.: SMOOTH - A Distributed Multimedia Database System, VLDB 2001,
    Rome, Italy, uri: http://ftp2-itec.uni-klu.ac.at/~harald/demo/demo/, last visited: 15<sup>th</sup> April
    2004
12. Infotrend Research Group, Inc., 2004, Internet, www.infotrends-rgi.com
13. Sabol Vedran, "Visualisation Islands", IICM, Graz University of Technology: Graz, Aus-
    tria, 2001.

# KM-SISO: An Approach for Knowledge Management in Civil Engineering

Knut Hinkelmann[1], Fabian Probst[1], and Benoît Stempfel[2]

[1] University of Applied Sciences Solothurn Northwestern Switzerland,
Department of Economics, Riggenbachstrasse 16, 4600 Olten, Switzerland
{knut.hinkelmann,fabian.probst}@fhso.ch
[2] SISO SA, Rte du Levant 8, 1709 Fribourg, Switzerland
info@sisonet.ch

**Abstract.** Construction site projects are characterised by high complexity, cost intensiveness and tight deadlines. Access to knowledge and experiences from actual and previous projects is from essential importance. The building construction site is a place, where knowledge intensive tasks are performed and information from high importance is generated. In a feasibility study different technologies and methodologies have been evaluated, always considering the special requirements of civil engineering projects. This report shows the main points of this study. It introduces a scenario and generalises the requirements for a practical approach for knowledge management. The report focuses on the process from the appearance of an incident, over documentation and storage in the system, to the reuse of this knowledge in a related case.

## 1 Introduction

Construction projects are typically very complex in execution and have tight deadlines. Construction companies are faced with cost pressure and high market competition. Due to the concentration on the core business, however, knowledge management did not enter this domain for a long time.

A construct is always a prototype as most of the objects are unique and need an individual planning. Nevertheless, experiences or lessons learned might be very helpful if similar cases occur at a later stage of the project or on another construction site. Since construction projects are long-lasting projects with many people from various fields of activities working together, knowledge transfer and reuse should be supported by organisational and technical means. To identify these means was the objective of the KM-SISO[1] research project.

We concentrated on tunnel and road construction projects. In particular we analyzed the project and knowledge management activities at the Alptransit Gotthard Base Tunnel (56.7 km) and the Lötschberg Base Tunnel (34.6 km), two of the world's largest tunnel projects. Both belong to AlpTransit which is a key tunnel construction project on the way to build up a high-speed railway line through Europe.

---

[1] KM-SISO was a research project funded by the soft[net] initiative of the Swiss Federal Office for Professional Education and Technology, with partners being Centre CIM de Suisse Occidentale, PERSS Ingénieurs-conseils SA, Fédération Fribourgeoise des entrepreneurs, Swiss Federal Railways, and the University of Applied Sciences Solothurn.

D. Karagiannis and U. Reimer (Eds.): PAKM 2004, LNAI 3336, pp. 353–364, 2004.
© Springer-Verlag Berlin Heidelberg 2004

Knowledge management must not be seen as an isolated management task but must be integrated with the "ordinary" project work. It is well recognized that project management is of utmost importance. In KM-SISO we identified technologies that are needed to enhance the already existing SiSO project management systems towards a knowledge management system. In a feasibility study we investigated various aspects of knowledge management and showed how they can be transferred into a practical solution. The outcome of KM-SISO, however, is not only a software component but also guidance for organisational improvement.

The following section gives a short description of the SiSO project management software that is in use in the projects we analyzed. It then describes the scenario on the construction site and defines the needs and the goals that were gathered in interviews with different stakeholders like construction site managers, construction supervisor or foreman. In a further section these requirements are converted into a practical solution.

## 2  Problem Description

When problems on the construction site arise, solutions often are developed without considering already acquired experience from the actual or from previous projects. Moreover, knowledge from previous projects is not used for complex planning tasks like site installation or calculation, as it is often not performed by the same person. External experts are consulted for problems which could be solved by internal personnel and faults are made because they were not or badly documented when they first occurred. These and other problems should be solved by an integrated knowledge management approach, resulting in cost and complexity reduction, improved quality of service and–as a consequence–a competitive advantage on the market.

It became clear rather quickly that knowledge management on the construction site requires some kind of information technology, because people from different companies and fields (politician, designer, geologists, civil engineers, construction workers) are involved at different times and places.

### 2.1  SiSO – A Project Management Information System

Knowledge management must not be seen as an isolated management task but must be integrated with the "ordinary" project management. Thus, we first investigated the technical and organisational means that are in use for project management.

At AlpTransit the project management system SiSO is used both in the design and the construction world. SiSO is an integrated management tool for construction site supervision. It was designed to specially meet the requirements of all the parties involved in large construction engineering projects. SiSO has been particularly suited for linear projects, such as roads, bridges or underground works like tunnels. SiSO records all project-related documents, activities and events. Among others, it allows to schedule activities, to calculate estimated and supervise effective costs, to manage quality assurance and to automatically create periodic reports. It has a special module for visualising plans and work progress.

SiSO is very well suited for project management and supervision. Consequently, today the usage of the system is limited to the office and the main operator is the building site manager. The lack for information acquisition directly on construction sites by foremen and the missing possibilities to reuse knowledge in related cases are the basis for the integrated approach which was developed in KM-SISO. KM-SISO should be an integrated information system that supports the process from information acquisition to information distribution.

## 2.2 Scenario

The following scenario description emphasises the characteristics of the construction domain and defines the requirements regarding knowledge acquisition, storage and distribution. The scenario illustrates the most important knowledge-intensive tasks (KIT) [1] as they arose from the various interviews with site managers, civil engineers and construction supervisors:

- problem solving on the construction site,
- knowledge acquisition from previous projects,
- setting up a new construction site.

*The construction supervisor periodically makes an inspection of the construction site of tunnel A in order to control the work process, to supervise the consumption of building material and also to solve problems that occurred since the last inspection. To keep the project management system up-to-date, the construction supervisor collects all the necessary information. Nowadays the information is written on a paper form and later entered into the information system SiSO, when the construction supervisor is back in the office.*

*Let's assume that a serious problem arises, that stops work progress. In this case it is not possible to wait for the next inspection. The problem must be solved immediately by the available persons. The problem solving process requires decisions, which have to be communicated to the involved partners in order to keep transparency and traceability.*

*Assume further, that on another construction site a construction site manager plans a section of a new tunnel – call it tunnel B. According to the main attributes (structure of rock, machines, size, etc.), the construct seems to be similar to tunnel A. Therefore the construction site manager of tunnel B would like to have access to the lessons learned from tunnel A. He analyses the notes of the project A and makes some phone calls to the involved construction supervisors in order to get the required information. The manager elaborates which of these advices are applicable to the new site and implements them to the construction site project B.*

*A few weeks after the project B has started, the tunnel drilling machine crosses a zone of highly toxic asbestos. Fortunately, the building site manager remembers the occurrence of asbestos in a previous project, which was managed by one of the subsidiary companies five years ago. With an enormous effort he gets at the end the information he was looking for. But in the meantime the company management has called an external expert: they would not risk interrupting the work for too long.*

## 2.3 Requirements

The above described scenario exemplarily shows some problems of the current situation which should be generalised in this section:

- **Mobility:** On a civil engineering construction site information and knowledge is accumulated and required not only at the office but outside at the working place. In addition, a tunnel, bridge or road construction site usually is a moving installation, starting at one point and moving its location while work progresses. Since information should be available at any time, a kind of *mobile device* is necessary. For information acquisition this mobile device has been pen and paper for the past. In combination with information systems like SiSO this demands that information has to be acquired twice, once on paper outside and again electronically in the office. It is obvious, that this discontinuity of media could be resolved by using any kind of mobile electronic device. However, one of the major points, why the construction industry is not seen as early adaptor for these technologies, might be the rough environment. Dust and dirt are permanently existent on construction sites. Thus, a device needs to be resistant against these emissions.
- **Convenience:** A solution should allow the user to access and store experiences without having a deep understanding of a system. It arose from interviews with construction workers, that an *easy-to-use interface* supporting simple forms, natural text or speech and graphics are regarded suitable, while scrolling through long scroll-down menus is cumbersome.
- **Traceability:** Non-predictable events often require to refine planning or to apply ad-hoc solutions. In civil engineering projects it is important to communicate these decisions to the involved partners and to make them transparent and traceable in order to record the *decision making process*.
- **Structure:** Once the information is stored in the system the problem arises, how to search for a specific knowledge object[2]. Information overload often causes a waste of time and cost and additionally discourages the employees. The key question is: How can knowledge objects be managed in an accurate way- supporting easy storage and direct access? A simple full text search does not meet the users' requirements and browsing through long result lists is not satisfying. Obviously information has to be classified by meta-data but users should not be harassed to fill in several fields. *Automatic indexing* methods that are based on predefined knowledge structures (like taxonomies or ontologies) seem to be a promising alternative.
- **Reusability:** Propagation of experiences to *similar situations* is characteristic for learning and knowledge transfer. Full text and attribute-based search offer insufficient possibilities to find appropriate cases; therefore a more powerful technology has to be adopted. The goal is, to provide lessons learned of a specific situation when problems or difficulties arise. Or it should be possible to use relevant experiences form previous constructs to plan and to *build up a new construction site*.

## 3 Approach

Tiwana describes in [11] the role of information technologies (IT) for knowledge management. IT is seen primarily as enabler for explicit knowledge, whereas the management of tacit knowledge can only marginally be supported by providing chan-

---

[2] A knowledge object is the set of information, used to describe a incidend that has a potentially high value for other users.

nels to exchange knowledge. As the KM-SISO project forces the enhancement of an existing IT-platform, the following approach will concentrate on explicit knowledge.

There are various definitions of knowledge management. Since we concentrate on explicit knowledge in informations systems, we follow the approach of Benjamins et al. [2], where knowledge management is regarded as a process divided in four phases: (1) gathering, (2) organisation and structuring, (3) refinement and (4) distribution of knowledge.

In the following subsections we first outline the process of knowledge acquisition (phase 1). In the next subsection we introduce an ontology-based approach for structuring knowledge objects in the information system (phase 2). Then we explore the validation process for new knowledge objects (phase 3) and the last subsection we show how case-based reasoning methodology could be applied to our approach (phase 4).

### 3.1 Knowledge Acquisition on the Construction Site

Starting point is the need for simple information gathering, as there is rarely time on construction sites and input structures should be as simple as possible.

To guide the user in the acquisition step, the 5W2H method has been elaborated as a potential option. Originally this method was developed for analysing processes and detecting potential improvement in the organisations' structure. The method defines a set of interrogative pronouns beginning with the letter "w" (what, why, where, when, who) or h (how, how much). The goal of this method is to act as a guideline for asking questions that are covering the main aspects for understanding a problem. The table below gives an impression, how the method could be used in the field of construction sites.

| What | What are the characteristic actions, elements and operations of the problem? |
|------|------|
| Why | Why is it a problem? |
| Where | Where has the problem occurred? |
| When | When, in which activities/phases of the project did the problem occur? What are date and time of the occurrence? |
| Who | Which persons are involved into the situation? Who is responsible? Who is the actor? What is the actors' function? |
| How | How could the problem be solved? Which resources were used (machines, documents, instructions)? |
| How much | How long did it take to solve the problem? What quantity of material was needed to solve the situation? |

Another important aspect of our approach is the need for information acquisition on the place where a problem occurs. As stated in the previous section, a civil engineering construction site is often a moving environment. For this reason it is obvious to investigate the possibilities of mobile data collection. Although the use of mobile devices is not directly connected to knowledge management issues, the use of these technologies can be viewed as a facilitator, as it provides a simple possibility for information acquisition.

Various devices have been evaluated, always taking into consideration the requirements of the end-user: notebooks, table PCs, PDAs, mobile phones, and a digital pens[3]:

1. PORTABILITY: Notebooks and tablet PCs are limited in portability. On one hand this is given by the capacity of the accumulator and on the other hand by the size of the device. PDA and digital pen do not need much electrical power, the digital pen is not much bigger than a conventional pen.
2. USABILITY: The digital pen can be used like conventional hand writing as it converts notes to machine-readable text. Thus it is easy to use and does not prerequisite any knowledge about the structure of any application behind. Additionally the pen allows preparing drawings of any kind of objects, but it prerequisites a well-readable handwriting and currently the products need a scaling paper to write on.

   PDAs, however, have the advantage that they combine input and output in the same device. Since photographs are an important and widely used information source, any of the above mentioned devices would have been supplemented by a digital camera (which, however, is part of modern mobile phones and PDAs).
3. COST: Compared to other devices, a digital pen is available for a lower price.

At an early stage it became obvious that notebooks and tablet PCs are not operable in the rough environment of a construction site. In addition they are not suitable in terms of usability, portability and cost for a broad use. The evaluation came to the result to further evaluate the digital pen – potentially in combination with mobile phones/PDAs – in a field test.

Documents, such as instructions guidelines, contracts, protocols, quality control or working procedures often contain highly valuable information. This information has to be managed by the system in a way; it can be retrieved at any time. Therefore the following section introduces an approach for managing various text documents - hand-written notes as well as documents from text processing software. Not part of this report are deliberations concerning the management of visual information carrier such as images or movies.

## 3.2  Management of Knowledge Objects

Once text is collected it has to be stored and managed in the system. SiSO already has a sophisticated structure for organising the information. Since we plan to enhance SiSO to KM-SISO, additional meta-data and structural information seem to be necessesary. It appeared, however, that many of the users already find it difficult to adequately store the information in SiSO. Thus, we had to find a way to support the user by automated indexing technologies. In the ideal case the user writes the information and the KM-SISO system automatically stores is way to be suitable for a context-specific retrieval mechanism

In the first step, the collected data has to be transmitted to a workstation. The pen captures data with an optical sensor and stores it as an image. In the next step the

---

[3]  Concretely, we investigated the Logitec® io™ Digital Pen and Paper, see
http://www.logitech.com/index.cfm?page=products/features/digitalwriting&crid=1545&countryid=18&languageid=1

image has to be converted by handwriting recognition software. These two steps can be based on established technologies that are offered by various vendors. At this stage, the information has reached the same stage like unformatted text from documents. Input from PDAs is directly available in digital form.

The most challenging task is to map a text with a knowledge structure. In other words, the meta-data has to be added to the text. This process should be supported by algorithms of linguistical text normalisation and text mining [5] and consists of the following steps [9]:

- PREPROCESSING: It includes linguistic processing like the normalisation of terms, expanding abbreviations or correcting errors, caused by the text recognition software.
- MINING: In this step, a domain-specific structure acts as backbone when assigning automatically text to different nodes. In this step the multiple existing relations between terms have to be taken into consideration.
- POSTPROCESSING: This step includes the refinement of the automated process by a person in order to ensure a correct classification of the node.

Figure 1 shows the above described process.

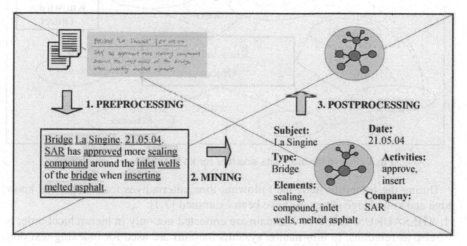

**Fig. 1.** Structure mapping of a handwritten text

To get the most satisfying result from an automatic mapping, it is required to describe the structure of the subjects, used in the application, in a formal and expressive model. Hotho et al. describe how background knowledge can improve text mining [9].

In our application, every knowledge object[4] is described by meta-data (cf. figure 2). The attributes of the meta-data can be associated to the questions of the 5W2H approach (see section 3.2). Each question type refers to specific aspects of background knowledge.

- For example, the analysis of the WHAT part needs background knowledge about types of construction elements and associated activities.

---

[4] In our approach a „knowledge object" is information with a potential high value for reuse in other contexts. Examples are: Decisions, problem solving descriptions, instructions, etc.

– For the WHEN question background knowledge about project phases is needed.
– To analyse the input of the WHO part, the system requires knowledge about typical roles (construction site manager, supervisor, designer, geologists, civil engineer, construction worker, buidlling owner etc.) and their responsibilities in a project, as well as machines used.

In Section 2.3 we outlined the importance of traceability of decisions in civil engineering projects. The proposed structure allows to "attach" any kind of knowledge object, that was previously defined, to a new knowledge object. The connection between the objects is represented by a reason statement. This method provides a possibility to build complex decision processes when problems occur. On the other hand it enhances audit and tracking of decision processes at a later stage of a project or in another project. This approach is based on a technique defined by Conklin et al. [6], where different positions respond to an issue. Positions are supported by arguments which support or object to positions.

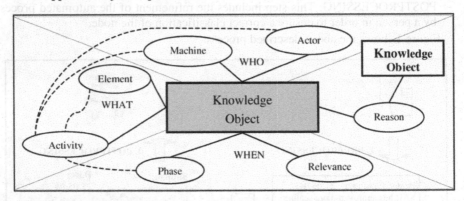

**Fig. 2.** Part of the meta-data structure for knowlede object (simplified)

During the feasbility study the following three alternatives for background knowledge and knowledge structures have been examined [7,1]:

1. THESAURUS: Terms of a domain are collected not only in hierarchical order but also as relations. In information systems thesauri are used for indexing text documents in order to assure consistent document descriptions (use of only one synonym to create the index). Another possibility is to provide the user with additional terms for defining a query for full text search. The third application of a thesaurus is to provide a hierarchy which helps the user to specialise or to generalise a query. In contrast to taxonomy and ontology, a thesaurus does not manage concepts but words or terms.
2. TAXONOMY: A taxonomy can be viewed as a hierarchical classification schema. Knowledge objects should always be assigned to one subject (node). All subjects are ordered in generalisation/specialisation hierarchy.
3. ONTOLOGY: Ontologies are providing possibilities to define any kind of semantic relationships between subjects and to state rules which can be used for a systematic search.

The result of the evaluation was that the taxonomy as well as the thesaurus are not expressive enough to represent the complex relations and mutual dependencies that are needed for the attribute mapping (indicated by dashed lines in figure 2). For example, there is a relation between construction elements and possible actions taken on them: not every activity can be taken for every construction element. As another example, note that a system should be able to process the following kind of statement which comes from the attributes given by the application:

*"If a knowledge object occurred in activity A it was applied in element X, Y or Z. Activity A is always performed in phase 1. As a consequence elements X, Y and Z are elements that are used in phase 1"*

Every activity should be assigned to a specific phase. Orientation on the project phases allows a person to filter the database with knowledge objects of a certain period of time in the project. Regarding the planning process this might be helpful, when for example the manager prepares the site installation for a new phase of a project and would like to prohibit faults which were made in previous projects.

Figure 3 shows the schema of the knowledge structure. This approach is closely related to business-process oriented knowledge [1], since projects can be seen as weakly structured processes [8]

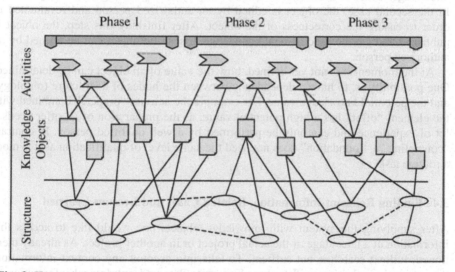

**Fig. 3.** Knwowledge objects are assigned to subjects of the structure and also to phases and activities

Moreover, attributes must be available in different languages. This enables a person to search for a text which was not written in his mother tongue (a common situation in the multilingual culture of Switzerland), as the search is based on the metadata of a text and not on the text itself.

## 3.3 Validating and Refining Knowledge

Users have stressed the importance of a validation process, which has the purpose to ensure the correctness of collected knowledge objects. In addition, the process facilitates the enhancement and refinement of knowledge objects.

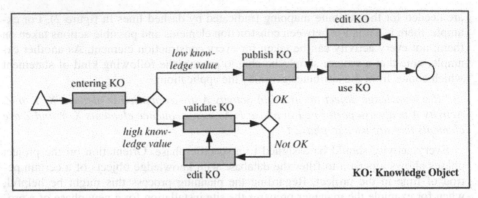

**Fig. 4.** Validation process

The process is instantiated when a new knowledge object is entered into the system. The potential value of the object determines, whether it is published directly (low knowledge value) or it needs further validation by an expert (high knowledge value). In the second case, the object is edited by an authorized person and revalidated in order to ensure the correctness of the object. After finishing this step, the object is published and can be used. If new knowledge arises, the object can be refined by an authorized person.

At the moment it is not yet defined, how the value of an object can be determined. One possibility is, to have a dependency between the nodes of a structure (ontology) and the potential knowledge value. For example the activity "prepare" combined with the element "offer" has a high potential value, as the preparation of an offer needs a lot of experience and can only be performed by a well qualified person. In contrast "concreting" a "foundation" does not need the same level of qualification as it is more a routine task.

### 3.4  Finding Relevant Information, Related Cases and Lessons Learned

After supplying the system with knowledge objects one would like to access this information at a later stage of the actual project or in another project. As already mentioned, fulltext search is not suffient. To take into account any context information, the retrieval mechanism will be based on meta-data and ontological information as described in [10]

To apply lessons learned and to transfer experiences we have to deal with the fact that problem situations usually occur again in slightly different form. As we have already developed a well-defined structure for meta-data, it should be reused for information retrieval. Among other methods, case-based reasoning (CBR; comp. [4]) provides an approach for retrieving objects based on a structure. Bergmann [3] describes how CBR can be applied for experience management and for transferring knowledge to similar cases. The idea of CBR is derived from the method of human problem solving. Humans solve problems on one hand by remembering former similar cases and assigning them to the current problem. CBR allows defining the similarity between existing knowledge objects as well as the similarity between a search query and the existing objects.

By applying this approach to a system, the problem of imprecision must somehow be solved. One approach is, to combine CBR and ontological reasoning by defining similarity values between the nodes of a given structure. Imaging a hierarchical structure, the similarity can be applied as shown in figure 5.

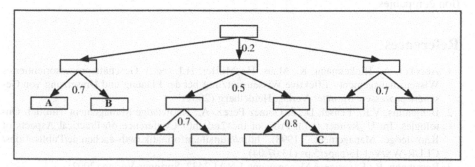

**Fig. 5.** Similarity quotes in a hierarchy

Every parent node of the structure defines the similarity of its child nodes. For example the nodes A and B have a similarity value of 0.7. Accordingly the similarity between A and C has the value 0.2 because their shared node is the root node.

## 4 Conclusion

This paper shows an approach for knowledge management in civil engineering; meeting the special requirements of this domain. It uses various technologies and methods that were developed in different contexts and combines them to a practical solution. The focus of the paper is primarily on technical issues and the management of explicit knowledge. The project, however, also revealed other important topics we had to deal with, particular strategic and organisational ones.

The authors are convinced that knowledge management has more dimensions of high importance that have to be considered when developing a knowledge-based organisation.

Knowledge management has to be an integral part of an enterprise's strategy. Knowledge as a resource has to be managed like any other resource in an organisation. Moreover the culture and leadership of an organisation has to encourage knowledge transfer between employees.

But in civil engineering projects with many involved companies there may be discrepancies between the ambition to share knowledge in the project and the resistance of participating companies who want to save there own knowledge. Additional reservations were expressed, if the owner of the KM-SISO organisational memory would be a competitor in future projects. We suggested a possible solution along the following criteria:

All the information about to the construction belongs to the building owner, who paid for the construction and thus also for the information about it. Also the project-related information, e.g. problems and solutions, have to be stored in the system.

In the meanwhile, a new company has been founded that develops and maintains the KM-SISO system. A first ontological extension of SiSO has already been implemented. The company, however, not only provides and maintains the system but also the content. Since it gathers information from multiple projects, it is possible to analyse them in order to find best practices and to act as a broker of problem solutions. This is possible, because the new company is not a competitor of any of the construction companies.

# References

1. Abecker, A., Hinkelmann, K., Maus, H.; Müller, H.J. (ed..): Geschäftsprozessorientiertes Wissensmanagement - Effektive Wissensnutzung bei der Planung und Umsetzung von Geschäftsprozessen. Springer-Verlag, Heidelberg (2002)
2. Benjamins, V.R., Fensel, D., & Gómez Pérez. A.: Knowledge Management Through Ontologies. In: U. Reimer (ed.): Proc. of the 2nd Int'l Conference on Practical Aspects of Knowledge Management. (1998), http://sunsite.informatik.rwth-aachen.de/Publications/CEUR-WS/Vol-13/paper5.ps (13.07.04)
3. Bergmann, R.: Experience Management. LNAI 2432, Springer-Verlag (2002)
4. Bergmann, R., Althoff, K.-D., Breen, S., Göker, M., Manago, M., Traphöner, R., Wess, S.: Developing Industrial Case-Based Reasoning Applications. LNAI 1612, Springer-Verlag (2004) 21-34
5. Berry, M., W.: Survey of Text Mining: Clustering, Classification, and Retrieval. Springer-Verlag (2003)
6. Conklin, J., Begeman, M.: gIBIS – A Hypertext Tool for Exploratory Policy Discussion. Proceedings of CSCW98 (1998) 140-152
7. Daconta, M. C., Obrst, L. J., Smith, K. T.: The Semantic Web. A Guide to the Future of XML, Web Services and Knowledge Management. Wiley Publishing, Indianapolis (2003) 145-238
8. Fünffinger, M., Rose, T., Rupprecht, C., Schott, H., Sieper, A.: Management von Prozesswissen in projekthaften Prozessen. In Abecker, A., Hinkelmann, K., Maus, H.; Müller, H.J. (ed..): Geschäftsprozessorientiertes Wissensmanagement - Effektive Wissensnutzung bei der Planung und Umsetzung von Geschäftsprozessen. Springer-Verlag, Heidelberg (2002) 293-320
9. Hotho, A., Maedche, A., Staab, S., Zacharias, V.: On Knowledgeable Unsupervised Text Mining. (2002), http://www.aifb.uni-karlsruhe.de/WBS/aho/pub/txt_mining_ws_2002.pdf (13.07.04)
10. Moench, E., Ulrich, M., Schnurr H.-P., Angele, J.: SemanticMiner - Ontology-Based Knowledge Retrieval. Journal of Universal Computer Science, Volume 9, Issue 7 (2003), 682-696
11. Tiwana, A.,: Knowledge Management Toolkit, The Practical Techniques for Building a Knowledge Management System, 1st Edition, Prentice Hall PTR (2000) S. 295 et sqq.
12. Ulrich, M., Maier, A., Angele, J.: Taxonomie, Thesaurus, Topic Map, Ontologie – Ein Vergleich. (2003) 3-11, http://www.ullri.ch/ullri_ch/download/Ontologien/ttto13.pdf (13.07.04)

# SemanticLIFE Collaboration:
# Security Requirements and Solutions –
# Security Aspects of Semantic Knowledge Management

Edgar R. Weippl, Alexander Schatten, Shuaib Karim, and A. Min Tjoa

Vienna University of Technology
{weippl,schatten,karim,tjoa}@ifs.tuwien.ac.at

**Abstract.** SemanticLIFE is a project that stores all information an individual works with in a semantically enriched form. Ontologies are used to improve the search process and to express queries in the way humans think – e.g. "Find the draft I've been working on when traveling home from the conference in Chicago". When people cooperate on projects they obviously need to share information without spending time on entering keywords and thinking about who should be able to access which data; the issue is to correctly configure access controls so that only required information is shared with the appropriate people. Using a combination of the Chinese Wall and the Bell LaPadula model we show how access controls can be configured correctly with little effort by the users.

## Introduction

The SemanticLIFE system is designed to store, manage and retrieve an individual's digital information accumulated over years. The system enables the acquisition and storage of data and creates semantic annotations to email messages, browsed web pages, phone calls, images, contacts, and other resources. SemanticLIFE also provides an intuitive and effective search mechanism based upon stored semantic knowledge [Ahmed].

While the first approach was to provide people with a tool to manage their personal (digital) life, we quickly recognized that individuals rarely work alone; instead, they permanently collaborate with others. Many emails and phone calls received by a person originate in the fact that the sender requires information. If the sender and the receiver work together on a regular basis, i.e. within a project, it would be more efficient if the information accumulated in the SemanticLIFE data base could be shared.

This paper presents security implications of allowing people to share their "Semantic Lives" (SemanticOFFICE); Two issues need to be addressed: (1) Access rights for new documents need to be set. (2) People join and leave projects teams or have informal contact with teams as expert advisors. Their access rights have to be dynamically managed. We thus show possible solutions to common issues of knowledge management in team processes: A combination of well-established access control models can be adapted to automatically assign access rights to new content. Users do not have to manually specify who may access which file. Based on semantic annotations and content analysis access rights can be set similar to those of existing documents.

D. Karagiannis and U. Reimer (Eds.): PAKM 2004, LNAI 3336, pp. 365–377, 2004.

# Related Work

In this area, a lot of work has already been carried out in some major projects. In this section we highlight their significant features and limitations.

## MyLifeBits (Microsoft Research)

It is a system for storing all of one's lifetime data on a PC. The guiding principles are: (a) collections and search must replace hierarchy for organization, (b) multiple visualizations, (c) easy annotations (d) the authoring tool should support reuse of external references [Gemmel2]. As an experiment, G. Bell has captured all his articles, books, cards, etc, and stored them digitally. He is now paperless, and is beginning to capture phone calls, IM transcripts, television, and radio [Gemmel1]. They have successfully incorporated multiple annotation types, and creation of stories which are helpful for the short term memory. Facility for logical schemas modification and extension is at experimental stage.

They are still trying to explore features such as versioning, document similarity ranking and faceted classification. Until now, they were more concerned with functionality, but now the future work is related with UI, advanced visualization techniques, data mining for search, new capture mode and devices, shared usage, security, privacy and social issues.

**Comparison with SemanticLIFE:** Primarily it is perceived as a data store and not a retrieval box. The architecture is apparently compact and not open source. In contrast, the use of ontologies right from visualizations to storage, EDS support, and open source, make SemanticLIFE architecture more flexible, scalable and accessible. Currently, MyLifeBits does not offer any access control mechanisms beyond traditional access control lists (ACLs) for files and role-based access control (RBAC) for the database. It seems that "sharing of life experiences" has not yet been considered.

## Haystack (MIT)

Haystack uses ontologies for information management [Huynh]. Its ultimate goal is to provide high-quality retrieval. Primarily it is designed as a single machine single user tool so as to give a psychological illusion of privacy and security. The guiding design principles are: (a) generic handling of all types of information, (b) flexibility to define additional information types by the user, (c) ability to define the interaction objects and associated operations directly by the user and (d) ability to delegate certain information processing tasks to the agents.

Haystack has a typical three tier architecture [Adar], i.e., a database layer, service layer and client layer. The focus of the database layer is more on augmenting its power by personalizing off-the-shelf information retrieval and database tools to individual user needs and preferences. They have also done some implementation at the Trust layer of Semantic Web by using reification mechanism for RDF storage, and identifier strings as digital signatures during storage of RDF statements. The future developments include ontology conversion, enhanced query mechanisms using machine learning tools to improve retrieval, provide better interface for hybrid search, recommender system based upon user's interests derived from the user interaction, collaborative working, security, access control and privacy.

Haystack is an Open Source RDF-based information management environment, written in Java and is built into the Eclipse platform.

**Comparison with SemanticLIFE:** Haystack is primarily perceived as a system to provide improved user experience using standard semantic web technology. Its architecture is based upon RDF and the components are service oriented using Agents. Though it lacks support for EDS plugins at present, however it seems to be a strong, flexible and scalable architecture coherent with the Semantic web vision. Major emphasis is given on semantic UI and visualization and interaction ontologies which make its design stand out from others. They plan to implement the trust layer just beneath the UI and RDF store. Then it will be possible to manage the list of trusted users by the users themselves. Consequently only those RDF statements which are duly signed by these trusted users will provide information to UI, and not all. Haystack is implemented using a pull strategy. If the user selects an item available option are evaluated and presented. SemantifLIFE is a system that pushes the information into a semantic data store as soon as the data is available from the source system.

### e-Person (HP)

Developed by HP, an ePerson is a personal representative on the net that is trusted by a user to store personal information, and make it available under appropriate controls for shared working environments. A test application 'SnippetManager' is developed, which allows users to manage collections of information items, annotate them and then share them with the community. HP's approach is focused on three principals, i.e., social filtering of information by the users themselves, structured knowledge in terms of ontologies mutually agreed upon by the communities, and person-centric instead of being corporate-centric in terms of ownership, vocabularies and scaling [Dave].

The ePerson infrastructure is designed as a series of layers, transport layer (TCP/UDP and Jabber transports), KB access layer (remote access to RDF stores and services), Structure layer (modeling of RDF vocabularies using DAML), Knowledge sources layer (provides specific knowledge services such as classification servers, importing profiles from the history server and a discovery server), and Applications layer (reusable UI components, viewing tools for knowledge based access during development and the SnippetManager application itself). Each of these provides an external API which abstracts the implementation details away from the client application. The testbed application SnippetManager, is based upon two guiding design principles. Firstly, to use RDF for storing all types of information, such as for the item metadata itself, the user's profile, the addressing and capability description of services, the user's preferences and configurations and the current state of the application UI. This way, the same set of data manipulation and query tools can be used for exploiting every part of the architecture. Secondly, to clearly separate the details of messaging layer and physical hosting of services from the application code making free relocation of services across different networks and connection types.

They have successfully implemented a functional infrastructure for personal and shared information management, based upon semantic web techniques. ePerson project also highlights the fact that peer-to-peer knowledge sharing is different from other types, like peer-to-peer music sharing. In the later case, the information is readily usable. But in the first case, the contents of a knowledge worker's PC are not so much an archive as it is a workbench. A lot of this information is not readily sharable with others because it is still information under process [Jennifer].

**Comparison with SemanticLIFE:** ePerson is basically an information infrastructure in a shared environment. Unlike MyLifeBits, ePerson's focus is on sharing information. Therefore the work is highly relevant, especially the access control part and security implementation at the transport layer. A role based access control (RBAC) is used for hosting services,. Message communication at transport layer supports message signing and verification without using a full public key infrastructure (PKI), authority, authentication and end-to-end security. But it also creates problems when there are slight changes at transport layer message format. Statement level access control is provided for RDF store. Roles associated with allowable information patters, are assigned to trusted users.

### Lifestreams (Yale University)

Lifestreams [Eric], is an academic project from Yale University. It is a personal store that uses a simple organizational metaphor, a time-ordered stream of documents combined with several powerful operators that replaces many conventional computer constructs (such as named files, directories, and explicit storage). Their work on the client side includes an x windows client, command line interface and a PDA client.

The motivating ideas were, (a) storage should be transparent, (b) directories are inadequate as an organizing device, (c) archiving should be automatic, (d) the system should provide sophisticated logic for summarizing or compressing a large group of related documents on one screen, (e) reminding should be made more convenient, and (f) personal data should be accessible anywhere and compatibility should be automatic. Consequently, they implemented a model incorporating document creation and storage, directories on demand, overviews and chronology as a storage model.

While their current prototype is for managing personal information, in future a "lifestream" could also be used as a natural framework for managing enterprise information and web sites. Other future directions include shared usage, UI design, system integration, indexing and retrieval, usage of agents, network access, security, and performance issues.

**Comparison with SemanticLIFE:** In our opinion the system provides a good visualization of your lifetime information items and is a good substitute for the desktop metaphor. The project is perceived more from UI point of view; thus issues in storing and analyzing data storage using semantic information is not their main focus.

### Edutella (The SUN Project JXTA)

Edutella [Nejdl] is an RDF based metadata infrastructure for P2P applications. It is a useful project for getting an insight into shared usage of SemanticLIFE project. Its service oriented architecture supports querying RDF metadata, persistent data storage, mapping between different set of metadata vocabularies, and annotation services.

Edutella is based upon JXTA, an open source project with a layered architecture (core, services and applications layer) and XML based protocols to cover typically

P2P functionality. This layered approach fits nicely for the Edutella infrastructure. Applications like repositories, annotation tools and GUI interfaces connected to and accessing the Edutalla network are implemented in the Application layer. Exchange of query, query results and other metadata between Edutella peers is carried out at Services layer. Peers register the query at the services layer by specifying the supported metadata in a standardized way. Queries are sent through Edutella network to the subset of peers who have registered with the service. For this purpose QEL (Query Exchange Language) is defined. Queries can be expressed in RDF form, and thus can be visualized by a query graph. Data persistency, availability and work load balancing is achieved by replicating metadata in additional peers. Mapping between RDF schemas at different locations is provided in such a way that queries across peers are also translated accordingly.

**Comparison with SemanticLIFE:** The comprehensive query language, mediation and registration services for P2P access can be very beneficial for interconnecting SemanticLIFE between different people. The added functionalities of cascaded analysis of information items, knowledge refinement in ontologies, aggregation, ranking of query results, interactive visualizations and accessibility for people with special needs clearly distinguish our project. Edutella uses the underlying transport layer security (TLS) which is common to JXTA framework. Secure communication between the peers is done by public key cryptography.

**Semagix Freedom (Ex. Protégé)**

Semagix Freedom architecture which is nicely tiered between schema, business logic and the use of extractor agents for knowledge source data access is based upon ontologies. These provide automated categorization, cataloguing and extraction of semantically enhanced metadata from content sources [Sheth2]. Agents can extract content from web sites and file repositories, as well as trusted data from unstructured (news articles), semi structured (web sites, Intranets) and structured sources (databases, spreadsheets etc). Knowledge Agents extract trusted data and resolve ambiguities before inserting or merging data into the ontology. Content Agents retrieve data for extraction of semantic metadata. The Semantic Enhancement Server classifies aggregated content into the appropriate topic/category, and subsequently performs entity extraction and content enhancement with semantic metadata from the Freedom ontology. Metabase index resides in main memory all the time, to accelerate the retrieval process. Adapters are implemented for exchange of metadata with other applications. Semantic query server enables users to make search in text, execute ambiguous queries, retrieve relevant and personalized content that is actionable and in context. On top of all this, semantic visualization is provided for easy and intuitive exploration [Sheth1].

Applications can be implemented in a modular, phased manner to allow incremental scaling. Open APIs provide external access to a rich set of ontology and metabase features. The approach is successfully used in different domains such as airline passenger risk assessment for airports, anti-money laundering solutions and market segmentation and resource allocation model for the music industry. Based on an XML orientated architecture, support of multiple metadata standards and Web Services is provided. It also provides automatic document format conversion to XML, to facilitate metadata extraction. A flexible scheduling mechanism is provided to take into account any database changes dynamically.

**Comparison with SemanticLIFE:** The architecture is designed for corporate content management systems; it covers corporate content only. SemanticLIFE stores an individual's entire digital life and makes the relevant parts available to coworkers.

## Security Aspects of Semantic Knowledge Management

As mentioned before, the SemanticLIFE project captures an individual's activities while working with her computer, PDA and cell phone. The sophisticated mechanisms to retrieve information empower users to work much more efficiently.

However, today's knowledge workers usually work in teams. Team work can only be efficient if sharing of knowledge works efficiently, too. Therefore the knowledge stored in the SemanticLIFE database should be accessible by coworkers. The obvious security issue resulting from this feature is that coworkers should not have access to an individual's entire digital life, for three reasons:

1. People often work on more than one project and coworkers should only have access to data that is related to a project in which they participate.
2. Within a certain project, some information should not be freely distributed. For instance, notes indicating that the project manager intends to terminate an employee should remain confidential – or, another example, the whistle blower who uncovers illegal transactions needs to collect confidential data to prove the accusations.
3. Even when using a company's equipment, people will communicate privately, e.g. receive private phone calls.

### Secrecy Requirements

The first step in every security risk analysis is to identify the assets that need to be protected. Looking at the data stored in the SemanticLIFE database two separate entities can be distinguished: (1) the ontology and (2) the instances.

In this paper we only focus on secrecy requirements of instances. We do neither consider security implications of sharing the ontology definitions nor other security requirements such as integrity or availability. The mechanism used to implement secrecy requirements is access control. Access control is used to allow only authenticated users perform authorized operations on data item.

### Hierarchical Organization of Projects

We thus need to identify who should be granted access to data under which conditions. Users working on the same project should be able to share data; however, based on their job description, they should not be able to access all data. Most projects are organized hierarchically.

In multi-level security (MLS) systems, data is categorized according to its level of secrecy, e.g. into 'project management', 'work package lead', 'unclassified'. Users then receive clearance to access data on certain levels. Thus, users are authorized to view

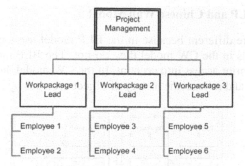

**Fig. 1.** Hierarchical Project Structure

all documents found on their own level or below. In this way it can be guaranteed that users cannot access information that does not correspond to their level. Write access, however, is only permitted on the same level. That is to say, a user who is authorized to access 'secret' data, may produce documents exclusively on the 'secret' level (during one session). In this way, users are prevented from (mistakenly) copying 'secret' data into a 'public' file. The above-mentioned security model was developed by Bell LaPadula (BLP). The levels are ordered so that

1. 'unclassified' $\leq$ 'work package lead'
2. 'project management' $\leq$ 'work package lead'

A simplified version of the ss-property (a.k.a no-read-up property) states that a user S can read a data object O if and only if $L_O \leq L_S$.

## Conflict of Interest

The Chinese Wall model (CW) [Brewer] implements both confidentiality and integrity. It primarily addresses the issue of conflict of interest: if a consultancy works for two competing clients (company A and company B), consultants should not be able to transfer information from one client to its rival (see Fig 2).

We follow Bishop's notation [Bishop] that a company dataset (CD) stores data objects (O) related to a single company and a conflict of interest (COI) contains all CDs pertaining to competing companies. PR(S) is the set of objects that a user S has read.

CW-simple security property: A user (S) can read O only if either one of the following two conditions is true:

1. $\exists O'$: S has previously accessed O' and CD(O') = CD(O).
2. $\forall O'$: O' $\in$ PR(S) $\Rightarrow$ COI(O') $\neq$ COI(O).

This policy works fine; however, it is too strict since it assumes that all data of a company must not be used by the competitor. By introducing a third condition this can be relaxed:

3. O is a data object that does not contain sensitive data (i.e. sanitized object).

Looking at write operations, the user S can write a data object O if following two conditions are both met:

1. S is granted read access on O by the previous three conditions
2. For all sanitized objects O', S can read O' $\Rightarrow$ CD(O') = CD(O).

## Comparison of BLP and Chinese Wall Model

The two models are different because in the BLP model users have associated clearance labels whereas in the CW model they do not. The BLP model is a static model that does not take prior access into account. In the CW model, however, the set PR(S) changes over time and reflects the history of object accesses by a user S.

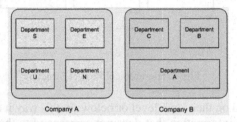

**Fig. 2.** Classes showing conflicts of interests (COIs) [Bishop]

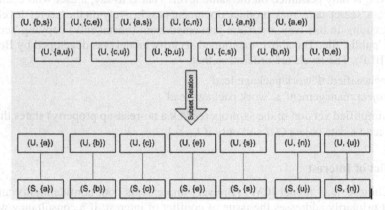

**Fig. 3.** BLP levels and compartments can be used to emulate a Chinese Wall model at any given (static) state [Bishop]

The BLP model can be used to emulate the CW model [Bishop] in a given state. A security category is assigned to each (COI, CD) pair and two security levels are defined: S = sanitized, U = unsanitized. S dominates U. However, the modification of the access rights over time that characterize the CW model cannot be expressed in the BLP model.

As previously shown, the CW model and the BLP model represent different requirements that are both relevant to sharing semantically enriched information between coworkers: the CW model can be used to implement the dynamic component and the BLP model the hierarchical approach.

## Reference Monitor

According to Bishop [Bishop] "a *reference monitor* is an access control concept of an abstract machine that mediates all accesses to objects by subjects. A *reference validation mechanism* (RVM) is an implementation of the reference monitor concept. An RVM must be tamperproof, must always be invoked and can never be bypassed, and must be small enough to be subject to analysis and testing, the completeness of which can be assured." (p 502).

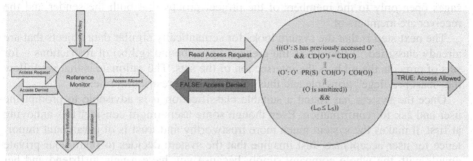

**Fig. 4.** Reference monitor [Povey]          **Fig. 5.** Evaluation of the proposed security policy

We propose to use the CW model's CW-simple security property to check in a first step whether a user may access data or whether a conflict of interest occurs. If the CW-simple security property would grant the user access, a second check is performed. The BLP model's ss-property is used to evaluate whether a user should be granted access. A user is permitted access to data object only if both the CW-simple security property and the ss-property grant access (Fig 5).

## Automatic Classification

For the aforementioned system to work in a real-world scenario two major issues have to be addressed:

1. How can the system know which data object is sanitized and if it is not sanitized which project it relates to.
2. How can the system downgrade data objects within the BLP model?

## Determining the State of Sanitation

If a new data object is created by a user, the system first needs to determine whether the data is sensitive or not. Based on a small set of rules, a decision can be made for many data objects. For instance, if a new email is received, a couple of rules (Fig 6) are evaluated.

| Domain | Rule | Result | Type |
|--------|------|--------|------|
| Email | If receiver = "all@company.com" | Sanitized | Company-wide rule |
| Email | If sender = "susan" | Not sanitized (private) | Individual rule |
| Email | If body contains \<cell phone number> | Not sanitized (\<project group sender> ∩ \<project group receiver>) | Individual rule |

**Fig. 6.** Rules to determine conflicts of interests

The first rule in Fig 6 states that if an email is sent to the company-wide mailing list it does not contain sensitive information for one or more projects. The second rule indicates that all emails received from Susan are considered private emails. The third rule is used to classify all emails that contain a cell phone number as sensitive messages open only to the members of the project groups that both the sender and the receiver are members of.

The next step is that the system looks for semantically similar data objects that are already classified. It then takes the greatest lower bound (g.l.b.) of restrictions – for sets of projects the g.l.b. is the intersection of the sets. The rationale is that we follow the "least privilege" principle and thus select the most restricting rule.

Once the system has found a suitable classification it is advisable to prompt the user and ask for confirmation. Even though some users might consider this annoying at first, it makes the system much more trustworthy and trust is of paramount importance for user acceptance. Just imagine that the system decides to share your private emails with the whole company simply because you have a new girlfriend and her emails do not yet match a rule and are too different from emails sent by your previous girlfriend for the matching to work reliably.

## Setting BLP Levels

After establishing which project a data item is related to, we need to determine the level (Project Management (PM) – Work package Lead (WL) or unclassified) a data object pertains to. Weippl [Weippl] proposes to use a SOM-based approach to find similar data objects and to classify the new item accordingly. This process can be improved by taking the underlying ontology into account. We expect that this approach will work especially well in our setting because all texts pertain to the same project and the SOM will thus not separate according to projects but to other differences in the content.

## Integrity Checking

The integrity and "correctness" of the ontological model is an important issue in most applications of the semantic office. As ontologies can become arbitrary complex, with no formal boundary conditions, a complete integrity check is not possible automatically. However the SOM-based classification algorithm (as suggested in the previous section) can be used to give the user hints about possible inconsistencies in the model.

Consider the following example: users build an ontology/taxonomy, where two categories (A and A') are actually semantically similar. This can happen as models grow and continuously undergo refactoring processes. As new objects are entered into the system, the SOM algorithm will suggest for certain objects the category A *and* A'. If such "double or multiple categorizations" occur repeated, the system would suggest the user, that a potential simplification of the model could be possible.

# Actor and Organisational Models for a SemanticOFFICE – A Knowledge Management Approach

Access control is a tedious task in most enterprise systems. Often access control lists or similar mechanisms are used to control which user/user group might access which resources. Often this type of model is too simple and moreover is not a direct representation of the "business reality".

As our SemanticOFFICE should capture individual as well as organization wide information objects, and the system information management is based on semantic web standards, it stands to reason to capture also the access control logic in a semantic way.

First of all, we want to avoid, keeping parallel models of the enterprise: a "business model" and a "access control model". The same is true for the actual information objects. Hence the first step is to build an ontology that captures the structure of the business (organization), essentially the actors involved. In the second step, the business processed and activities are modeled and expressed in an ontology schema.

The main idea now is this: the connection between the actor ontology and the process/activity ontology can be formally described and can be used to determine access control logic. To give a concrete example:

An enterprise may have (among other activities) projects and processes. The first step is, to define an ontology for these types of activities. E.g., a project has a project manager, who is a person. A project consists of tasks. Each task may have subtasks. Tasks may be dependent. Each task has attributes like start date, end date, man hours and so on. Each project must be authorized by a board of directors and the finance department and so on. The same has to be done for the process specification. A process has a process owner, has tasks, and so on...

The next step is to define the ontology for actors. This is essentially a map of the companies' hierarchy, but not only. Customers are actors, associate and business partners are actors; systems as web services might be actors and so on. As a matter of fact, all persons, organizational units or systems that have an active or passive role in a business activity have to be taken into consideration.

As soon as these models are prepared, the connection, the glue between these two has to be defined. E.g., one could define, that a person who is director has read access to all objects that are defined in the activity ontology except to such, that are private property of some other person.

A customer might use specific web services, whereas a associate partner may use other web services to modify data. A particular web service itself might have access to specific data objects according to the definition.

Up to now, these definitions are merely schemes, templates. Every actual entity must be an instance of one of these categories defined. As soon as this categorization is done, the access control is defined by implicit rules. No further definition of access control lists is required! E.g., a person who is assigned as project manager of a specific project automatically has the appropriate access rights to, e.g., read, write and modify all objects in the projects.

New information objects that entered into the system are now categorized by two boundary conditions: first of all, following the ontological rules according to the person or system who/which enters the object, and secondly by the automatically suggested category following the SOM algorithm.

Still we have to face two problems: First of all, the business and actor ontologies themselves are subject of continuous change. This has significant consequences: an object which was accessible to a specific person might become inaccessible according to a changed policy. Several options are conceivable: The policy change might only be applied for objects that are entered after the change, or the policy change might apply to all available objects. Most probably, this will be an option that has to be defined in changing the policy.

The second more general issue is the fact that many access policies will not be clear in defining the business and actor ontologies, or might depend on the concrete boundary conditions. These boundaries typically change over time, which is addressed by the CW model. Hence the logic that defines the implicit access control has to have rules of different types: first of all strict rules will be necessary like: "a project manager may change basic attributes of all project tasks". Then also weak rules must be possible such as: "Depending on the information object, the project manager may decide whether a specific object is accessible by a specific group or not". Here the SOM categorization comes again into play. The SOM can find similar documents and suggest to use the previous documents' rules for the new document.

## Conclusion

Information secrecy is crucial for building the trust layer for a shared SemanticOF-FICE. Combining easy-to-understand models allows users to really understand what content they share. Even though models such as the BLP may seem a little outdated they have the obvious advantage that they are easy to understand. In many cases the model will be implemented using RBAC controls since RBAC is supported by all major databases systems. The next step is to address additional requirements such as integrity and availability and to expand the level of protection from the instances to the ontology itself.

## References

[Ahmed] Ahmed M., Hoang H.H., Karim M.S., Khusro S., Lanzenberger M., Latif K., Michlmayr E., Mustofa K., Nguyen H.T, Rauber A.,Schatten A., Tho M. N. and Tjoa A M, 'SemanticLIFE' - A Framework for Managing Information of A Human Lifetime, The Sixth International Conference Information Integration and Web-based Applications and Services., 27-29th Sep, 2004, Jakarta-Indonesia.

[Adar] Eytan Adar, David Karger, and Lynn Andrea Stein, Haystack: Per-user information environments, Conference on Information and Knowledge Management., 1999.

[Bishop] Matt Bishop. *Computer Security: Art and Science*. Addison-Wesley-Longman, 2002.

[Brewer] D. Brewer and M. Nash, The Chinese Wall Security Policy, Proc. Of the 1989 IEEE Symposium on Security and Privacy pp 206-214, May 1989

[Dave] Banks Dave, Cayzer Steve, Dickinson Ian, and Reynolds Dave, The ePerson snippet manager: a semantic web application, Tech. report, HP Laboratories Bristol, HPL-2002-328.

[Eric] Freeman Eric and Gelernter David, Lifestreams: A storage model for personal data, ACM SIGMOD Record, Bulletin 25,1, March 1996, pp. 80–86.

[Gemmel1] Jim Gemmel, Gordon Bell, and Roger Lueder, Mylifebits: Living with a lifetime store, ATR Workshop on Ubiquitous Experience Media, Sept. 9-10 2003.

[Gemmel2] Jim Gemmel, Gordon Bell, Roger Lueder, Steven Drucker, and Curtis Wong, Mylifebits: Fulfilling the Memex vision, ACM Multimedia '02, December 2002, pp. 235–238.

[Huynh] David Huynh, David Karger, and Dennis Quan, Haystack: A platform for creating, organizing and visualizing information using RDF, Semantic Web Workshop, 2002.

[Jennifer] Hyams Jennifer and Sellen Abigail, Gathering and sharing web-based information: Implications for "ePerson" concepts, Tech. report, HP Laboratories Bristol, HPL-2003-19.

[Nejdl] Wolfgang Nejdl, Boris Wolf, Changtao Qu, Stefan Decker, Michael Sintek, Ambjorn Naeve, Mikael Nilsson, Matthias Palmer, and Tore Risch, Edutella: A P2P networking infrastructure based on RDF, WWW, ACM, May 2002.

[Povey] Dean Povey, Enforcing Well-formed and Partially-formed Transactions for Unix, Proceedings of the 8th USENIX Security Symposium, August 23-36, 1999, Washington, D.C. pages 47-62

[Quan] Dennis-Quan-and-David-Karger, How-to-make-a-semantic-web-browser, Proceedings of the 13th Conference on World Wide Web, May 17-20 2004.

[Sheth1] Amith Sheth and David Avant, Semantic visualization: Interfaces for exploring and exploiting ontology, knowledgebases, heterogeneous content and complex relationships, NASA Virtual Iron Bird Workshop, CA (2003).

[Sheth2] Amith Sheth and Cartic Ramakrishnan, Semantic (web) technology in action: Ontology driven information systems for search, integration and analysis, IEEE Data Engineering Bulletin, Special issue on Making the Semantic Web Real (2003).

[Weippl] Edgar Weippl, Ismail Khalil Ibrahim, and Werner Winiwarter. Content-based management of document access control. In The Proceedings of the 14th International Conference on Applications of Prolog, pages 78-86. Prolog Association of Japan, November 2001.

# Issues in Moving to a Semantic Web for a Large Corporation

Gary Wills[1], David Fowler[2], Derek Sleeman[2], Richard Crowder[1],
Simon Kampa[1], Leslie Carr[1], and David Knott[3]

[1] Intelligence, Agents, Multimedia Group, University of Southampton, Southampton,
SO17 1BJ, England, UK
{gbw,rmc,srk,lac}@ecs.soton.ac.uk

[2] Department of Computing Science, University of Aberdeen,
Aberdeen, AB24 3UE, Scotland, UK
{dfowler,sleeman}@csd.abdn.ac.uk
http://www.csd.abdn.ac.uk

[3] Rolls-Royce plc, Derby, UK
david.knott@rolls-royce.com

**Abstract.** In many large engineering design organizations the information systems have developed over time into a set of heterogeneous resources. This makes it difficult for engineers to follow a trail through the resources. This situation becomes particular difficult when the Engineer is new to a company; unfamiliar with the systems and unaware of the history of the designs. This paper presents a demonstrator system developed with a major aerospace company to aid engineers, through the use of knowledge technologies, to locate the documentation they require. The paper presents the systems and lessons learnt to enable the organisation to move towards a more semantically enriched document repository.

## 1 Introduction

In many large organisations which perform a substantial amount of engineering design, information systems have developed over time into a set of heterogeneous resources. This makes it difficult for engineers to follow a trail through these resources. This situation becomes particular difficult when the engineer is new to a company; unfamiliar with the systems and unaware of the history of the designs.

The challenge for organisations is to develop an information system that is both comprehensive and will satisfy the increasing demands from industry for up-to-date and easily accessible information. In addition, technical documentation is frequently highly cross-referenced, often to documents in different formats. The process of locating information then becomes time-consuming, frustrating users as they open and close applications looking for essential information as they move between information systems. Conventional information management techniques are not considered sufficient to satisfy these requirements [18].

A hypermedia system allows associations to be made between information in different media in a manner similar to that naturally undertaken by people. The concept and requirements for industrial strength hypermedia were initially presented by Malcolm *et al* [16]. Due to the increase in  virtual enterprises, lean and agile manufactur-

D. Karagiannis and U. Reimer (Eds.): PAKM 2004, LNAI 3336, pp. 378–388, 2004.
© Springer-Verlag Berlin Heidelberg 2004

ing, the demands for correct and easily accessible information have not abated. Wills *et al* have demonstrated the effective application of open hypermedia to industrial applications [22].

## 1.1 Background

The Advance Knowledge Technologies (AKT) project is one of the UK government's funded Interdisciplinary Research Collaborations (IRCs). The AKT project involves five universities from the UK. The AKT project aims to develop and extend a range of technologies providing integrated methods and services for the capture, modelling, retrieval, publishing, reuse and maintenance of knowledge [1]. As well as the academic expertise, AKT benefits from a close relationship with industrial collaborators. One such collaborator is Rolls-Royce, a major aerospace company based in the UK.

Rolls-Royce takes seriously the need to keep accurate records of design, manufacture and test; in part this is due to the nature of their aerospace business and in part due to the recognition that their main method of capturing corporate memory is through such documentation. As with many organisation's information systems, the system at Rolls-Royce has evolved over time, resulting in a number of document and information management systems.

Rolls-Royce is organised into Business Units (BU). Each BU is staffed with a number of engineers from different specialisations. A single component is usually designed by a number of specialists. This creates an additional requirement on any information system in that there is now a requirement for a federated (multi-perspective) view of the same information space. That is, the system should be able to provide different contextual slices (views) through the same information space to present appropriate information to the several designers/engineers who often have distinct perspectives.

## 2 Development of the Demonstrator

Like many organisations in the early 1990s Rolls-Royce outsourced the management of their IT systems. This has greatly influenced the scope of the type of demonstrator that could be build, as it was not possible for AKT to integrate prototype systems quickly in order to investigating alternative designs, or to carry out software trials. As a result AKT has focussed on using Rolls-Royce's data and providing demonstrators to show how advanced knowledge technologies can be applied in an international manufacturing company.

The AKT project aims to demonstrate how advanced knowledge technologies can be use to present a federated perspective on the documentation relating to a specific component, that is to provide Intelligent Document Retrieval.

The federated representation (multi-perspective view) will be represented by different ontologies for each of the engineering specialisms:

- Designer,
- Stress engineer,
- Thermodynamics analyst,
- Methods specialist.

Rolls-Royce issues most design related documents from a document repository. Rolls-Royce also record the document type, authors, abstract, and keywords related to each document in a central database, for over 300,000 documents.

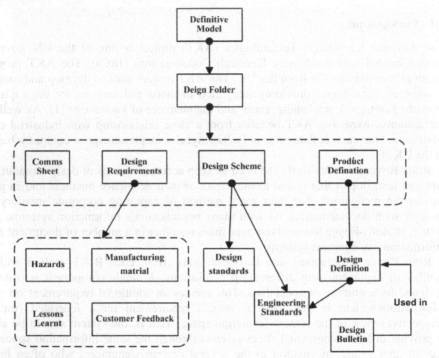

**Fig. 1.** A example of the result of a card sort, detailing the documents referred during a partial task in the methods process

## 2.1 Knowledge Acquisition

The first phase in building the demonstrator was to carry out a number of Knowledge Acquisition (KA) interviews at Rolls-Royce with carefully selected engineers (domain experts), from which a simple ontology of terms and concepts for each specialist was derived. During these interviews the 'card sort' technique was used to help the engineer show how they used different document types and the relationships between these documents [15]. In addition to the card sort, a number of semi-structured interviews were carried out in order to understand the working environment and the difficulty encountered when designing a product.

The result of these interviews enabled the AKT team to identify, by specialism, the main concepts and the associated keyword for these concepts used by the particular type of engineer when searching for information. The interviews also enable the AKT team to produce the initial set of cards for the 'card sort' technique. Each expert was free to discard cards and to add any they felt was missing. A number of sessions were carried out with engineers from different specialisms within the same BU. Figure 1 represents the typical result from a card sort session.

## 2.2 Background Technology

The term hypertext was first proposed by Ted Nelson in the late 1960s [7]. Nelson applied it to unstructured text, where associations between the text was made with links. Many 'closed' hypermedia applications embed links into the structure of the document, i.e early and conventional world-wide-web pages. In contrast, an open hypermedia system can be defined as follows [9], [13]:

- A system which does not impose any mark-up upon the data that will prevent the data from being accessible to other processes that do not belong to the system.
- A system in which there is a separation of links from data objects.
- A system that can integrate with any tool that runs under the host operating system.
- A system in which data and processes may be distributed across a network and across hardware platforms.
- A system in which there is no artificial distinction between readers and authors.
- A system in which it is possible to add new functionality easily.

Within the open hypermedia philosophy, the hypermedia links are themselves a valuable store of knowledge. If this knowledge is bound too tightly to the documents, then it cannot be applied to new data. Therefore, no information about the links is held in the document data files in the form of mark-up. Instead, all data files remain in the native format of the application that created them, whilst the link information is held in link databases (linkbases). Research into open hypermedia has been undertaken at the University of Southampton since 1989. The philosophy of open hypermedia was instantiated in the development of a software package, called Microcosm, which is still being used in teaching and research today [13].

With the advent of the Web, the open hypermedia principles and the Microcosm philosophy were embodied in a system called the Distributed Link Service (DLS) [4]. At the heart of the DLS is a proxy Web-server. All requests to and from and Web pages sent to the user must all go through the proxy server (see Figure 2). The proxy server can then manipulate the HTML and add additional links to the content of the web pages. The philosophy of Microcosm is also acknowledged to have influenced the new open linking standard for the Web, X-Link [10].

Hypertext is just one example of the use of a family of techniques that are intended to transcend the limitations of static, sequential presentations of text [19]. Hypertext uses computer effects (such as linking, indexing and interaction) to improve familiar textual communication for human beings; it is a form of human communication augmented by computer-manipulated media, databases and links. By contrast, the Semantic Web is an application of the World Wide Web aimed at computational agents, so that *programs,* and not just humans, can interpret the meaning of the information stored in the WWW hypertext [2]. The basis of this interpretation is an ontology, a structure which forms the backbone of the knowledge interpretation for an application.

An ontology is *"a specification of a conceptualization"* [14]; Gruber explains that a common ontology defines the vocabulary with which queries and assertions are exchanged among agents (people or software). The ontology sets out all the entities (objects or concepts) that we are interested in and the relationships that connect these entities together. This is intended to be a *pragmatic* definition, i.e. it defines the vo-

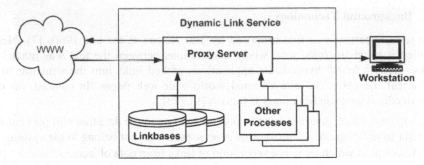

**Fig. 2.** Dynamic Link Service

cabulary that is actually *in use*, and the concepts that are *useful* in problem-solving. It does not give the deep underlying philosophical vision of the fundamental entities in the field. Hence, in Knowledge Management (KM), an ontology is a tool, whose quality is entirely dependent on its usefulness.

Carr *et al* describes the use of ontologies to model and capture domain knowledge, and to provide a shared and commonly agreed understanding of a particular domain [5]. The COHSE project (Conceptual OHS Environment) produced an experimental ontological hypermedia system by combining an existing open hypermedia link service with an ontological reasoning service to enable documents to be linked via the concepts referred to in their contents. Previous attempts to improve the linking through simple lexical matching had serious limitations due to the uncontrolled method of adding links: many keywords turn up in many contexts and there is no simple lexical basis for discriminating important terms and significant links. The aim of the COHSE project therefore was to combine the OHS architecture with an ontological model to provide linking on the *concepts* that appear in Web pages, as opposed to linking on *simple uninterpretted text fragments*.

COHSE used a standard Web browser controlled by an adapted *link service* which in turn used three independent services to manipulate the exposed DOM of the Web page, resulting in the effect of ontologically-controlled hypertext.

An **ontology service** manages ontologies (sets of concepts related according to some schema) and answers specific queries about them. The **metadata service** annotates regions of a document with a concept, rather than the familiar case of annotating a document with a simple piece of text. The **resource service** is a simple librarian which is used to lookup Web pages which are examples of a particular concept (*i.e.* which can be used to *illustrate* a concept).

When a web page is loaded, the ontology service provides a complete listing of all the language terms that are used to represent the concepts in the relevant ontology. Each language term is searched for in the document, and, if found, its associated concept is looked up. Having identified the significant concepts in the document, the resource service provides a list of documents that are about instances of this concept.

At this point, a number of potential link anchors and destinations have been identified for the page and decisions can be taken about whether the document contains too many or too few links. In those circumstances, alternative links may be chosen from the broader or narrower concepts in the ontology in order to expand or cull the set of link anchors. The decisions about link culling and presentation are controlled by be-

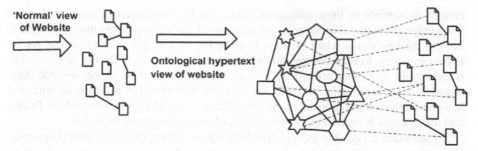

**Fig. 3.** An ontology allows a weakly linked Website to be enriched through the meta-layer provided by the ontology

haviour modules which define the navigation and interaction semantics of the resulting ontological hypertext.

The Ontoportal framework was initially developed in the Ontoportal project, and was used to build a web portal for the metadata research community, Metaportal [6]. It has now been extended to a generic application framework for building web portal applications based on domain ontologies. The Ontoportal system is the result of integrating ontologies, as conceptual models of knowledge, with hypertext to provide a powerful application environment. Which taking advantage of the various benefits of ontological hypertext and which also augments the breadth of hypertext with more meaningful links.

Once a domain ontology has been created, specific *ontoportals* are generated by populating the knowledge base with specific metadata, this process is referred to as instantiation of the ontology. That is, the resources have been identified as belonging to one or more of the concepts within the ontology. New *portals,* each representing a different view on the same set of resources, are generated by the Ontoportal framework from the instantiated domain ontology.

Woukeu *et al* have shown how ontologies and open hypermedia can be used to enrich a weakly linked resource, see Figure 3, using the Ontoporal framework [21].

### 2.3 Demonstrator

A web-based demonstrator was built that showed how, by using a simple ontology, appropriate documents can be retrieved from the document repository. The demonstrator used techniques developed from:

- The ontological hypertext system Conceptual Open Hypermedia Services Environment (COHSE)
- A framework for developing ontologically driven portals (Ontoportal) which allows different ontologies to be used on the same document set

The resulting list of document is ordered according to the engineering task and the related concepts (identified by keywords).

Depending on the designers main responsibility (Stress analysis, Thermodynamics, manufacturing Methods, or Design, see Figure 4) being undertaking, they are presented with appropriate job functions from the ontology, see Figure 5.

The AKT team also recognized that sometimes people found a particular document extremely useful for a certain task, so the system allowed Engineers to recommend certain documents to their colleagues. This can be considered as another form of knowledge elicitation. Similarly it was recognized that the engineers may also want to browse the key words when they are hunting for information. Therefore the system allows engineers to look through all the key words regardless of design function. The search could be further refined by looking for the occurrence of the concept (key-word) in any combination of Title, Abstract and Keyword fields. Once the engineer has chosen the job function, as in the case of Figure 4 and Figure 5 the role is *Design* and the function is *Input requirements*, a list of tasks is returned, Figure 6.

By selecting a task, the system will look-up the appropriate concepts (keywords) and returns a list of appropriate documents (title, author and date) from the database. The documents are returned by document type and the order of the document types is governed by the results of the card sort obtained during the knowledge acquisition phase. That is the document types the engineers most commonly used to undertake the task. In addition to ensure that information is not missed documents types not identified in the card sort are listed by type alphabetically at the end. In addition peer recommended documentation is listed first. The engineer can get further information on any document by clicking on the document in the list and the full record including the abstract/summary is returned.

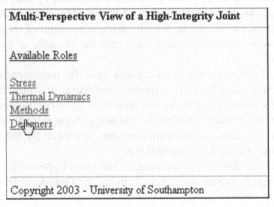

**Fig. 4.** The engineer selects the role they are undertaking

Occasionally, more documents are returned than is practical to browse through. Therefore it is necessary to cull the list in a meaningful way; the method chosen is to present the engineer with an interactive image of the card sort, see Figure 7, which allows the engineer to view the returned list by just one document type at a time and then switch to another type. By using the pictorial representation of the card sort the engineer can browse the results with some understanding as how the document type relates their role or their perceived role.

## 3  Lessons Learnt

As with many knowledge management projects, the knowledge acquisition phase took a considerable time. We were aided in this process by having a team that consisted of mechanical engineers (who acted as domain experts), computer scientist and knowledge management engineers.

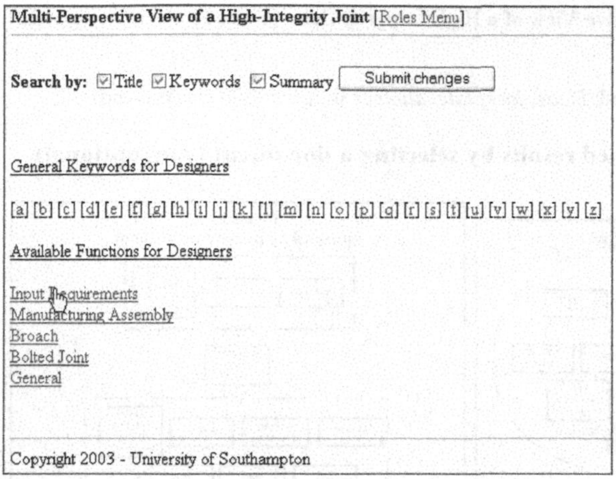

**Multi-Perspective View of a High-Integrity Joint** [Roles Menu]

Search by:  ☑ Title  ☑ Keywords  ☑ Summary  [ Submit changes ]

General Keywords for Designers

[a] [b] [c] [d] [e] [f] [g] [h] [i] [j] [k] [l] [m] [n] [o] [p] [q] [r] [s] [t] [u] [v] [w] [x] [y] [z]

Available Functions for Designers

Input Requirements
Manufacturing Assembly
Broach
Bolted Joint
General

Copyright 2003 - University of Southampton

**Fig. 5.** The engineer can choose which function to follow when undertaking the design role

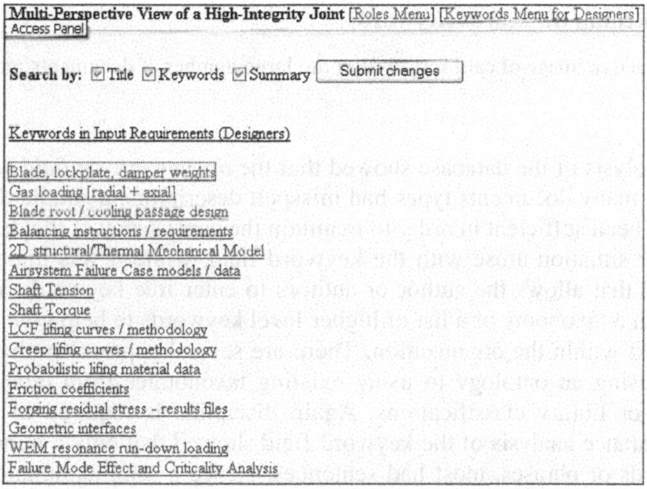

**Multi-Perspective View of a High-Integrity Joint** [Roles Menu] [Keywords Menu for Designers]
Access Panel

Search by:  ☑ Title  ☑ Keywords  ☑ Summary  [ Submit changes ]

Keywords in Input Requirements (Designers)

Blade, lockplate, damper weights
Gas loading [radial + axial]
Blade root / cooling passage design
Balancing instructions / requirements
2D structural/Thermal Mechanical Model
Airsystem Failure Case models / data
Shaft Tension
Shaft Torque
LCF lifing curves / methodology
Creep lifing curves / methodology
Probabilistic lifing material data
Friction coefficients
Forging residual stress - results files
Geometric interfaces
WEM resonance run-down loading
Failure Mode Effect and Criticality Analysis

**Fig. 6.** The engineer selects a requirements task associated with the design role

One of the aims of the system was to provide intelligent document retrieval, for example retrieval based more on the semantics than simply keywords. In many ways this can be likened to data mining [3], in that to facilitate this knowledge mining it was important to ensure that there is a clearly defined and well structured warehouse. This was achieved by using ontologies to give the warehouse structure and a triple store to hold the content [20].

Intelligent document retrieval relies on machine readable data that is fairly clean (nothing is ever perfect and the system must allow for this). Hence, it is important to maintain information discipline throughout the organization. This is partly a social issue as well as an engineering matter; people often do not understand the importance of it or see it as their responsibility to ensure that the data entered is correct. From an engineering perspective a system can be designed to help maintain the discipline. For

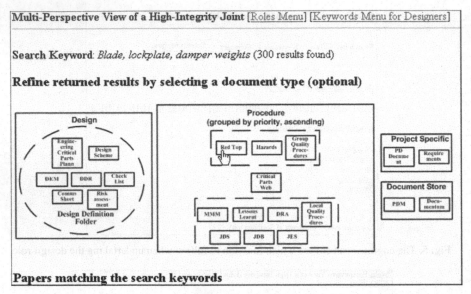

**Fig. 7.** Interactive image of card sort to filter the large number of documents returned by type

instance, analysis of the database showed that the *document type field* was a free text field, hence many documents types had misspelt descriptors; a simple drop down list would have been sufficient in order to maintain the consistency of the database.

A similar situation arose with the keyword field, while it was understandable to have a field that allows the author or authors to enter free keywords, it needs to be coupled with a taxonomy or a list of higher level keywords to help give the document some context within the organization. There are several approaches that can be used here from using an ontology to using existing taxonomies from other professional institutions or library classifications. Again discipline is required in any free text field, for instance analysis of the keyword field showed that only a minority of fields had keywords or phrases, most had sentences. Hence a semi-automatic process was applied to produce sensible keywords (a set of 9000 in total) from the meaningless information held in the keyword field.

Some of the above problems encountered could have been alleviated if much of the metadata for a document did not have to be manually entered in the database. Most if not all the information could be 'stripped out' of document automatically as most of the information is on the front sheet of the document. This was achieved practically by using document templates.

It is important to provide a controlled but flexible means for people to share their knowledge eg through a company wide intranet. As this is not yet available many of the BU's have their own website, which is used to collate knowledge on how to carry out the design. These pages are manually maintained and all links are button type links. Although only a few years old these several intranet are growing larger by the day and already are becoming unmanageable; dangling links are appearing [8], with knowledge being lost as pages disappear into hyperspace never to be found again.

# 4 Conclusions and Future Work

To help overcome the difficulty engineers find locating the correct information whilst designing components for the aerospace industry, a system was developed that demonstrated how knowledge technologies can be used to help solve this problem. While the system was only a demonstrator, feedback from the focus group was very encouraging; we had to frequently remind them that this was a demonstrator and it could not be brought into service next week. There are considerable benefits to the organisation [17], other that the engineer getting less frustrated at not being able to locate the information they know is there. We discovered during the KA interviews that experiments and associated costs (design and build of test rigs) were being repeated as engineers did not know that similar experiments had been carried out a few years earlier.

The lessons learnt from developing this system are now to be applied to the next system; a semantic web service environment [2][11]. As many of the Business Units now have their own website, we believe that semantically enriching the metadata of the Web pages and documents held on these sites, would provide the organisation with a method of improving the interconnectivity of the knowledge. Thereby stopping the growth in small disconnected islands of knowledge within the organisation. In addition the ontologies developed will aid automatic linking of the concepts held in the documents and Web pages.

The engineers require a flexible and easy method of capturing knowledge and sharing this with colleagues. This was the reason given for the development of these group websites. It is our aim in the next phase to develop Intelligent Editors to provide tools to support the capture, reuse and maintenance of this knowledge, For instance the Designers Workbench [11]. Fundamental to this being achieved is the warehousing of the knowledge, using the ontologies and structure, knowledgebases as the containers and a set of tools that will:

- Provide a means by which engineers can refine the information extraction techniques and retrieval mechanism, with respect to an ontology for a Business Unit or by specialisation.
- Provide searchable semantically enriched meta-data for each BU's intranet pages.
- Aid the maintenance of the ontologies.
- Allow Designers to customize their User Models.

# Acknowledgements

The author thanks Rolls-Royce engineers Gary Nicholson and Tamsyn Thorpe, for participating, advice and organizing the interviews.

# References

1. AKT Manifesto, http://www.aktors.org/publications/
2. Berners-Lee, T., Hendler, J., Lassila, O. (2001) The Semantic Web, *Scientific American, May 2001 34-43*
3. Berson A, Smith S, thearling K. (2000) Building Data Mining Applications for CRM, McGraw-Hill ISBN 007134446

4. Carr, Les A. and De Roure, David C. and Hall, Wendy and Hill, Gary J. (1995) The Distributed Link Service: A Tool for Publishers, Authors and Readers. *In Proceedings Fourth International World Wide Web Conference: The Web Revolution, Boston, Massachusetts, US).*, pages 647--656.
5. Carr L., Bechhofer S., Goble C., Hall W. (2001 )Conceptual Linking: Ontology-based Open Hypermedia. *In Proceedings WWW10, Hong-Kong, May 2001.*
6. Carr. L, Kampa S, and Miles-Board T. (2001) MetaPortal Final report: Building Ontological Hypermedia with the Ontoportal Framework. Technical Report,ECSTR-01-005 University of Southampton, May 2001 ISBN 085432 7371
7. Conklin J. Hypertext: An Introduction and survey. *IEEE Computing Vol. 20, 17-41, 1987*
8. Davis HC. Data integrity problems in an Open Hypermedia Link. *PhD Thesis University of Southampton November 1995.*
9. Davis, HC, Knight, S. and Hall, W.. Light Hypermedia Link Services: A Study of Third Party Application Integration. *Proceedings of the ACM European Conference on Hypermedia Technology. ECHT'94, Edinbough, Scotland, September 18-23, 1994, pp 41-45*
10. DeRose S, Maler E, Orchard D. 2001 XML Linking Language (XLink) Version 1.0 W3C Recommendation 27 June 2001,
11. de Roure, D., Jennings, N. R. and Shadbolt, N. (2003) *The Semantic Grid: A future e-Science infrastructure*, in Berman, F., Fox, G. and Hey, A. J. G., Eds. *Grid Computing - Making the Global Infrastructure a Reality*, pages pp. 437-470. John Wiley and Sons Ltd.
12. Fowler D, Sleeman D, Wills G, Lyon T, Knott D. (2004) The Designers' Workbench: Using Ontologies and Constraints for Configuration. *AI-2004. The Twenty-fourth SGAI International Conference on Innovative Techniques and Applications of Artificial Intelligence Queens' College, Cambridge, UK 13th-15th December 2004*
13. Fountain AM, Hall W, Heath I, Hill G. MICROCOSM: An Open Model for Hypermedia with Dynamic Linking. *In Rizk A, Streitz N & Andre J. eds. Hypertext: Concepts, Systems and applications. The Proceedings of the European Conference on Hypertext, INRIA, France, pp 298-311. Cambridge University Press 1990.*
14. Gruber T. R. (1993). A translation approach to portable ontologies. *Knowledge Acquisition, 5(2):199-220*
15. Kelly G, (1955)The Psychology of Personal Constructs, W.W. Norton, New York, 1955
16. Malcolm K., Poltrock S., Schuler D. Industrial Strength Hypermedia: Requirements for a Large Engineering Enterprise. *In Hypertext '91. The Third ACM Conference on Hypertext, San Antonio, Texas, December 1991, pp 13-24. ACM Press 1991*
17. Mika P, Iosif V, Sure Y, Akkermans H. (2004) Handbook on Ontologies, Eds. Staab S, Studer R. Springer-Verlag.
18. Marinheiro R M N, Hall W. "Expanding a Hypertext Information Retrieval System to Incorporate Multimedia Information", *Proceedings of the 31st Annual Hawaii International Conference on System Sciences, Vol. II, pp 286-295, 6-9 January, 1998, IEEE Computer Society.*
19. Nelson, T. (1987). Literary Machines. 87.1 edn. Computer Books.
20. schraefel, m. c., Shadbolt, N. R., Gibbins, N., Glaser, H. and Harris, S. (2004) CS AKTive Space: Representing Computer Science in the Semantic Web. In *Proceedings of World Wide Web Conference 2004* .
21. Woukeu A, Wills G, Conole G, Carr L, Kampa S, Hall W. Ontological Hypermedia in Education: A framework for building web-based educational portals. *Ed-Media, Hawaii 23-28 June 2003*
22. Wills GB, Sim YW, Crowder RM, Hall W (2002) Open Hypermedia for Product Support *International Journal of Systems Science 33(6):421-432*

# Picture Languages in Intelligent Retrieval of Visual Data Semantic Information

Marek R. Ogiela and Ryszard Tadeusiewicz

AGH University of Science and Technology
Institute of Automatics
Al. Mickiewicza 30, PL-30-059 Kraków, Poland
{mogiela,rtad}@agh.edu.pl

**Abstract.** In recent years knowledge engineering has become one of the most dynamically developing branches of intelligent IT systems, including PACS, CAD and medical databases. Medical databases storing data in visual form constitute a huge group among multimedia specialist databases, and contain patterns originate from numerous diagnostic examinations of practically all organs of the human body. One of the main problems in the fast accessing and analysis of information collected in this way, is transformation the visual information of those patterns into a form enabling intelligent semantic analysis and understanding of medical meaning of these patterns. In the paper we describe some examples presenting ways of applying graph picture languages techniques in the creation of intelligent cognitive multimedia systems for selected classes of medical images.

## 1 Introduction

One the main problems in accessing information collected in medical databases is the way to transform efficiently the visual information of patterns into a form enabling intelligent selection of cases obtained as an answer to queries directed at selected elements of contents of searched-for images. Therefore this paper will present the possibilities of application of context-free and graph grammars used as the ordering factor indexing and supporting commitment and semantically-oriented search for visual information in multimedia medical databases.

It is worthwhile to emphasise the very essence of semantic analysis which allows for content-based grouping of images sometimes differing in form though conveying similar diagnostic information about the disease. Generally speaking, we have to consider a great variety of examined medical cases [4, 5].

In medical images an actual shape of anomalies or lesions can vary between the cases due to the fact that human organs vary between individuals, differing in shape, size and location while the forms and progress of pathological lesions (e.g. caused by neoplasm or chronic inflammation process) are unforeseeable [6, 7]. On the other hand, every type of disease leads to some characteristic changes in the shapes of visualised organs; therefore this type of information, obtained owing to the application of the method of structural pattern analysis, will constitute information label determining the image content. Techniques proposed in [6] allow the change of a pattern into its syntactic description in such a way that the automatically generated language formula transforms precisely the basic pattern content: the shape of the examined organ and its anomaly caused by disease. Those formalised, automatically generated descriptions of

D. Karagiannis and U. Reimer (Eds.): PAKM 2004, LNAI 3336, pp. 389–396, 2004.

shapes of objects seen on a pattern placed or searched-for in a database, allow for separating the indexing process from the secondary formal features of the recorded patterns. Accordingly, the description is focused on the most important contents.

## 2 Image Understanding as a Tool for Semantic Searching in Databases

A tool described in this paper consisting of a set of automatic medical image understanding methods may have one more application in indexing of multimedia medical databases tasks. This application results from the fact, that more and more information resources collected and processed in medical information systems are multimedia resources. They consist not only of text information which are normally collected and looked up in all databases (in case of medical databases, the typical data are: patient's particulars, epicrisis, description of diagnostic and therapeutic procedures, case record, etc.), and, apart from easily computer processed numerical data (i.e. results of physical measurements and biochemical analyses), various signals. Specifying, it may be indicated that various bioelectric signals, sounds, and especially, a variety of images collected and analyzed both in medical research and routine treatment of patients constitute the aforementioned non-alphanumerical medical data. The characteristic feature of these signals is that they are usually very difficult from the point of view of intelligent service, as their ontologies have not been well developed.

However, multimedia resources of medical information collected in the numerical form are still growing, and this growth will accelerate because of future development of telemedicine. Difficulties in usage of such multimedia data may be considered from various points of view, but we shall focus on searching techniques with special consideration of semantic searching oriented to the meritorious content. Semantic searching is somehow inconvenient, because it may be very difficult to find multimedia information meeting the defined and meritorious criteria not supported with precise (and properly made!) verbal description, but based only on the registered signal itself (i.e. image bitmap). Now, we may signal the next application of the technique of automatic image understanding described further treated as a tool for intelligent indexation.

Concept of automatic image understanding creates interesting possibilities. Having a tool not only analyzing but also semantically describing an image, we can follow such model of procedure. A computer equipped with an automatic image understanding program systematically views accessible multimedia medical databases and tries "to understand" the content of each image. Certainly, this should be a background task performed only in time when there are no perpetual commendations of the user. Upon such review of certain images located in databases it will be possible to create their semantic descriptions automatically. When the semantic meaning of an automatically analyzed image is found out, a record identifier containing such a "decoded" image will be linked to the record containing the whole "deducted" semantic description of the image.

This description usually consists of a series of symbols denoting the semantic content of the image, usually illegible and incomprehensible for a human. Principles of creating such descriptions and methods of operation will be based on the methods of mathematical linguistics using specifically constructed graph grammars.

An automatically generated semantic description should be located in a special index file of a computer, which scans the base. The description should be always located outside the base in order not "clutter" the original database (automatically generated semantic descriptions of an image may contain errors!), and searching of separate index files is much more faster than searching the whole base expanded with large volume digital image records. A relevant record should appear in the index file for each image with the code representing its meaning settled in result of the automatic analysis. A number of images understandable for a computer vary, and probably, for a very long time, we will not be able to create semantic indexation mechanism able to refer automatically the adequate description to each medical image in any database. However, taking into account designation of the whole process, this defect is not very significant.

Naturally, all the images with distinct legible features will be the first to be indexed efficiently. In case of such images semantic analysis will be successful and consequently they will be unambiguously classified with the automatic indexation procedure. Searching process applied in this connection will find such "clear-cut" cases first. Taking into account the purpose of searching, it cannot be considered as a defect. We must remember that semantic searching database for medical images usually is focused on finding images that may serve as didactic examples or reference objects in the process of finding the optimal diagnosis – here the usefulness of "good" images seems to be indisputable. In this respect, finding the most distinct and the most typical images, neglecting ambiguous or highly atypical cases should be consider not as a drawback but as an advantage of the automatic image indexation procedure. The only problem is that not all the objects of the database will be indexed in result of such indexation. Namely, some objects, too difficult for the automatic understanding procedure, will not have an automatically settled semantic description of their content. In result, they will be of no use for automatic reasoning process. However, if such a database is rich enough the process of automatic indexation will provide us with quite a large number of identified records that we will not face the problem of deficit.

The mechanism of indexation and semantic searching the required medical images may be organized according to two patterns. The first pattern is designed for a client of the database. In this pattern, indexation of objects in databases and conversions of requests sent to databases in the semantic form described in this paper take place in the client's computer. In other words, users who want semantic-oriented access to information resources, request the computer to carry out the indexation of relevant databases. Indexation is run according to the pattern shown in fig. 1., however, it must be taken under consideration that the database is located at a server, and the tool for image intelligent understanding and the index file created by this tool are in the client's computer. The strong point of this approach is that any user having access to the scanned database and a tool for automatic understanding of the image content may realize it at any time. The weak point is the high cost of indexation resulted from the fact that practically each image contained in database must be transmitted via the web to a client's computer, which will try to understand the content In case many clients want to use the same server, the same job will be unnecessarily repeated many times.

Indexation performed by the owner of the database is a complementary solution. In this case automatic image understanding program must be located both in a server (for continual indexation of the database, which, of course, keeps changing its content all the time) and in the client's computer (to convert images displayed during requests).

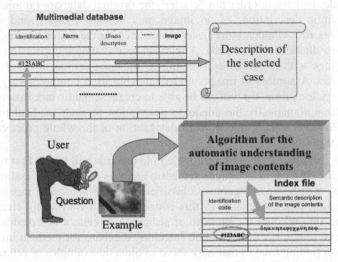

**Fig. 1.** Context related searching for required information in the semantically indexed multimedia database

## 3   Stages of Interpretation in the Indexing Task

The presented idea associated with creating indexing keys allows for an efficient search and categorisation of both information specifying the type of medical imaging or the examined structure and meaningful semantic information specifying the looked-for object within the framework of one database. In a special case, apart from the main indexing key allowing the search or archiving of a specified type of medical images (especially ERCP, urograms, coronograms or spinal cord images – fig. 2), it is possible to create additional indexing labels specifying successive layers of semantic details of image contents. First of all, this information tells us about the progress of a disease (e.g. neoplasm lesions or inflammation) detected with the use of the above-described grammars and semantic actions defined in them. The indexing information is also a description of the external morphology of the imaged organ. This type of description takes the form of a terminal symbol sequence introduced while grammars are defined for individual types of images and organs visible on them. The shape morphology described in this way requires a much smaller memory and computation input for the execution of the archiving operations and for searching for a given pattern. Finally, the lowest level of information useful for a detailed search are the types of recognised lesions (irregular ramifications or stenoses etc.) and sequences of production numbers leading to the generation of a linguistic description of those lesions. Such productions are defined in the sequential and graph grammars introduced in papers [4, 5]. Their sequences describing successive patterns of morphological lesions can constitute important information useful for a quick search for such irregularities on image data. Also graph grammars are applied for the task of description of important shape morphology features for the structure of the renal sinus (renal pelvis and renal calyx). The application of the description created in this way is analogous. Apart from the general diagnostic assessment, this grammar allows to create an indexing key specifying the number of smaller and bigger calyxes occurring in a renal pelvis. The general structure of semantic information and indexing keys is presented in Figure 2.

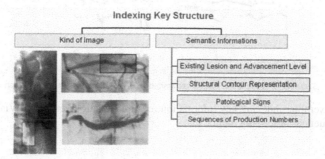

**Fig. 2.** General scheme of semantic information and indexing key structure

## 4  Semantic Description of Selected Visualization

The semantic approach to indexing and searching of multimedia medical databases seems to be a more efficient and appropriate method than the traditional indexing methods [1, 2, 3] due to the presence of distinguishable objects visible in the discussed medical patterns, which by virtue of their shape define pathological disease symptoms. A structural description of medical image contents becomes easier and more unambiguous than an analogous description applied to a different category of patterns, for examples scenes. Nevertheless, after defining an appropriate graph grammar, the methodology described here can be utilised to describe any patterns. It will enable therefore the creation of object-oriented semantic description of contents of those data and it will also constitute the key to their indexation and search. An additional advantage of structural description methods is a potential of additional analysis of the examined images in the course of archiving and defining the semantic meaning of lesions visible on them; this is performed by imitating a qualified professional's understanding of medical images.

Syntactic information, together with contour representation in the form of terminal symbols as well as production number sequences describing discovered pathologies, constitute the representation of patterns placed in the database or searched-for. An example of information constituting such indexing key for a pancreatic duct image is presented in Figure 3.

In the course of the analysis of selected images in each case we obtain a type of recognized symptom and a sequence of production numbers, which lead to grammar derivation of shape description of such lesions. Such sequences create the proper description of analyzed shapes and are stored in indexing record. In every case those spots are highlighted where any irregularities have been identified. For each of them there are detailed descriptions in the program representation relating to the previously listed information used as indexing keys. For an pancreatic duct image the said information is presented in more detail on the image shown in Figure 3.

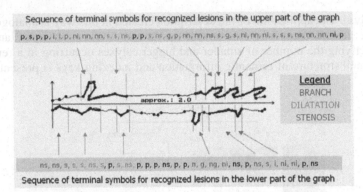

**Fig. 3.** An exemplar indexing key information for a pancreatic duct image. Visible lesions and terminal sequences describing them

The approach to the generation of structural-semantic representation of medical patterns in multimedia databases with the use of context-free and EDT graph grammars [5] presented in this study is an entirely new solution. Preliminary research reveals that such approach proves to be an extremely efficient and universal tool enabling visual data compression and unambiguous data representation. An important point is that the proposed indexation technique has been optimised with an aim to find diagnostic information, easily observed in the shape of organs visible on patterns and dependent on disease symptoms.

The main strength of the proposed structural methods for indexation and search for data in medical visual databases is its high efficiency due from small memory complexity of semantic representation generated to represent patterns; besides algorithms used to search for similar patterns are not time-consuming. Accordingly, such search boils down to comparing the sequences of symbols representing the semantic content of analyzed images, involving the search for the descriptions most similar to that of a given object in database (it is done as visual query). This type of search operations are unaffected by minor disturbances or geometrical transformations of patterns as these factors are independent of the generated syntactic and semantic representation.

In the presented on the figs. 2 and 4 examples of coronography, urogram patterns, pancreas and spinal cord visualization, a semantic descriptor created by the described methodology allows not only the diagnosis of a disease on the basis of a single pattern, but it serves also as a key for indexation in searching for data in the database. Those properties result from unambiguity of representation generated for various semantic contents. In practical terms the result of computer implementation of the syntactic analysis algorithms provided here is a developed system allowing for structural analysis of the discussed medical patterns targeted at creation of semantic representation defining various disease symptoms. The research confirmed the highest potential of developing the description of visible deformations of shapes as well as semantic categorisation and database mining of various disease symptoms. Those descriptions are arrived at as a result of intelligent lesions recognition. Yet, from the point of view of knowledge engineering, they may also serve as data for deeper reasoning and be used by Computer-Aided Diagnosis systems.

## 5  Selected Results

As a result of cognitive multimedia analysis using linguistic approach it is possible to quite efficiently describe, mine and search pathogenesis information of the deformations viewed on x-ray images of the organs under consideration, what means the possibility of recognize and quick search some kind of diseases even on images absolutely not similar one to other.

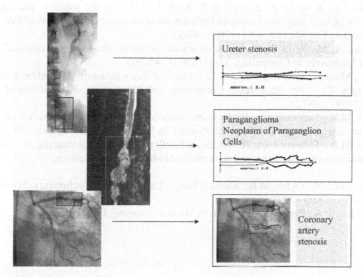

**Fig. 4.** Results of lesion description and understanding using linguistic methods. Width diagrams show the place in which the looked-for lesion was described

In particularly applications of the picture languages and grammars deliver almost complete information concerning the visual morphological irregularities of investigated organs [6]. An analysis of the efficiency of semantic information retrieval using syntactic methods was carried out on the basis of a set containing few dozens of medical images (urograms, coronarograms, and spinal cord images). The efficiency of gaining recognition of information with semantic character exceeded the threshold of 93%. In Fig. 4 are presented examples which show the description of the changes in question for ureter duct, coronary arteries, and spinal cord images.

In order to solve the problem of automatic analysis of the data, advanced techniques of artificial intelligence must be applied. Thus the aim of the presented algorithms was to show an innovative concept of the application of structural algorithms of artificial intelligence in the creation of cognitive vision systems aimed at understanding and determining the semantic meaning of medical images of certain classes. It is worth mentioning that machine perception using such methods may lead to an automatic interpretation of medical images in the way it is done by a specialist. It may enable the determination of not only crucial changes but also the consequences of existing irregularities and finally the optimal directions and methods of conducting a suitable therapy.

## Acknowledgement

This work was supported by the AGH University of Science and Technology under Grant No. 10.10.120.39.

## References

1. Berchtold S., Keim D. A., Kriegel H-P., Seidl T., Indexing the solution space: a new technique for nearest neighbor search in high-dimensional space, IEEE Transactions on Knowledge & Data Engineering, 12(1) (2000) 45-57
2. Martinez A. M., Serra J. R., A new approach to object-related image retrieval, Journal of Visual Languages & Computing, 11(3) (2000) 345-363
3. Niu Y., Mtamer Ozsu, Xiaobo Li, 2-D-S tree: An index structure for content-based retrieval of images, The 1999 Multimedia Computing and Networking, Proceedings of SPIE, Vol. 3654 (1999) 110-121
4. Ogiela, M.R., Tadeusiewicz, R.: Syntactic reasoning and pattern recognition for analysis of coronary artery images, Artificial Intelligence in Medicine, 26 (2002) 145-159
5. Ogiela, M.R., Tadeusiewicz, R.: Artificial Intelligence structural imaging techniques in visual pattern analysis and medical data understanding, Pattern Recognition, 36 (2003) 2441-2452
6. Tadeusiewicz R., Ogiela M.R.: Medical Image Understanding Technology, Springer Verlag, Berlin-Heidelberg (2004)
7. Meyer-Baese A.: Pattern Recognition in Medical Imaging, Elsevier (2003)

# Towards an Ontology for Data in Business Decisions

Wilfried Grossmann and Markus Moschner

Faculty of Computer Science
University of Vienna

**Abstract.** Correct usage of data in business decisions depends on additional knowledge about the data represented in metadata. In order to develop a conceptual model for metadata representation, which allows operational usage of the information in data processing, one has to consider not only the dataset itself but also a number of other data objects occurring in connection with the dataset. The paper proposes a unified description framework for all these data objects. Usage of this description in connection with standard set algebra operations for the dataset is outlined.

## 1 Introduction

Business decisions as well as economic decisions rely many times on the information contained in data. Usually such data encompass aggregations from transactional data as well as data collected under different conditions and for different purposes. In ideal case all these data are assembled as a coherent information base in a data warehouse. A crucial activity in building the data warehouse are the so called ETL processes for preparation and loading the data into the warehouse according to the required specifications. Unfortunately description of these processes is many times based only on a number of rather vague guidelines together with a description of possible methods for the different ETL steps. A similar situation occurs in case of data preparatory steps for data mining in order to set up an appropriate empirical information base for the mining activities (cf. Tamraparni and Johnson [16]).

In both cases building and using the empirical information base needs besides the data also additional information about the data captured usually under the topic meta-information. In order to get an idea about the meta-information requirements let us consider three different examples. The first one considers the case of using survey information. If one wants to use such data for decision making some information about the "representativity" of the data for the entire population is needed. Usually such informatiOn is represented as weights for the survey units. Another example is merging of data sets which differ slightly with respect to some aspects. In that case we have to do some alignment operations, which require information about the possible value domains. Another example is data provenance, which requires appropriate documentation of the data history for prospective users.

Keeping these examples in mind it is not surprising that in the last years there was considerable effort to formalize the meta-information accompanying the data in various areas. A rather formal treatment about metadata models in connection with data warehouses can be found in Jarke et al. [10]. As a more context oriented perspective onto the problem in case of data about the global economic background we want to

D. Karagiannis and U. Reimer (Eds.): PAKM 2004, LNAI 3336, pp. 397–407, 2004.

mention the SDDS initiative [15]. This approach proposed by a consortium of international organizations (IMF, OECD, ECB) aims for definition of a coherent data description which allows also evaluation of data quality. In the area of social sciences the DDI initiative [5] for a description of socioeconomic survey data has got a lot of popularity in particular in connection with NESSTAR [13] which offers an Internet platform for data and metadata access. Due to the fact that all these approaches have different goals and different end users in mind they stress different aspects of the documentation problem. Hence, mapping of different descriptions is rather difficult because it needs not only a (in most cases existing) unified formal specification as XML schemes but also a lot of substantive knowledge about data processing.

In order to overcome these problems the METANET project tried to put all these efforts into a coherent framework by setting the first steps towards an ontology for data description (Froeschl et al., [8]). Such an ontology is based on a number of fundamental concepts for data collection and processing used in the context of applied statistics. These concepts can be utilized as building blocks for representation of the information occurring in connection with data. Moreover the ontology encompasses also a methodological framework for processing the information in connection with data processing activities. Probably the most important issue in connection with processing is the fact that data and metadata have to be processed rather simultaneously in order to guarantee accurate information about the data. Furthermore it seems worth to mention that the METANET approach resembles some ideas occurring in connection with issues of data interoperability, data provenance and data annotation, which were developed in connection with management of scientific databases (cf. Bose and Frew, [3]). A first proposal of a data and metadata structure within this ontological framework is outlined in Denk et al. [7]. A concrete application for the case of weighting has been considered in Grossmann and Ofner [9]. In this paper we proceed further in this direction and show how this model can be applied in context of classical set operations for data. The organisation of the paper is as follows: In section 2 we outline the essentials of the ontology for dataset descriptions and in section 3 we consider processing aspects. Section 4 is devoted to a critical evaluation of the approach and some issues of further investigations.

## 2 Basic Elements of the Ontology

Proper usage of data in business decision requires different types of information units related to the dataset itself. A sketch of the information structure at the top level is shown in figure 1. The information units *Population* and the *Units* represent the universe from which the data stem from. This universe is a set of units, which are the carriers of the information contained in the dataset. Many times these data are the result of a survey and cover only a small subset of the universe. The dataset itself is built of a number of *Variables*, which represent the operational device for measuring the properties of interest for the units. In that sense the variables define the attributes for the relation describing the dataset and the description of the values for the attributes is captured in the information unit denoted by value domain. The information unit *Additional Attributes* is used for capturing results occurring in connection with computations. For example in case of a regression model applied to the data this information would contain at least values of the regression coefficients.

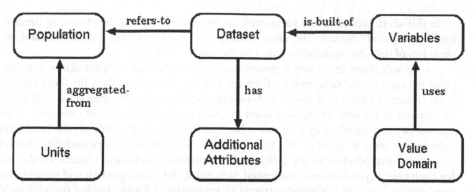

**Fig. 1.** Information units in connection with a dataset

Starting from the structure in figure 1 it seems quite obvious to consider not only the dataset itself as object of interest in connection with the development of the meta-data ontology, but also the other information units accompanying the dataset. This idea is important for various reasons. First of all we have to be aware that an arbitrary number of information units of a specific type can occur in connection with the dataset. In case of variables this is quite obvious but also with respect to populations different types of populations may occur: for example one population for the universe and a slightly different one for drawing the sample. Another reason for considering the different information units as objects of interest of their own stems from processing: sometimes one is interested in modifications of these information units rather independent from an existing dataset. For example a variable may be transformed or a new unit is defined from existing units (e.g. households from persons).

Taking the objects *Dataset, Population, PopulationUnit, Variable* and *ValueDomain* as basic object types for the ontology one has to define a description framework for these objects. Although these objects are rather different from its nature one can define at the top level a unified description format. This format uses the idea of facet classification, well known in the librarian comunities, and distinguish four different *description views*:

1. The *conceptual description view* is defined by a (usually) verbal definition of the object, a temporal reference for the object and a geospatial reference as well as a description of the relations between the objects under consideration (this corresponds to conceptual data modelling in the traditional way).
2. The *structural description view* contains a general characterization of the object structure by a number of type and role parameters, a description of the data structure for the objects and the relations to other objects. With respect to the parameters we distinguish between type and role parameters. Roughly speaking type parameters are independent of usage of objects whereas role parameters depend on context (cf. the example below). The parameter concept seems to be more appropriate than classical data modelling approaches because it supports better multiple inheritances between objects.
3. The data management view is geared towards machine-supported manipulation, storage and retrieval.
4. The administrative view addresses aspects of management and bookkeeping of all the structures.

In this short exposition we focus only on the conceptual and the structural description view, mainly because the other description views resemble rather standard approaches of data documentation based on the Dublin Core [6].

As we will show in section 3 proper usage of the dataset in applications may depend not only on the description of the objects but also on the data for these objects itself. Hence we have to define a uniform representation for the objects as well as the description of the objects. As described in Denk et al. [7] a so called *composite* is an appropriate and simple way to do this. Basically a composite pools all the necessary information into a number of *data buckets* described by corresponding *bucket schemes*. Corresponding to the different description views for the objects we discern for each object type between conceptual, structural, data management and administration buckets. In order to support retrieval of processing a further bucket for additional attributes is defined.

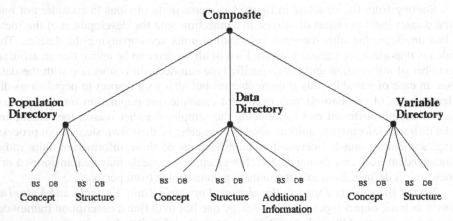

**Fig. 2.** Overview for composite structur

Figure 2 sketches the structure at the top level. BS denotes bucket schemes and DB data buckets. For sake of simplicity we have considered only those buckets which are of main interest for processing logic and left out the administration and data management buckets. Moreover we have omitted the value domains, mainly because processing in connection with value domains is already treated in a number of other papers (see for example McClean et al. [11] or Papageorgiou et al. [14]). In order to make the ideas more clear let us consider the following simple example.

**Example**
Suppose we have a survey from a universe of persons structured according to a classification of the persons by sex and three age groups. The survey data itself are based on a person survey with the variables PersonID, Sex, AgeGroup and Income measured as annual income. Figure 3 shows the data for the population as well as the data of the survey, which will be captured in the structural data buckets of the population and the data.

In order to describe these data in the composite we have to specify first of all the variables. Figure 4 shows the conceptual bucket data containing all the variables used for the population as well as the dataset. The VarConcepts refers to the names in the

|        | AgeGroup1  | AgeGroup2  | AgeGroup3  |
|--------|------------|------------|------------|
| female | 185.000,00 | 324.000,00 | 287.000,00 |
| male   | 196.000,00 | 387.000,00 | 253.000,00 |

| PersonID | Sex    | AgeGroup | Income    |
|----------|--------|----------|-----------|
| 1        | male   | 2        | 23.600,00 |
| 2        | female | 3        | 12.870,00 |
| ...      | ...    | ...      | ...       |

Fig. 3. Example for population data and survey data

tables of figure 3, PersonCount is used as variable for the number in the different population groups. Note that PersonID is based on a person register for Austria established in 2001, the variables Sex, AgeGroup and PersonCount are defined without any specific spatial reference and the used grouping of age was established in 1990. The variable Income is defined according to EU-regulations.

| VariableID | VarConcept  | VarSpatRef | VarTempRef |
|------------|-------------|------------|------------|
| V1         | PersonID    | AUT        | 2001       |
| V2         | Sex         | universal  | na         |
| V3         | AgeGroup    | universal  | 1990+      |
| V4         | Income      | EU         | 1995+      |
| V5         | PersonCount | universal  | na         |

Fig. 4. Conceptual bucket for variables

The structural bucket schemes for the variables are shown in figure 5.

| BucketNr | VariableID | VarType      | Structure   | Role       |
|----------|------------|--------------|-------------|------------|
| 1        | V1         | integer      | RegisterAUT | Identifier |
| 2        | V2         | qualitative  | SexScale1   | rossclass  |
| 3        | V3         | ordered      | AgeScale1   | crossclass |
| 4        | V4         | quantitative | real        | survey     |
| 5        | V5         | integer      | na          | count      |

Fig. 5. Structural bucket schemes for the variables

The type shows well known variable types and the structure column refers to the structure of the bucket data for each variable, i.e. the value domains of the variables. The role indicates the status of the variables inside the composite: Sex and AgeGroup are used as cross-classification variables, PersonCount is a count variable and Income the only survey variable.

Using this variable specification one can define for the datasets shown in figure 3 the corresponding conceptual and structural bucket schemes. Figure 6 shows the conceptual bucket data for the population and the survey. Again, the schemes for the buckets follow the standard form of conceptual buckets. The concept for the population holds universally over the EU whereas the concept for the survey has a specific spatial and temporal stamp. Obviously the temporal and the spatial reference of the dataset must lie within the ranges of corresponding references for the population.

| BucketNr | PopID | PopConcept | ConSpatRef | ConTempRef |
|----------|-------|------------|------------|------------|
| 1 | Pop1 | Person in LF | EU | 1990 + |

| BucketNr | DatasetID | DsConcept | ConSpatRef | ConTempRef |
|----------|-----------|-----------|------------|------------|
| 1 | DS1 | Income Survey | Austria | 1996+ |

**Fig. 6.** Conceptual bucket data for population and dataset

The structural bucket schemes describing the data shown in figure 3 are shown in figure 7. According to the different format of the data for population and dataset we have in the former case the structural type macro (i.e. a table) and in the latter the type micro (i.e. data for each observation). The temporal type is in both cases cross-sect identifying the data as representative for a specific time point or period specified in the columns PopTempRef and DSTempRef. The main information about the layout of the tables of figure 3 is captured in the structure column. In case of population we have a relation describing the data as cross-classified data, whereas in case of the dataset we have a classical table. The role column identifies the population as a sample population, i.e. the counts refer exactly to the size of the groups from which the sample was drawn.

| Bucket Nr | PopID | Struc Type | Temp Type | Pop SpatRef | Pop TempRef | structure | role |
|-----------|-------|------------|-----------|-------------|-------------|-----------|------|
| 1 | Pop1 | macro | cross-sect | Vienna | 2002 | R(V2*V3,V5) | sample |

| Bucket Nr | DSID | Struc Type | Temp Type | DS SpatRef | DS TempRef | structure | role |
|-----------|------|------------|-----------|------------|------------|-----------|------|
| 1 | DS1 | micro | cross-sect | Vienna | 2002 | R(V1...V4) | survey |

**Fig. 7.** Structural bucket schemes for population data and dataset

Also in this case one has to take into account a number of integrity conditions between the two schemes. For example it is obvious that in a valid composite the spatial reference for the sample population and the dataset must coincide and the temporal reference of the dataset must be within the range of the temporal reference of the population. Another integrity condition is that the cross-classification variables of the population must be contained in the relation for the dataset.

## 3  Processing of Composites

Processing of composites can be seen as a sequence of transformations $T$ of composites producing new composites out of already existing composites i.e.

$$\left(C_1, C_2, \ldots C_p\right) \rightarrow \left(T_1(C_1, C_2, \ldots C_p), \ldots, T_k(C_1, C_2, \ldots C_p)\right)$$

For formal specification it is obviously sufficient to consider only the case of a single transformation. Formally a transformation $T(C_1, C_2, \ldots, C_p)$ is described by definition of the origin composites, the output composites and the operators for computation, together with specification of operator parameters. Typically unary or binary operations are the building blocks for more complex operations. Imputation of missing values or weighting are frequently used examples for unary operations and set theoretic operations for the data sets are well known examples for binary operations.

Usually a transformation starts with a request for a necessary operation onto the dataset. Within the composite one can question the semantic correctness of the operations, which depends on the information contained in the composite. Moreover one has to take into account that the operation requires usually a number of additional operations for the other parts of the composite. Hence, depending on the specific entries in the various bucket schemes and data buckets of the composite one obtains a detailed transformation script which encompasses the following three main steps:

1. Metadata Processing. Admissibility of the transformation is checked by using the information available in the composites. In case of admissibility one obtains also a description of the implied side effects of the operation, i.e. operations for other parts of the composite.
2. Data Processing. The operations for the various data buckets of the composite are executed according to the specification of Metadata Processing in step 1.
3. Output Generation. In order to keep the results a new composite is generated. In case of unary operations it may be sufficient to augment the already existing composite with a bucket for additional attributes. In case of binary operations one has to define a new composite.

Let us show how such a transformation plan looks like in case of binary set operations for two data sets. We start with the assumption that the composites for the two datasets have a structure as outlined in the example of section 2 and that the two composites are valid with respect to the integrity constraints. Figure 8 shows the transformation plan in a rather conventional form as flowchart. Roughly speaking the metadata operations may be grouped into two blocks.

In the first block we investigate the composites at the population level. Here we have to check first of all whether the conceptual buckets of the two populations are identical. This operation is denoted by the operator PC in figure 8. If this condition is not satisfied any operation on the data would be infeasible, hence we need some special intervention.

The next step is checking of equality of the structural bucket schemes of the population, i.e. the data have been obtained from the population by comparable methods. If this is not the case we have to set up a new bucket scheme for the output composite. This is represented in figure 8 by the GNB-operator. The operator generates not only the structural bucket scheme of the population but also that part of the structural bucket scheme of the dataset which corresponds to the population scheme according to the integrity constraints. Note that in this case the resulting dataset will contain blocks of missing values, but this case may be of interest as start point for some imputation activities.

In case of equivalent structural bucket schemes for the populations we have to check next the coverage of the populations, i.e. whether the value domains of the variables defining the cross-classification coincide. This check corresponds to the VDS-operator in the figure. If the value domains coincide we can simply overtake the structural bucket scheme for the population of the result composite. A mismatch may occur in cases where the used grouping structures for some of the cross-classifications differ, for example in case of age groups slightly different grouping methods are used. In such cases one needs a partition operation for the bucket schemes which means designation of the common and disjoint parts of the two populations. Again this partition applies not only to the structure of the populations but also to the structure of the datasets. The operations are done by the RBS operator. See also McClean et al. [11] for details of such an operation.

Having done the metadata computations implied by the population structure we can proceed to the checks at the dataset level. Here we have to investigate first of all the structural bucket schemes of the two composites using the BSD operator. A mismatch would mean that we have different survey variables, hence a set operation would be doubtful and we need again special intervention.

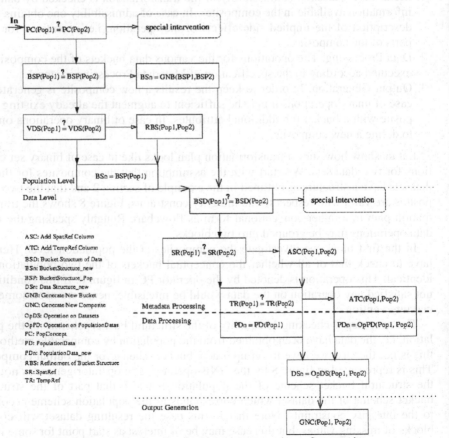

**Fig. 8.** Transformation plan for binary set operations of composites

The next step of metadata processing at the dataset level considers the spatial and the temporal coverage of the data. In case of equality of temporal and spatial component one can overtake the population data for the composite representing the results. In case of mismatch in the temporal or the spatial entries of the structural bucket schemes we have to update ones more the structural bucket scheme for the populations and the dataset by introducing an additional geospatial respectively temporal classification variable. The corresponding operations are denoted in the figure by the ATC and the ASC operator. Note that temporal augmentation occurs quite frequently in case of building time series.

After all processing activities we can proceed to data processing, which corresponds to the standard set operation. The results are put into the output composite, which contains in the bucket for additional information necessary the details of the transformation. Basically this can be done by keeping the input composites and the applied transformation. Using this information one can generate a description of the processing history as directed graph (see also Bose and Frew [3] for a similar approach in connection with satellite data).

# 4  Evaluation and Further Development

The above outlined methodology addresses a number of issues treated also in other areas of knowledge management.

## 1.  Formal Metadata Descriptions

Obviously it is not sufficient to have some (ad hoc) descriptions of data – as today's pain with the situation in even simple operations shows. For automatic and interoperable use one needs machine readable forms of descriptions, which are accepted and\or observed by larger communities. There can be no doubt on the usefulness and advantages of natural language but its ambiguous character and sloppy use renders it impossible for such matters. There is a trade-off between expressibility and automatizability. The proposed form of the conceptual (standard) bucket scheme for different object types makes this clear. We have not tried to formalize the conceptual descriptions up to now, although this could be useful in some of the proposed operators. The additional problem of efficiency goes along each of these issues.

Due to the fact that data processing makes heavy use of mathematical notions and methods in data processing one needs certainly a strong expressibility. The discipline of mathematical knowledge management (MKM) tackles such questions from the pure mathematicians viewpoint. First steps in usage of description logic in connection with efforts to characterize mathematical services such that clients could choose automatically can be found in [2, 4]. These ontologies are used for formulating service descriptions and queries (see also the MONET project [12]). By such an approach detection of impossible or unavailable processing steps may be possible. Another application in mathematics are guiding tools for formalizing descriptions Such an approach mirrors that of proof checkers in MKM – like Mizar [1]. The original aim was support for writing mathematical texts. However, until today the MKM people are still fighting to understand even smaller questions. Maybe it turns out that today methods are sufficient, but who knows? By the way, it is very likely that we do not need full mathematics, yet again: we do not even know how 'small' that amount is.

Maybe things are still easier in matters of metadata because we are speaking about mathematics. Yet again there is as good as no knowledge on that issue ( it seems even by no ways clear what serious methods of ontology could help).

Better descriptions can be achieved by formalizing 'ontologies' (in the sense of the logico-philosophers). Todays 'ontologies' within knowledge representation resemble such a methodological approach (in a restricted sense). As we have mentioned in the introduction one faces the development of many different ontologies for data, analogous to the diversification of XML. This seems to be an unavoidable development where humans are working, but this does not make things easier. Yet, we hope that the proposed first steps towards an ontology offers a 'wider' class of ontology, which allows translation of other data ontologies into that scheme.

## 2.  Usage of Descriptions in Formal Processing

With respect to usage of the descriptions one can distinguish in our case two possible applications: Automated checking for incompatibilities between datasets and interpretation of such incompatibilities in the context of analysis.

We have considered the problem of constraints only in the example. This is sufficient in the first steps of the development of the ontology. If automatic processing comes into play things change dramatically. One needs forms of efficiently treatable knowledge representations, as already pointed out in 1. Such a requirement gives at least some exclusive conditions. In the area of data analysis such conditions are treated in a very informal way under the heading 'good practice'. Some reflection on the 'naive' way of data collection and representation could be more helpful than at first view, and if it would only be in form of exclusion and avoidance criteria. Sometimes special conditions of interest give rise to special formalisms or processing methods.

It can (and will) happen that there are different descriptions. Thus the detection of differences is a goal itself. Different methods as foundation may lead to differences requiring translation procedures. Requirements of translatability act as additional demand for accurate conceptions of metadata descriptions and methodologies. Sometimes not the full conceptions are used. That raises the question when non-equivalence need not be a failure (in sense of classical logic especially). Thus subsumption properties need a handling. Furthermore such challenges require keeping an eye on matters of decision and algorithm issues which may dramatically change with slight changes. There are two foundational issues: on the one hand realizability and on the other hand efficiency (or lucidity).

There are (sometimes important) cases within interest into the failure data for special investigations. Here certain exclusion properties might be of interest (with interest into a smaller part of the data). Or graded forms of non equivalence could make sense. What could lead away from classical logic approaches. Graduated forms of evaluation (as in fuzzy logic) can lead to classifications of deviations. Such refinements could be another source of information about the quality of the underlying data (respectively its relative state of quality).

## References

1. Asperti, A., Buchberger, B., Davenport, J.H. (Eds.):  Mathematical Knowledge Management, Second International Conference, MKM 2003, Bertinoro, Italy, February 16-18, 2003, Proceedings. Springer, Lecture Notes in Computer Science 2594.

2. Bechhofer, S., Patel-Schneider, P.F., Turi, D.: OWL Web Ontology Language Concrete Abstarct Syntax. Technical Report, University of Manchester, December 2003.
3. Bose, R., Frew, J.: Composing Lineage Metadata with XML for Custom Satellite-Derived Data Products. In: Hatzopoulos, M. Manolopoulos, Y. (eds.): Proc. 16th International Conference on Scientific and Statistical Database Management, IEEE Los Alamitos, California (2004), 275 – 284.
4. Caprotti, O. Dewar, M., Turi, D.: Mathematical Service Matching Using Description Logic and OWL. In: Asperti, A., Bancerek, G., Trybulec, A. (Eds.): Mathematical Knowledge Management, Third International Conference, MKM 2004, Bialowieza, Poland, September 19-21, 2004, Springer, Lecture Notes in Computer Science 3119, 73 – 87.
5. DDI Data Documentation Initiative – A Project of the Social Science Community – Codebook. http://www.icpsr.umich.edu/DDI/codebook/index.html
6. DCMI Usage Board, DCMI Metadata Terms, 2003, Dublin Core Metadata Initiative (DCMI), http://dublincore.org/documents/2003/03/04/dcmi-terms/
7. Denk, M. Froeschl, K.A., Grossmann, W.: Statistical Composites: A Transformation Bound Representation of Statistical datasets. In: Kennedy, J. (ed.): Proc. 14th International Conference on Scientific and Statistical Database Management, IEEE Los Alamitos, California (2002), 217 – 226.
8. Froeschl, K.A., Grossmann, W., delVecchio, V.: The Concept of Statistical Metadata. MetaNet (IST-1999-29093) Work Group 2, Deliverable 5 (2003)
9. Grossmann, W., Ofner, P.: A Self Documenting Programming Environment for Weighting. In: Härdle, W., Rönz, B. (eds.): Proceedings in Computational Statistics –COMPSTAT 2002, Physica Verlag, Heidelberg (20022), 129 – 136.
10. Jarke, M., Lenzerini, M., Vassiliou, Y., Vassiliadis, P.: *Fundamentals of Data Warehouses.* Springer Verlag, Berlin 2000.
11. McClean, S., Scotney, B., Rutjes, H., Hartkamp, J. Karali, I., Hatzopolous, M., Lamb, J., Ma, D.: MISSION: An Agent Based System for Semantic Integration of Heterogeneous Distributed Statistical Information Systems. In: Hatzopoulos, M. Manolopoulos, Y. (eds.): Proc. 16th International Conference on Scientific and Statistical Database Management, IEEE Los Alamitos, California (2004), 337 – 340.
12. MONET – Mathematics on the Net. http://monet.nag.co.uk/cocoon/monet/index.html.
13. NESSTAR – Networked Social Science Tools and Resources. http://www.nesstar.org/
14. Papageorgiou, H., Pentaris, F., Theodorou, E., Vardaki, M., Petrakos, M.: A Statistical Metadata Model for Simultaneous Minipulation of Both Data and Metadata. Journal of Intelligent Information Systems 17, 2001, 169 – 192.
15. SDDS – Special Data Dissemination Standard, Dissemination Standards Bullentin Board. http://dsbb.imf.org/Applications/web/sddshome/#metadata
16. Tamraparni Dasu, Theodore Johnson: Exploratory data Mining and Data Cleaning. Wiley Interscience 2003.

# FCA-Based Ontology Augmentation
# in a Medical Domain

In-Cheol Kim

Department of Computer Science, Kyonggi University
San 94-6 Yiui-dong, Paldal-gu, Suwon-si, Kyonggi-do, 442-760, Korea
kic@kyonggi.ac.kr

**Abstract.** Building an ontology in a specific domain is a difficult and time-consuming task. We sometimes prefer augmenting an existing ontology to building a new entire ontology from scratch. A simple way to augment and enrich the existing ontology is to derive new hybrid subconcepts of the existing concepts and find new relationships among them. In this paper, we explore the potential role of FCA in augmenting an existing ontology in medical domain. We assume that instances of existing concepts can be extracted from a given set of domain-specific text documents by applying natural language processing techniques. We explain the three steps of FCA-based ontology augmentation, and then present the details of our experience on MeSH ontology augmentation.

## 1 Introduction

An ontology is a model of a particular field of knowledge-the concepts and their attributes, as well as the relationships between the concepts. Many ontologies have been established for knowledge sharing and are widely used as a means for conceptually structuring domains of interest. But building an ontology in a specific domain is still a difficult and time-consuming task. We sometimes prefer augmenting an existing ontology to building a new entire ontology from scratch. A simple way to augment and enrich the existing ontology is to derive new hybrid subconcepts of the fundamental ones and find new relationships among them. Formal Concept Analysis(FCA) has been advocated to find a lattice of formal concepts by grouping objects with shared attributes[1]. In this paper, we explore the potential role of FCA in augmenting an existing ontology in medical domain. In general, instances of existing concepts can be extracted from a given set of domain-specific text documents by applying natural language processing techniques[4,6,7]. However, there remain some issues in applying the FCA to ontology augmentation:

- How can we obtain instances of existing concepts in practical?
- What should be taken as attributes for FCA?
- Which part of the derived concept lattice can be used for ontology augmentation?

In the remaining part of this paper, we will address these issues through augmenting a medical ontology as an example.

## 2 Formal Concept Analysis

Formal Concept Analysis(FCA) is a mathematical approach to data analysis based on the lattice theory. It provides a way to identify groupings of objects with shared prop-

D. Karagiannis and U. Reimer (Eds.): PAKM 2004, LNAI 3336, pp. 408–413, 2004.
© Springer-Verlag Berlin Heidelberg 2004

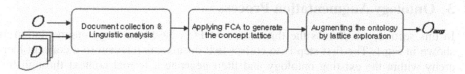

**Fig. 1.** Three steps of FCA-based ontology augmentation

erties[1]. We summarize briefly the basics of FCA as far as they are needed for this paper. The basic notions of FCA are those of a formal context and a formal concept[2].

**Definition 1.** A *formal context* is a triple $K := (G, M, I)$, where $G$ is a set of objects, $M$ is a set of attributes, and $I$ is a binary relation between $G$ and $M$. That means $I \subseteq G x M$. $(g, m) \in I$ is read *"object g has attribute m"*.

**Definition 2.** For a set $A \subseteq G$ of objects we define $A' := \{m \in M \mid \forall g \in A : (g, m) \in I\}$. Correspondingly, for a set $B \subseteq M$ of attributes we define $B' := \{g \in G \mid \forall m \in B : (g, m) \in I\}$.

**Definition 3.** A *formal concept* of the context $K := (G, M, I)$ is a pair $(A, B)$, with $A \subseteq G$, $B \subseteq M$, $A' = B$ and $B' = A$. We call $A$ the *extent* and $B$ the *intent* of the concept $(A, B)$. $\beta(G, M, I)$ denotes the set of all concepts of the context $K := (G, M, I)$.

**Definition 4.** If $(A_1, B_1)$ and $(A_2, B_2)$ are concepts of a context, $(A_1, B_1)$ is called a *subconcept* of $(A_2, B_2)$, provided that $A_1 \subseteq A_2$ or $B_2 \subseteq B_1$. In this case, $(A_2, B_2)$ is a *superconcept* of $(A_1, B_1)$, and we write $(A_1, B_1) \leq (A_2, B_2)$. The relation $\leq$ is called the *hierarchical order* of the concepts. The set of all concepts of $K := (G, M, I)$ ordered in this way is called the *concept lattice* of $K$ and denoted by $\underline{\beta}(K)$.

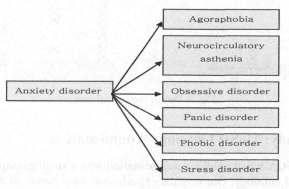

**Fig. 2.** A concept hierarchy within MeSH ontology

## 3   Ontology Augmentation Process

In this section, we discuss the three steps of FCA-based ontology augmentation as shown in Fig.1. The first step is to collect text documents relevant to a concept hierarchy within the existing ontology and then generate a formal context through linguistic analysis. For example, assume we try to augment a concept hierarchy within MeSH ontology shown in Fig.2. First we should retrieve documents relevant to the concept "Anxiety disorder" and its subconcepts from literature databases like MEDLINE. This may be accomplished simply by submitting a query containing the keyword "Anxiety disorder" along with some constraints to the retrieval system. Then through linguistic analysis of the retrieved documents, we build a formal context in which each object corresponds to a document and each attribute to a feature keyword, respectively. The feature keywords may be constrained to the names of existing concepts, or not.

The second step of FCA-based ontology augmentation is to derive a lattice of formal concepts from the context by applying the FCA. This step is somewhat straightforward as it follows the FCA process itself. The last step of ontology augmentation is to find out new useful concepts and ordering relationships from the derived concept lattice and then incorporate them into the existing ontology. Most of newly generated concepts may be more specific subconcepts of existing fundamental concepts or hybrid concepts sharing the properties of two or more distinct concepts. New ordering relationships between concepts may be also discovered within the concept lattice. According to the domain expert's decision, only useful ones of them can be selectively incorporated into the ontology. This methodology for FCA-based ontology augmentation can be widely applied in a variety of domains. In this paper, however, we illustrate the potential of this methodology in a medical domain – specifically psychopathologic domain dealing with mental disorder problems.

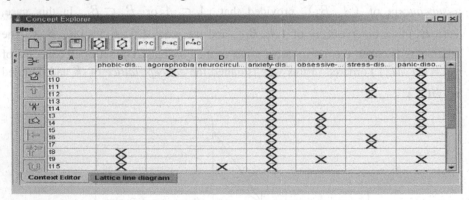

**Fig. 3.** Part of the formal context

## 4   Case Study: MeSH Ontology Augmentation

We illustrate FCA-based ontology augmentation with a small example taken from the MeSH medical ontology. Our original experiments were based on a subset of MeSH ontology containing about 43 psychological concepts and about 320 corresponding documents retrieved from MEDLINE. However, for demonstration purposes, we restrict ourselves to a very small subset of MeSH ontology as shown in Fig.2. We concentrate on the concept hierarchy containing the concept "Anxiety disorder" and its subconcepts. As mentioned above, we submitted a query like ("Anxiety disorder" AND (Agoraphobia OR "Neurocirculatory asthenia" OR ... OR "Stress disorder")) to MEDLINE system, and obtained about 24 text documents relevant to these concepts. After that, the tokenizer scans the text in order to identify boundaries of words and 2-gram expressions like "Neurocirculatory asthenia". Lexical analysis associates single words or complex expressions with a concept from the existing MeSH ontology if a corresponding entry in the domain-specific part of the lexicon exists. For example, the expression "Agoraphobia scale" is associated with the concept "Agoraphobia". If the concept "Agoraphobia" is in the MeSH ontology and document $g$ contains the expression "Agoraphobia scale", then the relation $(g, Agoraphobia) \in I$ holds. In this way, we generate a formal context $K := (G, M, I)$. The set of documents $D$ is taken as object set $(G := D)$, and the set of concepts $C$ is taken as attribute set $(M := C)$. The relation $(g, m) \in I$ shall hold whenever document $g$ contains an instance of $m$. Fig.3 shows a part of the formal context extracted from relevant documents. Based upon the formal context $K := (G, M, I)$, we compute the concept lattice $\underline{\beta}(K)$. The resulting concept lattice is shown in Fig. 4. The top node of the lattice represents the concept "Anxiety disorder". This result can be implied from the fact that the expression "Anxiety disorder" is contained in all documents.

The top part of the concept hierarchy on the derived lattice is isomorphic to that of the original MeSH ontology. From the middle and bottom parts of the lattice, we can find many interesting subconcepts and ordering relationships between them. For example, we can find two subconcepts of both "Panic disorder" and "Stress disorder" in Fig.4 (a). These subconcepts have the properties of the concept "Stress disorder" as well as those of the concept "Panic disorder". This implies the existence of patients feeling both panic disorder and stress disorder simultaneously. This special subconcept, denoted by "Panic-stress disorder", can be considered as a kind of hybrid concepts. Many consulting domain experts, that is, psychopathologists, confirm that in fact there are a significant number of patients suffering from both panic disorder and stress disorder simultaneously. In Fig.4 (b), we can also find a new ordering relationship between the concept "Phobic disorder" and the concept "Neurocirculatory asthenia". The derived lattice tells us that the concept "Phobic disorder" is the superconcept of the concept "Neurocirculatory asthenia". Within the existing MeSH ontology, however, there is no such ordering relationship between two concepts. Many consulting psychologists also confirm that this new ordering of two concepts is meaningful to some extent. Therefore, these useful concepts and relationships found within the concept lattice can be incorporated into the existing MeSH ontology for the purpose of augmentation and enrichment.

## 5  Conclusions

In this paper, we explored the potential role of FCA in augmenting an existing ontology in medical domain. We assumed that instances of existing concepts can be

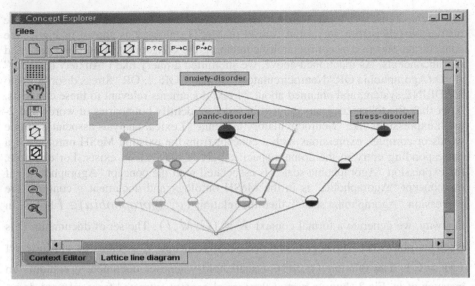

(a) Derived subconcepts

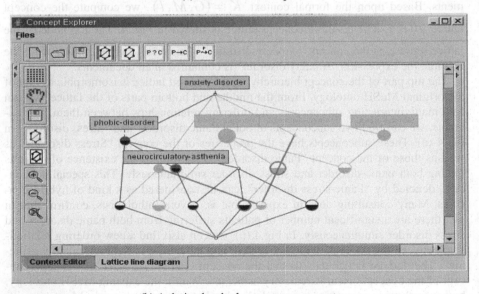

(b) A derived order between two concepts

**Fig. 4.** The concept lattice

extracted from a given set of domain-specific text documents by applying natural language processing techniques. We discussed the three steps of FCA-based ontology augmentation, and then presented the details of our experience on MeSH ontology augmentation. Based upon our work, we believe FCA can be an effective means for ontology augmentation.

# References

1. B. Diaz-Agudo, P.A. Gonzalez-Calero: Formal Concept Analysis as a Support Technique for CBR, Knowledge-Based Syst. Vol.14, (2001) 163-171.
2. B. Ganter, R. Willer: Formal Concept Analysis: Mathematical Foundations, Springer, Berlin, (1997).
3. T. Gruber: Toward Principles of the Design of Ontologies Used for Knowledge Sharing, Knowledge Systems Laboratory, Stanford University, (1993).
4. A. Maedche, R. Volz: The TEXT-TO-ONTO Ontology Extraction and Maintenance System, ICDM Workshop on Integrated Data Mining and Knowledge Management, San Jose, CA, USA, (2001).
5. E.A. Mendonca, J.J. Cimino: Automated Knowledge Extraction from MEDLINE Citations, Proc. AMIA Symp. (2000) 575-579.
6. S.L. Moigno, J. Charlet, D. Bourigault, P. Degoulet, M. Jaulent: Terminology Extraction from Text to Build an Ontology in Surgical Intensive Care, Proc. AMIA Symp. (2002) 430-434.
7. G. Stumme, A. Maedche: Merging Ontologies by Means of Formal Concept Analysis, First International Workshop on Databases, Documents, and Information Fusion, Magdeburg, Germany, (2001).

# An Approach for the Efficient Retrieval
# in Ontology-Enhanced Information Portals

Nenad Stojanovic

Institute AIFB, University of Karlsruhe, Germany
nst@aifb.uni-karlsruhe.de

**Abstract.** In this paper we present an application of the logic-based query refinement in the searching for information in an information portal. The refinement approach is based on discovering causal relationships between queries regarding the inclusion relation between the answers of these queries. We define a
formal model for the query-answering pairs and use methods from inductive
logic programming for the efficient calculation of a (lattice) order between
them. In a case study regarding searching a bibliographic database we demonstrate the benefits of using our approach in the traditional information retrieval
tasks, especially the combination of the free-text based querying and the logic-
based query refinement.

## 1 Introduction

The growing nature of the (public available) information content implies a users behavior's pattern that should be treated in a more collaborative way in the modern
retrieval systems: users tend to make short queries which they refine (expand) subsequently. Indeed, in order to be sure to get any answer to a query, a user forms as short
as possible query and depending on the list of answers, he tries to narrow his query in
several refinement steps. The main problem in modeling an efficient retrieval process
is that a user cannot express his information need straightforwardly in a query posted
to an information repository, i.e. a user's query represents just an approximation of
his information need [1]. Consequently such a query should be refined in order to
ensure the retrieval of as much as relevant products. Unfortunately, most of the retrieval systems do not provide a cooperative support in the query refinement process,
so that a user is "forced" to change his query on his own in order to find the most
suitable results. Indeed, although in an interactive query refinement process [2] a user
is provided with a list of terms that appear frequently in retrieved documents, the
explanation of their impact on the retrieval process is completely missing. Consequently, some redundant and/or failing refinements can be suggested to a user, what
decreases the efficiency of the refinement process drastically.

In our previous work we developed a logic-based approach for refining queries that
uses an ontology for modeling an information repository [3]. The approach enables a
user to navigate through the information content incrementally and interactively. In
each refinement step a user is provided with a complete but minimal set of
refinements, which enables him to develop/express his information need in a step-by-
step fashion.

In this paper we present an application of this approach for refining queries in a
traditional bibliographic database. Since the data are structured according to a schema

D. Karagiannis and U. Reimer (Eds.): PAKM 2004, LNAI 3336, pp. 414–424, 2004.
© Springer-Verlag Berlin Heidelberg 2004

defined by a database provider, we migrated this schema into an ontology. By using this ontology the content of the database is translated into a knowledge base. Each user's query is mapped into an ontology-based query and the logic-based query refinement is performed. The refinements are ranked according to their informativeness and displayed to the user.

This approach supports the so called step-by-step query refinement, which enables a novel user to inspect the content of the bibliographic database in a more systematic manner. Our evaluation study shows two main advantages of such a refinement: (i) a user can find relevant documents faster and (ii) he is more satisfied with the relevance of the documents for his information need.

The paper is structured in the following manner: In Section 2 we outline the problems that could arise in an information retrieval process and motivate the research. In Section 3 we give the basic terminology we use in this paper as well as an overview of the logic-based query refinement approach. In Section 4 we present a bibliographic case study that illustrates how our query refinement approach can be used in resolving these problems. Section 5 contains discussion about related work. In Section 6 we give concluding remarks.

## 2  Challenges for an Information Retrieval Process

Information retrieval is usually considered as a querying process in which a user makes a query (Querying) and tries to find information resources that are relevant for his information need (Browsing results). However, this simplificated treatment of the retrieval process causes many drawbacks in its implementation in an information portal, which, finally, leads to an unsatisfactory usage of the portal. Firstly, since a query is just an approximation of a user's information need, the process of creating a query is very important for the retrieval. A query depends not only on the cognitive gap of a user (which information he is searching for), but also his preferences (e.g. which format of the information does he prefer) and the task at hand. Fig. 1 sketched these factors. Therefore, a process of the *conceptualization* of a user's need in a query is needed in order to take into account this issue.

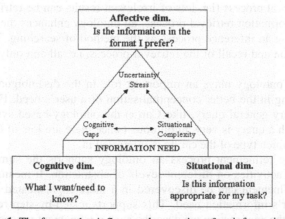

**Fig. 1.** The factors that influence the creation of an information need

However, this issue is completely neglected in searching traditional information portals.

Another problem is that users try to make as short as possible queries so that in the first querying step more relevant results are retrieved, which in subsequent query steps should be filtered. Therefore, an efficient retrieval system should support such a *query refinement* process, by providing a user enough information for deciding how to refine his query. For example an efficient clustering of results can be very useful for the user. Moreover, the system can ask a user some questions in order to acquire the user's preference and consequently to provide the best possible refinements. As mentioned in Introduction, this issue is very weakly supported in traditional portals.

Therefore, an efficient access to information requires an extended view on the information retrieval process. One such view is presented in Fig. 2.

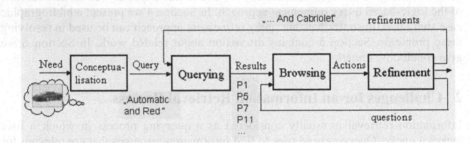

**Fig. 2.** An extended Information Retrieval process

However, this extension of the retrieval process requires more connection between particular phases, e.g. (i) the query language should be able to represent users preferences and users tasks and (ii) the refinements should summarize the browsing history of a user. Therefore, the need for a more conceptual description of the domain model is inevitable. The ontologies seem to be a very promising technologies for modeling information retrieval tasks. For example, in traditional IR, the Querying process is usually implemented as a free-text search, that causes some degradation in the precision of the retrieval process (i.e. lots of irrelevant results can be retrieved). In an ontology-based information retrieval process, an ontology enhances the Querying process by performing an inference process as the method of searching. This ensures the maximal precision and recall of the retrieval process, i.e. all and only relevant results are retrieved.

However, an ontology plays an important role in the disambiguation of a user's query [4], helping in the better conceptualisation of a user's need. For example, if a user makes a very general query, like Car(x) the ontology-based system can advice the user that such a query is very ambiguous (since there are lots of cars) and that he should specify which type of the car he is interested in.

Finally, in the refinement process an ontology supports the summarization of a user's browsing activities on different levels of abstraction. It means that the candidates for the refinement can be discovered in a more sophisticated manner and tailored to the user's information need. This supports a step-by-step refinement of the user's query. In the next section we describe such a refinement process.

## 3  The Approach

As a response to a user's query a search engine retrieves a set of resources (documents) that are in some way relevant for that query. Usualy the documents are described using the terms that appear frequently in them [5], such that the documents retrieved for a query contain the terms from the user's query. However, such a syntactical retrieval model often leads to a semantic mismatch between a query and the documents, which results in a low precision of the retrieval system. Moreover, the query refinement that is based on such a model suffers from the same problem, such that the refinements provided to a user do not reflect his need in an approproate manner.

In this section we present an approach that uses more semantic in order to support the query refinement process. Domain ontology is used as the conceptual backbone of the approach. The approach consists of three phases:

(1) Filtering, in which the initial set of relevant documents is retrieved by a search engine,
(2) Disambiguation (Contextualization), in which the domain ontology is used for clarifying the contexts in which the retieved documents appear in order to define the model for refinement (based on the language model [6]) and
(3) Clustering, in which the set of most appropriate refinements is derived from the refinement model.

Fig. 3 illustrates the whole process.

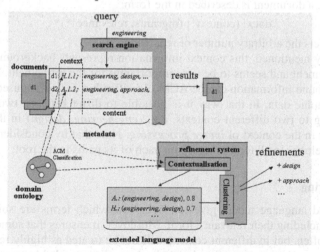

**Fig. 3.** The query refinement "workflow"

Since the Filtering phase is done by a search engine, in the next two subsections we describe other two phases in the refinement process.

### 3.1  Disambiguation

The main problem in defining an efficient refinement system is that the vector space model, usually used for indexing documents, is not adequate for the query refinement task. Namely, the vector space model treats document terms in the isolation (i.e. it represent the content of a document as a set of terms). For example, regarding Fig. 3, the document d1 is indexed with terms *engineering* and *design* whereas it can be possible that these two terms do not appear in the same context in that document. On the other hand, the task of the query refinement is to find some terms that are correlated with the terms from the query, which means that these terms can clarify the meaning of a query in a very efficient way. Regarding Fig. 1, it is important to find terms that appear in the same context with the term *engineering*. For example, the terms *design* and *approach* can be treated as relevant for the refinement only if they constraint the meaning of the term *engineering* directly. Note that regarding the vector space model such a discussion is not possible.

Therefore, we introduce a novel model for representing documents in order to support query refinement process. It is based on the language model for information retrieval [6] and consists of sets of bigrams in the form (term1, term2). Moreover, these bigrams are extended by a relevance factor that describes the strength of the correlation, as well as by a information about the context in which this bigram exists (c.f. Fig. 3, left-hand part).

Such a format enables us to define two types of metadata for a document (c.f. Fig. 1): (i) content-based metadata that represent traditional indexes, which can be created by a search engine and (ii) context-based metadata that represent the preclasification of a document regarding ACM classification and usually is treated as background knowledge about a document.

Therefore, a document is described in the form:

docx: (context*; (bigrams, relevance)*)* ,

where * depicts the arbitrary number of repetitions.

As already mentioned, this context information represents background knowledge about a document and seems to be very importanmt for the refinement. For example, this backgrpound information can be ACM classification very often used for describing bibliographic data. In that way it is possible to differ between two correlations which belong to two different contexts, e.g. (*engineering*, *design*) in the context of *databases* or in the context of *image processing*. Note that by condsidering inferencing a topic belongs to all topics that are on each of its paths to the root.

### 3.2 Clustering

The extended language model gives an overview which terms are suitable for the refinement including their relevance for it. Moreover, it ensures that some refinements that appear often, but in different context will not be treated as highly relevant. However, we assume that context-related metadata, usually provided by manual indexing, can contain some mistakes in terms of the wrong classification of documents. Inorder to bias such problems we do not constraint refinements derived from extended language model to the context information, i.e. the queryies are extended only by content related terms.

The second task of the Clustering process is to ensure the minimality of the proposed refinements. It is possible that a potential refinement is subsumed by another refinement regarding list of results (e.g. all the documents retrieved for the query *engineering and design* are retrieved for the query *engineering and approach*). In such a case the more general results should be only presented. Subsumed refinement will be presented if the user requires refinement of the subsuming refinements.

## 4   Case Study

In this section we present a case study regarding the bibliographic search we have done in the scope of the project SemIPort[1].

*CompuScience*[2] is a bibliographic database covering literature in the field of computer science, information- and communication technology, information management and science with about 160.000 citations. Citations are in English and contain bibliographic information and indexing terms. Many records also include an abstract. The citations are classified according to the Computing Reviews Classification Scheme of ACM. Therefore, for a publication not only the "traditional" bibliographic data (i.e. administrative, like author, publication year) but also the metadata w.r.t. ACM classification are given.

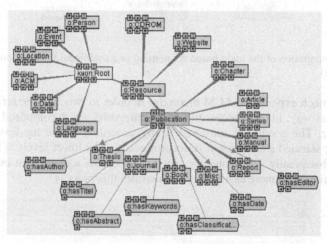

**Fig. 4.** A part of the SemIPort ontology

Since the data are structured according to a schema defined by a database provider, we migrated this schema into an ontology using the approach described in [7]. By using this ontology the content of the database is translated into a knowledge base.

The ontology is which is partially presented in Fig. 4. As the ontology modelling language we use KAON (kaon.semanticweb.org).

Fig. 5 presents the simplified integration architecture. A user's query is executed against a full-text search engine (in this case Lucene  - http://jakarta.apache.org/ lucene/docs/index.html). In the case that a user requires refinement of his query, the query string is transformed into an ontology based query (the task of the "conceptuali-

---

[1]  SemIPort (http://km.aifb.uni-karlsruhe.de/semiport/) is a Semantic Web related project, funded by the BMBF, whose task is the development of semantic methods for the traditional information portals.

[2]  http://www.fiz-informationsdienste.de/en/DB/compusci/index. html

sation" module in Fig. 5) and processed using the approach presented in this paper (the task of the "query refinement" module in Fig. 5). The generated refinements are translated into a set of query strings and retrieved to the user.

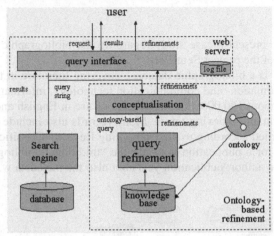

**Fig. 5.** The integration of the logic-based refinement in a traditional information portal (a simplified model)

Our approach exploits the ACM hierarchy in order to structure the refinements in a more abstract way. In that process the ACM categories are decomposed in a step-by-step manner. The results are clustered firstly according to the top-level categories. After a user selected a category, it is decomposed on the lower levels. This process is repeated subsequently. Consequently, a user can define a query that corresponds to his information need more easily. Fig. 6 illustrates this process.

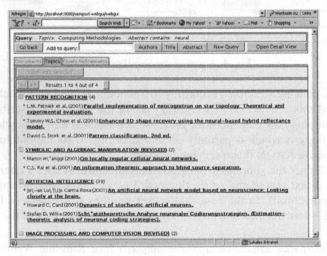

**Fig. 6.** A screenshot from the test portal. The usage of the ACM Classification for the query refinement: the second level of the decomposition. In the first level the top-level category "Computing Methodologies" was selected

Finally, Fig. 7 represents the result of applying the approach presented in Section 3 on the *CompuScience* dataset. A user is provided with a complete and minimal list of refinements that can help him to refine his query according to his information need.

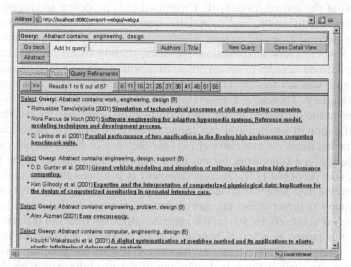

**Fig. 7.** A screenshot from the test portal. The list of the refinements generated for the query "engineering and design"

## 5  Related Work

Using lattices for query refinement process is not new, as some lattice representations were used in early IR [8] and even more recently [9] for refining queries containing Boolean operators. However as these approaches typically rely on a Boolean lattice formalization of the query, the number of proposed refinements may grow too large even for a very limited number of terms and they may easily become semantically meaningless to the user. These limitation can be overcomed by using concept lattices. In [10] the authors described an approach, named REFINER, to combine Boolean information retrieval and the content-based navigation with concept lattices. For a Boolean query REFINER builds and displays a portion of the concept lattice associated with the documents being searched centred around the user's query. The cluster network displayed by the system shows the result of the query along with a set of minimal query refinements/enlargements. A similar approach is proposed in [11], by adding the size of the query result as an additional factor of the navigation. Moreover, the distance between queries in the lattice is used for similarity ranking.

Conceptually, the most similar approach to our query refinement system is the Query By Navigation [12], an approach for the navigation through a hyperindex of query terms. The hyperindex search engine [13] aims users to add, delete or substitute a term from the initial query by providing the minimal query refinements/enlargements. It is designed specifically to (i) help user to express a precise description of their information need and (ii) reduce information overload by presenting the search result at a higher level of abstraction. Moreover, in [14] the analogy between the lithoid, a crystalline structure which organizes document descriptions (and may be used to support searchers in formulating their information demands via Query by Navigation) and the formal concept lattice is shown and used in the phrase searching. However, all of presented approaches are related to Boolean queries.

In terms of the formal framework, Chaudhuri [15] proposed an elegant one to describe query modification, and especially query generalization, for the relational model. He defined extended queries which express additional constraints on the answer set. Several query modification operators, mainly based on the structure of a query, are defined in order to model constraints which can be added to a query. However, the goal was not to support the refinement of a user's need, but just the extension of the query. Therefore, a generalization contains only one way to modify the query. Beside the difference in defining modification operators, we enable a step-by-step modification in which a user can define on his own which of modification can be relevant for his need. An extension of [15] for the case of XML dataset can be found in [16]. Recently, a framework for the refinement of SQL queries in the multimedia databases was proposed [17]. Query refinement is achieved through relevance feedback where the user judges individual result tuples and the system adapts and restructures the query to better reflect the users information need. In that way a kind of similarity search is achieved. However, the approach does not treat the refinement process formally, but rather as a set of heuristics (like predicate addition or removal) described as query refinement strategies. Moreover, it does not generate a set of refinements which can support a user in developing ill-defined information needs.

Regarding searching in product catalogues the most similar approach is presented in [18]. It is an extension of a mediator architecture that supports the relaxation or tightening of query constraints when no or too many results are retrieved from the catalogue. The query language is a type of Boolean queries suitable for the (web) form based querying against product catalogues. The query tightening is enabled when the cardinality of the resulted set has reached a predefined threshold and it is realized by selecting the most informative, not yet constrained product features. The information content of a feature is defined by measuring its entropy. Like previous one, this approach does not treat the problem of query refinement on an ontology-based level.

Finally, our approach can be seen as a method for Interactive Query Refinement for the case of logic-based information retrieval. In that sense our recommendations can be treated as a combination of subject thesauri and co-occurrence term lists [19].

## 6 Conclusion

In our previous work we developed a logic-based approach for refining queries that uses an ontology for modeling an information repository. The approach is based on the model-theoretic interpretation of the refinement problem, so that the query refinement process can be considered as the process of inferring all queries which are subsumed by a given query. In this paper we extend that approach for a traditional information repository, i.e. for the case that the resources are not well structured. However, the approach requires some background information about the domain at hand. For example, the hierarchical organisation of a taxonomy used for describing content of resources in an information repository can be treated as a light-weight ontology. This information is used for defining context of the refinement information which is extracted from the content of the repository. In that way the refinements that are more appropriate for a user's query are produced. Moreover, the approach enables a user to navigate through the information content incrementally and interactively. In each refinement step a user is provided with a complete but minimal set of refinements, which enables him to develop/express his information need in a step-by-step fashion. More precise tailoring to a user's need can be obtained by introducing user's relevance feedback in the query refinement process.

## Acknowledgement

Research for this paper was partially financed by BMBF in the project "SemIPort" (08C5939) and EU in project "KnowledgeWeb" (507482). Special thanks to Eric Schwarzkopf from DFKI Saarbrücken, Germany for the useful comments and implementation of graphical user interface.

## References

1. Saracevic, T.: Relevance: A Review of and a framework for the thinking on the notion in information science. Journal of the American Society for Information Science, 26, (6), (1975) 321-343
2. Efthimiadis, E.N.: User choices: A new yardstick for the evaluation of ranking algorithms for interactive query expansion. Information Processing and Management, 31(4), (1995) 605-620
3. Stojanovic, N, Studer, R., Stojanovic, Lj.: A logic-based approach for query refinement, Web Intelligence WI 2004, IEEE/ACM (2004)
4. Stojanovic, N.: An Approach for Using Query Ambiguity for Query Refinement: The Librarian Agent Approach. 22$^{nd}$ International Conference on Conceptual Modeling (ER 2003), Chicago, Illinois, USA, Springer (2003)
5. Baeza-Yates, R.: Modern Information Retrieval. Addison Wesley (1999)
6. Song, F., Croft, W.B.: A general language model for information retrieval. In Proceedings of Eighth International Conference on Information and Knowledge Management (CIKM'99), (1999)
7. Stojanovic, Lj,. Stojanovic N., Volz R.: Migrating data-intensive Web Sites into the Semantic Web. ACM SAC 2002 (2002)
8. Soergel, D.: Mathematical analysis of documentation systems. Information storage and retrieval, (1967) 3:129-173
9. Spoerri, A.: Infocrystal: Integrating exact and partial matching approaches through isualization. In Proceedings of RIAO 94, New York (1994) 687-696,
10. Carpineto, C., Romano, G.: Effective re formulation of boolean queries with concept lattices. In Flexible Query Answering Systems FQAS'98, Berlin, Springer, 277-291 (1998)
11. Becker, P., Eklund, P.: Prospects for Document Retrieval using Formal Concept Analysis. Proceedings of the Sixth Australasian Document Computing Symposium, Coffs Harbour, Australia, December 7 (2001)
12. Bruza, P., van der Weide, T. Stratified Hypermedia Structures for Information Disclosure. The Computer Journal 35(3) (1992) 208-220
13. Bruza, P., Dennis, S.: Query Reformulation on the Internet: Empirical Data and the Hyperindex Search Engine. In: Proceedings of RIAO97, Computer-Assisted Information Searching on Internet, Montreal (1997)
14. Grootjen, F.: Employing semantic issues in syntactical navigation. Proceedings of BCS-IRSG 2000 Colloquium on IR Research, 5th-7th April 2000 (2000)

15. Chaudhuri, S.: Generalization and a Framework for Query Modification. In IEEE ICDE, Los Angeles, CA (1990)
16. Lee, D: Query Relaxation for XML Model. In *Ph.D Dissertation,* University of California, Los Angeles, June 2002 (2002)
17. Ortega-Binderberger, M., Chakrabarti, K., Mehrotra, S.: An Approach to Integrating Query Refinement in SQL. 2002 Conference on Extending Database Systems (EDBT), (2002) 15-33
18. Ricci, F., Venturini, A., Cavada, D., N. Mirzadeh, Blaas, D., Nones, M.: Product Recommendation with Interactive Query Management and Twofold Similairty. In proceedings of the 5th International Conference on Case-Based Reasoning (ICCBR 2003) (2003)
19. Schatz, B. R., Johnson, E.H., Cochrane, P.A., Chen, H.: Interactive Term Suggestion for Users of Digital Libraries: Using Subject Thesauri and Co-occurrence Lists for Information Retrieval. Digital Libraries (1996) 126-133

# Assessing Knowledge Management with Fuzzy Logic

Gholamreza Khoshsima[1], Caro Lucas[2], and Ali Mohaghar[3]

[1] M. Sc, Instructor, Department of Management,
Vali-e-Asr University of Rafsanjan, Rafsanjan, Iran
Khoshsima@mail.vru.ac.ir
[2] Professor, Department of Electrical and Computer Engineering, University of Tehran, Iran
Lucas@ipm.ir
[3] Assistant Professor, Department of Management, University of Tehran, Tehran, Iran
Mohaghar@moi.gov.ir

**Abstract.** The role of knowledge management as the key source for competitive advantage in our organizations has become a hotly debated topic. Indeed, it is a core competency for creating competitive advantage. In this environment that knowledge management is vital, therefore, at first we should determine knowledge management situation, and then to achieve a desired point, formulate a knowledge management strategy. In this paper we are going to explain a model for assessment knowledge management along with a fuzzy logic methodology. Knowledge management is a multidimensional concept and a vague notion. For this reason, fuzzy logic and a knowledge-based methodology for the measurement and assessment of knowledge management in Iranian television manufacturers were used. At first, we explain knowledge management components (Strategic Alignment, People, Process and Technology). In the next step from the knowledge that is presented via IF {Fuzzy antecedents} THEN {Fuzzy consequents} rules, to assess knowledge management in Iranian television manufacturers was used.

## 1 Introduction

With increased levels of competition in the marketplace, high costs associated with human resources, increase in employee transience, and shortage of qualified knowledge workers, organizations have actively pursued the notion of making more effective use of the knowledge and expertise, and this notion of managing knowledge as a corporate resource has been looked to as one of the few foundational weapons that promise to deliver sustainable core competencies in the future (Khoshsima, 2003, Janz and Prasarnphanich, 2003). Companies today are facing important challenges such as the need to reduce the time-to-market, the development and manufacturing costs, or to manage products with more and more technology. As a result, this current situation is encouraging the implementation of new management techniques such as knowledge management to increase competitive advantages. Knowledge is an intangible asset, and measuring the effectiveness of knowledge management solutions, is challenging and this paper attempts to address the challenges. The velocity and dynamic nature of the new marketplace has created a competitive incentive among many companies to consolidate and reconcile their knowledge assets as a means of creating value that is sustainable over time. In order to achieve competitive sustainability, many firms are launching extensive knowledge management efforts. To compete effectively, firms must leverage their existing knowledge and create new knowledge that favorably positions them in their chosen markets (Gold et al, 2001). The first step

D. Karagiannis and U. Reimer (Eds.): PAKM 2004, LNAI 3336, pp. 425–432, 2004.

in developing knowledge management is to determine the current position of knowledge management systematically or, more activities and organizational conditions.

## 2    Theoretical Background

Sveiby (1997) defined knowledge management as "leveraging the intellectual assets of the company to meet defined business objectives"(Del-Rey-Chamorro et al, 2003). Nonaka and Takeouchi (1995), Nonaka (1995), and Alavi & Leidner, (2001) defined knowledge as "Justified true belief" and as the set of justified beliefs that enhance an entity's capability for effective action (Becerra-fernandez. and Sabherwal, 2001; Sabherwal and Becerra-Fernandez, 2003). Dovenport and Prusak (1998) have defined organizational knowledge as ranging from "complex, accumulated expertise that resides in individuals and is partly or largely inexpressible" to much more structured and explicit content". The types of organizational knowledge are reflected in several classification schemes. For example, Venzin et al (1998) identify a number of categories of knowledge-including tacit, embodied, encoded, embrained, embedded, event, and procedural. Kogut and Zander (1992) distinguish between "information" and "know-how" as two types of knowledge, viewing them as "what something means" and "knowing how to do something". Singley and Anderson (1989) also identify the parallel distinction between declarative knowledge (facts) and procedural knowledge (how to ride a bicycle). Another classification of knowledge views it as tacit or explicit as presented by Polnyi (1966). Explicit knowledge can be expressed in numbers and words and shared formally and systematically in the form of data, specifications, manuals, and the like. In contrast, tacit knowledge which includes insights, intuitions, and hunches is difficult to express and formalize, and therefore difficult to share (Becerra-fernandez. and Sabherwal, 2001). Lee and Choi attempts to find relationships among knowledge management factors such as enablers, processes, and organizational performance. An integrative research model is built from a process-oriented perspective and then tested empirically (Lee and Choi, 2003). Some specific work has been done in the particular domain of assessment related to Knowledge management. Bohn (1994) in his article proposes a framework for levels of technological knowledge. Moore (1999) developed a set of metrics for measuring and forecasting knowledge work. His set of measures was oriented to software companies, evaluating knowledge work with respect to the software characteristics. Hendriks et al (1999) have developed a framework in which companies can measure their current situation with respect to intellectual capacity and related management structure, in other words, measure how good their Knowledge management is. Chandler (1999) proposed a six-step framework to align macro knowledge management (where how the business will achieve the knowledge management targets is determined at this level) to micro knowledge management (what to target in knowledge management activities according to the company's mission statement and other strategies). Roy et al (2003) proposed a framework using to BSC in which the way to develop performance indicators for knowledge management solutions is presented.

## 3    Conceptual Model

Many researchers have emphasized four factors for managing knowledge separately: Strategic alignment (Hayes and Wheelwright, 1979; Henderson and Venkatraman,

1999; Del-Rey-Chamorro et al, 2003; Young, 2001; Smith et al, 2003; Buckley and Carter, 2002; Alazmi and Zairi, 2003), processes (Perez and Hynes, 1999; Soo et al, 2002; Del-Rey-Chamorro et al, 2003; Sabherwal and Becerra-Fernandez, 2003; Buckley and Carter, 2002; Sarvary, 1999; Lee and Choi, 2003; Becerra-fernandez and Sabherwal, 2001; Alazmi and Zairi, 2003), technologies (Gold et al, 2001; Perez and Hynes, 1999; Alazmi and Zairi, 2003; Schultze and Boland, 2000; Lee and Choi, 200; Moffett et al, 2003), and people (Perez and Hynes, 1999; Alazmi and Zairi, 2003; Lee and Choi, 2003; Soo et al, 2002; Holsapple and Joshi, 2000; Moffett et al, 2003). To assess knowledge management into an organization at first an NGM model and its components were used (see figure 1). Knowledge management was clustered into four elements of the NGM model and then operationalized by constructing indices of extensiveness of (1) strategic alignment, (2) people, (3) process and (4) technology.

*Strategic Alignment:* Concept of fit or alignment has been discussed and investigated in different approaches. Indices of strategic alignment are derived from a series of questions that relate to two items (Henderson and Venkatraman, 1993):

1. At first integration between business and knowledge management domains; is the link between business strategy and knowledge management strategy.
2. At the second deals with the corresponding internal domains, namely, the link between organizational infrastructure and processes and knowledge management infrastructure and processes.

*Process:* Knowledge management processes (knowledge management activities) can be thought of as a structured coordination for managing knowledge effectively (Gold et al, 2001). Typically these processes include activities such as identification, acquisition, development, sharing and distribution, utilization, and retention (Probest et al, 2000). In studying knowledge management processes, Nonaka proposed four knowledge management processes-internalization, externalization, socialization, and combination. Knowledge management processes are the broad approaches through which knowledge is discovered, captured, shared, or applied (Sabherwal and Becerra-Fernandez, 2003).

*People:* Includes of employees (Holsapple and Joshi, 2000) and managers (Andersen and APQC, 1996). A particular instance of knowledge activities in an organization can be carried out by a human-processor (e.g. an individual knowledge worker, a group). An organization's knowledge workers use their knowledge handling skills, plus the knowledge at their disposal, in performing an assortment of knowledge activities. Such activities can be examined at various levels of analysis and characterized in various ways. Managerial influences emanate from organizational participants responsible for administering the management of knowledge. The framework partitions these influences into four main factors: exhibiting leadership in the management of knowledge, coordinating the management of knowledge, controlling the management of knowledge, and measuring the management of knowledge. Human participants' personal beliefs and experiences can affect their approaches to sharing. (Holsapple and Joshi, 2000).

*Technology:* A particular instance of knowledge activities in an organization can be carried out by a computer-based processor (e.g. an intelligent agent) (Holsapple and Joshi, 2000). Technology advances can affect the modes and channels of sharing. It

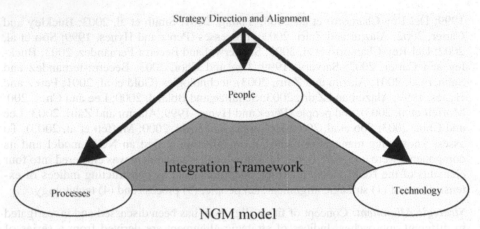

**Fig. 1.** Next Generation Manufacturing model

can create means to break knowledge-sharing barriers such as geographically dispersed locations (Holsapple and Joshi, 2000). Degree of support for collative work, for communication, for searching and accessing, for simulation and prediction, and for systematic storing (Lee and Choi, 2003). Through the linkage of information and communication systems in an organization, previously fragmented flows of information and knowledge can be integrated. These linkages can also eliminate barriers to communication that naturally occur between different parts of the organization (Gold et al, 2001).

## 4   Methodology and Assessment

Knowledge management is a multidimensional, inherently vague notion and because of involvement of human perception and beliefs its assessment is essentially required. In the processes of assigning values a Likert scale is used which is fuzzy by nature. The present paper uses the Likert scale turned into fuzzy number by Hwang and Lai (1994). The key idea of our model in assessment is the involvement of all distinct types and corresponding operational parameters in the determination of the overall knowledge management. This is implemented via multi-antecedent fuzzy If-Then rules, which are conditional statements that relate the observations concerning the allocated types (If-part) to the value of knowledge management (Then-part).

In addition, each component breaks into some measurable indices. Suppose $KM_i$, $i = 1,2,3,4$ is the set of knowledge management components and $LC_i$ the linguistic value of each component; then the expert knowledge general rule is:

If $KM_1$ is $LC_1$ AND $KM_2$ is $LC_2$ AND $KM_3$ is $LC_3$ AND $KM_4$ is $LC_4$

Then $KM_{ORGKM}$ is $ORGKM$

Where $ORGKM$ representing the set of linguistic values for organizational knowledge management $KM_{ORGKM}$. All linguistic values $KM_i$ and $ORGKM$ are fuzzy sets. To pre-test the mail questionnaire, a pilot study was undertaken. First, the questionnaire was subjected to critical review by six academics from within the fields of Strategic, Business, Management, Production, Technology, and Information Technology and by twelve experts from within Iran television manufactures.

**Table 1.** Results after aggregating data for company A, B, and C

|  | Company A | | | Company B | | | Company C | | |
|---|---|---|---|---|---|---|---|---|---|
|  | L | M | U | L | M | U | L | M | U |
| People | 0.124 | 0.266 | 0.413 | 0.247 | 0.394 | 0.531 | 0.154 | 0.271 | 0.347 |
| Process | 0.05 | 0.198 | 0.31 | 0.228 | 0.348 | 0.434 | 0.213 | 0.351 | 0.414 |
| Strategic Alignment | 0.13 | 0.297 | 0.425 | 0.159 | 0.27 | 0.339 | 0.297 | 0.404 | 0.547 |
| Technology | 0.182 | 0.324 | 0.436 | 0.286 | 0.37 | 0.423 | 0.294 | 0.44 | 0.609 |

From among Iranian television manufacturers six companies were selected from which three companies (A, B, and C) responded to questionnaires. Because of the number of questions included, the questionnaires were distributed between the following departments: information system department, planning and production department, engineering and R&D department, marketing department to determine the degree of each component and another questionnaire among industry experts to design Fuzzy Systems. Figure 3 illustrates the steps followed.

**Table 2.** Crisp number

|  | Companies | | |
|---|---|---|---|
|  | A | B | C |
| People | 0.26725 | 0.3915 | 0.26075 |
| Process | 0.189 | 0.3395 | 0.33225 |
| Strategic Alignment | 0.28725 | 0.2595 | 0.413 |
| Technology | 0.3165 | 0.36225 | 0.44575 |

At first level one system is designed to assess knowledge management, which has four components, at IF-part a 3-point Likert scale and at Then-part a 9-point Likert scale is used, therefore with respect to four linguistic variables and three linguistic terms, we have $3^4=81$ rule. After the data of questionnaires was aggregated degree of each component was determined (Table 1). At table 1: L is the most pessimistic state possible, M is the most possible state and U is the most optimistic state possible. The aggregate data (table 1) can enter Fuzzy system as either crisp or fuzzy. In the first procedure, fuzzy numbers were translated into crisp numbers through Minkowsky(Table 2) and then entered fuzzy system designed at MATLAB and the following results were acquired (Fig 4).

$$X = m + \left( \frac{\beta - \alpha}{4} \right)$$

At the second procedure, fuzzy systems were designed with MATLAB and Simulink. Then fuzzy triangular numbers entered fuzzy system (data entered as a signal, can be seen at figure 4) and the following results were acquired.

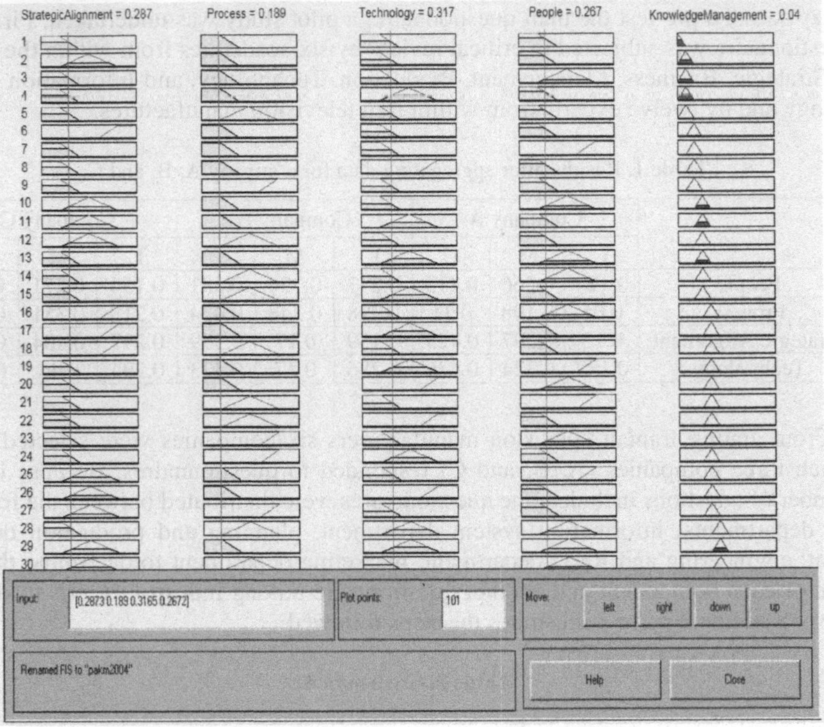

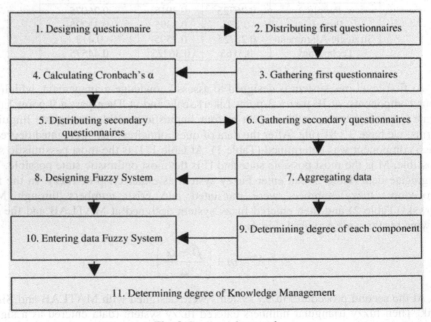

**Fig. 2.** Results for company A with crisp number

**Fig. 3.** Process of research

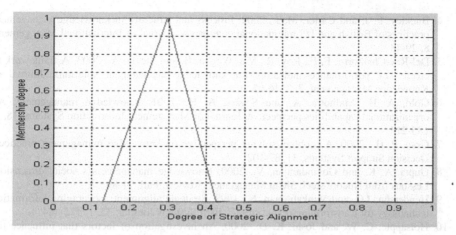

**Fig. 4.** Degree of Strategic Alignment

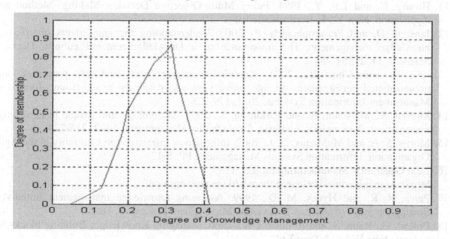

**Fig. 5.** Final result of company A

As figure 2 illustrate we have just one number for decision making, but at figure 5 we have a set of numbers with its membership degrees for decision making. Therefore, at figure 5 we have L that is the most pessimistic state possible, M is the most possible state and U is the most optimistic state possible for decision making.

## References

1. Alazmi, M. and Zairi, M., 2003, Knowledge management critical success factors. Total Quality Management, 14, 2, 199-204
2. Anderen, A. and APQC., 1996, The knowledge management assessment tool: External benchmarking version, Winter
3. Becerra-fernandez, I. And Sabherwal, R., 2001, Organizational knowledge management: A contingency perspective. Journal of Management Information Systems, 18, 1, 23-55

4. Buckley, P, J. and Carter, M. J., 2002, Process and structure in knowledge management practices of British and US mutinational enterprises. Journal of International Management, 8, 29-48
5. Del-Rey-Chamorro, F, F., Roy, R., Van Wegen, B. and Steele, A., 2003, A framework to create key performance indicators for knowledge management solutions. Journal of Knowledge Management, 7, 2, 46-62
6. Gold, A. H., Malhotra, A. and Segars, A. H., 2001, Knowledge management: An organizational capabilities perspective. Journal of Management Information Systems, 18, 1, 185-214
7. Gray, P. H., 2000, A problem-solving perspective on knowledge management practices. Decision Support Systems, 31, 87-102
8. Gupta, A. K. and Govindarajan, V., 2000, Knowledge management's social dimension: Lessons from Nucore steel. Sloan Management Review, Fall, 71-80
9. Henderson, J.C. and Venkatraman, N., 1999, Strategic alignment: Leveraging information technology for transforming organizations. IBM Systems Journal, 32, 1, 472-484
10. Holsapple, C. W. and Joshi, K. D., 2000, An investigation of factors that influence the management of knowledge Systems, 9, 193-212
11. Hwang, C. and Lai, Y., 1994, Fuzzy Multi Objective Decision Making: Method and Application. New York, Berlin Heidelberg.
12. Jans, B. D. and Prasarnphanich, P., 2003, Understanding the antecedents of effective knowledge management: The importance of a knowledge-centered culture. Decision Sciences, 34, 2, 351-384
13. Lee, H. and Choi, B., 2003, Knowledge management enablers, processes, and organizational performance: An integrative view and empirical examination.. Journal of Management Information Systems, 20, 1, 179-228
14. Moffett, S., McAdam, R. and Parkinson, S., 2003, Technology and people in knowledge management: An empirical analysis. Total Quality Management, 14, 2, 215-224
15. Morris, S. A. and McManus, D. J., 2002, Information Infrastructure Centrality in the Agile Organization. Information Systems Management, PP: 8-12
16. Next Generation Manufacturing project, 1997: http://apage.mit.edu/rkt/research/themes/rktgroup9/ngm.pdf
17. Perez, R. R. and Hynes, M. D., 1999, Assessing knowledge management initiatives: Sowing the seeds of success. Knowledge Management Review, 8, 16-21
18. Protest, G., Raub, S. and Romhardt, K., 2000, Managing Knowledge: Building blocks for success. John Wiley & Sons Ltd
19. Sabherwal, R. and Becerra-Fernandez,I., 2003, An empirical study of the effect of knowledge management processes at individual, group, and organizational levels. Decision Sciences, 34, 2, 225-260
20. Sarvary, M., 1999, Knowledge management and competition in the consulting industry. California Management Review, 41, 2, 95-107
21. Smith, H. A. and McKeen, J. D., 2003, Developing and aligning a KM strategy.Queen's center for knowledge-based enterprises, http://www.business.queensu.ca/kbe, WP 03-03
22. Soo, C., Devinney, T., Midgley, D. and Deering, A., 2002, Knowledge management: Philosophy, processes, and pitfalls. California Management Review, 44, 4, 129-150
23. Young, R., 2001, The relationship between strategic planning IT planning and context-driven knowledge management strategies. 4 th Westwrn Australian Workshop on Information Systems Research (WAWISR 2001)
24. Khoshsima, G., 2003, A model for measuring organizational agility in Iran television manufacturing industry: a fuzzy logic framework, Proceedings of International Engineering Management Conference 2003, Albany, New York USA 2-4 November 2003., 354- 358

# A Meta-service Framework for Knowledge Management

Robert Woitsch[1], Peter Höfferer[2], and Dimitris Karagiannis[2]

[1] BOC, Bäckerstraße 5, 1010 Vienna, Austria
Robert.Woitsch@Boc-eu.com
http://www.boc-eu.com

[2] University of Vienna, Institute for Computer Science and Business Informatics
Department of Knowledge Engineering, Bruenner Strasse 72, 1210 Vienna, Austria
{peter.hoefferer,dk}@dke.univie.ac.at

**Abstract.** This paper introduces KM-Services as a new basic concept for Knowledge Management. It discusses the vision of service oriented knowledge management (KM) as a realisation approach of process oriented knowledge management.

In the following process oriented knowledge management as it was defined in the EU-project PROMOTE (IST-1999-11658) is presented. Then the KM-Service approach to realise process oriented knowledge management is explained with special emphasis on semantic services. The Meta-Service-Framework that defines the KM-Service Framework will be introduced and a realization scenario is pointed out. This concept is used in the EU Project Akogrimo to merge Knowledge Management and Mobile Grid.

## 1 Introduction

Knowledge Management (KM) evolved to a serious management discipline that aims to integrate in the orchestra of existing management approaches. Current knowledge management approaches merge only partly with other management disciplines like strategic management (in the context of business intelligence), process management (in the context of process oriented knowledge management) or human resource management (in the context of skill and competence management). In contrast to rather weak integration on the management level the technological integration of knowledge- and information management is well advanced.

This can be explained by the historical development of this rather young (starting point around 1995) research discipline, as the root of knowledge management is seen in the artificial intelligence. Therefore the strong technical focus is still manifested in knowledge management.

Current status of knowledge management is therefore a tight coupling on the technical layer but a rather loose and weak integration at the management layer. The challenge of today's research is to integrate knowledge management not only at the technical but also on the management layer.

Integration on the management layer requires a homogenous concept; therefore a third layer – the conceptual layer – is defined that resides between the management and the technical layer. This conceptual layer has the task to connect the management view of knowledge management with the underlying technology. Process-oriented knowledge management belongs to the conceptual layer with the aim to integrate management issues and technological specifications.

D. Karagiannis and U. Reimer (Eds.): PAKM 2004, LNAI 3336, pp. 433–440, 2004.
© Springer-Verlag Berlin Heidelberg 2004

The aim of this text is to introduce a new viewpoint on knowledge management – Knowledge Management Services – that is seen as an implementation approach for process-oriented knowledge management.

To gain more flexibility the Knowledge Management Service is defined within a Meta-Service-Framework. This Meta-Service-Framework can then be adapted to various implementations of knowledge management.

## 2  Process Oriented KM: A Conceptual Approach

Process oriented KM (POKM) is an entry point into KM independent on the used technology under the umbrella of organisational management. Process oriented knowledge management is based on the following thoughts [3]:

- Knowledge has to be embedded in business processes.
- Knowledge processes can be modelled.
- A knowledge management system has to be a "Meta-tool".

PROMOTE® is a homogeneous process-oriented approach for knowledge management [12] that comes up to the requirements mentioned above by satisfying the following premises:

**Processes as knowledge:** The first step is to define processes as knowledge. PROMOTE® enables to model and analyse organisational sequences and points out knowledge intensive tasks.

**Processes as an entry point:** The second step is to define processes as the starting point to collect requirements for knowledge management.

**Processes as management approach:** The third step is to define management processes for knowledge.

PROMOTE® enables the combination of knowledge management with other management disciplines. In the following service-based KM is introduced as an implementation approach for process oriented knowledge management.

## 3  Service-Based KM: An Implementation Approach

Process oriented KM as realised in PROMOTE® uses a special modelling language that focuses on business processes in order to depict KM aspects. This modelling language contains the concept of KM-activities and KM-processes that are performed with the help of KM-tools.

The challenge is that existing KM-tools can hardly be classified, compared or selected regarding the requirements of the task to be performed. This is because today's KM solutions suffer from the following factors:

- a chaotic market situation, that makes it very difficult especially for decision makers to select the appropriate tool;
- often several different KM-tools are required to perform one single KM-task which means that the tools have to work cooperatively;
- holistic KM needs both social and technical services, but to date there is no concept that treats these services similar and
- global operating companies need KM-solutions that are location independent.

The idea of KM-Services is to enable a clear definition of KM-tools on a conceptual level that is independent of the underlying technology. Such a service-based view would enable the classification of KM-tools, make decision easier, enable a better cooperation between KM tools and would treat social and IT-based services equally.

## 3.1 Literature on KM-Services

It is reasonable that KM-platforms follow the trend of service oriented programming (SOP) as realised in the KM-platform of CSC [2] mentioned in [9] and discussed within the concept of nine keys in [10] introducing Knowledge Services.

These platforms define services on a technological level. As pointed out in [6] and [4] it is not sufficient to only emphasise the technological integration but it is also necessary to enhance the conceptual integration. In this case the conceptual integration would be a KM integration.

Such a KM integration is rarely discussed. [14] mentions a two dimensional framework for KM services whereas [8] introduces a business-driven classification for KM-tools in [5].

## 3.2 Web-Services: The Technological Basis

There are various different definitions of Web-Services that are either

Business-oriented like:

"Web-services are loosely coupled reusable software components that semantically encapsulate discrete functionality and are distributed and programmatically accessible over standard Internet protocols." [11]

Technical oriented as:

"A Web service is a software system designed to support interoperable machine-to-machine interaction over a network. It has an interface described in a machine-processable format (specifically WSDL). Other systems interact with the Web service in a manner prescribed by its description using SOAP-messages, typically conveyed using HTTP with an XML serialization in conjunction with other Web-related standards." [15]

When considering Web-Services in more detail the following characteristics stand out:

*Location-independence:* As Web-Services can be invoked via the use of standard Internet protocols (e.g. SOAP over HTTP) the existing Web architecture with slight extensions - mainly on server side - can be used, which allows for location-independent access.

*Standardized interface* descriptions for Web-Services exist (e.g. WSDL).

*Service registries* (e.g. UDDI registries) can be created that contain information on how Web-Services can be accessed and which functionalities they provide. This fact together with standardized interface definitions enable the following aspect of:

*Interoperability* of Web-Services. Recently much effort is given to enable workflows on the Internet in which complex services that consist of several smaller tasks are executed by smaller grained services that interact with one another. In this context the Web-Services stack which nowadays is commonly seen to be made up of SOAP, WSDL and UDDI only has to be extended with layers that deal with issues like choreography, transactions and contracts. [13]

KM-Services of different vendors that are implemented as Web-Services can interact smoothly to solve complex knowledge tasks. The following example shall give an impression of this.

Imagine the task of finding different kinds of knowledge resources according to one or more key words. These resources could be human contact persons, documents on file servers within a company, Internet resources or books in a library. Now different Web-Services can be used to perform this task: Two Web-Services of the company's own could run a search for human experts and classified files, whereas external Web-Services could be used for finding resources in the Internet or in libraries. All these services could be called by a superior Web-Service that consolidates the discrete search results and presents them to the user.

### 3.3    Knowledge Management Services: The Implementation Approach

The KM-Service is a semantic Web-Service that is defined in the context of KM. This means that semantic services are defined by a KM-Framework consisting of KM-Dimensions and algorithms to classify and select services.

The following KM-Dimensions can be distinguished: Representation of Knowledge, Medium of Knowledge, Knowledge User, Time of Knowledge, Origin of Knowledge, Sophistication, Life Cycle of Knowledge, Relevance of Knowledge, Applicability of Knowledge, Level of Knowledge, Dynamic of Knowledge, Expression of Knowledge, Service Boundaries, Knowledge Abstraction, Knowledge Action, and Knowledge Structure. [16], [17]

These KM-Dimensions depict a KM-Vector that describes the KM-requirements of users in the business layer. A bundle of KM-Services defines therefore the functional requirements for an enterprise KM system in the business layer.

Following five parameters are used to describe the KM-Service "Full Text Search":

*Name*: is a unique identifier.

*Description*: is a short description of the service.

*Benefit*: points out the characteristics of the service.

*Models*: gives the knowledge model types that can be used to manage this service.

*Vector:* semantic representation of the service vector.

Using such a formal description like the KM-Service vector, a semantic service repository can be built, that overcomes the drawbacks of current existing Web-Service UDDIs. The enrichment of service repositories with semantic information has been discussed by [7]. In the following the implementation of such a semantic enriched service framework will be discussed.

**Table 1.** Presents a description of the KM-Service Full Text Search by using a KM-Service vector for a formal description

| Name | Full Text Search |
|------|------------------|
| Description | The full text search searches for the occurrence of a string without relevance of content or semantics. |
| Benefit | The full text search is an easy to use and easy to implement search feature. The technological differences are the type of implementation, the index and therefore the speed of the results. This service strongly depends on the information carrier and if the service can use adapters to this information carrier. |
| Models | Knowledge Resource Model |
| Vector | $(v_r{=}e, v_m{=}e, v_u{=}i, v_{tu}{=}pre, v_{ts}{=}pre, v_o{=}c, v_s{=}hs, v_{lc}{=}\text{-}, v_{rel}{=}r,$ $v_{app}{=}o, v_l{=}o,\ v_d{=}s, v_{ex}{=}\text{-}, v_b{=}r, v_{abs}{=}i, v_{act}{=}i, v_{str}{=}ns)$ |

### 3.4 KM-Meta-Service-Framework: A Context Independent Implementation

The previously described KM-Service framework is based on selected KM-Dimensions. To enable a more flexible approach that allows for the definition of any KM-Dimensions by the organisation a Meta-Service-Framework has to be used.

Such a framework is semantically independent which means that dimensions can be easily adapted or exchanged therefore enabling the definition of individual KM-Frameworks and providing standard algorithms for analysing, simulating or verifying a KM-System.

The above-mentioned method is completely independent from the type and domain of KM-Dimensions. The Meta KM-Framework therefore defines an Enterprise KM-Ssystem (E-KMS) entirely on the basis of KM-Services.

The concrete value of the vector is represented by the object value. The value allows for storing semantic description and the mapping into a computable number.

The following figure 1 describes the Meta-Service-Framework by presenting the major UML classes.

## 4   Service-Based KM-Platform: A Realisation Scenario

This section gives an overview on a service-based realisation of an IT-based E-KMS. The KM-Service framework is seen as the classification concept of the UDDI repositories. It is reasonable that the organisations will develop their own KM-Service-Framework and will therefore install an organisational UDDI. The necessary KM-Services will be registered in the organisational UDDI.

The Web-Services implementing KM-Services are deployed by vendors and categorised using UDDI Services (KM-Framework). The KM-Dimensions are used to classify these KM-Services in the organisational service repository (UDDI). All user requests are coordinated by the KM-portal that uses a special service selection algorithm to find the most appropriate KM-Service either in the organisational service repository or in external service repositories.

The PROMOTE® platform contains special process models to manage KM-Services. Each user has access rights to certain knowledge management processes and knowledge services. When performing a knowledge intensive task, the user gets support by KM-services that are either related to the person, or related to the knowledge intensive task.

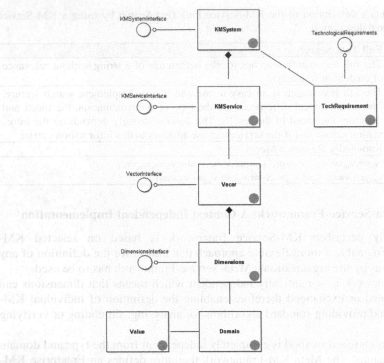

**Fig. 1.** The Meta-Service-Framework: The value class is concerned with the mapping of the domains to computable numbers. The domain class defines the possible state per dimension, whereas a bundle of dimensions defines the service vector. The KMservice is described by the service vector which is compared to the requirement vector. Technical requirements are listed in an own class

This leads to the definition of the business process that identifies the knowledge intensive tasks, the semantic framework that instantiates the semantic service framework and the knowledge management services that indicate Web-Services fulfilling the required operations.

KM-Services therefore support the execution of knowledge management processes in a user centric and flexible way. This architecture enables a very dynamic KM-approach by separating the technical implementation from the semantic requirements.

## 5  Summary

This paper introduces a new viewpoint on knowledge management – the service based approach – to enable the integration of KM into existing management approaches and discusses the possible implementation using a Meta-Service-Framework.

The process-oriented knowledge management of PROMOTE® has been used as a concept to define knowledge management requirements on the basis of business needs. The KM-Services approach has been introduced to implement the KM-system on basis of the processes oriented knowledge management.

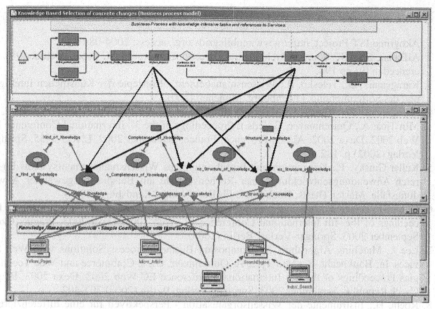

**Fig. 2.** Shows the definition of the semantic context of a business process at the top, the semantic framework using knowledge dimensions in the middle and Knowledge Management Services at the bottom of the picture

The KM-Service-Framework has been introduced to enable analysis, simulation and evaluation of KM-requirements and KM-solutions.

A Meta-Service-Framework has been defined to make the KM-Service-Framework adaptable.

Interesting questions for the future can be the identification of different knowledge management strategies in selecting KM-Services. New KM-Service-selection algorithms like heuristics could enable a usable configuration process for very dynamic future KM-platforms.

These ongoing questions are covered in the current running EU-project Akogrimo (FP6-2003-IST2-004293) [1] where a Next Generation Grid Framework will be developed strongly coupled with mobile networks. The above mentioned approach is used for the semantic distinction of different services and for the maintenance of the service repositories.

## Acknowledgement

We thank our partners FIDUCIA and INTERAMERICAN for the fruitful cooperation in the PROMOTE project providing test beds in the field of software development and legal case management. Both partners influenced the development of the PROMOTE-approach by providing end user requirements and business objective for Knowledge Management.

The EC-Project run within the European Knowledge Management Forum (EKMF) exchanging experiences on the KnowledgeBoard.

# References

1. Akogrimo IST Project, http://www.mobilegrids.org/, access: 2004-08-03
2. AlBanna, S.: CSC Sources Architectural Directions, internal CSC paper (October 98), referenced in [9] pp 198.
3. Karagiannis, D., Telesko, R.: Wissensmanagement - Konzepte der Künstlichen Intelligenz und des Softcomputing. Oldenbourg, München (2001)
4. Karagiannis, D., Kühn, H.: Metamodelling Platforms. Invited Paper. In: Bauknecht, K., Min Tjoa, A., Quirchmayer, G. (eds.): Proceedings of the 3rd International Conference EC-Web 2002. Dexa 2002, Aix-en-Provence, France, September 2002, LNCS 2455, Springer-Verlag (2002) p. 182.
5. Keller Ginsky, P.: Konzeption und Einführung eines Wissensmanagementsystems im Bereich Anwendungsentwicklung einer Rechenzentrale am Beispiel ausgewählter Anwendungsfälle. Master Thesis, Hochschule für Berufstätige, Rendsburg (2000)
6. Kühn, H., Bayer, F., Junginger, S., Karagiannis, D.: Enterprise Model Integration. In: Proceedings of the 4th International Conference EC-Web 2003. Dexa 2003, Prague, Czech, September 2003, Springer-Verlag, Berlin (2003)
7. Lee J.: Matching Algorithms for Composing Business Process Solutions with Web Services. In: Bauknecht, K., Min Tjoa, A, Quirchmayr, G.: E-Commerce and Web Technologies Proceedings of the 4th International Conference EC-Web 2003. Dexa 2003, Prague, Czech Republik, September 2003, Springer-Verlag, Berlin (2003) 393-402
8. Roehl, H.: Instrumente der Wissensorganisation - Perspektiven für eine differenzierende Interventionspolitik. PhD Thesis, Wiesbaden (2000)
9. Schwendenwein, G.: Wissensmanagment in der Beratung. PhD-thesis, Vienna University of Technology, Vienna (1999)
10. Sivan, Y.: Nine Keys to a Knowledge Infrastructure: A Proposed Analytic Framework for Organizational Knowledge Management. Harvard University (March 2001) http://www.pirp.harvard.edu/publications/pdf-blurb.asp?id=474, access: 2004-08-04
11. Sleeper, B.: Defining Web Services. The Stencil Group (June 2001) http://www.perfectxml.com/Xanalysis/TSG/WebServices.asp, access: 2004-08-03
12. Telesko, R., Karagiannis, D., Woitsch, R.: Knowledge Management Concepts and Tools: The PROMOTE Project. In: Gronau, N.: Wissensmanagement Systeme-Anwendungen-Technologien, Shaker Verlag, Aachen (2001), 95-112
13. Turner, M., Budgen, D., Brereton, P.: Turning Software into a Service. In: IEEE Computer (Oct. 2003) 38-44
14. Valente, A., Housel T.: A Framework to Analyze and Compare Knowledge Management Tools. In: Proceedings of the Knowledge-Based Intelligent Information Enineering Systems and Allied Technologies (KES2001), IOS Press, Ohmsha (2001)
15. W3c Web-Service Activity, http://www.w3.org/TR/ws-gloss/, access: 2004-08-04
16. Woitsch, R., Karagiannis, D.: Knowledge Management Service Based Organisation. In: Gronau N.: Wissensmanagement: Potentiale – Konzepte – Werkzeuge. GITO Verlag, Berlin (2003) 141 - 155
17. Woitsch, R.: Knowledge Management Services as a Basic Concept for Enterprise Knowledge Management Systems. In: Tochtermann, K., Maurer, H. (eds): Proceedings of the 3rd International Conference on Knowledge Management (I-Know03), July 2-4 2003, Graz (2003) 523-531

# Natural Language Expansion
# of Web Service Interoperability

Kurt Englmeier[1], Josiane Mothe[2], and Fionn Murtagh[3]

[1] LemonLabs GmbH, Munich, Germany
KurtEnglmeier@computer.org
[2] Université Paul Sabatier, Institut de Recherche en Informatique de Toulouse, France
Mothe@irit.fr
[3] Royal Holloway University of London, Department of Computer Science, UK
fionn@cs.rhul.ac.uk

**Abstract.** This paper presents the Web Service (WS)-Talk interface Layer, a structured natural language interface for the inter-service communication that extends service virtualization to strengthen consumer self-service. While providers will concentrate more on the technical levels of activation and communication within a service network, the users, i.e. the service consumers, will form ad-hoc collaborations between services at the semantic level that suit their own specific needs. We present the Web Service (WS)-Talk layer as a structured-language interface for Web services. This "open building block" can be implemented by both the service designers who as providers are more concerned with the architecture of the underlying service model and the service consumers who as users will seek to specify Web services as solutions to specific problems. Through a semantic layer, WS-Talk creates an abstraction layer that enables views on services expressed in natural language.

## 1 Introduction

Web services is the second generation of Internet tools to connect people to things they are dealing with. They are not connecting people with HTML Web pages; they are connecting their business applications with those of their colleagues, customers, partners and suppliers. By employing Web services people expect to respond quickly to customer demands and to capitalize on new market opportunities. Web services could in fact revolutionize the way we develop applications like the Internet itself changed our life [1]. And the rapid adoption of Web services is spurred on by the benefits they bring to collaborative communities. Connecting, however, exploits human relationships; service designers and service consumers (or requesters) working as a community define the architecture of their Web services collaboratively but each for their own benefit. Technologies used to set up and maintain Web services, help such communities create small, task-specific applications with software modules that can be used and re-used.

Standards are undoubtedly critically important for Web service technologies. They are a pre-requisite for interoperability. Users want their Web services to link and interact with those of their partners and colleagues in a standardized way, yet, personalized to their needs and preferences. The launch of XML opened avenues for a completely new type of interoperability of software across networks. The desire to use

D. Karagiannis and U. Reimer (Eds.): PAKM 2004, LNAI 3336, pp. 441–452, 2004.

each other's applications in order to develop new ad-hoc services and appliances seemed to be within reach. In the meantime the sobering truth about semantic Web standards is that they are not the silver bullet they were once conceived to be. Even though they support interoperability, developing large and complex domain-specific applications is still complicated and time consuming. Once implementation commences, it is often difficult to retract back to the specification in order to correct problems [2].

Service virtualization is one of the staple features of Web service interoperability. It typically creates a proxy of the Web service that hides implementation details from service consumers. Service virtualization includes a lot of tasks such as encryption, signature validation and message transformation, just to name a few. Its main focus, however, is the importance of consumer self-service. From the growing proliferation of Web service networks arises a growing network complexity typically comprising lot of details specified by different people and exposed to frequent changes over time. Consumer self-service intends to involve users on the basis of their past experience and competence in the specification of service identification and communication. Consumer self-provisioning, service selection, and service monitoring makes it possible for an organization to manage many consumers without blowing the budget of a large technical support staff. With the integration of natural language, WS-Talk drives this aspect even further. The definition of resources [3] benefits more from the direct involvement of all those creating and using Web services. At the organizational and market levels it is easier to reach an agreement on a suitable vocabulary than to design complicated XML models that can not be understood by users.

The paper is organized as follows: section 2 outlines the rationale and advantages of extending service virtualization by natural language (NL). Section 3 explains how natural language can be applied in service lookup and discovery. It introduces the concept of "enterprise talk" that reflects a certain domain, the organizational business or a market sector, for instance, including its respective tasks, processes, and operations. Section 4 describes how organization of Web services takes place in a semantic context. Design details of WS-Talk enriched with examples from its first prototypical realization are presented in section 5. Section 6 concludes.

## 2   Consumer Self-service: A Scenario

The conceptual business model or the business architecture [4] is a formal description of business processes established in a certain domain. Typically it is derived from a set of use cases that illustrate processes as they appear in domains such as production, customer relationship management or market analysis, just to name a few. A simple example of such a process could be the on-line reservation system of a cinema which includes the selection of a particular performance of a movie and of the number of required seats, and confirming the reservation back to the filmgoers. In this example a reservation manager co-operates with a performance manager that knows about the different movies and the dates they are shown and with a room manager that knows about the cinema's rooms and their capacities and availability of seats. The different managers and their interaction schema are defined in the conceptual business model or in the conceptual service model if the cinema resorts to Web service for the realization of its reservation system.

The conceptual service model maps the organizational schema of (business) processes into an architecture of Web services and, that is, it composes adequately Web services to realize the required processes [5]. The whole model is typically broken down into a hierarchical structure of sub-models on different levels of granularity. The different Web services emerge from their corresponding sub-model and are orchestrated according to the conceptual model's layout. Throughout this paper we concentrate on the design of the conceptual model and how natural language could enhance the efficiency in designing the model and its mapping features. Designing the conceptual model is realized under the assumption that the domain is completely known *a priori*. "Completely" means both in this case: the designers creating an application have a comprehensive understanding of the business or of the problem domain and they have to know how the problem domain may evolve into the future. Neither is usually the case.

For the time being the development of the conceptual service model is by large in the hands of service designers and providers. The very last details of the model, however, are quite often unknown to the designers. The end users, the service consumers, for instance, are not always in the position to explain all the facets of their tasks including those that are supposed to be represented in the conceptual model. This phenomenon is not new. It has been well-known in application development for decades. In addition, the future evolution of the application can hardly be foreseen comprehensively in advance. Both factors provoke a continuous re-design process to specify the very last details of the model. WS-Talk's approach of consumer self-service is well within the spirit of Participatory Design [6] that advocates a strong involvement of end users in application design which helps to reveal important but often tacit issues of domain knowledge. Of course, the user's competence ends when design comes closer to specifications of fine-grained services (like processing of time series) and interfaces. Fine-grained models are the area of service designers that develop and agree on XML structures for the service interfaces and implement these services.

## 3 Web Service Lookup and Discovery

In principle, a user contacts a registry service for getting information about a type of service he or she wishes to use. The registry returns all services available that matches the criteria stated by the user. In a standard situation as shown in figure 1 the user just chooses which service to use, binds it over a transport, and executes its methods based on the description of the service provided by the registry [5]. In a Web service environment for the cinema, the system as service consumer leases ad hoc the different managers from service providers. The choice among competing providers is based on service quality and price. The data to be transported, such as name and telephone number of the filmgoer, seat lay-out of the room, and information about the performance are wrapped into (i.e. represented by) XML which describes structure and "meaning" of data. This wrapping process is typically defined in the transport layer of the Web services. A service consumer (or service requester) requiring a particular service describes this service and retrieves (i.e. "finds") useful services using this description. Using a pointer from the registry the consumer "binds" to the provider of the retrieved service. The service description contains all the necessary instructions for executing the service and handling its interfaces. The consumer then formats its instructions following the descriptions of the service, binds these instructions to a certain type of transport medium used by the underlying transport layer and sends the service the wrapped instructions over the transport. On the same way the consumer gets a reply from the execution of the service.

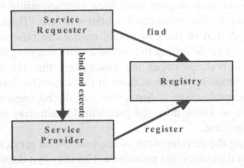

**Fig. 1.** The "find-bind-execute" paradigm in a standard situation of a service request

Hence, the situation depicted in figure 1 is simplified because in reality a service consumer is a hierarchy of different services that represent the conceptual service model at different levels of granularity. The registry then decomposes the request in accordance with the service model. This process is repeated top-down to the lowest level of granularity. The service consumer may also use a service proxy as shown in figure 2.

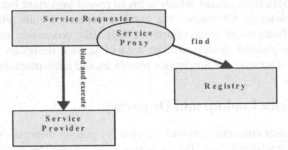

**Fig. 2.** A user proxy service orchestrates service composition and find-bind-execute processes

The proxy knows about the conceptual service model and is therefore in the position to compose correctly the services into the required application. It resides at the user's site which may be more convenient as the users may wish not expose organizational details of a company to the outside world, details that are well-described in the conceptual model.

We advocate now that the service proxy acts as "translator" proxy having automatic text analysis capabilities and being linked to the UDDI Registry. This enables the user to define in a flexible way and on a high level of granularity an application and eventually its composition out of a number of services on to the next lower level of granularity. This means the composition logic of the application is wrapped into natural language. For decomposition purposes the proxy analyses the request (query description) and transforms it into standard descriptions for service requests. The objective of the WS-Talk wrapper is exactly to endow the proxy with automatic text analysis capabilities. This means the communication with the UDDI Registry is wrapped into natural language.

This capability puts the end users in the position to express in their own language the application they require. Each company, and each industrial sector, has its specific domain talk used to describe products, services, objectives, processes, tasks, and so on. First of all we distil from this domain talk a structured representation and take the resulting condensed enterprise talk as quasi-standard for inter-application communication. Quite often domain talk is represented in taxonomies. More and more organizations are making a comprehensive taxonomy of the organization's content a high priority. Taxonomies as well as controlled vocabularies organize content and context of the organization's subject by grouping similar items into broad categories which themselves can be grouped onto ever-broader concept hierarchies. In essence, taxonomies provide a degree of structure to the organization's unstructured content. Because of a taxonomy reflecting the most important business categories, organizations that carry out the same business activities tend to have similar taxonomies. This fact and the rising importance of taxonomies to organizations brought us to the idea to harness this structured information as quasi-standard for the composition of a Web service network applied within an organization's scope, and beyond if similar taxonomies allow this expansion.

Strictly speaking the WS-Talk "translator" proxy consists of an interpreter interacting with a taxonomy maintained by a WS-Talk tool for capturing the enterprise talk. Through the structured-language interface, Web services can be implemented by both the software developer and technology end users who operate on the natural language interface. The objectives and advantages of this wrapper are:

1. a high availability for ad-hoc solutions for small technology user communities,
2. a high flexibility in responding to the dynamics of the community's environment to which it is applied,
3. fostering the proliferation of Web services as flexible means to construct complex and dynamic applications, and
4. passing on the design to technology users who are aware of the application area rather than technical people.

The objective of representing a domain context in natural language is to enable a flexible and easy management of enterprise "standards" necessary for domain-specific Web service composition. Such inner-enterprise "standards" have their origin in the enterprise talk, in its traditional way to represent business processes, products and resources. Sometimes the enterprise talk is reflected down to the labeling of functions and parameters in their software codes. Enterprise talk includes also descriptions of products and services. For external observers, it is sometimes hard to catch up on a discussion by car manufacturers, while the latter have problems to follow food producers, and so on. The issue becomes worse when it comes in combination with production details or IT-details.

Proprietary message-oriented middleware is currently the backbone of enterprise interoperability. Its interfaces and protocols reflect IT-specifics within the enterprise talk. The enormous amount of specific detail makes creating even intra-enterprise standards extremely complicated using a high level specification of a Web service standard. And in turn, this fact sheds light on the extreme complexity of establishing industry-wide standards. The situation looks equally grim on the side of industry-wide specifications. The problem of standardized specifications in capturing the complexity of the enterprise's reality is a severe technical limitation that hampers the broad proliferation of a technology that in fact could revolutionize our way of building applications. Facilitating the development of an architecture of context through sophisticated design tools eventually mitigates this problem, but cannot tackle it completely.

The reflection on this enterprise reality brought us to the idea of taking the enterprise talk as quasi-standard for inter-application communication. However, it is obvious that the approach can be applied as well in a context that is different from that of an enterprise. The definition of an open building block then consists of a transport layer representing a typical Web service interface and a context layer resorting to WS-Talk features for capturing the enterprise talk. The possibility to express a service description in natural language offers enormous flexibility.

## 4   Task Organization in WS-Talk

Natural language (NL) itself is not appropriate for programming, but NL referentiality is a key factor for the design of program instructions that are both machine-processable and understandable to humans [7]. For information retrieval and speech recognition systems [8] NL referentiality is essential and aspect-oriented programming shows how powerful program organizations can be realized based on instructions and structures expressed in NL [9], [10], [11]. In a Web service environment, services are propagated and identified through descriptions. To avoid ambiguity the descriptions have to be mapped correctly into a coherent context map that allows, at the same time, to locate the required service. Semantic co-ordinates – i.e. controlled vocabularies derived from taxonomies and structured according to concept hierarchies – are elements of orientation that can be communicated. Concept hierarchies representing semantic co-ordinates enable to develop a context map for the respective application domain. And, in addition, these hierarchies can be mapped into different natural languages in parallel [12]. To ensure that the descriptions are machine-processable (i.e. are interpreted correctly) we apply robust text mining methods that map descriptions into a suitable controlled vocabulary. From a different angle our solution resembles the current successful application of natural language processing in speech recognition systems where command languages are combined with NLP interfaces to provide for robustness.

Localizing a service in the context of WS-Talk is a two-step process. First a linguistic interface layer ensures that the service proxy "understands" a phrase expressed in an ad-hoc way in natural language. "Understanding" means mapping an information item like a Web service request into an appropriate request description that is developed by terms of the target language, the controlled vocabulary derived from taxonomies, and structured along concept hierarchies. The WS-Talk interpreter contains thus features to "translate" a service request or a service description (source language) into the target language generating automatically a request description that contains only terms of the controlled vocabulary. The request description can be a mixture of natural language and command language (see example below). The second step can be the translation of the respective standards as required by the Web services on a lower level of granularity. The "translation" of the essential content of a Web service – the automatic generation of service requests – thus has to contend with text mining methods that translate unambiguously service descriptions into suitable terms of the target language.

A robust text analysis method has to rely on predefined templates and pattern-based extraction rules to extract meaning. TFIDF (weighting-based) and LSI (latent semantic indexing) are the most prominent methods for the classification of content in unstructured textual data. The problem with such methods is that they can estimate the importance of the relevance of a term only in the shadow of global information about a larger corpus. And in addition, they cannot solve sufficiently the problem of ambiguity. This is a crucial drawback when the relevance estimation cannot or should not resort to a larger corpus because of performance purposes. To circumvent this problem in WS-Talk, we resort to the "vector voting method" [13]. In principle, each term in a text "votes" for a concept of the concept hierarchy if it contains a matching term. The more "votes" a concept receives, the stronger is the link between the text and that concept. In fact, the method is more complex as concept terms are not only those from the concept itself, but also those from related synonyms and terms associated with the concept ancestors. In the end, the technique uses the whole corresponding concept as index term.

A semantic co-ordinate system helps to determine the correct location of an information item like a service description or a user request within a domain-specific context. If we now deploy this approach in the context of Web services we implement the same features as presented above for service description and identification:

1. A Web service is described in the same way as a user defines a query using the concepts of the controlled vocabulary. This description is in any case easier and faster to specify than developing a corresponding XML or WSDL structure expressing the functionality of the service,

2. The matching mechanism to find a suitable service operates locates a document at the semantic co-ordinates that match a user query or a similar request from an intermediary service,

3. Instructions how to handle data that are passed from one service to another are also expressed in terms of the controlled vocabulary and may include command language components, and

4. The NLP part of the Web service hides unnecessary implementation details from service consumers, the non-technical end users.

Providing the controlled vocabulary in different languages in parallel has the advantage of exchanging service descriptions even across language boundaries, and this avoids the users having to apply a language they are not familiar with or having to be trained in a formal description language.

An exclusively private network eventually bypasses the installation of an UDDI Registry. In this case a WS-Talk "Translator" Service simply communicates with a WSDL interface to its "outside" world and to a network of facilitators with each one acting like a registry for a certain group of services. Facilitators and services can simply be implemented as independent program components of a more traditional application environment. The "inner" architecture of this web service network resembles that of a peer-to-peer network.

## 5   An Example of a Scenario from the WS-Talk Prototype

The following example scenario addresses a data mining environment supporting the economic analysis of an enterprise. An analyst may be interested in creating a Web service that searches time series related to economic activities (like the amount of incoming orders, productivity, exports, etc.) of all economic sectors that show a certain impact on a specific sector. The principal idea behind this analysis is that present activities in one industrial sector have an impact on the future economic situation of other sectors. In economic analysis, usually such an analysis helps to determine forecast indicators.

The analyst would create a Web service with the following specification: "Search for time series in our own and the OECD databases that represent all economic activities of all industrial sectors that have an impact on the products from the lubricants section of our company." This service doesn't exist so far. The service definition tool of WS-Talk "translates" the description into key words of the company's enterprise talk, i.e. transforms the original phrase in source language into terms of the target language, the company's controlled vocabulary. The "translation" process may include term replacements or query expansions. The concept of "products from the lubricants section of our company" may be replaced by a list of concrete product definitions. The subsequent localization process identifies the semantic co-ordinates corresponding to the key words resulting from the "translation" and searches for one or more existing services that have the same semantic co-ordinates. It is quite plausible that the required Web service has to be constructed from a number of services that exist within the company or located outside.

Let's assume, in our example there is a service available at OECD that enables the access to its time series database, a further one of the company that presents these time series in business charts, and a third one that identifies impact relationships between time series using time-warping as known from speech recognition and recently also applied in economic analysis. The latter service may come from the company's consultant. If the requested service is available, it will be propagated when its description is fully matched by the semantic co-ordinates of the existing services.

The services themselves have some co-ordination capabilities. From the localization they know which is the superior process they are related to and know, thus, the components they are co-operating with. The time-warping tool knows that it requires input from the OECD tool, and the OECD tool may at first confirm if this Web service of this specific company is authorized to retrieve OECD data. The exchange of data may be based on XML-specifications and further meta-data descriptions. We shall extend the above example with implementation details from the actual prototype of WS-Talk that also shows how the semantic co-ordination system is instrumented and how interfacing is developed. For the ambience of economic information, for instance, a powerful taxonomy has been produced that merges two of the most important structures in this field: Eurostat's NACE (Nomenclature des Activités dans la Communauté Européenne -systematic of the economic activities of the European Union) and the industry systematic of the ifo Institute for Economic Research.

Figure 3 shows how the unified taxonomy creates a semantic co-ordinate system that enables exact and automatic positioning of coherent information items like documents or service descriptions. The concept hierarchies presented make up the domain-talk of economic analysts. The concept hierarchies can be regarded as a con-

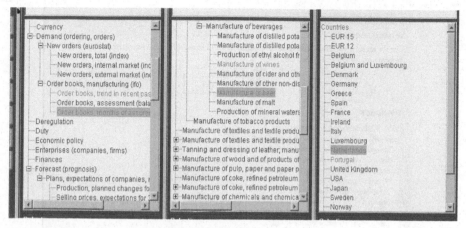

**Fig. 3.** Unified taxonomy

trolled vocabulary of the thematic area a European economic research institute is dealing with. They are constantly checked for completeness against the content covered by the text and time series documents reflecting comprehensively and in detail the organization's business. This approach can be extended easily towards descriptions of tasks that are related to economic analysis and to Web services performing or supporting these tasks.

The following table shows a part of a description of a service as being used for accessing and processing time series. A well-formulated description usually reflects precisely the nature of the essentials of the service and the way how to use it.

**Table 1.** Description section of a Web service that retrieves and processes time series

```
<Svc>
  ...
  <Desc>
    TimeSeries service
    (Retrieves time series specifies processing methods)
    Parameters:
    Types of processing methods:
    moving averages, smoothing::SMOOTH-MA::int
    period-on-period::PERIOD-ON-PERIOD
    ...
    Time scope, recent n periods::SCOPE::int
    Time scope, from a to b::SCOPE::Calendar::Calendar
    Time scope, from a on::SCOPE::Calendar
  </Desc>
</Svc>
```

A concept hierarchy containing an arrangement of task concepts and commands can then be used to analyze a service description and to represent its purpose by its most significant concepts. Commands are added to the title of the respective function like synonyms. The same holds for database specific codes of thematic concepts. In our example "Chemical Industry" is represented by the code "b25000" in the Eurostat database. In the same way a request expressed in natural language can be distilled to its most significant concepts from the same controlled vocabulary. This "translation

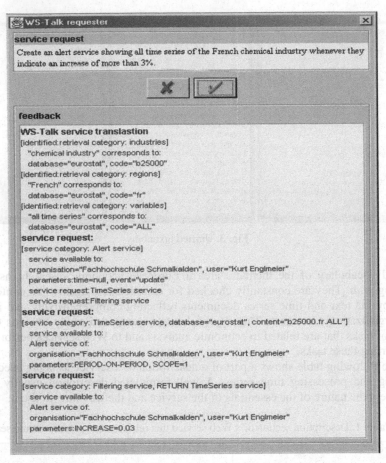

**Fig. 4.** Translation of a user request into the target language

process" is a preparatory step for the subsequent matching process that identifies service(s) necessary and suitable for the request. Figure 4 shows a user request for a service and the machine-processable "translation" of the request as feedback.

Concept hierarchies related to the tasks of economic analysis are organized in the same way. Like the entries of those hierarchies reflecting the thematic domain they are arranged according to main tasks and sub-tasks. In addition, the respective nodes point to the code or command necessary for the Web service specification.

## 6   Conclusions

Despite advances in the development of semantic Web standards, natural-language processing methods still form part of many techniques for enabling computers to understand and engage in human communication [8]. This is not at all a paradox since much information is passed or stored in natural language. Semantic Web standards do not replace NLP and vice versa, and the synthesis of both disciplines offers an enormous potential for a new generation of Web service technology. WS-Talk emerges from the cross-fertilization between semantic Web technologies and text mining methods. The idea behind this approach to support consumer self-service, i.e. to enable small communities to set up ad-hoc Web services using their own language instead of resorting to tools too complicated for them to define or modify their own context architecture.

A crucial component of such a design environment is the automatic and precise transformer of a Web service description into the catalogue logic of the respective application domain. This transformer resorts to methods supporting semantic context-awareness. It resides on the users' side putting them in the position to describe the services they require in their ambience.

Allowing software developers and service consumers to write an interface specification in their own words (i.e. allowing all to become context architectures), to avoid the complicated process of reaching an enterprise-wide agreement on this interface standard, sounds first of all like shutting a Pandora's box in favor of opening another one. However, as we harness only the most stable part of Web service specifications we also embark only on text analysis and information mapping methods that are in the position to tackle adequately the problem of ambiguity in interpreting service request and correctly locating the adequate services.

Future applications will emerge from networks of Web services that are defined within an organization and are used across the organizations' boundaries and the architects will be service providers and service consumers. The example of WS-Talk shows that, beside semantic Web specifications, natural language processing has a powerful role in these networks as it allows non-technical people to set up and maintain essential parts of a company's palette of services.

## Acknowledgement

Research outlined in this paper is part of the project WS-Talk that is supported by the European Commission under the Sixth Framework Programme (COOP-006026). However views expressed herein are ours and do not necessarily correspond to the WS-Talk consortium.

## References

1. Filman, R.E.: Semantic Services. IEEE Internet Computing 7(4) (2003) 4-6
2. Shirky, C.: Web Services and Context Horizons. IEEE Computer 35(9) (2002) 98-100
3. WebServices.Org: New Specifications Intended to Harmonzie Grid and Web Service Standards. http://www.webservices.org/ index.php/article/view/1314/ January (2004)
4. Fowler, M.: UML Distilled: Applying the Standard Object Modelling Language. Addison-Wesley, Reading USA (1997)
5. McGovern, J., Tyagi, S., Stevens, M., Mathew, S.: Java Web Service Architecture. Morgan Kaufmann Publishers, San Francisco USA (2003)
6. Winograd, T.: Bringing Design to Software. ACM Press, New York USA (1996)
7. Lopes, C.V., Dourish, P., Lorenz, D.H., Lieberherr, K.: Beyond AOP: toward naturalistic programming. ACM SIGPLAN Notices 38(December) (2003) 34-43
8. Ciravegna, F., Harabagiu, S.: Recent Advances in Natural Language Processing. IEEE Intelligent Systems 18(1) (2003) 12-13

9. Kiczales, G., Lamping, J., Mendhekar, M., Maeda, C., Lopes, C., Loingtier, J.-M., Irwin, J.:
   Aspect-Oriented Programming. In: proc. of the European Conference on Object-Oriented
   Programming (ECOOP'97) (1997)
10. Miller, L.A.,: Natural Language Programming: Styles, Strategies, and Contrasts. IBM Sys-
    tems Journal 20(2) (1981) 184-215
11. Nardi, B.: A Small Matter of Programming: Perspectives on End User Computing. MIT
    Press, Cambridge USA (1993)
12. Englmeier, K., Mothe, J.: Natural language meets semantic web.
    http://www.ktweb.org/doc/Englmeier-NLP-SW.pdf July (2003)
13. Mothe, J., Chrisment, C., Dousset, B., Alaux, J.: DocCube: Multi-Dimensional Visualisa-
    tion and Exploration of Large Document Sets. Journal of the American Society for Infor-
    mation Science and Technology 54(March) (2003) 650-659

# Developing Cooperative Environment Web Services Based on Action Research

Renate Motschnig-Pitrik, Michael Derntl, and Juergen Mangler

University of Vienna
Department of Computer Science and Business Informatics
Rathausstrasse 19/9, 1010 Vienna, Austria
{renate.motschnig,michael.derntl,juergen.mangler}@univie.ac.at

**Abstract.** Current technology has disappointed many users of cooperative learning environments by its complexity and only slow and tough adaptability to specific users' requirements. In order to compensate for these deficiencies, we use Action Research to guide us in a process in which we co-develop and improve open source, Web service based modules that directly and intuitively support learning, cooperation, and facilitation processes based on users' experiences. In this paper we characterize selected services, sketch our environment and propose an accompanying research procedure that allows us to assess and cyclically improve and extend our tools to closely match both their underlying didactics and users' needs.

## 1 Introduction

Several commercial tools supporting cooperative learning do not fully perform as expected. They tend to offer extensive functionality and hence are sophisticated in both their use and installation in a given environment. Often, they fail to support their users in their specific didactic designs or cooperative endeavors. Based on this observation, our goal is to develop a pool or toolbox of open source modules that support cooperative, blended learning in academic as well as industrial environments. Appropriate web support modules (such as discussion forums, shared workspaces, or collaborative text production) have the potential to improve cooperation and communication in these knowledge-based environments and the potential to include some of the tacit and informal knowledge. In general the proposed models support organizational knowledge gathering and management processes. By intention, we resist the temptation to implement an extensive set of services that are universally applicable. Instead, we focus on a well-defined set of interpersonal and educational values that we strive to support in our facilitative way of conducting courses. In brief, these values stem from a Person-Centered [15, 16], humanistic perspective and can be acquired through self-initiated learning, experiential learning, whole-person learning, solving authentic problems, learning from peers, active involvement of participants in all aspects of teaching/learning [12].

In this paper we focus on the strategy and accompanying research procedure while developing *Cooperative Environment Web Services* (*CEWebS*) [9] incrementally. Each service module is based on the practice gained from conducting academic courses, e.g. on Web Engineering, Project Management, etc., modeling them as scenarios and reusable patterns [5], and deriving the required support to be shared be-

D. Karagiannis and U. Reimer (Eds.): PAKM 2004, LNAI 3336, pp. 453–462, 2004.
© Springer-Verlag Berlin Heidelberg 2004

tween Web service and facilitator [4]. Since typically courses are repeated each year or semester, there is potential for improvement, redesign, and extension, if instructors view themselves both as practitioners and researchers. This process results in a methodology that has become known as *Participatory Action Research* (e.g., [14]).

The paper is organized as follows. The next Section introduces our extended Action Research framework that we employ and appreciate in the context of developing, extending, and customizing our Web service based environment. Section three briefly sketches the characteristics of our approach and tracks a selected Web service module through the individual phases in the Action Research process. Section four presents the resulting CEWebS architecture and describes its current status and open source availability. We conclude by sharing our plans for future practice and research in the realm of creative and effective cooperation and learning.

## 2    A Framework for Participatory Action Research

Besides the development of a clean technical solution, our goal is to propose a thoughtful confluence of methods and tools from the social and technical sciences to allow for systematic research and assessment of blended cooperation and learning across organizations. Since, typically, educators or project coordinators themselves research their innovative blended learning practices and apply their learning and insight iteratively in successive course cycles, participatory Action Research (AR), if carefully adopted, qualifies in providing the overall research framework. We propose to base this framework on visual, conceptual models of cooperation and learning processes and to complement it with a mix of qualitative and quantitative methods for evaluation, specifically designed to overcome the shortcomings of sole AR.

According to Baskerville [2], the ideal domain of AR is characterized by a social setting where:

- The researcher is actively involved, with expected benefit for research and organization,
- The knowledge obtained can be immediately applied, based on a clear conceptual framework,
- The research is a (typically cyclical) process linking theory and practice.

In general, AR is appreciated for integrating and concurrently advancing both practical and theoretical aspects. It accompanies real change effected by real actions in real organizations and thus has immediate validity for the hosting organization. All three characteristics fully apply in our setting. AR, however, is also criticized [8] for:

- lacking methodological precision,
- lacking controllability, due to the complexity and fuzziness of real environments,
- being subjective or biased, due to the researchers' deep personal involvement,
- delivering results that are difficult to generalize.

Although this criticism seems to be inherent in the nature of AR, we have begun to compensate this by complementing AR with a mix of empirical methods. This combined procedure, as will be illustrated below, re-establishes controllability and objectivity to a significant degree and, through the use of explicit conceptual models, provides paths for generalization of results across organizational boundaries.

According to the prevalent AR description by [18], five phases are iterated:
1. *Diagnosing,*
2. *Action planning,*
3. *Action taking,*
4. *Evaluating,* and
5. *Specifying learning.*

In order to overcome most of the difficulties of AR mentioned above, we propose to complement these basic phases by situated investigation methods that contribute empirical studies regarding those aspects that are amenable to traditional investigation. The resulting framework is sketched in Fig. 1 and elaborated below.

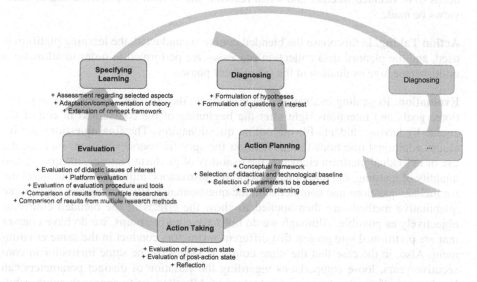

**Fig. 1.** Proposed extensions to the basic Action Research cycle [10]

In each phase we – as practitioners and researchers – consider three interrelated aspects:

- Didactic baseline,
- Learning platform (technological support), and
- Evaluation process.

**Diagnosing.** Initially, the problems that shall be overcome by the desired change are investigated. In the context of blended learning we ask questions such as: What is the organization's/department's current situation regarding the use of New Media? Who are the persons we deal with? Where do we want to get? What didactic baseline underlies teaching/learning? Which tools could we use? What are we interested in?

**Action Planning.** Based on a conceptual framework, the actions that lead to the desired future state are planned. Since, in our case the desired future state is quite complex, namely "improved teaching/learning", it requires controlled experimentation and can only be approached in each cycle. First, the didactic baseline or, in other words, the learning paradigm (humanistic education in our case) needs to be selected.

Second, we suggest using visual scenarios that model the activity flows in educational processes as the conceptual framework. This is because such scenarios are formal enough to allow for comparisons and specifications of learning platform elements, and are sufficiently intuitive to be understood by educators. Regarding the platform, the elements/features needed to support the selected didactical approach need to be selected and adapted and/or implemented (or at least prototyped). Regarding the evaluation, we need to formulate research questions, select the parameters to be observed along with appropriate methods and tools, and plan the evaluation process. For example, the questions to be included in online questionnaires need to be formulated as well as the time frames, in which the questionnaires shall be completed. Further, it needs to be decided whether and when reaction sheets shall be collected and/or interviews be made.

**Action Taking.** In this phase the blended course is conducted, the learning platform is used, and the planned data collection processes are performed in order to allow for a multi-perspective evaluation in the subsequent phase.

**Evaluation.** Regarding evaluation, we investigate the students' motivation, expectations, goals and intentions right after the beginning of the course and in end of the course by having students fill out online questionnaires. The final questionnaire includes additional questions that depend on the specific course situation, such as: the use of individual platform elements, the usability of platform features, the quality and quantity of learning, the role of team work, the instructors' attitudes, etc. Furthermore, we include questions and comments on the questionnaire. Histograms and appropriate quantitative methods are then applied to show the effects of the blended course as objectively as possible. Although we do not have control groups, we do have courses that are partitioned into groups that different instructors conduct in the same environment. Also, in the case that the same course is taught by the same instructor in consecutive years, loose comparisons regarding the variation of distinct parameters can be obtained. Thus, iterations, a core feature of AR, allow us to approach comparability between groups, although not as rigidly as in a classical experimental design employing control groups. It is our goal that open source learning platform modules that support reusable learning scenarios will enable comparability of parameters and results across organizations.

**Specifying Learning.** Learning ideally should be amenable to generalization in order to have more effect. In our case, most learning, clearly, comes from our own experience, both successes and failures, and from discussing one's practices with colleagues. Successful course designs are included in a repository of scenarios and reusable components thereof are specified as patterns [3]. The evaluation results further indicate which of the goals have been achieved, how the learning platform has been used and in which ways it was/was not found helpful. For example, the histogram in Fig. 2 shows that Web Engineering students preferred working with the CEWebS platform than with the commercial learning platform that was used to host the document workspaces. All of these results iteratively flow into the next cycle. As a side effect, the histograms indicate the influence of individual instructors on platform usage in general (see also [11]).

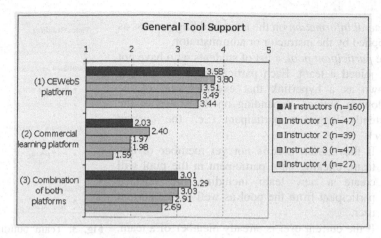

**Fig. 2.** General tool support in Web Engineering (1 = *low* ... 5 = *high*)

## 3   CEWebS Sample: From User Requirements to Web Services

**Diagnosing.** In the blended learning courses we conduct students collaboratively solve problems or elaborate contributions in small teams of about 2 – 5 members. These teams are usually formed at an early stage during each course. In previous years, the instructors asked the students in the initial "course kickoff" meeting to build their desired team constellations. Each team wrote the resulting constellation on a piece of paper and handed it over to the instructor or to one of the tutors either directly after the meeting or during a subsequent meeting. On this basis the instructor or a tutor had to manually "import" the hand-written team sheets (including student identifiers, names, and e-mail addresses) into the learning platform. In a course with 15 or 25 students this may not be a problem, but:

- What about courses with several hundred students?
- What about team sheets with unreadable or erroneous handwriting?
- What about students who want to switch their team during the initial phases?
- What about team sheets getting lost?
- What about typing errors while entering team data?

In one specific case, the Web Engineering lab course conducted last year, we had over 350 students organized in 12 lab groups, each with about 8 teams. The lesson we learned was that we never wanted to have to manually enter any team constellation into a learning platform again. Therefore we unanimously decided to conceive and to implement a CEWebS module for *Online Team Building* for the next iteration.

**Action Planning.** From the problems observed the requirements were clear: we had to include an online module where students could build and manage their team constellations on their own. During the following semester students of another course were involved in elaborating a list of usability requirements they expected from the team building module.

The resulting specification is sketched in Fig. 3. The figure shows a generic visual template that is capable of supporting the complete team building process on one single, interactive Web page. The page consists of three major sections:

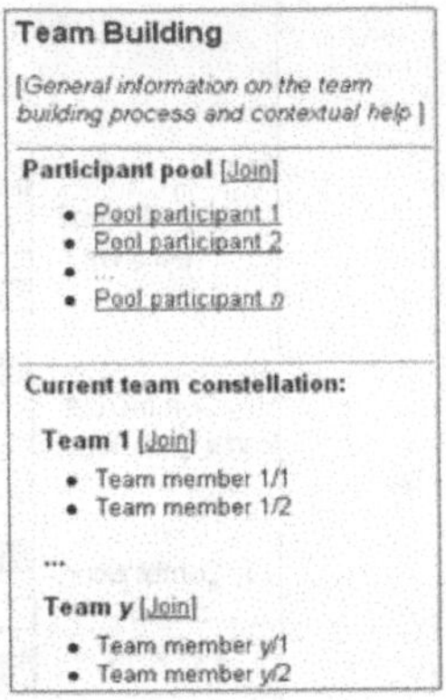

- *General information* on the team building process as supplied by the instructor or administrator.
- The *participant pool*, a list of students who have not yet joined a team. Each participant in the pool is shown as a hyperlink that executes one of the following actions, depending on the status of the currently logged-in participant (i.e., the *current user*):
  - If the current user is not yet member of any team, clicking on a participant in the pool will create a new team including the selected participant from the pool as well as the current user.
  - If the current user is already member of a team, the pool participant is added to the current user's team. Basically, this resembles an invitation to join the team.
- A list of currently existing teams (the current *team constellation*): Each team carries a hyperlink that, when clicked, makes the current user join that team.

**Team Building**

[*General information on the team building process and contextual help* ]

Participant pool [Join]
  - Pool participant 1
  - Pool participant 2
  - ...
  - Pool participant *n*

Current team constellation:

Team 1 [Join]
  - Team member 1/1
  - Team member 1/2

...

Team *y* [Join]
  - Team member *y*/1
  - Team member *y*/2

**Fig. 3.** Team building Web template

**Action Taking.** The learning platform module was then developed according to the above specification. This year, students in all teamwork-based courses that employed our learning platform were instructed to use the online team building module. Due to its simplicity, this took no more than about five minutes during the course. They immediately adopted the new module, producing smooth and quick team building processes in all courses and groups (for an example see the screenshot in Fig. 4).

**Evaluation and Specifying Learning.** As all instructors agreed to ask students to form teams online and we received neither negative feedback on the online module nor suggestions for improvement, we intend to keep its basic working principle for the next application cycle. However, there was one problem that caused confusion: Each time a team was formed for a specific learning activity, it was assigned a new team number. If the same team constellation is built for different learning activities within the same course, two equal team constellations may get different numbers assigned. This issue naturally produced some confusion among all concerned. It will be resolved for the upcoming semester by patching the team number generator to produce equal team numbers for equal team constellations.

These results motivate us to further develop CEWebS since it precisely confirms our thinking and experiences with learning platform usability. In the next questionnaires we plan to include questions regarding individual platform Web services to guide and prioritize future implementation and maintenance activities.

Currently, the following CEWebS modules are available and in use:

- *Contributions*: allows students to upload contributions and assignments online.
- *Diary*: enables students to keep track of their work, and facilitators to monitor teamwork progress online.
- *Discussion forum*: enables threaded discussions in online forums that may be dedicated to specific activities, instructors, or issues of interest.

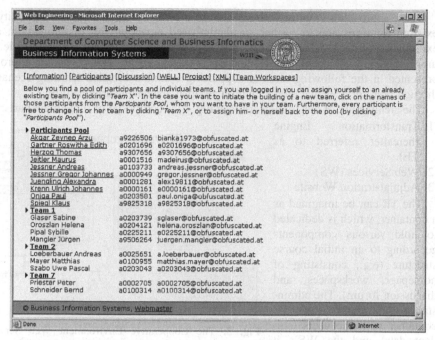

**Fig. 4.** Screenshot taken from the online team building module in Web Engineering

- *Evaluation*: a generic service that allows collecting feedback in the form of questionnaires, reaction sheets, or written evaluations.
- *Learning contract*: enables management of online learning contracts.
- *Participants & teams*: service for displaying course participants and collaborative building of student teams (compare the example above).
- *Wiki* [23]: allows administrative staff to collaboratively edit and structure the information pages on the learning platform.
- *Workspaces*: virtual document storage that enables students and teams to manage documents for particular learning activities (e.g., learning contracts) online.
- *XML Tools*: provides simple online tools for experimenting with different XML technologies (e.g., Schema, DTD, XPath, XSL, WSDL, etc.).

## 4 The CEWebS Architecture

Recently, Web services have drawn the attention of learning technology researchers and practitioners. Current approaches include for example:

- Decentralized, integrated support of Web-based learning processes [19],
- Personalization of such processes in intelligent tutoring systems through Web-service-based agents [7],
- Contract-based provision and discovery of distributed Reusable Learning Object (RLO) repositories [17], or
- Enhancing the functionality and interoperability of existing learning technology applications [1].

These approaches employ Web services to increase extensibility and flexibility of existing solutions and to further standards-based development, dissemination, and exploitation of desired functionality. Thereby, using Web services for blended learning purposes is all about sharing and open development. The particular approach presented in the following aims at supporting common blended learning scenarios through Web services that interact within an open, extensible architecture.

The architecture of our framework (see Fig. 5) is composed of three main parts:

1. Transformation Engine (hereafter referred to as TE)
2. Web Services (WS)
3. Administration Website

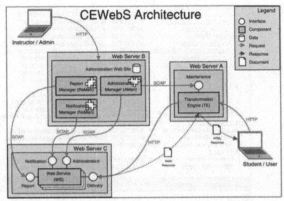

**Fig. 5.** The Cooperative Environment Web Services (CEWebS) architecture

The TE can be imagined as a container, which is dedicated to hold various components according to an initial course structure (e.g., consisting of homepage, workspaces, and discussion forum). The administrator initializes the TE container with the users (student data) and the WS's it should contain. Then he or she initializes and configures every WS with the user information and additional configuration data that may be required. That data is collected from the administrator via auto-generated, Web-based initialization wizards.

As the TE just consists of a simple, standardized SOAP (Simple Object Access Protocol) [21] interface, any existing learning platform can exploit the CEWebS architecture by implementing that interface. Thereby, the TE acts as the "link" component between the host platform, the users, and the WS's, by providing two main functionalities:

- Translating users' HTTP requests into Web service invocations
- Transforming the WS response via stylesheets (XSL, CSS) to meet the user interface guidelines given by the "surrounding" environment (e.g., some commercial learning platform such as WebCT [22]). The response from a WS is required to be a "raw" XML document that is defined as a subset of XHTML 1.0 [20].

The WS's are the central parts of the CEWebS architecture. Every TE can talk to an arbitrary number of WS's through a well-defined SOAP interface that has to be implemented by each WS. Each WS can hold multiple instances of user / configuration data, allowing it to be used by more than one TE. Additionally, each WS provides a formal description (XML Schema) of its configuration capabilities, enabling the Administration Manager to automatically generate user-friendly configuration wizards.

Finally, the Administration Website is a centralized service and user repository that additionally holds information about all TE's available. The Report Manager, which is part of the Administration Website, allows administrators to collect reports (e.g., a list of users that missed the submission deadline for some contribution) from each WS instance that implements the Report interface. Through the report interface the administrator or instructor always receives binary data, e.g. simple HTML pages, spreadsheets, PDF's, or pictures containing the solicited information.

The core of the architecture as described above is already working stably. Driven by additional requirements and conclusions drawn from each research/application cycle, several components – especially the Web services and the Administration Website – are still under development and perfective maintenance.

## 5  Discussion and Future Work

We have sketched a framework for cooperative blended learning and an accompanying research methodology that aims at developing and maintaining open-source, usable Web services that stem from and keep particularly close to the users' needs. These services can either be used in the form of a configurable toolbox, or equally be interlinked with commercial platforms. Initial experiences, users' reactions and empirical studies substantiate the effectiveness of our approach to facilitating cooperative blended learning [13]. From the social or psychological perspective we base our approach on the Person-Centered Approach stemming from humanistic psychology. This approach has proven to be most effective in furthering interpersonal relationships along with cooperation and significant learning.

Further research will take several directions. First, we are conceptually modeling generic learning processes that support Person-Centered educational values. We call the resulting conceptual models PCeL patterns [5] in order to support them with appropriate Web design elements in CEWebS [4]. These are intended to provide the computerized framework for deep and persistent learning on the one hand and to support and simplify the organization, administration, and evaluation of PCeL courses on the other hand. Second, we continue with case studies and Action Research on PCeL and, concurrently, improve the test instruments in order to be able to observe the effects of changes. Third, we are in the process of populating a virtual community of persons interested in the Person-Centered Approach in higher education (http://elearn.pri.univie.ac.at/pca) in order to have a medium to share experiences and coordinate research aiming to promote a science that is authentic [6] in so far as it inherently addresses the genuine questions of the researchers as persons involved in knowledge management and learning processes. Everybody interested in joining is welcome. Last but most challenging and influential is the field of staff development in the spirit of co-developing media-, personal-, and interpersonal competences in order to facilitate cooperative, blended learning most effectively.

## References

1. S. Apelt, "Using web services to extend an application to meet new requirements," IEEE Learning Technology Newsletter, vol. 6, 2004, pp. 19-20.
2. R. L. Baskerville, "Investigating Information Systems with Action Research," Communications of the Association for Information Systems, vol. 2, 1999, pp. http://cais.isworld.org/articles/2-19/.
3. M. Derntl, "The Person-Centered e-Learning Pattern Repository: Design for Reuse and Extensibility," Proc. ED-MEDIA'04 - World Conference on Educational Multimedia, Hypermedia, & Telecommunications, Lugano, Switzerland, 2004, pp. 3856-3861.

4. M. Derntl and J. Mangler, "Web Services for Blended Learning Patterns," Proc. IEEE International Conference on Advanced Learning Technologies, Joensuu, Finland, 2004
5. M. Derntl and R. Motschnig-Pitrik, "Patterns for Blended, Person-Centered Learning: Strategy, Concepts, Experiences, and Evaluation," Proc. 2004 ACM Symposium on Applied Computing (SAC), Nicosia, Cyprus, 2004, pp. 916-923.
6. R. Hutterer, "Authentic Science - Some Implications of Carl Rogers's Reflections on Science," Person-Centered Review, vol. 5, 1990, pp. 57-76.
7. K. Kabassi and M. Virvou, "Using Web Services for Personalised Web-based Learning," Educational Technology & Society, vol. 6, 2003, pp. 61-71.
8. N. Kock, "The three threats of action research: a discussion of methodological antidotes in the context of an information systems study," Decision Support Systems, vol. 1062, 2003, pp. 1-22.
9. J. Mangler and M. Derntl, "CEWebS - Cooperative Environment Web Services," Proc. 4th International Conference on Knowledge Management (I-KNOW '04), Graz, Austria, 2004
10. R. Motschnig-Pitrik, "An Action Research-Based Framework for Assessing Blended Learning Scenarios," Proc. ED-MEDIA'04 - World Conference on Educational Multimedia, Hypermedia, & Telecommunications, Lugano, Switzerland, 2004
11. R. Motschnig-Pitrik, M. Derntl, and J. Mangler, "Web-Support for Learning Contracts: Concept and Experiences," Proc. Second International Conference on Multimedia and Information & Communication Technologies in Education (m-ICTE'03), Badajoz, Spain, 2003
12. R. Motschnig-Pitrik and A. Holzinger, "Student-Centered Teaching Meets New Media: Concept and Case Study," IEEE Educational Technology & Society, vol. 5, 2002, pp. 160-172.
13. R. Motschnig-Pitrik and K. Mallich, "Effects of Person-Centered Attitudes on Professional and Social Competence in a Blended Learning Paradigm," IEEE Educational Technology & Society, to appear.
14. S. Ottosson, "Participation action research - A key to improved knowledge of management," Technovation, vol. 23, 2003, pp. 87-94.
15. C. R. Rogers, On Becoming a Person - A Psychotherapists View of Psychotherapy. Constable, London, 1961.
16. C. R. Rogers, Freedom to Learn for the 80's. Charles E. Merrill Publishing Company, Columbus, OH, 1983.
17. S. Sanchez, J. Parra, O. Sanjuàn, and M. A. Sicilia, "Learning object repositories as contract-based Web services," IEEE Learning Technology Newsletter, vol. 6, 2004, pp. 16-18.
18. G. I. Susman and R. D. Evered, "An assessment of the scientific merits of action research," Administrative Science Quarterly, vol. 23, 1978, pp. 582-603.
19. J. Torres, J. M. Dodero, and C. L. Padrón, "A Framework Based on Web Services Composition for the Adaptability of Complex and Dynamic Learning Processes," IEEE Learning Technology Newsletter, vol. 6, 2004, pp. 7-11.
20. W3C, "XHTML 1.0 The Extensible HyperText Markup Language (Second Edition)," available at http://www.w3.org/TR/xhtml1/ [accessed Jul 20, 2004], 2002.
21. W3C, "SOAP Specifications," available at http://www.w3.org/TR/soap [accessed Oct 8, 2003], 2004.
22. WebCT Inc., "WebCT - Learning without Limits," available at http://www.webct.com/ [accessed Apr 2, 2004], 2004.
23. Wikipedia, "Wiki," available at http://en.wikipedia.org/wiki/Wiki [accessed May 10, 2004], 2004.

# Acquiring and Refining Class Hierarchy Design of Web Application Integration Software

Satoshi Minegishi[1], Naoki Fukuta[2], Tadashi Iijima[3], and Takahira Yamaguchi[3]

[1] School of Science for Open and Environmental Systems, Keio University, 3-14-1 Hiyoshi
Kohoku-ku, Yokohama-shi Kanagawa-ken 223-8522, Japan
mine@ae.keio.ac.jp
[2] Department of Computer Science, Shizuoka University, 3-5-1 Johoku,
Hamamatsu-shi Shizuoka-ken 432-8011, Japan
fukuta@cs.inf.shizuoka.ac.jp
[3] Department of Administration Engineering, Keio University, 3-14-1 Hiyoshi, Kohoku-ku,
Yokohama-shi Kanagawa-ken 223-8522, Japan
{iijima,yamaguti}@ae.keio.ac.jp

**Abstract.** Classes and their hierarchy are one of important artifacts of software development. In contrast of ontology development, the base concepts of classes do not exist even in the mind of software designer at the first time of development. Therefore, software development process needs not only to support externalization of concepts, but also to support the conceptualization process of the design. In this paper, we investigate a class diagram design support method that is suitable for web application integration software. We discuss features and drawbacks of the method through a case study in a development process of a business support system.

## 1 Introduction

Web applications have become sufficiently comprehensive and stable to provide various services. These Web applications include not only services to make the Web itself more accessible (e.g., Google [1], a Web search engine), but also emerging services that are closely related to the real world in terms of weather information (e.g., Weather.com [2]) and product merchandising (Amazon.com [3]). Web applications integration software (WAIS) is a kind of software that integrates such useful Web applications [16]. WAIS will enable us to develop more advanced applications to meet user needs. WAIS also offers cost reduction for application developments.

In WAIS development, respective Web applications have their own input and output parameter types. WAIS should treat such I/O types appropriately inside the system. Construction of a WAIS may impose strong constraints against the system design, such as the type of I/O objects accompanying a Web application. Design of WAIS requires that many elements that are essential as the software components (parameters required for the I/O of a Web application) be provided before starting to design its class diagram. Conventional class diagram design support methods have proposed a procedure for creating a class diagram from a use-case diagram with robustness analysis [4], and a measure for evaluating the design appropriateness of the finished class diagram [5]. The problem is that no methodology has been well studied

D. Karagiannis and U. Reimer (Eds.): PAKM 2004, LNAI 3336, pp. 463–474, 2004.

for properly designing a class diagram that necessarily contains elements that is given before beginning the class diagram design. Accordingly, a design support procedure of a model should be developed that is applicable to design of a biased model affected by constraints of Web applications or similar frameworks.

Classes and their hierarchy are one of important artifacts of software development. In contrast of ontology development, the base concepts of classes do not exist even in the mind of software designer at the first time of development. Therefore, software development process needs not only to support externalization of concepts, but also to support the conceptualization process of the design.

In this paper, we investigate a class diagram design support method that is suitable for WAIS. We discuss features and drawbacks of the method through a case study in a development process of a business support system.

This paper is organized as follows: Section 2 proposes a design support method of a class diagram. Section 3 presents discussion of a business trip support system developed as a case study and applies the proposed class diagram design support method. In Section 4, we show some related studies and clarify the advantages of our proposed method. Section 5 concludes this paper and discuss about the relationship between knowledge management and our proposed method.

## 2 Class Diagram Design Support

This section proposes a design support method of a class diagram for WAIS development. Two types of support are proposed as the method: support by superficial information (syntactic information) and support using information on a semantic level. Lattice is used as the former support. We investigate the use of Lattice structure to by comparing distance and depth between elements.

The left end of Lattice is the shallowest and the right end of Lattice is the deepest. The depth is equivalent to the attribute number. We presume that it would be wrong to treat the attributes collectively in one class when the depth of each attribute of a certain class indicates a great difference. The difference in the depth was regarded as the difference in the attribute number. We inferred that the depth could be used as an index. Regarding the distance between elements, classes separated by a small distance were considered to be correlated. However, when few elements are available, a root element is routed and there is little actual correlation. Repeated up-and-down in small distances on Lattice also implies little correlation. For that reason, it was considered that two classes were correlated when they shared common multiple attributes, were in a parent-child relationship, and were located within a small distance. We assumed that this index would support the discovery of inclusion and succession relations.

Ontology is used for support using information on a semantic level. Ontology expresses the definition of conceptual relations. This study created Ontology according to DAML [6] and WordNet [7]. It was presumed that errors in a semantic level could be pointed out by matching Ontology and Lattice.

### 2.1 Model Design Support Method

This study employs the following two approaches of the class diagram design support method for software development incorporating a Web application:

**Approach A.**

Port information of a given Web application is set as an initial class diagram.

**Approach B.**

The conceptual definition structure of domain Ontology is applied to the class diagram.

## 2.2 Approach A

Approach A has multiple Web applications, as shown in Fig. 1; it defines their I/O ports as respective classes to produce an initial class diagram. An I/O port is a set of elements required for input and output. For example, we define the input ports of the Web application A in Fig. 1 (a, b, f, g) and the output ports (a, b, d, e, j, k) as the input class $A_i$ and the output class $A_o$, respectively. For all Web applications, ports required for input and output are used as attributes, and the class is designed for each of them. The initial class diagram is defined as a unified class comprising all these classes and an attribute set required in order to acquire the attribute value for the I/O of a Web application. This study defines a Web application as a service provided on the Web. Such service released at one site having multiple functions is considered as one Web application. For example, Tabi-no-Madoguchi [14] (we will call this as "Mytrip" henceforth), having the two functions of searching for a hotel and making a hotel reservation, is considered as one Web application.

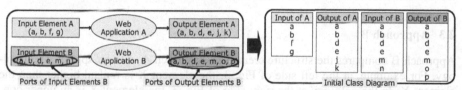

**Fig. 1.** An initial Class Diagram from I/O ports

A structure that is derived from a lattice is employed to implement Approach A. This study defines lattice as one space that includes a whole process from an empty set to a universal set by the gradual increase of elements. Lattice is constituted using the I/O port of a Web application. A class of Lattice is created according to the following procedure:

1. All attributes of the class is added as elements of the lattice.
2. When other classes are referred as a type in the attribute of the class (e.g. has associations to another class), the attributes of the referred classes are also added as elements of the lattice.
3. Repeat 2 until all the attributes included in the class become an atom.

   Then, a structure is constructed from the lattice by marking nodes as follows:

1. All nodes that only have elements as the same attributes of a class are marked.
2. All nodes that only have elements of a subset of a marked node are marked, and the nodes are linked. (Here, we call the newly marked node as a 'parent node'.)
3. Apply procedure 2 recursively.
4. The node that has no elements (empty node) is marked, and used as a root node of the structure.
5. Here, when a parent node has only one child, the parent node is unmarked.

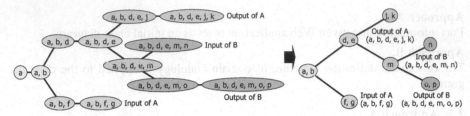

**Fig. 2.** A structure derived from the attribute lattice

Applying the above procedures from 1 to 4 to the initial four classes in Fig. 1, we get the structure in the left side of Fig. 2. The structure shows us the tree from generic nodes with common attributes to specific nodes with particular attributes. Furthermore, procedure 5 generates the right side of Fig. 2 from the left side of Fig. 2. It has property inheritance where the attributes in parent nodes are inherited to child nodes.

The total attribute number in a class diagram usually reaches several tens or more. Therefore, when all attributes are used as lattice elements, they are incomputable if they are to be used after computing the whole lattice. This study comprehends lattice as a mode of expression that represents the degree of refinement of a class diagram. It limits computation only to the required section. Here, extracted within four levels from the common parent marked nodes as candidates for the new class, where the level is distance of links between marked nodes.

## 2.3  Approach B

Approach B compares the structure created in Approach A with an appropriate ontology. For example, at the left side of Fig. 3, the element X is ranked higher than the element Y. In the ontology at the right side of Fig. 3, the element Y is an upper concept of the element X. Comparison between a class diagram and ontology can trigger a model designer to consider whether the conceptual definition is wrong or a wrong label is attached. Therefore it is supposed that comparison of a class diagram and ontology is effective in refinement of a class diagram.

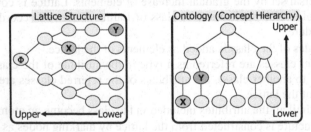

**Fig. 3.** Comparison with Ontology

## 3  Case Study

In the present business trip support system, when a user logs in, the system acquires his personal information. When the user enters a business trip schedule, the system proposes an appropriate train schedule and candidate hotels using his personal information; it makes necessary seat and hotel reservations. This business trip support system preserves, in its database, any changes made by the user against the system recommendation, such as changes in departure/arrival stations and departure/arrival times, alternative searches and new proposals, and previous use of the history of this system by the present user. This accumulated history enables the system to search again for a required item and thereafter propose a new schedule. The system employs a database to acquire the nearest station of origin or destination. When a previously visited place is input as the Origin or Destination, the system inputs its attribute value automatically using the database. This system cooperates with a business trip application system of a certain company. It has a mechanism for supporting the input of a schedule generated by this system to that business trip application system.

Search and reservation of trains or hotels are implemented using personal information such as the user's ID and password for using the Web application acquired at login, and using existing Web applications. The Web applications to be used include Jorudan [13] (train search), Mytrip (hotel search and reservation), JR Eki-Net [15] (train reservation), and the business trip application system mentioned above. Because this study aims at the design support of a class diagram when developing a system using a Web application, this business trip support system is presumed to be suitable as a case study.

## 3.1  Application of Model Design Support Method

A class is assigned to each of the input and output of a Web application as an initial class diagram of the business trip support system mentioned above. The proposed method stated in Section 2 is applied to this initial class diagram. It is verified whether a refined class diagram can be generated.

In system development, I/O attributes are extracted for every required Web application. In addition to this, although it is not the I/O attribute of Web application, attributes used for acquiring input attribute values for Web applications are 1) Business trip description, 2) Starting date, 3) Ending date, and 4) Origin. The initial class diagram produced from above-mentioned attributes is shown in Fig. 4.

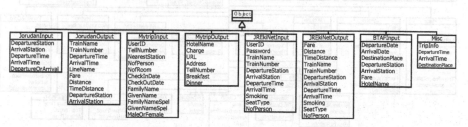

**Fig. 4.** The Initial Class Diagram

The system has 35 attributes, which include the I/O attributes of the above-mentioned Web applications and attributes for acquiring the input attribute values of the Web applications. Lattice was created with these 35 elements. Then, the initial class diagram was formulated for every Web application, defining each attribute set required for input and output as one class respectively. Fig. 5 shows in which position of Lattice these classes are located. Circles and triangles denote input classes and output classes, respectively. This Lattice indicates that classes are generally positioned in the left side of Lattice.

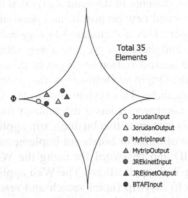

Total 35
Elements

○ JorudanInput
△ JorudanOutput
◎ MytripInput
▲ MytripOutput
● JREkinetInput
▲ JREkinetOutput
● BTAFInput

**Fig. 5.** Configuration of I/O Ports on Lattice

Next, attributes included in the final class diagram in the business trip support system (Fig. 6) were used as elements without using the above-mentioned method. Fig. 7 shows Lattice thus obtained. Squares and diamonds denote input classes and output classes, respectively. The section surrounded with a red curve is the class set up as the initial class diagram. The classes not surrounded with the red curve are classes related to the I/O of Web applications extracted out of the final class diagram designed at the development of the business trip support system (Fig. 6). The figure shows where of Lattice these classes correspond. In some cases, multiple classes share the attributes of the input or output of a Web application, so that one service has multiple inputs or outputs.

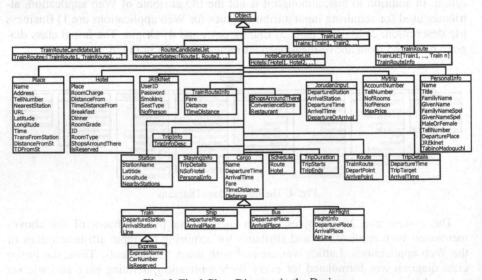

**Fig. 6.** Final Class Diagram in the Design

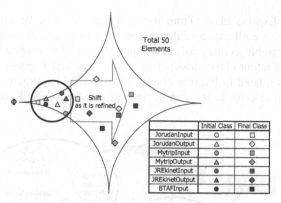

| | Initial Class | Final Class |
|---|---|---|
| JorudanInput | ○ | □ |
| JorudanOutput | △ | ◇ |
| MytripInput | ◉ | ▣ |
| MytripOutput | △ | ◆ |
| JREkinetInput | ● | ■ |
| JREkinetOutput | ▲ | ◆ |
| BTAFInput | ● | ■ |

**Fig. 7.** Shift on Lattice by Refinement

Comparison between the set of the initial classes (section surrounded by the red curve) with the set of the final classes (section outside the red curve) indicates that the former has fewer attributes per class than the latter. Therefore, the former tends toward the left side. That is, the last class has shifted to the right-hand side as compared with the first class. Fig. 7 implies that adding attributes to the initial class creates the final class. Because the initial class is a set of classes that are vital for use of a Web application, no attribute (element) would be deleted during refining into the final class diagram. If attributes (elements) on the interim class diagram are positioned on Lattice similarly, it is likely that attributes (elements) created during refinement from the initial to the interim may be judged unnecessary and deleted during refinement into the final class. However, we will treat only the change in refinement to the final class diagram from the initial class in this paper.

In output information on Jorudan, new elements were added by structuring on refining to the final class diagram from the initial class diagram. In addition, in the output of other Web applications such as Mytrip and JR Eki-Net, structuring caused the addition of new elements. For example, Train class that was newly created serves as the next input of JR Eki-Net. Thereby, coding was facilitated because only one class must necessarily be managed. Moreover, classifying outputs by type may improve maintainability and expandability. We conclude that elements that are added to the output information on each Web application are generated by structuring, which improves implementation efficiency.

The initial class diagram (Fig. 4) is then expressed with Lattice. Fig. 8 represents Sub-Lattices extracted from the common parent node, based on the above-mentioned proposition method – "Sub-Lattices extracted within four levels from the common parent node are assumed as candidates for the new class." JorudanOutput class, such as Departure station, Arrival station, Departure date/time, Arrival date/time, Fee, Distance, Time required, and Route name are inferred to be the classes that represent a train. When this system was actually developed, Express train class and Standard train class were separated finally, as shown in Fig. 6. Although a train had its Train number and Train name and an express train had its Route name in reality, they were deleted at this time because they were unimportant at the time of search or reservation. However, as Fig. 8 indicates, as Train name and Train number are classified in one common node, they can be separated into two classes. Therefore, Train class was inherited to be Express class (Train name, Train number). Because Fee, Time required, and Distance all express information on a train and its route, they were presumed to be separable as one class. Consequently, the class diagram was modified so that the JorudanOutput class consisted of Train class and Express class, and JREkiNetOutput class related to Express class. Because JREkiNetInput class had most attributes of Express class as its own attributes, as shown Fig. 8, it was replaced by Express class.

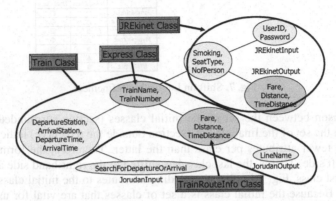

**Fig. 8.** Sub Lattices within Four Levels from the Common Parent Node

Because the MytripOutput class has information related with hotels, it changed into Hotel class. As TripStarts (at the time of a business trip opening day) and TripEnds (business trip end time) are common attributes in BTAFInput (BTAF means BusinessTripApplicationForm) class and Misc class, we can put together two attributes into a new class named TripDuration. Thus we get modified class diagram shown in Fig. 9 where gray classes are newly generated.

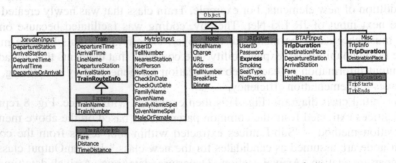

**Fig. 9.** Modified Class Diagram (After Approach A)

Ontology allows us to separate MytripInput class (the left side in Fig. 11). Because the Family name, Given name, Family name reading, Given name reading, and MaleOrFemale are classified as subordinate concepts of personal information in the Ontology in Fig. 10, these attributes can be collected into one class as personal information. For that reason, the class diagram is modified as the right side in Fig. 11.

**Fig. 10.** Ontology on Personal Information

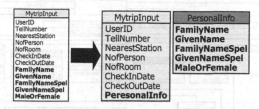

**Fig. 11.** Example of Class Diagram Restructuring

This study created Ontology as shown in Fig. 10 based on the ontology currently released by DAML (DARPA Agent Markup Language) [6]. DAML provides ontology on travel, which has no concepts regarding personal information. Instead, some ontology on a person was used to create the Ontology in this study. The Family name reading and Given name reading are expressions that are intrinsic to Japanese language: no currently-published existing ontology includes them. We added them considering that they are treated as a Family name or Given name.

When the output and input of cooperating Web applications (i.e., the output of train search and input of train reservation) have common attributes, they will be a part of a role. A role is a set of the I/O that defines one specific function when a Web application has multiple functions. Although not directly related to the refinement of a class diagram, a role, if known, may cancel the polysemy of a Web application.

The modified class diagram after Approach B is shown in Fig. 12. Gray classes are newly created classes; attributes changed in connection are shown in red. This class diagram was compared with the final class diagram (Fig. 13) designed when the business trip support system was developed. Classes in light gray and dark gray in Fig. 13 denote classes partially and completely supported with the presently proposed method, respectively.

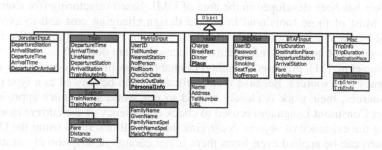

**Fig. 12.** Modified Class Diagram (After Approach B)

Therefore, it is considered that the presently proposed method can support discovery of inclusion and succession relations and separation of attribute sets commonly shared by others or close in a semantic sense. On the other hand, it cannot separate information that is intrinsic to each Web application. Furthermore, although architecture matching the user interface and objects was constructed in this case study, no framework for it could be prepared.

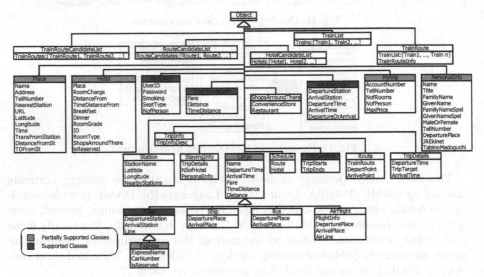

**Fig. 13.** Correlation with class diagram developed without using support method

## 4   Related Work

*Restructuring* [8] is a technique to refine the internal software structure. In the object oriented software development domain, we use the word *refactoring* [9] instead. In refactoring process, classes, variables, and methods are redistributed in order to facilitate future adaptations and extensions. Because it covers very wide area of incrementally development software process, our proposed method can be viewed as a variant of refactoring techniques. In last part of section 3, we demonstrated that our method can be applied to the refactoring process. But that is not our prior goal. Some methods and tools has been developed in the area of UML-based refactoring (for example, see [10]). Most of those tools tend to reduce design changing cost and to avoid errors caused by the change, not to improve the quality of refinement itself. We focus the improvement of quality of refinements for class diagram design.

Nytun et al. [11], proposed a method to enable modeling and consistency checking for legacy data sources. Because Web applications can be viewed as a type of legacy data sources, their work is closely related to our work. In Nytun's approach, OCL (Object Constraint Language) is used to check consistency of the current model. They assume the existence of objects' constrains that is well described using the OCL. Our approach can be applied even when there is not enough description of constraints. In that reason, our approach is mainly used in the initial stage of the development.

Egyed [12] proposed a method to abstract lower-level classes into higher-level classes by using relational reasoning approach. In Egyed's approach, relationships of inclusion among input and output parameters of a method, is used. Although using inclusion relationships of input and output parameters is a key feature of our approach, the goals are different. Egyed's method is developed for hiding complexity of class diagram that is designed in detail. In such diagram, because of implementation-related restrictions, one abstract class is often represented by several lower-level classes that contain same or similar features. For example, one distributed object is represented by three different classes in the implementation of J2EE framework. The goal of Egyed's method is to reproduce the higher-level class structure that is lost by the detailed design. Our method tends to be used in the initial stage of class diagram design where there is less detailed design.

## 5  Conclusions

This study specifically addressed the class diagram, especially in terms of the model design. It was assumed that many elements that are essential as the software components (attributes required for the I/O of a Web application) are provided by a Web application before starting to draw its class diagram. We proposed a class diagram design support method for designing the class diagram that implements these restrictions.

We adopted an approach to define the upper part of ports of a given application (service) into the initial class diagram. We then applied the conceptual definition structure of regional ontology to the class diagram. Specifically, the I/O ports of a Web application were treated as respective classes to create an initial class diagram. This class diagram was expressed using Lattice and Sub-Lattice extracted within four levels from the common parent node to be candidates for a new class. The semantic structure was verified by matching Lattice with ontological structure.

The business trip support system is itself supported using the presently proposed method in discovery of inclusion and succession relations, separation as a class of attributes shared commonly by others, and correction of the semantic structure with a wrong label attached. The presently proposed method cannot separate information that is intrinsic in each Web application. Furthermore, although architecture matching the user interface and objects was constructed in this case study, no framework for it could be prepared.

When software house takes our proposed method, we can find some relationship between knowledge management and our proposed method. From the point of tacit knowledge and explicit knowledge, the proposed method is the process of creating UML class diagrams based on pre-defined ontology, and so is to support the externalization from tacit knowledge to explicit knowledge. Moreover, after getting more UML class diagrams with the externalization, they work to refine the pre-defined ontology. Thus the refined ontology could support the externalization better. To refine the above-mentioned spiral of externalization, the future work is to establish the method of refining ontology from accumulated UML class diagrams.

## References

1. Google: http://www.google.com
2. Weather.com: http://www.weather.com/
3. Amazon.com: http://www.amazon.com/
4. G. Booch: Object-Oriented Analysis and Design with Applications, Benjamin Commings, 1994.

5. Shyam R. Chidamber and Chris F. Kemerer: A Metrics Suite for Object Oriented Design, IEEE transaction on Software Engineering, Vol.20, no.6, June 1994.
6. DAML: http://www.daml.org/
7. WordNet: http://www.cogsci.princeton.edu/wn/
8. Robert S. Arnold: An introduction to software restructuring, IEEE Press, 1986.
9. M. Fowler: Refactoring – Improving the Design of Existing Code, Addison-Wesley, 1999.
10. P. Van Gorp, H. Stenten, T. Mens, and S. Demeyer: Towards Automating Source-Consistent UML Refactorings, P. Stevens et al. (Eds.) <<UML>> 2003 – The Unified Modeling Language, Lecture Notes on Computer Science, Vol.2863, pp.144–158, Springer-Verlag, 2003.
11. J. P. Nytun and C. S. Jensen: Modeling and Testing Legacy Data Consistency Requirements, P. Stevens et al. (Eds.) <<UML>> 2003 – The Unified Modeling Language, Lecture Notes on Computer Science, Vol.2863, pp.341–355, Springer-Verlag, 2003.
12. Alexander Egyed : Compositional and Relational Reasoning during Class Abstraction, P. Stevens et al. (Eds.) <<UML>> 2003 – The Unified Modeling Language, Lecture Notes on Computer Science, Vol.2863, pp.121–137, Springer-Verlag, 2003.
13. Jorudan: http://www.jorudan.co.jp/
14. Tabi-no-Madoguchi (Mytrip): http://www.mytrip.net/
15. JR Eki-net: http://www.tabi.eki-net.com/;
16. A. Eyal and T. Milo: Integrating and customizing heterogeneous e-commerce applications, The VLDB Journal, Volume 10, Issue 1, pp.16–38, 2001.

# Implementation of Customer Service Management System for Corporate Knowledge Utilization

Thomas Hinselmann[1], Alexander Smirnov[2], Mikhail Pashkin[2], Nikolai Chilov[2], and Andrew Krizhanovsky[2]

[1] Festo AG & Co. KG, Plieninger Str. 50, D - 73760 Ostfildern-Scharnh, Germany
HNM@Festo.com
[2] St.Petersburg Institute for Informatics and Automation of the Russian Academy of Sciences, 39, 14th Line, St Petersburg, 199178, Russia
{Smir,Michael,Nick,Aka}@iias.spb.su

**Abstract.** Modern trends in knowledge-dominated economy are (i) from "capital-intensive business environment" to "intelligence-intensive business environment" and (ii) from "product push" strategies to a "consumer pull" management. This requires close contact between corporations and customers. Currently it is not enough to provide an access to corporate knowledge resources and gather feedback from the customers because very often customers do not know what they really need and what they can find. It is required to bridge a gap between the model of customer interests and corporate knowledge sources to transfer the right knowledge from distributed sources in the right context to the right person in the right time for the right purpose. The paper is devoted to knowledge logistics which with regard to individual user requirements, available knowledge sources, and current situation analysis in an open information environment addresses problems of intelligent support of user activities. Applicability of the approach to industrial system is illustrated through a released prototype of the customer service management system.

## 1 Introduction

Modern market opportunities require a continuous increase of product quality and decrease of its cost in rapidly changing environment. In fact, manufacturing companies need to introduce new strategic objectives and tools. In order to cope with these requirements, companies need to deeply transform both their product development structure and the structure of their business processes.

To increase competitive advantages and benefits companies need to contact with customers closely. This can be done by involving customers into industrial processes, R&D, production processes, etc. to improve the level of customization [1, 2]. One of the modern research and applied topic to improve the above needs is a concept of Customer Service Management (CSM) [3 - 5]. Currently it is not enough to provide an access to corporate knowledge resources and gather feedback from the users because very often customers do not know what they really need and what they can find. It is required to bridge a gap between model of customer interests and corporate knowledge sources (KSs) to transfer of the right knowledge from distributed sources in the right context to the right person in the right time for the right purpose. This can improve customer relationship management systems and provide for additional benefits to an industrial company.

D. Karagiannis and U. Reimer (Eds.): PAKM 2004, LNAI 3336, pp. 475–486, 2004.
© Springer-Verlag Berlin Heidelberg 2004

Usually, the first step for building a dialog with a customer is to open an access to corporate knowledge repository. This can be done via specially designed software, e-mailing, corporate Web site, etc. But such strategy does not allow understanding which information is the most interesting for the customer, which modifications can improve proposed services and products and has other drawbacks. The next step is in providing feedback tools: e.g., questionnaires, fields for results estimations, etc. But the experience shows that users prefer not to participate in such actions without stimulation from the side of a company. The further step is to gather history of user requests and learn it. Based on the results of the learning it is possible to increase customizability of existing information systems, improve their advantages and facilitate navigation of users in the ocean of corporate knowledge memory.

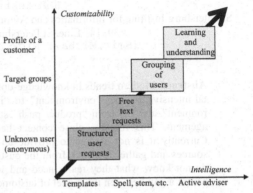

**Fig. 1.** Evolution of the CSM system based on the KSNet approach

Fig. 1 presents the evolution of the CSM system developed by the authors of the paper with regard to (i) intelligence of such systems in providing interface forms: from inflexible templates for special structured inputs and precise results for specific tasks, via free text inputs for KSs search, to learning-based intelligent adviser and (ii) customizability: from unknown unspecified user, via building and supporting target groups (e.g., by job titles, area of interests etc.) to personal profile-based support.

In the framework of research and the applied project devoted to implementation of CSM system all the above tasks were solved. The paper presents results concerning tasks depicted in the grey boxes: (i) gathering information from different sources, (ii) usage of templates for specific tasks, and (iii) intelligent information search.

Knowledge logistics (KL) is a new direction of knowledge management dealing with activities on acquisition, integration, and transfer of knowledge from distributed sources to decision makers/knowledge customers by demand for complex tasks solving [6 - 8]. KL with regard to individual user requirements, available KSs, and current situation analysis in an open information environment addresses problems of intelligent support of user activities. KL focuses on development of methods and tools allowing to turn distributed information into useful knowledge.

The paper briefly describes the approach to KL based on the ontology-driven methodology and presents its usage in a CSM system for an industrial company that has more than 300.000 customers in 176 countries supported by more than 50 companies worldwide with more than 250 branch offices and authorised agencies in further 36 countries. Here proposed approach considers the KL problem as a problem of a knowledge source network configuration that includes end-users / customers, loosely coupled knowledge sources / resources, and a set of tools and methods for information / knowledge processing. The approach is referred to as KSNet-approach. The CSM system implementing the approach is referred to as the system "Intelligent

Access to Catalogue and Documents" (IACD). Current version of the system provides for customers a common way for search and presentation of information about different applications: (i) technical data of company's articles, (ii) selection of project-specific solutions based on tasks' conditions given by a user and (iii) search through corporate documents and available Web sites taking into account users' interests and constraints stored in the corporate ontology. It helps to find the solution easily for planning simple methods, for alternative comparison. It focuses on topics related to information gained.

The customers of the software are sales manages and planning and design engineers. The list of customers can vary during the evolution of the system: its extension against types and content of KSs.

The paper is organized as follows. Section 2 describes the framework of the KSNet-approach. Section 3 depicts details of adaptation of the KSNet-approach to a CSM system. Applicability of the approach to corporate knowledge utilization is presented in section 4.

## 2  KSNet Approach to Knowledge Logistics

The developed approach is based on the idea that knowledge can be represented by two levels. The first level describes the structure of knowledge. It is made up of knowledge describing how to solve a problem. Knowledge represented by the second level is an instantiation of the first level knowledge. This knowledge describes the problem situation or holds object instances.

The approach is oriented to the use of a common notation for structured knowledge description (ontology) and for representation of the knowledge by instantiated object-oriented constraint network. In this notation an ontology is defined as a set of *object classes* ("*classes*"); each of the entities in a class is considered as an *instance* of the class; a set of class attributes ("*attributes*"); a set of attribute domains ("*domains*"); and a set of *constraints* [9].

Structured knowledge is stored in ontology libraries. Instantiated knowledge is stored in distributed KSs. Usually, knowledge stored in one KS is not sufficient to solve real life problem. Hence, methodology of knowledge integration based on synergistic use of knowledge from different sources was selected as a basis for KL.

Problem solving may require knowledge from various application domains. Integration of the knowledge results in a description of methods of the current problem solving (knowledge how to solve the problem). Integration of the knowledge from KSs gives instantiated knowledge meeting the requirements of the solution.

KL is oriented to an identification of user needs and a provision for the user with an appropriate (up-to-date, relevant, and accessible) knowledge. The methodology considers the problem of KL by an example of user request processing. User needs are introduced by a user request (Fig. 2). The request formulates the problem to be solved. The requested knowledge for the solution is provided by a set of KSs.

A part of the user request related to the problem solving knowledge is represented by the structural constituent. This constituent determines what kind of domain knowledge is to be used during the problem solving. The part of the user request containing problem situations is represented by the parametric constituent. Knowledge providing methods of the problem solving is formed based on the knowledge represented by the

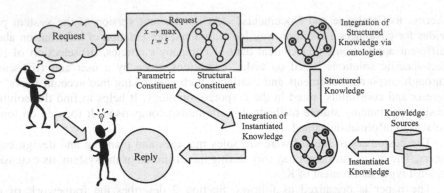

**Fig. 2.** Knowledge integration support of user request processing

structural request constituent through integration of the knowledge from various application domains. The parametric request constituent determines requirements that the solution has to meet. Thereby, the problem solving involves fused domain knowledge, instantiated knowledge fused from KSs, and additional restrictions imposed by the user request.

The proposed approach is based on the following components:

1. Ontology library: to describe industrial applications using application ontology (AO), provide vocabulary (terms and synonyms), structure of application area, methods for task solving, etc.
2. Knowledge map: to describe correspondence between AO and knowledge sources and store the characteristics of KSs. Monitoring tools perform checking of KSs availability and perform appropriate changes in the knowledge map. The knowledge map is meant to facilitate and speed up the process of the KSs choice.
3. User profile: to accumulate information about a user and prepare a slice of AO corresponding to model of user's interests. It includes an organized storage of information about a user, requests history, etc.
4. Wrappers to KSs (to extract information from KSs).

## 3    Adaptation of the KSNet Approach to an Industrial Application

The goal of the CSM system design is to extend facilities of existing company's user-oriented applications and to increase the level of customizability for the end users. One of the possible ways to achieve this goal is integration of such applications in a new one. This integration has to provide for customers with different skills of computer use an access to heterogeneous information in the common way and should offer the following advantages: (i) fast reaction time combined with high reliability of the results, (ii) re-use of data generated before, (iii) easy access by structured or full text search, and (iv) the same interface for access of focused information via Web site or on a stand alone PC not connected to Internet.

The main goal of the approach is to provide information about solutions to customers as well as own personnel in addition to existing product catalogue and to find products and solutions by means expressing customer's task. Therefore, besides company's documents two other data sources were selected for integration (Fig. 3.): (i) the product catalogue containing information about 20'000 items produced by the company: technical data, price, etc. for different languages, and (ii) the application "Project" containing a set of rules for configuration of handling system projects, structured data for industry segment and automation function description, and technical data of carried out products. These applications are oriented to industrial engineers and designers. Extension of these target groups with new ones allows increasing the number of potential clients and providing additional benefits to the company.

The following scenario of the customer access to corporate information was developed: the customer passes authentication procedure, selects an appropriate interface form and enters a request into the system. The system recognizes the request and defines which data the user needs. If the user needs to solve a certain problem the system defines load conditions (parameters describing a certain problem: e.g. mass to be moved, direction of the transportation, environmental conditions etc.) and looks for handling system projects. The system checks information in product catalogue, database storing technical data of standard handling systems and searches through company's documents. Among the major tasks that had to be solved the following should be outlined:

1. Keep existing facilities of the applications and avoid doubling of data;
2. Extend opportunities of fast provision of information about the company's products by new features (like free text search, feature prioritisation and other);
3. Provide multilingual interface;
4. Implement local and Web versions of the software;
5. Index existing documents against information stored in the database.

To adopt the developed approach to the company's requirements the following tasks were solved:

1. KSs were selected and interfaces for accessing them were developed;
2. AO which is a part of the company's ontology based on available structured data was built and extended by user-defined elements and synonyms;
3. Special methods to convert documents into appropriate formats were developed. An interface to other corporate databases was developed. Documents were indexed against the AO vocabulary and the knowledge map was created.
4. Methods for calculation of the results relevance, fuzzy string comparison, and document ranking were developed.

### 3.1 Knowledge Sources

The following existing KSs were selected:

1. Rule bases and databases with information about characteristics of company articles, compatibility and dependencies for configuration of industrial products (e.g., handling system projects). They were a foundation for the AO (vocabulary and structure). These databases contain heterogeneous data in different languages.
2. Corporate documents (e.g., technical documentation, price lists, etc.) in different formats: MS Word, Excel, PowerPoint, Rich text format, text data, portable documents, HTML;
3. Internet sites.

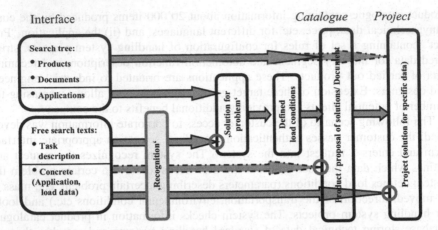

**Fig. 3.** Integration of different software systems into CSM system

Each document was described by the system administrator. The following characteristics were filled out: type of the document, document's location (physical path for local application and URL for Web access), languages of content, availability to be downloaded or ordered by e-mail, etc. For each type of documents, procedures to convert their content into appropriate format were developed. E.g., there were developed procedures (i) to convert MS Office documents and Adobe Acrobat documents into text format, (ii) to fetch data from databases and convert them into readable by a user view and other procedure to access, recognize, convert, fuse, integrate and present data from different sources.

## 3.2  Application Ontology Creation

AO, which is a basis for corporate knowledge description, was built using structured information from databases and rule bases in the following three steps (Fig. 4).

- A structure of the system database was created. It includes a set of auxiliary tables and relations between them.
- Program modules to import and export names of notions describing application area from different sources were prepared. These modules use ADO technology, and SQL queries for databases access and XML format for data exchange with rule bases. They compare and synchronize data in the system databases against data in external sources. Result of work of these modules is structured description of the application area and vocabulary in different languages. To provide flexible mechanism for string comparison the stemmed forms of terms from the AO vocabulary are also stored in the system database for each supported language.
- Information in the AO was modified manually - new ontology elements and synonyms were introduced by experts based on their experience, requests analysis, etc.

AO can be modified during the system operation time. It can be extended with new elements after request log analysis or by demand. An example of AO usage is given in sec. 4.

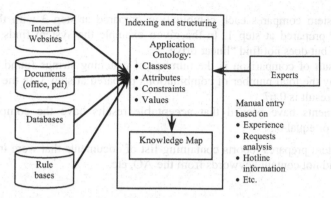

**Fig. 4.** Relation between application ontology and knowledge sources

### 3.3  Knowledge Map Creation

Knowledge map is built during indexing of corporate documents and Internet sites against the vocabularies of the AO and content of the databases. The following characteristics are significant for this process: (i) type of the document to extract its content and (ii) language of the content to compare against the right vocabulary. The structure of the system database was extended with new tables. Relations between them and tables presenting AO and describing documents were added.

The process of knowledge map creation was done in accordance with the following sequence:

- Content of the system tables was deleted.
- The described document were converted into appropriate format and stored in a temporary folder.
- Information from corporate databases was extracted and stored in the system's auxiliary structure.
- Stemmed text extracted from the documents and databases was compared against stemmed versions of vocabularies of AO. Algorithms for fuzzy string comparison were developed and implemented. The result is a filled out structure containing (i) correspondence between AO elements (pairs of class and attribute belonging to the class) and KSs and (ii) correspondence between corporate documents and primary keys of objects described in the corporate databases.

Algorithm for fuzzy string comparison works in accordance with the following sequence:

1. The system extracts content of documents to be indexed containing only stemmed versions of significant words (all the nonsignificant words, numbers and special symbols are removed or replaced). E.g., the systems transfer a phrase "Linear cylinders and drives" into "linear cylind and drive".
2. The system reads stemmed names of classes and attributes from the AO. E.g., a stemmed name of the class "Linear drives" is "linear drive".
3. The system builds all the possible combinations of words composing the name of the AO element. In the given example they are: "linear", "drive" and "linear drive".

4. The system compares each combination prepared at step 3 with the document content prepared at step 1. In the given example the system finds "linear" and "drive" but does not find "linear drive".
5. The result of comparison is the number of matching strings found at step 4 divided by the total number of combinations prepared at step 3. In the given example the result is 0.67.
6. Experiments have proved that acceptable results have the comparison value greater or equal 0.3.

The system prepares reports containing list of documents that were indexed, inaccessible, did not contain keywords from the AO, etc.

## 4    Usage of Developed Framework for User Request Processing

As it was mentioned above, one of the major tasks of the developed CSM systems is an intelligent processing of user requests. There are two types of user requests: structured and free form. For structured requests templates are used.

Template is a standard interface form designed to provide an easy access for customers to standard specific information (tree-like hierarchy, typical task solving, etc.). E.g., an example of template is a form to quickly find all the company products of certain type with restriction on price. List of variables, possible values, rules and triggers for template elements are individual for each template.

The user can select a template from a list, input constraints or select information to be found; and receive an answer via specially designed presentation form.

Templates provide quick access to information since they are designed for a restricted problem area. But they do not provide flexible tools for information access. So, to increase the system intelligence and customizability, recognition of requests in free form is required.

Currently there exist different commercial software packages for natural language text recognition (e.g., [10]). But most of them are oriented to defining the structural constituent of request and full-text search. Definition of the parametric constituent of the user request increases reliability of the found results by search of synonyms, units of measures, relational symbols and other. Below the steps of the developed algorithm for free text recognition are presented. The example of a user request is "*I am looking for a device to move mass 2 kg vertical 100 mm horizontal 150 mm*" (Fig. 5). The upper part of the figure presents the request and its constituents. The lower part presents a part of AO: class "Projects" with several subclasses. Sub class "*Pick&Place*" was found as a synonym to the word "*move*". It has a several attributes. Three of them were found in a request using synonyms: attributes "*Stroke Z*" by the synonym "*vertical*" attribute "*Stroke Y*"by the synonym "*horizontal*"and attribute "*Pay load*" by the synonym "*mass*" Analysis of the ontology structure allows to understand if the request can be processed.

The following steps are passed:

- *Tokenization*. Identification of borders of words, numbers, etc. Recognition of unique words. The following elements were recognized: words "I", "am", "looking", "for", "a", "device", "to", "move", "mass", "kg", "mm", "vertical", and

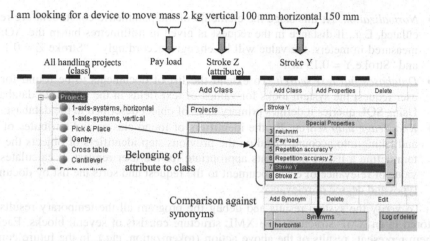

**Fig. 5.** Example of correspondence between user request and ontology elements

"horizontal"; numbers "2", "100", and "150". This process is unique for each supported language due to different special symbols can be recognized as native characters.

- *Stop-words finding.* This step is based on a list of stop words that should be omitted during the request recognition (e.g., articles, some prepositions, etc.) the system reduces a number of significant words. The following words were omitted: "I", "am", "for", "a", and "to". List of stop words is unique for each supported language.
- *Spelling.* This step helps to identify misspelled words that can be later matched with ontology elements. This procedure is unique for each supported languages.
- *Stemming.* This operation makes it possible to identify ontology elements even if they are written in different forms. The following conversions were done: "looking" → "look", "device" → "devic", "vertical" → "vertic", and "horizontal" → "horizont". This procedure is unique for each supported language.
- *Search of units of measures.* All supported units of measures are stored in the system database. Regular expressions are used to recognize them. The following units of measures were recognized: "kg", and "mm". The regular expressions are unique for each supported language.
- *Ontology search* taking into account synonyms. Here all found so far significant words are matched with stemmed names of the AO elements. Usage of synonyms allows to identify classes and attributes. Threshold depending on different rules allows to reject ontology elements with low degree of similarity to the user request. If the system can not recognize any class from the AO or finds ambiguity in the request it asks the user to correct the request.
- *Definition of constraints on values of attributes.* Using regular expressions for recognition of relational symbols (like ">", "<", etc.) and analyzing the found ontology attributes and identified numbers, the systems builds restriction to values of attributes to which to be found information should satisfy – "Pay load = 2", "Stroke Z = 100 mm", and "Stroke Y = 150 mm".

- *Normalization.* At this stage the elements of the parametric constituent are recalculated. E.g., if distance in the request is given in millimetres but in the AO it is measured in meters, the value will be changed accordingly - "Stroke Z = 0.1 m", and "Stroke Y = 0.15 m".
- *Databases full text search.* To extend the list of documents to be found for the user request the system looks for values of text fields in the corporate databases. Using SQL queries it defines primary keys of object described in the database.
- *Knowledge map search.* By the identifiers of found classes and attributes of AO and taking into account found on the previous step identifiers of objects the system define a list of documents appropriate for the user request. It calculates the value of relevance of each document to the request and sorts the list by document types and degree of relevance.

To verify the system results and debug the program all the temporary results are stored in an XML structure. The XML structure consists of several blocks. Each of them represents results of the above action (tokenization, etc.). In the future content of results will be used for user clustering, search of similarities in the customer requests to increase the system intelligence and customizability.

The following types of interactions with the user are possible:

1. Proposition to repeat the request and check of found misspellings. The user will be returned to the request input form, the request will be put into the input field and a text with the found misspellings will be presented.
2. Proposition to add insufficient information into the request. The user will be returned to the request input form, the request will be put into the input field and a text informing the user about the insufficient information will be presented.
3. Possibility to enter degree of satisfaction by the system answer, to select the best matching document (from the user's view point) and to enter text comment. The system saves this information, and the list of documents checked by the user. Documents rating will be calculated based on this information and will be taken into account during request processing.

All the adopted elements of the KSNet-approach were used during the user request processing. User profile stores requests log, user's preferences and user's feedback. AO is used to recognize and refine the user request. Knowledge map is used to find appropriate documents and calculate the degree of relevance of a document to the user request. Calculation of documents' relevance allows for a customer to find the most appropriate documents quickly.

## 5  Conclusion and Future Work

The paper presents an adaptation of the developed theoretical KSNet-approach to knowledge logistics to industrial application (implementation of a CSM system for certain problem area).

CSM systems provide good opportunities for companies to increase their competitive advantages due to unification of interfaces to different KSs for users with different skills in computer use. Currently companies have accumulated huge amount of heterogeneous information and developed a lot of tools to access it. To build a dialog with customers it is necessary to provide them with an effective tool for utilizing of corporate knowledge. Users do not need a new system to find all the available information. They need a system which will assist them in the search and will find the right information.

Application ontology which is a part of the company's ontology provides a common vocabulary for corporate knowledge sources indexing for different languages. Its extension by synonyms increases facilities of the system to find reliable information for user requests containing words different from the company's terminology. Knowledge map which is a result of above indexing allows to find knowledge sources quickly. Usage of user profile allows to accumulate request log and study it to better understand user needs and increase the system customizability (e.g., reduce space of search, etc.).

Current work under the project consists of development a tool for target user group ontology building based on the application ontology, learning of user requests and prioritisation of input components and clustering of users based on slices of application ontology.

## Acknowledgements

Some parts of the research were done by the Contract titled "Intelligent Access to Catalogues and Documents" between Festo and SPIIRAS and as parts of the project # 16.2.44 of the research program "Mathematical Modelling and Intelligent Systems", the project # 1.9 of the research program "Fundamental Basics of Information Technologies and Computer Systems" of the Russian Academy of Sciences, the grant # 02-01-00284 of the Russian Foundation for Basic Research.

## References

1. Caddy, I.: Moving from Mass Production to Mass Customization: the Impact on Integrated Supply Chains. In: proceedings of the Workshop on Mass Customization Management (MCM 2000), University of Wollongong, Australia. (2000) (Electronic Proceedings).
2. Rautenstrauch, C., Turowski, K.: Manufacturing Planning and Control Content Management in Virtual Enterprises Pursuing Mass Customization. In proceedings of the International NAISO Congress on Information Science Innovations (ISI'2001), Symposium on Intelligent Automated Manufacturing (IAM'2001). Dubai, U.A.E. (2001) (Electronic Proceedings).
3. Baumeister, H.: Customer relationship management for SMEs. In Proceedings of the 2nd Annual Conference eBusiness and eWork e2002. Prague, Czech Republic, October 16-18, (2002).
4. Piller, F., Schaller, C.: Individualization Based Collaborative Customer Relationship Management: Motives, Structures, and Modes of Collaboration for Mass Customization and CRM. In: Working Paper No. 29 of the Dept. of General and Industrial Management, Technische Universität München, ISSN 0942-5098, May 2002. URL: http://www.mass-customization.de/download//TUM-AIBWP029.pdf (2004).
5. Fjermestad,J., Romano, N.,C.,Jr.: An Integrative Implementation Framework for Electronic Customer Relationship Management: Revisiting the General Principles of Usability and Resistance. In: proceedings of the 36th Hawaii International Conference on System Sciences (HICSS'03), Big Island, HI, USA January 6-9, (2003) ISBN 0-7695-1874-5 – Track 7.

6. Smirnov, A., Pashkin, M., Chilov, N., Levashova, T.: Knowledge Logistics in Information Grid Environment In: Zhuge, H. (ed.): The special issue "Semantic Grid and Knowledge Grid: The Next-Generation Web" of International Journal on Future Generation Computer Systems. Vol. 20, Issue 1 (2004) 61–79.

7. Smirnov, A., Pashkin, M., Chilov, N., Levashova, T., Krizhanovsky, A.: Continuous Business Engineering for Virtual Enterprise Configuration Based on Adaptive Services, In: proceedings of the 10th International Conference on Concurrent Enterprising. Sevilla, Spain, June 14–16, (2004) 385–393.

8. Smirnov, A., Pashkin, M., Chilov, N., Levashova, T.: Agent-based support of mass customization for corporate knowledge management. In: Engineering Applications of Artificial Intelligence, 16(4), (2003) 349-364.

9. Smirnov, A., Pashkin, M., Chilov, N., Levashova, T., Krizhanovsky, A.: Ontology-Driven Knowledge Logistics Approach as Constraint Satisfaction Problem. In: Meersman, R., Tari, Z., Schmidt, D.C. et al. (eds.): On the Move to Meaningful Internet Systems 2003: CoopIS, DOA, and ODBASE. Lecture Notes in Computer Science, Vol. 2888. Springer Verlag, Berlin Heidelberg New York (2003) 535–652.

10. Inxight Software Inc. Corporate Web site. URL: http://www.inxight.com/ (2004).

# Constraint-Rules for Configuration Problems

Ulrich Geske

Fraunhofer FIRST, Berlin
Ulrich.Geske@first.fhg.de

**Abstract.** In this paper[1], we outline our constraint-based model for
configuring industrial products and treat some aspects of its use of
constrained-based rules as well as some model extensions for product
reconfiguration and for the efficient solution of large configuration problems. The resulting model realizes a substantial reduction of the search
space and allows the efficient configuration of industrial products. Correctness and completeness of the solution process are ensured with respect to the problem specification. Unlike most other configuration models, the proposed model offers almost unlimited user freedom to interact
with the solution process.

## 1 Introduction

Product-configuration software is still a hot topic in research and development.
The reasons for this are the shortcomings of existing configuration processes and
the fast-growing possibilities for shifting business marketing and sales activities
to the web. The importance of the shift to e-commerce becomes evident if we
consider the fact that, e.g., in the United States, 40 % of the average manufacturer's operating budget is spent on sales and marketing (cf. [9]).

In the last twenty years, with the introduction of the well-known rule-based
configuration system XCON for configuring DEC computers, different approaches
have been proposed and investigated for the knowledge-based configuration of
products and technical systems. These include various rule-based, case-based
and, recently, more and more constraint-based approaches. Overviews of different approaches and systems are given in [14], [13] and [12]. If research approaches
as well as commercial systems are considered, the following general shortcomings
are found. The problem specification is nondeclarative and hard to maintain. Often, the sequence of interactions during the configuration process is fixed. Thus,
a flexible configuration process, as supported by *ConBaCon*, is impossible. The
simulation of different effects resulting from alternative interactive decisions is
rare and the support of good reconfigurations, which is needed by industry, is
insufficient or nonexistent. Furthermore, finding optimal or near-optimal configurations is impossible, and there are other problems like the fact that the
underlying algorithms sometimes fail to terminate.

---

[1] This paper is based on former work and fruitful discussions with Ulrich John now
working at DaimlerChrysler Research, Berlin

D. Karagiannis and U. Reimer (Eds.): PAKM 2004, LNAI 3336, pp. 487–495, 2004.

It is generally accepted that high-quality configuration systems can be realized, especially by using *constraint programming* (cf. [3], [11]). Successful commercial configuration systems are always dubbed "constraint-based", but this is usually misleading because such systems do not use integrated constraint solvers to reduce the search space; they merely process a constraint-based problem specification by simple checking of constraints. As for genuine constraint-based configuration systems or research prototypes, we find that relevant publications on these approaches are often of a very general nature or exhibit limitations in terms of the quality of search-space reduction and the problem class they can handle.

Our prototypical configuration system ConBaCon, based on the CLP language[2] CHIP, attempts to overcome the above shortcomings/problems.

## 2   Modelling

By analyzing the results of design problems for industrial control systems, we developed a formal problem model and, based on this, a largely declarative specification language, which allows the specification of relevant configuration problems. Such specifications are composed of two parts: *an object hierarchy* and *constraint-rules*. Every technical object that can play a part in the configuration problem must be specified in terms of its structure in the object hierarchy (see, e.g., Fig. 1). An object can consist of several components in the sense of the *consist_of*-relation, where components may be optional, or the object has some specializations in the sense of the *is_a*-relation. In addition, all attributes of the technical objects are specified. If the attribute values of a technical object are explicitly known, they will be enumerated.

$configuration\_space\_specification([\%selection$
  $[system, [components([net, ground\_converter])]],$
  $[mains, [components(or([mains1, mains2])), constraints([[nominal\_voltage, \_]])]],$
  $[mains1, [components([]), constraints([[nominal\_voltage, [400]]])]],$
  $[mains2, [components([]), constraints([[nominal\_voltage, [690]]])]],$
  $[ground\_converter, [components([main\_converter, adjacent\_converter,$
                          $opt([main\_relay, commutation\_inductor])])]],$
  $[mains\_relay, [components([])]],$
  $[commutator\_choke, [components([])]],$
  $[adjacent\_converter, [components([])]],$
  $[main\_converter, [components(or([s101, s102, s103, s104, ..., s203]))]],$
  $[s101, [components([])]],$
  $[s103, [components([])]],$
  $[s203, [components([])]]]).$

**Fig. 1.** Configuration space

A visualization of the product model partly described in Fig. 1 is represented in Fig. 2.

---

[2] CLP=Constraint Logic Programming

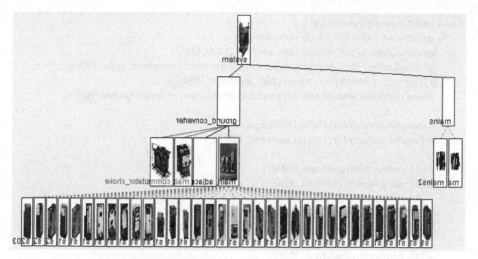

**Fig. 2.** Product model of a technical system

A correct internal representation of the configuration problem is created from the object-hierarchy specification by adding the specification of the constraints concerning different attribute value sets on the one hand, and the existence or nonexistence of technical objects in the problem solution on the other. Context constraint rules are added dealing with a specific problem of a costumer, e.g., customer-specific demands concerning energy consumption or resource-oriented constraints. A distinction between problem-specific and context-independent constraint rules is useful because the technical correctness of the problem solution is ensured if all context-independent constraint rules are fulfilled. Some examples for context-indepent constraint-rules in the field of power-supply systems for large electric motors are presented in Fig. 3.

## 2.1   Configuration Process

Based on the problem-solution model, a flexible and efficient problem-solution process was realized within the prototypical configuration system ConBaCon using the CLP language CHIP. In particular, the object-based data management and the existence of *Conditional Propagation Rules*[3] in CHIP facilitated the implementation.

The specified configuration problem is transformed into objects of the problem-solution model. This means that the objects of the solution model are generated, corresponding consistency-ensuring constraints are inferred and set, and the specified constraints are transformed into corresponding constraints of the problem-solution model. The value one is assigned to the $Ex\_Var$-attribute of the target object because the target object must exist in each solution. Thanks

---

[3] Similar language elements exist in other CLP languages, e.g., Constraint-Handling Rules in ECLIPSE

*constraint_rules([%selection*
  % constraint rules for single components
    [*ground_converter, connection_voltage,* [400, 690]],
    [*ground_converter, current_adjacent_converter,* [*mainnet, separately*]],
    [*if*([[*ground_converter, connection_voltage,* [690]]]),
      *then*([[*ground_converter, current_adjacent_converter,* [*separately*]]])],

    [*adjacent_converter, initial_voltage,* [310]],
    [*adjacent_converter, initial_current,* [25]]],

    [*s*101, *connection_voltage,* [500]],
    [*s*101, *measuered_current,* [630]]],

    [*s*103, [*connection_v oltage,* [500]]],
    [*s*103, [*measuered_current,* [1200]]])]],

    [*s*203, *connection_voltage,* [500]],
    [*s*203, *measuered_current,* [1200]]],

  % constraint rules between components
    [*iff*([[*ground_converter, initial_current,* [1400, 1600]]]),
      *then*([*noexist*([*mains_relay*])])],
    [*iff*([[*ground_converter, initial_current,* [1600]]]),
      *then*([*noexist*([*commutation_inductor*]])]),
    [*eq*([*mains, nominal_voltage*], [*ground_converter, connection_voltage*])],
    [*lt*([*ground_converter, peak_current*], [*main_converter, measuered_current*])]]).
% end of constraint_rules_definition

**Fig. 3.** Constraint rules

to the generated model with the model-specific consistency ensuring constraints, a substantial reduction of the search space is guaranteed. We call the set of the currently active module objects of the problem-solution model *Configuration Space*. Now, interactive user constraints can be given (one by one) relating to the existence or nonexistence of objects of the configuration space or to the shape of the corresponding attribute value sets (e.g., see Fig. 4).

*demands*([*value*(*peak_current*, 1000)]).

**Fig. 4.** Problem specific constraint rule

The user's freedom to decide which object or attribute value set of the configuration space should be restricted by an interactively given user constraint is an outstanding feature compared with most other configuration models/tools. Governed by the constraints of the problem-solution model, this results in a new configuration space (e.g., the result of the constraint rule in Fig. 5 given by the user is the new configuration space presented in Fig. 5).

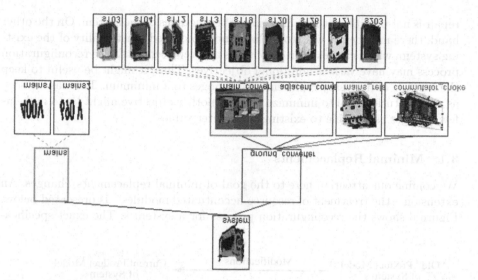

**Fig. 5.** Configuration space of the technical system as result of an additional problem-specific constraint rule

Then, a new cycle can start. Users can either give a new interactive constraint or they can delete previously given interactive user constraints. This allows the simulation of several user decisions, which is the prerequisite for a highly flexible configuration process. If no further interactive constraints are required, the generation of a solution can be started. This is done by labeling the $Ex\_Var$-attributes of the (still) active objects of the problem-solution model. Such labeling can be controlled by heuristics. This allows us to take into account preferences in the form of preference rules for controlling the labeling process. If the solution found is not suitable or fails to pass the solution quality check, further solutions can be created by backtracking. If a partial improvement of the solution suffices, a specific solution improvement can be started by specification and processing of a constraint hierarchy, i.e., the constraints that must be satisfied unconditionally will be specified as *hard* constraints, and the solution parts that should, if possible, be in the new solution or desired attribute values will be fixed as *weak* constraints. The weak constraints can be marked with several weights. The specified constraint hierarchy will be processed in an error-minimization process, which results in the generation of a set of equivalent (hard) constraints of the problem-solution model.

At second sight, it becomes obvious that the improvement process using a constraint-hierarchy transformer provides a sound basis for reconfiguration, which is needed by industry. Such a reconfiguration approach (cf. [5, 6]) within the ConBaCon model is presented in the following section.

## 3    Reconfiguration

There are two possible reasons for reconfiguring existing systems/products. On the one hand, parts/components sometimes break down and have to be replaced, repair is not possible without affecting other modules of the system. On the other hand, there may be the wish to realize a new/modified functionality of the existing system, which can result in extensions and replacements. The reconfiguration process may have various additional objectives. Thus, it might be useful to keep the number of necessary replacements/changes to a minimum. This can be seen as a substitution goal to minimize costs. Another objective might be to make as few changes as possible to existing parameter values[4].

## 3.1   Minimal Replacements

We confine our attention here to the goal of minimal replacements/changes. An extension – the treatment of resource-accentuated modules – is presented below. Figure 6 shows the reconfiguration process for a system $s$. The exact specifica-

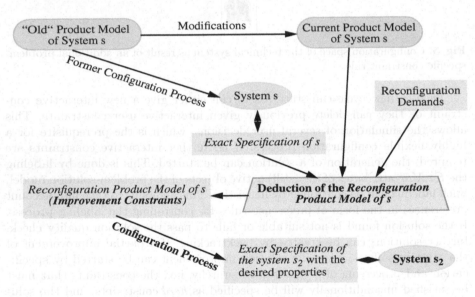

**Fig. 6.** Reconfiguration of a Technical System

tion of the existing system $s$ has to be merged with the current product model of $s$ in the following way. Starting with the current product model, all technical modules/objects of the system s *which are not out of order* and *which do not need replacing to meet explicit reconfiguration demands* should now be marked as valid if they were labeled as obsolete before. They are available because they are already integrated in $s$. Specified context-independent constraints were processed in a similar way. A *weak existence constraint* is generated for each technical module of $s$ that is not out of order and that does not need replacing to meet explicit

---

[4] For instance, in the field of safety control engineering, a large number of parameter value changes would necessitate expensive field simulations

reconfiguration demands. A *weak nonexistence constraint* is deduced for each optional object of the resulting product model that is not part of *s* and whose existence is not explicitly demanded by reconfiguration demands. The resulting *reconfiguration product model*, which also contains the reconfiguration demands (ConBaConL-specified constraints) and the generated weak constraints, is the *new problem specification*.

After transforming the specification into an adequate problem-solution model as described in the previous section, the weak nonexistence constraints and existence constraints are transformed into the sum over the existence variables $Ex\_Var$ of the objects in question or the terms "$1 - Ex\_Var$" for the weak existence constraints. The resulting sum is minimized by "restricted forward labeling" of the existence variables in question. After backjumping, the value of the (non labeled) sum term is set to the determined minimum. Thus, a configuration space is given that can be further reduced as described above. For each solution, the minimal number of replacements is ensured with respect to the system *s*, the current product model and the reconfiguration demands.

## 3.2   Resource-Accentuated Reconfiguration

Where a new/extended functionality of an existing system or parts of the system is demanded/necessary, it is not always reasonable to replace elements of the existing system. Instead, it might be cheaper to add only certain elements. For instance, if the capacity of the power supply is to be increased, it may be a better idea to add an additional power supply in parallel to the existing one than to replace it by a biger one. In order to allow such *resource-accentuated reconfigurations*, we would have to extend ConBaConL and our problem-solution model by adding so-called *generative objects*. We define generative objects as complex objects consisting of similar components that are connected in a specified manner. If the component number is not restricted by special ConBaConL constraints, it remains unknown initially. The property values of the generative object are calculated from the property values of its components by specified formulas.

The configuration model requires partial reorganization for proper treatment of generative objects in the initial configuration process. At the beginning of the configuration process, each generative object has one component. If no problem solution can be found, a new configuration cycle is started in which each generative object contains two similar components. In each case, one of them is optional and is attached to a weak nonexistence constraint. If this model instance does not allow a solution either, a new optional component with an attached weak nonexistence constraint is generated for each generative object, and so on. This cycle is repeated until a solution can be found or until the number of components of the generative objects becomes unrealistic.

Since, in most practical configuration problems a limit on the number of similar objects is known, and can be specified by a fixed number of optional components in the initial problem specification, the use of generative objects is reasonable, particularly for reconfiguration tasks.

Resource-accentuated reconfiguration begins by creating the reconfiguration model as described above. In addition, each component of a generative object is complemented by a similar optional component and a weak nonexistence constraint for the added component. The property formulas between each generative object and its components have to be adapted. The resulting model is the problem specification for the resource-accentuated reconfiguration of the existing system and is processed as described above. If the addition of more than one similar component per generative object is desired, further analogous extensions of the generated reconfiguration-problem specification would have to be made.

# 4   Conclusion / Future Work

Our constraint-based problem-solution model ConBaCon for the configuration and reconfiguration of technical systems/industrial products was presented.

So far, the prototypical realization in the CLP language CHIP has proved successful in the field of industrial control systems for the configuration of power-supply systems for large electric motors. By substantially reducing the search space by constraint rules, the problem-solution model – together with the underlying CLP system – allows an efficient configuration process that can be flexibly controlled by user interactions. It is ensured that each solution found is correct with respect to the problem specification and the underlying constraint solver. In addition, the completeness of the solution process is guaranteed. The use of constraint rules results in a high efficiency and dead-end free configuration. The first one is needed for a truely interactive configuration process and the second one is important to avoid restarts of the system and repeated input of the sequence of interactive actions.

When applying ConBaCon to larger generated problems (more than 10,000 module objects in the object-hierarchy specification), we recognized the need for model improvements because of the performance problems encountered. A clustering approach could allow the efficient solution of large configuration problems.

By integrating a graphical problem editor into ConBaCon, the system supports innovative design processes, which is essential for many practical design problems. An interesting extension would be the closer integration of selective alteration of the configuration-problem specification within the problem-solution model, making an innovative alteration possible each time during the interactive configuration phase without losing the whole set of interactively given constraints and their consequences.

Another important extension of the presented problem-solution model is distribution, which is motivated by two concerns. On the one hand, it is useful to develop DPS-oriented approaches[5] for the near-optimal solution of very large complex problems. More specifically, we have to develop proper problem-decomposition methods and models of corresponding agent systems. On the

---

[5] DPS = Distributed Problem Solving

other hand, it is useful to support existing team structures in configuration-related companies.

# References

1. E. C. Freuder: The Role of Configuration Knowledge in Business process. IEEE-Int. Systems 4/ 1998.
2. L. Gupta, J.F. Chionglo, Mark S. Fox: A Constraint Based Model of Coordination in Concurrent Design Projects. www.ie.utoronto.ca/EIL/DITL/WET-Ice96/ProjectCoordination/. 1996.
3. P. van Hentenryck, V. Saraswat: Constraint Programming: Strategic Directions. J. of Constraints, 2/ 1997.
4. John, U., Geske, U.: Reconfiguration of Technical Products Using ConBaCon. Proceedings of the AAAI'99 Workshop on Configuration. Orlando (1999)
5. John, U.: Configuration and Reconfiguration with Constraint-based Modelling (in German). PhD Thesis Technical University of Berlin. DISKI 255, Aka-Verlag, Berlin (2001)
6. John, U., Geske, U.: Constraint-Based Configuration of Large Systems. In: Bartenstein, O. et al: Web Knowledge Management and Decision Support. Revised Papers of 14th International Conference on Applications of Prolog, INAP 2001. Lecture Notes in Artificial Intelligence, Vol. 2543, Springer-Verlag, Berlin Heidelberg New York (2003)
7. U. John: Solving Large Configuration Problems Efficiently by Clustering the ConBaCon Model. Proc. of IEA/AIE-2000. LNCS, Springer.
8. Van Parunak et al: Distributed Component-centered Design as Agent-Based Distributed Constraint Optimization. Proc. of WS Constraints and Agents on AAAI'97.
9. A. J. Pasik: The Configuration Invasion. Report, Lazard Frères & Co. LLC, www.selectica.com/html/articles/Lazard1.html. New York, September 1998.
10. D. Sabin: www.cs.unh.edu/ccc/config. 1996.
11. D. Sabin, E.C. Freuder: Configuration as Composite Constraint Satisfaction. Proc. of AAAI'96.
12. D. Sabin, R. Weigel: Product Configuration Frameworks - A Survey. IEEE Int. Systems 4/ 1998.
13. M. Stumptner: An Overview of Knowledge-Based Configuration. AI Communications. Vol. 10 No. 2, 1997.
14. J. Tiihonen, T. Soininen, T. Männistö, R. Sulonen: State-of-the-Practice in Product Configuration - A Survey of 10 Cases in the Finnish Industry. In [15], 1996.
15. T. Tomiyama, M. Mäntylä, S. Finger (Eds.): Knowledge Intensive CAD. Capman & Hall, 1996.

# Using Hierarchical Knowledge Structures to Implement Dynamic FAQ Systems

David Camacho[1], Maria Dolores Rodriguez-Moreno[2],
Alberto López[1], and César Castro[1]

[1] Universidad Carlos III de Madrid, Departamento de Informática, Madrid, Spain
dcamacho@ia.uc3m.es
[2] Universidad de Alcalá de Henares, Departamento de Automática, Madrid, Spain
mdolores@aut.uah.es

**Abstract.** This paper presents a knowledge representation that allows building hierarchical structures that can be used to build dynamically solutions to solve a particular user question. The goal of this work is to show how it is possible to define (and handle) a new knowledge representation that allows the integration of Case-based Knowledge into a graph-based representation that can be easily learned and managed. The combination of both, Case-based Knowledge and graphs allows to implement a flexible hierarchical structures (or *learning graphs*) that have been applied to implement a new kind of Frequently Asked Questions Systems. In these systems the output is dynamically built from the user query, using as basis structures the knowledge retrieved from a Case Base. The paper shows how the management of these cases allow enriching the knowledge base. Finally, the paper shows a specific application of this technique, in particular a Web system named DynJAQ (Dynamic Java Asked Questions). DynJAQ is a FAQ system that is able to generate dynamically several HTML guides that can be used to answer any possible question about a particular programming language (Java).

**Keywords:** Knowledge Representation, Case-Based Reasoning, Intelligent Web Systems.

## 1 Introduction

Knowledge representation and management performs crutial aspects in most of the software applications. Both topics become specially important when Artificial Intelligence techniques are used. Several features such as flexibility, adaptability, reasoning, or learning are directly related to the knowledge representation used in those systems [7].

The aim of this work is to define a knowledge representation that must be able to integrate predefined knowledge about a particular topic (cases) into a common solution. These solutions will be built using this knowledge as the basis (or atomic) knowledge structures. The interaction with the system (when a problem, or question is proposed) will generate different solutions using several parameters provided by the users. Therefore the solution will be dynamically adapted to the

D. Karagiannis and U. Reimer (Eds.): PAKM 2004, LNAI 3336, pp. 496–507, 2004.

user skills. To show our knowledge-based approach, the next problem will be addressed: when any student needs to learn concepts about how to program in a particular language usually some books, manuals or distribution lists are used to solve his/her problems. When these problems are very usual it is possible to build a Frequently Asked Questions (FAQ) repository to answer these questions.

The Knowledge Based approach presented in this paper allows to obtain a solution *adapted* to the user skills, using stored knowledge. We have instantiated our knowledge representation into a particular Web system. The implemented system (named DynJAQ) allows to ask questions such as: *"I want to know how to define classes, and define variables and constants, in Java"*, and gives to the user one or several solutions for this particular question.

The paper is structured as follows. Section 2 shows the Related Work. Section 3 describes the hierarchical knowledge representation proposed. Section 4 shows a Dynamic Web FAQ System, named DynJAQ, that has been implemented using the previous knowledge representation. Finally, Section 5 summarizes the conclusions of this work.

## 2    Related Work

This section addresses some related systems to our approach. We briefly describe the main features of those systems in areas such as: FAQ Web systems, Questions Answering systems, and Case-Based Reasoning systems.

### 2.1    FAQ Web Systems

Usually a FAQ works in the following way: any user can consult a pre-existing list of questions with their answers in order to found a similar question that can answer his/her own problem. The user is the responsible of both, to analyse all the items in the FAQ (usually searching through previous questions asked by other users), find the most similar solutions and "reuse" or "adapt" to his/her problem. There is a huge number of Web sites that provides FAQ repositories, some interesting examples are:

- The Dynamic FAQ Database (http://products.dynamicwebdevelopers.com) is a Web Application that allows to Construct a Frequently Asked Questions Database for a particular Website. Therefore, the users may search in the FAQ Database, as well as submit questions for support. This application simply builds a database query access using a simple Web interface.
- The Hope Resource Center Dynamic FAQ (http://www.stmarys.org/ cancer/ faq/ default.asp). This FAQ provides a dynamic access through the selection of a particular issue in a list. Once any item is selected some static FAQ documents are shown.
- Web sites like *The Collection of Computer Science Bibliographies* (http:// liinwww.ira.uka.de/ bibliography/ index.html), is a traditional static FAQ based on a set of questions and their related solutions.

– Other Web sites like The Internet FAQs Archives (http://www.faqs.org/faqs/) allow to find different FAQ documents from repositories using a set of keywords.

However, developing a simple FAQ repository has several problems that could be summarized in:

1. Not all the users have the same knowledge about a particular topic. Therefore, if only a static FAQ is implemented, the questions could be over specific and the user could not understand correctly the solution proposed, or very general so the user does not find what s/he is really looking for.
2. If a Web system is implemented using only a static repository of solutions, this repository will grow up quickly and the number of documents retrieved could be very large. Therefore, the users could not find the information, or it could be very hard.
3. None FAQ system takes into account the user features, or skills, about a particular topic.
4. These kind of systems are not flexible because they store a set of predefined problems and their related solutions.

## 2.2   Question Answering Systems

There is an important research work related to the *Question answering* (QA) systems [5]. A question answering system provides directly an answer to the user question by accessing and consulting its Knowledge Base. These type of systems are related to the research in Natural Language Processing (NLP) [6].

In recent years, and due to the evolution of the Web, has originated a new interest in the application of QA systems to the Web. In [9] is defined what is required to implement a web-based QA system. Any QA system based on a document collection typically has three main components. The first is a retrieval engine that sits on top of the document collection and handles retrieval requests. In the context of the web, this is a search engine that indexes web pages. The second is a query formulation mechanism that translates natural-language questions into queries for the Information Retrieval engine in order to retrieve relevant documents from the collection, i.e., documents that can potentially answer the question. The third component, answer extraction, analyzes these documents and extracts answers from them.

Perhaps the most popular information retrieval system, based on NLP techniques is FAQ Finder [3–5]. FAQ Finder (http://faqfinder.ics.uci.edu/) is a system that retrieves answers to natural language questions from USENET FAQ files. The system integrates symbolic knowledge and statistical data in doing its question-matching. Part of the challenge was to pre-compile as much of the system knowledge, therefore the answers could be found fast enough to satisfy the constraints of the Web use. One issue raised by this research is the need to have the system correctly identify that a question cannot be answered.

However, the difficulty of NLP based systems has limited the scope of question answering systems to *domain specific* systems. In our approach this problem is relaxed using a general graph-based search technique integrated with a domain dependent Case-based Knowledge.

## 2.3   Case-Based Reasoning Systems

Case-based reasoning (CBR) [1, 2, 8] solves new problems by adapting previously successful solutions to similar problems. This problem solving technique does not require an explicit domain model, so elicitation becomes a task of gathering case histories. The implementation is reduced to identifying significant features that describe a case. This case is then stored and managed by means of database techniques, and CBR systems can learn by acquiring new knowledge as new cases.

Figure 1 shows the processes involved in CBR. This general CBR cycle may be described by the following four processes: [1]

- RETRIEVE the most similar case, or cases.
- REUSE the information and knowledge stored in the case, or cases, that solve the problem.
- REVISE the proposed solution (if necessary).
- RETAIN the new solution as a part of a new case.

**Fig. 1.** The CBR Cycle.

A new problem is solved by retrieving one or more previously experienced cases, reusing the case in one way or another, revising the solution based on reusing a previous case, and retaining the new experience by incorporating it into the existing Knowledge Base (Case Base).

This cycle rarely occurs without human intervention. For example, many CBR tools act primarily as a case retrieval and reuse systems. Case revision (i.e., adaptation) is often being undertaken by managers of the case base. However, it should not be viewed as weakness of the CBR that it encourages human collaboration in decision support. Our approach allows implementing a new way to manage the cases stored in the Case Base through the use of two different kind of cases, atomic and complex (see the following Section).

## 3   Hierarchical Learning Graphs

This section describes how to combine a graph-based representation and case-based knowledge into a hierarchical representation that can be used to build new flexible and adaptive QA systems.

### 3.1   Integrating Case-Based Knowledge into a Graph Structure

The proposed knowledge structure uses a graph representation as the main knowledge integration structure. The combination of graph structures and CBR knowledge implements the concept of the *learning graph*. Any learning graph can be characterized as follows:

- The *nodes* in the graph are cases extracted from the case base. Those nodes can be: *atomic*, if they only represent simple concepts, or *complex*, if they are implemented using other learning graphs.
- Any node (case) in the graph uses pre-connectors and post-connectors to represent what concepts are necessary to understand the knowledge stored in the node (pre-connectors), and what concepts are acquired if this node is learned by the user (post-connectors). Those connectors are used to define the *transitions* between the nodes in the graph.

Therefore, any learning graph is a hierarchical nested structure, where each node can be decomposed into several learning graphs, and where the leafs of this structure are implemented by simple knowledge structures (or atomic cases). Figure 2 shows a schematic representation of this structure.

To build an initial learning graph, it is necessary to define how to obtain the initial and final nodes in the graph, and how to generate from those nodes the

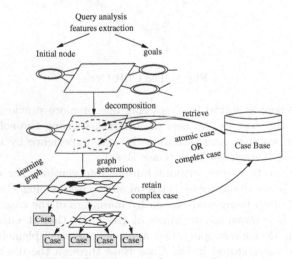

**Fig. 2.** Learning graph representation.

rest of the graph. In our approach, the initial and final nodes are obtained from the user interaction. Once those nodes are defined a simple searching algorithm is used to build the learning graph. The algorithm can be summarized as follows:

1. Using the user query (and other user characteristics), the initial and final nodes are defined (see Section 4).
2. While it does not exist a path from the initial node to all the final nodes do:
   - 2.1 Retrieve from the Case Base all the cases that match with all the post-connectors of the initial node.
   - 2.2 From the retrieved cases select those whose pre-connectors connect completely all the post-connectors in the previous node.
     - 2.2.1 If there are more than one case that could be used to connect a particular node, then generate one learning graph for each node.
     - 2.2.2 Insert those nodes in the graph.
   - 2.3 If does not exist any case that match with all the post-connectors for a particular node, retrieve a set of nodes that partially match with those connectors, until all the post-connectors are connected.
     - 2.3.1 For each selected node verify that all of its pre-connectors are connected, if don't, look for other nodes (cases) that can be used to join this node with the previous node.
     - 2.3.2 Insert those nodes in the graph.
3. For each learning graph generated, look for a path (solution) from the initial node to the final node (or nodes).

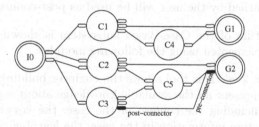

**Fig. 3.** Schematic Learning Graph.

Figure 3 shows a simple learning graph example that uses five (atomic) cases retrieved from the Case Base.

In this example, two concepts ($G_1$ and $G_2$) will be learned. From this learning graph, the next solutions (or *learning paths*) are possible:

- concepts to be learned: $G_1 \wedge G_2$
- **solution 1**: $I_0$—$C_1$—$C_4$—$G_1$ $\wedge$ $I_0$—$C_2$—$C_5$—$G_2$
- **solution 2**: $I_0$—$C_1$—$C_4$—$G_1$ $\wedge$ $I_0$—$C_2$—$C_3$—$G_2$
- **solution 3**: $I_0$—$C_1$—$C_4$—$G_1$ $\wedge$ $I_0$—$C_2$—$C_3$—$C_5$—$G_2$

The following learning paths: $I_0—C_1—G_1$, $I_0—C_2—G_2$, or $I_0—C_3—G_2$ cannot be considered as correct solutions because if they were considered, some pre-connectors in the goal nodes ($G_1$ and $G_2$) will be unconnected. This means that some concepts that the user needs to achieve for his/her (learning) goals, will never be acquired. The post-connectors that are not connected in the learning graph represent those extra concepts that have been acquired by the student in his/her learning process.

## 3.2   Case Model

Cases can be represented in a variety of forms using the full range of AI representational formalisms including frames, objects, predicates, semantic nets and rules.

The frame/object representation is currently used by the majority of CBR software. A case is a contextualised piece of knowledge representing an experience. It contains the past lesson that is the content of the case and those features, or characteristics, in which the lesson can be used [8]. Typically a case comprises:

- The *problem* that describes the state of the world when the case occurred. In our approach several keywords are used as pre-connectors to represent what concepts are necessary to understand the information stored in the case.
- The *solution* which states the derived solution to that problem. In our approach the case stores the information related to a particular programming topic.
- And/or the *outcome* which describe the state of the world after the case is applied. In our approach several keywords that represent those concept that have been learned by the user will be used as post-connectors.

The architecture of the Case-Based subsystem is shown in Figure 4. This subsystem is implemented using the following modules:

- *Case Creator Tool.* This tool allows the engineer building the initial *atomic* cases that represent all the available knowledge about a particular topic. It also allows including the content of the case, the keywords used to characterize the store information in the case, the learning connectors that are "learned" by the user once the content is studied, and the complexity of the case.
- *NLP module.* Although initially some cases characteristics like the keywords, or *connector* will be included by the engineer, a NLP analysis will be achieved by this module to suggest the characteristics that could represent the case.
- *Retrieving module.* This module implements one or several matching functions that are used to retrieve the most promising stored cases.
- *Retain module.* Once one or several solutions are successfully found, they will be stored as new cases. Therefore, the NLP module will be used to obtain the keywords and connectors that will be used to represent the case.

The Case Base is made by two different types of cases: atomic and complex.

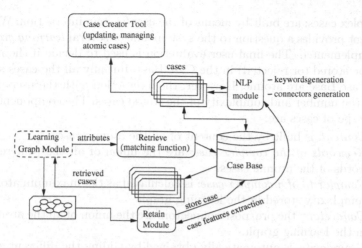

**Fig. 4.** CBR subsystem in DynJAQ.

- Atomic cases: are built by the engineer, and represent the specific knowledge about a particular topic. For instance, if we consider the problem of learning Java programming, these atomic cases represent the specific information about a particular topic in the language, i.e. an atomic case could be created to provide information about *how to define a variable*, other could represent *how to define a method* in Java Language, etc. Any atomic case is built by the next components:

  - *Content*: stores the knowledge (in natural language) about one or several concepts.
  - *Keywords*: represent a list of words that represent the semantic information stored in the content of the case.
  - *Complexity*: this attribute is actually fixed by the engineer and represents the complexity of the concept, or concepts stored in the case.
  - *Connectors*: pre and post connectors represent the learned concepts by the students if the content of the case is completely understandable.
  - *Granularity*: represents how detailed is the information stored by the case. The granularity is fixed by the engineer when builds the case. It is possible to measure the granularity of a particular atomic case using the number of keywords and connectors used by the case. Therefore, a thin granularity will use few keywords and connectors, because the knowledge stored is very specific. However, if a rough granularity is used the number of keywords and connectors will grow up.

The concept of granularity is very important because this feature could not be homogeneous. Therefore it is possible to store different atomic cases with different granularities. Our approach allows managing different granularities into a common solution. The number of stored cases in the Knowledge Base are related to this feature.

– Complex cases: are built by means of the user/system interaction. When any student provides a question to the system, one or several *learning graphs* will be implemented. The final user evaluation is used to decide if the new case will be stored (or rejected) in the Case Base. Initially all the cases stored in the Case Base are atomic. However, the interaction with the users modifies both the number and complexity of the stored cases. The components of this new type of cases are:

- *Content*: is built by the content of all the atomic cases.
- *Keywords of the complex case*: are the union of all the (different) keywords of the atomic cases.
- *Complexity of a complex case*: is calculated as the maximum atomic case complexity stored in the learning graph.
- *Connectors*: the pre/post-connectors are the union of all the atomic cases in the learning graph.
- *Granularity*: is automatically obtained by adding the different granularities of those atomic cases that build the case.

## 4   DynJAQ: A Dynamic Web FAQ System

This section describes how our approach has been instantiated into a particular implementation. We have designed and implemented a Dynamic Web FAQ System named DynJAQ (Dynamic Java Asked Question). DynJAQ is able to solve questions about how to programm in Java and it can be used like a Java-related FAQ repository. However, the answer(s) given by DynJAQ will be adapted to the user characteristics (like his/her programming level). Figure 5 shows the different modules that implements the DynJAQ architecture. The functionality of these modules can be summarized as follows:

– *User/system interaction*. The interaction between the users and the system has been carried out using Web Services technologies. The system uses a module (called $LearningGraph_{TO}HTML$) that is the responsible to generate an user-friendly representation (an HTML guide) for each possible solution. The set of Graphical User Interfaces (GUIs) provides the following information:

- The question that represents the concepts that the user wish to learn about Java Programming.
- The expertise knowledge, or skill programming of the user.
- The maximum number of possible solutions (answers) found for his/her question.

– *NLP module*: performs the analysis of the query. Our approach uses a simple NLP technique to extract the keywords from the user query (only a list of stop words are used to extract the keywords from the question). This module is used to extract other features (like the user characteristics) from the question. This module provides the necessary information to build the initial and final nodes.

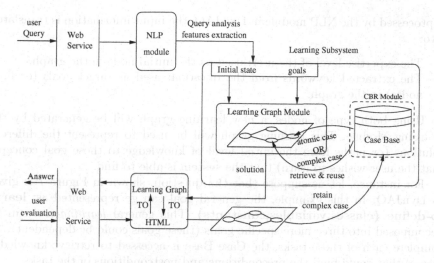

**Fig. 5.** DynJAQ architecture.

- *Learning Subsystem*: has been implemented using two related submodules:
  - *Learning graph module*: a hierarchical graph is built using the information obtained from the NLP module and the CBR module.
  - *CBR module*: is used by the previous module to retrieve the most promising cases stored in the Case Base.

Finally, the interaction with the user is used to learn those solutions that he/she marks as a success. The graphs used to build those successful solutions will be stored as new cases in the Case Base.

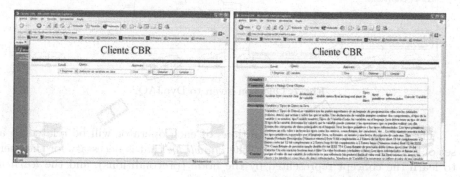

**Fig. 6.** (a) Question about how to define a variable in Java Language programming,(b) DynJAQ answer for a simple question.

Figure 6 (a) and (b) show a possible input to the system given by a beginner (Java programmer) user and the request given by the system. When a question is processed by the NLP module in DynJAQ, the input information is translated into:

- The expertise level of the user: used as the initial node in the graph.
- The extracted keywords from the question: used as target goals (or final nodes) in the graph.

Using both type of nodes, a new learning graph will be generated by the Learning Module. This learning graph will be used to represent the different solutions (or paths from the initial level of knowledge to those goal concepts that the user wishes to learn) that the system is able to find.

For instance, let us suppose that the question, shown in Figure 7 is given to DynJAQ. In this example, the general goal can ge represented as: **learn-to-define (classes,variables,constants)**. This general *learning-goal* can be decomposed into three more specific goals (these goals could be dependent). To complete each of those tasks, the Case Base is accessed to retrieve knowledge (cases) that could bind the preconditions and postconditions of the tasks.

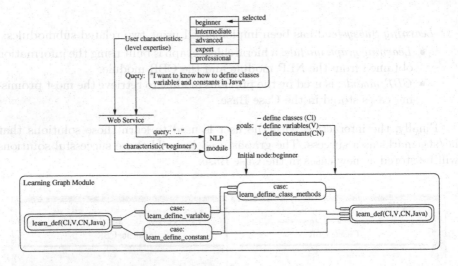

**Fig. 7.** Question given to DynJAQ.

The preconditions and postconditions of each operator will be related to a set of keywords that represent both, the *knowledge* that is necessary for the user to learn the concept represented by the node (preconditions), and the *learned concepts* if the node is applied (postconditions).

## 5   Conclusions

The main contribution of this work is to define a hierarchical knowledge representation that can be applied to build a new type of FAQ systems based on techniques like NLP [6], CBR [1, 2], or Web Services in order to allow the implementation of flexible question answering systems.

With the hierarchical knowledge representation proposed in this paper in a particular kind of Web systems such as the FAQ Systems, features like adaptability or flexibility, can be improved if several AI techniques are adequately used. We have used in DynJAQ those techniques as follows:

- NLP techniques are used to analyse the user query (to *extract* the keywords from this query), and to manage the *keywords* and *connectors* that are stored in the Case Base.
- CBR is used to represent and manage the knowledge about a particular topic or domain.
- The hierarchical learning graphs are used to build an adaptive solution to the user question. Using the keywords (and other user information) like "learning-goals", a new graph can be generated for each query.
- Web Services technologies are used (HTML, XML, SOAP, etc...) to implement an interoperable and flexible Web System.

# References

1. A. Aamodt and E. Plaza. Case-based reasoning: Foundational issues, methodological variations, and system approaches. *AICom-Artificial Intelligence Communications. IOS Press*, 7(1):39–59, 1994.
2. D. W. Aha, L. Breslow, and H. Muñoz-Avila. Conversational case-based reasoning. *To appear in Applied Intelligence*, 2000.
3. R. Burke, K. Hammond, V. Kulyukin, S. Lytinen, N. Tomuro, and S. Schoenberg. Natural language processing in the faq finder system: Results and prospects, 1997.
4. R. D. Burke, K. J. Hammond, and E. Cooper. Knowledge-based information retrieval from semi-structured text. In *In AAAI Workshop on Internet-based Information Systems*, pages 9–15. AAAI, 1996.
5. R. D. Burke, K. J. Hammond, V. A. Kulyukin, S. L. Lytinen, N. Tomuro, and S. Schoenberg. Question answering from frequently asked question files: Experiences with the FAQ finder system. *AI Magazine*, 18(2):57–66, 1997.
6. C. L. A. Clarke, G. V. Cormack, and T. R. Lynam. Exploiting redundancy in question answering. In *Research and Development in Information Retrieval*, pages 358–365, 2001.
7. R. Davis, H. Shrobe, and P. Szolovits. What is a knowledge representation? - an introductory critical paper. *AI Magazine*, 14(1):17–33, 1993.
8. J. Kolodner. *Case-Based Reasoning*. Morgan Kaufmann, 1993.
9. C. C. T. Kwok, O. Etzioni, and D. S. Weld. Scaling question answering to the web. In *World Wide Web*, pages 150–161, 2001.

# Knowledge Management in Eco-tourism: A Case Study

Stefanos Karagiannis[1] and Apostolos Apostolou[2]

[1] Technological Educational Institute of Crete, Heraklion Crete, Greece
Tel: +30 2810 379600
skaragianis@sdo.teiher.gr
[2] Technological Educational Institute of Crete, Heraklion Crete, Greece
Tel: +30 2810 379600
mgp@otenet.gr

**Abstract.** Ecotourism has been marketed as a form of nature-based tourism, in response to a number of local and regional initiatives associated with marketing nature conservation, local traditions and culture, as alternatives to mass tourism and the need for businesses that can be managed by people without large amounts of money. In this paper we try to apply the principles and methodologies of Knowledge Management in the development of integrated strategic plans concerning ecotourism, in regions with particular natural beauty, examining the case of the National Park and the Gorge of Samaria's in Crete.

## Introduction

The growth of the conservation and Eco-tourism movement is a logical one for the period of transition we are leaving in. Both developed in response to concerns for environmental quality. Biodiversity conservation, cultural heritage and Eco-tourism are logical partners, as each is needed to realize their individual aims. From the other side the significance of Knowledge Management gains continuously ground and finds a row of applications in a wide spectrum of industries, between these and the tourist industry, and appear reasonable questions for the possibility of the application of the principles and the methodology of Knowledge Management in the sector of ecotourism.

Knowledge Management can contribute in an important way to the consolidation of Eco-tourism as practised, especially in areas of protected natural beauty, and to the integration of Eco-tourism into national tourism development agendas.

Knowledge Management can help to the development of an integrated strategic plan for such destinations, acknowledging that Eco-tourism is a significant part of protected natural beauty areas sustainable development agenda, providing them with a framework for developing Eco-tourism policy and for linking eco-tourism with integrated land use and land use planning. It provides them with a tool to galvanize local social and political elements of tourism development and relate them immediately to income generation, economic growth, and improvements in rural economies. Eco-tourism gives value to local practices and traditions, and embraces scales of economic growth and business performance that are sustainable.

In this paper we try to apply the principles and methodologies of Knowledge Management in the development of integrated strategic plans concerning ecotourism, in regions with particular natural beauty, examining the case of the National Park and the Gorge of Samaria's in Crete.

D. Karagiannis and U. Reimer (Eds.): PAKM 2004, LNAI 3336, pp. 508–521, 2004.
© Springer-Verlag Berlin Heidelberg 2004

# Eco-tourism

Eco-tourism has been marketed as a form of nature-based tourism [1]; however, since 1990, non-governmental organizations (NGOs), development experts, and academics have studied it as a sustainable development tool. The term eco-tourism refers on the one hand to a concept based on a set of principles, and on the other hand to a specific market segment. In 1991, the International Eco-tourism Society produced one of the definitions we use: "Eco-tourism is responsible travel to natural areas that conserves the environment and sustains the well being of local people".

In 1996, the World Conservation Union said that eco-tourism: "...is environmentally responsible travel and visitation to relatively undisturbed natural areas, in order to enjoy and appreciate nature (and any accompanying cultural features - both past and present) that promotes conservation, has low negative visitor impact, and provides for beneficially active socio-economic involvement of local populations."

In all cases, eco-tourism aims to achieve sustainable development results. It is important to stress that all tourism activities, be they geared to holidays, business, conferences, congresses or fairs, health, adventure or eco-tourism, should aim to be sustainable. This means that the planning and development of tourism infrastructure, its subsequent operation, and its marketing should focus on environmental, social, cultural and economic sustainability criteria [2].

The strong orientation of eco-tourism toward principles, guidelines, and certification based on sustainability standards gives it an unusual position in the tourism field. In the years since the concept was first defined, a consensus has formed on the basic elements of eco-tourism [3]:

- Contributes to conservation of biodiversity
- Sustains the well being of local people
- Includes an interpretative/learning experience
- Involves responsible action on the part of tourists and the tourism industry
- Is delivered primarily to small groups by small- scale businesses
- Requires the lowest possible consumption of non-renewable resources
- Stresses local participation, ownership and business opportunities, particularly for rural people

Only if someone escapes from the artificial environment, then he recognizes how strong the human need for contact with the world of nature is. There, someone finds his roots, his space and the study of the universe. There, someone could find energy for the soul. The model of ecotourism appeared firstly to materialise responsible principles for the environment, however it appears that later the economic profits played the fundamental role in concrete countries, in order that consciously and for clearly economic reasons they cultivate the ecological tourism as an economic activity [4]. The importance of industry of ecological tourism consists into the fact that above 25 billions dollars are transported by the north in the south hemisphere each year, while it is forecasted that in year 2010 the arrivals are going to increase in 937 millions movements, from 456 that was been in 1994. According to the World Tourism Organization (WTO), which sets the eco-tourism as "a travel in order to enjoy and appreciate the nature", the 40% to 60% of world eco-tourists were tourists which their basic motive were the love to the nature and 20% to 40% were tourists which attract them the wild nature.

In the 20 century the travels near the nature have gone through a dramatic change. Africa is a good example. The safari of photograph became more popular than hunting, based in the "Big Five" (big mammals, which were and are more popular for the sightseers). Thus, until the 1970, the tourism in the wild nature was absorbed from the big mammals, while at the same time was destroyed the natural environment, the animals were tortured, and was despoiled the wild nature [5]. Today, this type of behaviour has changed. More and more visitors realise the damage that can cause in the value of wildly nature and in the social - economic environment of region. For this reason were created specialised tours - safari, distant travels or walks in the nature with drivers, but under strict control. This increasing tendency to this direction recommends the eco-tourism, a tendency which renders entire the tourist industry more sensitive opposite the environment. However, ecotourism means also something more from activities of some small teams of chosen persons who are showing devotion and love to the nature. It is really a "platform" that carries all the interests that emanate from environmental economic and social concerns. Finally, eco-tourism offers a powerful engagement in the nature with a sense of social responsibility [6]. This responsibility reaches the sensitivity of each traveller. For this reason the growth of eco-tourism, which presents enormous prospects, should be organised. In this frame is investigated the application of the principles of Knowledge Management in the development of integrated strategic plans for the growth of eco-tourism.

## Knowledge Management

In today's fast-changing global markets, success is no longer tied to the traditional inputs of labour, capital or land. The new critical resource is inside the heads of people: knowledge. What an organization knows, and how it leverages that knowledge, has never been more essential for success. Knowledge management is the new industry buzzword, but it is not something really new, it is just how best to help people share and leverage their expertise [7].

Knowledge management is an evolving technology area and it's very difficult to find a standard definition of what it is. The following are two possible definitions:

"Knowledge management is the strategy and processes to enable the creation and flow of relevant knowledge through the business to create organizational, customer and consumer value", (David Smith, Unilever).

"Knowledge management is the broad process of locating, organizing, transferring, and using the information and expertise within an organization. The overall knowledge management process is supported by four key enablers: leadership, culture, technology and measurement", (American Productivity and Quality Center).

Although many of the essential elements of knowledge management are not new, the integration of those elements into an overall strategy for effectively managing knowledge to achieve strategic business advantage is still an evolving science [8].

As Garvin [9] states, learning organizations are skilled at five main activities: systematic problem solving, experimentation with new approaches, learning from their own experiences and past history, learning from the experiences and best practices of others, and transferring knowledge quickly and efficiently throughout the organization. Each is accompanied by a distinctive mindset, tool kit, and pattern of behaviour. Many companies practice these activities to some degree. But few are consistently successful because they rely on happenstance and isolated examples. By creating systems and processes that support these activities and integrating them into the fabric of daily operations, companies can manage their learning more effectively.

Many companies are beginning to feel that the knowledge of their employees is their most valuable asset. They may be right, but few firms have actually begun to actively manage their knowledge assets on a broad scale [10]. Knowledge management has thus far been addressed at either a philosophical or a technological level, with little pragmatic discussion on how knowledge can be managed and used more effectively on a daily basis. At this early stage of knowledge management in business, the most appropriate form of dialogue is not detailed tactics, but rather high-level principles. When an organization decides what principles it agrees upon with respect to knowledge management, it can then create detailed approaches and plans based upon the principles [11].

Knowledge is an asset, but its effective management requires investment of other assets. There are many particular knowledge management activities requiring investment of money or labour, including the following [12]:

- Knowledge capture, i.e., creation of documents and moving documents onto computer systems
- Adding value to knowledge through editing, packaging, and pruning
- Developing knowledge categorization approaches and categorizing new contributions to knowledge;
- Developing information technology infrastructures and applications for the distribution of knowledge;
- Educating employees on the creation, sharing, and use of knowledge.

It is important to address and improve the generic knowledge management process, but knowledge is generated, used, and shared intensively in a few specific knowledge work processes. The specific processes vary by firm and industry, but they include market research, product design and development, and even more transactional processes like order configuration and pricing. If real improvements are to be made in knowledge management, improvements must be made in these key business processes [13].

## Knowledge Management and Eco-tourism

Knowledge management is beginning to make the transition from an intellectual area of study to a more pragmatic approach that can be implemented in actual practice to drive business results. It is becoming recognized that an effective knowledge management system must be based on the following concepts [14]:

- A way of capturing and organizing explicit as well as tacit knowledge of how the business operates including an understanding of how current business processes function.
- A "system-approach" to management that facilitates assimilation of new knowledge into the business system and is oriented toward continuous improvement / innovation.
- A common framework for managing knowledge and some way of validating and synthesizing new knowledge as it is acquired.

- A culture and values that support collaborative sharing of knowledge across functions and encourages full participation of all employees in the process.

Without those basic elements as a foundation, it is unlikely that any knowledge management effort would succeed.

The key to understand how both knowledge management and eco-tourism fit together is to see the operation of the destination as a "system". The value of treating the destination as a system is that it helps to break down the complexity and provides a framework for understanding cause – and effect relationships within the system [15].

Figure 1 shows a simplified model for eco-tourism.

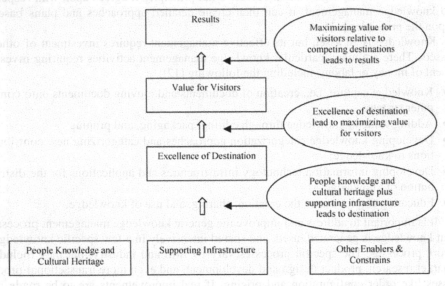

**Fig. 1.** Simplified model for Eco-tourism (adaptation from Cobb, 2000)

This model is based on the "balanced scoreboard" approach. The idea behind it is that a combination of financial and non-financial metrics is essential for effective management.

As Kaplan [16] states, financial measures are inadequate for guiding and evaluating organization's trajectories through competitive environments. They are lagging indicators that fail to capture much of the value that has been created or destroyed by managers' actions in the most recent accounting period. The financial measures tell some, but not all, of the story about past actions and they fail to provide adequate guidance for the actions to be taken today and the day after to create future financial value.

Understanding the cause-and-effect relationships within the destination as a system allows developing a more proactive and planned approach designed for prevention of problems and anticipation of visitor and market requirements as opposed to constant "fire-fighting" mode reacting to problems and taking corrective actions.

Knowledge management has to be defined in the context of the area it serves and, in fact, it can take on different meanings in different areas that have different needs and goals of what they want to achieve with it [17]. They should be aligned with driving results and that requires an understanding of how the cause-and-effect relationships of how the destination operates as a system. A good strategy should answer the following questions [18]:

* What is our strategy? Who are the customers? What are their needs and expectations? Who are the competitors? How does the destination seek to differentiate itself to gain competitive advantage?
* What are the customer values that have the most important impact on the results and what are the internal factors that have the greatest impact on maximizing customer value?
* What role does knowledge play in achieving those results? What kind of approach is appropriate?

## Case Study: The National Park and the Gorge of Samaria in Crete [2]

The region of Samaria is found in southern slope of Leuka Ori and belongs administratively in the province of Sfakia, at the county of Chania. Its particular characteristics are the rocky region, the small gorges that are linked with the mainly gorge, the sources with clean waters, the particular climate, the rich flora with the endemic species, the forests from cypresses and pines and unique in the world appearance of the Cretan wild goat. It is generally a region with rare natural beauties and rich history, but also a unique biotope, and it justifies why it was declared National Park.

The expanse of the park and its core, according to the decree in 1962, amounted in 33000 acres, while with the modification of limits of the park it amounted in 48000 acres. After its declaration as a National Park, in the Gorge of Samaria is prohibited every agricultural activity, the farming, the hunting etc.

*Geographical elements:* The gorge of Samaria is found in the West Crete, in the Southern department of Chania, between Leuka Orh and Volakia. It starts from the south of the mount of Omalos, it has length 18 Km, width 10-40m and height of sides 500-600m$^2$. There is not doubt that the gorge of Samaria constitutes the most imposing gorge of Europe, because of the closeness and his big length. Begins from the place of Ksilokastro (elevation 1227m.) to the south-eastern part of historical mount of Omalos and it leads to the blue sea of Libico. The medium elevation is calculated in the 1000m and his extent is amount in the 48485 square metres. The area of the core of the park amounted in the 28500 square metres.

*Demographic elements:* The villages of that region are: Kares, Karanos, Lakkoi, Askordalos, Omalos, Ag. Roymeli and Xora Sfakion. The villages Kares and Karanos have a population of 235 persons in total, from which the 114 are considered "active population" with the significance that they are workers. Lakkoi, Askordalos and Omalos have in total 425 residents, from which the 172 belong in the active population. Finally Ag.Roymeli and Xora Sfakion have 247 residents from which the 193 is active population. The basic professions of that region are: farmers, woodman, fishermen and self-employing.

*Climatic conditions:* The annual height of rainfalls fluctuates from 600–1800 m.m. The summer period lasts 5–6 months. The minimal temperature is 5 degrees C while biggest reaches 40 degrees C. The days of sunlight /year: 280–310, while the days of rainfall per year fluctuate from 55 to 76.

*Geomorphology of the region:* The gorge has unique geomorphology. It has 4 m width and sides almost boldly, which reach 300–400 m. Other characteristics of the region are, the lateral ravines that lead to the gorge, the impressive hypsometric differentiation (in 6,5 hm length the altitude increases from the 0 in the 2100m, while exist four tops above the 2000m), the characteristic precipices of height as 400m, the characteristics geomorphology elements of the great landscape of Crete, as calcareous stones, caves (most by which have not been explored), and a lot of sources, as well as regions with abandoned steps, important element of human action. The forest of Pinus Brutia is found mainly in low altitudes by 0 to 600m approximately.

*The flora and the fauna of the Park:* Crete is particularly known for her endemic plants with Asiatic characteristics, that number more than 57 types, but also for the 213 species of plants that flourish here only and no in rest Greece. Many of them present precious therapeutic attributes as diktamos that flourish in the wild and abrupt slopes of mountain Dikti, in the precipices and in gorges. It contains ethereal oil, diktamelaio that is constituted by small quantities cymolis, karvakrolis etc. and has many antiseptic, anthelmintic and other attributes. The main type of flora is the forest of pine and cypress. Also, clumps of holly and Cretan sfendamo exist in bigger elevation. Apart from the forest, which cover a percentage of 60–70% of total extent, exist also frygana as well as many plants. As for the fauna the national park, first it will be reported the much known Cretan wild goat, holy animal of Greek mythology, which is endemic animal of Crete, known and as "kri - kri". The main characteristic is that it walks comfortably, with big certainty in utmost of the rocks and clambers with facility and amazing agility. The wild goats that live today here find itself under the protection of the special provisions of Forestall Legislation.

Finally, remarkable it is that a lot of traditions by the antiquity (Aristotle) report that this animal when it is wounded noshes the plant of Crete diktamo and puts it in his wounds.

It should also be reported, that here live also other rare species of animals (badger, arkalos, kounavi, muoksos, wild cat), but also rapaciously and singing birds (vulture, eagle, nightingale goldfinch k.a.). Their existence, in combination with the steep natural landscape that causes the awe, composes the uniqueness of Gorge of Samara and the rendering most powerful pole of attraction for Greeks and other foreigner visitors.

*The honours of Gorge:* The Gorge of Samaria - National Park of Samaria, had a lot of honours and rewards up to today. For example, in 1989 there was new renewal of the European Diploma. In 1981 was declared by UNESCO as "Reserve of Biosphere", with international recognition of the enormous ecological importance of the region. Finally, European Union included the Park in the list of the most "Important on the fowl fauna of the Regions". In 1980 is granted by the Council of Europe, the European Diploma of Protection of Natural Environment – category A.

The National Park and the Gorge of Samaria selected as an ideal area to apply the principles of Knowledge Management for the development of an integrated strategic plan to support the growth of ecotourism in the region, for the fact that it is a region of a particular and unique wild natural beauty, and at the same time our interest was attracted by the fact that lately is observed a progressive reduction of many of the traditional occupations of residents of the wider region of the Gorge, something means that the locals are looking for new economic activities. Economic, mainly, are the reasons that led progressively to the alleviation of agricultural employment and naturally, the exacerbation of the problems which face the farmers. Also, because of wider changes, today has resulted to various environmental problems, as the "exhaustion of" the ground and the pollution of horizon.

In this ominous climate, a source of optimism is the growth of tourism of a particular form, the eco-tourism, because of the virgin natural beauty of the region.

## Using Knowledge Management for the Development of Eco-tourism in Samaria Gorge

Many attempts have been made to practice various forms of ecological, cultural, and other forms of sustainable tourism in the wider area of Samaria Gorge [19]. To date, there has been no systematic approach and strategic consistency to these efforts. A sustainable, eco-tourism development strategy will help to guide the area's tourism development efforts. The Strategy will further area's efforts to provide regional leadership, and to give the country a competitive edge in both the expanding domestic and international tourism markets. Eco-tourism provides once important opportunity for the area around the Samaria Gorge to recover economically. Natural and cultural resources are available for development and significant investments are not required. And since eco-tourism is usually developed as a small or family business, it can provide more local people with the incentives to stay and work in rural areas, stem emigration, and create many more centres of local economic prosperity [20].

An older research [2] which made in the region with basic aim the investigation of prospects for the growth of ecotourism activities, led to the following conclusions - problems, with regard to the planning for the growth of the region:

1. Wide use of pesticides in agriculture which destroy the flora.
2. Exceeding pasturing and fires.
3. Problems of accessibility and infrastructures.
4. Primitive means of mass transport.
5. Manufactures by materials foreigner in the region which degrade the environment.
6. Lack of spaces of sanitary burial and general problems of cleanness.
7. Problems of noise pollution.
8. Destruction of natural beauties.
9. Non-existence of single strategic plan in the level of Local Government.

These defined problems constitute threats external to eco-tourism that can detract from its development in the area. The eco-tourism sector cannot affect these factors, or attempt to circumvent them.

Protected areas of natural beauty, like Samaria Gorge, have to consistently develop policy and basic legislation necessary to support the implementation of modern nature management practices. Two elements are critical to sustain these achievements. The first is that protected area management must include benefits for the people living around them; and the second is that financial mechanisms must be developed to sustain both conservation activities and rural improvements in livelihood. The area around Samaria Gorge is faced with the same challenge. It must provide benefits to the people who preserve the region's important cultural heritage, and it must develop the financial mechanisms and incentives that allow individuals and the Local Government to preserve the diversity of the local cultural heritage.

In recent years information and knowledge has gained new importance for all the areas of economic and social life. This development is mainly based on the facts that due to the new technologies access to information is available immediately and rather unrestricted and that the efficient use of this information allows the establishment of a significant competitive advantage [21]. Awareness has increased that the efficient use of knowledge and the avoidance of errors improves performance by reducing problems and enhancing satisfaction among all stakeholders. The awareness of the consequences of not using existing knowledge or information has increased the efforts of consciously handling it. But due to the fast increase of information available rather immediately via internet or other media new strategies have to be set up for handling such amount of information [22].

In the course of most activities people face problems that they cannot solve alone. Their natural response is to study past experiences and re-use previously acquired knowledge, either from their own experience or from resources within their social environment [23].

For organizations the managing of knowledge constitutes a strategic perspective. If knowledge and know-how are not under control, they represent an element of weakness. On the other hand, if they are under control, they become a resource and a strategic factor for continues improvement and for the development of new knowledge [24].

Knowledge Management is the group of processes that transform intellectual capital of an organization or group of people into a value [25]. (Figure 2)

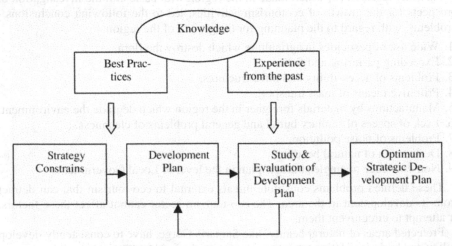

**Fig. 2.** Strategic Development Plan Process

If we analyze the problems that face a destination concerning the development of the area, we conclude that the same problems occur in other destinations, they are well known and they have been faced from others in the past. In most of the cases there is no need for new solutions. It should be noted that who are in charge of planning the development strategy of the destination, fail to prevent the problems because knowledge on such problems had not been acquired and accumulated so that it could be widely reused for the study and evaluation of the development plan. As a result, the quality of the development plan does not reach the proper level that could do in itself.

For an integrated strategic development plan for an eco-tourism destination we need the combination between knowledge and experience. The strategic development plan has to be based on the following factors:

1. protection of the local natural and socio-economic environment in combination with the imposition of penalties
2. co-operation of all levels of Local Government in an integrated plan of establishing the necessary infrastructure and road network
3. rules for noise pollution
4. rules for cleaning – sanitation
5. rules for construction using local materials
6. fire protection
7. prohibition of using agro-poisons in protected areas
8. new environmental friendly means for public transportation
9. alternative environmental friendly energy resources

Eco-tourism is a cornerstone of the area around Samaria Gorge tourism development strategy. More importantly it is a tool for improving local livelihoods in the region, and it is a sound mechanism for biodiversity conservation inside and outside of the protected areas system. Eco-tourism is the natural choice for the area around Samaria Gorge in its desire to develop sustainable livelihoods and land use, and conserve its natural assets. Thus, the Regional Eco-tourism Strategy reflects the number and diversity of public and private initiatives throughout the region. The continued engagement and focus on these achievements and the role of local government and local people is crucial for eco-tourism development.

In developing the strategic development plan for Samaria Gorge as an Eco-tourism destination we have to use a factor that is referred to the maximum number of visitors a destination can accept, without the alteration of the natural and socio-economic environment.

This factor plays a central role in the design phase. It is used to examine the following parameters:

1. the number of visitors
2. the type of visitors
3. the stage of tourism development of the destination
4. the difference in economic development between the destination and the origin countries of visitors
5. the cultural differences between the destination and the origin countries of the visitors
6. the total area of destination in combination with the density of the population
7. the size of services provided by local people
8. the size of services provided by foreigners
9. the percentage of ownership of local business between local and foreigners

10. the size of acquisition of land and buildings by the foreigners
11. the technological advance of the destination
12. the actual marketing strategies
13. the cohesion between local people
14. the approach of the destination and the road network

Using the principles and methodologies of knowledge management we can extract the knowledge and experience from local people, but also the experience from other similar case as well, in the design phase of the development plan, and use them in order to avoid problems [26].

The objective of the design development plan process is to create the conditions and provide the basis for sustainable, high-quality tourism and competitive tourism businesses. The strategy for achieving this is based on a number of points, with most important of all to follow a knowledge-driven approach, to know how to better exploit existing information, to acquire and develop know-how, to innovate by developing new processes and to benefit from best practices [27]. This also requires better understanding of the organisation of the stakeholders, their interrelation and their interdependence.

The area around Samaria Gorge shall offer high quality tourism products throughout the year, taking advantage of the diversity, uniqueness, and authenticity of its natural and cultural resources. These products will be targeted to national and international visitors who are responsible, caring and supportive of nature protection, biodiversity conservation and region's cultural heritage.

Eco-tourism for Samaria Gorge, therefore, is a brand of tourism that:

- Contributes to local economic growth and social development;
- Becomes an important tool in local government planning and development;
- Serves as the basis for strong regional, sustainable tourism associations and networks;
- Attracts international tourists at higher expenditure levels, and for longer periods of time throughout the year;
- Contributes to the domestic tourism market throughout the year;
- Expands trips and tours involving regional cooperation and linkages;
- Develops positive attitudes and knowledge in communities towards biodiversity conservation and cultural preservation and interpretation;
- Perpetuates and develops environmental friendly livelihoods;
- Expands the number of tools and financial mechanisms for preserving natural and cultural resources;
- Drives infrastructure development in appropriate, environment-friendly ways.

The general context for the evaluation of the integrated strategic development plan for Samaria Gorge and the area around, should address the following matters:

1. the scientific description
2. the specification of administrative objectives
3. the building of consensus and priorities setting
4. description of actions needed for accomplishing the goals set
5. definition and description of the system that will control the effectiveness of the administrative processes

6. the preservation and continuity of administration
7. the contribution in finding founds
8. the establishment of means concerning effective communication between all the stakeholders

Using the principles and methodologies of knowledge management in developing a strategic development plan for an Eco-tourism destination we avoid the detachment and usual contradiction of various measures taken [28]. We succeed in the existence of a broader and integrated view of the consequences from the implementation of actions and we provide the best possible result with respect to the development of eco-tourism.

The implementation of such a strategy is expected to lead to the following results:

* A process and procedures for decentralized eco-tourism planning and fiscal management with strong local accountability;
* The commitment and support of the local people towards natural and cultural heritage conservation and eco-tourism development;
* Regional networks of institutions and organizations that serve as the basis for ecotourism marketing, product development, financial investments, and business development;
* Eco-tourism, sustainable tourism, and environmental management systems will embraced as part of local government planning and operations;
* Eco-tourism and cultural tourism revenue-generating mechanisms will established and evaluated as fair and supportive of natural, cultural and historic resources, as well as of infrastructure and services attached to this sector;
* Eco-tourism will contribute to a policy of rural development that both develops the capacity of rural communities, protected areas and cultural sites and makes them equitable partners in realizing this national strategy.

## Conclusions

To succeed as part of a sustainable development agenda, eco-tourism must be regarded as a strategic planning and development tool. For the local government to understand its application and to nurture its values, eco-tourism must become a spatial planning tool for what can be done, where, and how. The benefits of it should be demonstrated to protected areas management authorities and to municipal and regional authorities – when they begin to use eco-tourism as part of their development strategies, eco-tourism will allow them eventually to gain new positions.

Eco-tourism planning and development must have a common approach. The approach must provide an equal playing field for all who intend to engage in such enterprises, regardless of whether they are fortunate enough to be able to operate close to a protected area or cultural site, or they are part of other areas of high biodiversity and cultural value.

Using the principles and methodologies of knowledge management we can extract the knowledge and experience from local people, but also the experience from other similar case as well, in the design phase of the development plan, and use them in order to avoid problems.

# References

1. Karagiannis, Stefanos, and Lamprakis Kostantinos.: Internationally Protected Areas: The importance of promoting this model for Crete, *Kritologika Grammata*, 15-16, Rethimnon (2000)
2. Karagiannis, Stefanos.: Samaria Gorge: A study on the problems of the area and the perspectives for the development of eco-tourism, *Ereuna*, 28, April 2002, Athens.
3. Vliamos, Spiros, and Karagiannis Stefanos.: Eco-tourism and Local Government: A proposal, *The Step of Social Sciences*, 28, June 2000, Athens.
4. Karagiannis Stephanos.: *Tourism and the Environment:* Review of Decentralization Local Government and Regional Development, Revue de Decentralization d' administration Locale et de Development Regional, V. 17,p. 68-69 1999.
5. Karagiannis Stephanos-Papailias Theodoros.: *The Influence of Tourist development on the social ethics of local communities of Hersonisos Municipality, on the island of Crete, Greece,* Archives of Economic Historie, Volume XIX, No 2, p. 147-166, July –December 2002.
6. Karagiannis Stephanos-Tsoukatos Evangelos.: *Spinaloga Heritage as an Alternative Tourist Product: The Case of the Spinaloga Islet in Crete,* Anatolia, an International Journal of Tourism and Hospitality Research, Vol.14, No 2, Winter 2003, pg. 161-167,
7. Barquin, Ramon C.: What is Knowledge Management? KNOWLEDGE & INNOVATION: Vol1, No2 ©2001, Journal of the KMCI (Knowledge Management Consortium International) (http://www.kmci.oro/KI Journal/KI Article.gHome.htm)
8. Beckman, Thomas J.: Chapter 1[s1]: The Current State of Knowledge Management)) from "Knowledge Management Handbook" by L1EBOWITZ, JA[1] (Editor): ©1999, CRS Press LLC
9. Garvin, David A.: *Building a Learning Organization*, Harvard Business Review on Knowledge Management, 52 (1998)
10. Drucker, Peter F.: "Knowledge-Worker Productivity: The Biggest Challenge", CMR (California Management Review) Vol41, No2 (Winter 1999)
11. Beijerse, Roelof P. UIT.: Questions in Knowledge management defining and conceptualising a phenomenon», Journal of Knowledge Management Vol.3, No2, ©1999 MCB University Press
12. Clarke, Thomas.: «The knowledge economy», Education & Training Vol.43, No4/5, ©2001
13. Bender, Silke & Fish, Alan.: «The transfer of knowledge and the retention of expertise: the continuing need for global assignments, Journal of Knowledge Management, Vol.4, No2, ©2000 MCB University Press
14. Davenport, Thomas H.: *Some Principles of Knowledge Management,* in www.mccombs.utexas.edu/kman/kmprin.htm (2000)
15. Cobb, Chuck. *Knowledge Management and Quality Systems*, ASQ's 54th Annual Quality Congress Proceedings (2000)
16. Kaplan, Robert S., and David P. Norton.: *The Balanced Scoreboard*, New York, Harvard Business School Press (1996)
17. Choo, Chun Wei: "The Knowing Organization: How organizations use information to construct meaning, create knowledge, and make decisions", International Journal of Information Management, Vol.16, No5, ©1996 http://choo.fis.utoronto.ca/FIS/ResPub/KOart.htfnl)
18. Hansen, Mortem T & Nohria, Nitin & Tierney Thomas.: "What's your strategy for managing knowledge?", ©1999 HBR (Harvard Business Review) Mar-Apr 1999
19. Karagiannis Stephanos: *Economic Benefits and Perspectives in Tourism:* Review of Decentralization Local Government and Regional Development, Revue de Decentralization d' administration Locale et de Development Regional, p. 101-105 2000.

20. Karagiannis Stephanos: *Natur und Kultur Griechenlands als unerscoepfliche Grundlagen des Zukunftsfähigen Tourismus,* Review of AIST- International Association of Scientific Experts in tourism, Vol. 58, No 1., pg. 41-47, 2003.
21. Karagiannis, Dimitrios: *Einfuerung in die Informationstechnologie,* Universitaet Wien, Institut fuer Informatik-Department of Knowledge Engineering (2004)
22. Karagiannis, Dimitrios: *Betriebliche Informationssysteme,* Universitaet Wien, Institut fuer Informatik-Department of Knowledge Engineering (2004)
23. Bierly, Paul E. & Kessler, Erich. & Christensen, Edward W.: "Organizational learning, knowledge and wisdom», Journal of Organizational Change Management, Vol.13, No6, ©2000 MCB University Press
24. Firestone, Joseph M.: "Key Issues In Knowledge Management" KNOWLEDGE & INNOVATION: VoM, No3 ©2001, Journal of the KMCI (Knowledge Management Consortium International) (httD://www.macroinnovation.com/papers_pitches.htrn)
25. Tamura, Yasuhiko, and Iizuka Yoshinori: *Systematization of Design Knowledge on Failures and Construction of Knowledge Base for Aiding Design,* ASQ's 55th Annual Quality Congress Proceedings (2001)
26. Karagiannis, Dimitrios: *Theoretische Grundlagen der Kuenstlichen Intelligenz* und Softcomputing Vorlesung-Abteilung Knowledge Engineering (2004)
27. Karagiannis, Dimitrios - Telesko-Kaghofer: *Fach Data Engineering und Wissensverarbeitung Teil: Wissensverarbeitung* Uebung-Abteilung Knowledge Engineering (2004)
28. Choo, Chun Wei & Bontis, Nick (Editors): "The Strategic Management of Intellectual Capital and Organizational Knowledge", ©2002 Oxford University Press, New York. (Chapter 1. Knowledge, Intellectual Capital, and Strategy: Themes and Tensions) fhttp://choo.fis.utoronto.ca/oup/Chapter1.ritmli

# Author Index

# Lecture Notes in Artificial Intelligence (LNAI)